ABOUT THE AUTHORS

So you will know your authors a bit better, here is some information.

Anita Woolfolk Hoy was born in Fort Worth, Texas. She is a Texas Longhorn—all her degrees are from the University of Texas, Austin, the last one a Ph.D. in Educational Psychology. After graduating, she worked as a school psychologist with students and teachers in elementary and secondary schools in fifteen counties of central Texas. She began her career in higher education as a professor of educational psychology at Rutgers University, then moved to The Ohio State University in 1994.

Wayne Kolter Hoy was born in Lock Haven, Pennsylvania. He is a Nittany Lion—his Master's and Doctorate in educational administration were earned at The Pennsylvania State University. He has served on the faculties of Oklahoma State University and Rutgers University, where he was a Distinguished Professor and Associate Dean for Academic Affairs. In 1994, Wayne was appointed the Novice Fawcett Chair of Educational Administration, an endowed professorship at the Ohio State University. Anita joined the faculty as well. Their three children, now grown and living in San Francisco and Columbus, continue to keep them informed about technology and the modern world.

As to their professional lives, Anita's research focuses on teachers' thinking and beliefs, particularly teachers' sense of efficacy, and the role of educational psychology in the preparation of teachers. She is the editor of the journal *Theory Into Practice*, which brings the best ideas from research to practicing educators. With students and colleagues, she has published over 70 book chapters and research articles in journals such as *Teaching and Teacher Education, Contemporary Educational Psychology, The Journal of Educational Psychology, Educational Psychologist, American Educational Research Journal, Review of Educational Research, Educational Researcher, Journal of Consulting and Clinical Psychology, The Journal of Experimental Education, The Journal of School Psychology,* and the *Elementary School Journal,* among others. She received the Alumni Award for Professional Research from the Rutgers University Graduate School of Education. Anita has served as Vice-President for Division K (Teaching & Teacher Education) of the American Educational Research Association and President of Division 15 (Educational Psychology) of the American Psychological Association. Her textbook, *Educational Psychology* (Allyn & Bacon), is moving into its eleventh edition and has been translated into over ten different languages.

Wayne's primary professional interests are theory and research in administration and leadership, the sociology of organizations, and the social psychology of administration. He is the co-editor with Michael DiPaola of a book series, *Theory and Research in Educational Administration.* With students and colleagues, he has published over 120 book chapters and research articles in journals such as *Educational Administration Quarterly, The Journal of Educational Administration, Journal of School Leadership, Sociology of Education, Journal of Educational Psychology, American Educational Research Journal, Review of Educational Research, Teaching and Teacher Education, Educational Researcher, The Journal of Experimental Education,* and *The Elementary School Journal,* among others. He also has served as President of the University Council for Educational Administration (UCEA) and Secretary-Treasurer of the National Conference for Educational Administration. He has received the Lindback Foundation Award for Distinguished Teaching from Rutgers University; the Alumni Award for Professional Research from the Rutgers University Graduate School of Education; the Excellence in Education Award from The Pennsylvania State University; and in 1996, he became an Alumni Fellow of The Pennsylvania State University. In 2003, he was awarded the Roald Campbell Lifetime Achievement Award in Educational Administration. Wayne has coauthored ten books on educational administration and leadership; his text with Cecil Miskel is in its eighth edition.

THIRD EDITION

Instructional Leadership

A Research-Based Guide to Learning in Schools

Anita Woolfolk Hoy
The Ohio State University

Wayne Kolter Hoy
The Ohio State University

Boston ▪ New York ▪ San Francisco
Mexico City ▪ Montreal ▪ Toronto ▪ London ▪ Madrid ▪ Munich ▪ Paris
Hong Kong ▪ Singapore ▪ Tokyo ▪ Cape Town ▪ Sydney

Vice President, Editor in Chief: *Paul A. Smith*
Executive Editor: *Stephen Dragin*
Series Editorial Assistant: *Christina Certo*
Marketing Manager: *Darcy Betts*
Production Editor: *Annette Joseph*
Editorial Production Service: *Kathy Smith*
Composition Buyer: *Linda Cox*
Manufacturing Buyer: *Linda Morris*
Electronic Composition: *Omegatype Typography, Inc.*
Cover Administrator: *Elena Sidorova*

For related titles and support materials, visit our online catalog at www.pearsonhighered.com.

Between the time website information is gathered and then published, it is not unusual for some sites to have closed. Also, the transcription of URLs can result in typographical errors. The publisher would appreciate notification where these errors occur so that they may be corrected in subsequent editions.

Printed in the United States of America

10 9 8 7 6 5 4   RRD-VA   12 11 10

Allyn & Bacon
is an imprint of

www.pearsonhighered.com

ISBN-10: 0-205-57844-6
ISBN-13: 978-0-205-57844-3

Dedicated to Our Brothers

Thomas C. Hoy, Principal
Robert M. Pratt, Artist
Eric W. Pratt, Engineer

Abiding friends

CONTENTS

6 Teaching   191

9 **Assessing and Changing School Culture and Climate   317**

PREFACE

Instructional Leadership is predicated on the assumption that teachers and principals need to work together as colleagues to improve teaching and learning in schools. Traditional supervision in which the principal rates the effectiveness of teachers is an outmoded concept, one that was always more ritual than reality. We believe that this is the first text of its kind, one written for principals to help them understand current theories of teaching and learning as well as the practical applications of these perspectives. The text uses a learning-centered approach that emphasizes making decisions based on what supports student learning.

We don't believe that instructional supervision can be effective unless the parties involved have a good understanding of how students learn. Although principals may take the lead in cooperative and professional endeavors, in the end it is the teachers who determine their success. Perhaps just as important as taking the lead in instructional matters is to develop a school climate where instructional leadership flourishes and emerges spontaneously from teachers themselves.

The text addresses the critical aspects of the teaching–learning process: student differences, learning, motivation, teaching, classroom management, assessing student learning, and assessing and changing school climate and culture. Each chapter is grounded in the latest research and theory in that area and provides specific suggestions for applying that knowledge to practice. After the Introduction, each chapter begins with a *Preview of Key Points* and a *Leadership Challenge,* an actual teaching problem, and ends with suggestions of projects to relate theory to practice in the form of professional *Portfolio* exercises. Moreover, throughout the chapters, *Theory into Action Guidelines* provide concrete suggestions. Also, each chapter includes an *Instructional Leader's Toolbox,* a collection of contemporary readings, useful websites, and helpful organizations. Finally, the text concludes with *Appendices,* which include instruments for assessing your school learning environment.

New to this edition is the extended coverage of students—the ultimate recipients of principals' and teachers' efforts to enhance learning. There are now two chapters on students: Chapter 2 considers diversity with new sections on fostering student resilience, culturally relevant pedagogy, and student sexual orientation. Chapter 2 also includes a *Point/ Counterpoint: Should Teachers Focus on Students' Learning Styles?* Chapter 3 addresses student abilities and learning challenges, with new sections on emotional intelligence, autism spectrum disorders, and the decision-making process in assessing students and ensuring they get the appropriate educational services. Chapter 3 also includes a new **Principal's Perspective.** We are again grateful to Thomas Reed, a successful former principal, superintendent, and Fawcett Scholar at The Ohio State University, for sharing his knowledge for the Principal's Perspectives. Finally, over 200 new studies and analyses enriched our examination of the crucial topics in this text. Following are specific changes to this edition:

CHAPTER 1: Introduction to Teaching and Learning
- Expanded coverage of No Child Left Behind Act
- New Point/Counterpoint: *Has NCLB Been a Positive Force in Schools?*
- New and expanded Internet sites
- New and revised suggested readings

CHAPTER 2: Student Diversity
- New Leadership Challenge
- New section: *Poverty and School Achievement*
- New section: *Teaching to Overcome Poverty and Foster Resilience*
- New Point/Counterpoint: *Should Teachers Focus on Students' Learning Styles?*
- New Figure 2.1: Creating a Resilient Classroom
- Revised discussion on dialects
- Revised discussion of second language learning and bilingual education
- New discussion of cultural practices and values; added discussion of Lisa Delpit's work
- New section on gender and sexual identity
- New and expanded Internet sites
- New and revised suggested readings

CHAPTER 3: Student Abilities and Challenges
- Completely revised discussion of intelligence and of Flynn effect
- New discussion of emotional intelligence
- New *A Principal's Perspective* on student differences
- Revised discussion of flexible grouping
- New section: *Autism Spectrum Disorders and Asperger Syndrome*
- New section: *Theory of Mind*
- Updated section on individual education programs
- New section: *The Decision-Making Process in Special Education*
- New and expanded Internet sites
- New and revised suggested readings

CHAPTER 4: Learning
- New section: *Functional Behavioral Assessment and Positive Behavior Support*
- Revised discussion of working memory and flashbulb memories
- Revised discussion of inquiry and problem-based learning
- New section: *What Can Go Wrong: Misuses of Group Learning*
- New section: *Dilemmas of Constructivist Practice*
- New and expanded Internet sites
- New and revised suggested readings

CHAPTER 5: Motivation
- New description of learning communities
- New discussion of what makes motivation a challenge in classrooms
- New discussion of social support and motivation
- Revised discussion of goals and goal acceptance
- Revised discussion of teachers' sense of efficacy
- New discussion of catching and holding student interests
- New section: *Diversity in Motivation to Learn*
- New section on classroom strategies that support motivation (see Table 5.5)
- New and expanded Internet sites
- New and revised suggested readings

CHAPTER 6: Teaching
- New section on quality teaching
- New description of an expert inclusive teacher
- New section on lesson study
- Revised discussion of criteria for good instructional objectives
- Revised discussion of teacher knowledge
- New discussion of the curriculum wars in reading, mathematics, and science
- New section on summer setbacks in learning
- New and expanded Internet sites
- New and revised suggested readings

CHAPTER 7: Classroom Management
- Revised section on student self-management
- New section on setting up natural consequences and encouraging student responsibility
- New section: *Planning for Computer Uses,* including Table 7.3: Tips for Managing a Computer Lab
- New section on social skills and caring in classroom management
- New section: *Positive Behavior Supports: Schoolwide Programs*
- New section: *Culturally Responsive Management*
- New and expanded Internet sites
- New and revised suggested readings

CHAPTER 8: Assessing Student Learning
- New discussion of problems with high-stakes testing
- Updated discussion of stereotype threat
- New section: *Helping Students with Disabilities Prepare for High-Stakes Tests*
- Revised section on performance-based assessment
- New section: *Informal Assessments*
- Updated research on retention in grade
- Updated section on grades and motivation

- Revised section on the effects of grades on students, including Table 8.6: The Assessment Experience
- New and expanded Internet sites
- New and revised suggested readings

CHAPTER 9: Assessing and Changing School Culture and Climate
- New section: *A Culture of Academic Optimism*
- Revised and expanded section on collective efficacy
- New and expanded Internet sites
- New and revised suggested readings

Our colleagues and students are important sources of ideas and criticism. We would like to thank and acknowledge them for their suggestions and encouragement in this project:

Jana Alig-Mielcarek, The Ohio State University
Michael DiPaola, College of William & Mary
Harry Galinsky, Superintendent, Paramus, NJ
Pamela J. Gaskill, The Ohio State University
Roger D. Goddard, University of Michigan
Sarah D. Kozel, The Ohio State University
Eileen McMahon, The Ohio State University
Thomas Reed, The Ohio State University
Page A. Smith, The University of Texas, San Antonio
Scott R. Sweetland, The Ohio State University
C. John Tarter, University of Alabama
Megan Tschannen-Moran, College of William & Mary

In addition, we thank the following reviewers for their helpful suggestions: Eric Glover, East Tennessee State University; Ken Hancock, Northeastern State University, Oklahoma; Thomas Livingston, Superintendent of Atwood Heights District, Alsip, Illinois; Stephen F. Midlock, University of St. Francis; P. J. Powers, University of Wisconsin, Superior; and Jan Walker, Drake University.

1 Introduction to Teaching and Learning

Schools are about teaching and learning; all other activities are secondary to these basic goals. Teaching and learning are elaborate and complex processes; this book is about understanding those processes. It is not a book about administration, but it is a book for administrators because the fundamental purpose of schooling is student learning. School leaders are responsible for creating learning organizations. Even though we focus on principals, this text is for all school leaders who are interested in improving teaching and learning whether they are teachers, curriculum and instructional specialists, or administrators; in the end, instructional leadership is a shared responsibility.

The centrality of student learning in the school is irrefutable; in fact, preparation standards for school leaders embrace this fundamental truth in their second standard (Council of Chief State School Officers, 1996, p. 12):

> A school administrator is an educational leader who promotes the success of all students by advocating, nurturing, and sustaining a school culture and instructional program conducive to student learning and staff professional growth.

We argue that school leaders cannot achieve this purpose without a clear and deep understanding of teaching, learning, motivation, assessment, and a nurturing school culture. Our book deals with issues pertaining to all six Interstate School Leaders Licensure Consortium (ISLLC) Standards. The inside front cover presents a matrix that lists and matches the ISLLC Standards with the chapters in this book.

The Role of the Instructional Leader

A critical role for all principals is that of instructional leader. We are not suggesting that principals alone are responsible for leadership in instruction. Clearly that is not the case. Leadership in instructional matters should emerge freely from both principals and teachers. After all, teachers deliver the instruction in the classroom; they have expertise in curriculum and teaching, and they have mastered a substantive body of knowledge. Principals, however, are responsible for developing school climates that support the very best instructional practices. Thus, it is principals who should forge a partnership with teachers, with the primary goal of the improvement of teaching and learning.

There is no one way to engage in such cooperation, but instructional leaders need to spend time in classrooms as colleagues and engage teachers in conversations about learning and teaching. Improvement is a continuous process, not merely a ritual observation that principals make once or twice a year. Professional conversations and professional development should revolve around the improvement of instruction, how students learn, and appropriate teaching strategies for different situations. Cooperation, colleagueship, expertise, and teamwork are hallmarks of successful improvement and are substitutes for traditional supervision.

Although principals may take the lead in cooperative and professional endeavors, in the end teachers are the ones who determine their success. Perhaps just as important as taking the lead in instructional matters is developing a school climate where instructional leadership flourishes and emerges spontaneously from teachers. Above all, principals must communicate clear visions of instructional excellence and continuous professional development consistent with the goal of the improvement of teaching and learning. What does this mean? How does it get translated into action?

1. Academic excellence should be a strong motivating force in the school. Increasingly the research is affirming that a school's academic emphasis is critical to student achievement (Goddard, Sweetland, & Hoy, 2000; Hoy & Sabo, 1998; Hoy, Tarter, & Woolfolk Hoy, 2006). The instructional leader should ensure a learning environment that is orderly, serious, and focused on high but achievable academic goals. The principal must demonstrate in both words and actions an optimistic belief that all students can achieve, while developing a school culture in which teachers and students alike respect hard work and academic success.

2. Instructional excellence and continuous improvement are ongoing and cooperative activities by instructional leaders and teachers. Activities such as student growth and achievement, school climate, teacher and student motivation, and faculty morale should be monitored and assessed regularly with the aim of improvement.

3. Teachers are at the center of the instructional improvement; in the end, only the teachers can change and improve their instructional practice in the classroom; hence, teacher motivation and self-regulation are critical to improvement. Teachers must decide that they want to improve.

4. Principals must provide constructive support and obtain the resources and materials necessary for teachers to be successful in the classroom; indeed, resource support is a basic principal role.

5. Principals should be intellectual leaders who keep abreast of the latest developments in teaching, learning, motivation, classroom management, and assessment, and share best practices in each area with teachers.

6. Principals should take the lead in recognizing and celebrating academic excellence among students and teachers because such activities reinforce a vision and culture of academic excellence.

Wang, Haertal, and Walberg (1993, 1997) did a meta-analysis of more than 10,000 statistical findings on the most significant influences on learning and found a reasonable consensus; in general, direct influences have a greater impact on student learning than indirect ones. Fifty years of research contradicts the current reliance on school restructuring as the key to school reform. Classroom management, student metacognitive and cognitive processes (e.g., study skills, background knowledge, work habits), instruction, motivation, and assessment have a greater impact on learning than indirect influences such as restructuring, district policy, and school policy. One exception to the general finding was school culture. School culture does seem to make an important difference by providing a school context that reinforces important teaching and learning practices. Increasingly the research suggests that the *key to improving student learning rests with what happens in the classroom:* The teacher is critical. Instructional leadership calls for principals to work with teacher colleagues in the improvement of instruction by providing a school culture and climate where change is linked to the best knowledge about student learning.

A Principal's Perspective

C. R. prided himself on being a visionary leader. An optimist who saw the good in every person in every situation, he was an inspiring, energetic, and creative principal who thrived on facing the seemingly impossible. Late in his career he was recruited by a failing school district to deliver its once proud high school from a malaise of underachievement and apathy by students and faculty alike. Driven by the personal improvement writing of Steven Covey (2004)*, C. R. set out to change the climate of the school one teacher at a time. He invigorated professional growth of the staff by focusing on their personal goals, ambitions, and needs. Personal mission statements and action plans dominated faculty meetings in the first semester. Predictably confronted with skepticism early on, C. R. persisted, modeling his trust of his teachers by frequently seeking authentic feedback from them through nonthreatening methods. He openly shared his own personal goals and demonstrated self-regulation as he genuinely assessed his progress. To foster cooperation and instill ownership of the school's achievement record, he enlisted committees of teachers to review all facets of the educational program, from budget allocations to curricular programming. Open to all suggestions, he harbored no sacred cows and honored the committees' work by adopting their recommendations as his own. In a short time, a talented but once divisive and uncommitted collection of teachers transformed into a trusting, efficacious faculty that systematically propelled the school toward excellence. Responding likewise to the newly enhanced culture and climate of the school, student achievement rose steadily while community perception and confidence in the district returned to its previously high levels.

*Covey, S. R. (2004). *The 7 habits of highly effective people: Powerful lessons in personal change.* New York: Free Press. Based on a true story.

Instructional Leadership after No Child Left Behind

On January 8, 2002, President George W. Bush signed into law the No Child Left Behind (NCLB) Act. Actually NCLB was the most recent authorization of the Elementary and Secondary Education Act (ESEA), first passed in 1965. The reauthorization had a new name to reflect the sweeping changes that came with it. In a nutshell, NCLB requires that all students in grades 3 through 8 and once more in high school must take standardized achievement tests in reading and mathematics every year. In addition, starting in 2007, a science test was added—one test a year in each of three grade spans (3–5, 6–9, 10–12). Based on these test scores, schools are judged to determine if their students are making adequate yearly progress (AYP) toward becoming proficient in the subjects tested. States have some say in defining proficiency and in setting AYP standards. But no matter how states define these standards, NCLB requires that all students in the schools must reach proficiency by the end of the 2013–2014 school year. In addition, schools must develop AYP goals and report scores separately for several groups, including racial and ethnic minority students, students with disabilities, students whose first language is not English, and students from low-income homes. See Figure 1.1 for the NCLB timeline from 1965 to 2014.

FIGURE 1.1   NCLB Timeline

1965   The Elementary and Secondary Education Act (ESEA) is enacted by Congress. ESEA provides support for low-income students.

1968   ESEA is extended by Congress to bilingual education.

1970   ESEA funds must "supplement, not supplant" other state and local education funding.

1978   ESEA permits Title I money to be spent schoolwide when 75 percent of students are low income.

1988   ESEA requires districts to use standardized tests to evaluate schools.

1994   ESEA is reauthorized as the Improving American Schools Act, which requires states to identify schools that are not making "adequate yearly progress."

2002   No Child Left Behind (NCLB) Act
NCLB is signed into law by President George Bush, and NCLB accountability begins.

2002–2003   NCLB provisions now include:

- Annual reading and math tests must be given (once a year in each grade span: 3–5, 6–9, 10–12).
- Newly employed teachers and paraprofessionals must meet NCLB requirements.
- Title I schools "in need of improvement" for two consecutive years must offer parents the option of transferring their children in such schools to higher-performing schools.
- Title I schools "in need of improvement" for three consecutive years must offer supplementary aid and service to eligible students.
- Over 19,000 schools nationwide fail to make "adequate yearly progress," and more than 11,000 schools are identified as ones "in need of improvement."

2004   NCLB—new Secretary of Education, Margaret Spellings, promises more flexibility.

2005   NCLB consequences:

- Utah rules that in cases of conflict, its own state assessment has priority over NCLB results.
- Some states are given permission to develop modified assessments for students from disadvantaged groups.
- Texas is fined $444,282 for exempting from the tests too many students with disabilities. Connecticut files a lawsuit to preserve its own state testing every other year.

2005–2006   NCLB: Reading and math tests must be administered annually (grades 3–8 and once in 10–12).

2006   NCLB

- All teachers should be highly qualified by June 30, 2006, but some states are given extensions.
- Tennessee and North Carolina take part in a model pilot program to measure student progress.

2007   ESEA is due for reauthorization; science testing added (once a year in each grade span: 3–5, 6–9, 10–12).

2013–2014   NCLB—All students must be proficient.

Source: Adapted from "NCLB: Is There Life Beyond Testing?" by C. Guilfoyle, *Educational Leadership*, November 2006, 64(3), pp. 10-11. Used by permission of the Association for Supervision and Curriculum Development. Copyright © 2006 by the Association for Supervision and Curriculum Development. Reprinted with permission. All rights reserved, www.ascd.org.

The effects on you as a principal, teacher, or parent are profound. James Popham (2005), an assessment expert, puts it this way:

> Testing—*and teaching*—following the passage of the NCLB Act are certain to be different than testing —*and teaching*—before the law's enactment. Today's public school teachers are now obligated to take part in an educational game whose rules have been dramatically altered because of a significant federal law. The NCLB Act, almost literally, seems likely to trump almost everything it touches. (p. 4)

We start the first chapter of this text describing NCLB because, as Popham notes, it will affect teaching life every day. What does NCLB mean for schools? Words that come to mind are *accountability*, *student achievement*, *closing achievement gaps*, *raising expectations*—but the first word that comes to mind for most principals and teachers is *testing*. To fully comply with NCLB in the 2007–2008 academic year, states will need to give about 68 million tests (Guilfoyle, 2006). Has NCLB helped schools, teachers, and students succeed? You can see in the Point/Counterpoint that this is a hotly debated question.

Let's turn now to those people we are trying not to leave behind—the students.

Student Differences

We begin our analysis of teaching and learning with the students. Chapters 2 and 3 discuss the broad range of differences students bring to schools and classrooms. Students differ in culture, learning styles, gender, and intelligence. Each of these differences has implications for teaching and learning.

In Chapter 2, "Student Diversity," we note that in less than two decades over half of the students in public schools will be students of color. Many of these will speak a language that is different from the teacher's. Teachers and administrators will have to work together to create classrooms that are good for all students. The challenge will be creating tolerance, respect, and understanding among a diverse student and teacher school community.

The number of children in poverty in the United States is almost 50% higher than in *any other developed Western nation* and five to eight times higher than in many prominent industrialized nations. Compared to children from affluent families, children growing up in poverty have lower average scores on achievement tests, are at least twice as likely to be kept back in school, and drop out more often. We examine some ways to foster resilience in students faced with these challenges.

Cultural differences often are associated with diversity in learning styles. Although students may have different learning styles or preferences, the consequences for teaching and learning are not clear; in fact, popular programs have far outrun what we know about how to deal with such differences. Indeed, the research gives one pause. There is promising work on visualizer/verbalizer differences, but applications to teaching have not been fully tested.

Gender differences and sex stereotyping are two other problems that face most teachers and administrators. Gender discrimination in the classroom, as well as students' concerns about sexual orientation, are just a few of the challenges facing school leaders. To act wisely is to first understand the facts and consequences, but the

POINT/COUNTERPOINT

Has NCLB Been a Positive Force in Schools?

POINT

Yes, scores are up; students are learning.
In many ways, No Child Left Behind was the product of frustration with administrators and teachers. Educators have known for years about achievement gaps and the poor test performance of students in poverty, yet, according to policymakers in Washington, no one was taking responsibility to make things better.

> Democrats and Republicans grew increasingly angry with state and local officials whom they saw as endlessly demanding more money, committed to explaining all the reasons why high expectations were unrealistic, and overly occupied with explaining why standards, testing, pay-for-performance, and accountability systems were incredibly difficult to implement. In a real sense, NCLB was a mighty yawp of frustration uttered by Washington policy makers tired of nicely asking educators to cooperate—and ready to ruffle some feathers. (Hess & Petrilli, 2004, p. 14)

U.S. Secretary of Education Margaret Spellings often notes that "what gets measured gets done." Even educators who criticize NCLB concede that the law has made it more difficult to ignore the learning needs of students who too often were overlooked—racial minorities, students in poverty, students with special needs, and English language learners. So the successes and failures of schools, especially the failures with particular groups of students, have become much more transparent. Concern with achievement gaps has grown. Low-achieving schools are receiving greater attention, and there is more accountability in every school. And schools have worked harder to align state and national content standards with their curricula. The idea of getting better qualified teachers into all classrooms, especially classrooms for the poorest students, is important too. More schools started creating data systems to follow students over several years (Jennings & Rentner, 2006; Lewis, 2007).

Are students learning more? The answer seems to be yes; at least some students are learning more of the basics that are tested. The scores of the lowest-achieving students are coming up (Lewis, 2007). Scores are up in reading and math for about 75% of states and districts—achievement gaps are generally narrowing (Jennings & Rentner, 2006). For example, the June 29, 2005, issue of the *New York Times* reported that English test scores for fourth graders in New York State were up from 50% to 60% proficiency (Winerip, 2005).

COUNTERPOINT

No, NCLB has hurt schools, teachers, and students.
Few educators question that what gets measured gets done. But that, say many, is the problem. More and more, the tests determine the curriculum—if it is not on the test, then there is no time or money for teaching it. That means social studies, art, music, physical education, languages, drama, and literature are not high priorities. As the educational sociologist, David Labaree, said over a decade ago, "Whatever is not on the test is not worth knowing, whatever is on the test need be learned only in the superficial manner that is required to achieve a passing grade" (1997, p. 46). Sarah Butzim, director of the Institute for Innovation, says, "NCLB has been stifling innovation, rather than encouraging it, as the law had intended. And it needs to be fixed" (2007, p. 768).

Another problem is that rather than getting better at helping students learn, some schools have gotten better at getting around the rules by lowering standards, excluding students who do not test well, teaching directly to the test, or encouraging low-scoring students to be absent on testing day. This temptation to "get around the rules" should not be surprising to anyone who knows the unintended consequences of systems that rely on punishment to control children or adults—humans are clever and often find ways to avoid the punishment, including cheating and manipulating the system. Any undergraduate psychology major knows that punishment is a bad way to change behaviors.

In some schools, administrators and teachers are targeting the "bubble kids," students who are almost at mastery level, and just ignoring the lower-achieving students who are far from mastery. This makes the school's numbers look better as more "bubble" students pass, but leaves the lowest-achieving

(Continued)

POINT/COUNTERPOINT   Continued

students even further behind. In addition, there is evidence that the higher-achieving students of all income levels and racial groups are regressing back to the mean as attention and resources are directed to lower-performing students (Lewis, 2007).

Other critics of NCLB have complained that the required focus on basic skills for everyone has taken money and attention away from the advanced STEM subjects (Science, Technology, Engineering, Mathematics) that are the foundation for innovation. The ability of any country to compete in the global economy rests on knowledge and skills in these subjects (Hess & Rotherham, 2007).

Finally, there are critics who claim that students spend only part of their time in schools and much more time in homes, in neighborhoods, and

in front of televisions. Schools cannot overcome all these other influences without massive changes in social policies such as health care and employment opportunities (Hess & Rotherham, 2007).

Guilfoyle (2006) sums up many people's thinking about the complex puzzle of NCLB: "The transparency that NCLB has brought is a welcome change, but we can put this transparency to better use by gathering more data to paint a more accurate picture of both students and schools" (p. 13). NCLB has to be reauthorized in 2007 or 2008. One suggestion has been to replace the AYP goals with a growth measurement model that looks at each individual child's progress to give useful information about both school success and how to help the child move ahead (Lewis, 2007).

---

issues are complex and often there are two sides. Consider the Point/Counterpoint on the differences in learning styles between boys and girls.

In Chapter 3, "Student Abilities and Challenges," we explore the meaning of intelligence, dealing with differences in student academic abilities, and the learning challenges that many students face. Intelligence is one dimension of student difference that clearly has implications for schools. There are many different conceptions about intelligence, as well as some misconceptions. We examine both. We also look at how intelligence has been measured and the best ways of using the information from those assessments. Beliefs about intelligence influence the structure and design of the curriculum. Administrators invariably confront practical issues such as ability grouping and programs for the gifted when they try to organize the school for effective learning.

There are continuing concerns about the requirements of legislation that mandate the inclusion of students with learning and behavior problems in the classroom. We discuss three of the most common challenges—students with attention deficit hyperactive disorder (ADHD), learning disabilities, and autism spectrum disorders—then look at effective assessment and teaching for these students.

Learning

Because learning is a complex cognitive process, there is no single best explanation of learning. Different theories of learning offer more or less useful explanations depending on what is to be explained. We examine three general theories of learning—behavioral, cognitive, and constructivist—each with a different focus.

POINT/COUNTERPOINT

Do Boys and Girls Learn Differently?

According to the National Association for Single Sex Public Education, in 2007 nationwide at least 253 public schools offered single-sex classes, and 51 schools were entirely single sex. In 1995 only 3 public schools offered single-sex classes (Bauer, 2007). Is this a good idea? There are a few documented sex differences in mental abilities. Do these translate into different ways of learning and, thus, different needs in the classroom?

POINT

Yes, boys and girls learn differently.
Since at least the 1960s, there have been questions about whether schools serve boys well. Accusations that schools were trying to destroy "boys' culture" and forcing "feminine, frilly content" on boys caused some public concern (Connell, 1996). More recently, according to Connell:

> Discrimination against girls has ended, the argument runs. Indeed, thanks to feminism, girls have special treatment and special programs. Now, what about the boys? It is boys who are slower to learn to read, more likely to drop out of school, more likely to be disciplined, more likely to be in programs for children with special needs. In school it is girls who are doing better, boys who are in trouble—and special programs for boys that are needed. (p. 207)

In their book, *Boys and Girls Learn Differently*, Michael Gurian and Patricia Henley (2001) make a similar argument that boys and girls need different teaching approaches. Reviewing the book for the Men's Resource Network, J. Steven Svoboda (2001) writes:

> Our schools seem to be creating overt depression in girls and covert depression in boys. Through violence, male hormones and brains cry out for a different school promoting closer bonding, smaller classes, more verbalization, less male isolation, better discipline, and more attention to male learning styles. Most of all, boys need men in their schools. (90% of

elementary teachers are female.) They need male teachers, male teaching assistants, male volunteers from the parents or grandparents, and older male students. Peer mentoring across grades helps everybody involved.

For girls, Gurian and Henley (2001) recommend developing their leadership abilities, encouraging girls to enjoy healthy competition, providing extra access to technology, and helping them understand the impact of the media on their self-images.

COUNTERPOINT

No, differences are too small or inconsistent to have educational implications.
Many of Gurian and Henley's (2001) claims about sex differences in learning are based on sex differences in the brain. But John Bruer (1999) cautions that

> although males are superior to females at mentally rotating objects, this seems to be the only spatial task for which psychologists have found such a difference. Moreover, when they do find gender differences, these differences tend to be very small. . . . The scientific consensus among psychologists and neuroscientists who conduct these studies is that whatever gender differences exist may have interesting consequences for the scientific study of the brain, but they have no practical or instructional consequences. (p. 655)

In fact, there are boys who thrive in schools and boys who do not; girls who are strong in mathematics and girls who have difficulties; boys who excel in languages and those who do not. There is some evidence that the activities used to teach math may make a difference for girls. Elementary-age girls may do better in math if they learn in cooperative as opposed to competitive activities. Certainly it makes sense to balance both cooperative and competitive approaches so that students who learn better each way have equal opportunities (Fennema & Peterson, 1988).

Behavioral theories of learning stress observable changes in behaviors, skills, and habits. Attention is clearly on behavior. Learning is seen as a change in behavior brought about by experience with virtually no concern for the mental or internal processes of thinking. Behavior is what people do. The intellectual underpinnings of behavioral theory rest with Skinner's (1950) operant conditioning; functional behavioral assessment and positive behavior supports are applications of this theory of learning. When specific skills and behaviors need to be learned, teaching approaches consistent with behavioral learning theory are quite effective.

Cognitive theories of learning deal with thinking, remembering, creating, and problem solving. How information is remembered and processed as well as how individuals use their knowledge to regulate their thinking are critical in this perspective. Some of the most important applications of cognitive theories are teaching students how to learn and remember by using learning tactics such as note taking, mnemonics, and visual organizers. Teaching strategies based on cognitive views of learning, particularly on information processing, highlight the importance of attention, organization, practice, and elaboration in learning. They also provide ways to give students more control over their own learning by developing and improving their self-regulated learning strategies. The emphasis of the cognitive approach is on what is happening "inside the head" of the learner.

Constructivist theories of learning are concerned with how individuals make meaning of events and activities; hence, learning is seen as the construction of knowledge. In general, constructivism assumes that people create and construct knowledge rather than internalize it from the external environment, but there are different approaches to constructivism. Some constructivist views emphasize the shared and social construction of knowledge while others see social forces as less important. Constructivist perspectives on learning and teaching, which are increasingly influential today, are grounded in the research of Piaget, Bruner, Dewey, and Vygotsky. Inquiry and problem-based learning, cooperative learning, cognitive apprenticeships, and the integrated schoolwide program, Fostering Communities of Learners, are typical teaching strategies that are consistent with constructivist approaches. The essence of the constructivist approach is that it places the students' own efforts at the center of the educational process, thus the notion of student-centered teaching.

Each of these approaches to learning (Chapter 4) has much to offer; in fact, each brings with it advantages and disadvantages. We think of these main learning theories as three pillars for teaching. Students must first understand and make sense of the material (constructivist); then they must remember what they have understood (cognitive–information processing); and then they must practice and apply (behavioral) their new skills and understanding to make them more fluid and automatic, a permanent part of their repertoire. Failure to attend to any part of the process means lower-quality learning. It is not sufficient to know one perspective; indeed, knowledgeable teachers and administrators should understand, remember, and apply all of these perspectives appropriately. As a preview of what is to come, examine the Point/Counterpoint: "What's Wrong with Memorizing?"

POINT/COUNTERPOINT

What's Wrong with Memorizing?

For years students have relied on memorization to learn vocabulary, procedures, steps, names, and facts. Is this a bad idea?

POINT

Rote memorization creates inert knowledge.

Years ago William James (1912) described the limitations of rote learning by telling a story about what can happen when students memorize but do not understand:

> A friend of mine, visiting a school, was asked to examine a young class in geography. Glancing at the book, she said: "Suppose you should dig a hole in the ground, hundreds of feet deep, how should you find it at the bottom—warmer or colder than on top?" None of the class replying, the teacher said: "I'm sure they know, but I think you don't ask the question quite rightly. Let me try." So, taking the book, she asked: "In what condition is the interior of the globe?" And received the immediate answer from half the class at once. "The interior of the globe is in a condition of igneous fusion." (p. 150)

The students had memorized the answer, but they had no idea what it meant. Perhaps they didn't understand the meaning of *interior*, *globe*, or *igneous fusion*. At any rate, the knowledge was useful to them only when they were answering test questions, and only then when the questions were phrased exactly as they had been memorized. Students often resort to memorizing the exact words of definitions when they have no hope for actually understanding the terms or when teachers count off for definitions that are not exact.

Most recently, Howard Gardner has been a vocal critic of rote memorization and a champion of "teaching for understanding." In an interview in *Phi Delta Kappan* (Siegel & Shaughnessy, 1994), Gardner says:

> My biggest concern about American education is that even our better students in our better schools are just going through the motions of education. In *The Unschooled Mind*, I review ample evidence that suggests an absence of understanding—the inability

of students to take knowledge, skills, and other apparent attainments and apply them successfully in new situations. In the absence of such flexibility and adaptability, the education that the students receive is worth little. (pp. 563–564)

COUNTERPOINT

Rote memorization can be effective.

Memorization may not be such a bad way to learn new information that has little inherent meaning, such as foreign language vocabulary. Alvin Wang, Margaret Thomas, and Judith Ouellette (1992) compared learning Tagalog (the national language of the Philippines) using either rote memorization or the keyword approach. The keyword method is a way of creating connections and meaning for associating new words with existing words and images. In their study, even though the keyword method led to faster and better learning initially, long-term forgetting was *greater* for students who had used the keyword method than for students who had learned by rote memorization.

There are times when students must memorize, and we do them a disservice if we don't teach them how. Every discipline has its own terms, names, facts, and rules. As adults, we want to work with physicians who have memorized the correct names for the bones and organs of the body or the drugs needed to combat particular infections. Of course, they can look up some information or research certain conditions, but they have to know where to start. We want to work with accountants who give us accurate information about the new tax codes, information they probably had to memorize because it changes from year to year in ways that are not necessarily rational or meaningful. We want to deal with computer salespeople who have memorized their stock and know exactly which printers will work with our computer. Just because something was learned through memorization does not mean it is inert knowledge. The real question, as Gardner points out above, is whether you can *use* the information flexibly and effectively to solve new problems.

Motivation

Effective teaching and learning depend on motivated students; hence, teachers must know how to stimulate, direct, and maintain high levels of interest among students. Teachers can create intrinsic motivation by stimulating students' curiosity and making them feel more competent as they learn, but that is easier said than done because some tasks simply are not inherently interesting. Teachers cannot count on intrinsic motivation to energize all of their students all of the time. There are times when teachers must use such extrinsic means to motivate students without undermining intrinsic aspects of learning. To do this, teachers need to know the factors that influence motivation. Five approaches to motivation are important in this regard.

Behaviorists explain motivation with concepts such as rewards (attractive consequences) and incentives (promise of a reward). Thus, according to the behavioral view, understanding student motivation begins with a careful analysis of the incentives and rewards present in the classroom. Providing grades, stars, and so on for learning—or demerits for misbehavior—are attempts to motivate students by extrinsic means of incentives, rewards, and punishments, but there is much more to motivating students than manipulating rewards and incentives.

In fact, proponents of humanistic psychology such as Carl Rogers argue that such behavioral explanations do not adequately explain why people act as they do. These humanistic explanations are based on the belief that people are continually motivated by the inborn need to fulfill their potential. Thus, from the humanistic perspective, to motivate means to encourage people's inner resources: their sense of competence, self-esteem, autonomy, and self-actualization. When we examine the role of needs in motivation, we will see two examples of the humanistic approach: Maslow's theory of the hierarchy of needs and Deci's self-determination theory.

Cognitive explanations of motivation also developed as a reaction to behavioral views. These perspectives argue that our behavior is determined by our thinking, not simply by whether we have been rewarded or punished for the behavior in the past. Behavior is initiated and regulated by an individual's plans, goals, schemas, expectations, and attributions. People are seen as active and curious, searching for information to solve personally relevant problems; the focus of motivation is internal and personal.

Social cognitive theories of motivation are integrations of behavioral and cognitive approaches. They take into account both the behaviorists' concern with the effects or outcomes of behavior and the cognitivists' interest in the impact of individual beliefs and expectations. In other words, the important questions are, "If I try hard, can I succeed?" and "If I succeed, will the outcome be valuable or rewarding to me?"

Finally, sociocultural theories of motivation stress engaged participation in learning communities. Such theories focus on developing and maintaining group identities through authentic participation in the activities of the group.

Teachers and administrators must understand all these perspectives if they are to be effective in improving student learning. For example, goals that are specific, challenging, and realistic are effective in motivating students. Motivation is affected by such individual needs as self-esteem and achievement, but students have different needs at different times. Motivation is also affected by students' beliefs about the causes of successes and failures; for example, when students believe effort can improve their ability, they persist longer and reach higher levels of achievement. In fact, simply believing that they have the ability to be successful is a strong motivator.

In sum, student motivation to learn is enhanced when teachers use strategies that help students develop confidence in their ability to learn, see the value of the learning, and stay focused on learning without resorting to self-protective and self-defeating beliefs and actions. We will explore both the current explanations of motivation as well as the development of strategies to enhance motivation and performance, including strategies that capitalize on students' funds of cultural knowledge. How critical is the self-esteem of students? The Point/Counterpoint on the next page: "What Should Schools Do to Encourage Students' Self-Esteem?" illustrates that there are no simple answers to this question.

Teaching

Good teaching matters. It is the sine qua non of schooling. In fact, good teaching is what instructional leadership is about: finding ways to improve teaching and learning. There are no simple answers to what good teaching is, but we know it is anchored in expertise. Expert teachers work from integrated sets of principles instead of dealing with each new event as a new problem. They have broad professional knowledge in academic subjects, teaching strategies, curriculum, student characteristics, learning contexts, teaching goals, and pedagogical content knowledge. We will examine successful teachers from a variety of settings, trying to describe their similarities and differences.

Effective teachers are creative and organized, and the basis for their organization is planning. Planning influences what students will learn because planning transforms the available time and curriculum materials into activities, assignments, and tasks for students. There is, however, no one model for effective planning. For experienced teachers, planning is a creative problem-solving process of determining how to accomplish many lessons and segments of lessons. Experienced teachers know what to expect and how to proceed, so they don't necessarily follow the detailed lesson-planning models that are so useful for beginning teachers. For all teachers, regardless of experience, clear objectives—both cognitive and affective—are a key to successful planning.

Effective teachers are also warm and enthusiastic in their teaching. Warmth, friendliness, and understanding seem to be the teacher traits most strongly related to student attitudes. In other words, teachers who are warm and friendly tend to have students who like them and the class in general, but being warm, friendly, and enthusiastic is not enough to guarantee student achievement. Research has identified teacher knowledge, clarity, and organization as important characteristics of effective teachers. We will examine the practical implications of these findings for the classroom.

The "reading wars" have raged for years: phonics versus whole language. Again, there are no simple solutions, but we will examine the research and propose some sensible suggestions about the teaching of reading and writing. There is enough excellent research to make some clear recommendations.

POINT/COUNTERPOINT

What Should Schools Do to Encourage Students' Self-Esteem?

More than 2,000 books about how to increase self-esteem have been published. Schools and mental health facilities continue to develop self-esteem programs (Slater, 2002). James Beane (1991) begins his article on the school's role in self-esteem, "Sorting Out the Self-Esteem Controversy," with this statement: "In the '90s, the question is not whether schools should enhance students' self-esteem, but how they propose to do so" (p. 25). The attempts to improve students' self-esteem have taken three main forms: personal development activities such as sensitivity training; self-esteem programs in which the curriculum focuses directly on improving self-esteem; and structural changes in schools that place greater emphasis on cooperation, student participation, community involvement, and ethnic pride.

POINT

The self-esteem movement has problems.
Many of the self-esteem courses are commercial packages—costly for schools but without solid evidence that they make a difference for students (Crisci, 1986; Leming, 1981). As Beane notes, "Saying 'I like myself and others' in front of a group is not the same as actually feeling that way, especially if I am only doing it because I am supposed to. Being nice has a place in enhancing self-esteem, but it is not enough" (1991, p. 26). Some people have accused schools of developing programs in which the main objective is "to dole out huge heapings of praise, regardless of actual accomplishments" (Slater, 2002, p. 45).

Sensitivity training and self-esteem courses share a common conceptual problem. They assume that we encourage self-esteem by changing the individual's beliefs, making the young person work harder against the odds. But what if the student's environment is truly unsafe, debilitating, and unsupportive? Some people have overcome tremendous problems, but to expect everyone to do so "ignores the fact that having positive self-esteem is almost impossible for many young people, given the deplorable conditions under which they are forced to live by the inequities in our society" (Beane, 1991, p. 27). Worse yet, some psy-

chologists are now contending that low self-esteem is not a problem, whereas high self-esteem may be. For example, they contend, people with high self-esteem are more willing to inflict pain and punishment on others (Slater, 2002). And when people set self-esteem as a main goal, they may pursue that goal in ways that are harmful over the long run. They may, for example, avoid constructive criticisms or challenging tasks (Crocker & Park, 2004). In fact, Roy Baumeister and his colleagues—experts on the meaning and measure of self-esteem—note: "We have not found evidence that boosting self-esteem (by therapeutic interventions or school programs) causes benefits" (Baumeister, Campbell, Krueger, & Vohs, 2003, p. 1). In addition, high self-esteem does not prevent children from experimenting with drugs or alcohol, smoking, or engaging in early sexual activity. High self-esteem may even encourage this kind of experimentation.

Because many attempts to encourage self-esteem have been superficial, commercial, and filled with "pop psychology," the self-esteem movement has become an easy target for critics.

COUNTERPOINT

The self-esteem movement has promise.
Beyond the "feel-good psychology" of some aspects of the self-esteem movement is a basic truth: "Self-esteem is a central feature of human dignity and thus an inalienable human entitlement. As such, schools and other agencies have a moral obligation to help build it and avoid debilitating it" (Beane, 1991, p. 28). Baumeister and his colleagues (2003) found an important exception to the lack of connection between self-esteem and positive outcomes. Having high self-esteem reduces the chances that a girl will develop bulimia, a serious eating disorder. If we view self-esteem accurately as a product of our thinking and our actions—our values, ideas, and beliefs as well as our interactions with others—then we see a significant role for the school. Practices that allow authentic participation, cooperation, problem solving, and accomplishment should replace policies that damage self-esteem, such as tracking and competitive grading.

Beane (1991) suggests four principles to guide educators:

First, being nice is surely a part of this effort, but it is not enough. Second, there is a place for some direct instruction regarding affective matters, but this is not enough either. Self-esteem and affect are not simply another school subject to be placed in set-aside time slots. Third, the negative effect of "get tough" policies is not a promising route to self-esteem and efficacy. This simply blames young people for problems that are largely not of their own making. Fourth, because self-perceptions are powerfully informed by culture, comparing self-esteem across cultures without clarifying cultural differences is distracting and unproductive. (pp. 29–30)

Psychologist Lauren Slater (2002), in her article "The Trouble with Self-Esteem," suggests we rethink self-esteem and move toward honest self-appraisal that will lead to self-control:

Maybe self-control should replace self-esteem as a primary peg to reach for. . . . Ultimately, self-control need not be experienced as a constriction; restored to its original meaning, it might be experienced as the kind of practiced prowess an athlete or artist demonstrates, muscles not tamed but trained, so that the leaps are powerful, the spine supple and the energy harnessed and shaped. (p. 47)

Sources: From "The Trouble with Self-Esteem," by L. Slater, *The New York Times Magazine*, February 3, 2002, pp. 44–47, and "Sorting Out the Self-Esteem Controversy," by J. A. Beane, 1991, *Educational Leadership, 49*(1), pp. 25–30. Copyright © 1991 by the Association for Supervision and Curriculum Development. Reprinted with permission. All rights reserved, www.ascd.org. Baumeister, R., Campbell, J. D., Krueger, J. I., & Vohs, K. D. (2003). Does high self-esteem cause better performance, interpersonal success, happiness, or healthier lifestyles? *Psychological Science in the Public Interest, 4*(1), 1–44.

Wars have raged in math and science teaching too, between advocates of teacher-centered methods and proponents of constructivist approaches. Critics of teacher-centered instruction believe that traditional mathematics instruction often has unintended consequences: Students don't understand mathematics, or worse, they decide that mathematics doesn't have to make sense; you just have to memorize the formulas. In science, as in mathematics, for students to learn and understand, they must go through a number of stages: initial discomfort with their own beliefs, attempts to explain away inconsistencies between their understandings and evidence, attempts to adjust observations to fit personal explanations, doubt, vacillation, and finally conceptual change and understanding.

In the end, students have to do the learning, but teachers can create situations that guide, support, stimulate, and encourage learning, just as administrators can do the same for teachers. In spite of the debates and different viewpoints, it remains clear that there is no one best way to teach. Different goals require different methods. Teacher-centered instruction leads to better performance on achievement tests, whereas the open, informal methods like discovery learning or inquiry approaches are associated with better performance on tests of creativity, abstract thinking, and problem solving. In addition, open methods are better for improving attitudes toward school and for stimulating curiosity, cooperation among students, and lower absence rates.

Our goal is to help teachers and administrators understand the complexities of teaching and learning so that they can make better, more reasoned decisions in these areas. For example, should schools focus on process or content, that is, on problem-solving skills or core knowledge? What do you think? Consider the arguments in the Point/Counterpoint on teaching critical thinking and problem solving.

Should Schools Teach Critical Thinking and Problem Solving?

The question of whether schools should focus on process or content, problem-solving skills or core knowledge, higher-order thinking skills or academic information has been debated for years. Some educators suggest that students must be taught how to think and solve problems, while other educators assert that students cannot learn to think in the abstract. They must be thinking about something—some content. Should teachers focus on knowledge or thinking?

POINT

Problem solving and higher-order thinking can and should be taught.
An article in the April, 28, 1995, issue of the *Chronicle of Higher Education* makes this claim:

> Critical thinking is at the heart of effective reading, writing, speaking, and listening. It enables us to link together mastery of content with such diverse goals as self-esteem, self-discipline, multicultural education, effective cooperative learning, and problem solving. It enables all instructors and administrators to raise the level of their own teaching and thinking. (p. A–71)

How can students learn to think critically? Some educators recommend teaching thinking skills directly with widely used techniques such as the Productive Thinking Program or CoRT (Cognitive Research Trust). Other researchers argue that learning computer programming languages will improve students' minds and teach them how to think logically. For example, Papert (1980) believes that when children learn through discovery how to give instructions to computers in LOGO "powerful intellectual skills are developed in the process" (p. 60). Finally, because expert readers automatically apply certain metacognitive strategies, many educators and psychologists recommend directly teaching novice or poor readers how to apply these strategies. Michael Pressley's Good Strategy User model and Palincsar and Brown's (1984) reciprocal teaching approach are successful examples of direct teaching of metacognitive skills. Research on these approaches generally shows improvements in achievement and compre-

hension for students of all ages who participate (Pressley, Barkowski, & Schneider, 1987; Rosenshine & Meister, 1994).

COUNTERPOINT

Thinking and problem-solving skills do not transfer.
According to E. D. Hirsch (1996), a vocal critic of critical thinking programs:

> But whether such direct instruction of critical thinking or self-monitoring *does* in fact improve performance is a subject of debate in the research community. For instance, the research regarding critical thinking is not reassuring. Instruction in critical thinking has been going on in several countries for over a hundred years. Yet researchers found that students from nations as varied as Israel, Germany, Australia, the Philippines, and the United States, including those who have been taught critical thinking, continue to fall into logical fallacies. (p. 136)

The CoRT program has been used in over 5,000 classrooms in ten nations. But Polson and Jeffries (1985) report that "after 10 years of widespread use we have no adequate evidence concerning . . . the effectiveness of the program" (p. 445). In addition, Mayer and Wittrock (1996) note that field studies of problem solving in real situations show that people often fail to apply the mathematical problem-solving approaches they learn in school to actual problems encountered in the grocery store or home.

Even though educators have been more successful in teaching metacognitive skills, critics still caution that there are times when such teaching hinders rather than helps learning. Robert Siegler (1993) suggests that teaching self-monitoring strategies to low-achieving students can interfere with the students' development of adaptive strategies. Forcing students to use the strategies of experts may put too much burden on working memory as the students struggle to use an unfamiliar strategy and miss the meaning or content of the lesson. For example, rather than teach students strategies for figuring out words from context, it may be helpful for students to focus on learning more vocabulary words.

Classroom Management

Classrooms are distinctive environments that affect participants regardless of how students are organized for learning or what educational philosophy the teacher espouses (Doyle, 1986, 2006). Classrooms are crowded with people, tasks, and time pressures. There are many students—all with differing goals, preferences, and abilities—who must share resources, accomplish various tasks, and use and reuse materials. In addition, actions typically have multiple effects. Calling on low-ability students may encourage their participation and thinking, but it also may slow the discussion and lead to management problems if the students cannot answer. Moreover, events occur simultaneously; everything happens at once and the pace is fast. Teachers have literally hundreds of exchanges with students during a single day. In this rapid-fire existence, events are unpredictable and public. Finally, classrooms have histories. The meaning of a particular action depends in part on what has happened before. To manage these complex places is a challenge for all, but an especially major one for beginning teachers.

No productive activity can take place in a group without the cooperation of members; hence, a main task of teaching is to enlist students' cooperation in activities that will lead to learning, and the first step in achieving cooperation is to organize the learning environment in a productive way. But order for its own sake is a hollow ritual. There are at least three reasons why classroom management is important: to make more time for learning, to include everyone in learning, and to develop systems that help students better manage their own learning.

Research on effective elementary and secondary classroom managers shows that these teachers have carefully planned rules and procedures (including consequences) for their classes; they teach these rules and procedures early using explanations, examples, practice, correction, and student involvement. In fact, getting started with a careful system of rules and procedures the first week of school sets the tone for the rest of the year. One area that requires good rules and procedures today involves managing technology. We give some useful guidelines and considerations.

Rules and procedures are a start, but not enough. Teachers need to establish a climate of trust and respect to create a positive community for learning. Once a good classroom environment is established, it must be maintained by encouraging student engagement and by preventing management problems. "With-it-ness," overlapping, group focus, and movement management are the skills of good preventers of problems. For special or more difficult situations, positive behavior supports often are helpful in preventing disruptive classroom episodes.

Even with the best prevention, there will be discipline problems in the classroom. When a conflict arises, teachers can deal more effectively with the situation if they first determine who "owns" the problem, then respond appropriately with empathetic listening or problem solving. Conflicts between students, though potentially dangerous, can be the occasions for learning conflict negotiation and peer-mediation strategies. One possible source of conflict is management that is unresponsive to students' cultural background and perceptions of schools. Establishing a positive learning context includes understanding teachers' and students' beliefs about respect as well as attention to the

Lee Canter (1989), the developer of "assertive discipline," describes his observations of effective teachers:

> I found that, above all, the master teachers were assertive; that is, they *taught* students how to behave. They established clear rules for the classroom, they communicated those rules to the students, and they taught students how to follow them. (p. 58)

Is assertive discipline effective? There are strong opinions both against and in favor of the approach, as you will see. Researchers are skeptical, but some practitioners are committed to assertive discipline.

POINT

Research results do not support assertive discipline.
In an article entitled "What Research Really Shows about Assertive Discipline," Gary F. Render, Jenell M. Padilla, and H. Mark Krank (1989) note that very little unbiased information is available about the effectiveness of this approach. Even though reports claim that 500,000 people have been trained in assertive discipline, Render and his colleagues were able to find only sixteen systematic studies of assertive discipline. Their analysis of these studies led them to conclude that:

> The claims made by Canter (1988) . . . are simply not supported by the existing and available literature. We would agree that Assertive Discipline could be helpful in severe cases where students are behaving inappropriately more than 96% of the time, as in the study by Mandlebaum et al. (1983). We would also argue that teachers such as the one in that study would benefit from any intervention. However, we can find no evidence that Assertive Discipline is an effective approach deserving schoolwide or districtwide adoption. (p. 72)

A second criticism of assertive discipline is that, while it may stop misbehavior in the short run, the long-term effects on students are damaging. Richard Curwin and Allen Mendler (1988) remind teachers that classroom management systems not only manage behavior, they also teach students lessons about their own self-worth, their ability to act responsibly and solve problems, how much control they have over their own lives, and how to use that control. What lessons are taught by systems such as assertive discipline? "If Richard shapes up after the third mark on the chalkboard because the fourth means a call home to an abusive parent, did the program improve his self-control, or did it simply transfer the inner turmoil of a child caught in a dysfunctional family?" (Curwin & Mendler, 1988, p. 68). This concern is echoed by John Covaleskie (1992): "What helps children become moral is not knowledge of the rules, or even obedience to the rules, but discussions about the reasons for acting in certain ways" (p. 56). Covaleskie also believes that the simplicity of assertive discipline is one of its biggest shortcomings. He argues that children should obey the rules because that is the right thing to do, not because there is some reward associated with obeying, or some punishment for not obeying.

COUNTERPOINT

Practitioners know that assertive discipline works.
In response to the assertion by Render and his colleagues that research does not support assertive discipline, Sammie McCormack (1989) says, "The decision to implement a program should be based on many factors, in addition to research; from a practitioner's standpoint, Assertive Discipline works" (p. 77). McCormack reports the reactions of more than 8,700 teachers from four school districts and a confederation of schools in Oregon. In these schools, 78 to 99% of the teachers saw improvements in student behavior as a consequence of using assertive discipline. McCormack does not explain how these particular samples were selected or if teachers in other schools had different reactions.

In response to Curwin and Mendler's (1988) concerns that classroom management models such as assertive discipline may undermine students' self-worth and sense of responsibility, Lee Canter (1988) notes that several studies have found improvements in both teachers' and students' self-concepts after the introduction of assertive discipline. Further, Canter and Canter (1997) note that the basis of assertive discipline is giving students choices and that it is through making choices and accepting the consequences that students learn about responsibility. Helping students to learn responsibility should be a major objective of all teachers.

factors that support motivation to learn. Our goal is to give teachers and principals the tools to succeed in that endeavor. Is assertive discipline one of those tools? Before you answer the question, read and consider the Point/Counterpoint.

Assessing Student Learning

The teaching-learning cycle is not complete without evaluation and assessment; in fact, all teaching involves assessing and evaluating learning. Increasingly, evaluation and measurement specialists are using the term *assessment* to describe the process of gathering information about student learning. Assessment is broader than testing and measurement. Assessments can be designed by classroom teachers or by local, state, or national agencies such as school districts or the Educational Testing Service. Today's assessments can go well beyond paper-and-pencil exercises to observations of performances and the development of portfolios and artifacts.

Teachers and administrators are increasingly being called on to make assessments of student learning and interpret the results of tests. Hence, they need to know the difference between norm-referenced and criterion-referenced tests. They must understand the concepts and language of test makers—sample, mean, mode, median, standard deviation, reliability, validity, normal distribution, percentile scores, standard scores, grade-equivalent scores—because they will be called on to interpret test results to parents and policymakers.

Several kinds of standardized tests are used in schools today. There are three broad categories of standardized tests: achievement, diagnostic, and aptitude (including interest). Principals and teachers will probably encounter achievement and aptitude tests most frequently because they are important tools for diagnosing learning problems and measuring the success of schooling. Today, many important decisions about students, teachers, and schools are based in part on the results of standardized tests. Because the decisions affected by test scores are so critical, many educators call this process *high-stakes testing;* in fact, all states have statewide mandated testing for public school students under NCLB.

We will consider a number of critical questions about standardized tests. For example, what role should testing play in making decisions about people? What effects do high-stakes tests have on the curriculum? Do some students have an unfair advantage in taking tests? How can we help students with disabilities prepare for testing?

Although standardized tests are important and will likely increase in their significance, most tests given to students to evaluate their performance are teacher-made tests. In the end, teachers are the ones who give grades and decide who will be promoted and who will repeat, and what and how to teach. Teachers are concerned with *formative* assessment, that is, diagnosing the strengths and weaknesses of students so they can build an instructional program that will be effective. Teachers also must make *summative* assessments at the end of instruction to determine the level of accomplishment.

One of the main criticisms of standardized tests—that they control the curriculum, emphasizing recall of facts instead of thinking and problem solving—is a major criticism of classroom tests as well. What can be done? One proposed solution is authentic assessment. Authentic tests ask students to apply skills and abilities as they would in real life. For example, they might use fractions to design a floor plan for a student lounge. If our instructional goals for students include the abilities to write, speak, listen, create, think critically, solve problems, or apply knowledge, then our tests should ask students to write, speak, listen, create, think, solve, and apply. The concern with authentic assessment has led to the development of several new approaches based on the goal of *performance in context*. Facts are used in a context where they apply; for example, the student uses grammar facts to write a persuasive letter to a software company requesting donations for the class computer center.

Portfolios and exhibitions are two new approaches to assessment that require performance in context. With these new approaches, it is difficult to tell where instruction stops and assessment starts because the two processes are interwoven. A portfolio is a purposeful collection of student work that demonstrates the student's efforts, progress, and achievements. An exhibition is a performance test that has two additional features. First, it is public, so students preparing exhibitions must take the audience into account; communication and understanding are essential. Second, an exhibition often requires many hours of preparation, because it is the culminating experience of a whole program of study. Another alternative is informal assessments such as journals that gather information from multiple sources to help teachers make decisions.

Finally, it is important to consider the effects of grades and grading on students. Teachers and administrators need to learn how to take advantage of the positive functions of grading and feedback while avoiding their negative consequences. That is no mean feat, but it is possible. Which do you think are better, traditional tests or authentic assessments? Take a look at the Point/Counterpoint arguments. Chapter 8 deals with the issues of assessment and grading in more detail.

Assessing and Changing School Culture and Climate

The school is a complex social system. Teachers teach in classrooms, but classrooms are only a part of the broader social system of the school. Just as a positive classroom climate is critical for effective teaching and learning, so too are the culture and climate of the school. The concepts of culture and climate are two ways to capture the feel or atmosphere of the school workplace. These two approaches to examining the collective identity of the workplace, its culture and climate, come from different intellectual traditions, but both perspectives are attempts to understand the influence of social context on school life. Thus, both should be useful to teachers and principals as they grapple with how social conditions in the school affect teaching and learning.

Organizational culture is a pattern of shared orientations that binds the unit together and gives it a distinctive identity. To understand the culture of a school, one must comprehend the meanings and the shared orientations of the school at four levels: its artifacts, norms, values, and tacit assumptions. A culture of efficacy is one important school property that links shared beliefs of the faculty with student achievement.

Although there is no one culture that is best for every school, there are some tacit assumptions that facilitate the process of supervision as improvement of instruction.

POINT/COUNTERPOINT

Which Are Better: Traditional Tests or Authentic Assessments?

We have seen the advantages and disadvantages of standardized tests, but what about classroom testing? Are traditional multiple-choice and essay tests useful in classroom assessment?

POINT

Traditional tests are a poor basis for classroom assessment. In his article "Standards, Not Standardization: Evoking Quality Student Work," Grant Wiggins (1991) makes a strong case for giving students standards of excellence against which they can judge their accomplishments. But these standards should not be higher scores on multiple-choice tests. When scores on traditional tests become the standard, the message to students is that only right answers matter and the thinking behind the answers is unimportant. Wiggins notes:

> We do not judge Xerox, the Boston Symphony, the Cincinnati Reds, or Dom Perignon vineyards on the basis of indirect, easy to test, and common indicators. Nor would the workers in those places likely produce quality if some generic, secure test served as the only measure of their success in meeting a standard. Demanding and getting quality, whether from students or adult workers, means framing standards in terms of the work that we undertake and value. And it means framing expectations about that work which make quality a necessity, not an option. Consider:

- the English teacher who instructs peer-editors to mark the place in a student paper where they lost interest in it or found it slapdash and to hand it back for revision at that point;
- the professor who demands that all math homework be turned in with another student having signed off on it, where one earns the grade for one's work and the grade for the work that each person (willingly!) countersigned. (p. 22)

In a second article, Wiggins (1993) continues to argue for assessment that makes sense, that tests

knowledge as it is applied in real-world situations. Understanding cannot be measured by tests that ask students to use skills and knowledge out of context. "In other words, we cannot be said to understand something unless we can employ our knowledge wisely, fluently, flexibly, and aptly in particular and diverse contexts" (p. 200).

COUNTERPOINT

Traditional tests can play an important role. Most psychologists and educators would agree with Wiggins that setting clear, high, authentic standards is important, but many also believe that traditional tests are useful in this process. Learning may be more than knowing the right answers, but right answers are important. While schooling is about learning to think and solve problems, it is also about knowledge. Students must have something to think about—facts, ideas, concepts, principles, theories, explanations, arguments, images, opinions. Well-designed traditional tests can evaluate students' knowledge effectively and efficiently (Airasian, 1996; Kirst, 1991b). Some educators believe that traditional testing should play an even greater role than it currently does. Educational policy analysts suggest that American students, compared to students in many other developed countries, lack essential knowledge because American schools emphasize process—critical thinking, self-esteem, problem solving—more than content. In order to teach more about content, teachers will need to determine how well their students are learning the content, and traditional testing provides useful information about content learning.

Tests are also valuable in motivating and guiding students' learning. There is research evidence that frequent testing encourages learning and retention (Nungester & Duchastel, 1982). In fact, students generally learn more in classes with more rather than fewer tests (Dempster, 1991).

Consider the following set of basic assumptions that Schein (1992) labels the heart of a learning culture.

1. Teachers and students are proactive problem solvers and learners.
2. Solutions to problems derive from a pragmatic search; knowledge is found in many forms: scientific research, experience, trial and error, and clinical research in which teachers and supervisors work things out together.
3. Teachers are basically good and are amenable to change and improvement.
4. Creativity and innovation are central to learning.
5. Both individualism and teamwork are important aspects of human interaction.
6. Diversity is a resource that has the potential to enhance learning.

Schools anchored with such assumptions have created learning cultures that encourage learning and improvement among all participants—students, teachers, and administrators.

Another aspect of the school context that sets the scene for effective teaching and learning is organizational climate. Teachers' performance in schools is in part determined by the climate in which they work. Climate is a general concept that refers to teachers' perceptions of the school's work environment; it is affected by the formal organization, informal organization, and politics, all of which, including climate, affect the motivations and behavior of teachers. School climate is a relatively enduring quality of the school environment that is experienced by teachers, influences their behavior, and is based on their collective perceptions. Climate is to a school what personality is to an individual.

We examine organizational climate from several perspectives: *openness*, that is, the extent to which behaviors in the school are authentic and real; the *health* of the interpersonal dynamics among the students, teachers, and principal; and the *collective efficacy* of the school, that is, the extent to which the teachers as a group believe that they have the ability to organize and teach such that the school can overcome extant student difficulties and help students achieve academically. Each of these climate perspectives brings with it a set of reliable and valid measures that teachers and principals can use to assess the functionality of the climate of their school.

Organizations are in a constant state of flux. Their change can be progressive, regressive, or aimless. Schools can develop their own learning procedures to solve their problems. They can become places where teachers and principals can continually expand their capacity to create the results that they desire, where emergent patterns of thinking are nurtured, where collective aspiration is liberated and where people are constantly learning how to learn (Senge, 1990). We will illustrate how teachers and administrators can use the climate framework and its measures as bases for organizational change. Using an organizational development approach, we will demonstrate how one school identified a climate problem, established a problem-solving team, diagnosed potential causes of the problem, developed an action plan, and set the stage for improving teaching and learning. Not all educators believe that a culture that focuses on character development is desirable. Examine the Point/Counterpoint on teaching character and morality.

POINT/COUNTERPOINT — Should Schools Teach Character and Compassion?

Not all educators believe that schools should teach compassion, tolerance, or other aspects of character and morality. Here are the two contrasting opinions.

POINT

Schooling should include character education.
Proponents of character education point to violence in the schools, teenage pregnancy, and drug use among young people as evidence that educators need to address issues of morality and virtue. They argue that families are no longer doing a good job in this area, so schools must assume the burden. Thomas Lickona (2002) describes character education as the deliberate effort to cultivate personal qualities such as wisdom, honesty, kindness, and self-discipline. The goals of character education are to produce good people (who can work and love), good schools (that are caring and conducive to learning), and a good society (that deals effectively with problems such as violence and poverty). To accomplish these goals, Lickona believes that students need knowledge and moral reasoning capabilities, emotional qualities such as self-respect and empathy, and skills such as cooperation and communication. Character education strategies include modeling kindness and cooperation, creating a classroom community that is democratic and supportive, using

cooperative learning strategies, including reflection on moral issues in the curriculum, and teaching conflict resolution.

COUNTERPOINT

Character education is ineffective and dangerous.
Alfie Kohn (2002) cautions that the term *character education* has two meanings. The first is the general concern shared by most parents and educators that students grow into good, caring, honest people. The second is a narrow set of programs and strategies for teaching a particular set of values. Few people disagree with the general concern, but there is disagreement about the narrower programs. For example, Kohn (2002) says:

> What goes by the name of character education nowadays is, for the most part, a collection of exhortations and extrinsic inducements designed to make children work harder and do what they're told. Even when other values are also promoted—caring or fairness, say—the preferred method of instruction is tantamount to indoctrination. The point is to drill students in specific behaviors rather than engage them in deep, critical reflection about certain ways of being. (p. 138)

Kohn suggests that rather than try to "fix" students' character, we should fix the structure of schools to make them more just and caring.

Summary

This is a book about understanding and improving teaching and learning. We have provided an overview of our strategy for accomplishing that goal in this chapter. We began with a discussion of the role of instructional leadership and then examined the likely impact of the No Child Left Behind Act on instructional leadership. Then we turned to the students: how they differ in intelligence, emotion, learning styles, gender, and race. Each of these differences has implications for teaching and learning that are explored in some detail (Chapters 2 and 3). Most experts agree that learning occurs when there is a stable change in an individual's skill, knowledge, or behavior, but some emphasize behavior and skills while others emphasize cognition and knowledge. Because learning is a complex cognitive process, there is no single best explanation of learning. Different perspectives are more or less useful depending on what kind of learning is to be explained. We examine three general explanations of learning—behavioral, cognitive, and constructivist—each with a different focus and each with different consequences (Chapter 4).

Effective teaching and learning depend on motivated students; hence, teachers must know how to stimulate, direct, and maintain high levels of student engagement. Motivation to learn is enhanced when teachers use strategies that help students develop confidence in their ability to learn, see the value of the learning, and stay focused on learning without resorting to self-protective and self-defeating beliefs and actions. Five approaches to motivation are important in this regard: behavioral, humanistic, cognitive, social cognitive, and sociocultural theories. Each perspective has something to offer to improve teaching and learning (Chapter 5). In the end, students have to do the learning, but teachers must create situations that guide, support, stimulate, and encourage learning. Good teaching is critical to student learning, but there is no one best way to teach. Different goals require different methods. Teacher-centered, student-centered, discovery, and inquiry are all more or less effective depending on the task and goal (Chapter 6).

Teachers not only have to motivate and teach, but they also must be able to manage the classroom. Inevitably there will be discipline problems in the classroom. When conflicts arise, teachers can deal more effectively with the situation if they first determine who "owns" the problem and then respond appropriately with empathetic listening and problem solving. Establishing a positive learning context also includes attention to the factors that support motivation to learn, such as tasks, autonomy, recognition, grouping, evaluation, and time (Chapter 7). All teaching involves assessing and evaluating learning. Assessment involves standardized and teacher-made tests, objective and essay tests, local and national tests, reliability and validity, traditional and innovative tests, and portfolios and exhibitions. Appropriate assessment is becoming increasingly more important for teachers and administrators as pressure mounts for school accountability (Chapter 8).

Finally, teaching and learning are affected by the organizational context: the culture and climate of the school. Open, healthy, optimistic, and efficacious school environments are pivotal in improving teaching and learning. Administrators and teachers need to assess their school environment and then work together to develop and improve the learning environment (Chapter 9).

In sum, we will address the critical aspects of the teaching–learning process: student differences, learning, student and teacher motivation, teaching, classroom management, assessing student learning, and assessing and changing school climate and culture. Each chapter is grounded in the latest research and theory in that area and provides specific ideas for applying that knowledge to practice, including many *Theory into Action* guidelines with concrete suggestions and *A Principal's Perspective,* a true story of how one principal solved a problem of practice related to the ideas in the chapter. The following chapters begin with a *Preview of Key Points* and a *Leadership Challenge,* an actual school problem. They conclude with suggestions of projects to relate theory to practice in the form of professional *Portfolio* exercises and an *Instructional Leader's Toolbox,* a collection of contemporary readings, useful websites, and helpful organizations.

DEVELOPING YOUR PORTFOLIO

Portfolios are increasingly being used for the licensure, hiring, and evaluation of principals; thus portfolios serve many purposes. There are two major uses for portfolios. The first is for the professional growth and reflection of the individual who is developing the portfolio. The second is as an assessment for external audiences—college and university programs, state licensure boards, and districts that are hiring principals.

At the end of every chapter in this book you will read suggestions for possible entries into your professional portfolio. Each idea asks you to create a product that incorporates the knowledge from the chapter into a plan, newsletter, presentation, or policy statement. A portfolio is not a scrapbook of clippings, notes, transcripts, and awards. A portfolio is a planned collection that reveals your philosophy, skills, and accomplishments. Often portfolios are developed to demonstrate competence in the Interstate School Leaders Licensure Consortium (ISLLC) Standards: development and implementation of a vision of learning; creation of a school culture that supports student learning; management of a safe, efficient, and effective learning environment; appropriate collaboration with families and the community; ethical practice; and understanding of the larger context of schooling. The exercises in this book will help you, especially with the first two standards.

For your first exercise, decide how you will organize your portfolio. Examine other principal portfolios and develop ideas for your own.

INSTRUCTIONAL LEADER'S TOOLBOX

Readings

Alexander, P. A., & Murphy, P. K. (1998). The research base for APA's Learner-Centered Psychological Principles. In N. Lambert & B. McCombs (Eds.), *How students learn: Reforming schools through learner-centered education.* Washington, DC: American Psychological Association.

Darling-Hammond, L., & Bransford, J. (2005). *Preparing teachers for a changing world: What teachers should learn and be able to do.* San Francisco: Jossey-Bass.

Dietz, M. E. (2001). *Designing the school leader's portfolio.* Arlington Heights, IL: Skylight Professional Development.

Educational Leadership (November, 2006). Special issue on "NCLB: Taking stock, looking forward" (vol. 64, No. 3).

Good, T. L., & Brophy, J. E. (2008). *Looking in classrooms* (10th ed.). Boston, MA: Allyn & Bacon/Longman.

Kilbane, C. R., & Milman, N. B. (2003). *What every teacher should know about creating a digital portfolio.* Boston: Allyn & Bacon.

Kimball, M. (2003). *The web portfolio guide: Creating electronic portfolios for the web.* Boston: Allyn & Bacon.

Meece, J. L., & Daniels, D. H. (2008). *Child and adolescent development for educators* (3rd ed.). New York: McGraw-Hill.

Slavin, R. E., & Olatokunbo, S. F. (1998). *Show me the evidence: Proven and promising programs for America's schools.* Thousand Oaks, CA: Corwin.

Websites

www.bestevidence.org/
Best Evidence Encyclopedia, Johns Hopkins University

www.doe.state.in.us/htmls/states.html
The contact information and website address for every state's Department of Education

http://electronicportfolios.com/portfolios.html
Using Technology to Support Alternative Assessment and Electronic Portfolios

www.proteacher.com
The Vent—a discussion group for new teachers

Organizations

http://ascd.org
Association for Supervision and Curriculum Development (ASCD)

www.ccsso.org
Council of Chief State School Officers

www.iel.org
Institute for Educational Leadership

www.naesp.org
National Association of Elementary School Principals

www.nassp.org
National Association of Secondary School Principals

CHAPTER

2 Student Diversity

PREVIEW: KEY POINTS

1. By the year 2020 over 66% of the students in public school classrooms will be children of color, many of whom will speak a dialect or language that differs from the teacher's.

2. One in six American children lives in poverty, one in fourteen lives in extreme poverty; and nearly 50% of all African American children are poor.

3. A key to overcoming the educational problems of poverty is fostering resilience in students, in teachers, and in classrooms.

4. Academic self-efficacy is a belief in your own ability to learn, and it is one of the consistent predictors of academic achievement.

5. A dialect is a variety of language spoken by a particular group; it is important that teachers remember that differences in dialect are not errors.

6. Bilingualism is an asset, not a liability, provided that there is balance—equal fluency in both languages.

7. Learning styles are preferred ways of learning and processing information; teachers need to be aware of cultural differences in learning styles so teaching approaches are consistent with learning style.

8. Creating culturally compatible classrooms requires that teachers know, respect, and effectively teach all their students.

9. There appear to be some gender differences in spatial and mathematical abilities, but these do not hold in all cultures and situations.

10. Teachers are in positions to reinforce or challenge gender stereotypes through their choice of materials and interactions with students.

Leadership Challenge

You are the principal of a fairly homogeneous elementary school. In fact, most of your students are middle- or upper-middle class and white. In January, a new student enters your school, the daughter of an African American professor who recently moved to the nearby college. After a few weeks, one of your third-grade teachers comes to you with a potential problem. She has noticed that the new student is not being included in many activities. She sits alone in the library and plays alone at recess. All these things are troubling to your teacher, but most disturbing of all is that yesterday the teacher overheard two of her higher-achieving girls talking about their "White Girls Club." Your teacher is shocked and has turned to you for advice.

1. Would you investigate to learn more about this "club"? How?
2. What advice do you give this teacher?
3. Should you formulate a plan of action? What should you do? What should the teacher do?
4. If you find that the students have created a club that excludes nonwhite students, what would you do?
5. Do you need a school policy on this matter? If so, what should the policy be? If not, why not?

Schools and instructional leaders today must deal with a wealth of student differences. These differences pose challenges (as evident in the situation above) but provide opportunities as well. This chapter examines student differences in culture and gender. We begin with the differences the principal faces in dealing with the "White Girls Club."

Today's Diverse Classrooms

Who are the students in American classrooms today? Here are a few statistics:

One in six American children lives in poverty, and one in fourteen lives in extreme poverty.

Nearly 50% of all African American children are poor.

The number of children in poverty in the United States is almost 50% higher than in *any other developed Western nation* and five to eight times higher than in many prominent industrialized nations.

Children growing up in poverty are twice as likely to be retained in a grade, drop out of school, or experience a violent crime.

One child in three is born to unmarried parents. One in five is born to a mother who did not graduate from high school. One child in three lives with a single parent, usually a working mother.

One in 83 children will be in state or federal prison before age twenty; one in 1,339 will be killed by gunfire before age twenty.

Eighteen percent of the U.S. population speaks a language other than English at home; half of these families speak Spanish.

By the year 2020, over 66% of all school-age children in the United States will be African American, Asian, Hispanic, or Native American—many the children of new immigrants.

By 2050, there will be no majority race or ethnicity in the United States; every American will be a member of a minority group (Banks, 2002; Children's Defense Fund, 2007; Duncan & Brooks-Gunn, 2000; Halford, 1999; McLoyd, 1998; Meece & Kurtz-Costes, 2001; Payne & Biddle, 1999).

Even though students in classrooms are increasingly diverse in economic level, race, ethnicity, and language, teachers are less diverse—the percentage of white teachers is increasing (now about 91%) while the percentage of black teachers is falling, down to about 7%. Clearly, it is important for all teachers, no matter what their race or ethnicity, to understand and work effectively with all their students. In the following pages, we explore some dimensions of diversity among students today. Some of the most troubling statistics above have to do with poverty—let's consider economic differences first.

Poverty and School Achievement

About one in six Americans under the age of eighteen lives in poverty, defined in 2007 by the U.S. Department of Health and Human Services as an income of $20,650 for a family of four ($25,820 in Alaska and $23,750 in Hawaii). That means about 13 million children. And almost half of these children can be classified as living in deep poverty—in families with incomes 50% below the poverty threshold. In 2005, the absolute number of children who lived in poverty was about the same for non-Hispanic white children (4.2 million), Latino children (4.1 million), and black children (3.7 million). But the rate of poverty was higher for black and Latino children: 35% of black and 28% of Latino children lived in poverty in 2005, while 11% of Asian and 10% of non-Hispanic white children were poor. Contrary to many stereotypes, more poor children live in suburban and rural areas than in central cities (Fass & Cauthen, 2006).

Compared to students in poverty, students of all ethnic groups from wealthier homes show higher average levels of achievement on test scores and stay in school longer (Gutman, Sameroff, & Cole, 2003; McLoyd, 1998). Poor children are at least twice as likely as nonpoor children to be kept back in school. And the longer the child is in poverty, the stronger the impact on achievement. For example, even when we take into account parents' education, the chance that children will be retained in grades or placed in special education increases by 2% to 3% for every year the children live in poverty (Ackerman, Brown, & Izard, 2004; Bronfenbrenner, McClelland, Wethington, Moen, & Ceci, 1996; Sherman, 1994).

What are the effects of poverty that might explain the lower school achievement of these students? It is not low income itself, but the material hardships that come with poverty, that lead to greater parental stress and fewer resources for children's achievement (Gershoff, Aber, Raver, & Lennon, 2007). Material hardships include poor health care for the family; dangerous, unhealthy, or unstable housing; insecurity about getting enough food; and general financial trouble—too many bills and not enough money. Other factors that follow are family stress and instability, interruptions in schooling, overcrowding, homelessness, discrimination, tracking in school, lower-quality school resources—all of which can lead to school failures. Poor children have less access to books, computers, high-quality day care, libraries, trips, and museums (Evans, 2004). Home and neighborhood resources seem to have the greatest impact on children's achievement when school is not in session—during the summer or before children enter school. For example, Entwisle, Alexander, and Olson (1997) found that low-SES (SES stands for socioeconomic status) and high-SES students made comparable gains in reading and math when schools were open, but the low-SES students lost ground during summer while the high-SES students continued to improve academically.

Of course, not all low-income families lack resources. Many of these families provide rich learning environments for their children. In fact, "most disadvantaged children grow up in relatively stable and secure environments" (Ackerman & Brown, 2006, p. 92). As instructional leaders, you and your teachers can learn from these families to focus on and foster the strengths of your students, rather than dwelling on deficit thinking.

Teaching to Overcome Poverty and Foster Resilience

Many children at risk for academic failure not only survive, they thrive. They are resilient students. What can we learn from these students? What can teachers and schools do to encourage **resilience**?

Resilient Students.   People vary in their capacity to be resilient. Students who seem able to thrive in spite of serious challenges are actively engaged in school. They have good interpersonal skills, confidence in their own ability to learn, positive attitudes toward school, pride in their ethnicity, and high expectations (Borman & Overman, 2004; Lee, 2005). Also, students who have high intelligence or valued talents are more protected from risks. Being easy going and optimistic is associated with resilience as well. Factors outside the student—interpersonal relationships and social support—matter too. It helps to have a warm relationship with a parent who has high expectations and supports learning by organizing space and time at home for study. But even without such a parent, a strong bond with someone competent—grandparent, aunt, uncle, teacher, administrator, mentor, or other caring adult—can serve the same supportive function. Involvement in school, community, or religious activities can provide more connections to concerned adults and also teach lessons in social skills and leadership (Berk, 2005).

Resilient Classrooms.   You can't choose personalities or parents for your students. Even if you could, stresses can build up for even the most resilient students. Beth Doll and her colleagues (2005) suggest that we have to change classrooms instead of kids because "alternative strategies will be more enduring and most successful when they are integrated into naturally occurring systems of support [like schools] that surround children" (p. 3). In addition, there is some evidence that changes in classrooms—like reducing class size and supportive relationships with teachers—have a greater impact on the academic achievement of African American students compared to Latino and white students (Borman & Overman, 2004). So how can you create a classroom that supports resilience?

Borman and Overman (2004) identify two characteristics of schools associated with academic resilience: a safe, orderly environment and positive teacher-student relationships. In their book on resilient classrooms, Doll and her colleagues (2005) draw on research in education and psychology on best practices for children in poverty and children with disabilities to describe the characteristics of resilient classrooms. There are two strands of elements that bind students to their classroom communities. One strand emphasizes the self-agency of students—their capacity to set and pursue goals. The second strand emphasizes caring and connected relationships in the classroom and the school.

The *Self-Agency Strand* fosters three key beliefs:

- *Academic self-efficacy*, a belief in your own ability to learn, is one of the most consistent predictors of academic achievement. As you will see in Chapter 5, self-efficacy emerges when students tackle challenging, meaningful tasks with the support needed to be successful and they see other students do the same. Accurate and encouraging feedback from teachers also helps.
- *Behavioral self-control* or student self-regulation is essential for a safe and orderly learning environment. Chapters 5 and 7 will give you ideas for helping students develop self-regulation knowledge and skills.
- *Academic self-determination,* making choices, setting goals, and following through, is the third element in the Self-Agency Strand. As you will see in Chapter 5, students who are self-determined are more motivated and committed to learning.

The *Relationship Strand* includes three important relationships:

- *Caring teacher-student relationships* are consistently associated with better school performance, especially for students who face serious challenges. We will examine the power of caring teachers in Chapters 6 and 7.
- *Effective peer relations* also are critical in connecting students to school.
- *Effective home-school relationships* are the final element in building a caring, connected network for students. James Comer has found that when parents stay involved, their children's grades and test scores improve (Comer, Haynes, & Joyner, 1996). The Theory into Action Guidelines on the next page give some ideas for connecting with families.

Constructing a Resilient Classroom.   To build student self-agency and relationships, the two strands of resilience, use Doll et al.'s (2005) student questionnaires for gathering data about your classrooms. Figure 2.1 on page 33 is an example of the "teacher relationship" part of the student questionnaire. One teacher gave this questionnaire and found that almost half of her students did not listen carefully or have any fun in class. They said the teacher was not fair and did not help, respect, or believe in them. Figure 2.1 also shows part of the plan the teacher developed based on the results of the questionnaire.

Next we turn to another kind of diversity, one based on culture.

Cultural Diversity

There are many definitions of culture. Most include the knowledge, skills, rules, traditions, beliefs, and values that guide behavior in a particular group of people as well as the art and artifacts produced and passed down to the next generation (Betancourt & Lopez, 1993; Pai & Adler, 2001). The group creates a culture—a program for living—and communicates the culture to members. Cultural groups can be defined along regional, ethnic, religious, racial, gender, social class, or other lines. Each of us is a member of many groups, so we all are influenced by many different cultures. Sometimes the influences are incompatible or even contradictory. For example, if you are a feminist but also a Roman Catholic, you might have trouble reconciling the two different cultures' beliefs about the ordination of women as priests. Your personal belief on the issue will be based, in part, on how strongly you identify with each group (Banks, 1997, 2002).

There are many different cultures, of course, in every modern country. In the United States, students growing up in a small rural town in the Deep South are part of a cultural group that is very different from that of students in a large urban center or students in a West Coast suburb. In Canada, students living in the suburbs of Toronto certainly differ in a number of ways from students growing up in a Montreal high-rise apartment or on a farm in Quebec. Within those small towns in the Deep South or Quebec, the child of a convenience store clerk grows up in a different culture from the child of the town doctor or dentist. Individuals of African, Asian, Hispanic, Native American, or European descent have distinctive histories and traditions. The experiences of males and females are different in most ethnic and economic groups. Everyone living within a particular country shares many common experiences and values,

Partnerships with Families

Joyce Epstein (1995) describes six types of family/school/community partnerships. The following guidelines are based on her six categories:

Parenting partnerships: Help all families establish home environments to support children as students.

Examples

1. Offer workshops, videos, courses, family literacy fairs, and other informational programs to help parents cope with parenting situations that they identify as important.
2. Establish family support programs to assist with nutrition, health, and social services.
3. Find ways to help families share information with the school about the child's cultural background, talents, and needs—learn from the families.

Communication: Design effective forms for school-to-home and home-to-school communication.

Examples

1. Make sure communications fit the needs of families. Provide translations, visual support, large print—whatever is needed to make communication effective.
2. Visit families in their territory after gaining their permission. Don't expect family members to come to school until a trusting relationship is established.
3. Balance messages about problems with communications of accomplishments and positive information.

Volunteering: Recruit and organize parent help and support.

Examples

1. Do an annual postcard survey to identify family talents, interests, times available, and suggestions for improvements.
2. Establish a structure (telephone tree, etc.) to keep all families informed. Make sure families without telephones are included.

3. If possible, set aside a room for volunteer meetings and projects.

Learning at home: Provide information and ideas for families about how to help children with schoolwork and learning activities.

Examples

1. Provide assignment schedules, homework policies, and tips on how to help with schoolwork without doing the work.
2. Get family input into curriculum planning—have idea and activity exchanges.
3. Send home learning packets and enjoyable learning activities, especially over holidays and summers.

Decision-making partnerships: Include families in school decisions, developing family and community leaders and representatives.

Examples

1. Create family advisory committees for the school with parent representatives.
2. Make sure all families are in a network with their representative.

Community partnerships: Identify and integrate resources and services from the community to strengthen school programs, family practices, and student learning and development.

Examples

1. Have students and parents research existing resources—build a database.
2. Identify service projects for students—explore service learning.
3. Identify community members who are school alumni and get them involved in school programs.

For more ideas on partnerships with parents, see http://saskschoolboards.ca/EducationServices/EducationalIssues/ParentSchoolPartnership/Types.htm

Source: Excerpt from pp. 704–705, "School/Family/Community Partnerships: Caring for Children We Share," by J. L. Epstein, *Phi Delta Kappan,* 76, pp. 701–712. Reprinted with permission of the author.

FIGURE 2.1   Creating a Resilient Classroom

Here is an example of a student questionnaire about perceptions of relationships with the teacher. Using results from this questionnaire, one teacher, Ellie, made plans to improve her relationships with her students using the Plan Record Worksheet below.

QUESTIONNAIRE

Ellie's students circled YES, SOMETIMES, or NEVER in answer to these questions:

1. My teacher listens carefully to me when I talk.	YES	SOMETIMES	NEVER
2. My teacher helps me when I need help.	YES	SOMETIMES	NEVER
3. My teacher respects me.	YES	SOMETIMES	NEVER
4. My teacher believes that I am an important member of this class.	YES	SOMETIMES	NEVER
5. My teacher makes it fun to be in class.	YES	SOMETIMES	NEVER
6. My teacher is fair to me.	YES	SOMETIMES	NEVER

PLAN RECORD WORKSHEET

Classroom: *Ellie's third grade*   Record for week of: _____

		Did this happen?
Activity 1		
What will be done?	*Take turns giving "special time" at lunch to the three kids that are struggling most: Matthew, Lisette, Arnie.*	YES
Who will do it?	*Ellie.*	PARTLY
When?	*Every Tuesday and Thursday at lunch period.*	
Where?	*In the classroom.*	NO
Activity 2		
What will be done?	*Plan a fun learning game for the mid-morning break.*	YES
Who will do it?	*Ellie and the class.*	PARTLY
When?	*Every day from 10 to 10:20 a.m.*	
Where?	*In the classroom.*	NO
Activity 3		
What will be done?	*Make friendship bracelets to remind us to be kind to classmates.*	YES
Who will do it?	*Classroom students.*	PARTLY
When?	*Week 1.*	
Where?	*In the classroom.*	NO

Source: From *Resilient classrooms: Creating healthy environments for learning* by B. Doll, S. Zucker, & K. Brehm, 2004, Guilford Press.

especially because of the influence of the mass media. But other experiences are not common to all, so we should be cautious in making assumptions based on cultural memberships. The information we will examine reflects tendencies and probabilities. It does not tell you about a specific person. Each person is a unique product of many influences, a member of a variety of groups.

Language Differences in the Classroom

In the classroom, quite a bit happens through language. In this section, we will examine two kinds of language differences—dialect differences and bilingualism.

A **dialect** is any variety of a language spoken by a particular group. Eugene Garcia (2002) defines a dialect as "a regional variation of language characterized by distinct grammar, vocabulary, and pronunciation" (p. 218). The dialect is part of the group's collective identity. Actually, every person reading this book speaks at least one dialect, maybe more, because there is no one absolute standard English. The English language has several dialects, for example Australian, Canadian, British, and American. Within each of these dialects are variations. A few examples for American English are Southern, Bostonian, Cajun, and African American Vernacular (Garcia, 2002).

Dialects differ in their rules about pronunciation, grammar, and vocabulary, but it is important to remember that these differences are not errors. Each dialect is logical, complex, and rule-governed. An example of this is the use of the double negative. In many versions of American English, the double negative construction, such as "I don't have no more," is incorrect. But in many dialects, such as some varieties of African American Vernacular English, and in other languages (for instance, Russian, French, Spanish, and Hungarian), the double negative is part of the grammatical rules. To say "I don't want anything" in Spanish, you must literally say, "I don't want nothing," or "*No quiero nada.*"

Dialects and Teaching.   Although the various dialects of a language may be equally logical, complex, and rule-governed, should teachers show respect for the dialect and make learning easier for children by teaching in their dialect? To do this would rob children of the opportunity to learn the speech needed to take advantage of many social and occupational opportunities as adults. Moving between two speech forms is called **code switching,** something we all have learned to do. Sometimes the code is formal speech for educational or professional communication. Sometimes the code is informal for talk among friends and family. Sometimes the codes are different dialects. Even young children recognize variations in codes. Lisa Delpit (1995) describes the reaction of one of her first-grade students to her very first reading lesson. After she carefully recited the memorized introduction from the teacher's manual, a student raised his hand and asked, "Teacher, how come you talkin' like a white person? You talkin' just like my momma talk when she get on the phone."

The best teaching approach seems to be to focus on understanding the children and accepting their dialects as valid and correct language systems, but to teach formal English (or whatever the dominant language is in your country) as an alternative. Learning formal speech is easy for most children whose original language is a dialect, as long as they have good models. How can teachers cope with linguistic diversity in the classroom? First, they can be sensitive to their own possible negative stereotypes about children who speak a different dialect. Taylor (1983) found that teachers who held negative attitudes toward "black English" gave lower ratings for reading comprehension to students using that dialect, even when the accuracy of the students' performance was the same as that of speakers of formal English. Second, principals and teachers can ensure comprehension by repeating instructions using different words and by asking students to paraphrase instructions or give examples. The Theory into Action Guidelines give more ideas.

THEORY INTO ACTION GUIDELINES
Dialects

1. Become familiar with features of the students' dialect. This will allow you to understand students better and to distinguish a reading miscue (a noncomprehension feature) from a comprehension error. Students should not be interrupted during the oral reading process. Correction of comprehension features is best done after the reading segment.

2. Allow students to listen to a passage or story first. This can be done in two ways: (a) finish the story and then ask comprehension questions, or (b) interrupt the story at key comprehension segments and ask students to predict the outcome.

3. Use predictable stories, which can be familiar episodes in literature, music, or history. They can be original works or experiential readers.

4. Use visual aids to enhance comprehension. Visual images, whether pictures or words, will aid word recognition and comprehension.

5. Use "cloze procedure" deletions to focus on vocabulary and meaning. Cloze procedures are selected deletions of words from a passage in order to focus on a specific text feature. *Examples:* (a) The little red hen found an ear of corn. The little red _____ said, "Who will dry the ear of _____?" (vocabulary focus) (b) Today I feel like a (*noun*). (grammar focus) (c) There was a (*pain*) in the pit of his stomach. (semantic focus)

6. Allow students to retell the story or passage in various speech styles. Have students select different people to whom they would like to retell the story (family member, principal, friend), and assist them in selecting synonyms most appropriate to each audience. This allows both teacher and student to become language authorities.

7. Integrate reading, speaking, and writing skills whenever possible.

8. Use the computer (if available) as a time-on-task exercise. The microcomputer can effectively assist in teaching the reading techniques of skimming (general idea), scanning (focused reference), reading for comprehension (mastery of total message), and critical reading (inference and evaluation).

9. Teach students directly how to switch between home and school dialects.

10. Give practice with feedback and correction in using school dialect. All learning takes practice.

Sources: From Christine I. *Bennett, Comprehensive Multicultural Education: Theory and Practice, 6/e.* Published by Allyn & Bacon, Boston, MA. Copyright © 2007 by Pearson Education. Adapted by permission of the publisher. Ogbu, J. U. (1999). Beyond language: Ebonics, proper English, and identity in a Black-American speech community. *American Educational Research Journal, 36,* p. 178. Reprinted by permission.

Bilingualism.   The topic of **bilingualism** sparks heated debates and touches many emotions. One reason is the changing demographics mentioned earlier in this chapter. About 18% of the U.S. population speaks a language other than English at home—half of these families speak Spanish. In the past 10 years, there has been a 65% increase in the number of Spanish-speaking students and almost a 100% increase in students who speak Asian languages. In some states, almost 25% of all students speak a first language other than English—usually Spanish (Gersten, 1996a). Right now, there is one qualified teacher for every 100 English language learners (Hawkins, 2004). As a principal, you should be aware that there are a number of misconceptions about becoming bilingual; see Table 2.1 for a few.

Benefits of Bilingualism.   There is no cognitive penalty for children who learn and speak two languages. In fact, there are benefits. Higher degrees of bilingualism are

TABLE 2.1   Myths about Bilingual Students

In the following table, L1 means the original language and L2 means the second language.

Myth	Truth
Learning a second language (L2) takes little time and effort.	Learning English as a second language takes 2–3 years for oral and 5–7 years for academic language use.
All language skills (listening, speaking, reading, writing) transfer from L1 to L2.	Reading is the skill that transfers most readily.
Code switching is an indication of a language disorder.	Code switching indicates high-level language skills in both L1 and L2.
All bilinguals easily maintain both languages.	It takes great effort and attention to maintain high-level skills in both languages.
Children do not lose their first language.	Loss of L1 and underdevelopment of L2 are problems for second language learners (semilingual in L1 and L2).
Exposure to English is sufficient for L2 learning.	To learn L2, students need to have a reason to communicate, access to English speakers, interaction, support, feedback, and time.
To learn English, students' parents need to speak only English at home.	Children need to use both languages in many contexts.
Reading in L1 is detrimental to learning English.	Literacy-rich environments in either L1 or L2 support development of necessary prereading skills.
Language disorders must be identified by tests in English.	Children must be tested in both L1 and L2 to determine language disorders.

Source: From Alejandro E. Brice, *The Hispanic Child: Speech, Language, Culture, and Education.* Published by Allyn & Bacon, Boston, MA. Copyright © 2002 Pearson Education. Reprinted by permission of the publisher.

correlated with increased cognitive abilities in such areas as concept formation, creativity, and cognitive flexibility. In addition, these children have more advanced awareness about language; for example, they are more likely to notice grammar errors. These findings seem to hold as long as there is no stigma attached to being bilingual and as long as children are not expected to abandon their first language to learn the second (Bialystok , 2001; Bialystok, Majumder, & Martin, 2003; Galambos & Goldin-Meadow, 1990; Hamers & Blanc, 2000; Ricciardelli, 1992). In addition, speaking two languages is an asset for those graduates entering the business world (Mears, 1998).

Even though the advantages of bilingualism seem clear, many children and adults are losing their **heritage language.** In a large survey of eighth- and ninth-grade first- and second-generation immigrant students in Miami and San Diego, Portes and Hao (1998) found that only 16% had retained the ability to speak their heritage language well. And 72% said they preferred to speak English. The languages of Native Americans are disappearing as well. Only about one-third still exist, and nine out of ten of those are no longer spoken by the children (Krauss, 1992). Rather than losing one language to gain another, the goal for these children could be to become **balanced bilinguals**—equally fluent in both languages (Gonzalez, 1999).

Second Language Learning. Two terms that you will see associated with bilingualism are **English language learners (ELLs)**, describing students whose primary or heritage language is not English, and **English as a second language (ESL)** classrooms where these students learn English. The earlier people learn a second language, the more their pronunciation is near-native. After adolescence it is difficult to learn a new language without speaking with an accent (Anderson & Graham, 1994). Age is a factor in learning language, but not because of any critical period for language; adults can and do learn new languages (Marinova-Todd, Marshall, & Snow, 2000). Even overhearing a language as a child, without actually learning the language, can improve later learning. After studying college students learning Spanish, Terry Au and colleagues (2002) conclude that, "Although waiting until adulthood to learn a language almost guarantees a bad accent, having overheard the target language during childhood seems to lessen this predicament substantially" (p. 242). So the best time to acquire two languages on your own through exposure (and to learn native pronunciation for both languages) is early childhood.

Proficiency in a second language has two separate aspects: face-to-face communication (known as "contextualized language skills") and academic uses of language like reading and doing grammar exercises ("decontextualized language skills") (Hakuta, 2000; Hakuta, Butler, & Witt, 2000). It takes students about two years in a good program to be able to communicate face-to-face in a second language, but mastering decontextualized, academic language skills in the new language takes five to seven years. So students who seem in conversation to "know" a second language may still have great difficulty with complex schoolwork in that language (Bialystok, 2001; Bialystok, Majumder, & Martin, 2003; Cummins, 1994). And the situation can be made even more complex if students have to navigate competing curricula. The Principal's Perspective tells how a real principal improved reading instruction in her school for ESL students.

A Principal's Perspective

D. R. served approximately 720 students in preschool through fourth grades, including 65 special needs students and a widely diverse population of ESL students. Even before the No Child Left Behind mandates, there had been an ongoing district-wide goal to increase reading achievement scores at all grade levels and among all students. D. R. dedicated much of her first year as principal to carefully observing and evaluating her building's reading program. She was perplexed to find that, while the students in general were making significant gains in reading achievement, subgroups of students, specifically those in ESL and special education programs, were lagging in their performance scores.

After meeting with teachers she discovered an incompatibility in reading instruction for these students, referred to by Jim Shipley and associates (2000) as "random acts of improvement." Regular classroom teachers were trained in and used one particular research-based reading program while teachers of exceptional children used something different. The result was inconsistent and unsupported reading instruction for these children as they moved between their included classroom and the resource room.

Without declaring one program superior to the other, the principal emphasized the need for consistency in reading instruction and clarified that all teachers in the school must teach the same reading strategies. Rather than retraining 45 classroom teachers already using an identical program, the most cost-effective and efficient decision was to train and support all special needs teachers in the predominant reading framework. Even though it is widely accepted that no one set of teaching techniques will be effective for every exceptional student, maintaining alignment in instruction and assessment is critical to the success of emergent readers, especially those moving between regular and resource classrooms.

For more ideas, see the following resources:

Shipley, J., & Wescott, M. C. (2000). *Systems check: School improvement resource guide.* Seminole, FL: Jim Shipley & Associates.

Literacy Collaborative at the Ohio State University. www.lcosu.org/ (last visited October 8, 2007).

Research on Bilingual Programs.   It is difficult to separate politics from practice in the debate about bilingual education. It is clear that high-quality bilingual education programs can have positive results. Students improve in the subjects taught in their native languages, in their mastery of English, and in self-esteem as well (Gersten, 2006; Hakuta & Gould, 1987; Wright & Taylor, 1995). ESL programs seem to have positive effects on reading comprehension (Fitzgerald, 1995; Vaughn et al., 2006). But attention today is shifting from debate about general approaches to a focus on effective teaching strategies. As you will see many times in this book, the combination of clarity of learning goals, direct instruction in needed skills (including phonics, vocabulary, comprehension and story retelling, learning strategies and tactics), teacher- or peer-guided practice leading to independent practice, authentic and engaging tasks, interactions and conversations that are academically focused, and warm encouragement from the teacher seems to be effective. If both languages can be integrated into the classroom, ELL students may participate more actively, learn English faster, and be less frustrated (Crawford, 1996; Gersten, 1996b; Vaughn et al., 2006). Table 2.2 is a set of constructs for promoting learning and language acquisition that capture many of these ideas for effective instruction.

TABLE 2.2   Ideas for Promoting Learning and Language Acquisition

Effective teaching for students in bilingual and ESL classrooms combines many strategies—direct instruction, mediation, coaching, feedback, modeling, encouragement, challenge, and authentic activities.

1. Structures, frameworks, scaffolds, and strategies
   - Provide support to students by "thinking aloud," building on and clarifying input of students
   - Use visual organizers, story maps, or other aids to help students organize and relate information

2. Relevant background knowledge and key vocabulary concepts
   - Provide adequate background knowledge to students and informally assess whether students have background knowledge
   - Focus on key vocabulary words and use consistent language
   - Incorporate students' primary language meaningfully

3. Mediation/feedback
   - Give feedback that focuses on meaning, not grammar, syntax, or pronunciation
   - Give frequent and comprehensible feedback
   - Provide students with prompts or strategies
   - Ask questions that press students to clarify or expand on initial statements
   - Provide activities and tasks that students can complete
   - Indicate to students when they are successful

   - Assign activities that are reasonable, avoiding undue frustration
   - Allow use of native language responses (when context is appropriate)
   - Be sensitive to common problems in second language acquisition

4. Involvement
   - Ensure active involvement of all students, including low-performing students
   - Foster extended discourse

5. Challenge
   - Implicit (cognitive challenge, use of higher-order questions)
   - Explicit (high but reasonable expectations)

6. Respect for—and responsiveness to—cultural and personal diversity
   - Show respect for students as individuals, respond to things students say, show respect for culture and family, and possess knowledge of cultural diversity
   - Incorporate students' experiences into writing and language arts activities
   - Link content to students' lives and experiences to enhance understanding
   - View diversity as an asset, reject cultural deficit notions

Source: From "Literacy Instruction for Language-Minority Students: The Transition Years," by R. Gersten, 1996, *The Elementary School Journal, 96,* pp. 241–242. Copyright © 1996 by the University of Chicago Press. Adapted with permission.

We have touched on a wide range of differences in this chapter. How can schools provide an appropriate education for all their students? One response is to make classrooms compatible with students' cultural heritage. Such a classroom is described as being *culturally compatible* or *culturally inclusive*.

Creating Culturally Inclusive Classrooms

Rosa Hernandez Sheets (2005) uses the term *culturally inclusive* to describe classrooms that provide culturally diverse students equitable access to the teaching–learning process. The goal of creating **culturally inclusive classrooms** is to eliminate racism, classism, and prejudice while adapting the content and methods of instruction to meet the needs of all students. Almost 20 years ago, Roland Tharp (1989) outlined three dimensions of classrooms—social organization, learning styles, and participation structures—that can be tailored to adapt the classroom to the needs of students.

Social Organization

Tharp (1989) states that "a central task of educational design is to make the organization of teaching, learning, and performance compatible with the social structures in which students are most productive, engaged, and likely to learn" (p. 350). Social structure or social organization in this context means the ways people interact to accomplish a particular goal. For example, the social organization of Hawaiian society depends heavily on collaboration and cooperation. Children play together in groups of friends and siblings, with older children often caring for the younger ones. When cooperative work groups of four or five boys and girls were established in Hawaiian classrooms, student learning and participation improved (Okagaki, 2001). The teacher worked intensively with one group while the children in the remaining groups helped each other. But when the same structure was tried in a Navajo classroom, students would not work together. These students are socialized to be more solitary and not to play with the opposite sex. By setting up same-sex working groups of only two or three Navajo students, teachers encouraged them to help each other. If you have students from several cultures, you may need choices and variety in grouping structures.

Tharp's (1989) second classroom dimension that can be tailored to students is learning style—a topic that requires critical analysis.

Learning Styles

To look at **learning styles,** let's consider what Sheets (2005) has to say about teachers who design culturally inclusive classrooms. These teachers (1) recognize the various ways all their students display their capabilities—their cultural *practices* and *values;* (2) respond to students' *preferred styles of learning;* and (3) understand that a particular group's cultural practices, values, and learning preferences *may not apply* to everyone in that group.

Cultural Practices and Values.   Results of some research suggest that Hispanic American students are more oriented toward family and group loyalty. This may mean that these students prefer cooperative activities and dislike being made to compete with fellow students (Garcia, 1992; Vasquez, 1990). Four values shared by many Hispanic students (not all—remember Sheets' third characteristic above) are:

> **Familismo**—tightly knit families. Discussing family problems or business outside the family may be seen as disloyal.
>
> **Simpatia**—value of interpersonal harmony. Assertively voicing personal opinions or arguing may be seen as inappropriate.
>
> **Respecto**—respect for people in authority
>
> **Personalismo**—valuing of close interpersonal relationships; discomfort with distant, cold, professional relationships. (Dingfelder, 2005)

Cultural Differences in Learning Styles.   Learning styles are preferred ways of learning and processing information. The learning styles of many African Americans may be inconsistent with teaching approaches in most schools. Some of the characteristics of this learning style are a visual/global rather than a verbal/analytic approach; a preference for reasoning by inference rather than formal logic; a focus on people and relationships; a preference for energetic involvement in several activities simultaneously rather than routine, step-by-step learning; a tendency to approximate numbers, space, and time; and a greater dependence on nonverbal communication. Students of color who identify with their traditional cultures tend to respond to open-ended questions with more than one answer, as opposed to single, "right" answer questions. Questions that focus on meaning or the "big picture" may be more productive than questions that focus on details (Bennett, 1999; Gay, 2000; Sheets, 2005).

Native Americans also appear to have a more global, visual style of learning. For example, Navajo students prefer hearing a story all the way through to the end before discussing parts of the story. Teachers who stop to ask questions seem odd to these students and interrupt the learning process (Tharp, 1989). Also, these students sometimes show strong preferences for learning privately, through trial and error, rather than having their mistakes made public (Vasquez, 1990).

There has been little research on the learning styles of Asian Americans, perhaps because they are seen as "successful minorities." Some educators suggest that Asian children tend to value teacher approval and to work well in structured, quiet learning environments where there are clear goals and social support (Manning & Baruth, 1996). But there are dangers in stereotyping Asian and Asian American students as quiet, hardworking, and passive. Suzuki (1983) suggests that this practice

> tends to reinforce conformity and stifle creativity. Asian and Pacific American students, therefore, frequently do not develop the ability to assert and express themselves verbally and are channeled in disproportionate numbers into the technical/scientific fields. As a result, many Asian and Pacific American students are overly conforming, and have their academic and social development narrowly circumscribed. (p. 9)

Individual Learning Styles and Preferences.   Since the late 1970s, a great deal has been written about differences in students' **learning preferences** (Dunn & Dunn, 1978, 1987; Dunn & Griggs, 2003; Gregorc, 1982; Keefe, 1982). Learning preferences are often called *learning styles* in these writings, but we believe *preferences* is a more accurate label because it describes preferences for particular learning environments—for example, where, when, with whom, or with what lighting, food, or music you like to study. There are a number of instruments for assessing students' learning preferences: *Learning Style Inventory* (Dunn, Dunn, & Price, 1989), *Learning Styles Inventory* (Kolb, 1985), and the *Learning Style Profile* (Keefe & Monk, 1986). Are these useful tools? The answer is not simple, as you can see in the Point/Counterpoint: "Should Teachers Focus on Students' Learning Styles?"

Misuses and Uses of Learning Styles Research.   In considering this research on learning styles, particularly in relation to cultural groups, you should keep two points in mind. First, the validity of some of the learning styles research has been strongly questioned, as we saw in the Point/Counterpoint. Second, there is a heated debate today about whether identifying ethnic group differences in learning styles and preferences is a dangerous, racist, sexist exercise. In our society we are quick to move from the notion of "difference" to the idea of "deficits" and stereotypes (Gordon, 1991; O'Neil, 1990). If used with caution and common sense, these general guidelines can help teachers be more sensitive to individual and group differences. It is dangerous and incorrect, however, to assume that every individual in a group shares the same learning style. Get to know the individual.

Tharp's (1989) third classroom dimension that can be tailored to students is participation structures.

Participation Structures

The classroom is a special setting for communicating; it has its own set of rules for when, how, to whom, about what subject, and in what manner to use language. To be successful, students must know these communication rules. This is not such an easy task. As class activities change, rules change. Sometimes you have to raise your hand (during the teacher's presentation), but sometimes you don't (during storytime on the rug). Sometimes it is good to ask a question (during discussion), but other times it isn't so good (when the teacher is scolding you). The differing activity rules are called **participation structures.**

Some students are simply better than others at reading the classroom situation because the participation structures of school match the structures they have learned in their middle-class homes. These students often appear to be more competent because they know the unwritten rules. Students from different cultural backgrounds may have learned participation structures that conflict with the behaviors expected in school. For example, one study found that the home conversation style of Hawaiian children is to chime in with contributions to a story. In school, however, this overlapping style is seen as "interrupting." When the teachers in one school learned about these differences and made their reading groups more like their students' home conversation groups, the young Hawaiian children in their classes improved in reading (Au, 1980; Tharp, 1989). Another example, researchers found that Pueblo Indian

POINT/COUNTERPOINT

Should Teachers Focus on Students' Learning Styles?

POINT

Teaching to different learning styles has no strong research basis.

Tests of learning style have been strongly criticized for lacking evidence of reliability and validity (Snider, 1990; Wintergerst, DeCapua, & Itzen, 2001). In fact, in an extensive examination of learning styles instruments, researchers at the Learning Skills Research Centre in England concluded, "With regard to Dunn and Dunn (Section 3.2), Gregorc (Section 3.1) and Riding (Section 4.1), our examination of the reliability and validity of their learning style instruments strongly suggests that they should not be used in education or business" (Coffield et al., 2004, p. 127). As to most of the other research on learning preferences, even though results of some studies indicate that students learn more when they study in their preferred settings and manners (Dunn & Griggs, 2003), generally there is little hard evidence; most researchers are skeptical about the value of learning preferences. "The reason researchers roll their eyes at learning styles research is the utter failure to find that assessing children's learning styles and matching to instructional methods has any effect on their learning" (Stahl, 2002, p. 99).

Why are these ideas so popular? Part of the answer is, "A thriving commercial industry has also been built to offer advice to teachers, tutors and managers on learning styles, and much of it consists of inflated claims and sweeping conclusions which go beyond the current knowledge base and the specific recommendations of particular theorists" (Coffield et al., 2004, p. 127). The same is true for the claims that we should teach to both sides of the brain. Recent research on brain functioning makes it clear that "the practice of teaching to 'different sides of the brain' is not supported by the neuroscientific research" (Byrnes & Fox, 1998, p. 310). So beware of educational approaches based on simplistic views of brain functioning, what Keith Stanovich (1998) has called "the left-brain-right-brain nonsense that has inundated education through workshops, in-services, and the trade publications" (p. 420).

COUNTERPOINT

Some differences in learning styles do matter.

There is one learning styles distinction that has research support. Richard Mayer (e.g., Mayer & Massa, 2003) has been studying the distinction between visual and verbal learners, with a focus on learning from computer-based multimedia. He is finding that there is a visualizer–verbalizer dimension and that it has three facets: *cognitive spatial ability* (low or high), *cognitive style* (visualizer vs. verbalizer), and *learning preference* (verbal learner vs. visual learner), as shown in Table 2.3. So the picture is more complex

TABLE 2.3   Three Facets of the Visualizer–Verbalizer Dimension

Facet	Types of learners	Definition
Cognitive ability	High spatial ability	High proficiency in creating, holding, and manipulating spatial representations.
	Low spatial ability	Low proficiency in creating, holding, and manipulating spatial representations.
Cognitive style	Visualizer	Uses visual modes of thinking.
	Verbalizer	Uses verbal modes of thinking.
Learning preference	Visual learner	Prefers instruction involving pictures.
	Verbal learner	Prefers instruction involving words.

(Continued)

POINT/COUNTERPOINT   Continued

than simply being a visual or a verbal learner. A student might have a preference for learning with pictures, but low spatial ability could make using pictures to learn less effective. These differences can be reliably measured, but research has not identified the effects of teaching to these styles; certainly presenting information in multiple modalities might be useful.

Schools can make learning options available. Having quiet, private corners as well as large tables for working; comfortable cushions as well as straight chairs; brightly lighted desks along with darker areas; headphones for listening to music as well as earplugs; structured as well as open-ended assignments; information available on films and tapes as well as in books. All these options will allow students to work and learn in their preferred mode at least some of the time. Will making these alterations lead to greater learning? Here the answer is not clear. Very bright students appear to need less structure and prefer quiet, solitary learning (Torrance, 1986) and the visual–verbal distinction seems to be valid.

So before you encourage your teachers to accommodate all your students' learning styles, remember that students, especially younger ones, may not be the best judges of how they should learn. Preference for a particular style does not guarantee that using the style will be effective. Sometimes students, particularly poorer students, prefer what is easy and comfortable; real learning can be hard and uncomfortable. Sometimes students prefer to learn in a certain way because they have no alternatives; it is the only way they know how to approach the task. These students may benefit from developing new—and perhaps more effective—ways to learn.

---

students participated twice as much in classes where teachers waited longer to react. Waiting longer also helps girls to participate more freely in math and science classes (Grossman & Grossman, 1994).

Sources of misunderstanding can be very subtle. The families of racial and ethnic minority students often have to be vigilant about discrimination to protect their children. Teachers may unintentionally offend these families if they are not sensitive to possible messages of discrimination. For example, Carol Orange (2005) described a teacher who sent home a holiday worksheet that featured an alphabetical list of all the students in the class. Three students' names were not in the typed list, but were handwritten, out of order, and on the side of the sheet. Two of these students were Latino and one was African American. The mother of the African American student was very upset that her son was truly "marginalized" (written in the margins) on the list. The reason was that those three students were added to the class later in the year, after the list was set up. But the teacher could have avoided this insult (unintended on her part) by redoing the list to give every student a place—a small but important symbol that she valued each one of them.

What should principals and teachers do? Especially in the early grades, you and your teachers should make communication rules for activities clear and explicit. Do not assume students know what to do. Use cues to signal students when changes occur. Explain and demonstrate appropriate behavior. We have seen teachers show young children how to "talk in your inside voice" or "whisper so you won't disturb others." One teacher said and then demonstrated, "If you have to interrupt me while I'm working with other children, stand quietly beside me until I can help you."

Culturally Relevant Pedagogy

In the last twenty years, several researchers have focused on teachers who are especially successful with students of color and students in poverty (Bennett, 1999; Delpit, 1995; Ladson-Billings, 1994, 1995; Moll, Amanti, Neff, & Gonzalez, 1992). For example, for three years Gloria Ladson-Billings (1990, 1992, 1995) studied excellent teachers in a California school district that served an African American community. Ladson-Billings was able to examine in depth eight of the nine teachers who were nominated by *both parents and principals.* Based on her research, she developed a **culturally relevant pedagogy** that encompasses but goes beyond considerations of sociolinguistics or social organizations to include three elements: Students must

1. *Experience academic success.* "Despite the current social inequities and hostile classroom environments, students must develop their academic skills. The ways those skills are developed may vary, but all students need literacy, numeracy, technological, social, and political skills in order to be active participants in a democracy" (Ladson-Billings, 1995, p. 160).

2. *Develop/maintain their cultural competence.* "Culturally relevant teachers utilize students' culture as a vehicle for learning" (Ladson-Billings, 1995, p. 161). For example, one teacher brought in a community expert known for her sweet potato pies to work with students. Follow-up lessons included investigations of George Washington Carver's sweet potato research, numerical analyses of taste tests, marketing plans for selling pies, and research on the educational preparation needed to become a chef.

3. *Develop a critical consciousness to challenge the status quo.* Excellent teachers help students "develop a broader sociopolitical consciousness that allows them to critique the social norms, values, mores, and institutions that produce and maintain social inequities" (Ladson-Billings, 1995, p. 162). For example, in one school students mobilized to investigate the funding formulas that allowed middle-class students to have newer books, wrote letters to the newspaper editor to challenge these inequities, and updated their texts with current information from other sources.

Lisa Delpit (2003) describes three steps for teaching students of color that are consistent with culturally relevant pedagogy: (1) Teachers must be convinced of the inherent intellectual capability, humanity, and spiritual character of their students—they must believe in the children. There are many examples around the country of schools where low-income African American students are reading well above grade level and doing advanced math. When scores are low, the fault is not in the students but in their education. (2) Teachers must fight the foolishness that test scores or scripted lessons make for good learning. Delpit says that successful instruction is "constant, rigorous, integrated across disciplines, connected to students' lived cultures, connected to their intellectual legacies, engaging, and designed for critical thinking and problem solving that is useful beyond the classroom" (p. 18). (3) Teachers must learn who their children are and the legacies they bring. Then students can explore their own intellectual legacies and understand the important reasons for academic, social, physical, and moral excellence—not just to "get a job" but also "for our community, for your ancestors, for your descendents" (p. 19). In the past, discussions of teaching students from racial, ethnic, or language minority groups have focused on remediating problems or overcoming perceived deficits. But thinking today emphasizes teaching to the strengths and the resilience of these students. See the Theory into Action Guidelines for more ideas about creating culturally compatible classrooms.

THEORY INTO ACTION GUIDELINES
Culturally Compatible Classrooms

Experiment with different grouping arrangements to encourage cooperation.

Examples
1. Try "study buddies" and pairs.
2. Organize heterogeneous groups of four or five.
3. Establish larger teams for older students.

Provide a range of ways to learn material to accommodate a range of learning styles.

Examples
1. Give students verbal materials at different reading levels.
2. Offer visual materials—charts, diagrams, models.
3. Provide tapes for listening and viewing.
4. Set up activities and projects.

Teach classroom procedures directly, even ways of doing things that you think everyone will know.

Examples
1. Tell students how to get the teacher's attention.
2. Explain when and how to interrupt the teacher if students need help.
3. Show which materials students can take and which require permission.
4. Demonstrate acceptable ways to disagree with or challenge another student.

Learn the meaning of different behaviors for your students.

Examples
1. Ask students how they feel when you correct or praise them. What gives them this message?
2. Talk to family and community members and other teachers to discover the meaning of expressions, gestures, or other responses that are unfamiliar to you.

Emphasize meaning in teaching.

Examples
1. Make sure students understand what they read.
2. Try storytelling and other modes that don't require written materials.
3. Use examples that relate abstract concepts to everyday experiences; for instance, relate negative numbers to being overdrawn in your checkbook.

Get to know the customs, traditions, and values of your students.

Examples
1. Use holidays as a chance to discuss the origins and meaning of traditions.
2. Analyze different traditions for common themes.
3. Attend community fairs and festivals.

Help students detect racist messages.

Examples
1. Analyze curriculum materials for biases.
2. Make students "bias detectives," reporting comments from the media.
3. Discuss the ways that students communicate biased messages about each other and what should be done when this happens.
4. Discuss expressions of prejudice such as anti-Semitism.

For more ideas, see the Education Alliance at Brown University: www.alliance.brown.edu/tdl/tl-strategies/crt-principles.shtml

Gender Differences in the Classroom

The word *gender* usually refers to traits and behaviors that a particular culture judges to be appropriate for males and for females. Through their interactions with family, peers, teachers, and the environment in general, children begin to form **gender schemas,** or organized networks of knowledge about what it means to be male or female. These schemas help the children make sense of the world and guide their behavior. So a young girl whose schema for "girls" includes "girls play with dolls and not with trucks" or "girls can't be scientists" will pay attention to, remember, and interact more with dolls than trucks, and she may avoid science activities (Liben & Signorella, 1993; Martin & Little, 1990). In contrast to gender, *sex* refers to biological differences (Brannon, 2002; Deaux, 1993). Are there biological differences in mental abilities? Is gender discrimination a problem in schools? We will consider each question.

Differences in Mental Abilities

Only 23% of the scientists and engineers and just 10% of the physicists in the United States are women, even though women earn about half of the bachelor's degrees in chemistry, biology, and mathematics and about 20% of the bachelor's degrees in physics and engineering (Angier & Chang, 2005; Bleeker & Jacobs, 2004). Women earn 30% more bachelor's degrees overall than men and 50% more master's degrees. And African American women now earn twice as many college degrees as African American men (Hulbert, 2005). But let's not overlook the boys. The International Comparisons in Fourth-Grade Reading Literacy: Findings from the Progress in International Reading Literacy Study (Mullis, Martin, Gonzalez, & Kennedy, 2003) revealed that in thirty-four countries, fourth-grade boys scored below girls in reading literacy. Are all these differences between men and women due to ability, interest, culture, social pressure, discrimination, or some other factor? Let's see if we can make sense of this issue.

From infancy through the preschool years, most studies find few differences between boys and girls in overall mental and motor development or in specific abilities. However, during the school years, scores on some tests of specific abilities show sex differences. For example, from elementary through high school, girls score higher than boys on tests of reading and writing, and fewer girls require remediation in reading (Halpern, 2000; Hyde, 2005; Spelke, 2005). But academically gifted boys in the United States perform better than girls on advanced mathematics tests. In 2001, twice as many boys as girls scored over 700 on the math SATs, but boys also were more likely than girls to get all the answers wrong (Angier & Chang, 2005). In fact, the scores of males tend to be more variable in general, so there are more males than females with very high *and* very low scores on tests (Berk, 2005; Willingham & Cole, 1997). There also are more boys than girls diagnosed with learning disabilities, attention deficit hyperactive disorder (ADHD), and autism. Diane Halpern (2004) summarized the research:

> Females and males show different average patterns of academic achievement and scores on cognitive ability tests. Females obtain higher grades in school, score much higher on tests of writing and content-area tests on which the questions are similar to material that was learned in school, attain a majority of college degrees, and are closing the gap in

many careers that were traditionally male. By contrast, males score higher on standardized tests of mathematics and science that are not directly tied to their school curriculum, show a large advantage on visuospatial tests (especially those that involve judgments of velocity and navigation through three-dimensional space), and are much more knowledgeable about geography and politics. (p. 135)

There is a caution, however. In most studies of sex differences, race and socioeconomic status are not taken into account. When racial groups are studied separately, African American females outperform African American males in high school mathematics; there is little or no difference in the performance of Asian American girls and boys in math or science (Grossman & Grossman, 1994; Yee, 1992). And girls in general tend to get higher grades than boys in mathematics classes (Halpern, 2004). Also, international studies of fifteen-year-olds in forty-one countries show no sex differences in mathematics for half of the countries tested. In fact, in Iceland, girls significantly outperformed boys on all the math tests, just as they usually do on their national math exams (Angier & Chang, 2005).

What is the basis for the differences? The answers are complex. For example, males on average are better on tests that require mental rotation of a figure in space, prediction of the trajectories of moving objects, and navigating. Some researchers argue that evolution has favored these skills in males (Buss, 1995; Geary, 2006), but others relate these skills to males' more active play styles and to their participation in athletics (Linn & Hyde, 1989; Newcombe & Baenninger, 1990; Stumpf, 1995). The cross-cultural comparisons suggest that much of the difference in mathematics comes from learning, not biology. And studies showing that adults rated a math paper attributed to "John T. McKay" a full point higher on a 5-point scale than the same paper attributed to "Joan T. McKay" suggests that gender discrimination plays a role as well (Angier & Chang, 2005). This brings us to our next question: Is gender discrimination a problem in schools?

Gender Discrimination in Classrooms

There has been quite a bit of research on teachers' treatment of male and female students. One of the best-documented findings of the past 25 years is that teachers interact more with boys than with girls. This is true from preschool to college. Teachers ask more questions of males, give males more feedback (praise, criticism, and correction), and give more specific and valuable comments to boys. As girls move through the grades, they have less and less to say. By the time students reach college, men are twice as likely to initiate comments as women (Bailey, 1993; Sadker & Sadker, 2000; Wingate, 1986). The effect of these differences is that from preschool through college, girls on the average receive 1,800 fewer hours of attention and instruction than boys (Sadker, Sadker, & Klein, 1991). These differences are not evenly distributed. Some boys, generally high-achieving white students, receive more than their share. Minority-group boys, like girls, tend to receive much less attention from teachers.

Stereotypes are perpetuated in many ways, some obvious, some subtle. Guidance counselors, parents, and teachers often do not protest at all when a bright girl says she doesn't want to take any more math or science courses, but when a boy of the same ability wants to forget about math or science, they will object (Sadker & Sadker, 2000). But there are some aspects of school that may be biased against boys. For example, following rules and being neat are rewarded, and these behaviors are more often associated with girls. In addition, a majority of elementary teachers are women (DeZolt & Hull, 2001). It is a challenge to make schools responsive to both males and females.

Eliminating Gender Bias

There is some evidence that teachers treat girls and boys differently in mathematics classes. For example, some elementary school teachers spend more academic time with boys in math and with girls in reading. In one study, high school geometry teachers directed most of their questions to boys, even though the girls asked questions and volunteered answers more often. Several researchers have found that some teachers tend to accept wrong answers from girls but tell boys, in effect, to "try harder—you can do it." These messages, repeated time and again, can convince girls that they just aren't cut out for mathematics (Horgan, 1995). The activities used to teach math may make a difference as well. Elementary school girls may do better in math if they learn in cooperative as opposed to competitive activities (Fennema & Peterson, 1988). Certainly it makes sense to balance both cooperative and competitive approaches so that students who learn better each way have equal opportunities. The Theory into Action Guidelines on the next page provide ideas for your school about how to avoid sexism.

Sexual Identity

Sexual identity includes gender identity, gender-role behaviors, and sexual orientation (Patterson, 1995). *Gender identity* is a person's self-identification as male or female. *Gender-role behaviors* are those behaviors and characteristics that the culture associates with each gender, and *sexual orientation* involves the person's choice of a sexual partner. Relations among these three elements are complex. For example, a woman may identify herself as a female (gender-identity), but behave in ways that are not consistent with the gender role (play football), and may be heterosexual, bisexual, or homosexual in her orientation. So sexual identity is a complicated construction of beliefs, attitudes, and behaviors.

Sexual Orientation.   During adolescence, about 8% of boys and 6% of girls report engaging in some same-sex activity or feeling strong attractions to same-sex individuals. Males are more likely than females to experiment with same-sex partners as adolescents, but females are more likely to experiment later, often in college. Fewer adolescents actually have a homosexual or bisexual orientation—about 4% of adolescents identify themselves as gay (males who chose male partners), lesbian (females who chose female partners), or bisexual (people who have partners of both sexes). This number increases to about 8% for adults (Savin-Williams & Diamond, 2004; Steinberg, 2005).

Scientists debate the origins of homosexuality. Most of the research has been with men, so less is known about women. Evidence so far suggests that both biological and

THEORY INTO ACTION GUIDELINES

Avoiding Sexism

Check to see if textbooks and other materials you are using present an honest view of the options open to both males and females.

Examples

1. Are both males and females portrayed in traditional and nontraditional roles at work, at leisure, and at home?
2. Discuss your analyses with teachers, and ask them to help you find sex role biases in other materials—magazine advertising, TV programs, news reporting, for example.

Watch for any unintended biases in your teachers' classroom practices.

Examples

1. Do teachers group students by sex for certain activities? Is the grouping appropriate?

2. Do teachers call on one sex or the other for certain answers—boys for math and girls for poetry, for example?

Look for ways in which your school may be limiting the options open to male or female students.

Examples

1. What advice is given by guidance counselors to students in course and career decisions?
2. Is there a good sports program for both girls and boys?

For lessons that identify sexism in schools, see www.tolerance.org/teach/activities/activity.jsp?ar=299

---

social factors are involved, with biology probably playing the larger role. For example, sexual orientation is more similar for identical twins than for fraternal twins, but not all identical twins have the same sexual orientation (Berk, 2007). There are quite a few models describing the development of sexual orientation. Most focus on how adolescents develop an identity as gay, lesbian, or bisexual. Generally, the models include the following or similar stages (Berk, 2007; Yarhouse, 2001):

- Feeling different—beginning around age six the child may be less interested in the activities of other children who are the same sex. Some children may find this difference troubling and fear being "found out." Others do not experience these anxieties.
- Feeling confused—in adolescence, as they feel attractions for the same sex, students may be confused, upset, lonely, unsure of what to do. They may lack role models and try to change to activities and dating patterns that fit heterosexual stereotypes.
- Acceptance—As young adults, many of these youth sort through the identity issues and identify themselves as gay, lesbian, or bisexual. They may or may not make their sexual orientation public, but might share the information with a few friends.

The problem with these phase models of identity development is that the identity achieved is assumed to be final. Actually, newer models emphasize that sexual orientation can be flexible, complex, and multifaceted; it may change over the lifetime. For example, people may have dated or married opposite-sex partners at one point in their lives, but have same-sex attractions or partners later in their lives or vice versa (Garnets, 2002).

Teachers and administrators are seldom the first people to hear about the adolescent's sexual identity concerns. But if a student does seek you out, Table 2.4 has some ideas for reaching out.

TABLE 2.4   Reaching Out to Help Students with Sexual Identity

---

These ideas come from the *Attic Speakers Bureau,* a program of The Attic Youth Center, where trained peer educators reach out to youth and youth-service providers in schools, organizations, and health-care facilities.

Reaching Out

If a lesbian, gay, bisexual, or transgender youth or a youth questioning his or her own sexual orientation should come to you directly for assistance, remember the following simple, 5-point plan:

LISTEN It seems obvious, but the best thing that you can do in the beginning is allow that individual to vent and express what is going on in his or her life.

AFFIRM Tell them, "You are not alone."—this is crucial. A lot of l/g/b/t/q youth feel isolated and lack peers with whom they can discuss issues around sexual orientation. Letting them know that there are others dealing with the same issues is invaluable. This statement is also important because it does not involve a judgment call on your part.

REFER You do not have to be the expert. A referral to someone who is trained to deal with these issues is a gift you are giving to that student, not a dismissal of responsibility.

ADDRESS Deal with harassers—do not overlook issues of verbal or physical harassment around sexual orientation. It is important to create and maintain an environment where all youth feel comfortable and welcome.

FOLLOW-UP Be sure to check in with the individual to see if the situation has improved and if there is anything further you may be able to do.

There are also some things that you as an individual can do to better serve l/g/b/t/q youth and youth dealing with issues around sexual orientation:

■ Work on your own comfortability around issues of sexual orientation and sexuality.

■ Get training on how to present information on sexual orientation effectively.

■ Dispel myths around sexual orientation by knowing facts and sharing that information.

■ Work on setting aside your own personal biases to better serve students dealing with issues around sexual orientation and sexuality.

Source: From Figure 3. Copyright © The Attic Speakers Bureau and Carrie E. Jacobs, Ph.D. Reprinted with permission of Carrie E. Jacobs.

The most important individual differences for schools are the differences in students' academic abilities. These also are complex and often misunderstood. We turn to these differences in the next chapter.

Summary

Statistics point to increasing cultural diversity in American society. Everyone is a member of many cultural groups, defined in terms of geographic region, nationality, ethnicity, race, gender, social class, and religion. Membership in a particular group does not determine behavior or values but makes certain values and kinds of behavior more likely. Wide variations exist within each group. Compared to students in poverty, however, students of all ethnic groups from wealthier homes show higher average levels of achievement on test scores and stay in school longer. Nevertheless, many students at risk for academic failure survive and thrive when teachers and schools support resilience.

Language differences among students include dialects, bilingualism, and culture-based communication styles. Dialects are not inferior languages and should be respected, but formal English should be taught for academic contexts. Bilingual students may have some degree of limitation in English proficiency, and also must often struggle with social adjustment problems relating to biculturalism. While there is much debate over the best way to help bilingual students master English, studies show it is best if they are not forced to abandon their first language. The more proficient students are in their first language, the faster they will master the second. Mastering academic language skills in any new language takes five to seven years.

Learning preferences are individual preferences for particular learning modes and environments. Some of the most promising research is on verbalizer versus visualizer learning approaches. Even though cognitive styles and learning preferences are not related to intelligence or effort, they may affect school performance, but not all measures of learning styles and preferences are valid or reliable. Beware.

Culturally inclusive classrooms are free of racism, sexism, and ethnic prejudice and provide equal educational opportunities for all students. Dimensions of classroom life that can be modified to that end are social organization, learning-style formats, and participation structures. Teachers, however, must avoid stereotypes of culture-based learning styles and must not assume that every individual in a group shares the same style. Communication may break down in classrooms because of differences in sociolinguistic styles and skills. Teachers can directly teach appropriate participation structures and be sensitive to culture-based communication rules. To help create compatible multicultural classrooms, teachers must know and respect all their students, have high expectations of them, and teach them what they need to know to succeed. Culturally relevant pedagogy ensures that students experience academic challenge and success, maintain their cultural competence, and develop a critical consciousness to challenge the status quo.

Educational equity for females and males is also an issue. Research shows that gender-role stereotyping begins in the preschool years and continues through gender bias in the school curriculum and sex discrimination in the classroom. Teachers often unintentionally perpetuate these problems. Some measures on IQ and SAT tests have shown small sex-linked differences, especially in spatial abilities and mathematics. Research on the causes of these differences has been inconclusive, except to indicate that academic socialization and teachers' treatment of male and female students in mathematics classes do play a role. Principals and teachers can use many strategies for reducing gender bias as well as providing support for students who are dealing with questions of sexual orientation.

KEY TERMS

balanced bilingual (37)
bilingualism (36)
code switching (34)
culturally inclusive classroom (40)
culturally relevant pedagogy (45)

dialect (34)
English as a second language (ESL) (37)
English language learners (ELLs) (37)
gender schemas (47)
heritage language (37)

learning preferences (42)
learning styles (40)
participation structures (42)
resilience (29)
sexual identity (49)

DEVELOPING YOUR PORTFOLIO

1. Develop a plan for communicating with families of students who do not speak English at home. What kinds of information would you need to communicate to them? What information could they provide that would help you teach their children? What form would the communications take?

2. Develop a position statement and action plan on culturally relevant teaching. How could you support your teachers in examining and improving

their practices? What are your expectations? What resources would you provide?

3. Devise a plan to determine if your school's STEM subjects (Science, Technology, Engineering, Mathematics) are attracting a representative number of girls and minority group students. If the numbers are lower than you want, develop an action plan addressing the problem.

INSTRUCTIONAL LEADER'S TOOLBOX

Readings

Educational Leadership. (2006, February). Special section on "Helping struggling learners," pp. 56–75.

Educational Leadership. (2006, September). Special section on teaching "With boys in mind," pp. 8–78.

Ladson-Billings, G. (1995). But that is just good teaching! The case for culturally relevant pedagogy. *Theory into Practice, 34,* 161–165.

Loveless, T. (1999). Will tracking reform promote social equity? *Educational Leadership, 56*(7), 28–32.

Phi Delta Kappan, (2006, November). Special section on "Indian education for all: Montana takes the lead," pp. 184–222.

Pogrow, S. (2006). Restructuring high-poverty schools for success: A description of the Hi-Perform school design. *Phi Delta Kappan, 88,* 223–229.

Websites

www.cln.org/
>   Community Learning Network: a Canadian site with information on multiculturalism

www.edchange.org
>   EdChange: Professional Development, Scholarship & Activism for Diversity, Social Justice & Community Growth

www.woodrow.org/teachers/math/gender/
>   Modified Fennema-Sherman Attitude: assessment of attitudes toward mathematics

www.cln.org/subjects/mc.html
>   Multicultural curriculum and instructional resources

http://mathforum.org/social/math.women.html
>   Resources on Women and Mathematics

Organizations

www.al-anon.org
>   *Al-Anon/Alateen:* This organization provides support for the family members of alcoholics.

www.csos.jhu.edu/crespar/index.htm
>   Center for Research on the Education of Students Placed at Risk

www.nabe.org
>   *National Association for Bilingual Education*

http://nlchp.org/
>   National Law Center on Homelessness and Poverty

www.nmci.org/index.htm
>   National Multicultural Institute: The mission of this institute is to increase knowledge, awareness, and respect among people of different racial, ethnic, and cultural backgrounds.

www.nn4youth.org/
>   National Network for Youth

www.newhorizons.org
>   New Horizons

www.researchtopractice.info/
>   Research and Training Center on Early Childhood Development

http://spice.stanford.edu/
>   Stanford Program on International and Cross-Cultural Education

www.equipforequality.org/
>   Equip for Equality

CHAPTER

3   Student Abilities and Challenges

PREVIEW: KEY POINTS

1. Over the years there have been many theories about intelligence, but most current views emphasize abstract thinking, reasoning, and problem solving; some interpretations of intelligence emphasize multiple abilities, including emotional intelligence, whereas others stress the processes of analytical, creative, and practical thinking.

2. Emotional intelligence is the ability to process emotional information accurately and efficiently.

3. The Flynn effect is the fact that, in industrialized countries, in a generation the average IQ scores go up about 18 points as measured by standardized IQ tests.

4. Grouping students by ability seems to be advantageous for high achievers, but other approaches such as heterogeneous and cross-age grouping work better for other students.

5. Teachers are not always successful at identifying gifted students, but once identified both acceleration and enrichment may be necessary to give highly gifted students an appropriate education.

6. Students may have different cognitive styles (preferred ways of processing information) and different learning preferences; the research on learning preferences is weak, but the visualizer–verbalizer style shows promise.

7. Approximately 3 to 5% of elementary school students have attention deficit hyperactive disorder (ADHD): boys are three to four times more likely than girls to be identified as hyperactive.

8. Legal changes since the mid-1970s mean that regular teachers will be responsible for more students with learning and behavior problems; the largest group represented are students with learning disabilities.

9. To provide students with disabilities with the least restrictive placement and an individual educational program, the students may be taught in inclusive classrooms using collaborative or cooperative teaching models.

Leadership Challenge

Several of your teachers have asked to speak to you. They believe they are seeing a trend developing in the school. More than ever this year, or so it seems, parents are requesting that their children be tested for learning disabilities or assessed for 504 plans. In fact, the school psychologist is backlogged and behind by many months in completing scheduled tests. One of the teachers ventures an explanation for the sharp increase in testing requests. A group of parents has found out that children identified as learning disabled or eligible for Section 504 plans are allowed more time to complete standardized tests and have other accommodations, even for tests like the PSAT and SAT, that could open admission doors for the student. But another teacher suggests that the flood of requests is more likely due to new policies that have resulted in better communications with families about the options available for their children. Whatever the reason, you are beginning to get calls from parents wondering what's with the delay on their testing requests.

- How would you proceed? Would you investigate to learn why there are so many new testing requests? How?
- If you find out that some parents seem to be testing to give their children more time, what would you do?
- If the requests seem to be a result of better communications with families, how would you proceed?

The most important individual differences for schools are the differences in students' academic abilities and the challenges the students face. Intelligence is one of the most complex and misunderstood of the academic abilities.

Individual Differences in Intelligence

Because the concept of intelligence is so important in education, so controversial, and so often misunderstood, we will spend quite a few pages discussing it. Let us begin with a basic question: What is intelligence?

What Is Intelligence? Single, Multiple, Emotional, Triarchic

The idea that people vary in what we call **intelligence** has been with us for a long time. Plato discussed similar variations over 2,000 years ago. Most early theories about the nature of intelligence involved one or more of three themes: (1) the capacity to learn; (2) the total knowledge a person has acquired; and (3) the ability to adapt successfully to new situations and to the environment in general.

In 1986 at a symposium on intelligence, 24 psychologists offered 24 different views about the nature of intelligence (Neisser et al., 1996; Sternberg & Detterman, 1986). Over half of the experts did mention higher-level thinking processes such as abstract reasoning, problem solving, and decision making as important aspects of intelligence, but they disagreed about the structure of intelligence. Is it a single ability or many separate abilities (Gustafsson & Undheim, 1996)?

Intelligence: One Ability or Many?　　Because there are moderate to high correlations among all mental tests, some believe intelligence is a basic ability that affects performance on all cognitively oriented tasks, from solving mathematical problems, to analyzing poetry, to taking history essay examinations. In fact, this positive intercorrelation among scores for all cognitive tasks "is arguably both the best established and the most striking phenomenon in the psychological study of intelligence" (van der Mass et al., 2006, p. 855). What could explain these results? Charles Spearman (1927) suggested mental energy, which he called *g* or **general intelligence,** was used to perform any mental test, but each test also requires some specific abilities in addition to *g*. Today, psychologists generally agree that there is a mathematically derived common factor across cognitive tests, but knowing this isn't much help in understanding human abilities; the notion of *g* does not have much explanatory power (Blair, 2006).

Raymond Cattell and John Horn proposed a theory of fluid and crystallized intelligence that is more helpful in providing explanations (Cattell, 1963, 1987; Horn, 1998). Sometimes people assume that fluid intelligence is process—the ability to learn—and crystallized intelligence is content—what you have learned. But it isn't quite that simple. **Fluid intelligence** is mental efficiency and reasoning ability. The neurophysiological underpinnings of fluid intelligence may be related to changes in brain volume, myelinization (coating of neural fibers that makes processing faster), the density of dopamine receptors, or processing abilities in the prefrontal lobe of the brain such as selective attention and working memory. This aspect of intelligence increases until late adolescence (about age 22) because it is grounded in brain development, then declines gradually with age. Fluid intelligence is sensitive to injuries and diseases.

In contrast, **crystallized intelligence** is the ability to apply the problem-solving methods appropriate in your cultural context, so processes are involved here too. Fluid intelligence can increase throughout the life span because it includes the learned skills and knowledge such as how to read, hail a cab, make a quilt, or design professional development programs. By *investing fluid intelligence* in solving problems, we develop our *crystallized intelligence*, but many tasks in life such as mathematical reasoning draw on both fluid and crystallized intelligence (Ferrer & McArdle, 2004; Finkel, Reynolds, McArdle, Gatz, & Pederson, 2003; Hunt, 2000). The most widely accepted psychometric view today is that intelligence has many facets and is a hierarchy of abilities, with general ability at the top and more specific abilities at lower levels of the hierarchy (Carroll, 1997; Sternberg, 2000).

Multiple Intelligences.   In spite of the correlations among the various tests of different abilities, some psychologists insist that there are several separate mental abilities (Gardner, 1983; Guilford, 1988). According to Gardner's (1983, 2003) **theory of multiple intelligences** (see Figure 3.1), there are at least eight separate intelligences: linguistic (verbal), musical, spatial, logical-mathematical, bodily-kinesthetic (movement), interpersonal (understanding others), intrapersonal (understanding self), and naturalist (observing and understanding natural and human-made patterns and systems). Gardner stresses that there may be more kinds of intelligence—eight is not a magic number. Recently he has speculated that there may be a spiritual intelligence or an existential intelligence or the ability to contemplate big questions about the meaning of life (Gardner, 2003). Gardner bases his notion of separate abilities on evidence that brain damage (from a stroke, for example) often interferes with functioning in one area, such as language, but does not affect functioning in other areas. Also, individuals may excel in one of these eight areas but have no remarkable abilities in the other seven.

What are these intelligences? Gardner (1998, 2000, 2003) contends that an intelligence is the ability to solve problems and create products or outcomes that are valued by a culture. Varying cultures and eras of history have placed different values on the eight intelligences. A naturalist intelligence is critical in farming cultures, whereas verbal and mathematical intelligences are important in technological cultures. In addition, Gardner (1998) believes that intelligence has a biological basis. Intelligence "is a biological and psychological potential; that potential is capable of being realized to a greater or lesser extent as a consequence of the experiential, cultural, and motivational factors that affect a person" (p. 62). Gardner does not deny the existence of a general ability, but he does question how useful g is as an explanation for human achievements.

Gardner's multiple intelligence theory has not received wide acceptance in the scientific community, even though it has been embraced by many educators. Some critics suggest that several of the "intelligences" are not new at all. Many researchers have identified separate verbal and spatial abilities. In addition, the eight intelligences are not independent; there are correlations among the abilities. In fact, logical-mathematical and spatial intelligences are highly correlated (Sattler, 2001). Evidence linking musical and spatial abilities has prompted Gardner to consider that there may be connections among the intelligences (Gardner, 1998). Stay tuned for more developments.

FIGURE 3.1   Eight Intelligences

Howard Gardner's theory of multiple intelligences suggests that there are eight kinds of human abilities. An individual might have strengths or weaknesses in one or several areas.

Intelligence	End States	Core Components
Logical-mathematical	Scientist Mathematician	Sensitivity to, and capacity to discern, logical or numerical patterns; ability to handle long chains of reasoning.
Linguistic	Poet Journalist	Sensitivity to the sounds, rhythms, and meanings of words; sensitivity to the different functions of language.
Musical	Composer Violinist	Abilities to produce and appreciate rhythm, pitch, and timbre; appreciation of the forms of musical expressiveness.
Spatial	Navigator Sculptor	Capacities to perceive the visual-spatial world accurately and to perform transformations on one's initial perceptions.
Bodily-kinesthetic	Dancer Athlete	Abilities to control one's body movements and to handle objects skillfully.
Interpersonal	Therapist Salesman	Capacities to discern and respond appropriately to the moods, temperaments, motivations, and desires of other people.
Intrapersonal	Person with detailed, accurate self-knowledge	Access to one's own feelings and the ability to discriminate among them and draw on them to guide behavior; knowledge of one's own strengths, weaknesses, desires, and intelligence.
Naturalist	Botanist Farmer Hunter	Abilities to recognize plants and animals, to make distinctions in the natural world, to understand systems and define categories (perhaps even categories of intelligence).

Source: From "Multiple Intelligences Go to School," by H. Gardner and T. Hatch, *Educational Researcher*, 18(8), 1989, Figure p. 6. Copyright 1989 by the American Educational Research Association. Journals. Reproduced with permission of Sage Publications Inc. Journals in the format Textbook and E-book via Copyright Clearance Center. "Are There Additional Intelligences? The Case for the Naturalist, Spiritual, and Existential Intelligences," by H. Gardner (1999) in J. Kane (Ed.), *Educational Information and Transformation*, Upper Saddle River, NJ: Prentice-Hall, Inc.

Multiple Intelligences Go to School.   An advantage of the multiple intelligences perspective is that it expands our thinking about abilities and avenues for teaching, but the theory has been misused. Some teachers embrace a simplistic version of Gardner's theory. They include every "intelligence" in every lesson, no matter how inappropriate.

A better way to use the theory is to focus on six Entry Points—narrative, logical-quantitative, aesthetic, experiential, interpersonal, and existential/foundational—in designing a curriculum (Gardner, 1991). For example, to teach about evolution, teachers might use the Entry Points as follows (Kornhaber, Fierros, & Veenema, 2004):

> *Narrative:* Provide rich stories about Darwin's voyage to the Galapagos Islands or traditional folktales about the different plants and animals.
>
> *Logical-quantitative:* Examine Darwin's attempts to map the distributions of the species or pose logical problems about what would happen to the ecosystem if one species disappeared.
>
> *Aesthetic:* Examine Darwin's drawings of the species he studied on the Galapagos Islands.
>
> *Experiential:* Do laboratory activities such as breeding fruit flies or completing virtual simulations of evolutionary processes.
>
> *Interpersonal:* Form research teams or hold debates.
>
> *Existential/foundational:* Consider questions about why species die out or the purpose for variation in species.

Table 3.1 lists some other positive applications of Gardner's work, as well as some misuses.

Many educators and schools have embraced Gardner's ideas and believe that multiple intelligences practices increase achievement for all students and improve both student discipline and parent participation (Kornhaber, Fierros, & Veenema, 2004). But there is not yet strong research evidence that adopting a multiple intelligences approach will enhance learning. In one of the few carefully designed evaluations, Callahan, Tomlinson, and Plucker (1997) found no significant gains in either achievement or self-concept for students who participated in START, a multiple intelligences approach to identifying and promoting talent in students who were at risk of failing. Learning is still hard work, even if there are multiple entry points and paths to knowledge.

Emotional Intelligence.   Howard Gardner's theory of multiple intelligences includes intrapersonal and interpersonal intelligences, or intelligence about self and others. Here we look a related perspective—emotional intelligence.

We all know people who are academically or artistically talented, but unsuccessful. They have problems in school, in relationships, and on the job, but can't improve the situations. According to some psychologists, the source of the difficulties may be a lack of **emotional intelligence,** first defined by Peter Salovey and John Mayer as the ability to process emotional information accurately and efficiently (Mayer & Cobb, 2000; Mayer & Salovey, 1997; Roberts, Zeidner, & Matthews, 2001). Daniel Goleman (1995) popularized the idea of emotional intelligence (E-IQ or EQ) in his best-selling book based on the work of Salovey and Mayer.

What Is EQ?   At the center of emotional intelligence are four broad abilities: perceiving, integrating, understanding, and managing emotions (Mayer & Cobb, 2000). If you can't *perceive* what you are feeling, how can you make good choices about jobs,

TABLE 3.1   Misuses and Applications of Multiple Intelligence Theory

Recently Howard Gardner described these negative and positive applications of his theory. The quotes are his words on the subject.

Misuses:

1. **Trying to teach all concepts or subjects using all intelligences:** "There is no point in assuming that every subject can be effectively approached in at least seven ways, and it is a waste of effort and time to attempt to do this."
2. **Assuming that it is enough just to apply a certain intelligence, no matter how you use it:** For bodily-kinesthetic intelligence, for example, "random muscle movements have nothing to do with the cultivation of the mind."
3. **Using an intelligence as a background for other activities**, such as playing music while students solve math problems. "The music's function is unlikely to be different from that of a dripping faucet or humming fan."
4. **Mixing intelligences with other desirable qualities:** For example, interpersonal intelligence "is often distorted as a license for cooperative learning," and intrapersonal intelligence "is often distorted as a rationale for self-esteem programs."
5. **Direct evaluation or even grading of intelligences without regard to context:** "I see little point in grading individuals in terms of how 'linguistic' or how 'bodily-kinesthetic' they are."

Good uses:

1. **The cultivation of desired capabilities:** "Schools should cultivate those skills and capabilities that are valued in the community and in the broader society."
2. **Approaching a concept, subject matter, discipline in a variety of ways:** Schools try to cover too much. "It makes far more sense to spend a significant amount of time on key concepts, generative ideas, and essential questions and to allow students to become familiar with these notions and their implications."
3. **The personalization of education:** "The heart of the MI perspective—in theory and in practice—inheres in taking human difference seriously."

Source: "Reflections on Multiple Intelligences: Myths and Messages," by H. Gardner, 1998. In A. Woolfolk (Ed.), *Readings in Educational Psychology* (2nd ed.) (pp. 64–66), Boston: Allyn & Bacon. Used by permission of Howard Gardner, Harvard University.

relationships, time management, or even entertainment (Baron, 1998)? Individuals who can *perceive* and *understand* emotions in others (usually by reading the nonverbal cues) and respond appropriately are more successful in working with people and often emerge as leaders (Wood & Wood, 1999). If you can't *integrate* your emotions into your thinking about situations and *understand* your own emotions, how can you communicate your feelings to others accurately? Friends keep asking, "What's wrong?" and you keep saying, "Nothing!"

Finally, you must *manage* your emotions, particularly negative emotions such as anger or depression. The goal is not to suppress feelings, but not to be overwhelmed by them either. Managing emotions includes the ability to focus energy, persist, control impulses, and delay immediate gratification. Emotional management is critical in school. For example, compared to four-year-old students who act on their impulses immediately, four-year-old children who can delay instant gratification so they can work toward a goal become much better students in high school (Shoda, Mischel, & Peake, 1990).

Some researchers have criticized the notion of EQ. Does intelligence inform emotion so we are "smart" about managing our feelings and impulses, or does emotion inform intelligence so we make good decisions and understand other people? Probably both are true. The major point is that success in life requires more than cognitive skills, and schools are important influences in helping students develop all of these capabilities.

EQ Goes to School.   Some research suggests programs that help students build their emotional competencies have beneficial effects, including an increase in cooperative behaviors and a reduction in antisocial activities like the use of slurs and bullying. For example, Norma Feshbach (1989, 1997) developed a 36-hour program for helping elementary students become more empathetic. The program included exercises such as deciding what each person in your family would like most as a birthday present. Students also retold stories from the perspective of the different characters in a story and then played the role of each character on videotaped performances of the stories. Students learned to analyze how people looked and sounded as they played each role. Sandra Graham's (1996) program for helping aggressive boys learn to read the intentions of others also included role plays and practice in reading the emotions of others. The educational advantages of decreased student aggression and increased empathy are obvious, but these skills also prepare students for life outside the classroom.

Beware! One of the problems with innovations in psychology is that they are often inadvertently misinterpreted or ill-described in the popular media by writers and reporters who have limited backgrounds in both psychology and education. The concept of emotional intelligence is one innovation that seems to be facing that fate.

Intelligence as a Process.   As you can see, the theories of Spearman, Gardner, Salovey, and Mayer tend to describe how individuals differ in the content of intelligence—the different abilities. Recent work in cognitive psychology has emphasized instead the information processing that is common to all people. How do humans gather and use information to solve problems and behave intelligently? New views of intelligence are growing out of this work. For example, the debates in the 2006 issue of *Behavioral and Brain Sciences* emphasized working memory capacity, executive control processes such as the abilities to focus attention and inhibit impulses, and emotional self-regulation as aspects of fluid cognitive abilities.

Robert Sternberg's (1985, 2004) **triarchic theory of successful intelligence** is a cognitive process approach to understanding intelligence. *Successful intelligence* includes "the skills and knowledge needed for success in life, according to one's own definition of success, within one's own sociocultural context" (Sternberg, 2004, p. 326).

Sternberg prefers the term *successful intelligence* to stress that intelligence is more than what is tested by mental abilities measures: intelligence is about success in life. As you might guess from the name, this theory has three parts: analytic, creative, and practical. Analytic intelligence involves the mental processes of the individual that lead to more or less intelligent behavior. Some processes are specific; that is, they are necessary for only one kind of task, such as solving analogies. Other processes such as monitoring progress are very general and may be necessary in almost every cognitive task.

The second part of Sternberg's theory, creativity, involves coping with new experiences. Intelligent behavior is marked by two characteristics: (1) *insight*, or the ability to deal effectively with novel situations, and (2) *automaticity*, the ability to become efficient and automatic in thinking and problem solving. The third part, practical intelligence, highlights the importance of choosing an environment in which a person can succeed, adapting to that environment, and reshaping it if necessary. People who are successful often seek situations in which their abilities will be valuable and then work hard to capitalize on those abilities and compensate for any weaknesses. Thus, intelligence in this third sense involves practical matters such as career choice or social skills (Grigorenko & Sternberg, 2001; Sternberg, Wagner, Williams, & Horvath, 1995).

Principals, teachers, and parents are most familiar with intelligence as a number or score on an IQ test. Let's next consider an important question.

What Does an IQ Score Mean?

Most intelligence tests are designed so that they have certain statistical characteristics. For example, the average score is 100. Fifty percent of the people from the general population who take the tests will score 100 or above, and 50% will score below 100. About 68% of the general population will earn IQ scores between 85 and 115. Only about 16% of the population will receive scores below 85, and only 16% will score above 115. Note, however, that these figures hold true for white, native-born Americans whose first language is standard English. Whether IQ tests should even be used with ethnic minority group students is hotly debated.

Group versus Individual IQ Tests.   Individual intelligence tests (such as the Stanford-Binet or Wechsler Scales) have to be administered to one student at a time by a trained psychologist and take about two hours. Most of the questions are asked orally and do not require reading or writing. A student usually pays closer attention and is more motivated to do well when working directly with an adult. Psychologists also have developed group tests that can be given to whole classes or schools. Compared to an individual test, a group test is much less likely to yield an accurate picture of any one person's abilities. When students take tests in a group, they may do poorly because they do not understand the instructions, because their pencils break, because they are distracted by other students, or because they do not shine on paper-and-pencil tests. As an instructional leader, you should be very wary of IQ scores based on group tests. The Theory into Action Guidelines on the next page give ideas for helping teachers and parents interpret scores from intelligence tests.

THEORY INTO ACTION GUIDELINES

Interpreting Intelligence Test Scores

Check to see if the score is based on an individual or a group test. Be wary of group test scores.

Examples

1. Individual tests include the Wechsler Scales (WPPSI-III, WISC-IV, WAIS-III), the Stanford-Binet, the McCarthy Scales of Children's Abilities, the Woodcock-Johnson Psycho-Educational Battery, the Naglieri Nonverbal Ability Test—Individual, and the Kaufman Assessment Battery for Children.
2. Group tests include the Otis-Lennon School Abilities Tests, Slosson Intelligence Test, Raven Progressive Matrices, Naglieri Nonverbal Ability Test—Multiform, Differential Abilities Scales, and Wide Range Intelligence Test.

Remember that IQ tests are only estimates of general aptitude for learning.

Examples

1. Ignore small differences in scores among students.
2. Bear in mind that even an individual student's scores may change over time for many reasons, including measurement error.

3. Be aware that a total score is usually an average of scores on several kinds of questions. A score in the middle or average range may mean that the student performed at the average on every kind of question or that the student did quite well in some areas (for example, on verbal tasks) and rather poorly in other areas (for example, on visual–spatial tasks).

Remember that IQ scores reflect a student's past experiences and learning.

Examples

1. Consider these scores as predictors of school abilities, not measures of innate intellectual abilities.
2. If a student is doing well in your school, do not change your opinion or lower your expectations just because one score seems low.
3. Be wary of IQ scores for minority students and for students whose first language was not English. Even scores on "culture-free" tests are lower for disadvantaged students.

The Flynn Effect: Are We Getting Smarter?   Ever since IQ tests were introduced in the early 1900s, scores in twenty different industrialized countries and some more traditional cultures have been rising (Daley, Whaley, Sigman, Espinosa, & Neumann, 2003). In fact, in a generation, the average score goes up about 18 points on standardized IQ tests—maybe you really are smarter than your parents! This is called the **Flynn effect** after James Flynn, a political scientist who documented the phenomenon. Some explanations include better nutrition and medical care for children and parents, increasing complexity in the environment that stimulates thinking, smaller families who give more attention to their children, increased literacy of parents, more and better schooling, and better preparation for taking tests. One result of the Flynn effect is the norms used to determine scores (more about norms in Chapter 8) have to be continually revised. In other words, to keep a score of 100 as the average, the test questions have to be made more difficult. This increasing difficulty has implications for any program that uses IQ scores as part of the entrance requirements. For example, students who were not identified as having intellectual disabilities a generation ago might be identified as disabled now because the test questions are harder (Kanaya, Scullin, & Ceci, 2003).

Intelligence and Achievement. Scoring higher on IQ tests is related to school achievement for children in all ethnic groups. But what about life after school? Do people who score high on IQ tests achieve more in life? Here the answer is less clear because life success and education are intertwined. High school graduates earn over $200,000 more in their lifetime than nongraduates, college graduates earn over $800,000 more, and grads with professional degrees, over $1.6 million more (Ceci & Williams, 1997). People with higher intelligence test scores tend to complete more years of school and to have higher-status jobs. However, when the number of years of education is held constant, the correlation decreases between IQ scores and income and success in later life. Other factors such as motivation, social skills, and luck may make the difference (Goleman, 1995; Neisser et al., 1996; Sternberg & Wagner, 1993).

For all adults caring for children—parents, teachers, administrators, counselors, medical workers—it is especially important to realize that cognitive skills, like any other skills, are always improvable. *Intelligence is a current state of affairs,* affected by past experiences and open to future changes, as the Flynn effect demonstrates. Even if intelligence is a limited potential, the potential is still quite large. For example, Japanese and Chinese children know much more mathematics than American children, but their intelligence test scores are quite similar. This superiority in math probably is related to differences in the way mathematics is taught and studied in the three countries and to the self-motivation skills of many Asian students (Baron, 1998; Stevenson & Stigler, 1992).

A Principal's Perspective

"What's best for kids?" is a question that guides decision-making processes of many educators, principals and teachers alike, and also serves as an exhibition of their student-centered orientation. However, answering this rhetorical question with actions is not so straightforward as it may seem. T. R., a principal and superintendent for many years, shares his thoughts.

Obviously, educators make innumerable decisions daily that impact students. What is less obvious is how each decision a principal or a teacher makes regarding students in general impacts students individually. In fact, academic accountability prescribed in No Child Left Behind (NCLB, 2002; reauthorized 2007) states that solutions and strategies that might be best for most students *are not good enough* for all students. Rather, NCLB and its focus of ensuring the academic progress of every child has shifted the question to "What's best for this child in this subject in this specific situation at this point in time?"—no easy task when a single principal is charged with monitoring as many as 40 classroom teachers each serving 20 to 30 students of different ethnic backgrounds, often reading at five or more distinct levels, demonstrating varying degrees of independence and cognitive ability, and having widely varying nonschool experiences and family support structures.

However, the enormity of this task has not dissuaded student-focused leaders from implementing effective practices that attempt to address individual student needs. One example of how a principal can support meeting individual student needs is by bringing together teachers at the end of a school year to carefully consider individual characteristics when assigning students to class lists for the following school year. In most cases, teachers and principals strive to craft heterogeneous groupings of students that will allow teachers to efficiently and effectively meet students' needs based on cognitive ability, behavior, and the ability to work independently to name a few. In another example, principals may assemble classroom teachers and support staff regularly each week or each month to serve on intervention teams that review multiple data points of individual student progress, especially for students with identified cognitive deficits or challenges. Typically, these teams then identify the areas where each student has made insufficient progress, develop specific intervention strategies, determine action steps for implementing the strategies, and establish timelines for measuring and assessing the success of newly defined interventions.

Clearly, the principal's role as instructional leader has never been more important when considered in the context of meeting the needs of every child. As a result, reviewing, understanding, and effectively applying research regarding the emotional, social, academic, and physical development of individual students is an essential component of decision making when now considering the question, "What's best for kids—what's best for this particular child right now?"

For ideas about individualizing instruction, see: Tomlinson, C. (2005, Summer). Differentiated instruction. *Theory Into Practice, 44(3)* (special issue).

Teaching Students with Ability Differences

Ability grouping has moved in and out of favor since the early 1900s. Today, teachers are encouraged to use forms of cooperative learning and heterogeneous grouping to deal with ability differences in their classes (Hilgard, 1996). In this section we consider how to handle differences in academic ability. Is ability grouping a solution to the challenge of ability differences? If so, when and for whom?

Between-Class Ability Grouping

When whole classes are formed based on ability, the process is called **between-class ability grouping** or **tracking,** a common practice in secondary schools and some elementary schools as well. Most high schools have "college prep" courses and "general" courses or, for example, high-, middle-, and low-ability classes in particular subjects. Although on the surface this seems to be an efficient way to teach, research has consistently shown that segregation by ability may benefit high-achieving students, but it causes problems for low-achieving students (Castle, Deniz, & Tortora, 2005; Garmon, Nystrand, Berends, & LePore, 1995; National Research Council, Institute of Medicine, 2004; Oakes & Wells, 1998; Robinson & Clinkenbeard, 1998).

Low-ability classes seem to receive lower-quality instruction in general. Teachers tend to emphasize lower-level objectives and routine procedures, with less academic focus. Often there are more management problems and, with these problems, increased stress and decreased enthusiasm. These differences in instruction and the teachers' negative attitudes may mean that low expectations are communicated to the students. Attendance may drop. The lower tracks often have a disproportionate number of minority group and economically disadvantaged students, so ability grouping, in effect, resegregates schools. Possibilities for friendships become limited to students in the same ability range. Assignments to classes are often made on the basis of group IQ tests instead of tests in the subject area itself. Yet group IQ tests are not good guides for what someone is ready to learn in a particular subject area (Garmon, Nystrand, Berends, & LePore, 1995; Good & Brophy, 2003; Lucas & Berends, 2002).

There are two exceptions to the general finding that between-class ability grouping leads to lower achievement. The first is found in honors or gifted classes, where high-ability students tend to perform better than comparable students in regular classes. The second exception is the nongraded elementary school. In this arrangement, students are grouped by ability in particular subjects, regardless of their age or grade. A reading class might therefore have students from several grades, all working on the same level on reading. This *cross-grade grouping* seems to increase achievement and self-esteem for students of all abilities as long as the grouping allows teachers to give more direct instruction to the groups (Ong, Allison, & Haladyna, 2000). When cross-age grouping is used to implement individualized instruction, the effects are much less positive, probably because many individualized instruction programs leave students on their own too much of the time and many students (of all ages) cannot manage their own time without some supervision (Gutierrez & Slavin, 1992). But be sensible about cross-age grouping. Mixing third, fourth, and fifth graders for math or reading class based on what they are ready to learn makes sense. Sending a large fourth grader to the second grade, where he is the only older student and stands out like a sore thumb, isn't likely to work well. Also, when cross-age classes are created just because there are too few students for one grade, the results are not positive (Veenman, 1997).

Recently there has been a press for **untracking,** or teaching all students in mixed ability groups, then providing extra help for those who struggle and enrichment for those who learn quickly (Corno, 1995; Rubin, 2006). Jeannie Oakes and A. S. Wells (2002) describe several different ways to teach effectively in secondary schools without tracking:

- Eliminate remedial courses and have one regular and one advanced track.
- Offer honors assignment options or challenge pull out activities within each course.
- Require all students to take a common core of classes, then allow self-selection into advanced classes after the core.
- Encourage minority group students to enroll in advanced placement courses.
- Provide additional times during intercessions when struggling students can get extra help.
- Provide tutoring before and after school.
- Staff a homework help center with teachers, parents, and community volunteers.
- Instead of "dumbing down" content, teach students learning strategies for dealing with difficult material.

Not everyone agrees that untracking is a good idea. This movement has been more successful at the elementary than the secondary level. The Point/Counterpoint on the next page looks at both sides.

POINT/COUNTERPOINT   Is Tracking an Effective Strategy?

Tracking students into different classes or strands (college prep, vocational, remedial, gifted, and so on) has been standard procedure in many schools for a long time, but does it work? Critics say tracking is harmful while supporters claim it is useful, even though it presents challenges.

POINT

Tracking is harmful and should be eliminated.
According to Tom Loveless, writing in the April 1999 issue of *Educational Leadership*, "Prominent researchers and prestigious national reports have argued that tracking stands in the way of equal educational opportunity" (p. 28).

Loveless goes on to cite the work of Braddock and Slavin (1993); Carnegie Council on Adolescent Development (1995); and Wheelock (1992)—all of whom make the argument against tracking. What is the basis for these claims? Surprisingly, the evidence is not clear or direct. For example, a few well-done and carefully designed studies found that tracking increases the gap between high and low achievers by depressing the achievement of low-track students and boosting the achievement of high-track students (Gamoran, 1987; Kerckhoff, 1986). And Gamoran (1987) also found that the achievement gap between low- and high-track students is greater than the gap between students who drop out of school and students who graduate. Because low-income students and students of color are overrepresented in the lower tracks, they suffer the greatest harm from tracking and should benefit the most from the elimination of tracking (Oakes, 1990; Oakes & Wells, 2002). Is this likely?

COUNTERPOINT

Eliminating tracking will hurt many students.
Researchers who have looked closely at tracking believe that tracking may be harmful for some students some of the time, but not for all students and not all of the time. First, as most people agree, tracking seems to have positive effects for the high-track students. Gifted programs, honors classes, and advanced placement classes seem to work (Fuchs, Fuchs, Hamlett, & Karns, 1998; Robinson & Clinkenbeard, 1998). No one, especially parents, wants to eliminate the positive effects of these programs. And the chance of being assigned to a high track is 10% greater for African American students (Gamoran & Mare, 1989), so detracking could be a special disservice to these students.

What would happen if schools were detracked? Loveless (1999) identifies some possible hidden costs. First, results of a large national study suggest that when low-track 10th graders are assigned to heterogeneous classes rather than low tracks, they gain about 5 percentage points in achievement. So far, so good. But average students lose 2 percentage points when put into heterogeneous classes and high-ability students lose about 5 points.

> The achievement gap is indeed narrowed, but apparently at the expense of students in regular and high tracks, representing about 70% of 10th graders in the United States. (Loveless, 1999, p. 29)

Another consequence of detracking is *bright flight*—the withdrawal of the brightest students from the schools. Both African American and white parents distrust mixed-ability classes to meet the needs of their children (Public Agenda Foundation, 1994).

In some classes, using a mixed-ability structure seems to hinder the achievement of all students. For example, students in heterogeneous algebra classes don't learn as much as students in tracked classes—whatever the ability level of the students (Epstein & MacIver, 1992). And a meta-analysis of student self-esteem found that students in low-track classes did *not* have lower self-esteem than students in heterogeneous classes (Kulik & Kulik, 1997).

So what is the answer? As usual, it is more complicated than simply detracking versus tracking. Careful attention to every student's achievement may mean different answers at different times.

Within-Class and Flexible Ability Grouping

Today many elementary school classes are grouped for reading, and some are grouped for math, even though there is no clear evidence that this **within-class ability grouping** is superior to other approaches. Thoughtfully constructed and well-taught ability groups in math and reading can be effective, but other approaches such as cooperative learning are available too. The point of any grouping strategy should be to provide appropriate challenge and support—that is, to reach children within their "zone of proximal development" (Vygotsky, 1997). Flexible grouping is one possible answer.

Flexible Grouping.   The idea of **flexible grouping** is to group and regroup students based on learning needs. Assessment is continuous so that students are always working on challenging, but doable tasks. Arrangements might include small group, partners, individuals, and even whole class—depending on which grouping best supports the student in learning the particular academic content. Flexible grouping approaches often include high-level instruction and high expectations for all students, no matter what their group placement. One five-year longitudinal study of flexible grouping in a high-needs urban elementary school found 10% to 57% increases in students who reached mastery level, depending on the subject area and grade level (Castle et al., 2005). Teachers received training and support in the assessment, grouping, and teaching strategies needed, and by the end of the study, 95% of the teachers were using flexible grouping. The teachers in the study believed that some of the gains came because students were more focused on learning and more confident.

If you use ability groups in your school, the Theory into Action Guidelines on the next page should help your teachers make the approach more effective (Good & Brophy, 2008; Slavin, 1987). Many people are strongly against ability groupings of any kind.

What should instructional leaders do when they face more extreme differences in student ability? We turn to this question next.

Students Who Are Gifted and Talented

Consider this situation, a true story:

> Latoya was already an advanced reader when she entered first grade in a large urban school district. Her teacher noticed the challenging chapter books Latoya brought to school and read with little effort. After administering a reading assessment, the school's reading consultant confirmed that Latoya was reading at the fifth-grade level. Latoya's parents reported with pride that she had started to read independently when she was three years old and "had read every book she could get her hands on." (Reis et al., 2002)

In her struggling urban school, Latoya received no particular accommodations, and by fifth grade she was still reading at just above the fifth-grade level. Her fifth-grade teacher had no idea that Latoya had ever been an advanced reader.

Latoya is not alone. There is a group of students with special needs that is often overlooked by the schools: the **gifted and talented.** In the past, providing an enriched

THEORY INTO ACTION GUIDELINES

Ability Grouping

Form and reform groups on the basis of students' current performance in the subject being taught.

Examples

1. Use scores on the most recent reading assessments to establish reading groups, and rely on current math performance to form math groups.
2. Change group placement frequently when students' achievement changes.

Discourage comparisons between groups and encourage students to develop a whole-class spirit.

Examples

1. Don't seat groups together outside the context of their reading or math group.
2. Avoid naming ability groups—save names for mixed-ability or whole-class teams.

Group by ability for one or, at the most, two subjects.

Examples

1. Make sure there are many lessons and projects that mix members from the groups.

2. Experiment with learning strategies in which cooperation is stressed (described in Chapter 4).
3. Keep the number of groups small (two or three at most) so that you can provide as much direct teaching as possible—leaving students alone for too long leads to less learning.

Make sure teachers, methods, and pace are adjusted to fit the needs of the group.

Examples

1. Organize and teach groups so that low-achieving students get appropriate extra instruction—not just the same material again.
2. Experiment with alternatives to grouping. There are alternatives to within-class grouping that appear more effective for some subjects. Mason and Good (1993) found that supplementing whole-class instruction in math with remediation and enrichment for students when they needed it worked better than dividing the class into two ability groups and teaching these groups separately.

education for extremely bright or talented students was seen as undemocratic and elitist. Now there is a growing recognition that gifted students are being poorly served by most public schools. A national survey found that more than one-half of all gifted students do not achieve in school at a level equal to their ability (Tomlinson-Keasey, 1990).

Who Are the Gifted?   There are many definitions of gifted because individuals can have many different gifts. Remember that Gardner (2003) identified eight separate "intelligences," and Sternberg (1997) suggests a triarchic model. Renzulli and Reis (2003) have a different three-part conception of giftedness: above-average general ability, a high level of creativity, and a high level of task commitment or motivation to achieve. Truly gifted children are not the students who simply learn quickly with little effort. The work of gifted students is original, extremely advanced for their age, and potentially of lasting importance. These children may read fluently with little instruction by age three or four. They may play a musical instrument like a skillful adult, turn a visit to the grocery store into a mathematical puzzle, and become fascinated with algebra when their friends are having trouble with simple addition (Winner, 2000). Recent conceptions widen the view of giftedness to include attention to the children's culture, language, and exceptionalities (Association for the Gifted, 2001).

Identifying a gifted child is not always easy. Many parents provide early educational experiences for their children. Some students with intellectual gifts and talents also have learning problems such as difficulties hearing, learning disabilities, or attention deficit disorders, and their talents will be missed if the abilities as well as the problems are not properly assessed. And older students may actually try to hide their abilities from their friends and teachers.

The best single predictor of academic giftedness is still the individual IQ test, but these tests are costly and time-consuming, and far from perfect. Group achievement and intelligence tests tend to underestimate the IQs of very bright children. Group tests may be appropriate for screening, but they are not appropriate for making placement decisions. One answer is a case study approach: gathering many kinds of information, test scores, grades, examples of work, projects and portfolios, letters or ratings from teachers, self-ratings, and so on (Renzulli & Reis, 1991, 2003). Especially for recognizing artistic talent, experts in the field can be called in to judge the merits of a child's creations. Creativity tests may identify some children not picked up by other measures, particularly minority students who may be at a disadvantage on the other types of tests.

Teaching Gifted Students. Some educators believe that gifted students should be accelerated—moved quickly through the grades or through particular subjects. Other educators prefer enrichment—giving the students additional, more sophisticated, and more thought-provoking work, but keeping them with their age-mates in school. Actually, both may be appropriate (Torrance, 1986). One way of doing this is through *curriculum compacting*—assessing a student over the goals of the instructional unit, then teaching only for those goals not yet reached. The time saved can be used for learning goals that include enrichment, sophistication, and novelty (Reis & Renzulli, 2004).

Many people object to acceleration, but most careful studies indicate that truly gifted students who begin primary, elementary, junior high, high school, college, or even graduate school early do as well as, and usually better than, nongifted students who are progressing at the normal pace. Social and emotional adjustment does not appear to be impaired. Skipping grades may not be the best solution for a particular student, but it does not deserve the bad name it has been given (Jones & Southern, 1991; Richardson & Benbow, 1990). An alternative to skipping grades is to accelerate students in one or two particular subjects but keep them with peers for most classes. For students who are extremely advanced intellectually (for example, those scoring 160 or higher on an intelligence test), the only practical solution may be to accelerate their education (Gross, 1992; Hallahan & Kauffman, 2006; Keogh & MacMillan, 1996).

Teaching methods for gifted students should encourage abstract thinking, creativity, and independence, not just the learning of greater quantities of facts. In working with gifted and talented students, a teacher must be imaginative, flexible, and unthreatened by their capabilities. Instructional leaders must ask: What does this student need most? What does the student already know, and what is she or he ready to learn? Who can help me to help? Answers might come from faculty members at nearby colleges, retired professionals, books, museums, or older students. Strategies might be as simple as letting the child do math with the next grade. Increasingly, more flexible programs are being devised for gifted students: summer institutes or camps; courses at nearby colleges; classes with local artists, musicians, or dancers; independent research projects; selected classes in high school for younger students; honors classes; and special-interest clubs.

Reaching Every Student: Giftedness and Diversity.   There are three groups of students who are underrepresented in gifted education programs: women, students with learning disabilities, and students living in poverty (Stormont, Stebbins, & Holliday, 2001).

Girls and Giftedness.   "Gifted adolescent females are particularly at risk for under-achievement, social and emotional problems, and feelings of isolation" (Stormont et al., 2001, p. 415). As young girls develop their identities in adolescence, they often reject being labeled as gifted; being accepted and popular, "fitting in," may become more important than achievement (Basow & Rubin, 1999). As they grow older, girls may even deliberately score lower on standardized tests and take fewer challenging courses. How can teachers reach girls with gifts? Here are some ideas:

- Notice when girls' test scores in middle or high school seem to decline.
- Encourage assertiveness, achievement, high goals, and demanding work from all students.
- Provide models of achievement through speakers, internships, or readings.
- Look for and support gifts in arenas other than academic achievement.

Gifted Students with Learning Disabilities: Twice-Exceptional.   These twice-exceptional students may be more angry and frustrated than other students by the problems that they encounter (Stormont et al., 2001). Learning problems may be subtle, and the student is fine through elementary school but begins to have problems as academic work gets harder in the later grades. Learning problems may be severe and may mask the gifts, so these students are seldom identified for gifted programs. Or the student's gifts may be used to compensate for learning disabilities, so the student seems just average to teachers (McCoach, Kehle, Bray, & Siegle, 2001). Here are some ideas for supporting twice-exceptional students:

- Identify these students by looking longitudinally at achievement: who was a high achiever in elementary school but began having trouble as more and more reading was required in later grades?
- Remediate skill deficits but also identify and develop talents and strengths.
- Promote emotional support, especially for this group.

- Help students learn to compensate directly for their learning problems and help them "tune in" to their own strengths and difficulties.
- Find help for career planning that takes advantage of their gifts and talents.

Gifted Students Who Live in Poverty.   Health problems, lack of resources, homelessness, fears about safety and survival, frequent moves, responsibilities for the care of other family members—all make achievement in school more difficult. To identify students with gifts, do the following:

- Use alternative assessment, teacher nomination, creativity tests. Look for students who are expressive, good storytellers, able to improvise when they have limited materials. Try dynamic assessments that give students clues and observe how they solve problems using the clues.
- Be sensitive to cultural differences in values about cooperative or solitary achievement (Ford, 2000).
- Use multicultural strategies to encourage both achievement and the development of racial identities.

Students with Learning Challenges

Thus far we have focused mostly on schools' responses to the varying abilities and styles of students. For the rest of the chapter, we will consider problems that can interfere with learning. It is beyond this book to discuss all the exceptionalities, but there are three that are the source of much confusion in teaching: attention deficit disorder, learning disabilities, and autism spectrum disorders.

Hyperactivity and Attention Disorders

You have probably heard and may even have used the term *hyperactivity.* Today most psychologists agree that the main problem for children labeled hyperactive is directing and maintaining attention, not simply controlling their "hyper" activity. The American Psychiatric Association (APA) has established a diagnostic category called **attention deficit hyperactive disorder (ADHD)** to identify children with this problem. Table 3.2 on the next page lists some indicators of ADHD used by the APA.

Children with ADHD may be more physically active and inattentive than other children, but not necessarily. They often have difficulty responding appropriately and working steadily toward goals (even their own goals). A particular difficulty involves inhibitions. Instead of thinking before acting, they have problems delaying actions, so these students just act (Barkley, 2003). The problem behaviors are generally evident in all situations and with every teacher.

It is difficult to know how many children should be classified as hyperactive. The most common estimate is 3 to 5% of the elementary school population, with over half of these students having the combined attention and hyperactivity conditions (Hardman,

---

TABLE 3.2   Indicators of ADHD: Attention Deficit Hyperactivity Disorder

---

Do any of your students show these signs? They could be indications of ADHD.

Problems with *Inattention*
- Fails to give close attention to details or makes careless mistakes
- Has difficulty sustaining attention in tasks or play activities
- Does not seem to listen when spoken to directly
- Does not follow through on instructions and fails to finish schoolwork (not due to oppositional behavior or failure to understand instructions)
- Has difficulty organizing tasks or activities
- Avoids, dislikes, or is reluctant to engage in tasks that require sustained mental effort (such as schoolwork or homework)
- Loses things necessary for tasks or activities
- Is easily distracted by extraneous stimuli
- Is forgetful in daily activities

Problems with *Impulse Control*
- Blurts out answers before questions have been completed
- Has difficulty awaiting his/her turn
- Interrupts or intrudes on others in conversations or games

Hyperactivity
- Fidgets with hands or feet or squirms in seat
- Leaves seat in classroom or in other situations in which remaining seated is expected
- Runs about or climbs excessively in situations in which it is inappropriate (in adolescents may be limited to subjective feelings of restlessness)
- Has difficulty playing or engaging in leisure activities quietly
- Talks excessively
- Acts as if "driven by a motor" and cannot remain still

Source: Reprinted with permission from *Diagnostic Statistical Manual of Mental Disorders (DSM-IV-TR)*, Fourth Edition. Text revision, 1994, Washington, DC: American Psychiatric Association. Copyright © 2000 American Psychiatric Association.

Drew, & Egan, 2005; Sagvolden, 1999). About three to four times more boys than girls are identified as hyperactive, but the gap appears to be narrowing (Hallahan et al., 2005). Just a few years ago, most psychologists thought that ADHD diminished as children entered adolescence, but now there are some researchers who believe that the problems can persist into adulthood (Berk, 2007). Today there is an increasing reliance on drug therapy such as Ritalin (methylphenidate) for ADHD. In fact, from 1990 to 1998, there was a 700% increase in the production of Ritalin in the United States (Diller, 1998).

Ritalin and other prescribed drugs such as Dexedrine, Adderall, Concerta, and Cylert are stimulants, but in particular dosages they appear to stimulate the brain's frontal lobe, improving attention and the ability to inhibit distracting behaviors.

Research suggests that about 70% of hyperactive children are more manageable when on medication. But for many there are negative side effects such as increased heart rate and blood pressure, interference with growth rate, insomnia, weight loss, and nausea (Panksepp, 1998; Weiss & Hechtman, 1993). In addition, little is known about the long-term effects of drug therapy. So beware. Many studies have concluded that the improvements in behavior from the drugs *seldom* lead to improvements in academic learning or peer relationships, two areas where children with ADHD have great problems. Because children appear to improve dramatically in their behavior, parents and teachers, relieved to see change, may assume the problem has been cured. It hasn't. The children still need special help in learning (Doggett, 2004; Purdie, Hattie, & Carroll, 2002). One large study in Australia concluded:

> Multimodal approaches to intervention have been found to be most effective in terms of lasting change. For most, but not all children and adolescents, treatment with psychostimulants has beneficial effects, provided that it is accompanied by remedial tuition, counselling, and behaviour management by parents/teachers, as required. Thus, advice from several different professions may be necessary. (van Kraayenoord, Rice, Carroll, Fritz, Dillon, & Hill, 2001, p. 7)

David Nylund (2000) describes a therapy for ADHD, called SMART, that has important implications for educators. Rather than treating the problem child, Nylund's idea is to enlist the child's strengths to conquer the child's problems: put the child in control. New metaphors for the situation are developed. Rather than seeing the problems as inside the child, Nylund helps everyone see ADHD, "Trouble," "Boredom," and other enemies of learning as outside the child, demons to be conquered or unruly spirits to be enlisted in the service of what *the child* wants to accomplish. The focus is on solutions. The steps of the SMART approach are these:

Separating the problem of ADHD from the child
Mapping the influence of ADHD on the child and family
Attending to the exceptions to the ADHD story
Reclaiming special abilities of children diagnosed with ADHD
Telling and celebrating the new story (Nylund, 2000, p. xix)

Ask your teachers to look for times when the student is engaged, even short times, and to note what is different about these times. Discover the student's strengths and allow yourself to be amazed by them. Make changes in teaching that support the changes the student is trying to make. Students working with Nylund said these teaching strategies would help them gain control:

- Use lots of pictures (visual clues) to help me learn.
- Offer me choices.
- Recognize cultural and racial identity.

- Realize that I am intelligent.
- Don't just lecture—it's boring!
- Let me walk around the classroom.
- Know when to bend the rules.
- Don't give tons of homework.
- Notice when I am doing well.
- More recess!
- Don't tell the other kids that I am taking Ritalin.
- Be patient. (Nylund, 2000, pp. 202–203)

Learning Disabilities

How do you explain what is wrong with a student who has no developmental disabilities; who has normal vision, hearing, and language capabilities; and who still cannot learn to read, write, or compute? One explanation is that the student has a **learning disability.** This is a relatively new and controversial category of exceptional students. There is no fully agreed upon definition. A recent text on learning disabilities gives eight definitions (Hallahan et al., 2005), including the definition used in IDEA (Individuals with Disabilities Education Act): "a disorder in one or more of the basic psychological processes involved in understanding or using language, spoken or written" (p. 15). Most definitions agree that students with learning disabilities perform significantly below what would be expected, given their other abilities.

Students with Learning Disabilities.   Students with learning disabilities are not all alike. The most common characteristics are specific difficulties in one or more academic areas; poor fine motor coordination; problems paying attention; hyperactivity and impulsivity; problems organizing and interpreting visual and auditory information; disorders of thinking, memory, speech, and hearing; and difficulties making and keeping friends (Hallahan & Kauffman, 2006; Hallahan, Lloyd, Kauffman, Weiss, & Martinez, 2005). As you can see, many students with other disabilities (such as attention deficit disorder) and many normal students may have some of the same characteristics. To complicate the situation even more, not all students with learning disabilities will have these problems, and few will have all of the problems. These students may be well below average in some academic areas, but average or strong in others.

Most students with learning disabilities have difficulties reading and writing. Table 3.3 lists some of the most common problems and signs, although these problems are not always signs of learning disabilities. These difficulties appear to be due to problems with relating sounds to letters that make up words, which makes spelling hard as well (Stanovich, 1994; Willcutt et al., 2001). Math, both computation and problem solving, is the second most common problem for learning-disabled students. The writing of some learning-disabled students is virtually unreadable, and their spoken language can be halting and disorganized. Many researchers trace some of these problems to the students' inability to use effective learning strategies, which we discuss in Chapter 4. Students with learning disabilities often lack effective ways to approach academic tasks.

TABLE 3.3   Potential Signs of Learning Disabilities

Do any of your students show these signs? They could be indications of learning disabilities.

Reading
- Has difficulty recognizing and remembering sight words
- Frequently loses place while reading
- Reversing letters or words (e.g., *was* is read *saw*)
- Confuses similar looking words (e.g., *beard* and *bread*)
- Weak comprehension of ideas and themes
- Has significant trouble learning to read
- Guesses at unfamiliar words rather than using word analysis skills
- Slow, laborious reading, less than 20 to 30 words per minute
- Substitutes or leaves out words

Writing
- Writing is messy and incomplete
- Uneven spacing between words and letters
- Copies inaccurately
- Spells poorly and inconsistently
- Has difficulty proofreading and self-correcting work

Source: From *Child and Adolescent Development for Educators 3/e*, (p. 78–79), by J. L. Meece and D. H. Daniels. Published by McGraw-Hill. Copyright © 2008 by The McGraw-Hill Companies. Adapted with permission of The McGraw-Hill Companies.

They don't know how to focus on the relevant information, get organized, apply learning strategies and study skills, change strategies when one isn't working, or evaluate their learning. They tend to be passive learners, in part because they don't know how to learn. Working independently is especially trying, so homework and seatwork are often left incomplete (Hallahan et al., 2005).

Early diagnosis is important so that students with learning disabilities do not become terribly frustrated and discouraged or develop bad habits in an attempt to compensate. The students themselves do not understand why they are having such trouble, and they may become victims of **learned helplessness.** This condition was first identified in learning experiments with animals. The animals were put in situations where they received punishment (electric shocks) that they could not control. Later, when the situation was changed and they could have escaped the shocks or turned them off, the animals didn't even bother trying (Seligman, 1975). They had learned to be helpless victims. Learning-disabled students may also come to believe that they cannot control or improve their own learning. This is a powerful belief. The students never exert the effort to discover that they can make a difference in their own learning, so they remain passive and helpless.

Teaching Students with Learning Disabilities.   There is controversy over how best to help these students. In teaching reading, a combination of teaching letter-sound (phonological) knowledge and word identification strategies appears to be effective. For example, Maureen Lovett and her colleagues (Lovett et al., 2000) in Canada taught students with severe reading disabilities to use the four different word identification strategies: (1) word identification by analogy, (2) seeking the part of the word that you know, (3) attempting different vowel pronunciations, and (4) "peeling off" prefixes and suffixes in a multisyllabic word. Teachers worked one-to-one with the students to learn and practice these four strategies along with analysis of word sounds and blending sounds into words (phonological knowledge). Direct teaching of skills and strategies is especially important for students with reading disabilities. And the teaching does not have to focus on low-level skills. Here are some general strategies taken from Hardman, Drew, and Egan (2005):

Preschool Years

- Keep verbal instructions short and simple.
- Match level of content carefully to the child's developmental level.
- Give multiple examples to clarify meaning.
- Allow more practice than usual, especially when material is new.

Elementary School Years

- Keep verbal instructions short and simple; have students repeat directions back to you to be sure they understand.
- Use mnemonics (memory strategies) in instruction to teach students how to remember.
- Repeat main points several times.
- Provide additional time for learning and practice—reteach when necessary.

Secondary School and Transition Years

- Directly teach self-monitoring strategies, such as cueing students to ask, "Was I paying attention?"
- Connect new material to knowledge student already has.
- Teach students to use external memory strategies and devices (tape-recording, note taking, to-do lists, and so on).

You may be thinking that these are good ideas for many students who need more support and direct teaching of study skills. You are right.

Autism Spectrum Disorders and Asperger Syndrome

You may be familiar with the term "autism." In 1990 *autism* was added to the IDEA list of disabilities qualifying for special services. It is defined as "a developmental disability significantly affecting verbal and nonverbal communication and social interaction, generally evident before age three, that adversely affects the child's educational performance" (34 Federal Code of Regulations § 300.7). About 1 in every 150 children are born with autism. We have used the term preferred by professionals in the field, **autism spectrum disorders,** to emphasize that autism includes a range of disorders from mild to major. From early on, children with autism spectrum disorders may have difficulties in social relations. Children with autism do not form connections with others, avoid eye contact, or don't share feelings such as enjoyment or interest with others. Communication is impaired. About half of these students are nonverbal; they have no or very few language skills. Others make up their own languages. They may obsessively insist on regularity and sameness in their environments—change is very disturbing. They may repeat behaviors and have restricted interests, watching the same DVD over and over, for example. They may be very sensitive to light, sound, touch, or other sensory information. Sounds may be painful, for example, or the slight flickering of fluorescent lights may seem like constant bursts of light, causing severe headaches (Franklin, 2007). They may be able to memorize words or steps in problem solving, but not use them appropriately or be very confused when the situation changes or questions are asked in a different way (Friend, 2008).

   Asperger syndrome is one of the disabilities included in the autistic spectrum. These children have many characteristics described above, but have the greatest trouble with social relations. Language is less affected. Their speech may be fluent but unusual, mixing up pronouns of "I" and "you," for example (Friend, 2008). Many students with autism also have moderate to severe intellectual disabilities, but those with Asperger syndrome usually have average to above average intelligence.

Theory of Mind.   One current explanation for autism and Asperger syndrome is that children with these disorders lack a theory of mind—an understanding that they and other people have minds, thoughts, and emotions. They have difficulty explaining their own behaviors, appreciating that other people might have different feelings, and predicting how behaviors might affect emotions. So, for example, a student may not understand why classmates are bored by his constant repetition of stories or obscure facts about topics he finds fascinating. Or the student may stand too close or too far away when interacting, not realizing that she is making other people uncomfortable (Friend, 2008; Harris, 2006).

Interventions.   Early and intense interventions that focus on communications and social relations are particularly important for children with autism spectrum disorders. As they move into elementary school, some of these students will be in inclusive settings, others in specialized classes, and many in some combination of these two. Collaboration among teachers and the family is particularly important. Supports such as smaller classes, structured environments, finding a class "buddy" to give support, providing a safe "home base" for times of stress, consistency in instruction and transition routines, assistive technologies, and the use of visual supports may be part of a collaborative plan (Friend, 2008). Through adolescence and transition to adulthood, life, work, and social skills are important educational goals.

Integration, Mainstreaming, and Inclusion

No matter what grade or subject you supervise, your teachers will work with exceptional students in their classrooms. In the United States, beginning in 1975 with PL 94-142 (the Education of the Handicapped Act), a series of laws has led to revolutionary changes in the education of children with disabilities. The legislation, now called the **Individuals with Disabilities Education Act (IDEA),** was revised in 1990, 1997, and 2004. At the most general level, the law now requires states to provide a free, appropriate public education (FAPE) for all students with disabilities who participate in special education. There are no exceptions—the law requires **zero reject.** This policy also applies to students with communicable diseases such as AIDS. The expenses of meeting the special needs of these students are considered a public responsibility. Let's examine the requirements in these laws. There are three major points of interest to principals and teachers: the concept of "least restrictive placement," the protection of the rights of students with disabilities and of their parents, and the individualized education program (IEP).

Least Restrictive Placement.   The laws require states to develop procedures for educating each child in the **least restrictive placement.** This means a setting that is as close to the general education class setting as possible. Over the years, recommended approaches to achieve this have moved from **mainstreaming** (including special needs children in a few regular education classes as convenient), to integration (fitting the special needs child into existing class structures), to **inclusion** (restructuring educational settings to promote belonging for all students) (Avramidis, Bayliss, & Burden, 2000). Advocates of inclusion believe that students with disabilities can benefit from involvement with their nondisabled peers and should be educated with them in their regular home-district school, even if doing so calls for changes in educational requirements, special aids, services, and training or consultation for the regular teaching staff (Stainback & Stainback, 1992). But some researchers caution that inclusion classrooms are not the best placement for every child. For example, Naomi Zigmond and her colleagues (1995) report that, in their study of six elementary schools that had implemented full inclusion, only about half of the students with learning disabilities in these schools were able to benefit.

The Rights of Students and Parents.   Several stipulations in these laws protect the rights of parents and students. Schools must have procedures for maintaining the confidentiality of school records. Testing practices must not discriminate against students from different cultural backgrounds. Parents have the right to see all records relating to the testing, placement, and teaching of their child. If they wish, parents may obtain an independent evaluation of their child. Parents may bring an advocate or representative to the meeting at which the IEP is developed. Students whose parents are unavailable must be assigned a surrogate parent to participate in the planning. Parents must receive written notice (in their native language) before any evaluation or change in placement is made. Finally, parents have the right to challenge the program developed for their child, and are protected by due process of law. Because principals and teachers often have conferences with these families, we have provided some Theory into Action Guidelines to make the meetings more effective, but be aware that guidelines apply to all students and their parents.

Individual Education Program.   The drafters of the laws recognized that each student is unique and may need a specially tailored program to make progress. The **individualized education program (IEP)** is an agreement between parents and the school about the services that will be provided. The IEP is written by a team that includes the student's parents or guardians, a general education teacher who works with the student, a special education teacher, a qualified school representative who can interpret the student's evaluation results, and (if appropriate) the student. If the school and parents agree, the team could add other people who have special knowledge of the

---

THEORY INTO ACTION GUIDELINES

Productive Family Conferences

Plan and prepare for a productive conference.

Examples

1. Have a clear purpose and gather the needed information. If you want to discuss student progress, have work samples.
2. Send home a list of questions and ask families to bring the information to the conference. Sample questions from Friend and Bursuck (2006) are:
   - What is your child's favorite class activity?
   - Does your child have worries about any class activities? If so, what are they?
   - What are your priorities for your child's education this year?
   - What questions do you have about your child's education in my class this year?
   - How could we at school help make this the most successful year ever for your child?
   - Are there any topics you want to discuss at the conference that I might need to prepare for? If so, please let me know.
   - Would you like other individuals to participate in the conference? If so, please give me a list of their names.
   - Is there particular school information you would like me to have available? If so, please let me know. (p. 100)

During the conference, create and maintain an atmosphere of collaboration and respect.

Examples

1. Arrange the room for private conversation. Put a sign on your door to avoid interruptions. Meet around a conference table for better collaboration. Have tissues available.
2. Address families as "Mr." and "Ms.," not "Mom" and "Dad" or "Grandma." Use students' names.
3. Listen to families' concerns and build on their ideas for their children.

After the conference, keep good records and follow up on decisions.

Examples

1. Make notes to yourself and keep them organized.
2. Summarize any actions or decisions in writing and send a copy to the family and any other teachers or professionals involved.
3. Communicate with families on other occasions, especially when there is good news to share.

child (for example, a therapist). The program can be updated each year and must state in writing:

1. The student's present academic achievement and functional performance.
2. Measurable performance goal for the year. Parents must get reports of progress toward goals at least as often as report cards are sent home for all students.
3. A statement of specific special education and related services to be provided to the student and details of when those services will be initiated.
4. An explanation of how much of the student's program will not be in regular classroom and school settings.
5. A statement about how the student will participate in the state- and district-wide assessments, particularly those required by the No Child Left Behind accountability requirements.
6. Beginning at age fourteen and by age sixteen, a statement of needed transitional services to move the student toward further education or work in adult life.

Figure 3.2 is an example of an individual transition planning (ITP) form for employment.

Section 504 Protections for Students

As a consequence of the civil rights movement in the 1960s and 1970s, the federal government passed the Vocational Rehabilitation Act of 1973. Section 504 of that law prevents discrimination against people with disabilities in any programs, such as public schools, that receive federal money.

Through **Section 504,** all school-age children are ensured an equal opportunity to participate in school activities. The definition of *disability* is broad in Section 504. If a student has a condition that substantially limits participation in school, then the school must develop a plan for giving that student access to education, even though the school gets no extra funds. To get assistance through Section 504, students must be assessed, often by a team, and a plan developed. Unlike IDEA however, there are fewer rules about how this must happen, so individual schools design their own procedures (Friend, 2008). Look at Table 3.4 on the next page to see an example of the kinds of accommodations that might be made for a student. Many of these ideas seem to be "just good teaching." But we have been surprised to see how many teachers won't let students use calculators or tape recorders because "they should learn do it like everyone else!"

Two major groups are considered for Section 504 accommodations: students with medical or health needs such as diabetes, drug addictions, severe allergies, communicable diseases, temporary disabilities resulting from accidents, or alcoholism; and students with ADHD. We have already spent some time with the second group because teachers must spend quite a bit of time with them. Students with ADHD now also qualify for services under the "Other Health Impaired" category of IDEA, so your school district may serve these students under either IDEA or Section 504.

FIGURE 3.2   An Example of a Transition Planning Form in the Area of Employment

This ITP was developed for a student who is moving toward work in a grocery store. The plan describes the needed services so the student can transition into supported employment.

ILLUSTRATIVE TRANSITION PLANNING FORM IN THE AREA OF EMPLOYMENT

Student: *Robert Brown*

Meeting Date: *January 20, 2003*

Graduation Date: *June, 2004*

IDEA 2004

IEP/Transition Planning Team Members: *Robert Brown (student), Mrs. Brown (parent), Jill Green (teacher), Mike Weatherby (Vocational Education), Dick Rose (Rehabilitation), Susan Marr (Developmental Disabilities Agency)*

TRANSITION PLANNING AREA: *Employment*

Student Preferences and Desired Postschool Goals:
Robert would like to work in a grocery store as a produce stocker.

Present Levels of Performance:
Robert has held several work experience placements in local grocery stores (see attached placement summaries). He requires a self-management checklist using symbols to complete assigned work tasks. His rate of task completion is below the expected employer levels.

Need Transition Services:
Robert will require job placement, training, and follow-along services from an employment specialist. In addition, he needs bus training to get to his job.

ANNUAL GOAL: *Robert will work Monday through Friday from 1:00 to 4:00 p.m. at Smith's Food Center as a produce stocker, completing all assigned tasks without assistance from the employment specialist on ten consecutive weekly performance probes.*

Activities	Person	Completion Date
1. Place Robert on the state supported employment waiting list.	Susan Marr	May 1, 2003
2. Obtain a monthly bus pass.	Mrs. Brown	February 1, 2003
3. Schedule Robert for employee orientation training.		February 16, 2003

Source: From John J. McDonnell, Michael L. Hardman & Andres P. McDonnell, *Introduction to Persons with Moderate and Severe Disabilities: Educational and Social Issues,* 2/e. Published by Allyn & Bacon, Boston, MA. Copyright © 2003 by Pearson Education. Reprinted by permission of the publisher.

TABLE 3.4   Examples of Accommodations under Section 504

The types of accommodations that can be written into a Section 504 plan are almost without limit. Some accommodation may relate to physical changes in the learning environment (for example, air filters are installed to remove allergens). However, many students who have Section 504 plans have functional impairments related to their learning or behavior, and their needs are somewhat similar to those of students with disabilities. The following is a sample of instructional accommodations that could be incorporated into a Section 504 plan:

- Seat the student nearest to where the teacher does most of his/her instruction.
- Have the student sit next to a peer who can help as needed.
- Seat the student away from the distractions of doorways or windows.
- Fold assignments in half so that the student is less overwhelmed by the quantity of work.
- Make directions telegraphic, that is, concise and clear.
- Allow use of a calculator or tape recorder.
- Use voice recognition software on the computer for written assignments.
- Mark right answers instead of wrong answers.
- Send a set of textbooks to be left at home so that the student does not have to remember to bring books from school.
- Provide books on tape so that the student can listen to assignments instead of reading them.

If you review these items, you can see that many of them just make good instructional sense. They are effective instructional practices that help learners with special needs succeed in your classroom.

Source: From Marilyn Friend & William D. Bursuck, *Including Students with Special Needs: A Practical Guide for Classroom Teachers*, 3/e. Published by Allyn & Bacon, Boston, MA. Copyright © 2006 by Pearson Education. Adapted by permission of the publisher.

Effective Teaching in Inclusive Classrooms

Effective teaching for exceptional students is not a unique set of skills. It is a combination of good teaching practices and sensitivity to students. Students with disabilities need to learn the academic material, and they need to be full participants in the day-to-day life of the classroom. To accomplish the first goal of academic learning, Larrivee (1985) concludes that effective teachers do the following: Use time efficiently by having smooth management routines, avoiding discipline problems, and planning carefully. Ask questions at the right level of difficulty. Give supportive, positive feedback to students, helping them figure out the right answer if they are wrong but on the right track.

To accomplish the second goal of integrating students with disabilities into the day-to-day life of the classroom, Ferguson, Ferguson, and Bogdan (1987) give the following guidelines:

1. Mix students with disabilities into groups with nondisabled students. Avoid re-segregating students into separate groups.
2. Instead of sending students out for special services like speech therapy, remedial reading, or individualized instruction, try to integrate the special help into the

class setting, perhaps during a time when the other students are working independently too.

3. Make sure your language and behavior is a good model for everyone.

4. In addition, students with learning disabilities appear to benefit from extended practice distributed over days and weeks and from *advance organizers* such as focusing students on what they already know or stating clear objectives (Swanson, 2001).

5. Teach about differences among people as part of the curriculum. Let students become familiar with aids for people with disabilities, such as hearing aids, sign language, communication boards, and so on.

6. Have students work together in cooperative groups or on special projects such as role playing, biographical interviews, or lab assignments.

7. Try to keep the schedules and activity patterns of disabled and nondisabled students similar.

Decision Making.   Making decisions in the best interest of students is a complex job. Figure 3.3 on the next page guides you and your teachers through the process of identifying, assessing, and planning for students in your school.

Even though there are many good tests and careful procedures for making special education placement decisions, racial and ethnic minority students are overrepresented in the disability categories and underrepresented in gifted programs. For example, almost 20% of all students defined as having disabilities under IDEA are African American, but only 15% of all students attending school are African American. The overrepresentation is worse when we look at specific categories: 34% of all students identified as having intellectual disabilities/mental retardation and 27% of student identified as having emotional disturbance are African American—twice as high as we would expect based on the percent of African American students in the United States. And these students are more likely than white or Asian students to be placed outside of the general education system for most of their school day. In contrast, African American and Hispanic students make up only about 8% each of the students served in gifted and talented programs (Friend, 2008).

For almost four decades, educators have struggled to understand the causes of these over- and underrepresentations. Explanations include the higher poverty rates among African American and Hispanic families leading to poorer prenatal care, nutrition, and health care; systematic biases in teachers' attitudes, curriculum, instruction, and the referral process itself; and lack of preparation for teachers to work effectively with ethnic minority students (Friend, 2008). To deal with the referral problem, educators have recommended gathering more information about a student before a formal referral is made. How long has the student been in the United States? What about proficiency with English? Are there unusual stressors such as being homeless? Is the teacher knowledgeable about and respectful of the student's culture? Is the classroom culturally compatible and engaging (Chapter 2)? Can the student's abilities be assessed through alternative approaches such as creativity tests and portfolios or performances (Chapter 8)? Having more knowledge about the student and his or her circumstances outside of school should help teachers make better decisions about what programs are

FIGURE 3.3 The Decision-Making Process for Special Education

When a response to intervention (RTI) model is used, the data collected during that phase may be central to the assessment and decision-making process. MDT refers to a Multidisciplinary Team.

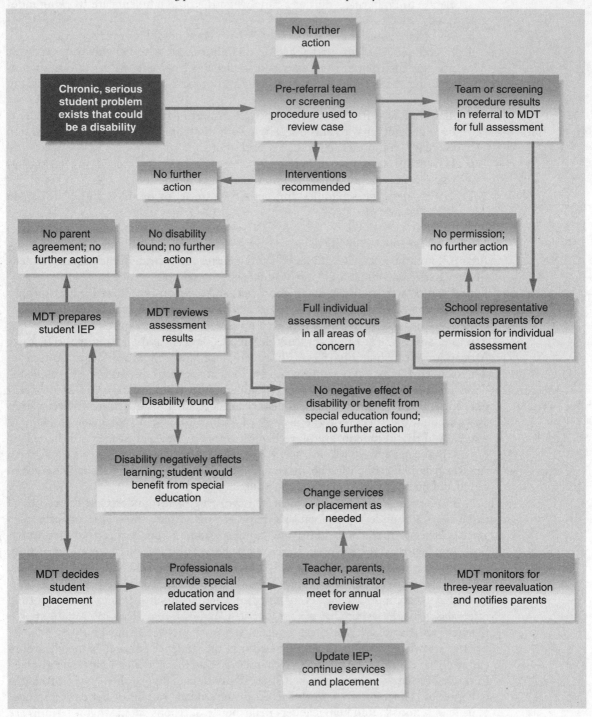

Source: From Marilyn Friend & William D. Bursuck. *Including Students with Special Needs: A Practical Guide for Classroom Teachers,* 3/e. Published by Allyn & Bacon, Boston, MA. Copyright © 2002 by Pearson Education. Reprinted by permission of the publisher.

appropriate (Friend, 2008; Gonzales, Brusca-Vega, & Yawkey, 1997; National Alliance of Black School Educators, 2002). In fact, instruction should be differentiated to better match the needs of all students.

Summary

Spearman suggests there is one mental attribute, which he called g, or general intelligence, that is used to perform on any mental test, but that each test also requires some specific abilities in addition to g. Gardner contends that an intelligence is a biological and psychological potential to solve problems and create products or outcomes that are valued by a culture. He identifies at least eight separate intelligences: linguistic, musical, spatial, logical-mathematical, bodily-kinesthetic, interpersonal, intrapersonal (these last two are similar to the idea of emotional intelligence), and naturalist; he now suggests perhaps existential as well. Gardner does not deny the existence of a general ability, but does question how useful g is as an explanation for human achievements. Recently, psychologists have also explored the notion of emotional intelligence—that is, perceiving, integrating, understanding, and managing emotions. Research suggests that helping students build their emotional competencies has beneficial effects on students' social and emotional development.

Sternberg's triarchic theory of intelligence is a cognitive process approach to understanding intelligence that has three parts: analytic, creative, and practical. Analytic intelligence involves the mental processes that lead to more or less intelligent behavior. Creative intelligence involves coping with new experiences through insight, or the ability to deal effectively with novel situations, and automaticity, or the ability to become efficient and automatic in thinking and problem solving. The third part is practical intelligence—choosing to live and work in a context where success is likely, adapting to that context, and reshaping it if necessary.

Intelligence is measured through individual tests (such as Stanford-Binet, Wechsler, Woodcock-Johnston, and Kauffman Assessment Battery) and group tests (such as Otis-Lennon School Abilities Tests, Slosson Intelligence Test, Raven Progressive Matrices, and Wide Range Intelligence Test). Compared to an individual test, a group test is much less likely to yield an accurate picture of any one person's abilities. The average score is 100; 50% of the people from the general population who take the tests will score 100 or above, and 50% will score below 100. About 68% of the general population will earn IQ scores between 85 and 115. Only about 16% of the population will receive scores below 85, and only 16% will score above 115. These figures hold true for white, native-born Americans whose first language is standard English. Intelligence predicts success in school, but is less predictive of success in life when level of education is taken into account.

Academic ability groupings can have both disadvantages and advantages for students and teachers. Low-ability classes seem to receive lower-quality instruction in general. Teachers tend to emphasize lower-level objectives and routine procedures, with less academic focus. Often there are more student behavior problems and, along with these problems, increased teacher stress and decreased enthusiasm. The lower tracks often have a disproportionate number of minority group and economically disadvantaged students, so ability grouping becomes segregation in school. Cross-age grouping by subject can be an effective way to deal with ability differences in nongraded elementary schools. Within-class ability grouping, if handled sensitively and flexibly, can have positive effects, but alternatives such as cooperative learning are also possible.

Ability grouping has benefits for gifted students, as does acceleration. Many people object to acceleration, but most careful studies indicate that truly gifted students who are accelerated do as well as, and usually better than, nongifted students who are progressing at the normal pace. Gifted students tend to prefer the company of older playmates and may be bored if kept with children of their own age. Skipping grades may not be the best solution for a particular student, but for students who are extremely advanced intellectually (160 or higher on an individual intelligence test), the only practical solution may be to accelerate their education.

Three common learning problems in the schools are attention deficit disorders, autism spectrum disorders, and specific learning disabilities. *Attention deficit hyperactivity disorder* (ADHD) is the term used to describe individuals of any age with hyperactivity and attention difficulties. Use of medication to address ADHD is controversial, but currently on the rise. About 70% of children with ADHD are more manageable when on medication. But for many there are negative side effects, and little is known about the long-term effects of drug therapy. There also is no evidence that the drugs lead to improvement in academic learning or peer relationships. *Autism* is a developmental disability that affects communication and social interaction. Autism spectrum disorders range along a continuum from mild to major disorders. Early interventions are particularly important for children with such disorders.

Specific learning disabilities involve significant difficulties in the acquisition and use of listening, speaking, reading, writing, reasoning, or mathematical abilities. These disorders are intrinsic to the individual, presumed to be due to central nervous system dysfunction, and may occur across the life span. Students with learning disabilities may become victims of learned helplessness when they come to believe that they cannot control or improve their own learning and therefore cannot succeed. A focus on learning strategies often helps students with learning disabilities.

IDEA, the Individuals with Disabilities Education Act, requires that each exceptional learner or special needs student be educated in the least restrictive environment according to an individualized education program. The law also protects the rights of special needs students and their parents. Recent legislation extends services to include transition programming for exceptional learners 16 years old and older.

KEY TERMS

attention deficit hyperactive disorder (ADHD) (73)
autism spectrum disorders (79)

between-class ability grouping (66)
crystallized intelligence (58)

emotional intelligence (EQ) (60)
flexible grouping (69)
fluid intelligence (57)

Flynn effect (64)

g (general intelligence) (57)

gifted and talented (69)

inclusion (80)

individualized education program (IEP) (81)

Individuals with Disabilities Education Act (IDEA) (80)

intelligence (57)

learned helplessness (77)

learning disability (76)

least restrictive placement (80)

mainstreaming (80)

Section 504 (82)

theory of multiple intelligences (58)

tracking (66)

triarchic theory of successful intelligence (62)

untracking (67)

within-class ability grouping (69)

zero reject (80)

DEVELOPING YOUR PORTFOLIO

1. Develop a position statement and action plan on the appropriate use of school-level student groupings.

   What is your philosophy about ability grouping and tracking? Be sure to support your perspective with the available research.

   What will you do? Develop a plan for implementing this philosophy in your school.

   How will you do it? Develop a realistic implementation strategy.

2. Develop a position statement and action plan on inclusion that complies with PL 94-142 and the subsequent modifications and extensions of the law.

   What is your philosophy about mainstreaming and inclusion? Be sure to support your perspective with the available research and the law.

Develop a plan for implementing this philosophy in your school. Be sure to include how you will comply with the "least restrictive placement" and other provisions of PL 94-142 as well as your district's policies on inclusion. Does the district policy facilitate or hinder your philosophy about inclusion? How?

Develop a framework and checklist to ensure that your school is in compliance with the relevant laws.

3. Develop a school policy on the use of results from intelligence tests. What sort of testing should be done? Who should have access? How should scores be used to support students' learning? Buttress your positions with current research and theory on intelligence.

INSTRUCTIONAL LEADER'S TOOLBOX

Readings

Benson, E. (2003). Intelligent intelligence testing. *Monitor on Psychology, 34*(2), 48.

Campbell, L., Campbell, B., & Dickinson, D. (2004). *Teaching and learning through multiple intelligences* (3rd ed.). Boston: Allyn & Bacon.

Kornhaber, M., Fierros, E., & Veenema, S. (2004). *Multiple intelligences: Best ideas for research and practice.* Boston: Allyn & Bacon.

Loveless, T. (1999). Will tracking reform promote social equity? *Educational Leadership, 56*(7), 28–32.

Neisser, U., et al. (1996). Intelligence: Knowns and unknowns. *American Psychologist, 51*, 77–101.

Meece, J. L., & Daniels, D. H. (2008). *Child and adolescent development for educators* (3rd ed.). New York: McGraw-Hill.

Panksepp, J. (1998). Attention deficit hyperactivity disorders, psychostimulants, and intolerance of playfulness: A tragedy in the making? *Current Directions in Psychological Science, 7*, 91–98.

Williams, W., Blythe, T., White, N., Li, J., Sternberg, R., & Gardner, H. (1996). *Practical intelligence in school.* New York: HarperCollins.

Videos

Educating Everybody's Children. The three-tape series shows how teachers set high expectations for learning, respond to the cultural differences of students, and create classroom environments that serve diverse learning styles. (ASCD Videos, 2000). Three 20- to 25-minute videotapes and a 92-page Facilitator's Guide. Order from: Association for Supervision and Curriculum Development (ASCD), 125 N. West St., Alexandria, VA 22314–2798. Telephone: (703) 549–9110; FAX: (703) 549–3891. http://shop.ascd .org/category.cfm?categoryid=video.

Websites

www.umaine.edu/edhd/
A collection of child development websites
www.cln.org/
Community Learning Network: a Canadian site with information on multiculturalism
www.thearc.org
Disability-related Resources on the Web
www.apa.org/monitor/sep99/sp.html
Emotional intelligence: Popular or scientific psychology?
idea.ed.gov/
IDEA (Individuals with Disabilities Education Act)
www.edwebproject.org/
Introduction to multiple intelligences
pzweb.harvard.edu
Project Zero

Organizations

www.al-anon.org
Al-Anon/Alateen: This organization provides support for the family members of alcoholics.

www.aacap.org/
American Academy of Child and Adolescent Psychiatry: This organization helps families understand the developmental, emotional, and behavioral disorders affecting children and adolescents.
www.aagc.org/
American Association for Gifted Children
www.chadd.org/
Children and Adults with Attention Deficit Disorders (C.H.A.D.D.)
www.cec.sped.org/
Council for Exceptional Children
www.ldanatl.org/
Learning Disabilities Association
www.nacd.org/
The National Academy of Child Development: An international organization of parents and professionals dedicated to helping children and adults reach their full potential. The site includes resources for parents and links to research articles.
www.add.org/
National Association for Attention Deficit Disorder
curry.edschool.virginia.edu/sped/projects/ose/ new.html
The Office of Special Education: You can find information on new legislation and new resources on this site. This is an excellent general resource.
www.ocecd.org/
Ohio Coalition for the Education of Children with Disabilities
www.researchtopractice.info/
Research and Training Center on Early Childhood Development

CHAPTER

4 Learning

PREVIEW: KEY POINTS

1. Learning occurs when experience leads to a relatively permanent change in an individual's knowledge or behavior.

2. There are many explanations for learning, but the most useful are the behavioral, cognitive, and constructivist perspectives.

3. Behavioral explanations of learning emphasize the importance of antecedents (cues and prompts) and consequences (reinforcement and punishment) in shaping behavior.

4. Functional behavioral assessments with positive behavior supports and homework are applications of the behavioral approach.

5. Cognitive explanations of learning highlight the importance of prior knowledge in focusing attention, making sense of new information, and supporting memory.

6. Information processing is a cognitive theory of memory that describes how information is taken in; processed (combined with prior knowledge); stored in long-term memory in the forms of episodes, productions, images and schemas, and retrieved.

7. Learning strategies (overall plans for learning) and learning tactics such as underlining, highlighting, and graphing are applications of the cognitive approach.

8. Constructivist views of learning explain learning in terms of the individual and social construction of knowledge; knowledge is judged not so much by its accuracy as by its usefulness.

9. Features of constructivist applications include complex real-life tasks, social interaction and shared responsibility, multiple representations of content, and student-centered teaching.

10. Three promising applications of the constructivist approach are inquiry or problem-based learning, cognitive apprenticeships, and cooperative learning. Fostering Communities of Learners is a system for integrating inquiry, collaborating, and learning deep disciplinary content.

Leadership Challenge

Your school's social studies department is highly regarded for its innovative approach to teaching. The program is oriented toward inquiry as a process, rather than the retention of historical facts. Typically, curriculum is developed by the department. The teachers are enthusiastic about their program, and it is well received by the students. You do not always agree with the direction of the curriculum, but there is little question that this is a highly skilled and professional group of teachers whom you respect.

Recent reform in the state has argued for back to basics and the use of curricular materials that stress recall of specific persons, places, and events in state and national history. The reform is supported by a battery of state tests. Although the state maintained that no invidious comparisons would be made, your community has made them. The superintendent has her feet to the fire on this issue, and now you, too, are feeling the heat. Recent test scores show that your students are not doing nearly as well in history as they are in science and mathematics. The superintendent has "requested" that you integrate the state curricular materials into the history program to correct the current deficiencies. Your history faculty, on the other hand, claim that this is exactly the wrong tack to take to develop inquiring minds. They are not overly concerned with the students' performance on the state tests because they claim the tests measure the wrong thing. Parents, however, cannot understand why their children are not doing as well in history as they are in math and science; in fact, at the last board meeting the superintendent promised that the history scores would rise.

What do students need to "know" about history?

What is the role of rote memory in learning?

What do the behavioral, cognitive, and constructivist perspectives on learning have to offer?

How does one achieve the right balance of teaching facts and teaching for discovery and understanding?

Source: The above situation has been adapted from Hoy, W. K., & Tarter, C. J. (1995). *Administrators solving the problems of practice: Decision making, concepts, cases, and consequences*: Boston: Allyn & Bacon.

What Is Learning?

Learning is at the center of schooling. Learning is a goal and a process—a noun and a verb. As a goal, learning (new knowledge and skills) is the outcome instructional leaders work toward as they interact with teachers. Learning is the teachers' goal with their students. But learning is also a process. In order to design useful learning environments in schools and classrooms, we must understand how people learn. The purpose of this chapter is to examine briefly what is known about learning so that your work with teachers and their work with students can be informed by and compatible with the ways that people learn. We will examine the contemporary contributions to education of three major perspectives on learning: behavioral, cognitive, and constructivist, noting specific strategies for teaching that are consistent with each perspective. Our goal is not to pick the "best" or most popular explanation of learning, but instead to use the best from each explanation, because each tells us something different and useful about the complex phenomenon that is human learning.

When we hear the word *learning*, most of us think of studying and school. We think about subjects or skills we intend to master, such as algebra, history, chemistry, or karate. But learning is not limited to school. We learn every day of our lives. Babies learn to kick their legs to make the mobile above their cribs move, teenagers learn the lyrics to all their favorite songs, and every few years we all learn to find a new style of dress attractive when the old styles go out of fashion. This last example shows that learning is not always intentional. We don't try to like new styles and dislike old; it just seems to happen that way. So what is this powerful phenomenon called learning?

In the broadest sense, **learning** occurs when practice or experience causes a relatively permanent change in an individual's knowledge, behaviors, or attitudes. The change may be deliberate or unintentional, for better or for worse (Hill, 2002). To qualify as learning, this change must be brought about by the interaction of a person with his or her physical or social environment. Changes due simply to maturation, such as growing taller or turning gray, do not qualify as learning. Temporary changes due to illness, fatigue, or hunger are also excluded from a general definition of learning. A person who has gone without food for two days does not learn to be hungry, and a person who is ill does not learn to run more slowly. Of course, learning plays a part in how we respond to hunger or illness.

Our definition specifies that the changes resulting from learning are in the individual's knowledge, attitudes, or behavior. Although most learning theorists would agree with this statement, some tend to emphasize changes in knowledge and attitudes, others the changes in behavior (Gredler, 2005; Swartz, Wasserman, & Robbins, 2002).

Behavioral psychologists emphasize observable changes in behaviors, skills, and habits.

Cognitive psychologists, who focus on changes in knowledge, believe learning is an internal mental activity that cannot be observed directly. Cognitive psychologists studying learning are interested in unobservable mental processes such as thinking, remembering, and solving problems.

Constructivist psychologists, more commonly known as constructivists, are interested in how people make meaning; learning is seen as the construction of knowledge.

Different theories of learning have had different impacts on education and have supported different practices. In the 1960s and early 1970s, behavioral views of learning dominated education. But beginning in the 1980s, cognitive and constructivist explanations became more prevalent. Even though there are differences in these explanations, each provides insights about some aspect of learning, in part because they focus on different kinds of outcomes. Each perspective provides instructional leaders with tools for improving instruction. We begin our explorations of learning with the behavioral perspective.

Behavioral Views of Learning

The behavioral approach to learning developed out of work by Skinner and others who emphasized the role of antecedents and consequences in behavior change. Learning was defined as a change in behavior brought about by experience, with little concern for the mental or internal aspects of learning. Behavior, like response or action, is simply a word for what a person does in a particular situation. Conceptually, we may think of a behavior as sandwiched between two sets of environmental influences: those that precede it (its antecedents) and those that follow it (its consequences) (Skinner, 1950). This relationship can be shown very simply as antecedent–behavior–consequence, or A–B–C. As behavior is ongoing, a given consequence becomes an antecedent for the next ABC sequence. Research shows that behavior can be altered by changes in the antecedents, the consequences, or both. Early work focused on consequences.

Types of Consequences

According to the behavioral view, consequences determine to a great extent whether a person will repeat the behavior that led to the consequences. The type and timing of consequences can strengthen or weaken behaviors. Consequences that strengthen behaviors are called *reinforcers*.

Reinforcement. Although reinforcement is commonly understood to mean "reward," this term has a particular meaning in learning theory. A **reinforcer** is any consequence that strengthens the behavior it follows. So, by definition, reinforced behaviors increase in frequency or duration. The **reinforcement process** can be diagrammed as follows:

CONSEQUENCE   EFFECT
Behavior $\longrightarrow$ reinforcer $\longrightarrow$ strengthened or repeated behavior

We can be fairly certain that food will be a reinforcer for a hungry animal, but what about people? It is not clear why an event acts as a reinforcer for an individual, but there are many theories about why reinforcement works. For example, some psychologists suggest that reinforcers satisfy needs, whereas other psychologists believe that reinforcers reduce tension or stimulate a part of the brain (Rachlin, 1991). Whether the consequences of any action are reinforcing probably depends on the individual's perception of the event and the meaning it holds for her or him (Landrum & Kauffman, 2006). For example, students who repeatedly get themselves sent to the principal's office for misbehaving may be indicating that *something* about this consequence is reinforcing for them, even if it doesn't seem desirable to their teachers.

There are two types of reinforcement. The first, called **positive reinforcement,** occurs when the behavior produces (adds) a new stimulus. Examples include wearing a new outfit producing many compliments, or, for a student, falling out of the chair producing cheers and laughter from classmates. When teachers claim that a student misbehaves "just to get attention," the teachers are applying a behavioral explanation based on positive reinforcement, assuming that attention is a positive reinforcer for the student.

Notice that positive reinforcement can occur even when the behavior being reinforced (falling out of a chair or disrupting math class) is not "positive" from the teacher's point of view. In fact, positive reinforcement of inappropriate behaviors occurs unintentionally in many classrooms. Teachers and principals help maintain problem behaviors by inadvertently reinforcing them. We once worked with a principal in a middle school who was concerned about a student. The boy had lost his father a few years earlier and was having trouble in a number of subjects, especially math. The student was sent to the office from math at least twice a week. When he arrived, the boy got the principal's undivided attention for at least ten minutes. After a scolding they talked sports because the principal liked the student and was concerned that he had no male role models. It is easy to spot the reinforcers in this situation, even though the principal did not mean to be part of the problem.

When the consequence that strengthens a behavior is the appearance (addition) of a new stimulus, the situation is defined as *positive* (+) reinforcement. In contrast, when the consequence that strengthens a behavior is the disappearance (subtraction) of a stimulus, the process is called **negative (−) reinforcement.** If a particular action leads to stopping, avoiding, or escaping an aversive situation, that action is likely to be repeated in a similar situation. A common example is the car seat belt buzzer. As soon as you attach your seat belt, the irritating buzzer stops. You are likely to *repeat* this "buckling up" action in the future (so the process is *reinforcement*) because the behavior made an aversive buzzing stimulus *disappear* (so the kind of reinforcement is *negative*).

The student who was repeatedly sent to the principal's office from math class not only spent time with the principal talking sports (positive reinforcement), he also escaped math class (negative reinforcement). Whatever the student did to get kicked out of math class is likely to continue (and it did) because the behavior led to both positive and negative reinforcers. The "negative" in negative reinforcement does not imply that the behavior being reinforced is necessarily bad. The meaning is closer to that of "negative" numbers—something is subtracted. Associate positive and negative reinforcement with adding or subtracting something following a behavior, leading to an increase in that behavior.

Punishment.   Negative reinforcement is often confused with punishment. In fact, when you understand the difference between negative reinforcement and punishment, you will know more than most of your colleagues. The process of reinforcement (positive or negative) always involves strengthening behavior. **Punishment,** on the other hand, involves decreasing or suppressing behavior. A behavior followed by a "punisher" is *less* likely to be repeated in similar situations in the future. Again, it is the effect that defines a consequence as punishment, and different people have different perceptions of what is punishing. One student may find suspension from school punishing, while another student wouldn't mind at all. The process of punishment is diagrammed as follows:

CONSEQUENCE   EFFECT
Behavior ⟶ punisher ⟶ weakened or decreased behavior

Like reinforcement, punishment may take one of two forms. The first type has been called Type I punishment, but this name isn't very informative, so we use the term **presentation punishment.** It occurs when the presentation of a stimulus following the behavior suppresses or decreases the behavior. When teachers assign demerits, extra work, running laps, and so on, they are using presentation punishment. The other type of punishment (Type II punishment) we call **removal punishment** because it involves removing a stimulus. When teachers or parents take away privileges after a young person has behaved inappropriately, they are applying removal punishment. With both types, the effect is to decrease or slow down the behavior that led to the punishment. Figure 4.1 summarizes the processes of reinforcement and punishment we have just discussed.

FIGURE 4.1 Kinds of Reinforcement and Punishment

Negative reinforcements and punishment are often confused. It may help you to remember that reinforcement is always associated with increases in behaviors, and punishment always involves decreasing or suppressing behavior.

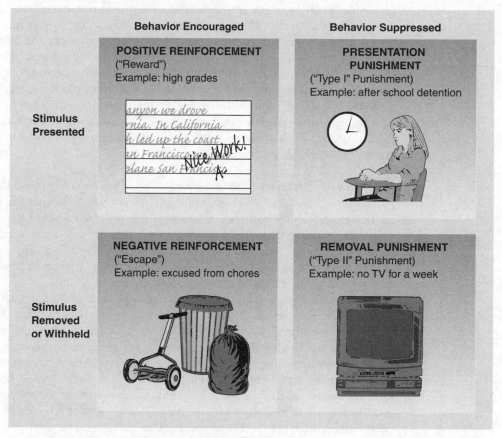

Source: From Anita E. Woolfolk, *Educational Psychology: Active Learning Edition*, 10/e. Published by Allyn & Bacon, Boston, MA. Copyright © 2008 by Pearson Education. Reprinted by permission of the publisher.

Antecedents and Behavior Change

Antecedents.   The events preceding behaviors, the **antecedents,** provide information about which behaviors will lead to positive consequences and which to negative. We all learn to discriminate—to read situations. When should a principal ask the board for additional resources, after a budget cut or when a good story about the school has appeared in the local paper? The antecedent cue of a school principal standing in the hall helps students discriminate the probable consequences of running or attempting to break into a locker. We often respond to such antecedent cues without fully realizing that they are influencing our behavior. But we can use cues deliberately.

Cueing.   By definition, **cueing** is the act of providing an antecedent stimulus just before a particular behavior is to take place. Cueing is particularly useful in setting the stage for behaviors that must occur at a specific time but are easily forgotten. In working with young people, teachers often find themselves correcting behaviors after the fact. For example, they may ask students, "When are you going to start remembering to . . . ?" But the mistake is already made, and the young person is left with only two choices, to promise to try harder or to say, "Why don't you leave me alone?" Neither response is very satisfying. Presenting a nonjudgmental cue, such as a checklist, can help prevent these negative confrontations. When a student performs appropriately after a cue, the teacher can reinforce the student's accomplishment instead of punishing the student's failure.

Prompting.   Sometimes students need help in learning to respond to a cue. One approach is to provide an additional cue, called a *prompt*, following the first cue. There are two principles for using a cue and a prompt to teach a new behavior. First, make sure the environmental stimulus that you want to become a cue occurs immediately before the prompt you are using, so students will learn to respond to the cue and not rely only on the prompt. Second, fade the prompt as soon as possible so students do not become dependent on it (Alberto & Troutman, 2006).

An example of cueing and **prompting** is providing students with a checklist or reminder sheet. Figure 4.2 is a checklist for the steps in peer tutoring. Working in pairs is the cue; the checklist is the prompt. As students learn the procedures, the teacher may stop using the checklist, but may remind the students of the steps. When no written or oral prompts are necessary, the students have learned to respond appropriately to the environmental cue of working in pairs; they have learned how to behave in tutoring situations. But the teacher should continue to monitor the process, recognize good work, and correct mistakes. Before a tutoring session, the teacher might ask students to close their eyes and "see" the checklist, focusing on each step. As students work, the teacher could listen to their interactions and continue to coach students as they improve their tutoring skills.

Principals and teachers can make good use of behavioral principles, particularly in their wise and caring applications of reinforcement and punishment. The Theory into Action Guidelines on page 100 give examples that will help your teachers apply the behavioral theory described above. Instructional leaders not only need to know the theory; they must be able to demonstrate and apply it as they work with their teachers.

Teaching Applications of Behavioral Theories

The behavioral approach to learning has made several important contributions to instruction, including systems for specifying learning objectives (we will look at this topic in Chapter 6 when we discuss planning and teaching) and class management systems such as group consequences, token economies, and contingency contracts. These

FIGURE 4.2   Written Prompts: A Peer-Tutoring Checklist
By using this checklist, students are reminded how to be effective tutors. As they become
more proficient, the checklist may be less necessary.

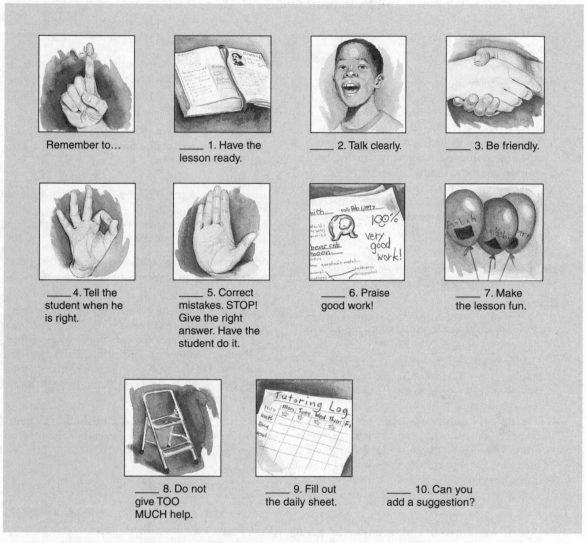

Remember to…

_____ 1. Have the lesson ready.

_____ 2. Talk clearly.

_____ 3. Be friendly.

_____ 4. Tell the student when he is right.

_____ 5. Correct mistakes. STOP! Give the right answer. Have the student do it.

_____ 6. Praise good work!

_____ 7. Make the lesson fun.

_____ 8. Do not give TOO MUCH help.

_____ 9. Fill out the daily sheet.

_____ 10. Can you add a suggestion?

Source: From *Achieving Educational Excellence: Behavior Analysis for School Personnel* (Figure, p. 89), by B. Sulzer-
Azaroff and G. R. Mayer, 1994, San Marcos, CA: Western Image, P. O. Box 427. Copyright © 1994 by Beth
Sulzer-Azaroff and G. Roy Mayer. Reprinted by permission of the authors.

approaches are especially useful when the goal is to learn explicit information or change
behaviors and when the material is sequential and factual (Alberto & Troutman, 2006;
Kazdin, 2001). As an example of a teaching approach, let's consider a system that supports students' positive behaviors rather than punishing mistakes.

THEORY INTO ACTION GUIDELINES

Using Reinforcement and Punishment

Associate positive, pleasant events with learning tasks.

Examples

1. Emphasize group competition and cooperation over individual competition. Many students have negative emotional responses to individual competition that may generalize to other learning.
2. Make division drills fun by having students decide how to divide refreshments equally, then letting them eat the results.
3. Make voluntary reading appealing by creating a comfortable reading corner with pillows, colorful displays of books, and reading props such as puppets (see Morrow & Weinstein, 1986, for more ideas).

Help students to risk anxiety-producing situations voluntarily and successfully.

Examples

1. Assign a shy student the responsibility of teaching two other students how to distribute materials for map study.
2. Devise small steps toward a larger goal. For example, give ungraded practice tests daily, and then weekly, to students who tend to "freeze" in test situations.
3. If a student is afraid of speaking in front of the class, let the student read a report to a small group while seated, then read it while standing, then give the report from notes instead of reading it verbatim. Next, move in stages toward having the student give a report to the whole class.

Be clear, systematic, and genuine in giving praise.

Examples

1. Make sure praise is tied directly to appropriate behavior.
2. Make sure the student understands the specific action or accomplishment that is being praised. Say, "You returned this poster on time and in

good condition," not, "You were very responsible."
3. Tie praise to students' improving competence or to the value of their accomplishment. Say, "I noticed that you double-checked all your problems. Your score reflects your careful work."

Attribute the student's success to effort and ability so the student will gain confidence that success is possible again.

Examples

1. Don't imply that the success may be based on luck, extra help, or easy material.
2. Ask students to describe the problems they encountered and how they solved them.

When students are tackling new material or trying new skills, give plenty of reinforcement.

Examples

1. Find and comment on something right in every student's first life drawing.
2. Reinforce students for encouraging each other. "French pronunciation is difficult and awkward at first. Let's help each other by eliminating all giggles when someone is brave enough to attempt a new word."

After new behaviors are established, give reinforcement on an unpredictable schedule to encourage persistence.

Examples

1. Offer surprise rewards for good participation in class.
2. Start classes with a short, written extra-credit question. Students don't have to answer, but a good answer will add points to their total for the semester.
3. Make sure the good students get compliments for their work from time to time. Don't take them for granted.

Make sure all students, even those who often cause problems, receive some praise,

(continued)

THEORY INTO ACTION GUIDELINES Continued

privileges, or other rewards when they do something well.

Examples

1. Review your class list occasionally to make sure all students are receiving some reinforcement.
2. Set standards for reinforcement so that all students will have a chance to be rewarded.
3. Let students suggest their own reinforcers or choose from a "menu" of reinforcers with "weekly specials."

Be consistent in your application of punishment.

Examples

1. Avoid inadvertently reinforcing the behavior you are trying to punish. Keep confrontations private, so that students don't become heroes for standing up to the teacher in a public showdown.
2. Let students know in advance the consequences of breaking the rules by posting major class rules for younger students or outlining rules and consequences in a course syllabus for older students.
3. Tell students they will receive only one warning before punishment is given. Give the warning in a calm way, then follow through.
4. Make punishment as unavoidable and immediate as is reasonably possible.

Focus on the students' actions, not on the students' personal qualities.

Examples

1. Reprimand in a calm but firm voice.
2. Avoid vindictive or sarcastic words or tones of voice. You might hear your own angry words later when students imitate your sarcasm.
3. Stress the need to end the problem behavior instead of expressing any dislike you might feel for the student.

Adapt the punishment to the infraction.

Examples

1. Ignore minor misbehaviors that do not disrupt the class, or stop these misbehaviors with a disapproving glance or a move toward the student.
2. Don't use homework as a punishment for misbehaviors like talking in class.
3. When a student misbehaves to gain peer acceptance, removal from the group of friends can be effective, since this is really time out from a reinforcing situation.
4. If the problem behaviors continue, analyze the situation and try a new approach. Your punishment may not be very punishing, or you may be inadvertently reinforcing the misbehavior.

Functional Behavioral Assessment and Positive Behavior Support

Teachers in both regular and special education classes have had success with a new approach that begins by asking, "What are students getting out of their problem behaviors—what functions do these behaviors serve?" The focus is on the why of the behavior, not on the what (Lane, Falk, & Wehby, 2006). The reasons for problem behaviors generally fall into four categories (Barnhill, 2005; Maag & Kemp, 2003). Students act out to:

1. receive attention from others—teachers, parent, or peers;
2. escape from some unpleasant situation—an academic or social demand;
3. get a desired item or activity;
4. meet sensory needs, such as stimulation from rocking or flapping arms for some children with autism.

If the reason for the behavior is known, then the teacher can devise ways of supporting positive behaviors that will serve the same "why" function. For example, in the situation we described earlier, the student who was repeatedly sent out of math class to the principal's office, it is easy to spot the function of the classroom disruptions—they always led to (1) escape from math class (negative reinforcement) and (2) one-on-one time with the principal (positive reinforcement after a little bit of reprimanding). Working with the principal and math teacher, we developed a way to support the student's positive behaviors in math by getting him some extra tutoring and by giving him time with the principal when he completed math problems instead of when he acted up in class. The new positive behaviors served many of the same functions as the old problem behaviors.

Discovering the "Why": Functional Behavioral Assessments.   The process of understanding a problem behavior is known as **functional behavioral assessment (FBA)**—"a collection of methods or procedures used to obtain information about antecedents, behaviors, and consequences to determine the reason or function of the behavior" (Barnhill, 2005, p. 132). Many different procedures might help you determine the functions of a behavior. You can simply interview students about their behaviors. In one study, students were asked to describe what they did that got them in trouble in school, what happened just before, and what happened right after they acted out. Even though the students were not always sure why they acted out, they seemed to benefit from talking to a concerned adult who was trying to understand their situation, not just reprimand them (Murdock, O'Neill, & Cunningham, 2005). You also can observe students with these questions in mind: When and where does the problem behavior occur? What people or activities are involved? What happens right before—what do others do or say and what did the target student do or say? What happens right after the behavior—what did you, other students, or the target student do or say? What does the target student gain or escape from—what changes after the student acts out? A more structured approach is shown in Figure 4.3—an observation and planning worksheet for functional behavioral assessment.

With information from a functional behavioral assessment, administrators and teachers can develop an intervention package of positive behavior supports, as we did with the math student.

Positive Behavior Supports.   The Individuals with Disabilities Education Act (IDEA, 1997) discussed in Chapter 2 requires positive behavior supports (PBS) for students with disabilities and those at-risk for special education placement. **Positive behavior supports** are interventions designed to replace problem behaviors with new actions that serve the same purpose for the student.

Positive behavior supports based on functional behavioral assessments can help students with disabilities succeed in inclusion classrooms. For example, the disruptive behavior of a five-year-old boy with mental retardation was nearly eliminated in a relatively short time through a PBS intervention that was based on a functional assessment conducted by the regular teaching staff and the special education teacher. The

FIGURE 4.3 A Structured Observation Guide for Functional Behavioral Analysis

Student Name: _____ Date: _____

Target Behavior: Operationally define the behavior that most interferes with the student's functioning in the classroom. Include intensity (high, medium, or low), frequency, and duration.

_____
_____

When, where, with whom, and in what condition is the target behavior *least* likely to occur?

_____

Setting Events or Context Variables (i.e., hunger, lack of sleep, medications, problems on bus):

_____

Immediate Antecedents & Consequences

Antecedents	*Problematic Settings*	*Consequences*
____ Demand/Request	____ Unstructured setting	____ Behavior ignored
____ Difficult task	____ Unstructured activity	____ Reprimanded
____ Time of day	____ Individual seat work	____ Verbal redirection
____ Interruption in routine	____ Group work	____ Time-out (duration: ____)
____ Peer tease/provoked	____ Specials	____ Loss of incentives
____ No materials/activities	____ Specific subject/task	____ Physical redirection
____ Could not get desired item	____ Crowded setting	____ Physical restraint
____ People _____	____ Noisy setting	____ Sent to office
____ Alone	____ Other _____	____ Suspension
____ Other _____	____ Other _____	____ Other _____

What function(s) does the target behavior seem to serve for the student?

____ Escape from: ____ demand/request   ____ person   ____ activity/task   ____ school   ____ other _____

____ Attention from: ____ adult   ____ peer   ____ other _____

____ Gain desired: ____ item   ____ activity   ____ area   ____ other _____

____ Automatic sensory stimulation: _____

Hypothesis:

When _____ occurs in the context of _____
           (antecedent)   (problematic setting)

the student exhibits _____ in order to _____ .
                   (target behavior)   (perceived function)

This behavior is more likely to occur when _____ .
                                                      (setting event/context variables)

Replacement or competing behavior that could still serve the same function for the student:

_____

Is the replacement behavior in the student's repertoire, or will it need to be taught directly?_____

If so, how will it be taught?_____

List some potential motivators for student: _____
_____

Source: From "Functional behavior assessment in schools" by G. P. Barnhill, *Intervention in School and Clinic,* 40, p. 138. Copyright 2005 by the Hammill Institute on Diversity. Reprinted with permission.

intervention included making sure tasks assigned were at the right difficulty level, providing assistance with these tasks, teaching the student how to request assistance, and teaching the student how to request a break from assigned work (Soodak & McCarthy, 2006; Umbreit, 1995). But these approaches are not only for students with special needs. Research shows that disciplinary referrals decrease when the whole school uses these approaches for all students (Lewis, Sugai, & Colvin, 1998). Because about 5% of students account for half of the discipline referrals, it makes sense to develop interventions for those students. Positive behavior interventions based on functional assessments can reduce these behavior problems by 80% (Crone & Horner, 2003).

Homework

One of the implications of the behavioral view is that learning requires practice of correct responses—practice makes permanent. Educators have been studying the effects of homework for over seventy-five years (Cooper, 2004; Cooper & Valentine, 2001; Corno, 2000; Trautwein & Koller, 2003). Homework is one form of practice, but the value of homework has been debated, as you can see in the Point/Counterpoint.

Cognitive Views of Learning

The cognitive perspective is both the oldest and youngest explanation of learning. It is old because discussions of the nature of knowledge, the value of reason, and the contents of the mind date back at least to the ancient Greek philosophers (Hernshaw, 1987). From the late 1800s until a few decades ago, however, cognitive studies fell from favor and behaviorism thrived. Then, research during World War II on the development of complex human skills, the computer revolution, and breakthroughs in understanding language development all stimulated a resurgence in cognitive research. Evidence accumulated indicating that people do more than simply respond to reinforcement and punishment. For example, we plan our responses, use systems to help us remember, and organize the material we are learning in our own unique ways (Miller, Galanter, & Pribram, 1960; Shuell, 1986). With the growing realization that learning is an active mental process, educational psychologists became interested in how people think, learn concepts, and solve problems (e.g., Ausubel, 1963; Bruner, Goodnow, & Austin, 1956).

Interest in concept learning and problem solving soon gave way, however, to interest in how knowledge is represented in the mind and particularly how it is remembered. Remembering and forgetting became major topics for investigation in cognitive psychology in the 1970s and 1980s, and the information-processing model of memory dominated research. Today, there are other models of memory besides information processing. In addition, many cognitive theorists have a renewed interest in learning, thinking, and problem solving.

POINT/COUNTERPOINT   Is Homework a Valuable Use of Time?

Like so many methods in education, homework has moved in and out of favor. In the early 1900s, homework was seen as an important path to mental discipline, but by the 1940s, homework was criticized as too much drill and low-level learning. Then in the 1950s, homework was rediscovered as a way to catch up with the Soviet Union in science and mathematics, only to be seen as too much pressure on students during the more laid-back 1960s. By the 1980s, homework was in again as a way to improve the standing of American children compared to students around the world (Cooper & Valentine, 2001). Everyone has done homework—were those hours well spent?

POINT

Homework does not help students learn.
No matter how interesting an activity is, students will eventually get bored with it, so why give them work both in and out of school? They will simply grow weary of learning. And important opportunities are lost for community involvement or leisure activities that would create well-rounded citizens. When parents help with homework, they can do more harm than good—sometimes confusing their children or teaching them incorrectly. And students from poorer families often must work, so they miss doing the homework; then the learning discrepancy between the rich and poor grows even greater. Be-

sides, the research is inconsistent about the effects of homework. For example, one study found that in-class work was better than homework in helping elementary students learn (Cooper & Valentine, 2001).

COUNTERPOINT

Well-planned homework can work for many students.
Harris Cooper and Jeffrey Valentine reviewed many studies of homework and concluded that there is little relationship between homework and learning for young students, but the relationship between homework and achievement grows progressively stronger for older students. There is recent evidence that students in high school who do more homework (and watch less television after school) have higher grades, even when other factors such as gender, grade level, ethnicity, socioeconomic status, and amount of adult supervision are taken into consideration (Cooper & Valentine, 2001; Cooper, Valentine, Nye, & Lindsay, 1999). Consistent with these findings, the National PTA makes these recommendations:

> [F]or children in grades K–2, homework is most effective when it does not exceed 10–20 minutes each day; older students, in grades 3–6, can handle 30–60 minutes a day; in junior and senior high school, the amount of homework will vary by subject. (Henderson, 1996, p. 1)

Knowledge and Learning

Current cognitive approaches suggest that one of the most important elements in the learning process is what the individual brings to the learning situation. What we already know determines to a great extent what we will pay attention to, perceive, learn, remember, and forget (Bransford, Brown, & Cocking, 2002; Bransford, Derry, Berliner, & Hammerness, 2005). Pat Alexander (1996) notes that what we already know—our knowledge base—"is a scaffold that supports the construction of all future learning" (p. 89). Thus knowledge is more than the end product of previous learning; it also guides new learning.

A study by Recht and Leslie (1988) shows the importance of knowledge in understanding and remembering new information. These researchers identified junior high school students who were either very good or very poor readers. They tested the students on their knowledge of baseball and found that knowledge of baseball was not related to reading ability. So the researchers were able to identify four groups of students: good readers/high baseball knowledge, good readers/low baseball knowledge, poor readers/high baseball knowledge, and poor readers/low baseball knowledge. Then all the subjects read a passage describing a baseball game and were tested in a number of ways to see if they understood and remembered what they had read.

The results demonstrated the power of knowledge. Poor readers who knew baseball remembered more than good readers with little baseball knowledge and almost as much as good readers who knew baseball. Poor readers who knew little about baseball remembered the least of what they had read. So a good basis of knowledge can be more important than good learning strategies in understanding and remembering, but extensive knowledge plus good strategies are even better.

There are different kinds of knowledge. Some is general—it applies to many different situations. For example, general knowledge about how to read or write or use a word processor is useful in and out of school. **Domain-specific knowledge,** on the other hand, pertains to a particular task or subject. For example, knowing that the shortstop plays between second and third base is specific to the domain of baseball. Another way of categorizing knowledge is as declarative, procedural, or conditional (Paris & Cunningham, 1996; Paris, Lipson, & Wixson, 1983). **Declarative knowledge** is "knowledge that can be declared, usually in words, through lectures, books, writing, verbal exchange, Braille, sign language, mathematical notation, and so on" (Farnham-Diggory, 1994, p. 468). Declarative knowledge is "knowing that" something is the case. The range of declarative knowledge is tremendous. You can know very specific facts (the atomic weight of gold is 196.967), generalities (leaves of some trees change color in autumn), personal preferences (we don't like lima beans), personal events (what happened at the last faculty meeting), rules (to divide fractions, invert the divisor and multiply). Small units of declarative knowledge can be organized into larger units; for example, principles of reinforcement and punishment can be organized in your thinking into a theory of behavioral learning (Gagné, Yekovich, & Yekovich, 1993).

Procedural knowledge is "knowing how" to do something such as divide fractions or clean a carburetor; procedural knowledge must be demonstrated. Notice that repeating the rule "to divide fractions, invert the divisor and multiply" shows declarative knowledge; the student can state the rule. But to show procedural knowledge, the student must act. When faced with a fraction to divide, the student must divide correctly. Students or teachers demonstrate procedural knowledge when they translate a passage into Spanish or correctly categorize a geometric shape or craft a coherent paragraph.

Conditional knowledge is "knowing when and why" to apply your declarative and procedural knowledge. Given many kinds of math problems, it takes conditional knowledge to know when to apply one procedure and when to apply another to solve each problem. It takes conditional knowledge to know when to read every word in a text

TABLE 4.1   Kinds of Knowledge

	General Knowledge	Domain-Specific Knowledge
Declarative	Hours the library is open	The definition of *hypotenuse*
	Rules of grammar	The lines of the poem "The Raven"
Procedural	How to use your word processor	How to solve an oxidation-reduction equation
	How to drive	How to throw a pot on a potter's wheel
Conditional	When to give up and try another approach	When to use the formula for calculating volume
	When to skim and when to read carefully	When to rush the net in tennis

Source: From Anita Woolfolk, *Educational Psychology*, 9/e. Published by Allyn & Bacon, Boston, MA. Copyright © 2004 by Pearson Education. Reprinted by permission of the publisher.

and when to skim or when to intervene when new teachers are struggling and when to hold back and let the teachers work it out for themselves. For many people, conditional knowledge is a stumbling block. They have the facts and can do the procedures, but they don't seem to apply what they know at the appropriate time. Table 4.1 shows that we can combine our two systems for describing knowledge. Declarative, procedural, and conditional knowledge can be either general or domain-specific.

To be used, knowledge must be remembered. What do we know about memory?

An Information-Processing Model

One widely used cognitive model of the structure and processes of memory is the information-processing model, based on the analogy between the mind and the computer (Ashcraft, 2006). This model (see Figure 4.4 on the next page) includes three storage systems: the sensory memory, working memory (also called short-term memory), and long-term memory. Let's look at this system in more depth.

Sensory Memory

As you can see, **sensory memory** is the initial processing that transforms incoming stimuli (sights, sounds, smells, and so on) into information so we can make sense of them. We hold information, in the form of images or sounds or other codes, for only a very few seconds. **Attention** (maintaining cognitive focus on something and resisting distractions) is critical at this stage. What is not attended to is lost. This is actually useful because if every variation in color, movement, sound, smell, temperature, and so on ended up in memory, life would be impossible. But attention is *selective*. What we pay attention to is guided to a certain extent by what we already know and what we need to know, so attention is involved in and influenced by all three memory processes—sensory, working, and long-term.

FIGURE 4.4 The Information-Processing Model
Information is encoded in sensory memory where perception and attention determine what will be held in working memory for further use. In working memory, new information connects with knowledge from long-term memory. Thoroughly processed and connected information becomes part of long-term memory, and can be activated to return to working memory. Implicit memories are formed without conscious effort.

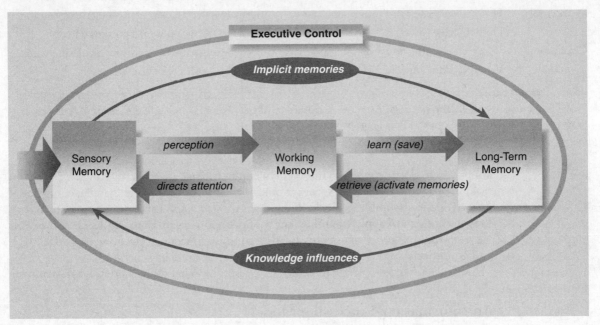

Source: From Anita E. Woolfolk, *Educational Psychology: Active Learning Edition*, 10/e. Published by Allyn & Bacon, Boston, MA. Copyright © 2008 by Pearson Education. Reprinted by permission of the publisher.

Attention also is a very limited resource. We can pay attention to only one demanding task at time. For example, if you learned to drive a stick shift, there probably was a time when you couldn't listen to the radio and drive at the same time. After some practice, you could listen, but might turn the radio off when traffic was heavy. After years of practice, some people shave or put on makeup as they drive. This is because many processes that initially require attention and concentration become automatic with practice (Bransford et al., 2005).

So the first step in learning is paying attention. Students cannot process something that they do not recognize or perceive (Lachter, Forster, & Ruthruff, 2004). Many factors in the classroom influence student attention. A teacher might begin a science lesson on air pressure by blowing up a balloon until it pops. Bright colors, underlining, highlighting of written or spoken words, calling students by name, surprise events, intriguing questions, variety in tasks and teaching methods, and changes in voice level, lighting, or pacing can all be used to gain attention. And students have to maintain attention; they have to stay focused on the important features of the learning situation.

THEORY INTO ACTION GUIDELINES

Capturing Attention

Use signals.

Examples

1. Develop a signal that tells students to stop what they are doing and focus on you. Some teachers move to a particular spot in the room, flick the lights, or play a chord on the class piano.
2. Avoid distracting behaviors such as tapping a pencil that interfere with both signals and attention to learning.
3. Give short, clear directions before, not during, transitions.

Make sure the purpose of the lesson or assignment is clear to students.

Examples

1. Write the goals or objectives on the board and discuss them with students before starting. Ask students to summarize or restate the goals.
2. Explain the reasons for learning, and ask students for examples of how they will apply their understanding of the material.
3. Tie the new material to previous lessons—show an outline or map of how the new topic fits with previous and upcoming material.

Emphasize variety, curiosity, and surprise.

Examples

1. Arouse curiosity with questions such as "What would happen if . . . ?"

2. Create shock by staging an unexpected event such as a loud argument just before a lesson on communication.
3. Alter the physical environment by changing the arrangement of the room or moving to a different setting.
4. Shift sensory channels by giving a lesson that requires students to touch, smell, or taste.
5. Use movements, gestures, and voice inflection—walk around the room, point, and speak softly and then more emphatically. (The second author has been known to jump up on his desk to make an important point in his college classes!)

Ask questions and provide frames for answering.

Examples

1. Ask students why the material is important, how they intend to study, and what strategies they will use.
2. Give students self-checking or self-editing guides that focus on common mistakes or have them work in pairs to improve each other's work— sometimes it is difficult to pay attention to your own errors.

How can instructional leaders help teachers develop strategies for capturing and maintaining students' attention? The Theory into Action Guidelines above provide some concrete examples.

Working Memory

Once noticed and transformed into patterns, the information in sensory memory is available for further processing. The working space of the memory system is called (surprise) **working memory.** It is the interface where new information is held temporarily (no more than 20 seconds or so) and combined with knowledge from long-term memory, to solve problems or understand a talk on leadership, for example. Working memory "contains" what you are thinking about at the moment. You may have heard the term *short-term memory*. This is similar to working memory but refers only to the storage space available. Working memory includes both temporary storage and active processing; it is the process or stage where active mental effort is applied to new and old information.

A current view of working memory is that it is composed of at least four elements: the central executive that controls attention and other mental resources (the "worker" of working memory), the phonological loop that briefly holds verbal and acoustical (sound) information, and the visuospatial sketchpad for visual and spatial information. Information from the phonological loop and the visuospatial sketchpad is integrated with information from long-term memory in an episodic buffer. This episodic buffer is the true workbench of working memory—the point where information from many sources is pulled together and processed (Alloway, Gathercole, & Pickering, 2006; Baddeley, 2006; Gathercole, Pickering, Ambridge, & Wearing, 2004).

Capacity and Contents.   Working memory capacity is limited. In experimental situations it appears that the capacity of working memory is only about five to nine separate new items at once (Miller, 1956). For example, if you get a phone number from information, you can remember it long enough to dial the number, but would you try to remember two numbers? Two new phone numbers (fourteen digits) probably cannot be stored simultaneously. We are discussing the recall of *new* information. In daily life we certainly can hold more than five to nine bits of information at once. While you are dialing that seven-digit phone number you just found, you are bound to have other things "on your mind" (in your memory), such as how to use a telephone, whom you are calling, and why. You don't have to pay attention to these things; they are not new knowledge. Some of the processes, such as dialing the phone, have become automatic. However, because of the working memory's limitations, if you were in a foreign country and were attempting to use an unfamiliar telephone system, you might very well have trouble remembering the phone number because you were trying to figure out the phone system at the same time.

It is clear that the duration of information in working memory is short, about 5 to 20 seconds. This is why working memory has been called short-term memory. It may seem to you that a memory system with a 20-second time limit is not very useful. But without this system, you would have already forgotten what you read in the first part of this sentence before you came to these last few words. This would clearly make understanding sentences difficult.

Retaining Information in Working Memory.   Because information in working memory is fragile and easily lost, it must be kept activated to be retained. When activation fades, forgetting follows. To keep information activated in working memory for longer than 20 seconds, most people keep rehearsing the information mentally.

There are two types of rehearsal. **Maintenance rehearsal** involves repeating the information in your mind. As long as you repeat the information, it can be maintained in working memory indefinitely. Maintenance rehearsal is useful for retaining something you plan to use and then forget, like a phone number. **Elaborative rehearsal** involves connecting the information you are trying to remember with something you already know, that is, with information from long-term memory. For example, if you meet someone at a party whose name is the same as yours, you don't have to repeat the name to keep it in memory, you just have to make the association. This kind of rehearsal not only retains information in working memory but helps move information from short-term to long-term memory. Rehearsal is thus an *executive control process* that affects the flow of information through the information-processing system.

The limited capacity of working memory can also be somewhat circumvented by the control process of **chunking.** Because the number of bits of information, not the size of each bit, is the limitation for working memory, you can retain more information if you can group individual bits of information. For example, if you have to remember the six digits 3, 5, 4, 8, 7, and 0, it is easier to put them together into three chunks of two digits each (35, 48, 70) or two chunks of three digits each (354, 870). With these changes, there are only two or three bits of information rather than six to hold at one time. Chunking helps you remember a telephone number or a Social Security number.

Long-Term Memory

Working memory holds the information that is currently activated, such as a telephone number you have just found and are about to dial. Long-term memory holds the information that is well learned, such as all the other telephone numbers you know.

Capacity and Duration of Long-Term Memory.   Information enters working memory very quickly. To move information into long-term storage requires more time and a bit of effort. Whereas the capacity of working memory is limited, the capacity of long-term memory appears to be, for all practical purposes, unlimited. In addition, once information is securely stored in long-term memory, it can remain there permanently. Theoretically, we should be able to remember as much as we want for as long as we want. Of course, the problem is finding the right information when it is needed. Our access to information in working memory is immediate because we are thinking about the information at that very moment. But access to information in long-term memory requires time and effort.

Contents of Long-Term Memory.   Most cognitive psychologists distinguish three categories of long-term memory: episodic, procedural, and semantic. Memory for information tied to a particular place and time, especially information about the events of your own life, is called episodic memory. **Episodic memory** keeps track of the order of things, so it is also a good place to store jokes, gossip, or plots from films. Memories for dramatic or emotional episodes in your life are called **flashbulb memories.** This kind of episodic memory is vivid and complete, as if your brain demanded "record this moment." Under stress, more glucose energy goes to fuel brain activity while stress-induced hormones signal the brain that something important is happening (Myers, 2005). So when we have strong emotional reactions, memories are stronger and more lasting. Many people have vivid memories of very positive or very negative events in school, winning a prize or being humiliated, for example. You probably know just where you were and what you were doing on 9/11.

Memory for how to do things is called **procedural memory.** It may take a while to learn a procedure—such as how to ski, serve a tennis ball, or factor an equation—but once learned, this knowledge tends to be remembered for a long time. Procedural memories are represented as condition–action rules, sometimes called *productions*. Productions specify what to do under certain conditions: if A occurs, then do B. A production might be something like, "If you want to snow ski faster, lean back slightly," or "If your goal is to increase student attention, and a student has been paying attention a bit longer than usual, then praise the student." People can't necessarily state all their condition–action rules, but they act on them nevertheless. The more practiced the procedure, the more automatic the action (Anderson, 1995). **Semantic memory** is memory for meaning. Two important ways that these memories are stored are images and schemas. Because these are very important concepts for teaching, we will spend some extra time on them.

Images are representations based on perceptions, on the structure or appearance of the information (Anderson, 1995). As we form images we try to remember or recreate the physical attributes and spatial structure of information. For example, when asked how many windowpanes are in their living room, most people call up an image of the windows "in their mind's eye" and count the panes—the more panes, the longer it takes to respond (Mendell, 1971). Images are useful in making many practical decisions such as how a sofa might look in your living room or how to line up a golf shot. Images may also be helpful in abstract reasoning. Physicists, such as Faraday and Einstein, report creating images to reason about complex new problems (Gagné, Yekovich, & Yekovich, 1993).

Schemas (sometimes called "schemata") are abstract knowledge structures that organize vast amounts of information. A schema (the singular form) is a pattern or guide for understanding an event, a concept, or a skill. The schema tells you what features are typical of a category, what to expect. The schema is like a pattern, specifying the "standard" relationships in an object or situation. And schemas are individual. For example, a museum curator and a salesperson may have very different schemas about antiques.

Another type of schema, a *story grammar* (sometimes called a schema for text or story structure) helps students to understand and remember stories (Gagné, Yekovich, & Yekovich, 1993; Rumelhart & Ortony, 1977). A story grammar could be something like this: murder discovered, search for clues, murderer's fatal mistake identified, trap set to trick suspect into confessing, murderer takes bait . . . mystery solved! In other words, a story grammar is a typical general structure that could fit many specific stories. To comprehend a story, we select a schema that seems appropriate. Then we use this framework to decide which details are important, what information to seek, and what to remember. It is as though the schema is a theory about what should occur in the story. The schema guides us in "interrogating" the text, filling in the specific information we expect to find so that the story makes sense. If we activate our "murder mystery schema" we may be alert for clues or a murderer's fatal mistake (Resnick, 1981). Without the appropriate schema, trying to understand a story, textbook, or classroom lesson is a very slow, difficult process, something like finding your way through a new town without a map.

Storing and Retrieving Information in Long-Term Memory

How can we make the most effective use of our practically unlimited capacity to learn and remember? The way you learn information in the first place—the way you process it at the outset—seems to affect its recall later. One important requirement is that you integrate new material with information already stored in long-term memory as you construct an understanding. Here elaboration, organization, and context play a role.

Elaboration is the addition of meaning to new information through its connection with already existing knowledge. In other words, we apply our schemas and draw on already existing knowledge to construct an understanding and often change our existing knowledge in the process. We often elaborate automatically. For example, a paragraph about a historic figure in the seventeenth century tends to activate our existing knowledge about that period; we use the old knowledge to understand the new. Material that is elaborated when first learned will be easier to recall later. First, as we saw earlier, elaboration is a form of rehearsal. It keeps the information activated in working memory long enough to have a chance for permanent storage in long-term memory.

Second, elaboration builds extra links to existing knowledge. The more one bit of information or knowledge is associated with other bits, the more routes there are to follow to get to the original bit. To put it another way, you have several "handles," or retrieval cues, by which you can recognize or "pick up" the information you might be seeking (Schunk, 2004). The more students elaborate new ideas, the more they "make them their own," the deeper their understanding and the better their memory for the knowledge. We help students to elaborate when we ask them to translate information into their own words, create examples, explain to a peer, draw the relationships, or apply the information to solve new problems. Of course, if students elaborate new information by making incorrect connections or developing misguided explanations, these misconceptions will be stored and remembered too.

Organization is a second element of processing that improves learning. Material that is well organized is easier to learn and to remember than bits and pieces of information, especially if the information is complex or extensive. Placing a concept in a structure will help you learn and remember either general definitions or specific examples. The structure serves as a guide back to the information when you need it. For example, Table 4.1 (on page 107) organizes information about kinds of knowledge.

Context is a third element of processing that influences learning. Aspects of physical and emotional context—places, rooms, how we are feeling on a particular day, who is with us—are learned along with other information (Ashcraft, 2002). Later, if you try to remember the information, it will be easier if the current context is similar to the original one. So studying for a test under "testlike" conditions may result in improved performance. Of course, you can't always go back to the same place you learned in order to recall something. But you can picture the setting, the time of day, and your companions, and you may eventually reach the information you seek.

Craik and Lockhart (1972) suggested that what determines how long information is remembered is how completely the information is analyzed and connected with other information. The more completely information is processed, the better our chances of remembering it. For example, according to the levels of processing theory, if you were asked to sort pictures of dogs based on the color of their coats, you might not remember many of the pictures later. But if asked to rate each dog on how likely it is to chase you as you jog, you probably would remember more of the pictures. To rate the dogs as dangerous you must pay attention to details in the pictures, relate features of the dogs to characteristics associated with danger, and so on. This rating procedure requires "deeper" processing and more focus on the meaning of the features in the photos.

Retrieving Information from Long-Term Memory.   When we need to use information from long-term memory, we search for it. Sometimes the search is conscious, as when you see a friend approaching and you search for her name. At other times locating and using information from long-term memory is automatic, as when you call your home or solve a math problem without having to search for each step. Think of long-term memory as a huge shelf full of tools and supplies ready to be brought to the workbench of working memory to accomplish a task. The shelf (long-term memory) stores an incredible amount, but it may be hard to quickly find what you are looking for. The workbench (working memory) is small, but anything on it is immediately available. Because it is small, however, supplies (bits of information) sometimes are lost when the workbench overflows or when one bit of information covers (interferes with) another (Gagné, 1985).

The size of the long-term memory network is huge, but only one small area is activated at any one time. Only the information we are currently thinking about is in working memory. Information is retrieved in this network through the spread of activation. When particular information is active—when we are thinking about it—other closely associated knowledge can be activated as well, and activation can spread through the network (Anderson, 1993; Gagné, Yekovich, & Yekovich, 1993). Thus, as you focus on the thought, "I'd like to go for a drive to see the fall leaves today," related ideas such as, "I should rake leaves," and "The car needs an oil change," come to mind. As activation spreads from the "car trip" to the "oil change," the original thought, or active memory, disappears from working memory because of the limited space.

In long-term memory the information is still available, even when it is not activated, even when you are not thinking about it at the moment. If spreading activation does not "find" the information we seek, then we might still come up with the answer through *reconstruction*, a problem-solving process that makes use of logic, cues, and other knowledge to construct a reasonable answer by filling in any missing parts. Sometimes reconstructed recollections are incorrect. For example, in 1932, F. C. Bartlett conducted a series of famous studies on remembering stories. He read a complex, unfamiliar Native American tale to students at England's Cambridge University and after various lengths of time, asked the students to recall the story. Students' recalled stories were generally shorter than the original and were translated into the concepts and language of the Cambridge student culture. The story told of a seal hunt, for instance, but many students remembered "a fishing trip," an activity closer to their experiences and more consistent with their schemas.

Forgetting and Long-Term Memory. Information lost from working memory truly disappears. No amount of effort will bring it back. But information stored in long-term memory may be available, given the right cues. Information appears to be lost from long-term memory through time decay and interference. For example, memory for Spanish–English vocabulary decreases for about three years after a person's last course in Spanish, then stays level for about 25 years, then drops again for the next 25 years. One explanation for this decline is that neural connections, like muscles, grow weak without use (Anderson, 1995). Finally, newer memories may interfere with or obscure older memories, and older memories may interfere with memory for new material.

Even with decay and interference, long-term memory is remarkable. In a review of almost 100 studies of memory for knowledge taught in school, Semb and Ellis (1994) concluded that, "contrary to popular belief, students retain much of the knowledge taught in the classroom" (p. 279). It appears that teaching strategies that encourage student engagement and lead to higher levels of initial learning (such as frequent reviews and tests, elaborated feedback, high standards, mastery learning, and active involvement in learning projects) are associated with longer retention. But initial learning is not enough; students have to practice their understanding. In fact, many cognitive psychologists believe that the failures of education, such as the inability of many Harvard graduates to explain why it is colder in winter than summer, are really failures to retain what was once understood (Pashler, 2006). What can instructional leaders do to use the principles of information processing to improve instruction? See the Theory into Action Guidelines on the next page.

Metacognition, Regulation, and Individual Differences

One question that intrigues many educators and cognitive psychologists is why some people learn and remember more than others. For those who hold an information-processing view, part of the answer lies in the **executive control processes** shown earlier in Figure 4.4 that guide the flow of information through the system. We have already discussed a number of control processes, including selective attention, maintenance rehearsal, elaborative rehearsal, organization, and elaboration. These executive control processes are sometimes called **metacognition,** defined as our awareness of our own "cognitive machinery and how the machinery works" (Meichenbaum, Burland, Gruson, & Cameron, 1985, p. 5). Metacognition literally means cognition about cognition, or knowledge about knowledge.

There are three essential metacognitive skills: planning, monitoring, and evaluation (Brown, 1987; Nelson, 1996). *Planning* involves deciding how much time to give to a task, which strategies to use, how to start, what resources to gather, what order to

THEORY INTO ACTION GUIDELINES

Applying Information Processing

Make sure you have the students' attention.

Examples

1. Develop a signal that tells students to stop what they are doing and focus on you. Make sure students respond to the signal—don't let them ignore it. Practice using the signal.
2. Move around the room, use gestures, and avoid speaking in a monotone.
3. Begin a lesson by asking a question that stimulates interest in the topic.
4. Regain the attention of individual students by walking closer to them, using their names, or asking them a question.

Help students separate essential from nonessential details and focus on the most important information.

Examples

1. Summarize instructional objectives to indicate what students should be learning. Relate the material you are presenting to the objectives as you teach: "Now I'm going to explain exactly how you can find the information you need to meet Objective One on the board—determining the tone of the story."
2. When you make an important point, pause, repeat, ask a student to paraphrase, note the information on the board in colored chalk, or tell students to highlight the point in their notes or readings.

Help students make connections between new information and what they already know.

Examples

1. Review prerequisites to help students bring to mind the information they will need to understand new material: "Who can tell us the definition of a quadrilateral? Now, what is a rhombus? Is a square a quadrilateral? Is a square a rhombus? What did we say yesterday about how you can tell? Today we are going to look at some other quadrilaterals."

2. Use an outline or diagram to show how new information fits with the framework you have been developing. For example, "Now that you know the duties of the FBI, where would you expect to find it in this diagram of the branches of the U.S. government?"
3. Give an assignment that specifically calls for the use of new information along with information already learned.

Provide for repetition and review of information.

Examples

1. Begin the class with a quick review of the homework assignment.
2. Give frequent, short tests.
3. Build practice and repetition into games, or have students work with partners to quiz each other.

Present material in a clear, organized way.

Examples

1. Make the purpose of the lesson very clear.
2. Give students a brief outline to follow. Put the same outline on an overhead so you can keep yourself on track. When students ask questions or make comments, relate these to the appropriate section of the outline.
3. Use summaries in the middle and at the end of the lesson.

Focus on meaning, not memorization.

Examples

1. In teaching new words, help students associate the new word to a related word they already understand: "*Enmity* is from the same base as *enemy.*"
2. In teaching about remainders, have students group twelve objects into sets of 2, 3, 4, 5, 6, and ask them to count the "leftovers" in each case.

follow, what to skim and what to give intense attention, and so on. *Monitoring* is the on-line awareness of "how I'm doing." Monitoring means asking, "Is this making sense? Am I trying to go too fast? Have I practiced enough?" *Evaluation* involves making judgments about the processes and outcomes of thinking and learning. Should I change strategies? Get help? Give up for now? Is this report (proposal, budget, painting, formula, model, poem, plan, etc.) finished yet, or does it need more work? Many planning, monitoring, and evaluation processes are not necessarily conscious. Especially in adults, these processes can be automatic. Because people differ in their metacognitive knowledge and skills, they differ in how well and how quickly they learn (Brown, Bransford, Ferrara, & Campione, 1983; Morris, 1990). Experts in a field may plan, monitor, and evaluate as second nature; they have difficulty describing their metacognitive knowledge and skills (Schraw & Moshman, 1995).

Some differences in metacognitive abilities are due to development. Metacognitive abilities begin to develop around ages five to seven and improve throughout school. Most children go through a transitional period when they can apply a particular strategy if reminded, but will not apply it on their own (Flavell, Green, & Flavell, 1995; Perner, 2000; Sigler, 1998). Nancy Perry found that asking students two questions helped them become more metacognitive. The questions were: "What did you learn about yourself as a reader/writer today?" and "What did you learn that you can do again and again and again?" When teachers asked these questions regularly during class, even young students demonstrated fairly sophisticated levels of metacognitive understanding and action (Perry, VandeKamp, & Mercer, 2000).

Not all differences in metacognitive abilities have to do with age or maturation. Some individual differences probably are caused by biological differences or by variations in learning experiences. In fact, many students diagnosed as having learning disabilities actually have attention disorders (Hallahan & Kauffman, 2006), particularly with long tasks (Pelham, 1981). Thus, there is great variability even among students of the same developmental level, but these differences do not appear to be related to intellectual abilities. In fact, superior metacognitive skills can compensate for lower levels of ability, so these metacognitive skills can be especially important for students who often have trouble in school (Swanson, 1990).

Cognitive Contributions: Learning Strategies and Tactics

Most teachers will tell you that they want their students to "learn how to learn." Years of research indicate that using good learning strategies helps students learn and that these strategies can be taught (Hamman, Berthelot, Saia, & Crowley, 2000). But were you taught "how to learn"? Powerful and sophisticated learning strategies and study skills are seldom taught directly until high school or even college, so students have little practice with these powerful strategies. In contrast, early on students usually discover repetition and rote learning on their own, so they have extensive practice with these strategies. And, unfortunately, some teachers think that memorizing is learning (Hofer & Pintrich, 1997; Woolfolk Hoy & Murphy, 2001). This may explain why many students cling to flash cards and memorizing; they don't know what else to do to learn (Willoughby, Porter, Belsito, & Yearsley, 1999).

Let's examine several good learning strategies and tactics.

Deciding What Is Important

Learning begins with focusing attention—deciding what is important. But distinguishing the main idea from less important information is not always easy. Often students focus on the "seductive details" or the concrete examples, perhaps because they are more interesting (Gardner, Brown, Sanders, & Menke, 1992). Finding the central idea is especially difficult if you lack prior knowledge in an area and the amount of new information provided is extensive. Teachers can give students practice in using signals in texts such as headings, bold words, outlines, or other indicators to identify key concepts and main ideas. Teaching students to summarize material can be helpful, too (Lorch, Lorch, Ritchey, McGovern, & Coleman, 2001).

Summaries.   Creating summaries can help students learn, but students have to be taught how to summarize (Byrnes, 1996; Dole et al., 1991; Palincsar & Brown, 1989). Jeanne Ormrod (1999, p. 333) summarizes these suggestions for helping students create summaries:

- Begin doing summaries of short, easy, well-organized readings. Introduce longer, less organized, and more difficult passages gradually.
- For each summary, ask students to find or write a *topic sentence* for each paragraph or section, identify *big ideas* that cover several specific points, find some *supporting information* for each big idea, and delete any *redundant information* or unnecessary details.
- Ask students to compare their summaries and discuss what ideas they thought were important and why—what's their evidence?

Two other study strategies that are based on identifying key ideas are *underlining* texts and *taking notes*.

Underlining and Highlighting.   Underlining and note taking are probably two of the most commonly used strategies among high school and college students. Yet few students receive any instruction in the best ways to take notes or underline, so it is not surprising that many students use ineffective strategies.

One common problem is that students underline or highlight too much. It is far better to be selective. In studies that limit how much students can underline—for example, only one sentence per paragraph—learning has improved (Snowman, 1984). In addition to being selective, students also should actively transform the information into their own words as they underline or take notes. Teach students not to rely on the words of the book. Encourage them to note connections between what they are reading and other things that they already know. Draw diagrams to illustrate relationships. Finally, look for organizational patterns in the material and use them to guide underlining or note taking (Irwin, 1991; Kiewra, 1988).

Taking Notes.   Research indicates that taking notes serves at least two important functions:

- Taking notes focuses attention during class. In order to record key ideas in your own words, you have to translate, connect, elaborate, and organize, which helps move information to long-term memory. Of course, if taking notes distracts you from actually listening to and making sense of the lecture, then note taking may not be effective (DiVesta & Gray, 1972; Kiewra, 1989; Van Meter, Yokoi, & Pressley, 1994).
- Notes provide extended external storage that allows students to return and review. Students who use their notes to study tend to perform better on tests, especially if they take many high-quality notes—more is better as long as the students are capturing key ideas, concepts, and relationships, not just intriguing details (Kiewra, 1985, 1989).

To help students organize their note taking, some teachers provide matrices or maps, such as the one in Figure 4.5 on the next page. When students are first learning to use these maps, teachers often fill in some of the spaces for them. Also, it is helpful for students to exchange their filled-in maps and explain their thinking to each other.

Mnemonics

Mnemonics are systematic procedures for improving memory (Atkinson et al., 1999; Levin, 1994; Rummel, Levin, & Woodward, 2003). If students need to remember information for long periods of time, an acronym may be the answer. An acronym is a form of abbreviation, a word formed from the first letter of each word in a phrase, for example HOMES to remember the Great Lakes (Huron, Ontario, Michigan, Erie, Superior). Another method forms phrases or sentences out of the first letter of each word or item in a list, for example, Every Good Boy Does Fine to remember the lines on the G clef—E, G, B, D, F. Because the words must make sense as a sentence, this approach also has some characteristics of chain mnemonics, methods that connect the first item to be memorized with the second, the second item with the third, and so on. In one type of chain method, each item on a list is linked to the next through some visual association or story. Another chain-method approach is to incorporate all the items to be memorized into a jingle like "i before e except after c."

The mnemonic system that has been most extensively researched in teaching is the **keyword method.** Joel Levin and his colleagues (Carney & Levin, 2000; Jones,

FIGURE 4.5   A Map to Guide Note Taking
The compare/contrast map allows students to organize their listening or reading as they consider two ideas, concepts, time periods, authors, experiments, theories, and so on.

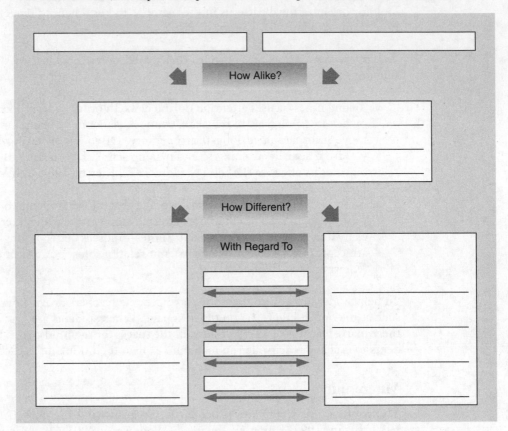

Source: From *Organizing Thinking: Book 1*, by S. Parks and H. Black, Critical Thinking Co. © 1992. Reprinted by permission. All rights reserved.

Levin, Levin, & Beitzel, 2000) use a mnemonic (the *3 Rs*) to teach the keyword mnemonic method:

> *recode* the to-be-learned vocabulary item as a more familiar, concrete keyword—this is the keyword;
>
> *relate* the keyword clue to the vocabulary item's definition through a sentence;
> *retrieve* the desired definition.

For example, to remember that the English word *carlin* means *old woman*, you might recode *carlin* as the more familiar keyword *car*. Then make up a sentence such as *The old woman was driving a car*. When you are asked for the meaning of the word *carlin*, you think of the keyword *car*, which triggers the sentence about the car and the *old woman*, the meaning (Jones, Levin, Levin, & Beitzel, 2000). A similar approach has been used to help students connect artists with particular aspects of their paintings. For example, students are told to imagine that the heavy dark lines of paintings by Rouault are made with a *ruler* (Rouault) dipped in black paint (Carney & Levin, 2000). Figure 4.6 is an example of using mnemonic pictures as aids in learning complicated science concepts (Carney & Levin, 2002).

One problem, however, is that the keyword method does not work well if it is difficult to identify a keyword for a particular item. Many words and ideas that students need to remember are quite a challenge to associate with keywords (Hall, 1991). Also, vocabulary learned with keywords may easily be forgotten if students are given keywords and images instead of being asked to supply the words and images. When the teacher provides the memory links, these associations may not fit the students' existing knowledge and may be forgotten or confused later, so remembering suffers (Wang & Thomas, 1995; Wang, Thomas, & Ouelette, 1992). Younger students have some difficulty forming their own images. For them, memory aids that rely on auditory cues—

FIGURE 4.6   Using Mnemonics to Learn Complex Content

This illustration tells a story that provides a frame for remembering and pegs for hanging the concept names in the biological subdivision of angiosperms.

To remember that the subdivision **angiosperms** includes the class **dicotyledons**, which in turn includes the three orders **rubales**, **sapindales**, and **rosales**, study the picture of the angel with the pet **dinosaur** that is walking up the **Rubik's cubes** so that he can lick the sweet **sap** that drips down from the **rose** tree.

Source: From "Scientific Mnemonomies: Methods of Maximizing More than Memory," by Mary E. Levin and Joel R. Levin. *American Education Research Journal, 27*(2), 1990, p. 305. Copyright 1990 by the American Educational Research Association. Reproduced with permission of Sage Publications Inc. Journals in the format Textbook and E-book via Copyright Clearance Center

rhymes such as "Thirty days hath September . . ."—seem to work better (Willoughby et al., 1999).

Reading Strategies

Effective learning strategies and tactics should help students focus attention, invest effort (elaborate, organize, summarize, connect, translate) so they process information deeply, and monitor their understanding. A number of strategies have been developed to support these processes in reading. Many use mnemonics to help students remember the steps involved. For example, one strategy for fourth grade or above is READS:

R   *Review* headings and subheadings.
E   *Examine* boldface words.
A   *Ask*, "What do I expect to learn?"
D   *Do* it—Read!
S   *Summarize* in your own words (Friend & Bursuck, 2006).

A strategy that can be used in reading literature is CAPS:

C   Who are the *characters*?
A   What is the *aim* of the story?
P   What *problem* happens?
S   How is the problem *solved*?

There are literally hundreds of strategies that can be taught. Ours has been a brief and selective look. The point for teachers is to teach subject-appropriate learning strategies directly and support strategic learning through coaching and guided practice. Teaching strategies based on cognitive views of learning, particularly information processing, highlight the importance of attention, organization, rehearsal (practice), and elaboration in learning and provide ways to give students more control over their own learning by developing and improving their own metacognitive skills. The focus is on what is happening "inside the head" of the learner. Using the cognitive theory just explicated, principals can give their teachers hands-on examples to develop more effective ways to teach learning strategies. The Theory into Action Guidelines illustrate both the principles and practices of such strategies for students.

Constructivist Theories of Learning

In this section we look beyond the individual to expand our understanding of learning and teaching. Consider this situation:

A young child who has never been to the hospital is in her bed in the pediatric wing. The nurse at the station down the hall calls over the intercom above the bed, "Hi Chelsea,

THEORY INTO ACTION GUIDELINES

Learning Strategies

Make sure you have the necessary declarative knowledge (facts, concepts, ideas) to understand new information.

Examples

1. Keep definitions of key vocabulary available as you study.
2. Review required facts and concepts before attempting new material.

Find out what type of test the teacher will give (essay, short answer), and study the material with that in mind.

Examples

1. For a test with detailed questions, practice writing answers to possible questions.
2. For a multiple-choice test, use mnemonics to remember definitions of key terms.

Make sure you are familiar with the organization of the materials to be learned.

Examples

1. Preview the headings, introductions, topic sentences, and summaries of the text.
2. Be alert for words and phrases that signal relationships, such as *on the other hand, because, first, second, however, since.*

Know your own cognitive skills and use them deliberately.

Examples

1. Use examples and analogies to relate new material to something you care about and understand well, such as sports, hobbies, or films.

2. If one study technique is not working, try another—the goal is to stay involved, not to use any particular strategy.

Study the right information in the right way.

Examples

1. Be sure you know exactly what topics and readings the test will cover.
2. Spend your time on the important, difficult, and unfamiliar material that will be required for the test or assignment.
3. Keep a list of the parts of the text that give you trouble and spend more time on those pages.
4. Process the important information thoroughly by using mnemonics, forming images, creating examples, answering questions, making notes in your own words, and elaborating on the text. Do not try to memorize the author's words—use your own.

Monitor your own comprehension.

Examples

1. Use questioning to check your understanding.
2. When reading speed slows down, decide if the information in the passage is important. If it is, note the problem so you can reread or get help to understand. If it is not important, ignore it.
3. Check your understanding by working with a friend and quizzing one another.

how are you doing? Do you need anything?" The girl looks puzzled and does not answer. The nurse repeats the question with the same result. Finally, the nurse says emphatically, "Chelsea, are you there? Say something!" The little girl responds tentatively, "Hello, Wall—I'm here."

Chelsea encountered a new situation—a talking wall. The wall is persistent. It sounds like a grown-up wall. She shouldn't talk to strangers, but she is not sure about walls. She uses what she knows and what the situation provides to *construct* meaning and to act.

Here is another example of constructing meaning taken from Berk (2001, p. 31). This time a father and his four-year-old son co-construct understandings as they walk along a California beach, collecting litter after a busy day:

BEN: (*running ahead and calling out*) Some bottles and cans. I'll get them.

MEL: If the bottles are broken, you could cut yourself, so let me get them. (*Catches up and holds out the bag as Ben drops items in*)

BEN: Dad, look at this shell. It's a whole one, really big. Colors all inside!

MEL: Hmmm, might be an abalone shell.

BEN: What's abalone?

MEL: Do you remember what I had in my sandwich on the wharf yesterday? That's abalone.

BEN: You eat it?

MEL: Well, you can. You eat a meaty part that the abalone uses to stick to rocks.

BEN: Ewww. I don't want to eat it. Can I keep the shell?

MEL: I think so. Maybe you can find some things in your room to put in it. (*Points to the shell's colors*) Sometimes people make jewelry out of these shells.

BEN: Like mom's necklace?

MEL: That's right. Mom's necklace is made out of a kind of abalone with a very colorful shell—pinks, purples, blues. It's called Paua. When you turn it, the colors change.

BEN: Wow! Let's look for Paua shells!

MEL: You can't find them here, only in New Zealand.

BEN: Where's that? Have you been there?

MEL: No, someone brought Mom the necklace as a gift. But I'll show you New Zealand on the globe. It's far away, halfway around the world.

Look at the knowledge being co-constructed about sea creatures and their uses for food or decoration, safety, environmental responsibility, and even geography. Constructivist theories of learning focus on how people make meaning, both on their own like Chelsea and in interaction with others like Ben.

Different Versions of Constructivism

Constructivism, that "vast and woolly area in contemporary psychology, epistemology, and education" (von Glaserfeld, 1997, p. 204), is a broad term used by philosophers, curriculum designers, psychologists, educators, and others. Most people who use the term emphasize "the learner's contribution to meaning and learning through both individual and social activity" (Bruning, Schraw, & Ronning, 1999, p. 215). Constructivist perspectives are grounded in the research of Piaget, Vygotsky, the Gestalt psychologists (e.g., Kohler and Duncker), Bartlett, and Bruner as well as the educational philosophy of John Dewey, to mention just a few intellectual roots.

There is no one constructivist theory of learning, but "most constructivists share two main ideas: that learners are active in constructing their own knowledge and that social interactions are important to knowledge construction" (Bruning, Schraw, Norby, & Ronning, 2004, p. 195). Constructivism views learning as more than receiving and processing information transmitted by teachers or texts. Rather learning is the active and personal construction of knowledge (de Kock, Sleegers, & Voeten, 2004). There are constructivist approaches in science and mathematics education, in educational psychology and anthropology, and in computer-based education. Even though many psychologists and educators use the term *constructivism*, they often mean very different things (Driscoll, 2005; McCaslin & Hickey, 2001; Phillips, 1997).

One way to organize constructivist views is to talk about two forms of constructivism: psychological and social construction (Palincsar, 1998; Phillips, 1997). We could oversimplify a bit and say that psychological constructivists focus on how individuals use information, resources, and even help from others to build and improve their mental models and problem-solving strategies. In contrast, social constructivists see learning as increasing our abilities to participate with others in activities that are meaningful in the culture (Windschitl, 2002). Let's look a bit closer at each type of constructivism.

Psychological/Individual Constructivism. The **psychological constructivists** "are concerned with how *individuals* build up certain elements of their cognitive or emotional apparatus" (Phillips, 1997, p. 153). These constructivists might be interested in individual knowledge, beliefs, self-concept, or identity, so they are sometimes called *individual* constructivists; they all focus on the inner psychological life of people. Chelsea talking to the wall in the previous section was making meaning using her own individual knowledge and beliefs about how to respond when someone (or something) talks to you. She was using what she knew to impose intellectual structure on her world (Piaget, 1971; Windschitl, 2002).

Using these standards, the most recent information-processing theories are constructivist (Mayer, 1996). Information-processing approaches to learning regard the outside world as a source of input, but once the sensations are perceived and enter working memory, the important work is assumed to be happening "inside the head" of the individual (Schunk, 2004; Vera & Simon, 1993). But even though information-processing theorists talk about meaning and knowledge construction, many psychologists believe that information processing is "trivial constructivism" because the individual's only constructive contribution is to build accurate representations of the outside world (Derry, 1992; Garrison, 1995; Marshall, 1996).

In contrast, Piaget's psychological constructivist perspective is less concerned with "correct" representations and more interested in meaning as constructed by the individual. Piaget proposed a sequence of cognitive stages that all humans pass through.

Thinking at each stage builds on and incorporates previous stages as it becomes more organized and adaptive and less tied to concrete events. Piaget's special concern was with logic and the construction of universal knowledge that cannot be learned directly from the environment, knowledge such as conservation of volume or mental reversibility of actions (Miller, 2002). Such knowledge comes from reflecting on and coordinating our own thoughts, not from mapping external reality. Piaget saw the social environment as an important factor in development, but did not believe that social interaction was the main mechanism for changing thinking (Moshman, 1997).

Some educational and developmental psychologists have referred to Piaget's kind of constructivism as **"first wave constructivism"** or "solo" constructivism, with its emphasis on individual meaning-making (DeCorte, Greer, & Verschaffel, 1996; Paris, Byrnes, & Paris, 2001).

At the extreme end of individual constructivism is the notion of **radical constructivism.** This perspective holds that there is no reality or truth in the world, only the individual's perceptions and beliefs. Each of us constructs meaning from our own experiences, but we have no way of understanding or "knowing" the reality of others (Woods & Murphy, 2002). A difficulty with this position is that, when pushed to the extreme of relativism, all knowledge and all beliefs are equal because they are all valid individual perceptions. There are problems with this thinking for educators. First, teachers have a professional responsibility to emphasize some values, such as honesty or justice, over others, such as bigotry and deception. All perceptions and beliefs are not equal (Schunk, 2000).

Vygotsky's Social Constructivism.   Vygotsky believed that social interaction, activity, and cultural tools shape individual development and learning, just as Ben's interactions on the beach with his father shaped Ben's learning about sea creatures, safety, environmental responsibility, and geography. By participating in a broad range of activities and using tools with others (both actual tools such as calculators and psychological signs and symbols such as language and number systems), learners *appropriate* (take for themselves) the outcomes produced by working together (Gredler, 2005; Palincsar, 1998). Putting learning in social and cultural context is **"second wave constructivism"** (Paris, Byrnes, & Paris, 2001).

Because his theory relies heavily on social interactions and the cultural context to explain learning, most psychologists classify Vygotsky as a **social constructivist** (Palincsar, 1998; Prawat, 1996), but some theorists categorize Vygotsky as a psychological constructivist because he was primarily interested in development within the individual (Moshman, 1997; Phillips, 1997). In a sense, he is both. One advantage of his theory of learning is that it gives us a way to consider both the psychological and the social; he bridges both camps. For example, Vygotsky's concept of the zone of proximal development—the area where a child can solve a problem with the help (scaffolding) of an adult or more able peer—has been called a place where culture and cognition create each other (Cole, 1985). Culture creates cognition when the adult uses tools and practices from the culture (language, maps, computers, looms, music, etc.) to steer the child toward goals the culture values (reading, writing, weaving, dance). Cognition creates culture as the adult and child together generate new practices and problem solutions to add to the cultural group's repertoire (Serpell, 1993). One way of integrating individual and social constructivism is to think of knowledge as individually constructed and socially mediated (Windschitl, 2002).

The term *constructivism* is sometimes used to talk about how public knowledge is created. Although this is not our main concern, it is worth a quick look.

Sociological Constructivism. Sociological constructivists (sometimes called constru*ctionists*) do not focus on individual learning. Their concern is how public knowledge in disciplines such as science, math, economics, or history is constructed. Beyond this kind of academic knowledge, sociological constructivists also are interested in how commonsense ideas, everyday beliefs, and commonly held understandings about the world are communicated to new members of a sociocultural group (Gergen, 1997; Phillips, 1997). Questions raised might be who determines what constitutes history or the proper way to behave in public or how to get elected class president. There is no true knowledge, according to these theorists. All of knowledge is socially constructed, and, more important, some people have more power than others do in defining what constitutes such knowledge. Relationships between and among teachers, students, families, and the community are the central issues. Collaboration to understand diverse viewpoints is encouraged, and traditional bodies of knowledge often are challenged (Gergen, 1997). The philosophies of Jacques Dierrida and Michel Foucault are important sources for constructionists. Vygotsky's theory, with its attention to how cognition creates culture, has some elements in common with constructionism.

We think of the three main learning theories as three pillars for teaching. Students must first understand and make sense of the material (constructivist); then they must remember what they have understood (cognitive—information processing); and then they must practice and apply (behavioral) their new skills and understanding to make them more fluid and automatic, a permanent part of their repertoire. Failure to attend to any part of the process means lower-quality learning. Table 4.2 on the next page presents the behavioral and selected constructivist perspectives on learning.

Teaching Applications of
Constructivist Perspectives

We have looked at some areas of disagreement among the constructivist perspectives, but what about areas of agreement? All constructivist theories assume that knowing develops as learners, like Chelsea and Ben, try to make sense of their experiences. "Learners, therefore, are not empty vessels waiting to be filled, but rather active organisms seeking meaning" (Driscoll, 2005, p. 487). These learners construct mental models or schemata and continue to revise them to make better sense of their experiences. Their constructions do not necessarily resemble external reality; rather they are the unique interpretations of the learner, like Chelsea's friendly persistent wall. This doesn't mean that all constructions are equally useful or viable. Learners test their understandings

TABLE 4.2 Four Views of Learning

There are variations within each of these views of learning that differ in emphasis.
There is also an overlap in constructivist views.

	Cognitive		Constructivist	
	Behavioral	Information Processing	Psychological/Individual	Social/Situated
	Skinner	J. Anderson	Piaget	Vygotsky
Knowledge	Fixed body of knowledge to acquire Stimulated from outside	Fixed body of knowledge to acquire Stimulated from outside Prior knowledge influences how information is processed	Changing body of knowledge, individually constructed in social world Built on what learner brings	Socially constructed knowledge Built on what participants contribute, construct together
Learning	Acquisition of facts, skills, concepts Occurs through drill, guided practice	Acquisition of facts, skills, concepts, and strategies Occurs through the effective application of strategies	Active construction, restructuring prior knowledge Occurs through multiple opportunities and diverse processes to connect to what is already known	Collaborative construction of socially defined knowledge and values Occurs through socially constructed opportunities Co-construct knowledge with students
Teaching	Transmission Presentation (Telling)	Transmission Guide students toward more "accurate" and complete knowledge	Challenge, guide thinking toward more complete understanding	
Role of Teacher	Manager, supervisor Correct wrong answers	Teach and model effective strategies Correct misconceptions	Facilitator, guide Listen for student's current conceptions, ideas, thinking	Facilitator, guide Co-participant Co-construct different interpretations of knowledge; listen to socially constructed conceptions
Role of Peers	Not usually considered	Not necessary but can influence information processing	Not necessary but can stimulate thinking, raise questions	Ordinary part of process of knowledge construction
Role of Student	Passive reception of information Active listener, direction-follower	Active processor of information, strategy user Organizer and reorganizer of information Rememberer	Active construction (within mind) Active thinker, explainer, interpreter, questioner	Active co-construction with others and self Active thinker, explainer, interpreter, questioner Active social participator

Source: From *Reconceptualizing Learning for Restructured Schools* by H. H. Marshall. Paper presented at the Annual Meeting of the American Educational Research Association, April 1992. Copyright © Hermine H. Marshall. Adapted with permission.

against experience and the understandings of other people—they negotiate and co-construct meanings like Ben did with his father.

Constructivists share similar goals for learning. They emphasize knowledge in use rather than the storing of inert facts, concepts, and skills. Learning goals include developing abilities to find and solve ill-structured problems, critical thinking, inquiry, self-determination, and openness to multiple perspectives (Driscoll, 2005).

Elements of Constructivist Teaching

Even though there is no single constructivist theory, many constructivist teaching approaches recommend

1. authentic tasks and complex, challenging learning environments;
2. social negotiation and shared responsibility as a part of learning;
3. multiple representations of content;
4. understanding that knowledge is constructed;
5. student-centered instruction (Driscoll, 2005; Marshall, 1992).

Let's look more closely at these dimensions of constructivist teaching.

Authentic Tasks. Constructivists believe that students should not be given stripped down, simplified problems and basic skills drills, but instead should deal with complex situations and "fuzzy," ill-structured problems. The world beyond school presents few simplified problems or step-by-step directions, so schools should be sure that every student has experience solving complex problems. These problems should be embedded in authentic tasks and activities, the kinds of situations that students will face as they apply what they are learning to real-world problems (Needles & Knapp, 1994).

Social Negotiation. Many constructivists share Vygotsky's belief that higher mental processes develop through social interaction, so collaboration in learning is valued. The Language Development and Hypermedia Group (1992) suggests that a major goal of teaching is to develop students' abilities to establish and defend their own positions while respecting the positions of others. To accomplish this exchange, students must talk and listen to each other.

Multiple Representations. When students encounter only one representation of content—one model, analogy, or way of understanding complex content—they often oversimplify as they try to apply that one approach to every situation. Rand Spiro and his colleagues (1991) suggest that "revisiting the same material, at different times, in rearranged contexts, for different purposes, and from different conceptual perspectives is essential for attaining the goals of advanced knowledge acquisition" (p. 28). This idea is not entirely new. Years ago Jerome Bruner (1966) described the advantages of a spiral curriculum. This is a way of teaching that introduces the fundamental structure of all subjects—the "big ideas"—early in the school years, then revisits the subjects in more and more complex forms over time.

Understanding Knowledge Construction. The assumptions we make, our beliefs, and experiences shape what each of us comes to "know" about the world. Different assumptions and different experiences lead to different knowledge. Constructivists stress the importance of understanding the knowledge construction process so that students will be aware of the influences that shape their thinking; thus they will be able to choose, develop, and defend positions in a self-critical way while respecting the positions of others.

Student-Centered Instruction. The last characteristic of constructivist teaching listed by Driscoll (2005) is student-centered instruction. Following are four examples of student-centered instruction that are consistent with the other dimensions of constructivist teaching as well—inquiry learning, problem-based learning, cognitive apprenticeships, and cooperative learning.

Inquiry Learning

John Dewey described the basic **inquiry learning** format in 1910. There have been many adaptations of this strategy, but the form usually includes the following elements (Echevarria, 2003; Lashley, Matczynski, & Rowley, 2002): The teacher presents a puzzling event, question, or problem. The students

1. formulate hypotheses to explain the event or solve the problem;
2. collect data to test the hypotheses;
3. draw conclusions;
4. reflect on the original problem and on the thinking processes needed to solve it.

Shirley Magnusson and Annemarie Palincsar have developed a teachers' guide for planning, implementing, and assessing different phases of inquiry science units (Palincsar, Magnusson, Marano, Ford, & Brown, 1998). The model, called Guided Inquiry Supporting Multiple Literacies (or GIsML), is shown in Figure 4.7.

The teacher first identifies a curriculum area and some general guiding questions, puzzles, or problems. For example, an elementary teacher chooses communication as the area and asks this general question: "How and why do humans and animals communicate?" Next several specific focus questions are posed. "How do whales communicate? How do gorillas communicate?" The focus questions have to be carefully chosen to guide students toward important understandings. One key idea in understanding animal communication is the relationship between the animal's structures, survival functions, and habitat. Animals have specific *structures*, such as large ears or echo-locators, that *function* to find food or attract mates or identify predators, and these structures and functions are related to the animals' *habitats*. So focus questions must ask about animals with different structures for communication, different functional needs for survival, and different habitats. Questions about animals with the same kinds of structures or the same habitats would not be good focus points for inquiry (Magnusson & Palincsar, 1995).

The next phase is to engage students in the inquiry, perhaps by playing different animal sounds, having students make guesses and claims about communication, and asking the students questions about their guesses and claims. Then the students con-

FIGURE 4.7   Learning Community: Program of Study

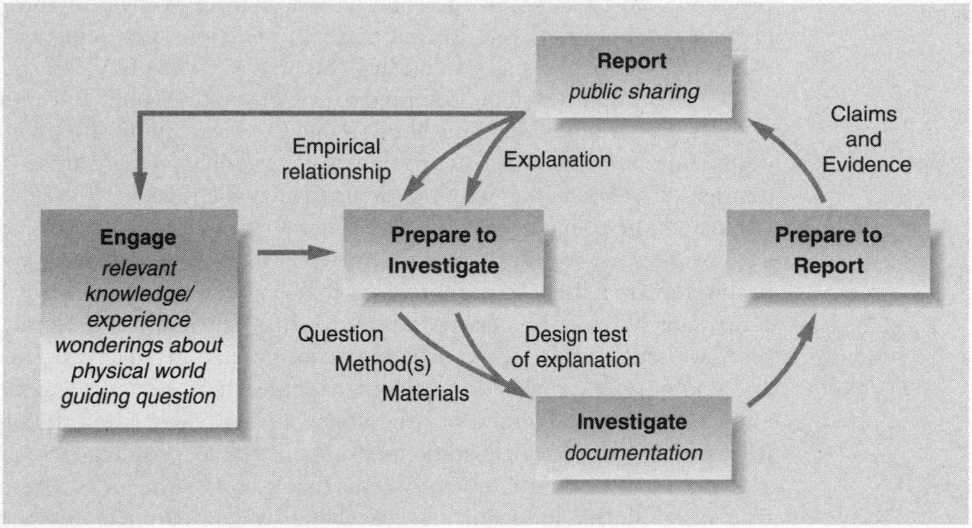

Source: Adapted from "Designing a Community of Practice: Principles and Practices of the GIsML Community," by A. S. Palincsar, S. J. Magnusson, N. Marano, D. Ford, and N. Brown, *Teaching and Teacher Education*, 14, 1998, p. 12. Reprinted by permission from Elsevier.

duct both first-hand and second-hand investigations. *First-hand investigations* are direct experiences and experiments, for example, measuring the size of bats' eyes and ears in relation to their bodies (using pictures or videos, not real bats!). In *second-hand investigations*, students consult books, the Internet, interviews with experts, and so on to find specific information or get new ideas. As part of investigating, the students begin to identify patterns. The curved line in Figure 4.7 shows that cycles can be repeated. In fact, students might go through several cycles of investigation, pattern identification, and reporting results before moving on to constructing explanations and making final reports. Another possible cycle is to evaluate explanations before reporting by making and then checking predictions, applying the explanation to new situations.

Inquiry teaching allows students to learn content and process at the same time. In the examples above, students learned about animal communication and habitats. In addition, they learned the inquiry process itself: how to solve problems, evaluate solutions, and think critically. Inquiry has much in common with guided discovery learning in that inquiry methods require great preparation, organization, and monitoring to be sure everyone is engaged and challenged (Kindsvatter, Wilen, & Ishler, 1988).

Problem-Based Learning

In **problem-based learning,** students are confronted with a real problem that has meaning for them. This problem launches their inquiry as they collaborate to find solutions. In true problem-based learning, the problem is real and the students' actions matter.

"Problem-based learning turns instruction topsy-turvy. Students meet an ill-structured problem before they receive any instruction. In place of covering the curriculum, learners probe deeply into issues searching for connections, grappling with complexity, and using knowledge to fashion solutions" (Stepien & Gallagher, 1993, p. 26).

An example problem presented to one group of seventh and eighth graders in Illinois is, "What should be done about a nuclear waste dump site in our area?" The students soon learn that this real problem is not a simple one. Scientists disagree about the dangers. Environmental activists demand that the materials be removed, even if this bankrupts the company involved, one that employs many local residents. Some members of the state assembly want the material taken out-of-state, even though no place in the country is licensed to receive the toxic materials. The company believes the safest solution is to leave the materials buried. The students must research the situation, interview parties involved, and develop recommendations to be presented to state experts and community groups. "In problem-based learning students assume the roles of scientists, historians, doctors, or others who have a real stake in the proposed problem. Motivation soars because students realize it's their problem" (Stepien & Gallagher, 1993, p. 26). Other authentic problems that might be the focus for student projects are tracking pollution in local rivers, resolving student conflicts in school, raising money for the school computer lab, or building a playground for young children.

The teacher's role in problem-based learning is summarized in Table 4.3.

TABLE 4.3   The Teacher's Role in Problem-Based Learning

Phase	Teacher Behavior
Phase 1 Orient students to the problem	Teacher goes over the objectives of the lesson, describes important logistical requirements, and motivates students to engage in self-selected problem-solving activity.
Phase 2 Organize students for study	Teacher helps students define and organize study tasks related to the problem.
Phase 3 Assist independent and group investigation	Teacher encourages students to gather appropriate information, conduct experiments, and search for explanations and solutions.
Phase 4 Develop and present artifacts and exhibits	Teacher assists students in planning and preparing appropriate artifacts such as reports, videos, and models and helps them share their work with others.
Phase 5 Analyze and evaluate the problem-solving process	Teacher helps students to reflect on their investigations and the processes they used.

Source: From *Classroom Instruction and Management* (p. 161), by R. I. Arends, New York: McGraw-Hill. Published by McGraw-Hill. Copyright © 1997 McGraw-Hill. Reproduced with permission of The McGraw-Hill Companies.

Research on Inquiry and Problem-Based Learning.   Inquiry methods are similar to discovery and share some of the same problems, so inquiry must be carefully planned and organized, especially for less prepared students who may lack the background knowledge and problem-solving skills needed to benefit. Some research has shown that discovery methods are ineffective and even detrimental for lower-ability students (Corno & Snow, 1986; Slavin, Karweit, & Madden, 1989). A distinction is usually made between pure discovery learning, in which the students work on their own to a very great extent, and **guided discovery,** in which the teacher provides some direction.

We know that working memory is severely limited when it is dealing with novel information from the outside, but almost unlimited when it is dealing with familiar, well-practiced and organized information from long-term memory. Because most inquiry and problem-based lessons require students to deal with the former—novel information and fuzzy problems—many educational psychology researchers believe that unguided discovery methods do not fit our information-processing capabilities and often put a strain on working memory (Kirschner, Sweller, & Clark, 2006, 2007). Reviewing thirty years of research on pure discovery learning, Richard Mayer (2004) concludes:

> Like some zombie that keeps returning from its grave, pure discovery continues to have its advocates. However, anyone who takes an evidence-based approach to educational practice must ask the same question: Where is the evidence that it works? In spite of calls for free discovery in every decade, the supporting evidence is hard to find. (p. 17)

Activity-based teaching in science appears to be better than traditional methods in terms of students' understanding of the scientific method and creativity, but about the same for learning science content (Bredderman, 1983).

In terms of problem-based learning, Cindy Hmelo-Silver (2004) reviewed the research and found good evidence that problem-based learning supports the construction of flexible knowledge and the development of problem solving and self-directed learning skills, but there is less evidence that participating in problem-based learning is intrinsically motivating or that it teaches students to collaborate. In addition, most of the research has been done in higher education, especially medical schools.

In medical school, students learning with problem-based methods as opposed to traditional approaches appear to be better at clinical skills such as problem formation and reasoning, but worse in their basic knowledge of science and less prepared in science (Albanese & Mitchell, 1993). And some students, those who are better at self-regulation, benefit more from problem-based methods (Evensen, Salisbury-Glennon, & Glenn, 2001). The best approach may be a balance of content-focused and inquiry or problem-based methods (Arends, 2004). For example, Eva Toth, David Klahr, and Zhe Chen (2000) tested a balanced approach for teaching fourth graders how to use the controlled variable strategy in science to design good experiments. The method had three phases: (1) in small groups, students conducted exploratory experiments to identify variables that made a ball roll farther down a ramp; (2) the teacher led a discussion, explained the controlled variable strategy, and modeled good thinking about experiment design; and (3) the students designed and conducted application experiments to isolate which variables caused the ball to roll farther. The combination of inquiry, discussion, explanation, and modeling was successful in helping the students understand the concepts.

Cognitive Apprenticeships

Over the centuries, apprenticeships have proved to be an effective form of education. By working alongside a master and perhaps other apprentices, young people have learned many skills, trades, and crafts. Why are they so effective? Apprenticeships are rich in information because the master knows a great deal about the subject. Working with more knowledgeable guides provides models, demonstrations, and corrections, as well as a personal bond that is motivating. The performances required of the learner are real and important and grow more complex as the learner becomes more competent (Collins, Brown, & Holum, 1991; Collins, Brown, & Newman, 1989; Hung, 1999).

Collins and his colleagues (1989) suggest that knowledge and skills learned in school have become too separated from their use in the world beyond school. To correct this imbalance, some educators recommend that schools adopt many of the features of apprenticeships. But rather than learning to sculpt or dance or build a cabinet, apprenticeships in school would focus on cognitive objectives such as reading comprehension or writing or mathematical problem solving. There are many **cognitive apprenticeship** models, but most share six features:

1. Students observe an expert (usually the teacher) model the performance.
2. Students get external support through coaching or tutoring (including hints, feedback, models, reminders).
3. Conceptual scaffolding (in the form of outlines, explanations, notes, definitions, formulas, procedures, etc.) is provided and then gradually faded as the student becomes more competent and proficient.
4. Students continually articulate their knowledge, putting into words their understanding of the processes and content being learned.
5. Students reflect on their progress, comparing their problem solving to an expert's performance and to their own earlier performances.
6. Students are required to explore new ways to apply what they are learning, ways that they have not practiced at the master's side.

One way to connect learning to the outside world is to include parents in students' learning. The Principal's Perspective tells how an actual elementary principal accomplished this goal.

A Principal's Perspective

Mindful of the research on the impact of home environment on student achievement (Marzano, 2003; Reeves, 2000), D. W. knew that, to make the academic gains in reading she envisioned for her elementary school, she would have to somehow enhance parental involvement at home. Combining the resources of a statewide reading grant and an established school-business partnership with a local hospital, D. W. purchased an assortment of books, games, and information cards to include in 150 book bags that students could take home for a couple of days at a time to read together with their parents, grandparents, babysitters, and even siblings. The bags also included a journal in which parents could share feedback and general comments with the school.

But D. W. also knew that making quality reading materials more accessible to families was not enough. If parents were to be true partners in their children's education they also would need strategies and techniques to most effectively use the reading materials at home. So she enlisted the expertise of her teaching staff and organized a series of family reading nights throughout the school year. At these events, teachers taught parents how to use decoding and questioning techniques familiar to the students from school and gave them the confidence and the strategies to be genuine partners in their children's reading development.

Marzano, R. J. (2003). *What works in schools: Translating research into action.* Alexandria, VA: Association of Supervision and Curriculum Development.

Reeves, D. B. (2000). *Accountability in action: A blueprint for learning organizations.* Denver, CO: Advanced Learning Press.

Group Work and Cooperation in Learning

Clearly, collaboration and cooperation are important in many visions of innovation and school reform. Teachers are expected to collaborate with parents, administrators, and each other. Cooperative learning structures and approaches are seen as valuable; interdependence, reciprocal learning, and learning communities are mentioned often as desirable features of teaching and learning. For example, the second of three recommendations for strengthening middle grades' teacher preparation published by the National Middle School Association (Scales & McEwin, 1994) is "greater variety of developmentally responsive teaching and assessment techniques, especially cooperative learning, interdisciplinary curriculum and team teaching, student exhibitions, and portfolios" (p. 5).

The History of Cooperative Learning.   Collaboration and cooperative learning have a long history in American education. In the early 1900s, John Dewey criticized the use of competition in education and encouraged educators to structure schools as democratic learning communities. These ideas fell from favor in the 1940s and 1950s, replaced by a resurgence of competition. In the 1960s, there was a swing back to individualized and cooperative learning structures, stimulated in part by concern for civil rights and interracial relations (Webb & Palincsar, 1996).

Today, evolving constructivist perspectives on learning fuel interest in collaboration and cooperative learning. Two characteristics of constructivist teaching—complex, real-life learning environments and social interaction (Driscoll, 2005)—are consistent with the use of cooperative learning structures. As educators focus on learning in real contexts, "there is a heightened interest in situations where elaboration, interpretation, explanation, and argumentation are integral to the activity of the group and where learning is supported by other individuals" (Webb & Palincsar, 1996, p. 844).

Theoretical Underpinnings of Cooperative Learning.   Advocates of different theories of learning find value in cooperative learning, but not for the same reasons.

In terms of *academic/cognitive goals*, information-processing theorists suggest that group discussion can help participants rehearse, elaborate, and expand their knowledge. As group members question and explain, they have to organize their knowledge, make connections, and review, all processes that support information processing and memory. Advocates of a Piagetian perspective assert that the interactions in groups can create the cognitive conflict and disequilibrium that lead an individual to question his or her understanding and try out new ideas or, as Piaget (1985) said, "to go beyond his current state and strike out in new directions" (p. 10). Educators who favor Vygotsky's theory suggest that social interaction is important for learning because higher mental functions such as reasoning, comprehension, and critical thinking originate in social interactions and are then internalized by individuals. Thus, cooperative learning provides the social support and scaffolding that students need to move learning forward. Table 4.4 summarizes the functions of cooperative learning from different perspectives, and describes some of the elements of each kind of group.

In terms of *interpersonal/social goals*, research indicates that cooperative learning has a positive impact on interracial friendships, prejudice reduction, acceptance of disabled students, self-esteem, peer support for academic goals, altruism, empathy, social perspective-taking, liking fellow classmates and feeling liked, sense of responsibility and control over learning, and time on-task. Positive effects often are attributed to the process of working toward common goals as equals, which was shown in laboratory studies years ago to increase liking and respect among individuals from different racial or social groups (Allport, 1954). The motivation growing from the praise and encouragement of peers working toward a common goal also brings positive effects (Deutsch, 1949). Thus, cooperative strategies have been touted as particularly useful in combating the detrimental social effects of cliques in middle school and high schools, the negative effects of competition on student self-esteem, and the alienation of students who are not members of popular social groups (Aronson, 2000; Aronson & Patnoe, 1997).

Elements of Cooperative Learning.   David and Roger Johnson (1999a) list five elements that define true **cooperative learning** groups. Students *interact face-to-face* and close together, not across the room. Group members experience *positive interdependence:* They need each other for support, explanations, and guidance. Even though they work together and help each other, members of the group must ultimately demonstrate learning on their own; they are held *individually accountable* for learning, often through individual tests or other assessments. *Collaborative skills* are necessary for effective group functioning. Often these skills, such as giving constructive feedback, reaching consensus, and involving every member, must be taught and practiced before the groups tackle a learning task. Finally, members monitor *group processes* and relationships to make sure the group is working effectively and to learn about the dynamics of groups. They take time to ask, "How are we doing as a group? Is everyone working together?"

What Can Go Wrong: Misuses of Group Learning.   Without careful planning and monitoring by the teacher, group interactions can hinder learning and reduce rather

TABLE 4.4   Different Forms of Cooperative Learning for Different Purposes

Different forms of cooperative learning (Elaboration, Piagetian, and Vygotskian) fit different purposes, need different structures, and have their own potential problems and possible solutions.

Considerations	Elaboration	Piagetian	Vygotskian
Group size	Small (2–4)	Small	Dyads
Group composition	Heterogeneous/ homogeneous	Homogeneous	Heterogeneous
Tasks	Rehearsal/integrative	Exploratory	Skills
Teacher role	Facilitator	Facilitator	Model/guide
Potential problems	Poor help-giving	Inactive	Poor help-giving
	Unequal participation	No cognitive conflict	Providing adequate time/dialogue
Averting problems	Direct instruction in help-giving	Structuring controversy	Direct instruction in help-giving
	Modeling help-giving		Modeling help-giving
	Scripting interaction		

Source: From "Learning from Peers: Beyond the Rhetoric of Positive Results," by A. M. O'Donnell and J. O'Kelly, 1994, *Educational Psychology Review,* 6, p. 327. Reprinted with kind permission of Springer Science and Business Media and Angela O'Donnell.

than improve social relations in classes. For example, if there is pressure in a group for conformity—perhaps because rewards are being misused or one student dominates the others—interactions can be unproductive and unreflective. Misconceptions might be reinforced or the worst, not the best, ideas may be combined to construct a superficial understanding (Battistich, Solomon, & Delucci, 1993). Students who work in groups but arrive at wrong answers may be more confident that they are right—a case of "two heads are worse than one" (Puncochar & Fox, 2004). Also, the ideas of low-status students may be ignored or even ridiculed while the contributions of high-status students are accepted and reinforced, regardless of the merit of either set of ideas (Anderson, Holland, & Palincsar, 1997; Cohen, 1986). The next sections examine how teachers can avoid these problems and encourage true cooperation.

Setting Up Cooperative Groups.   O'Donnell & O'Kelly (1994) note that determining the size of a group depends in part on the purpose of the group activity. If the purpose is for the group members to review, rehearse information, or practice, larger groups (between four and six students) are useful. But if the goal is to encourage each student to participate in discussions, problem solving, or computer learning, then groups of two to four members work best. Also, some research indicates that when there are just a few girls in a group, they tend to be left out of the discussions unless they are the most able or assertive members. By contrast, when there are only one or two boys in the group, they tend to dominate and be "interviewed" by the girls unless these boys are less able than the girls or are very shy. In general, for very shy and introverted students, individual learning may be a better approach (Webb, 1985; Webb & Palincsar, 1996).

In practice, the effects of learning in a group vary, depending on what actually happens in the group and who is in it. If only a few people take responsibility for the work, these people will learn, but the nonparticipating members probably will not. Students who ask questions, get answers, and attempt explanations are more likely to learn than students whose questions go unasked or unanswered. In fact, there is evidence that the more a student provides elaborated, thoughtful explanations to other students in a group, the more the *explainer* learns. Giving good explanations appears to be even more important for learning than receiving explanations (Webb, Farivar, & Mastergeorge, 2002; Webb & Palincsar, 1996). In order to explain, you have to organize the information, put it into your own words, think of examples and analogies (which connect the information to things you already know), and test your understanding by answering questions. These are excellent learning strategies (King, 1990, 2002; O'Donnell & O'Kelly, 1994).

Some teachers assign roles such as reporter or discussion manager to students to encourage cooperation and full participation. Such roles should be assigned with engagement and learning in mind. In groups that focus on practice, review, or mastery of basic skills, roles should support persistence, encouragement, and participation. In groups that focus on higher-order problem solving or complex learning, roles should encourage thoughtful discussion, sharing of explanations and insights, probing, brainstorming, and creativity. Teachers must be careful, however, not to communicate to students that the major purpose of the groups is simply to do the roles, in order to avoid having roles become ends in themselves (Woolfolk Hoy & Tschannen-Moran, 1999).

Jigsaw. An early format for cooperative learning, **Jigsaw** emphasized high interdependence. This structure was invented by Elliot Aronson and his graduate students in 1971 in Austin, Texas, "as a matter of absolute necessity to help defuse a highly explosive situation" (Aronson, 2000). The Austin schools had just been desegregated by court order. White, African American, and Hispanic students were together in classrooms for the first time. Hostility and turmoil ensued with fistfights in corridors and classrooms. Aronson's answer was the Jigsaw classroom.

In Jigsaw, each group member was given part of the material to be learned by the whole group and became an "expert" on his or her piece. Students had to teach each other, so everyone's contribution was important. A more recent version, Jigsaw II, adds expert groups where the students who have the same material from each learning group confer to make sure they understand their assigned part and then plan ways to teach the information to their learning group members. Next, students return to their learning groups, bringing their expertise to the sessions. In the end, students take an individual test covering all the material and earn points for their learning team score.

Teams can work for rewards or simply for recognition (Aronson & Patnoe, 1997; Slavin, 1995).

In his first test of Jigsaw, Aronson reports that teachers "spontaneously told us of their great satisfaction with the way the atmosphere of their classrooms had been transformed. Adjunct visitors (such as music teachers and the like) were little short of amazed at the dramatically changed atmosphere in the classroom" (Aronson, 2000). Students expressed less prejudice, were more confident, liked school better, and had higher scores on objective examinations. The overall improvements in test scores came mostly from increases in minority group children; Anglo students maintained their previous levels of performance. These findings are consistent with recent research on cooperative learning, as reviewed by Slavin (1995).

There are many other forms of cooperative learning used in schools today. It would be difficult to complete a teacher preparation program without encountering encouragement to use these methods. Kagan (1994) and Slavin (1995) have written extensively on the subject and developed many formats. No matter what the format, however, the key to learning in groups appears to be the *quality of the discussions* among the students. Talk that is interpretive—that analyzes and discusses explanations, evidence, reasons, and alternatives—is more valuable than talk that is merely descriptive. And teachers play an important role; they cannot leave the students unguided, but rather have to seed the discussion with ideas and alternatives that push and prod student thinking (Palincsar, 1998; Woolfolk Hoy & Tschannen-Moran, 1999).

Sometimes when schools adopt innovative teaching practices there are objections from families. The Theory into Action Guidelines for principals and teachers on the next page suggest ways of working with families and the community when schools adopt innovations.

Dilemmas of Constructivist Practice

Years ago, Larry Cremin (1961) observed that progressive, innovative pedagogies require infinitely skilled teachers. Today, the same could be said about constructivist teaching. We have already seen that there are many varieties of constructivism and many practices that flow from these different conceptions. We also know that all teaching today happens in a context of high-stakes testing and accountability. In these situations, constructivist teachers face many challenges. Mark Windschitl (2002) identified four teacher dilemmas of constructivism in practice, summarized in Table 4.5 on page 141. The first is conceptual: How do I make sense of cognitive versus social conceptions of constructivism and reconcile these different perspectives with my practice? The second dilemma is pedagogical. How do I teach in truly constructivist ways that honor my students' attempts to think for themselves but still ensure that they learn the academic material? Third are cultural dilemmas about what activities, cultural knowledge, and ways of talking will build a community in a diverse classroom. How do I build on students' cultural funds of knowledge while acknowledging but seeing beyond my own past experiences? Finally there are political dilemmas. How can I teach for deep understanding and critical thinking but still satisfy the accountability demands of parents and the requirements of No Child Left Behind?

THEORY INTO ACTION GUIDELINES

Explaining Innovations

Be confident and honest.

Examples

1. Write out your rationale for the methods you are using—consider likely objections and craft your responses.
2. Admit mistakes or oversights—explain what you have learned from them.

Treat parents as equal partners.

Examples

1. Listen carefully to parents' objections, take notes, and follow up on requests or suggestions. Remember, you both want the best for the child.
2. Give parents the telephone number of an administrator who will answer their questions about a new program or initiative.
3. Invite families to visit your room or assist in the project in some way.

Communicate effectively.

Examples

1. Use plain language and avoid jargon. If you must use a technical term, define it in accessible ways. Use your best teaching skills to educate parents about the new approach.

2. Encourage local newspapers or television stations to do stories about the "great learning" going on in your classroom or school.
3. Create a lending library of articles and references about the new strategies.

Have examples of projects and assignments available for parents when they visit your class.

Examples

1. Encourage parents to try math activities. If they have trouble, show them how your students (and their child) are successful with the activities and highlight the strategies the students have learned.
2. Keep a library of students' favorite activities to demonstrate for parents.

Develop family involvement packages.

Examples

1. Once a month, send families, via their children, descriptions and examples of the math, science, or language to be learned in the upcoming unit. Include activities children can do with their parents.
2. Make the family project count, for example, as a homework grade.

Source: From M. Meyer, M. Delgardelle, and J. Middleton. "Addressing parents' concerns over curriculum reform." *Educational Leadership*, *53*(7), p. 57. Adapted by permission of the Association for Supervision and Curriculum Development. Copyright © 1996 by ASCP. All rights reserved.

Summary

Although theorists disagree about the definitions of *learning*, most would agree that learning occurs when experience causes a change in a person's knowledge or behavior.

Behavioral views of learning focus on the role of external events—antecedents and consequences—in changing observable behaviors. Consequences that increase behaviors are called reinforcers, and consequences that decrease behaviors are called punishers. A behavioral perspective is most useful in understanding and dealing with classroom management issues. For example, positive behavior supports are an application of

TABLE 4.5 Teachers' Dilemma of Constructivism in Practice

Teachers face conceptual, pedagogical, cultural, and political dilemmas as they implement constructive practices. Here are explanations of these dilemmas and some representative questions that teachers face as they confront them.

Teachers' Dilemma Category	Representative Questions of Concern
I. *Conceptual dilemmas:* Grasping the underpinnings of cognitive and social constructivism; reconciling current beliefs about pedagogy with the beliefs necessary to support a constructivist learning environment.	Which version of constructivism is suitable as a basis for my teaching? Is my classroom supposed to be a collection of individuals working toward conceptual change or a community of learners whose development is measured by participation in authentic disciplinary practices? If certain ideas are considered correct by experts, should students internalize those ideas instead of constructing their own?
II. *Pedagogical dilemmas:* Honoring students' attempts to think for themselves while remaining faithful to accepted disciplinary ideas; developing deeper knowledge of subject matter; mastering the art of facilitation; managing new kinds of discourse and collaborative work in the classroom.	Do I base my teaching on students' existing ideas rather than on learning objectives? What skills and strategies are necessary for me to become a facilitator? How do I manage a classroom where students are talking to one another rather than to me? Should I place limits on students' construction of their own ideas? What types of assessments will capture the learning I want to foster?
III. *Cultural dilemmas:* Becoming conscious of the culture of your classroom; questioning assumptions about what kinds of activities should be valued; taking advantage of experiences, discourse patterns, and local knowledge of students with varied cultural backgrounds.	How can we contradict traditional, efficient classroom routines and generate new agreements with students about what is valued and rewarded? How do my own past images of what is proper and possible in a classroom prevent me from seeing the potential for a different kind of learning environment? How can I accommodate the worldviews of students from diverse backgrounds while at the same time transforming my own classroom culture? Can I trust students to accept responsibility for their own learning?
IV. *Political dilemmas:* Confronting issues of accountability with various stakeholders in the school community; negotiating with key others the authority and support to teach for understanding.	How can I gain the support of administrators and parents for teaching in such a radically different and unfamiliar way? Should I make use of approved curriculums that are not sensitive enough to my students' needs, or should I create my own? How can diverse problem-based experiences help students meet specific state and local standards? Will constructivist approaches adequately prepare my students for high-stakes testing for college admissions?

Source: From "Framing constructivism in practice as the negotiation of dilemmas: An analysis of the conceptual, pedagogical, cultural, and political challenges facing teachers." M. Windschitl, 2002, *Review of Educational Research*, 72, p. 133. Copyright © 2002 by the American Educational Research Association. Reproduced with permission of Sage Publications, Inc. Journals in the format Textbook and E-book via Copyright Clearance Center.

behavioral learning. Another example you may have used is contracts. The teacher draws up an individual contract with each student, describing exactly what the student must do to earn a particular privilege or reward. In some programs, students participate in deciding on the behaviors to be reinforced and the rewards that can be gained. A teacher must use these programs with caution, emphasizing learning and not just "good" behavior.

Cognitive views of learning focus on the human mind's active attempts to make sense of the world. Knowledge is a central force in cognitive perspectives. The individual's prior knowledge affects what he or she will pay attention to, recognize, understand, remember, and forget. Knowledge can be general or domain-specific and declarative, procedural, or conditional, but to be useful, knowledge must be remembered. One influential model of memory is information processing, which describes how information moves from sensory memory (which holds a wealth of sensations and images very briefly) to working memory (where the information is elaborated and connected to existing knowledge) to long-term memory (where the information can be held for a long time, depending on how well it was learned in the first place and how interconnected it is to other information). People vary in how well they learn and remember based in part on their metacognitive knowledge, their abilities to plan, monitor, and regulate their own thinking. There are many teaching applications of cognitive views including mnemonics, imagery, and other learning strategies to help organize and elaborate material.

Constructivist views of learning emphasize the importance of students' construction of knowledge; however, there are many different constructivist explanations of learning. Psychological constructivists are concerned with how *individuals* make sense of their worlds. These constructivists might be interested in individual knowledge, beliefs, self-concept, or identity, so they are sometimes called *individual* constructivists; they all focus on the inner psychological life of people. Social constructivists believe that social interaction, cultural tools, and activity shape individual development and learning. By participating in a broad range of activities with others, learners appropriate (take for themselves) the outcomes produced by working together; they acquire new strategies and knowledge of their world. Finally, sociological constructivists are interested in how public knowledge in disciplines such as science, math, economics, or history is constructed as well as how everyday beliefs and commonly held understandings about the world are communicated to new members of a sociocultural group.

Constructivist approaches to teaching recommend complex, challenging learning environments; social negotiation and collaboration; multiple representations of content; understanding that knowledge is a human construction; and student-centered methods such as inquiry learning, problem-based learning, cognitive apprenticeships, and cooperative learning.

Each of these three perspectives provides valuable insights into learning; hence, the issue is not which perspective is best but rather what each perspective brings to bear in understanding a variety of teaching and learning problems. Just as there is no one best way to teach (Chapter 6), this is no one best way to learn. Behavioral, cognitive, and constructivist viewpoints of learning complement each other and enhance our understanding of learning.

KEY TERMS

antecedents (97)
attention (107)
chunking (111)
cognitive apprenticeship (134)
conditional knowledge (106)
constructivism (124)
cooperative learning (136)
cueing (98)
declarative knowledge (106)
domain-specific knowledge (106)
elaboration (113)
elaborative rehearsal (111)
episodic memory (111)
executive control processes (115)
first wave constructivism (126)
flashbulb memory (111)

functional behavioral assessment (FBA) (102)
guided discovery (133)
inquiry learning (130)
Jigsaw (138)
keyword method (119)
learning (93)
maintenance rehearsal (110)
metacognition (115)
mnemonics (119)
negative reinforcement (96)
positive behavioral supports (102)
positive reinforcement (95)
presentation punishment (96)
problem-based learning (131)
procedural knowledge (106)
procedural memory (112)

prompting (98)
psychological constructivists (125)
punishment (96)
radical constructivism (126)
reinforcement process (95)
reinforcer (95)
removal punishment (96)
schemas (112)
second wave constructivism (126)
semantic memory (112)
sensory memory (107)
social constructivist (126)
working memory (109)

DEVELOPING YOUR PORTFOLIO

1. As principal, you have decided that your elementary school needs a writing program that is a good balance of skills and composition. Prepare a short position paper on the advantages and disadvantages of each approach. Then prepare a plan that incorporates the best of both approaches. Support your argument with current research and theory on learning.
2. Prepare a PowerPoint presentation on the strengths and weaknesses of each of the learning perspectives discussed in this chapter: behavioral, cognitive, and constructivist. Be sure to discuss the situations for which each perspective is most appropriate. For example, list the tasks or situations for which the behavioral approach is best. Give at least one example for each approach.
3. Reread the Leadership Challenge at the beginning of this chapter and assume you are the principal in that school.
   a. Develop a plan for working with the history department to resolve the issue such that both extremes (the traditionalists and the constructivists) are satisfied.
   b. Consult the Theory into Action Guidelines about explaining innovations and devise a process for introducing the new plan to the community.

INSTRUCTIONAL LEADER'S TOOLBOX

Readings

Bransford, J., Derry, S., Berliner, D., Hammerness, K., with Beckett, K. L. (2005). Theories of learning and their roles in teaching. In L. Darling-Hammond & J. Bransford (Eds.), *Preparing teachers for a changing world: What teachers should learn and be able to do* (pp. 40–87). San Francisco: Jossey-Bass.

John-Steiner, V., & Mahn, H. (1996). Sociocultural approaches to learning and development: A Vygotskian framework. *Educational Psychologist, 31,* 191–206.

Pashler, H. (2006). How we learn. *APS Observer, 19*(3), 24–34.

Perkins, D. (1992). *Smart schools: From training memories to educating minds.* New York: Free Press.

Phillips, D. (1995). The good, the bad, and the ugly: The many faces of constructivism. *Educational Researcher, 24*(7), 5–12.

Wiggins, G., & McTighe, J. (2005). *Understanding by design: Expanded 2nd edition.* Alexandria, VA: Association for Supervision and Curriculum Development.

Videos

Memory: Fabric of the mind. 28 minutes. What kind of brain chemistry can explain memory? Are different types of memory located at different areas of the brain? What is the process of forgetting? Is it possible to improve memory? This program seeks answers to these and other fascinating questions about the brain and memory at several internationally renowned memory-research labs. Order from Films for the Humanities & Sciences, Inc., P.O. Box 2053, Princeton, NJ, 08543, or 800–257–5126.

Websites

www.ericdigests.org/pre-924/critical.htm
    Critical Thinking in the Social Studies
www.eric.ed.gov/ERICDocs/data/ericdocs2sql/content_storage_01/0000019b/80/15/45/88.pdf
    Improving the Quality of Student Notes
edweb.sdsu.edu/courses/ET650_online/MAPPS/Strats.html
    Learning Strategies Matrix
www.tutorials.com/fd/tutorials.asp
    Learn To: provides thousands of step-by-step tutorials on a variety of skills
www.indiana.edu/~reading/ieo/digests/d96.html
    Metacognition and Reading to Learn

www.eric.ed.gov/ERICDocs/data/ericdocs2sql/content_storage_01/0000019b/80/11/0a/c3.pdf
    Metacomprehension
www.psychwww.com/mtsite/
    Mindtools
www.ericdigests.org/1993/early.htm
    Problem Solving in Early Childhood Classrooms
www.ericdigests.org/pre-9212/problem.htm
    Teaching Problem Solving—Secondary School Science

Organizations

www.wolftrap.org/institute/
    Wolf Trap Institute for Early Learning through the Arts: Organization to help early childhood professionals use the arts as part of their care and instruction of young children. The Institute is accessible on the Web by going to the main site for Wolf Trap and then selecting "education."
www.ascd.org/
    Association for Supervision and Curriculum Development
www.ciera.org/
    Center for the Improvement of Early Reading Achievement

CHAPTER

5 Motivation

PREVIEW: KEY POINTS

1. Motivation is the spring of action, an internal state that arouses, directs, and maintains behavior.

2. Whether motivation is intrinsic or extrinsic is determined by the individual's perception of causality for the action: internal causality → intrinsic motivation; external causality → extrinsic motivation.

3. Five major approaches to motivation are behavioral (rewards and incentives); humanistic (self-actualization); cognitive (beliefs, attributions, and expectations); social cognitive (outcomes combined with beliefs, goals, expectations, and self-efficacy); and sociocultural (engaged participation in learning communities).

4. Goals that are specific, are moderately challenging, and can be reached in the near future with reasonable effort are the most motivating goals; in schools, goals that focus on learning (not performance) are the most powerful.

5. If they are to be strong motivators, goals, in addition to being specific and challenging, must be accepted by the individual and feedback concerning progress must be continuous.

6. Motivation is affected by the individual's need for safety, self-esteem, connections to others, self-determination, achievement, and self-actualization; people have different needs at different times.

7. Motivation also is affected by the individual's beliefs about the causes of successes and failures and whether ability can improve; believing that effort can improve ability leads to greater persistence and achievement in school.

8. Self-efficacy, the belief that you have the ability to orchestrate the actions to manage a particular situation, is a significant source of motivation.

9. Anxiety can interfere with motivation and learning by affecting attention, information processing, and performance.

10. Motivation to learn is enhanced when teachers employ strategies that help students have confidence in their abilities to learn, see the value of the learning task, and stay focused on learning without resorting to self-protective and self-defeating beliefs and actions.

Leadership Challenge

For some reason this year, many of the students in your middle school classes seem defeated about learning. At a recent faculty meeting, teachers started to complain about their students: "They look at an assignment and protest: 'This is too long (too hard, too much)!' and 'We can't do this by tomorrow (Monday, next week)!' Because they don't exert much effort, of course, they prove themselves right every time; they can't do the work." Your teachers claim that neither pep talks nor punishments for incomplete work are making a dent in the students' defeatist attitudes. And the "I can't" attitude seems contagious. Even the better students are starting to drag their feet, protest longer assignments, and invest minimal effort in class. Teachers also maintain that more students have started to cheat on tests to save their sinking grades. A few teachers blame the negative attitudes on students from the "projects" who are in school this year because the other middle school in the district was closed and those students had to be redistributed. A cloud of despair seems to be hovering over the whole school. You are starting to dread Mondays. You need to show some leadership, and you begin by asking yourself these questions:

- Are these students "unmotivated"?
- Why might they be so pessimistic about learning?
- How can you help your teachers get a handle on this problem?
- What can you and your teachers do to change student attitudes toward school work?
- How can teachers get students to believe in themselves?
- What perspectives on motivation seem most useful?

Motivation: A Definition

Motivation is usually defined as *an internal state that arouses, directs, and maintains behavior.* Psychologists studying motivation have focused on five basic questions. First, what choices do people make about their behavior? Why do some students, for example, focus on their homework while others watch television? Second, having made a decision, how long is it before the person actually gets started? Why do some students start their homework right away, while others procrastinate? Third, what is the intensity or level of involvement in the chosen activity? Once the book bag is opened, is the student absorbed and focused or just going through the motions? Fourth, what causes a person to persist or to give up? Will a student read the entire Shakespeare assignment or just a few pages? Finally, what is the individual thinking and feeling while engaged in the activity? Is the student enjoying Shakespeare, worrying about an upcoming test, or daydreaming (Graham & Weiner, 1996; Pintrich, Marx, & Boyle, 1993)?

Intrinsic and Extrinsic Motivation

We all know how it feels to be motivated, to move energetically toward a goal. We also know what it is like to work hard, even if we are not fascinated by the task. What energizes and directs our behavior? The explanation could be drives, needs, incentives, fears, goals, social pressure, self-confidence, interests, curiosity, beliefs, values, expectations, and more. Some psychologists have explained motivation in terms of personal *traits* or individual characteristics. Certain people, so the theory goes, have a strong need to achieve, a fear of tests, or an enduring interest in art, so they behave accordingly. They work hard to achieve, avoid tests, or spend hours in art galleries. Other psychologists see motivation more as a *state*, a temporary situation. If, for example, you are reading this paragraph because you have an examination tomorrow, you are motivated (at least for now) by the situation. Of course, the motivation we experience at any given time usually is a combination of trait and state.

As you can see, some explanations of motivation rely on internal, personal factors such as needs, interests, curiosity, and enjoyment. Other explanations point to external, environmental factors: rewards, social pressure, punishment, and so on. Motivation that stems from factors such as interest or curiosity is called **intrinsic motivation.** Intrinsic motivation is the natural tendency to seek out and conquer challenges as we pursue personal interests and exercise capabilities (Deci & Ryan, 1985; Reeve, 1996). When we are intrinsically motivated, we do not need incentives or punishments because the activity itself is rewarding. James Raffini (1996) states simply that intrinsic motivation is "what motivates us to do something when we don't have to do anything" (p. 3). In contrast, when we do something to earn a merit increase, to avoid criticism from parents, to please the superintendent, or for some other reason that has very little to do with the task itself, we experience **extrinsic motivation.** We are not really interested in the activity for its own sake; we care only about what it will gain us.

It is impossible to tell just by looking if a behavior is intrinsically or extrinsically motivated. The essential difference between the two types of motivation is the person's reason for acting, that is, whether the **locus of causality** for the action (the location of the cause) is internal or external. Students who read or practice their backstrokes or paint may be reading, stroking, or painting because they freely chose the activity based on personal interests (internal locus of causality/intrinsic motivation), or because someone or something else outside is influencing them (external locus of causality/extrinsic motivation).

Is your motivation for reading this page intrinsic or extrinsic? Is your locus of causality internal or external? As you try to answer this question, you probably realize that the dichotomy between intrinsic and extrinsic motivation is too simple, too all-or-nothing. Human activities fall along a continuum from fully self-determined (internal causality/intrinsic motivation) to fully determined by others (external causality/extrinsic motivation). For example, teachers may freely choose to work hard on activities that they don't find particularly enjoyable because they know the activities are important in reaching a valued goal, like spending hours studying or preparing a portfolio in order to earn National Board Certification. Is this intrinsic or extrinsic motivation? Actually it is in between: The person is freely choosing to respond to outside causes such as certification requirements. The person has *internalized* an external cause.

Recently, the notion of intrinsic and extrinsic motivation as two ends of a continuum has been challenged. An alternative explanation is that motivation can include both intrinsic and extrinsic factors. Intrinsic and extrinsic tendencies are two independent possibilities; at any given time we can be motivated by some of each (Covington & Mueller, 2001). This makes sense because in school, both intrinsic and extrinsic motivation are useful. Teaching can create intrinsic motivation by connecting to students' interests and supporting growing competence, but you know this won't work all the time. Did you find long division inherently interesting? Was your curiosity piqued by irregular verbs? If teachers count on intrinsic motivation to energize all of their students all of the time, they will be disappointed. There are situations when incentives and external supports are necessary. Principals and teachers must encourage and nurture intrinsic motivation while making sure that extrinsic motivation supports learning

(Brophy, 1988; Deci, Koestner, & Ryan, 1999; Ryan & Deci, 1996). To do this, they need to know about the factors that influence motivation.

Five General Approaches to Motivation

Motivation is a vast and complicated subject with many theories developed in laboratories, through games and simulations, and in clinical or industrial settings. Our examination of the field will be selective; otherwise we would never finish the topic. As with learning, there are several general explanations for motivation. Each has something to offer principals and teachers.

Behavioral Approaches to Motivation.   Behaviorists explain motivation with concepts such as "reward" and "incentive." A **reward** is an attractive object or event supplied as a consequence of a particular behavior. An **incentive** is an expected object or event that encourages or discourages behavior, the promise of a reward. Thus, according to the behavioral view, understanding motivation begins with a careful analysis of the incentives and rewards present in the school and classroom. Providing grades, stickers, certificates, and so on for learning—or demerits for misbehavior—are attempts to motivate students by extrinsic means of incentives, rewards, and punishments. Of course, in any individual case, many other factors will affect how a person behaves.

For years educators and psychologists have debated whether students should be rewarded for schoolwork and academic accomplishments. In the early 1990s, Paul Chance and Alfie Kohn exchanged opinions in several issues of *Phi Delta Kappan* (March 1991; November 1992; June 1993). What are the arguments? Kohn (1993) argues that "applied behaviorism, which amounts to saying, 'do this and you'll get that,' is essentially a technique for controlling people. In the classroom it is a way of doing things *to* children rather than working *with* them" (p. 784). He contends that rewards are ineffective because when the praise and prizes stop, the behaviors stop too. But Chance (1993) disagrees:

> Skinner, unlike Kohn, understood that people learn best in a responsive environment. Teachers who praise or otherwise reward student performance provide such an environment. . . . If it is immoral to let students know they have answered questions correctly, to pat students on the back for a good effort, to show joy at a student's understanding of a concept, or to recognize the achievement of a goal by providing a gold star or a certificate—if this is immoral, then count me a sinner. (p. 788)

Do rewards undermine interest? Even psychologists such as Edward Deci (1975) and Mark Lepper (1988), who suggest that rewards might undermine intrinsic motivation, agree that rewards can also be used positively. When rewards provide students with information about their growing mastery of a subject or when the rewards show appreciation for a job well done, then the rewards bolster confidence and make the task more interesting to the students, especially students who lacked ability or interest in the task initially. Nothing succeeds like success. If students master reading or mathematics with the support of rewards, they will not forget what they have learned when the praise stops. Would they have learned without the rewards? Some would, but some might not. Would you continue working for a school that didn't pay you, even though you liked the work? Will freelance writer Alfie Kohn, for that matter, lose interest in writing because he gets paid fees and royalties?

Humanistic Approaches to Motivation.   In the 1940s, proponents of humanistic psychology such as Carl Rogers argued that neither of the dominant schools of psychology, behavioral or Freudian, adequately explained why people act as they do. Humanistic interpretations of motivation emphasize such intrinsic sources of motivation as a person's needs for "self-actualization" (Maslow, 1968, 1970), the inborn "actualizing tendency" (Rogers & Freiberg, 1994), or the need for "self-determination" (Deci, Vallerand, Pelletier, & Ryan, 1991). From the humanistic perspective, to motivate means to encourage peoples' inner resources, their sense of competence, self-esteem, autonomy, and self-actualization. When we examine the role of needs in motivation, we will see two examples of the humanistic approach: Maslow's theory of the hierarchy of needs and Deci's self-determination theory.

Cognitive Approaches to Motivation.   In many ways, cognitive theories of motivation also developed as a reaction to the behavioral views. Cognitive theorists believe that behavior is determined by our thinking, not simply by whether we have been rewarded or punished for the behavior in the past (Stipek, 2002). Behavior is initiated and regulated by plans (Miller, Galanter, & Pribram, 1960), goals (Locke & Latham, 1990), schemas (Ortony, Clore, & Collins, 1988), expectations (Vroom, 1964), and attributions (Weiner, 1992, 2000). One of the central assumptions in cognitive approaches is that people respond not to external events or physical conditions like hunger, but rather to their interpretations of these events. In cognitive theories, people are seen as active and curious, searching for information to solve personally relevant problems. Thus, cognitive theorists emphasize intrinsic motivation. We will see examples of cognitive theories of motivation when we examine Bernard Weiner's attribution theory.

Social Cognitive Approaches to Motivation.   Social cognitive theories of motivation are integrations of behavioral and cognitive approaches: They take into account both the behaviorists' concern with the consequences of behavior and the cognitivists' interest in the impact of individual beliefs and expectations. Many influential social cognitive explanations of motivation can be characterized as **expectancy-value theories.** This means that motivation is seen as the product of two main forces: the individual's expectation of reaching a goal and the value of that goal to him or her. In other words, the important questions are, "If I try hard, can I succeed?" and "If I succeed, will the outcome be valuable or rewarding to me?" Bandura's self-efficacy theory, discussed later in this chapter, is an example of a social cognitive motivation (Pintrich & Schunk, 2002).

Sociocultural Approaches to Motivation.   Sociocultural theories of motivation emphasize participation in communities of practice. People engage in activities to maintain their identities and their interpersonal relations within the community. Thus, students are motivated to learn if they are members of a classroom or school community that values learning. Just as we learn to speak and dress and conduct ourselves in restaurants or shopping malls by being socialized—watching and learning from more capable members of the culture—we also learn to be students by watching and learning from members of our community. In other words, we learn by the company we keep (Hickey, 2003; Rogoff, Turkanis, & Bartlett, 2001). The concept of identity is central in sociocultural views of motivation. When we see ourselves as soccer players, or sculptors, or engineers, or teachers, or principals, we have an identity within a group. Part of our socialization is moving from peripheral to central participation in that group, much like going from an internship to the actual role with increased responsibility. We are motivated to learn the values and practices of the community to keep our identity as community members (Lave & Wenger, 1991; Wenger, 1998). The challenge in schools is to be sure that all students and teachers are fully participating members of the community because motivation comes from identity, and identity comes from participation.

Some classrooms are intentionally structured as learning communities. For example, Brown and Campione (1996) developed learning communities for middle school students around research projects in science, as we saw in Chapter 4. Scardamalia and Bereiter (1996) designed a learning community using a computer system called CSILE—Computer-Supported Intentional Learning Environment—that encourages collaboration among students about questions, hypotheses, and findings. The challenge in these approaches is to be sure that all students are fully participating members of the community because motivation comes from both identity and legitimate participation.

The behavioral, humanistic, cognitive, social cognitive, and sociocultural approaches to motivation are summarized in Table 5.1. These general theoretical perspectives differ in their answers to the question "What is motivation?" but each contributes in its own way to a comprehensive understanding of human motivation.

TABLE 5.1 Five Views of Motivation

	Behavioral	Humanistic	Cognitive	Social Cognitive	Sociocultural
Source of Motivation	Extrinsic	Intrinsic	Intrinsic	Intrinsic and Extrinsic	Intrinsic
Important Influences	Reinforcers, rewards, incentives, and punishers	Need for self-esteem, self-fulfillment, and self-determination	Beliefs, attributions for success and failure, expectations	Goals, expectations, intentions, self-efficacy	Engaged participation in learning communities: maintaining identity through participation in activities of group
Key Theorists	Skinner	Maslow Deci	Weiner Graham	Locke & Latham Bandura	Lave Wenger

Source: From Anita E. Woolfolk, *Educational Psychology: Active Learning Edition*, 10/e. Published by Allyn & Bacon, Boston, MA. Copyright © 2008 by Pearson Education. Reprinted by permission of the publisher.

Motivation to Learn in School

Instructional leaders are concerned about developing a particular kind of motivation in their schools, the motivation to learn. Jere Brophy (1988) describes student **motivation to learn** as "a student tendency to find academic activities meaningful and worthwhile and to try to derive the intended academic benefits from them" (p. 205). Motivation to learn can be construed as both a general trait (some students or teachers have more than others) and a situation-specific state (some situations encourage motivation to learn more than others). What makes student motivation a challenge in classrooms? In an interview, Jere Brophy (2003) listed five obstacles:

> First, school attendance is compulsory and curriculum content and learning activities are selected primarily on the basis of what society believes students need to learn, not on the basis of what students would choose to do if given the opportunity. . . . Second, teachers usually work with classes of 20 or more students and therefore cannot always meet each individual's needs, so some students are often bored and others are often confused or frustrated. Third, classrooms are social settings in which much that occurs is public, so that failures often produce not only personal disappointment but public embarrassment. Fourth, students are graded, and periodic reports are sent home to their parents. Finally, teachers and students often settle into familiar routines that become the "daily grind." School reduces to covering content (for the teachers) and completing assignments (for the students). (pp. 206–207)

It would be wonderful if all students came to school filled with the motivation to learn, but they don't. And even if they did, schoolwork might still seem boring or unimportant to some students some of the time. Instructional leaders have three major goals. The first is to get students productively involved with the work of the class: in other words, to create a *state* of motivation to learn. Second, teachers want students to move beyond simple participation to cognitive engagement, to think deeply about what they study. Finally, the long-term goal is to develop in students the *trait* of being motivated to learn so they will be able to educate themselves for their entire lives (Blumenfeld, Puro, & Mergendoller, 1992).

As you can already see, motivation is a complex subject. But principals and teachers need working knowledge. What can they do to support motivation to learn in their schools and classrooms? We will draw from a number of theories to examine four key elements that "build" motivation to learn: *goals*, *needs*, *beliefs*, and *emotions*. By keeping in mind these four important aspects of motivation, you can greatly enhance learning in your school.

Goals and Motivation

A **goal** is what an individual is striving to accomplish. Goals motivate people to act in order to reduce the discrepancy between "where they are" and "where they want to be." There are four main reasons why goal setting improves performance. First, goals direct our attention to the task at hand. Second, goals mobilize effort. (The harder the goal, to a point, the greater the effort.) Third, goals increase persistence. (When we have a clear goal, we are less likely to be distracted or to give up until we reach the goal.) Finally, goals promote the development of new strategies when old strategies fall short (Locke & Latham, 2002).

Types of Goals and Goal Orientations

The types of goals we set influence the amount of motivation we have to reach them. Goals that are specific, moderately difficult, and likely to be reached in the near future tend to enhance motivation and persistence (Pintrich & Schunk, 2002; Stipek, 1996). Specific goals provide clear standards for judging performance. If performance falls short, we keep going. Moderate difficulty provides a challenge, but not an unreasonable one. Finally, goals that can be reached fairly soon are not likely to be pushed aside by more immediate concerns. Groups like Alcoholics Anonymous show they are aware of the motivating value of short-term goals when they encourage their members to stop drinking "one day at a time."

Goals are specific targets. **Goal orientations** are patterns of beliefs about goals related to achievement in school. Goal orientations include the reasons why we pursue goals and the standards we use to evaluate progress toward goals. For example, your target might be to make an A in this course. Are you doing so in order to master the content—to learn all about it—or to perform—to look good in the eyes of your friends and family? In classrooms there are four main goal orientations: mastery (learning), performance (looking good), work-avoidance, and social (Murphy & Alexander, 2000; Pintrich & Schunk, 2002).

The most common distinction in research on students' goals is between learning goals (also referred to as task goals or mastery goals) and performance goals (also called ability goals or ego goals). The point of a **learning goal** is to improve, to learn, no matter how many mistakes you make or how awkward you appear. Students who set learning goals tend to seek challenges and persist when they encounter difficulties. Nicholls and Miller (1984) call these students **task-involved learners** because they are concerned with mastering the task and are not worried about how their performance "measures up" compared to others in the class. We often say that these people "get lost in their work." In addition, task-involved learners are more likely to seek appropriate help, use deeper cognitive processing strategies, and apply better study strategies (Butler & Neuman, 1995; Young, 1997).

The second kind of goal is a **performance goal.** Students with performance goals care about demonstrating their ability to others. They may be focused on getting good test scores and grades or they may be more concerned with winning and beating other students (Wolters, Yu, & Pintrich, 1996). Students whose goal is outperforming others may do things to look smart, such as reading easy books in order to "read the most books" (Young, 1997). If winning is impossible, they may adopt defensive, failure-avoiding strategies: they pretend not to care, make a show of "not really trying," or cheat (Jagacinski & Nicholls, 1987; Pintrich & Schunk, 2002). The evaluation of their performance by others, not what they learn or how hard they try, is what matters. Nicholls and Miller (1984) refer to these students as **ego-involved learners** because they are preoccupied with themselves. Deborah Stipek (2002) lists these behaviors as indicative of a student who is ego-involved with classwork:

1. Cheats/copies from classmates' papers
2. Seeks attention for good performance
3. Works hard only on graded assignments
4. Is upset by and hides papers with low grades
5. Compares grades with classmates
6. Chooses tasks that are most likely to result in positive evaluations
7. Is uncomfortable with assignments that have unclear evaluation criteria and repeatedly checks with the teacher

Are performance goals always bad? There is a similarity between intrinsic versus extrinsic motivation and mastery versus performance goal orientations. Mastery-oriented students tend to be motivated by intrinsic factors whereas performance-oriented students tend to respond to extrinsic motivation. Earlier research indicated that performance goals generally were detrimental to learning, but, like extrinsic motivation, a performance goal orientation may not be all bad all of the time. In fact, some recent research indicates that both mastery and performance goals are associated with using active learning strategies and high self-efficacy (Stipek, 2002). And, like intrinsic and extrinsic motivation, students can pursue mastery and performance goals at the same time, and often do.

Some students, however, don't want to learn or to look smart, they just want to avoid work. These students try to complete assignments and activities as quickly as possible without exerting much effort (Pintrich & Schunk, 2002). Nicholls called these **work-avoidant learners:** They feel successful when they don't have to try hard, when the work is easy, or when they can "goof off."

A final category of goals becomes more important as students get older—**social goals.** As students move into adolescence, their social networks change to include more peers. Nonacademic activities such as athletics, dating, and "hanging out" compete with schoolwork (Urdan & Maehr, 1995). Social goals include a wide variety of needs and motives with different relationships to learning; some help but some hinder learning. For example, adolescents' goal of maintaining friendly relations in a cooperative learning group can get in the way of learning when group members don't challenge wrong answers or misconceptions because they are afraid to hurt other members' feelings (Anderson, Holland, & Palincsar, 1997). Certainly, pursuing goals such as having fun with friends or avoiding being labeled a "nerd" can get in the way of learning. But goals of bringing honor to your family or team by working hard can support learning (Urdan & Maehr, 1995).

We talk about goals in separate categories, but students have to coordinate their goals so they can make decisions about what to do and how to act. As noted above, sometimes social and academic goals are incompatible. For example, if students do not see a connection between achievement in school and success in life, particularly because discrimination prevents them from succeeding, then those students are not likely to set academic achievement as a goal. Such anti-academic students and groups of students probably exist in every high school (Committee on Increasing High School Students' Engagement and Motivation to Learn, 2004; Wentzel, 1999). Sometimes, succeeding in the peer group means not succeeding in school—and succeeding in the peer group is important. The need for social relationships is basic and strong for most people.

Feedback and Goal Acceptance

Besides having specific goals and creating supportive social relationships, there are two additional factors that make goal setting in the classroom effective. The first is *feedback*. In order to be motivated by a discrepancy between "where you are" and "where you want to be," you must have an accurate sense of both your current status and how far you have to go. There is evidence that feedback emphasizing progress is the most effective. In one study, feedback to adults emphasized either that they had accomplished 75% of the standards set or that they had fallen short of the standards by 25%. When the feedback highlighted accomplishment, the subjects' self-confidence, analytic thinking, and performance were all enhanced (Bandura, 1997).

The second factor affecting motivation to pursue a goal is *goal acceptance*. If students reject goals set by others or refuse to set their own goals, then motivation will suffer. Generally, students are more willing to commit to the goals of others if the goals seem realistic, reasonably difficult, and meaningful—and if good reasons are given for the value of the goals (Grolnick, Gurland, Jacob, & Decourcey, 2002). Commitment matters—the relationship between higher goals and better performance is strongest when people are committed to the goals (Locke & Latham, 2002).

Goals: Lessons for Teachers and Principals

Students and teachers are more likely to work toward goals that are clear, specific, reasonable, moderately challenging, and attainable within a relatively short period of time. If teachers focus on student performance, high grades, competition, and achievement, they may encourage students to set performance goals. This will undermine the students' ability to learn and could encourage cheating or self-defeating actions (Anderman & Maehr, 1994). If any reward or incentive systems are used, make sure participants (teachers or students) understand that the goal is to learn and improve in some area, not just to perform well or look smart. And be sure the goal is not too difficult. Individual students or teachers may not yet be expert at setting their own goals or keeping the goal in mind, so encouragement and accurate feedback are necessary. The Theory into Action Guidelines on the next page give ideas to principals and teachers for involving families in goal setting in schools.

THEORY INTO ACTION GUIDELINES

Family and Community Partnerships

Understand family goals for children.

Examples

1. In an informal setting, around a coffee pot or snacks, meet with families individually or in small groups to listen to what they want for their children.
2. Mail out questionnaires or send response cards home with students, asking what skills the families believe their children most need to work on. Pick one goal for each child and develop a plan for working toward the goal both inside and outside school. Share the plan with the families and ask for feedback.

Identify student and family interests that can be related to goals.

Examples

1. Ask a member of the family to share a skill or hobby with the class.

2. Identify "family favorites"—favorite foods, music, vacations, sports, colors, activities, hymns, movies, games, snacks, recipes, memories. Tie class lessons to interests.

Give families a way to track progress toward goals.

Examples

1. Provide simple "progress charts" or goal cards that can be posted on the refrigerator.
2. Ask for feedback (and mean it) about parents' perceptions of your effectiveness in helping students reach goals.

Needs and Motivation

A **need** can be defined as "a biological or psychological requirement; a state of deprivation that motivates a person to take action toward a goal" (Darley, Glucksberg, & Kinchla, 1991, p. 743). Our needs are seldom satisfied completely and perfectly; improvement is always possible. People are thus motivated by the tensions the needs create to move toward goals that could satisfy the needs. Let's look at one very influential humanistic theory of motivation that deals with this central concept.

Maslow's Hierarchy

Abraham Maslow has had a great impact on the psychology of motivation. Maslow (1970) suggested that humans have a **hierarchy of needs** ranging from lower-level needs for survival and safety to higher-level needs for intellectual achievement and finally self-actualization. **Self-actualization** is Maslow's term for self-fulfillment, the realization of personal potential.

Maslow (1968) called the four lower-level needs—survival, safety, belonging, and self-esteem—**deficiency needs.** When these needs are satisfied, the motivation for fulfilling them decreases. He labeled the three higher-level needs—intellectual achievement, aesthetic appreciation, and self-actualization—**being needs.** When they are met, a person's motivation does not cease; instead, it increases to seek further fulfillment. For example, the more successful you are in your efforts to develop professionally, the harder you are likely to strive for even greater improvement. Unlike the deficiency needs, these being needs can never be completely filled. The motivation to achieve them is endlessly renewed.

Maslow's theory has been criticized for the very obvious reason that people do not always appear to behave as the theory would predict. Most of us move back and forth among different types of needs and may even be motivated by many different needs at the same time. Some people deny themselves safety or friendship in order to achieve knowledge, understanding, or greater self-esteem.

Criticisms aside, Maslow's theory does give us a way of looking at the whole person, whose physical, emotional, and intellectual needs are all interrelated. This has important implications for education. A child whose feelings of safety and sense of belonging are threatened by divorce may have little interest in learning to divide fractions. If a school is a fearful, unpredictable place where neither teachers nor students know where they stand, they are likely to be more concerned with security and less with learning or teaching. Students' desires to fill lower-level needs may at times conflict with a teacher's desire to have them achieve higher-level goals. Belonging to a social group and maintaining self-esteem within that group, for example, are important to students. If doing what the teacher says conflicts with group rules, students may choose to ignore the teacher's wishes or even defy the teacher.

A great deal has been written about needs and motivation. For teaching, the most fully developed and relevant work involves the need to achieve.

Achievement Motivation

David McClelland and John Atkinson were among the first to concentrate on the study of achievement motivation (McClelland, Atkinson, Clark, & Lowell, 1953). People who strive for excellence in a field for the sake of achieving, not for some reward, are considered to have a high need for achievement. There are two general explanations for the source of achievement motivation (Stipek, 2002). Some psychologists see achievement motivation as a stable and unconscious trait, something the individual has more or less of. The origins of high achievement motivation are assumed to be in the family and cultural group of the child. If achievement, initiative, and competitiveness are encouraged and reinforced in the home, and if parents let children solve problems on their own without becoming irritated by the children's initial failures, children are more likely to develop a high need for achievement (McClelland & Pilon, 1983). Children who see that their actions can have an impact and who are taught how to recognize a good performance are more likely to grow up with the desire to excel (Schunk, 2000).

Other theorists see achievement motivation as a set of conscious beliefs and values shaped mainly by recent experiences with success and failure and by factors in the immediate situation such as the difficulty of the task or the incentives available. Thus, you might have high achievement motivation when working with teachers in one subject because you know it well and value it, but low achievement motivation when working in another area because you are less familiar with that subject and you question the real value of the material (Stipek, 2002).

Atkinson (1964) added a new consideration to the theory of achievement need when he noted that all people have a need to avoid failure as well as a need to achieve. If the need to avoid failure is greater than the need to achieve in a particular situation, the risk will be threatening rather than challenging, and the resultant motivation will be to avoid the situation. If students' motivation to achieve is greater than their motivation to avoid failure, a moderate amount of failure can often enhance their desire to pursue a problem. They are determined to achieve, so they try again. On the other hand, success gained too easily can actually decrease motivation for those with high achievement needs. In contrast, students motivated by the need to avoid failure are usually discouraged by failure and encouraged by success.

A Principal's Perspective

T. G. was a service-oriented principal who constantly sought input from his faculty, staff, students, and parents regarding ways to improve his middle school and his leadership. Using a variety of nonthreatening methods to gather feedback, he heard this recurring concern from the classified staff: Cooks, custodians, bus drivers, secretaries, and teacher aides were growing increasingly disconnected from the school's mission. T. G. realized that the intense focus on academic achievement was crowding out the contributions of the support staff. These employees were beginning to feel uncelebrated, unwelcome, and undervalued. He also knew that if he didn't act to reverse the deteriorating morale, ultimately they would feel unmotivated. Mindful of the importance of the support staff to the overall educational climate of the school, T. G. decided to dedicate the first five minutes of every monthly staff meeting to the recognition of classified workers. He called it "The Curtain Call" and invited *all* employees to stay for the brief recognition. Selecting two or three names in advance, he asked them to stand, identified their positions and years of service to the school, and added some interesting facts about the work they do, such as "These cooks served over 12,000 hot lunches to our students last month" or "Every night these custodians sweep around 400 desks and carry out one thousand pounds of trash." In the end, teachers applauded, the workers smiled, and everyone was reminded that while academic achievement was the most important thing, it wasn't the only thing.

A more recent approach to motivation that focuses on human needs is self-determination theory (Deci & Ryan, 2002).

The Need for Self-Determination

Self-determination is the need to experience choices to have our own wishes, rather than external rewards or pressures, determine what we do and how we do it. People constantly struggle against pressure from external controls such as the rules, schedules, deadlines, orders, and limits imposed by others. Sometimes help is even rejected so that the individual can remain in command, a possible problem for principals striving to be instructional leaders (Deci & Ryan, 2002; Reeve, Deci, & Ryan, 2004; Ryan & Deci, 2000).

Classroom environments that support student self-determination and autonomy are associated with greater student interest, sense of competence, creativity, conceptual learning, and preference for challenge. These relationships appear to hold from first grade through graduate school (Deci & Ryan, 2002; Williams, Wiener, Markakis, Reeve, & Deci, 1993). When students can make choices, they are more likely to believe that the work is important, even if it is not "fun." Thus, they tend to internalize educational goals and take them as their own. In contrast to autonomy-supporting classrooms, controlling environments tend to improve performance only on rote recall tasks. When students are pressured to perform, they often seek the quickest, easiest solution.

The Need for Social Support

The need for relatedness is the desire to establish close emotional bonds and attachments with others. When adults are responsive and demonstrate that they care about the students' interests and well-being, the students show high intrinsic motivation. But, when students are denied the interpersonal involvement they seek from adults—when adults, for example, are unresponsive to their needs—the students lose intrinsic motivation (Solomon, Battistich, Watson, Schaps, & Lewis, 2000). Students who feel a sense of relatedness to administrators, teachers, parents, and peers are more emotionally engaged in school (Furrer & Skinner, 2003). In addition, emotional and physical problems—ranging from eating disorders to suicide—are more common among people who lack social relationships (Baumeister & Leary, 1995).

Relatedness has two components, *involvement* and *autonomy support*. Involvement is the degree to which teachers and parents are interested in and knowledgeable about their children's activities and experiences and devote time to them. When students feel a sense of belonging and personal support from their teachers, they are more interested in class work and find it more valuable (Goodenow, 1993; Stipek, 1996). Autonomy support is the degree to which teachers and parents encourage children to make their own choices rather than applying pressure to control the children's behavior. The Theory into Action Guidelines on the next page give principals and teachers ideas about how to support students' self-determination and autonomy.

Needs and Motivation: Lessons for Teachers and Principals

All people need to feel safe, secure, accepted, competent, effective, connected, and in charge of their own behavior. Some people may have developed a particularly strong need to achieve. Most people are more motivated when they are involved with tasks that give them a sense of achievement and a chance to form positive relationships with others. No one enjoys failure, and for some people it is crushing. Students, like adults, are unlikely to stick with tasks or respond well to teachers who make them feel insecure or incompetent. They are less likely to take responsibility for learning if they believe that the teacher doesn't really care about them. The same can be said for teachers: If they feel like faceless workers or if they believe that the principal doesn't really care about them or their problems, they are not likely to respond well to help.

THEORY INTO ACTION GUIDELINES

Supporting Self-Determination

Allow and encourage students to make choices.

Examples

1. Design several different ways to meet a learning objective (e.g., a paper, a compilation of interviews, a test, a news broadcast) and let students choose one. Encourage them to explain the reasons for their choice.
2. Appoint student committees to make suggestions about streamlining procedures such as caring for class pets or distributing equipment.
3. Provide time for independent and extended projects.

Help students plan actions to accomplish self-selected goals.

Examples

1. Experiment with goal cards. Students list their short- and long-term goals and then record three or four specific actions that will move them toward the goals. Goal cards are personal—like credit cards.
2. Encourage middle school and high school students to set goals in each subject area, record them in a goal book or on the computer, and check progress toward the goals on a regular basis.

Hold students accountable for the consequences of their choices.

Examples

1. If students choose to work with friends and do not finish a project because too much time was spent socializing, grade the project as it deserves and help the students see the connection between lost time and poor performance.
2. When students choose a topic that captures their imagination, discuss the connections between their investment in the work and the quality products that follow.

Provide rationales for limits, rules, and constraints.

Examples

1. Explain reasons for rules.
2. Respect rules and constraints in your own behavior.

Acknowledge that negative emotions are valid reactions to teacher control.

Examples

1. Communicate that it is OK (and normal) to feel bored waiting for a turn, for example.
2. Communicate that sometimes important learning involves frustration, confusion, weariness.

Use noncontrolling, positive feedback.

Examples

1. See poor performance or behavior as a problem to be solved, not a target of criticism.
2. Avoid controlling language—*should, must, have to.*

Sources: Adapted from J. P. Raffini (1996). *150 ways to increase intrinsic motivation in the classroom.* Boston: Allyn & Bacon; and J. Reeve (1996). *Motivating others: Nurturing inner motivational resources.* Boston: Allyn & Bacon, pp. 29–31.

Attributions, Beliefs, and Motivation

Thus far, we have talked about goals and needs, but there is another factor that must be considered in explaining motivation to learn. Success will not encourage motivation if you believe it was "just lucky" and probably won't happen again. Failure is not threatening unless you believe that it implies something is "wrong" with you. In other words, our beliefs and attributions about what is happening and why—about why we succeed and why we fail—affect motivation.

Attribution Theory

Cognitive explanations of motivation, called **attribution theories,** begin with the assumption that we all ask "Why?" in our attempts to understand our successes and failures. Attribution theories of motivation describe how the individual's explanations, justifications, and excuses influence motivation.

Dimensions: Locus, Stability, Responsibility.　　Bernard Weiner is one of the main educational psychologists responsible for relating attribution theory to school learning (Weiner, 1986, 1992, 1994; Weiner & Graham, 1989). According to Weiner, most of the causes to which students attribute their successes or failures can be characterized in terms of three dimensions: locus (location of the cause internal or external to the person), stability (whether the cause stays the same or can change), and responsibility (whether the person can control the cause). Table 5.2 shows how a student might explain failing a test using the eight possible combinations of these dimensions as causes.

Weiner believes that these three dimensions have important implications for motivation. The internal/external locus, for example, seems to be closely related to feelings of self-esteem (Weiner, 2000). If success or failure is attributed to internal factors, success will lead to pride and increased motivation, whereas failure will diminish self-esteem. The stability dimension seems to be closely related to expectations about the

TABLE 5.2　　Weiner's Theory of Causal Attribution

There are many explanations students give for why they fail a test. Below are eight reasons representing the eight combinations of locus, stability, and responsibility in Weiner's model of attributions.

Dimension Classification	Reason for Failure
Internal-stable-uncontrollable	Low aptitude
Internal-stable-controllable	Never studies
Internal-unstable-uncontrollable	Sick the day of the exam
Internal-unstable-controllable	Did not study for this particular test
External-stable-uncontrollable	School has hard requirements
External-stable-controllable	Instructor is biased
External-unstable-uncontrollable	Bad luck
External-unstable-controllable	Friends failed to help

Source: Human Motivation: Metaphors, Theories, and Research (p. 253), by B. Weiner. Copyright © 1992 by Sage Publications, Inc. Books. Reproduced with permission of Sage Publications, Inc. Books in the format Textbook and E-book via Copyright Clearance Center.

future. If, for example, students attribute their success (or failure) to stable factors such as the difficulty of the subject, they will expect to succeed (or fail) in that subject in the future. But if they attribute the outcome to unstable factors such as mood or luck, they will expect (or hope for) changes in the future when confronted with similar tasks. The responsibility dimension is related to emotions such as anger, pity, gratitude, or shame. If we fail at something that we believe is controllable, we may feel guilt; if we succeed, we may feel proud. Failing at an uncontrollable task may lead to shame or to anger toward the person or institution in control, while succeeding leads to feeling lucky or grateful. Also, feeling in control of your own learning seems to be related to choosing more difficult academic tasks, putting out more effort, and persisting longer in school-work (Schunk, 2000; Weiner, 1994).

Weiner (1994) summarizes the sequence of motivation when failure is attributed to lack of ability and ability is considered uncontrollable:

Failure → lack of ability → uncontrollable → not responsible → shame and embarrassment → performance declines in future

When failure is attributed to lack of effort, the sequence is:

Failure → lack of effort → controllable → responsible → guilt →performance improves in future

Weiner's locus and responsibility dimensions are closely related to locus of causality.

Learned Helplessness.   Whatever the label, most theorists agree that a sense of choice, control, and self-determination is critical if people are to feel intrinsically motivated. When people come to believe that the events and outcomes in their lives are mostly uncontrollable, they have developed **learned helplessness** (Seligman, 1975). To understand the power of learned helplessness, consider this experiment (Hiroto & Seligman, 1975). Subjects receive either solvable or unsolvable puzzles. In the next phase of the experiment, all subjects are given a series of solvable puzzles. The subjects who struggled with unsolvable problems in the first phase of the experiment usually solve significantly fewer puzzles in the second phase. They have learned that they cannot control the outcome, so why should they even try?

Learned helplessness appears to cause three types of deficits: motivational, cognitive, and affective. Students who feel hopeless will be unmotivated and reluctant to attempt work. They expect to fail so why even try, thus motivation suffers. Because they are pessimistic about learning, these students miss opportunities to practice and improve skills and abilities, so they develop cognitive deficits. Finally, they often suffer from affective problems such as depression, anxiety, and listlessness (Alloy & Seligman, 1979). Once established, it is very difficult to reverse the effects of learned helplessness. Learned helplessness is a particular danger for students with learning disabilities and students who are the victims of discrimination.

Attributions and Student Motivation. Most students try to explain their failures to themselves. When usually successful students fail, they often make internal, controllable attributions: They misunderstood the directions, lacked the necessary knowledge, or simply did not study hard enough, for example. When students see themselves as capable and attribute failure to lack of effort or insufficient knowledge—controllable causes—they usually focus on strategies for succeeding next time. This is an adaptive, mastery-oriented response, one that often leads to achievement, pride, a greater feeling of control, and a sense of self-determination (Ames, 1992).

The greatest motivational problems arise when students attribute failures to stable, uncontrollable causes. Such students may seem resigned to failure, depressed, and helpless, what we generally call "unmotivated" (Weiner, 1994; Weiner, Russell, & Lerman, 1978). These students respond to failure by focusing even more on their own inadequacy; their attitudes toward schoolwork may deteriorate even further (Ames, 1992). Apathy is a logical reaction to failure if students believe the causes are stable, unlikely to change, and beyond their control. In addition, students who view their failures in this light are less likely to seek help; they believe nothing and no one can help (Ames & Lau, 1982).

Cues about Causes. How do students determine the causes of their successes and failures? The behavior of their teachers is one cue. When teachers assume that student failure is attributable to forces beyond the students' control, they tend to respond with sympathy and to avoid giving punishments. If, however, the failures are attributed to a controllable factor such as lack of effort, the teacher's response is more likely to be anger, and punishments may follow. These tendencies seem to be consistent across time and cultures (Weiner, 1986).

What do students make of these reactions from their teachers? Graham (1991, 1996) gives some surprising answers. There is evidence that when teachers respond to students' mistakes with pity, praise for a "good try," or unsolicited help, the students are more likely to attribute their failure to an uncontrollable cause, usually lack of ability. Does this mean that teachers should be critical and withhold help? Of course not! But it is a reminder that "praise as a consolation prize" for failing (Brophy, 1985) or oversolicitous help can give unintended messages. Graham (1991) suggests that many minority group students could be the victims of well-meaning pity from teachers. Seeing the very real problems that the students face, teachers may "ease up" on requirements so the students will "experience success" and "feel good about themselves." But a subtle communication may accompany the pity, praise, and extra help: "You don't have the ability to do this, so I will overlook your failure." Graham says, "The . . . pertinent question for blacks is whether their own history of academic failure makes them more likely to be the targets of sympathetic feedback from teachers and thus the recipients of low-ability cues" (1991, p. 28). This kind of sympathetic feedback, even if well intended, can be a subtle form of racism.

Beliefs about Ability

Rate the following statements taken from Dweck (2000) on a scale from 1 (Strongly Agree) to 6 (Strongly Disagree).

_____ You have a certain amount of intelligence and you really can't do much to change it.

_____ You can learn new things, but you can't really change your basic intelligence.

_____ No matter who you are, you can change your intelligence a lot.

_____ No matter how much intelligence you have, you can always change it quite a bit.

Some of the most powerful beliefs affecting motivation in school are about *ability*. By examining these beliefs and how they affect motivation, we will understand why some people set inappropriate, unmotivating goals; why some students adopt self-defeating strategies; and why some students seem to give up altogether. Adults use two basic concepts of ability (Dweck, 1999, 2002). An **entity view of ability** assumes that ability is a *stable, uncontrollable* trait—a characteristic of the individual that cannot be changed. According to this view, some people have more ability than others, but the amount each person has is set. An **incremental view of ability,** on the other hand, suggests that ability is unstable and controllable—"an ever-expanding repertoire of skills and knowledge" (Dweck & Bempechat, 1983, p. 244). By hard work, study, or practice, knowledge can be increased and thus ability can be improved. What is your view of ability? Look back at your answers to the questions above—you can tell.

Young children tend to hold an exclusively incremental view of ability. Through the early elementary grades, most students believe that effort is the same as intelligence. Smart people try hard and trying hard makes you smart. If you fail, you aren't smart and you didn't try hard; if you succeed, you must be a smart, hard worker (Stipek, 2002). Children are age 11 or 12 before they can differentiate among effort, ability, and performance. About this time, they come to believe that someone who succeeds without working at all must be really smart. This is when beliefs about ability begin to influence motivation (Anderman & Maehr, 1994).

Students who hold an entity view of intelligence tend to set performance goals. They seek situations where they can look smart and protect their self-esteem. They keep doing what they can do well without expending too much effort or risking failure, because either one—working hard or failing—indicates (to them) low ability. And to work hard but still fail would be a devastating blow to their sense of competence. Another strategy is to make a point of not trying at all. If you don't try and then fail, no one can accuse you of being dumb. Just before a test a student might say, "I didn't study at all!" or "All I want to do is pass." Then, any grade above passing is a success. Procrastination is another self-protective strategy. Low grades do not imply low ability if the student can claim, "I did okay considering I didn't start the term paper until last night." Of course, even though these strategies may help students avoid the negative implications of failure, very little learning is going on. Students with learning disabilities are more likely to hold an entity view. Teachers who hold entity views are quicker to form judgments about students and slower to modify their opinions when confronted with contradictory evidence (Stipek, 2002).

Students who have an incremental notion of ability, in contrast, tend to set learning goals and seek situations in which they can improve their skills because improvement means getting smarter. Failure is not devastating; it simply indicates more work is needed, as the best athletic coaches know well. Ability is not threatened when failure signals simply that more effort is needed. Incremental theorists tend to set moderately difficult goals, the kind we have seen are the most motivating.

One of the most powerful influences on motivation to achieve is another kind of belief, self-efficacy.

Beliefs about Self-Efficacy

Albert Bandura (1986, 1997) suggests that critical sources of motivation are predictions about possible outcomes of behavior. "Will I succeed or fail? Will I be liked or laughed at?" We imagine future consequences based on past experiences and our observations of others. These predictions are affected by **self-efficacy,** our beliefs about our personal competence or effectiveness *in a given area*. Bandura (1997) defines self-efficacy as "beliefs in one's capabilities to organize and execute the courses of action required to produce given attainments" (p. 3).

Self-Efficacy, Self-Concept, and Self-Esteem.   Most people assume self-efficacy is the same as self-concept or self-esteem, but it isn't. Self-efficacy is distinct from other conceptions of self, in that it involves judgments of capabilities *specific to a particular task*. Self-efficacy is "a context-specific assessment of competence to perform a specific task" (Pajares, 1997, p. 15). Self-concept is a more global construct that contains many perceptions about the self, including self-efficacy. Self-concept is developed as a result of external and internal comparisons, using other people or other aspects of the self as frames of reference. But self-efficacy focuses on your ability to successfully accomplish a particular task with no need for comparisons; the question is can *you* do it, not would others be successful (Marsh, Walker, & Debus, 1991). Also, efficacy beliefs are strong predictors of behavior, but self-concept has weaker predictive power (Bandura, 1997).

Compared to self-esteem, self-efficacy is concerned with judgments of personal capabilities; self-esteem is concerned with judgments of self-worth. There is no direct relationship between self-esteem and self-efficacy. It is possible to feel highly efficacious in one area and still not have a high level of self-esteem, or vice versa (Valentine, DuBois, & Cooper, 2004). For example, if you have very low self-efficacy for singing, your self-esteem as an instructional leader probably won't be affected unless you believe that singing is a critical skill for educational administrators.

Sources of Efficacy.   Bandura identified four sources of efficacy expectations: mastery experiences, physiological and emotional arousal, vicarious experiences, and social persuasion. **Mastery experiences** are our own direct experiences, the most powerful source of efficacy information. Successes raise efficacy beliefs while failures lower efficacy. **Level of arousal** affects efficacy, depending on how the arousal is interpreted. As you face the task, are you anxious and worried (lowers efficacy) or excited and "psyched" (raises efficacy) (Bandura, 1997; Pintrich & Schunk, 2002)?

In **vicarious experiences,** accomplishments are modeled by someone else. The more closely the observer identifies with the model, the greater the impact on efficacy. When the model performs well, the observer's efficacy is enhanced, but when the model performs poorly, efficacy expectations decrease. Although mastery experiences generally are acknowledged as the most influential source of efficacy beliefs in adults, Keyser and Barling (1981) found that children (sixth graders in this study) rely more on modeling as a source of self-efficacy information.

Social persuasion may be a "pep talk" or specific performance feedback. Social persuasion alone can't create enduring increases in self-efficacy, but a persuasive boost in self-efficacy can lead a student or teacher to make an effort, attempt new strategies, or try hard enough to succeed (Bandura, 1982). Social persuasion can counter occasional setbacks that might have instilled self-doubt and interrupted persistence. The potency of persuasion depends on the credibility, trustworthiness, and expertise of the persuader (Bandura, 1986).

Efficacy and Motivation.   Greater efficacy leads to greater effort and persistence in the face of setbacks. Efficacy also influences motivation through goal setting. If we have a high sense of efficacy in a given area, we will set higher goals, be less afraid of failure, and find new strategies when old ones fail. If our sense of efficacy is low, however, we may avoid a task altogether or give up easily when problems arise (Bandura, 1993, 1997; Zimmerman, 1995).

Self-efficacy and attributions affect each other. If success is attributed to internal or controllable causes such as ability or effort, then self-efficacy is enhanced. But if success is attributed to luck or the intervention of others, then self-efficacy may not be strengthened. And efficacy affects attributions too. People with a strong sense of self-efficacy for a given task ("I'm good at math") tend to attribute their failures to lack of effort ("I should have double-checked my work"). But people with a low sense of efficacy ("I'm terrible at math") tend to attribute their failures to lack of ability ("I'm just dumb"). So having a strong sense of efficacy for a certain task encourages controllable attributions and controllable attributions increase efficacy. You can see that if a student held an *entity view* (ability cannot be changed) and a *low sense of self-efficacy*, motivation would be destroyed when failures were attributed to lack of ability ("I just can't do this and I'll never be able to learn") (Bandura, 1997; Pintrich & Schunk, 2002).

What is the most motivating level of efficacy? Should students be accurate, optimistic, or pessimistic in their predictions? There is evidence that a higher sense of self-efficacy supports motivation, even when the efficacy is an overestimation. Children and adults who are optimistic about the future are more mentally and physically healthy, less depressed, and more motivated to achieve (Flammer, 1995). After examining almost 140 studies of motivation, Sandra Graham concluded that these qualities characterize many African Americans. She found that the African Americans studied had strong self-concepts and high expectations, even in the face of difficulties (Graham, 1994, 1995).

Of course there are dangers in underestimating abilities because then students are more likely to put out a weak effort and give up easily. But there are dangers in continually overestimating performance as well. Students who think that they are better readers than they actually are may not be motivated to go back and repair misunderstandings as they read. They don't discover until it is too late that they did not really understand (Pintrich & Zusho, 2002). So slightly optimistic, but not unrealistic, is probably best.

Research on self-efficacy and achievement suggests that performance in school is improved and self-efficacy is increased when students (1) adopt short-term goals so it is easier to judge progress; (2) are taught to use specific learning strategies such as outlining or summarizing that help them focus attention; and (3) receive rewards based on quality of performance, not just engagement, because the former signal increasing competence (Graham & Weiner, 1996). Table 5.3 shows how the different elements we have been discussing combine to support motivation to learn.

Teacher Efficacy. Much of our own research has focused on a particular kind of self-efficacy, sense of efficacy in teaching (Hoy & Woolfolk, 1990, 1993; Tschannen-Moran, Woolfolk Hoy, & Hoy, 1998; Woolfolk & Hoy, 1990). **Teaching efficacy,** a teacher's belief that he or she can reach even difficult students to help them learn, appears to be

TABLE 5.3 Building a Concept of Motivation to Learn

Motivation to learn is encouraged when the sources of motivation are intrinsic, the goals are personally challenging, and the individual is focused on the task, has a mastery orientation, attributes successes and failures to controllable causes, and believes ability can be improved.

	Optimum Characteristics of Motivation to Learn	**Characteristics That Diminish Motivation to Learn**
Source of Motivation	INTRINSIC: Personal factors such as needs, interests, curiosity, enjoyment	EXTRINSIC: Environmental factors such as rewards, social pressure, punishment
Type of Goal Set	LEARNING GOAL: Personal satisfaction in meeting challenges and improving; tendency to choose moderately difficult and challenging goals.	PERFORMANCE GOAL: Desire for approval for performance in others' eyes; tendency to choose very easy or very difficult goals
Type of Involvement	TASK-INVOLVED: Concerned with mastering the task.	EGO-INVOLVED: Concerned with self in others' eyes.
Achievement Motivation	Motivation to ACHIEVE: mastery orientation.	Motivation to AVOID FAILURE: prone to anxiety
Likely Attributions	Successes and failures attributed to CONTROLLABLE effort and ability	Success and failures attributed to UNCONTROLLABLE causes
Beliefs about Ability	INCREMENTAL VIEW: Belief that ability can be improved through hard work and added knowledge and skills	ENTITY VIEW: Belief that ability is a stable, uncontrollable trait

one of the few personal characteristics of teachers that is correlated with student achievement. Self-efficacy theory predicts that teachers with a high sense of efficacy work harder and persist longer even when students are difficult to teach, in part because these teachers believe in themselves and in their students. Also, they are less likely to experience burnout (Fives, Hamman, & Olivarez, 2005).

We have found that prospective teachers tend to increase in their personal sense of efficacy as a consequence of completing student teaching. But sense of efficacy may go down after the first year as a teacher, perhaps because the support that was there for you in student teaching is gone (Woolfolk Hoy & Burke-Spero, 2005). Teachers' sense of efficacy is higher in schools where the other teachers and administrators have high expectations for students and where teachers receive help from their principals in solving instructional and management problems (Capa, 2005; Hoy & Woolfolk, 1993; Tschannen-Moran & Woolfolk Hoy, 2007). Another important conclusion from our research is that efficacy grows from real success with students, not just from the moral support or cheerleading of administrators and colleagues. Any experience or training that helps your teachers succeed in the day-to-day tasks of teaching will give them a foundation for developing a sense of efficacy.

Teachers' Sense of Efficacy and Student Achievement.   How does a strong sense of teacher efficacy work to increase student achievement? Teacher efficacy is context-specific; teachers do not feel equally efficacious for all teaching situations. Teachers can feel efficacious in one situation but not in others. Even from one class to another, teachers' level of efficacy can change (Raudenbush, Rowen, & Cheong, 1992; Ross, Cousins, & Gadalla, 1996). Efficacy judgments involve both the teaching task and the context.

In analyzing the *teaching task and its context*, the relative importance of factors that make teaching difficult are weighed against an assessment of the resources available that facilitate learning. In assessing *self-perceptions of teaching competence*, the teacher assesses personal capabilities such as skills, knowledge, and strategies balanced against personal weaknesses in a particular teaching situation. The key efficacy questions are:

Teaching Task Question: How difficult is the task at hand and what resources are available?

Teaching Competence Question: Given the situation, do I have the skills and knowledge?

The interaction of these two components leads to judgments of self-efficacy for the task at hand. The consequences of these efficacy judgments may be effort, persistence, and active teaching (higher efficacy) or minimal effort, helplessness, and weak teaching (low efficacy). With Megan Tschannen-Moran, we (Tschannen-Moran, Woolfolk Hoy, & Hoy, 1998) have developed a model that explains these relationships and that has received research support (Ebmeier, 2003). Our model is summarized in Figure 5.1.

One of the things that makes teacher efficacy so powerful is its cyclical nature. As noted in Figure 5.1, a successful performance creates a new mastery experience, which provides new information (feedback) that will be processed to shape future

FIGURE 5.1   A Model of Teacher's Perceived Efficacy

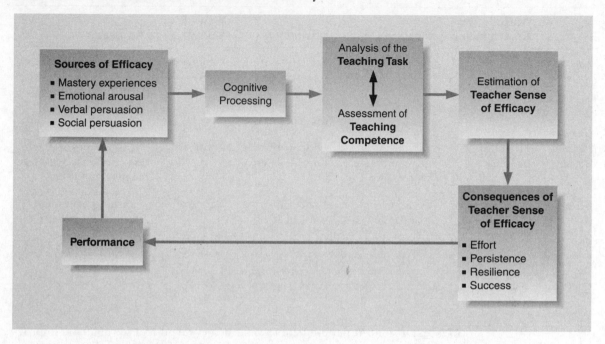

efficacy beliefs. Greater efficacy leads to greater effort and persistence, which leads to better performance, which in turn leads to greater efficacy. The reverse is also true. Lower efficacy leads to less effort, which leads to poor teaching outcomes, which then decreases efficacy. Over time this process stabilizes into a relatively enduring set of efficacy beliefs.

Teachers' efficacy beliefs influence their investment and level of aspiration, resilience, and persistence (Tschannen-Moran & Woolfolk Hoy, 2001). Teachers' efficacy is also related to commitment to teaching (Coladarci, 1992) and job satisfaction (Caprara, Barbaranelli, Borgogni, & Steca, 2003). Once established, efficacy beliefs seem resistant to change. A strong sense of efficacy can support higher motivation, greater effort, persistence, and resilience. Consequently, helping teachers develop strong efficacy beliefs early in their career will pay lasting dividends.

Attributions, Achievement Motivation, and Self-Worth

What are the connections between need for achievement, attributions for success and failure, beliefs about ability, self-efficacy, and self-worth? Covington and his colleagues suggest that these factors come together in three kinds of motivational sets: mastery-oriented, failure-avoiding, and failure-accepting, as shown in Table 5.4 on the next page (Covington, 1992; Covington & Mueller, 2001; Covington & Omelich, 1987).

TABLE 5.4   Mastery-Oriented, Failure-Avoiding, and Failure-Accepting Students

	Attitude toward Failure	Goals Set	Attributions	View of Ability	Strategies
Mastery-Oriented	Low fear of failure	Learning goals: moderately difficult and challenging	Effort, use of right strategy, sufficient knowledge is cause of success	Incremental; improvable	Adaptive strategies; e.g., try another way, seek help, practice/study more
Failure-Avoiding	High fear of failure	Performance goals: very hard or very easy	Lack of ability is cause of failure	Entity; set	Self-defeating strategies; e.g., make a feeble effort, pretend not to care
Failure-Accepting	Expectation of failure; depression	Performance goals or no goals	Lack of ability is cause of failure	Entity; set	Learned helplessness; likely to give up

Source: From Anita E. Woolfolk, *Educational Psychology: Active Learning Edition*, 10/e. Published by Allyn & Bacon, Boston, MA. Copyright © 2008 by Pearson Education. Reprinted by permission of the publisher.

Mastery-oriented people tend to value achievement and see ability as improvable, so they focus on learning goals in order to increase their skills and abilities. They are not fearful of failure because failing does not threaten their sense of competence and self-worth. This allows them to set moderately difficult goals, take risks, and cope with failure constructively. They generally attribute success to their own effort, and so they assume responsibility for learning and have a strong sense of self-efficacy. They perform best in competitive situations, learn fast, have more self-confidence and energy, are more aroused, welcome concrete feedback (it does not threaten them), and are eager to learn "the rules of the game" so that they can succeed. All of these factors make for persistent, successful learning for teachers or students (Alderman, 2004; McClelland, 1985).

Failure-avoiding people tend to hold an entity view of ability, so they set performance goals. They lack a strong sense of their own competence and self-worth separate from their performance. In other words, they feel only as smart as their last test grade or performance evaluation, so they never develop a solid sense of self-efficacy. In order to feel competent, they must protect themselves (and their self-images) from failure. If they have been generally successful, they may avoid failure simply by taking few risks and "sticking with what they know." If, on the other hand, they have experienced some successes but also a good bit of failure, they may adopt the strategies we discussed earlier: procrastination, feeble efforts, setting very low or ridiculously high goals, or claiming not to care.

Unfortunately, as we have seen, failure-avoiding strategies are self-defeating, generally leading to the very failure the person was trying to avoid. If failures continue and excuses wear thin, the students or teachers may finally decide that they are incompetent. This is what they feared in the first place, but they come to accept it. Their sense of self-worth and self-efficacy deteriorate. They give up and thus become **failure-accepting**

people. They are convinced that their problems are due to low ability, and they can no longer protect themselves from this conclusion. As we saw earlier, those who attribute failure to low ability and believe ability is set are likely to become depressed, apathetic, and helpless.

Teachers may be able to prevent some failure-avoiding students from becoming failure-accepting by helping them to find new and more realistic goals. Also, some students may need support in aspiring to higher levels in the face of sexual or ethnic stereotypes about what they "should" want or what they "should not" be able to do well. This kind of support could make all the difference. Instead of pitying or excusing these students, teachers and schools can teach them how to learn and then hold them accountable.

Attributions and Beliefs: Lessons for Teachers and Principals

At the heart of attribution theory is the notion of individual perception. If students believe they lack the ability to deal with higher mathematics, they will probably act on this belief even if their actual abilities are well above average. These students are likely to have little motivation to tackle calculus because they expect to do poorly in these areas. If students believe that failing means they are stupid, they are likely to adopt many self-protective, but also self-defeating, strategies. Just telling students to "try harder" is not particularly effective. Students need real evidence that effort will pay off, that setting a higher goal will not lead to failure, that they can improve, and that abilities can be changed. The Theory into Action Guidelines should help instructional leaders suggest ideas for teachers to encourage student self-worth and self-efficacy.

Interests and Emotions

How do you feel about learning? Excited, bored, curious, fearful? Today, researchers emphasize that learning is not only about the *cold cognition* of reasoning and problem solving. Learning and information processing also are influenced by emotion, so *hot cognition* plays a role in learning as well (Miller, 2002; Pintrich, 2003). Students are more likely to pay attention to, learn, and remember events, images, and readings that provoke emotional responses (Alexander & Murphy, 1998; Cowley & Underwood, 1998; Reisberg & Heuer, 1992) or that are related to their personal interests (Renninger, Hidi, & Krapp, 1992). Sometimes, emotions interfere with learning by taking up attention or working memory space that could be used for learning (Pekrun, Goetz, Titz, & Perry, 2002). How can we use these findings to support learning in school?

Tapping Interests

When Walter Vispoel and James Austin (1995) asked over 200 middle school students to rate reasons for their successes and failures in different school subjects, lack of interest in the topic received the highest rating as an explanation for failures. Interest was second only to effort as a choice for explaining successes.

THEORY INTO ACTION GUIDELINES

Encouraging Self-Worth and Self-Efficacy

Emphasize students' progress in a particular area.

Examples

1. Return to earlier material in reviews and show how "easy" it is now.
2. Encourage students to improve projects when they have learned more.
3. Keep examples of particularly good work in portfolios.

Make specific suggestions for improvement, and revise grades when improvements are made.

Examples

1. Return work with comments noting what the students did right, what they did wrong, and why they might have made the mistakes.
2. Experiment with peer editing.
3. Show students how their revised, higher grade reflects greater competence and raises their class average.

Stress connections between past efforts and past accomplishments.

Examples

1. Have individual goal-setting and goal-review conferences with students, in which you ask students to reflect on how they solved difficult problems.
2. Confront self-defeating, failure-avoiding strategies directly.

Set learning goals for your students, and model a mastery orientation for them.

Examples

1. Recognize progress and improvement.
2. Share examples of how you have developed your abilities in a given area and provide other models of achievement who are similar to your students—no supermen or women whose accomplishments seem unattainable.
3. Read stories about students who overcame physical, mental, or economic challenges.
4. Don't excuse failure because a student has problems outside school. Help the student succeed inside school.

There are two kinds of interests, personal and situational. *Personal interests* are more enduring aspects of the person, like an interest in sports, music, or ancient history. *Situational interests* are more short-lived aspects of the activity, text, or materials that catch and keep the student's attention. Both personal and situational interests are related to learning from texts—greater interest leads to more positive emotional responses to the material, then to greater persistence, deeper processing, better remembering of the material, and higher achievement (Ainley, Hidi, & Berndorf, 2002; Pintrich, 2003; Schraw & Lehman, 2001). And interests increase when students feel competent, so even if students are not initially interested in a subject or activity, they may develop interests as they experience success (Stipek, 2002).

Catching and Holding Interests.   Whenever possible, it helps to connect academic content to students' enduring personal interests. But given that the content you will teach is determined by standards in most classrooms today, it will be difficult to tailor lessons to each student's personal interests. You will have to rely more on situational interest. Here, the challenge is to not only *catch* but also *hold* students' interest (Pintrich, 2003). For example, Mathew Mitchell (1993) found that using computers, groups, and puzzles caught students' interest in secondary mathematics classes, but the interests did not hold. Lessons that held interests over time included math activities that were related to real-life problems and active participation in laboratory activities and projects (Anderman, 2004).

One source of interest is fantasy. For example, Cordova and Lepper (1996) found that students learned more math facts during a computer exercise when they were challenged, as captains of star ships, to navigate through space by solving math problems. The students got to name their ships, stock the (imaginary) galley with their favorite snacks, and name all the crew members after their friends. Principals can use the Theory into Action Guidelines to give teachers other ideas. However, there are cautions in responding to students' interests, as you can see in Point/Counterpoint on the next page.

THEORY INTO ACTION GUIDELINES

Building on Students' Interests

Relate content objectives to student experiences.

Examples

1. With a teacher in another school, establish pen pals across the classes. Through writing letters, students exchange personal experiences, photos, drawings, written work, and ask and answer questions ("Have you learned cursive writing yet?" "What are you doing in math now?" "What are you reading?"). Letters can be mailed in one large mailer to save stamps.
2. Identify classroom experts for different assignments or tasks. Who knows how to use the computer for graphics? How to search the Net? How to cook? How to use an index?
3. Have a "Switch Day" when students exchange roles with a school staff or support person. Students must research the role by interviewing their staff member, prepare for the job, dress the part for the day they take over, and then evaluate their success after the switch.

Identify student interests, hobbies, and extracurricular activities that can be incorporated into class lessons and discussions.

Examples

1. Have students design and conduct interviews and surveys to learn about each other's interests.
2. Keep the class library stocked with books that connect to students' interests and hobbies.

Support instruction with humor, personal experiences, and anecdotes that show the human side of the content.

Examples

1. Share your own hobbies, interests, and favorites.
2. Tell students there will be a surprise visitor, then dress up as the author of a story and tell about "yourself" and your writing.

Source: Adapted from J. P. Raffini (1996). *150 ways to increase intrinsic motivation in the classroom.* Boston: Allyn & Bacon.

POINT/COUNTERPOINT

Does Making Learning Fun Make for Good Learning?

When many beginning teachers are asked about how to motivate students, they often mention making learning fun. It is true that connecting to students' interests, stimulating curiosity, and using fantasy all encourage motivation and engagement. But is it necessary for learning to be fun?

POINT

Teachers should make learning fun.
When we searched "making learning fun" on Google.com, we found 10 pages of resources and references. Clearly there is interest in making learning fun. In 1987, Thomas Malone and Mark Lepper wrote a chapter on "Making Learning Fun: A Taxonomy of Intrinsic Motivations for Learning." Research shows that passages in texts that are more interesting are remembered better (Pintrich & Schunk, 2002). For example, students who read books that interested them spent more time reading, read more words in the books, and felt more positively about reading (Guthrie & Alao, 1997). Games and simulations can make learning more fun, too. For example, when one of our daughters was in the eighth grade, all the students in her grade spent three days playing a game her teachers had designed called ULTRA. Students were divided into groups and formed their own "countries." Each country had to choose a name, symbol, national flower, and bird. They wrote and sang a national anthem and elected government officials. The teachers allocated different resources to the countries. To get all the materials needed for the completion of assigned projects, the countries had to establish trade with one another. There was a monetary system and a stock market. Students had to work with their fellow citizens to complete cooperative learning assignments. Some countries "cheated" in their trades with other nations, and this allowed debate about international relations, trust, and war. Liz says she had fun—but she also learned how to work in a group without the teacher's supervision and gained a deeper understanding of world economics and international conflicts.

COUNTERPOINT

Fun can get in the way of learning.
As far back as the early 1900s, educators warned about the dangers of focusing on fun in learning. None other than John Dewey, who wrote extensively about the role of interest in learning, cautioned that you can't make boring lessons interesting by mixing in fun like you can make bad chili good by adding some spicy hot sauce. Dewey wrote, "When things have to be made interesting, it is because interest itself is wanting. Moreover, the phrase itself is a misnomer. The thing, the object, is no more interesting than it was before" (Dewey, 1913, pp. 11–12). There is a good deal of research now indicating that adding interest by adding fascinating but irrelevant details actually gets in the way of learning the important information. These "seductive details," as they have been called, divert the readers' attention from the less interesting main ideas (Harp & Mayer, 1998). For example, students who read biographies of historical figures remembered more very interesting but unimportant information compared to interesting main ideas (Wade, Schraw, Buxton, & Hayes, 1993). Shannon Harp and Richard Mayer (1998) found similar results with high school science texts. These texts added emotional interest and seductive details about swimmers and golfers who are injured by lightning to a lesson on the process of lightning. They concluded that, "in the case of emotional interest versus cognitive interest, the verdict is clear. Adjuncts aimed at increasing emotional interest failed to improve understanding of scientific explanations" (p. 100). The seductive details may have disrupted students' attempts to follow the logic of the explanations and thus interfered with comprehending the text. Harp and Mayer conclude that "the best way to help students enjoy a passage is to help them understand it" (p. 100).

Arousal: Excitement and Anxiety in Learning

Just as we all know how it feels to be motivated, we all know what it is like to be aroused. **Arousal** involves both psychological and physical reactions—changes in brain wave patterns, blood pressure, heart rate, and breathing rate. We feel alert, wide awake, even excited. To understand the effects of arousal on motivation, think of two extremes. The first is late at night. You are trying for the third time to finish reading materials for a meeting tomorrow, but you are so sleepy. Your attention drifts as your eyes droop, even though you have not finished your preparation. At the other extreme, imagine that you have a television interview tomorrow, one that is sure to be watched by many parents in your district. You feel tremendous pressure from everyone to do well. You know that you need a good night's sleep, but you are wide awake. In the first case, arousal is too low, and in the second, too high.

There appears to be an optimum level of arousal for most activities. Generally speaking, a higher level of arousal is helpful on simple tasks like organizing files, but lower levels of arousal are better for complex tasks such as taking the GRE. Let's look for a moment at how to increase arousal by arousing curiosity.

Curiosity: Novelty and Complexity.   Interest and curiosity are related. Curiosity could be defined as a tendency to be interested in a wide range of areas (Pintrich, 2003). Almost 40 years ago, psychologists suggested that individuals are naturally motivated to seek novelty, surprise, and complexity (Berlyne, 1966). Research on teaching has found that variety in teaching approaches and tasks can support learning (Brophy & Good, 1986; Stipek, 2002). For younger students, the chance to manipulate and explore objects relevant to what is being studied may be the most effective way to keep curiosity stimulated. For older students, well-constructed questions, logical puzzles, and paradoxes can have the same effect. But remember that you have to do more than catch students' interest. You have to hold it, so the questions and puzzles should be related to meaningful learning.

George Lowenstein (1994) suggests that curiosity arises when attention is focused on a gap in knowledge. "Such information gaps produce the feeling of deprivation labeled *curiosity*. The curious person is motivated to obtain the missing information to reduce or eliminate the feeling of deprivation" (p. 87). This idea, similar to Piaget's (1985) concept of disequilibrium, has a number of implications for teaching. First, students need some base of knowledge before they can experience gaps in knowledge leading to curiosity. Second, students must be aware of the gaps in order for curiosity to result. Asking students to make guesses, then providing feedback can be helpful. Also, mistakes, properly handled, can stimulate curiosity by pointing to missing knowledge. Finally, the more we learn about a topic, the more curious we may become about that subject. As Maslow (1970) predicted, fulfilling the need to know and understand increases, not decreases, the need to know more.

Sometimes arousal is too high, not too low. Because schools are places where students are tested and graded, anxiety can become a factor in classroom motivation.

Anxiety in the Classroom.   At one time or another, everyone has experienced **anxiety,** or "general uneasiness, a sense of foreboding, a feeling of tension" (Hansen,

1977, p. 91). The effects of anxiety on school achievement are clear. "From the time of the earliest work on this problem, starting with the pioneering work of Yerkes and Dodson (1908), to the present day, researchers have consistently reported a negative correlation between virtually every aspect of school achievement and a wide range of anxiety measures" (Covington & Omelich, 1987, p. 393). Anxiety can be both a cause and an effect of school failure: Students do poorly because they are anxious, and their poor performance increases their anxiety. Anxiety probably is both a trait and a state. Some students tend to be anxious in many situations (*trait anxiety*), but some situations are especially anxiety-provoking (*state anxiety*) (Covington, 1992).

Anxiety seems to have both cognitive and affective components. The cognitive side includes worry and negative thoughts—thinking about how bad it would be to fail and worrying that you will, for example. The affective side involves physiological and emotional reactions such as sweaty palms, upset stomach, racing heartbeat, or fear (Schunk, 2000; Zeidner, 1995). Whenever there are pressures to perform, severe consequences for failure, and competitive comparisons, anxiety may be encouraged (Wigfield & Eccles, 1989). Also, research with school-age children shows a relationship between the quality of sleep (how quickly and how well you sleep) and anxiety. Better-quality sleep is associated with positive arousal or an "eagerness" to learn (Meijer & van den Wittenboer, 2004). Poor-quality sleep, on the other hand, was related to debilitating anxiety and decreased school performance. You may have discovered these relationships for yourself in your own career.

How Does Anxiety Interfere with Achievement? Sigmund Tobias (1985) suggests a model to explain how anxiety interferes with learning and test performance at three points in the learning and performance cycle. When students are learning new material, they must pay attention to it. Highly anxious students evidently divide their attention between the new material and their preoccupation with how nervous they are feeling. Much of their attention is taken up with negative thoughts about performing poorly, being criticized, and feeling embarrassed. From the beginning, anxious students may miss much of the information they are supposed to learn because their thoughts are focused on their own worries (Hill & Wigfield, 1984; Paulman & Kennelly, 1984).

But the problems do not end here. Even if they are paying attention, many anxious students have trouble learning material that is somewhat disorganized and difficult, material that requires them to rely on their memory. Unfortunately, much material in school could be described this way. Anxious students may be more easily distracted by irrelevant or incidental aspects of the task at hand. They seem to have trouble focusing on the significant details (Hill & Wigfield, 1984). In addition, many highly anxious students have poor study habits. Simply learning to be more relaxed will not automatically improve these students' performance; their learning strategies and study skills must be improved as well (Naveh-Benjamin, 1991).

Finally, anxious students often know more than they can demonstrate on a test. They may lack critical test-taking skills, or they may have learned the materials but "freeze and forget" on tests. So anxiety can interfere at one or all three points: attention, learning, and testing (Naveh-Benjamin, McKeachie, & Lin, 1987).

Coping with Anxiety. When students face stressful situations such as tests, they can use three kinds of coping strategies: *problem solving, emotional management,* and *avoidance.* Problem-focused strategies might include planning a study schedule, borrowing good notes, or finding a protected place to study. Emotion-focused strategies are attempts to reduce the anxious feelings, for example, by using relaxation exercises or describing the feelings to a friend. Of course, the latter might become an avoidance strategy, along with going out for pizza or suddenly launching an all out desk-cleaning attack (can't study until you get organized). Different strategies are helpful at different points, for example, problem solving before and emotion management during an exam. Different strategies fit different people and situations (Zeidner, 1995).

Teachers should help highly anxious students to set realistic goals because these individuals often have difficulty making wise choices. They tend to select either extremely difficult or extremely easy tasks. In the first case, they are likely to fail, which will increase their sense of hopelessness and anxiety about school. In the second case, they will probably succeed on the easy tasks, but they will miss the sense of satisfaction that could encourage greater effort and ease their fears about schoolwork. Anxious students may need a good deal of guidance in choosing both short- and long-term goals. Goal cards, progress charts, or goal-planning journals may help here. On the next page are Theory into Action Guidelines for principals to help teachers deal with anxious students.

Now that we have a picture of some important building blocks of motivation, let's consider how to put this knowledge to work in classrooms. How will you help teachers deal with one of their greatest challenges, motivating their students?

Strategies to Encourage Motivation and Thoughtful Learning

Until four basic conditions are met, no motivational strategies will succeed. So your first step as an instructional leader working with teachers to improve their students' motivation is to determine if these basic conditions are met in your school. Once these requirements are in place, there are many strategies to help students gain confidence, value learning, and stay involved with the task (Brophy, 1988; Lepper, 1988).

Necessary Conditions in Classrooms

First, the classroom must be relatively organized and free from constant interruptions and disruptions. (Chapter 7 will give you the information you need to make sure this requirement is met.) Second, the teacher must be a patient, supportive person who never embarrasses students for making mistakes. Everyone in the class should see mistakes as opportunities for learning (Clifford, 1990, 1991). Third, the work must be challenging but reasonable. If work is too easy or too difficult, students will have little motivation to learn. They will focus on finishing, not on learning. Finally, the learning tasks must be authentic and not just busywork (Brophy, 1983; Brophy & Kher, 1986; Stipek, 2002).

THEORY INTO ACTION GUIDELINES

Dealing with Anxiety

Use competition carefully.

Examples

1. Monitor activities to make sure no students are being put under undue pressure.
2. During competitive games, make sure all students involved have a reasonable chance of succeeding.
3. Experiment with cooperative learning activities.

Avoid situations in which highly anxious students will have to perform in front of large groups.

Examples

1. Ask anxious students questions that can be answered yes or no, or some other brief reply.
2. Give anxious students practice in speaking before smaller groups.

Make sure all instructions are clear. Uncertainty can lead to anxiety.

Examples

1. Write test instructions on the board or on the test itself instead of giving them orally.
2. Check with students to make sure they understand. Ask several students how they would do the first question of an exercise or the sample question on a test. Correct any misconceptions.

3. If you are using a new format or starting a new type of task, give students examples or models to show how it is done.

Avoid unnecessary time pressures.

Examples

1. Give occasional take-home tests.
2. Make sure all students can complete classroom tests within the period given.

Remove some of the pressures from major tests and exams.

Examples

1. Teach test-taking skills; give practice tests; provide study guides.
2. Avoid basing most of a report card grade on one test.
3. Make extra-credit work available to add points to course grades.
4. Use different types of items in testing because some students have difficulty with certain types.

Develop alternatives to written tests.

Examples

1. Try oral, open-book, or group tests.
2. Have students do projects, organize portfolios of their work, make oral presentations, or create a finished product.

Once these four basic conditions are met, the influences on students' motivation to learn in a particular situation can be summarized in three basic questions: Can I succeed at this task? Do I want to succeed? What do I need to do to succeed? (Eccles & Wigfield, 1985). As reflected in these questions, we want students to have confidence in their ability so they will approach learning with energy and enthusiasm. We want them to see the value of the tasks involved and work to learn, not just try to get the grade or get finished. We want students to believe that success will come when they apply good learning strategies instead of believing that their only option is to use self-defeating, failure-avoiding, face-saving strategies. When things get difficult, we want students to try to solve the problem and stay focused on the task, not get so worried about failure that they "freeze" with anxiety.

Can I Do It? Building Confidence and Positive Expectations

Let's assume the four basic conditions are met in your school. What's next? One of the most important factors in building expectations for success is past success. No amount of encouragement or cheerleading will substitute for real accomplishment. To ensure genuine progress, teachers in your school should be encouraged to:

1. *Begin work at the students' level and move in small steps.* The pace should be brisk, but not so fast that students have to move to the next step before they understand the previous one. This may require assigning different tasks to different students. One possibility is to have very easy and very difficult questions on every test and assignment, so all students are sure to pass some questions and fail others. This provides both success and challenge for everyone. When grades are required, make sure all the students in class have a chance to make at least a C if they work hard.

2. *Make sure learning goals are clear, specific, and possible to reach in the near future.* When long-term projects are planned, break the work into subgoals and help students feel a sense of progress toward the long-term goal. For example, a big research paper could be broken down into identifying a topic and a few basic references, doing an outline, taking notes, finding additional references and learning the form for a bibliography, writing an introduction, doing a first draft, and finally writing the polished paper. If possible, give students a range of goals at different levels of difficulty and let them choose.

3. *Stress self-comparison, not comparison with others.* Help students see the progress they are making by showing them how to use self-management strategies. Give specific feedback and corrections. Tell students what they are doing right as well as what is wrong and *why* it is wrong. Periodically, give students a question or problem that was once hard for them but now seems easy. Point out how much they have improved. Show the connections between their efforts and their accomplishments.

4. *Communicate to students that academic ability is improvable and specific to the task at hand.* In other words, the fact that a student has trouble in algebra doesn't necessarily mean that geometry will be difficult or that he or she is a bad English student. Even when a task is hard, students can improve if they stick with it. Don't undermine efforts to stress improvement by displaying only the A+ papers on the bulletin board.

5. *Model good problem solving.* Students need to see that learning is not smooth and error-free, even for the teacher.

Do I Want to Do It? Seeing the Value of Learning

We can think of a task as having three kinds of value to the students (Eccles & Wigfield, 1985). *Attainment value* is the importance of doing well on the task. This aspect of value is closely tied to the needs of the individual (for example, the need to be competent, well-liked, masculine, etc.) and the meaning of success to that person. A second kind of value is intrinsic or *interest value*. This is simply the enjoyment one gets from the activity itself. Some people like the experience of learning. Others enjoy the feeling of hard physical effort or of solving puzzles. Finally, tasks have *utility value;* that is, they help us achieve a short-term or long-term goal.

Principals and teachers can use intrinsic and extrinsic motivation strategies to help students see the value of the learning task. In this process the age of the student must be considered. For young children, interest value is a greater determinant of motivation than attainment or utility value. Because younger students have a more immediate, concrete focus, they have trouble seeing the value of an activity that is linked to distant goals such as getting a good job or even preparing for the next grade. Older students, on the other hand, have the cognitive ability to think more abstractly and connect what they are learning now with goals and future possibilities, so utility value becomes important to these students (Eccles & Wigfield, 1985).

Attainment and Intrinsic Value.   To establish attainment value, we must connect the learning task with the needs of the students. First, it must be possible for students to meet their needs for safety, belonging, and achievement in our schools. The classroom should not be a frightening or lonely place. Second, we must be sure that sexual or ethnic stereotypes do not interfere with motivation. For example, if students subscribe to rigid notions of masculinity and femininity, we must make it clear that both women and men can be high achievers in all subjects and that no subjects are the territory of only one sex. It is not "unfeminine" to be strong in mathematics, science, shop, or sports. It is not "unmasculine" to be good in literature, art, music, or French. Students' beliefs about the value of a task seem to predict the choices they make, such as whether to enroll in advanced science classes or join a team. Efficacy expectations predict achievement in doing the task—how well the students actually perform in the advanced science class or on the team (Wigfield & Eccles, 2002). There are many strategies for encouraging intrinsic (interest) motivation. Several of the following are taken from Brophy (1988).

1. *Tie class activities to student interests* in sports, music, current events, pets, common problems or conflicts with family and friends, fads, television and cinema personalities, or other significant features of their lives (Schiefele, 1991). When possible, give students choices of research papers or reading topics so they can follow their own interests.

2. *Arouse curiosity.* Point out puzzling discrepancies between students' beliefs and the facts. For example, Stipek (2002) describes a teacher who asked her fifth-grade class if there were "people" on some of the other planets. When the students said yes, the teacher asked if people needed oxygen to breathe. Since the students had just learned this fact, they responded yes to this question also. Then the teacher told them that there is no oxygen in the atmosphere of the other planets. This surprising discrepancy between what the children knew about oxygen and what they believed about life on other planets led to a rousing discussion of the atmospheres of other planets, the kinds of beings that could survive in these atmospheres, and so on. A straight lecture on the atmosphere of the planets might have put the students to sleep, but this discussion led to real interest in the subject.

3. *Make the learning task fun.* Many lessons can be taught through simulations or games. Computers, problem-based learning, cable TV, and Web connections are just a

few possibilities. Students can create newspapers, videotaped debates, or learning materials for younger students

4. *Make use of novelty and familiarity.* Don't overuse a few teaching approaches or motivational strategies. We all need some variety. Varying the goal structures of tasks (cooperative, competitive, individualistic) can help, as can using different teaching media. When the material being covered in class is abstract or unfamiliar to students, try to connect it to something they know and understand. For example, talk about the size of a large area, such as the Acropolis in Athens, in terms of football fields. Brophy (1988) describes one teacher who read a brief passage from *Spartacus* to personalize the unit on slavery in the ancient world.

Instrumental Value. Sometimes it is difficult to encourage intrinsic motivation, and so teachers must rely on the utility or "instrumental" value of tasks. That is, it is important to learn many skills because they will be needed in more advanced classes or because they are necessary for life outside school.

1. When these connections are not obvious, educators should *explain the connections to their students.* Jeanette Abi-Nader (1991) describes one project, the PLAN program, that makes these connections come alive for Hispanic high school students. The three major strategies used in the program to focus students' attention on their future are (1) working with mentors and models—often PLAN graduates—who give advice about how to choose courses, budget time, take notes, and deal with cultural differences in college; (2) storytelling about the achievements of former students; sometimes the college term papers of former students are posted on PLAN bulletin boards; and (3) filling the classroom with future-oriented talk such as "When you go to college, you will encounter these situations" or, "You're at a parents' meeting—you want a good education for your children—and you are the ones who must speak up; that's why it is important to learn public speaking skills" (p. 548).

2. In some situations educators need to *provide incentives and rewards for learning.* Remember, though, that giving rewards when students are already interested in the activity may undermine intrinsic motivation. As Stipek (2002) has noted, if teachers began testing and grading students on their memory of the television programs they watched the previous evening, even television viewing would lose some of its intrinsic appeal.

3. *Use ill-structured problems and authentic tasks in teaching.* Connect problems in school to real problems outside: helping the homeless, improving traffic problems, protecting endangered species, creating safe playgrounds for children, or any current community concern.

What Do I Need to Do to Succeed?
Staying Focused on the Task

When students encounter difficulties, as they must if they are working at a challenging level, they need to keep their attention on the task. If the focus shifts to worries about performance, fear of failure, or concern with looking smart, then motivation to learn is lost. Here are some ideas principals can suggest to teachers for keeping the focus on learning.

1. *Give students frequent opportunities to respond* through questions and answers, short assignments, or demonstrations of skills. Make sure you check the students' answers so you can correct problems quickly. You don't want students to practice errors too long. Computer learning programs give students the immediate feedback they need to correct errors before they become habits.

2. When possible, *have students create a finished product.* They will be more persistent and focused on the task when the end is in sight. We all have experienced the power of the need for closure.

3. *Avoid heavy emphasis on grades and competition.* Competition will force students to be ego-involved rather than task-involved. Anxious students are especially hard hit by highly competitive evaluation.

4. *Reduce task risk without oversimplifying the task.* When tasks are risky (failure is likely and the consequences of failing are grave), student motivation suffers. For difficult, complex, or ambiguous tasks, provide students with plenty of time, support, resources, help, and the chance to revise or improve work.

5. *Model motivation to learn for students.* Teachers can talk about their interest in the subject and how they deal with difficult learning problems.

6. *Teach the particular learning tactics* that students will need to master the material being studied. Show students how to learn and remember so they won't be forced to fall back on self-defeating strategies or rote memory.

Diversity in Motivation to Learn

Because students differ in terms of language, culture, economic privilege, personality, knowledge, and experience, they will also differ in their needs, goals, interests, and beliefs. For example, self-efficacy is a central concept in motivation because it is a strong predictor of academic performance. But there are cultural differences as well. Males and African American students are more likely to be overconfident in their academic abilities, so their predictions of future achievement are less accurate than the predictions of Asian American students and female students who are much less likely to express overconfidence in their abilities. Gifted male students are less likely to be overconfident, and gifted female students are likely to underestimate their abilities, whereas special-education students tend to be overconfident in their sense of efficacy (Pajares, 2000).

Taking this diversity into account when designing tasks, supporting autonomy, recognizing accomplishments, grouping, making evaluations, and managing time can encourage motivation to learn. Take interest, for example. Embedding student writing tasks in cultural contexts is one way to catch and hold situational interest (Alderman, 2004; Bergin, 1999). When Hispanic immigrant students in junior high classes moved from writing using worksheets and standard assignments to writing about such topics as immigration, bilingualism, and gang life—factors that were important to them and to their families—their papers got longer and the writing quality was better (Rueda & Moll, 1994).

Language is a central factor in students' connections with the school. When bilingual students are encouraged to draw on both English and their heritage language, motivation and participation can increase. Robert Jimenez (2000) found in his study of bilingual Hispanic students that successful readers saw reading as a process of making sense; they used both of their languages to understand the material. For instance, they might look for Spanish word parts in English words to help them translate. Less-successful students had a different goal. They believed that reading just meant saying the words correctly in English. It is likely their interest and sense of efficacy for reading in English would be lower, too.

Encouraging students to capitalize on their cultural knowledge can increase motivation and meaning in school. But this doesn't happen often enough. "The lack of congruence between students' life experiences and instruction in most schools has been well documented, especially for low income students, students of color, and English language learners" (Committee on Increasing High School Students' Engagement and Motivation to Learn, 2004, p. 66).

Putting It All Together

We can see how these motivational elements come together in real classrooms. Sara Dolezal and her colleagues observed and interviewed third-grade teachers in eight Catholic schools and determined if their students were low, moderate, or high in their level of motivation (Dolezal, Welsh, Pressley, & Vincent, 2003). Table 5.5 on the next page summarizes the dramatic differences in these classrooms between strategies that support motivation and those that undermine it. Students in the low-engagement classes were restless and chatty as they faced their easy, undemanding seatwork. The classrooms were bare, unattractive, and filled with management problems. Instruction was disorganized. The class atmosphere was generally negative. The moderately engaged classrooms were organized to be "student friendly," with reading areas, group work area, posters, and student artwork. The teachers were warm and caring, and they connected lessons to students' background knowledge. Management routines were smooth and organized, and the class atmosphere was positive. The teachers were good at catching student attention and encouraging students to become more self-regulating, but they had trouble holding attention, probably because the tasks were too easy. Highly engaging teachers had all the positive qualities of student-friendly classrooms—positive atmosphere, smooth management routines, support for student self-regulation, and effective instruction—but they added more challenging tasks along with the support necessary to succeed at these tasks. These excellent motivators did not rely on one or two approaches to motivate their students; they applied a large repertoire of strategies from Table 5.5.

TABLE 5.5   Strategies That Support and Undermine Motivation in the Classroom

A Few Strategies That SUPPORT Motivation	
Strategy	**Example**
Messages of accountability and high expectations	The teacher asks students to have parents review and sign some assignments.
Teacher communicates importance of work	"We need to check it for at least 1 minute, which means looking over it carefully."
Clear goals/directions	The teacher explains exactly how the students are to separate into groups and complete their nominations for their favorite book.
Connections across the curriculum	The teacher relates the concept of ratios in math to compare/contrast skills in reading.
Opportunities to learn about and practice dramatic arts	After studying about historical figures, students write and produce their own plays.
Attributions to effort	During a word game, the teacher says to a student, "Did you study last night?" The student nods. "See how it helps?"
Encouraging risk-taking	"I need a new shining face. Someone I haven't called on yet. I need a risk-taker."
Uses games and play to reinforce concept or review material	During a math lesson using balance, students spend 5 minutes weighing the favorite toy they were asked to bring in that day.
Home–school connections	As part of a math/science unit, a recycling activity asks families to keep a chart of everything they recycle in a week.
Multiple representations of a task	The teacher uses 4 ways to teach multiplication: "magic multipliers," sing-along multiplication facts, whole-class flash card review, "Around-the-World" game.
Positive classroom management, praise, private reprimands	"Thumbs up when you are ready to work. Table 7 has thumbs up, table 7. I like the way table 7 is waiting patiently."
Stimulating creative thought	"We are going to use our imaginations today. We are going to take a trip to an imaginary theater in our heads."
Opportunities for choice	Students can choose to use prompts for their journal writing or pick their own topic.
Teacher communicates to students that they can handle challenging tasks	"This is hard stuff and you are doing great. I know adults who have trouble with this."
Value students—communicate caring	The teacher allows a new student to sit with a buddy for the day.

TABLE 5.5 (*Continued*)

A Few Strategies That UNDERMINE Motivation	
Strategy	**Example**
Attributions to intellect rather than effort	When students remark during a lesson, "I'm stupid" or "I'm a dork," the teacher says nothing, then replies, "Let's have someone who is smart."
Teacher emphasizes competition rather than working together	The teacher conducts a poetry contest where students read poems to class and the class members hold up cards with scores rating how well each student performed.
Few displays of student work	Public bulletin boards are used for posting grades.
No scaffolding for learning a new skill	The teacher is loud and critical when students have trouble: "Just look back in the glossary and don't miss it because you are too lazy to look it up."
Ineffective/negative feedback and the teacher moves on	"Does everyone understand?" A few students say yes.
Lack of connections	On Martin Luther King Day, the teacher leads a brief discussion of King, then the remainder of the activities are about Columbus.
Easy tasks	The teacher provides easy work and "fun" activities that teach little.
Negative class atmosphere	"Excuse me, I said page number. If you follow and listen, you would know."
Punitive classroom management	The teacher threatens bad grades if students do not look up words in the glossary.
Work that is much too difficult	The teacher assigns independent math work that only one or two students can do.
Slow pacing	The pace is set for the slowest students; others finish and have nothing to do.
Emphasis on finishing, not learning	The teacher communicates the purpose is to finish, not learn or use the vocabulary.
Sparse, unattractive classroom	There are no decorated bulletin boards, maps, charts, or displays of student work.
Poor planning	Missing handouts force the teacher to have large instead of smaller work groups.
Public punishment	All students stand, and the teacher reads a list of those who finished the assignment and they sit down. The teacher gives public lecture on responsibility to those left standing.

Source: Adapted from "How do nine third-grade teachers motivate their students?" by S. E. Dolezal, L. M. Welsh, M. Pressley, & M. Vincent. *Elementary School Journal*, 2003, 103, pp. 247–248.

Summary

Motivation is an internal state that arouses, directs, and maintains behavior. The study of motivation focuses on how and why people initiate actions directed toward specific goals, how intensively they are involved in the activity, how persistent they are in their attempts to reach these goals, and what they are thinking and feeling along the way. Explanations of motivation include both personal and environmental factors as well as intrinsic and extrinsic sources of motivation.

Intrinsic motivation is the natural tendency to seek out and conquer challenges as we pursue personal interests and exercise capabilities; it is motivation to do something when we don't have to. Extrinsic motivation is based on factors not related to the activity itself. We are not really interested in the activity for its own sake; we care only about what it will gain us. The essential difference between the intrinsic and extrinsic motivation is the person's reason for acting, that is, whether the locus of causality for the action (the location of the cause) is internal or external, inside or outside the person. If the locus is internal, the motivation is intrinsic, and if the locus is external, the motivation is extrinsic. Most motivation has elements of both.

Behaviorists tend to emphasize extrinsic motivation caused by incentives, rewards, and punishment. Humanistic views stress the intrinsic motivation created by the need for personal growth, fulfillment, and self-determination. Cognitive psychologists stress a person's active search for meaning, understanding, and competence, and the power of the individual's beliefs and interpretations. Social cognitive views are integrations of behavioral and cognitive approaches: They take into account both the behaviorists' concern with the consequences of behavior and the cognitivists' interest in the impact of individual beliefs and expectations. Sociocultural theories of motivation emphasize participation in communities of practice. People are motivated to learn the values and practices of the community to keep their identity as community members.

Teachers are interested in a particular kind of motivation—student motivation to learn. Student motivation to learn is both a trait and a state. It involves taking academic work seriously, trying to get the most from it, and applying appropriate learning strategies in the process. In order to encourage motivation to learn, instructional leaders can create environments that give students *goals* for learning, meet students' basic and higher-level *needs*, help students and teachers have *beliefs* that support learning, and arouse *interest* while avoiding *anxiety* in learning.

Many theories of motivation feature a prominent role for goals. *Goals* increase motivation if they are specific, moderately difficult, and able to be reached in the near future. Four kinds of goals influence classroom activities. A learning goal is the intention to gain knowledge and master skills. Students who set learning goals are not too concerned with setbacks because they are focused on the task. A performance goal is the intention get good grades or to appear smarter or more capable than others. Work-avoidant learners simply want to find the easiest way to handle the situation. Students with social goals can be supported or hindered in their learning, depending on the specific goal (i.e., have fun with friends or bring honor to the family). In order for goal setting to be effective in the classroom, students need accurate feedback about their progress toward goals, and they must accept the goals rather than reject them.

Needs are also an important component of many theories of motivation. Maslow has suggested that people are motivated by a hierarchy of needs, beginning with basic physiological requirements and moving up to the need for self-fulfillment. Lower-level needs must be met before higher-level needs can influence motivation. The need for achievement has been viewed as a personal characteristic nurtured by early experiences in the family and as a reaction to recent experiences with success or failure. The need to achieve is balanced by the need to avoid failure. Together, these are strong motivating forces. Several theorists emphasize the role of choice and self-determination in motivation and the need for positive relations with others. When students experience self-determination, they are intrinsically motivated: They are more interested in their work, have a greater sense of self-esteem, and learn more. In addition, teachers must acknowledge the students' perspective, offer choices, provide rationales for limits, and treat poor performance as a problem to be solved rather than a target for criticism.

The attribution theory of motivation suggests that the explanations people give for behavior, particularly their own successes and failures, have strong influences on future plans and performance. One of the important features of an attribution is whether it is internal and within a person's control or external and beyond control. Teachers may cue attributions by the way they respond to students' work. Surprisingly, praise, sympathy, and unsolicited help can communicate to students that they lack the ability to do the work. When people believe that ability is fixed, they tend to set performance goals and strive to protect themselves from failure. When they believe ability is improvable, however, they tend to set appropriate learning goals and handle failure constructively.

Bandura suggests that sense of self-efficacy, the belief that you will be effective in a given situation, is a powerful influence on motivation. If an individual has a strong sense of self-efficacy, he or she tends to set more challenging goals and to persist even when obstacles are encountered. Self-efficacy is distinct from other conceptions of self, in that it involves judgments of capabilities *specific to a particular task*. Self-concept is a more global construct that contains many perceptions about the self, including self-efficacy. Self-concept is developed as a result of external and internal comparisons, using others people or other aspects of the self as frames of reference. Compared to self-esteem, self-efficacy is concerned with judgments of personal capabilities; self-esteem is concerned with judgments of self-worth.

Attributions and beliefs about self come together in three possible student orientations. Mastery-oriented students tend to value achievement and see ability as improvable, so they focus on learning goals in order to increase their skills and abilities. They are not fearful of failure because failing does not threaten their sense of competence and self-worth. They attribute failure to controllable causes. This allows them to take risks and cope with failure constructively. A low sense of self-worth seems to be linked with the failure-avoiding and failure-accepting strategies intended to protect the individual from the consequences of failure. These strategies may seem to help in the short term, but are damaging to motivation and self-esteem in the long run.

Learning and information processing are influenced by emotion. Students are more likely to pay attention to, learn, and remember events, images, and readings that provoke emotional responses or that are related to their personal interests. However, there are cautions in responding to students' interests. "Seductive details"—interesting bits of information that are not central to the learning but distract from it—can hinder learning.

There appears to be an optimum level of arousal for most activities. Generally speaking, a higher level of arousal is helpful on simple tasks, but lower levels of arousal are better for complex tasks. When arousal is too low, teachers can stimulate curiosity by pointing out gaps in knowledge or use variety in activities. Severe anxiety is an example of arousal that is too high for optimal learning. Anxiety can be the cause or the result of poor performance; it can interfere with attention to, learning of, and retrieval of information. Many anxious students need help in developing effective test-taking and study skills.

What can teachers do to motivate students? Before any strategies to encourage motivation can be effective, four conditions must exist in the classroom. The classroom must be organized and free from constant disruption, the teacher must be a supportive person who never embarrasses students for making mistakes, the work must be neither too easy nor too difficult, and, finally, the tasks set for students must be authentic, not busywork.

Once these conditions are met, teachers can use strategies that help students feel confident in their abilities to improve (e.g., set challenging but reachable goals, stress self—not other—comparisons, communicate the belief that ability is improvable), strategies that highlight the value of the learning tasks (e.g., tie tasks to student interests, arouse curiosity, show connections to the future and to real-world problems, provide incentives), and strategies that help students stay involved in the learning process without being threatened by fear of failure (e.g., provide opportunities to create a finished product, teach learning tactics, model motivation to learn for students, avoid emphasizing grades, reduce risk without oversimplifying the task).

KEY TERMS

anxiety (175)
arousal (175)
attribution theories (161)
being needs (156)
deficiency needs (156)
ego-involved learners (154)
entity view of ability (164)
expectancy-value theories (150)
extrinsic motivation (148)
failure-accepting people (170)
failure-avoiding people (170)
goal (152)

goal orientations (153)
hierarchy of needs (156)
incentive (149)
incremental view of ability (164)
intrinsic motivation (148)
learned helplessness (162)
learning goal (153)
level of arousal (165)
locus of causality (148)
mastery experience (165)
mastery-oriented people (170)
motivation (147)

motivation to learn (152)
need (156)
performance goal (153)
reward (149)
self-actualization (156)
self-determination (158)
self-efficacy (165)
social goals (154)
social persuasion (166)
task-involved learners (153)
teaching efficacy (167)
vicarious experience (165)
work-avoidant learners (154)

DEVELOPING YOUR PORTFOLIO

1. As principal of your school, outline a one-day in-service program to help your teachers understand student motivation so they can apply it in the classroom.
   a. What motivational theories will be discussed? Why? How?
   b. What hands-on approaches to motivation will be demonstrated and discussed? Why? How?
   c. How will you and your teachers decide on a motivational program to be implemented in your school? Consider the pros and cons of various approaches, then develop a rationale for your choice(s).

2. Describe how you and your teachers will develop and design a comprehensive plan for working with parents and families to improve motivation and instruction in your school.
   a. Of what utility are the various motivation theories? Which theories seem most promising given the makeup of your student body?
   b. How can parents and teachers work cooperatively to set goals?
   c. Consider plans that have both intrinsic and extrinsic rewards.

3. Develop a 45-minute PowerPoint presentation to explain your three favorite motivation theories.
   a. What theories would you select? Why?
   b. What are the strengths and weaknesses of each theory?
   c. What are the practical applications of each perspective? Give some hands-on examples of each.
   d. Develop a series of questions for your teachers to discuss about student motivation. What end products do you expect from your teachers?

INSTRUCTIONAL LEADER'S TOOLBOX

Readings

Butterworth, B., & Weinstein, R. S. (1997). Enhancing motivational opportunity in elementary schooling: A case study of the ecology of principal leadership. *The Elementary School Journal, 97,* 57–80.

Childress, H. (1998). Seventeen reasons why football is better than high school. *Phi Delta Kappan, 79,* 616–619.

Committee on Increasing High School Students' Engagement and Motivation to Learn. (2004). *Engaging schools: Fostering high school students' motivation to learn.* Washington, DC, The National Academies Press.

Johnson, D., & Johnson, R. (1999). *Learning together and alone: Cooperation, competition, and individualization* (5th ed.). Boston: Allyn & Bacon.

Maehr, M. L., & Anderman, E. M. (1993). Reinventing schools for early adolescents: Emphasizing task goals. *The Elementary School Journal, 93,* 593–610.

Raffini, J. P. (1996). *150 ways to increase intrinsic motivation in the classroom.* Boston: Allyn & Bacon.

Stipek, D. (2002). *Motivation to learn* (4th ed.). Boston: Allyn & Bacon.

Paul Chance and Alfie Kohn exchanged opinions in several issues of *Phi Delta Kappan:*

Kohn, A. (1991, March). Caring kids: The role of the schools. *Phi Delta Kappan.*

Chance, P. (1991, June). Backtalk: A gross injustice. *Phi Delta Kappan.*

Chance, P. (1992, November). The rewards of learning. *Phi Delta Kappan.*

Kohn, A. (1993, June). Rewards versus learning: A response to Paul Chance. *Phi Delta Kappan.*

Chance, P. (1993, June). Sticking up for rewards. *Phi Delta Kappan.*

Videos

What I learned from not learning, 12 minutes. An insightful examination of what really goes on in a classroom. Teachers present accurate information in unintelligible ways to uninterested students or irrelevant answers to appropriate questions. Teachers may be so intent on what they are teaching that they are unable to distinguish between students who already know what they are being taught and those who are only pretending to understand. To purchase: #CC-1915. Order from Films for the Humanities & Sciences, Inc., P.O. Box 2053, Princeton, NJ 08543, or 800-257-5126.

Head of the class, 14 minutes. This story aroused tremendous interest when it was broadcast on *60 Minutes*. It reveals the high pressure of the Japanese educational system, where the goal is to gain admission to the university. American educators must decide which elements of the Japanese educational system they should draw upon to improve their own. Order from Films for the Humanities & Sciences, Inc., P.O. Box 2053, Princeton, NJ 08543, or 800-257-5126.

Websites

www.ericdigests.org/1999–2/theory.htm
    Creating Learning Centered Classrooms—What Does Learning Theory Have to Say? (talks about self-efficacy)
www.eric.ed.gov/ERICDocs/data/ericdocs2sql/content_storage_01/0000019b/80/15/a3/8b.pdf
    Herzberg's Theory of Motivation and Maslow's Hierarchy of Needs
www.jostens.com/edserv/renaissance/default.asp
    Josten's Renaissance School Academic Achievement and Recognition Program

www.ericdigests.org/1997–1/low.html
    Motivating Low Performing Adolescent Readers
www.ericdigests.org/1999–1/motivation.html
    Motivation and Middle School Students
www.bookitprogram.com/
    Reading Incentive Program from Pizza Hut to encourage K–6 students to read
www.ericdigests.org/1995–1/learn.htm
    Student Motivation to Learn

The following websites have interesting content that can be used for a variety of purposes related to motivation and instruction.
www.historyhouse.com
    History: The History House
www.particleadventure.org
    Science: The Particle Adventure
http://whyfiles.org/
    Science: The Why Files

Organizations

http://www.iasce.net/
    International Association for the Study of Cooperation in Education
www.successforall.net
    Success for All Foundation

CHAPTER

6 Teaching

PREVIEW: KEY POINTS

1. Teachers make a difference, but good teaching is only one of the key elements of successful student learning.

2. Successful student learning requires a mix of engagement, support, and opportunity, as well as good teaching.

3. Expert teachers work from integrated sets of principles instead of dealing with each new event as a new problem.

191

4. Shulman's seven areas of professional knowledge include academic subjects, teaching strategies, curriculum materials, student characteristics, learning settings, teaching goals, and pedagogical content knowledge.

5. There is no one model for effective planning, but having clear objectives is important.

6. Using taxonomies of objectives improves planning; a new taxonomy in the cognitive domain has just been developed. Constructivist planning often involves themes and integrated units.

7. Characteristics of effective teaching include knowledge, organization, clarity, warmth, and enthusiasm.

8. A balanced approach to reading, including both phonics and whole language, is effective.

9. Children growing up in poverty lag behind their affluent peers in reading and the gap widens each year in large part because children in poverty lose ground each summer.

10. Constructivist theories have inspired new ways of teaching mathematics and science.

11. There is no one best way to teach; different goals and students require different approaches.

Leadership Challenge

Your school district has adopted a whole-language, integrated curriculum approach for grades K–6. Quite a bit of time and money was spent on workshops for teachers; buying big books and multiple copies of good children's literature; developing manipulatives for mathematics; building comfortable reading corners; making costumes, puppets, and other reading props; designing science projects; and generally supporting the innovations. Students and teachers are mostly pleased with the program. There seems to be more reading and more enjoyment of reading, at least for many children, but some students seem lost. The students' written work is longer and more creative. However, standardized tests indicate a drop in scores. As principal you are getting worried; after all, it was your big project and you had worked hard to sell it to members of the PTA and school board. But now some parents of students in your school are complaining that they have had to hire tutors or buy commercial programs to teach their children to read.

1. What would you do about the parents' complaints?
2. What would you advise your teachers to do about such complaints?
3. Are changes necessary? How can you find out?
4. What information do you need to make good decisions?
5. Who should be involved in these decisions?
6. What is your stance on phonics versus whole language? Can you support your position?

Do Teachers Make a Difference?

Before we examine theory and practice about teaching, let's consider a basic question: Do teachers make a difference? We ask the question because, for a while, some researchers reported findings suggesting that wealth and social status, not teaching, were the major factors determining who learned in schools (e.g., Coleman, 1966). In fact, much of the early research on teaching was conducted by educational psychologists who refused to accept these claims that teachers were powerless in the face of poverty and societal problems (Wittrock, 1986).

Gary Fenstermacher and Virginia Richardson (2005) state that successful student learning requires four elements: student engagement, social support, opportunities to learn and teach, and good teaching. They note that

> good teaching is but one of four ingredients in this mix. The others are that the learner desires to learn and expends the necessary effort to do so; that the social surround of family, community, and peer culture support and assist in learning; and that there are sufficient facilities, time and resources (opportunities) to accomplish the learning that is sought. The point of introducing this list is to clarify that learning, if it is to be both good and successful, calls on a cluster of conditions, only one of which pertains to the nature of the teaching received by the learner. (p. 190)

We include this reminder because sometimes it seems that answers to the question, "Do teachers make a difference?" often fall at the extremes—no difference or all the difference. Both answers are wrong. Learning rests on at least the four foundations described above. In this chapter we look at good teaching, an element that instructional leaders can influence and improve. Our examination of the importance of teaching will cover social, affective, and cognitive dimensions. First, we look at the social and relationship side of teaching.

Teacher–Student Relationships

Bridgett Hamre and Robert Pianta (2001) followed all the children in a small school district who entered kindergarten one year and continued in the school district through the eighth grade. The researchers concluded that the quality of the teacher–student relationship in kindergarten (defined in terms of level of conflict with the child, the child's dependency on the teacher, and the teacher's affection for the child) predicted a number of academic and behavioral outcomes through the eighth grade, particularly for students with high levels of behavior problems. Even when the gender, ethnicity, cognitive ability, and behavior ratings of the student were accounted for, the relationship with the teacher still predicted aspects of school success. The researchers concluded that "the association between the quality of early teacher–child relationships and later school performance can be both strong and persistent" (p. 636). Based on the results of this carefully conducted study, it appears that students with significant behavior problems in the early years are less likely to have problems later in school if their teachers are sensitive to their needs and provide frequent, consistent feedback.

Teacher Preparation and Qualifications

Using data from a fifty-state survey of policies, state case study analyses, the 1993–94 Schools and Staffing Surveys, and the National Assessment of Educational Progress (NAEP), Linda Darling-Hammond (2000) examined the ways in which teacher qualifications are related to student achievement across states. Her findings indicated that the quality of teachers—as measured by whether the teachers were fully certified and had a major in their teaching field—was related to student performance. In fact, measures of teacher preparation and certification were by far the strongest predictors of student achievement in reading and mathematics, both before and after controlling for student poverty and English-language proficiency. Teacher subject matter knowledge and verbal ability are important in student learning, but teacher preparation and qualifications make a difference too (Darling-Hammond & Youngs, 2002).

Finally, Sanders and Rivers (1996) studied how students are affected by having several effective or ineffective teachers in a row. They looked at fifth graders in two large metropolitan school systems in Tennessee. Students who had highly effective teachers for third, fourth, and fifth grades scored an average of 83rd percentile on a standardized mathematics achievement test in one district and 96th percentile in the other (99th percentile is the highest possible score). In contrast, students who had the least effective teachers three years in a row averaged 29th percentile in math achievement in one district and 44th percentile in the other, a difference of over 50 percentile points in both cases! Students with average teachers or with a mixture of low, average, and high effectiveness teachers for the three years had math scores between these extremes. Sanders and Rivers concluded that the best teachers encouraged good to excellent gains in achievement for all students, but lower-achieving students were the first to benefit from good teaching. The effects of teaching were cumulative and residual; that is, better teaching in a later grade could make up *in part* for less effective teaching in earlier grades, but could not erase all the deficits. In fact, one study found that at least 7% of the differences in test score gains for students could be traced to their teachers (Rivkin, Hanushek, & Kain, 2001).

What Is a Good Teacher?

There are hundreds of answers to this question, including ideas based on your own experience. This question has been examined by educators, psychologists, philosophers, novelists, journalists, mathematicians, scientists, historians, policymakers, and parents, to name only a few groups.

Inside Five Classrooms

To begin our examination of good teachers, let's step inside the classrooms of several outstanding teachers. All the situations that follow are real. The first two are elementary teachers described by Weinstein and Mignano (2007). The next three are secondary school teachers who have been studied by other researchers.

A Bilingual First Grade.   There are 25 students in Viviana's class. Most have recently emigrated from the Dominican Republic; the rest come from Nicaragua, Mexico, Puerto Rico, and Honduras. Even though the children speak little or no English when they begin school, by the time they leave in June, Viviana has helped them master the normal first-grade curriculum for their district. She accomplishes this by teaching in Spanish early in the year to aid understanding, then gradually introducing English as the students are ready. Viviana does not want her students segregated or labeled as disadvantaged. She encourages them to take pride in their Spanish-speaking heritage while using every available opportunity to support their developing English proficiency.

Viviana's expectations for her students are high, and she makes sure the students have the resources they need. She provides materials—pencils, scissors, colors—so no child lacks the means to learn. And she supplies constant encouragement. "Viviana's commitment to her students is evident in her first-grade bilingual classroom. With an energy level that is rare, she motivates, prods, instructs, models, praises, and captivates her students. . . . The pace is brisk and Viviana clearly has a flair for the dramatic; she uses music, props, gestures, facial expressions, and shifts in voice tone to communicate the material" (Weinstein & Mignano, 2007, p. 21). Viviana's expectations for herself are high as well. She continually expands her knowledge of teaching through graduate work and participation in special training programs. To know more about her students each year, she spends hours in their homes. For Viviana, teaching is a not just a job; it is a way of life.

A Suburban Middle School.   Ken teaches fifth/sixth grade in a suburban middle school in central New Jersey. Ken emphasizes "process writing." His students complete first drafts, discuss them with others in the class, revise, edit, and "publish" their work. The students also keep daily journals and often use these to share personal concerns with Ken. They tell him of problems at home, fights, and fears; he always takes the time to respond in writing. The study of science is also placed in the context of the real world. They learn about ocean ecosystems by using a software program called *A Field Trip to the Sea* (Sunburst, 1999). For social studies, the class plays two simulation games that focus on history. One is on coming of age in Native American cultures and the other is on the colonization of America.

Throughout the year Ken is very interested in the social and emotional development of his students. He wants them to learn about responsibility and fairness as well as science and social studies. This concern is evident in the way he develops his class rules at the beginning of the year. Rather than specifying dos and don'ts, Ken and his students devise a "Bill of Rights" for the class, describing the rights of the students. These rights cover most of the situations that might need a "rule." On occasion, when classes are a real challenge, he has established some "laws."

An Inner City Middle School.   Another excellent teacher is described in the *Harvard Education Letter*:

> Robert Moses, founder of the Algebra Project at the Martin Luther King School in Cambridge, Massachusetts, teaches students the concept of number and sign through a physical event: they go for a ride on a subway. Choosing one subway stop as a starting point, students relate inbound and outbound to positive and negative numbers. They translate their subway ride into mathematical language by considering both the number of stops and their direction.
>
> By giving students such experiences before introducing the formal language of algebra, Moses . . . has made math more enjoyable and accessible. (Ruopp & Driscoll, 1990, p. 5)

An Inclusive Class.   Elliot was bright and articulate. He easily memorized stories as a child, but he could not read by himself. His problems stemmed from severe learning difficulties with auditory and visual integration and long-term visual memory. When he tried to write, everything got jumbled. Dr. Nancy White worked with Elliot's teacher, Mia Russell to tailor intensive tutoring that specifically focused on Elliot's individual patterns and his errors. With his teachers' help over the next years, Elliot became an expert on his own learning and an independent learner; he knew which strategies he had to use and when to use them. According to Elliot, "Learning that stuff is not fun, but it works!" (Hallahan & Kauffman, 2006, pp. 184–185).

An Advanced Math Class.   Hilda Borko and Carol Livingston (1989) describe Randy, an expert secondary school mathematics teacher. Randy's students were having trouble understanding integrals. Randy worked with his students' confusion to construct a review lesson about strategies for doing integrals. When one student said that a particular section in the book seemed "haphazard," Randy led the class through a process of organizing the material. He asked the class for general statements about useful strategies for doing integrals. He clarified their suggestions, elaborated on some, and helped students improve others. He asked the students to tie their ideas to passages in the text. Even though he accepted all reasonable suggestions, he listed only the key strategies on the board. By the end of the period, the students had transformed the disorganized material from the book into an ordered and useful outline to guide their learning. They also had a better idea about how to read and understand difficult material.

What do you see in these classrooms? The teachers are committed to their students. They must deal with a wide range of student abilities and challenges: different languages, different home lives, different needs. These teachers must understand their subjects and their students' thinking so well that they can spontaneously create new examples and explanations when students are confused. They must make the most abstract concepts, such as negative numbers, real and understandable for their particular students. And then there is the challenge of new technologies and techniques. The teachers must use them appropriately to accomplish important goals and not just to entertain the students. The whole time that these experts are navigating through the academic material, they also are taking care of the emotional needs of their students, propping up sagging self-esteem and encouraging responsibility. If we followed these individuals from the first day of class, we would see that they carefully plan and teach the basic procedures for living and learning in their classes. They can efficiently collect and correct homework, regroup students, give directions, distribute materials, collect lunch money, and deal with disruptions, while also making a mental note to check why one of their students is so tired.

Viviana, Ken, Mia, Robert, and Randy are examples of expert teachers, the focus of much recent research in education and psychology. For another perspective on the question "What is a good teacher?" let's examine this research on expertise in teaching.

Expert Teachers

What do expert teachers know that allows them to be so successful? How do they differ from beginners? Researchers are investigating how expert teachers think about their students, the subjects they teach, and the process of teaching itself.

Experts focus more than beginners on analyzing a problem and mentally applying different principles to develop a solution. In one study of solutions to discipline problems, the expert teachers spent quite a bit of time framing each problem, forming questions, deciding what information was necessary, and considering alternatives. Novices jumped to the first solution that came to mind (Swanson, O'Conner, & Cooney, 1990). Expert teachers have a sense of what is typical in classrooms, of what to expect during certain activities or times of the day. They also have a good sense of what students in their grade and school are like: their background, needs, concerns, abilities, and problems. Many of their teaching routines have become automatic; they don't even have to think about how to distribute materials, take roll, move students in and out of groups, or assign grades. This gives the teachers more mental and physical energy for being creative and focusing on their students' progress. In addition, expert teachers have clear goals and take individual differences into account when planning for their students. These teachers are **reflective** practitioners (Floden & Klinzing, 1990; Hogan, Rabinowitz, & Craven, 2003).

We saw with Randy that expert teachers can turn students' confusion into understanding by helping the students organize and expand on what they know. Expert teachers are not bound by their plans, but can follow the needs of the students. They begin teaching by assessing what their students know and need to know. Their starting point is not where the book starts or where the last teacher left off, but instead where the students are. Expert teachers read student cues as information for instruction whereas novices read student cues in terms of classroom management issues. Experts are less likely to take student misbehavior personally and are confident that they can handle most classroom interactions. Many experts continue their education, adding to their knowledge (Sabers, Cushing, & Berliner, 1991; Tochon & Munby, 1993). Finally, expert teachers know themselves—their biases, strengths, and blind spots as well as their own cultural identity. Only by having a clear sense of themselves can teachers understand and respect the cultural identity of their students. Jay Dee and Allan Henkin (2002) note that teachers must be willing to explore beyond their own zone of comfort as members of the majority cultural status quo.

So it seems that expert teachers, like expert dancers or gymnasts, have mastered a number of moves or routines that they can perform easily, almost without thinking. But they also know a great deal about their subjects, so they can create new moves, improvise, and avoid trouble. And they are analytical; they can take a situation apart, diagnose the source of the problem, consider alternatives, and make decisions about what will work.

Concerns of Teachers

A review of studies conducted around the world found that beginning teachers regard maintaining classroom discipline, motivating students, accommodating differences among students, evaluating student work, and dealing with parents as the most serious challenges they face (Conway & Clark, 2003). Many teachers also experience what has been called "reality shock" when they take their first job and confront the "harsh and rude reality of everyday classroom life" (Veenman, 1984, p. 143). One source of shock may be that teachers really cannot ease into their responsibilities. On the first day of their first job, beginning teachers face the same tasks as teachers with years of experience. When schools give beginning teachers a lighter load and limit outside class assignments, new teachers say that they do a better job of learning to teach. But schools seldom allow these arrangements. In addition, a full school day usually offers little chance for helpful contact between novice and experienced teachers, making mutual support and assistance difficult (Calderhead & Robson, 1991; Cooke & Pang, 1991; Duke, 1993).

With experience, however, most teachers meet the challenges that seem difficult for beginners. They have more time to experiment with new methods or materials. Finally, as confidence grows, seasoned teachers can focus on the students' needs. "The difference between a beginning teacher and an experienced one is that the beginning teacher asks, 'How am I doing?' and the experienced teacher asks, 'How are the children doing?'" (Codell, 2001, p. 191). Are my students learning? Are they developing positive attitudes? Is this the best way to teach the slower learners to write a persuasive essay? At this advanced stage, teachers judge their success by the successes of their students (Pigge & Marso, 1997). So advanced teachers need a different kind of support that gives them the tools to teach and assess students.

For the remainder of the chapter, we will look at the research on good teaching, beginning with planning.

The First Step: Planning

In the past few years, educational researchers interviewed teachers about how they plan, asked teachers to "think out loud" while planning or to keep journals describing their plans, and even studied teachers intensively for months at a time. What have they found?

First, planning influences what students will learn because planning transforms the available time and curriculum materials into activities, assignments, and tasks for students. When a teacher decides to devote 7 hours to language arts and 15 minutes to science in a given week, the students in that class will learn more language than science. In fact, differences as dramatic as this do occur. In one school the time allocated to mathematics ranged from 3 hours a week in one class to 6 hours a week in a class down the hall (Clark & Peterson, 1986; Clark & Yinger, 1988; Karweit, 1989).

Second, teachers engage in several levels of planning—by the year, term, unit, week, and day. All the levels must be coordinated. Planning done at the beginning of the year is particularly important, because many routines and patterns are established early. For experienced teachers, unit planning seemed to be the most important level, followed by weekly and then daily planning. For beginning teachers, the focus is more likely to be on isolated day-to-day lesson planning; often these inexperienced teachers have difficulty integrating discrete lessons into more comprehensive units (Koeppen, 1998; McCutcheon & Milner, 2002; Morine-Dershimer, 2006).

Third, plans reduce—but do not eliminate—uncertainty in teaching. Even the best plans cannot (and should not) control everything that happens in class; planning must allow flexibility (Calderhead, 1996). There is some evidence that when teachers "overplan"—fill every minute and stick to the plan no matter what—their students do not learn as much as students whose teachers are flexible (Shavelson, 1987). Beginning teachers may need to be reminded that they should not proceed with a scheduled new unit if their in-class review shows that many students still don't understand the material in the current unit.

In order to plan creatively and flexibly, teachers need to have wide-ranging knowledge about students, their interests, and abilities; the subjects being taught; alternative ways to teach and assess understanding; working with groups; the expectations and limitations of the school and community; how to apply and adapt materials and texts; and how to pull all this knowledge together into meaningful activities. The plans of beginning teachers sometimes don't work because they lack knowledge about the students or the subject: They can't estimate how long it will take students to complete an activity, for example, or they stumble when asked for an explanation or a different example (Calderhead, 1996).

In planning, collaboration can be helpful. Some educators think that a collaborative approach to planning used in Japan called *kenshu* or "mastery through study" is one reason why Japanese students do so well on international tests. A basic part of the process involves a small group of teachers developing a lesson, then videotaping one of the group members teaching the lesson. Next, all members review the tape, analyze student responses, and improve the lesson further. Other teachers try the revised lesson and more improvements follow. At the end of the school year, all the study groups may publish the results of their work. In the United States, this process is called **lesson study** (Morine-Dershimer, 2006). To learn about this approach, search the Internet using the keywords "lesson study."

But even great lesson plans taken from a terrific website on science have to be adapted to your situation. Some of the adaptation comes before teaching and some comes after. In fact, much of what experienced teachers know about planning comes from looking back—reflecting—on what worked and what didn't, so encourage your teachers to look back on their plans. Collaborative reflection and revising lessons are major components of the *lesson study* approach to planning.

Finally, there is no one model for effective planning. For experienced teachers, planning is a creative problem-solving process (Shavelson, 1987). Experienced teachers know how to accomplish many lessons and segments of lessons. They know what to expect and how to proceed, so they don't necessarily continue to follow the detailed lesson-planning models they learned during their teacher-preparation programs. Planning is more informal, "in their heads." But many experienced teachers think it was helpful to learn this detailed system as a foundation (Clark & Peterson, 1986).

The Principal's Perspective tells how a real principal helped a new teacher plan and teach more effectively by providing the resources she needed and giving some personal attention.

A Principal's Perspective

P. M. didn't need formal evaluations of one young teacher to realize she was in trouble. Periodic walks past her classroom early in the school year revealed a frustrated teacher floundering before uncharacteristically disinterested senior honor students. The situation deteriorated so quickly that students began seeking the principal out to complain. Oh, he had heard students complain about teachers before but never complaints that the teacher wasn't *rigorous* enough. Parents echoed their children's concerns that they were not receiving proper preparation for postsecondary pursuits. P. M. was an outstanding classroom teacher, but he understood it was not his role to model effective instruction for this teacher. After all, as is the case with most high school principals, he lacked the depth of content knowledge necessary to effectively teach such a specialized subject. However, he did understand it was his responsibility as an instructional leader to help her in any way possible.

Acting quickly, P. M. arranged nonthreatening, weekly meetings with the teacher during which they reviewed her lesson plans for the upcoming week, reflected on her classes from the previous week, discussed her assessment and evaluation strategies, and generally identified potential problems. Even though the teacher had been assigned a mentor at the school to assist her with the daily duties of teaching, P. M. also hired an external mentor, a content specialist, who could share specific strategies regarding the courses she was assigned to teach. This broad personal support combined with a personalized professional development plan of workshops and readings resulted in dramatic improvements in the teacher's knowledge, confidence, and sense of efficacy.

Glickman, C. D. (2002). *Leadership for learning: How to help teachers succeed.* Alexandria, VA: Association for Supervision and Curriculum Development.

No matter how your teachers plan, they must have a learning goal in mind. In the next section we consider the range of goals for your students.

Objectives for Learning

We hear quite a bit today about visions, goals, outcomes, and standards. At a very general, abstract level are the grand goals society may have for graduates of public schools such as, "We remain committed to ensuring that all students can read and do math at grade level or better by 2014" (Spelling, 2007, p. 6). But very general goals are meaningless as potential guidelines for instruction. States may turn these grand goals into standards, such as the Colorado standard that students will "[u]se comprehension skills such as previewing, predicting, inferring, comparing and contrasting, rereading and self-monitoring, summarizing, etc." At this level, the indicators are close to being instructional objectives (Airasian, 2005).

An **instructional objective** is a clear and unambiguous description of educational intentions for students. These specific statements describe what the students should know and be able to do at the end of the lesson or unit. Although there are many different approaches to writing objectives, each assumes that the first step in teaching is to decide what changes should take place in the learner: What are the goals of teaching?

Objectives written by people with behavioral views focus on observable and measurable changes in the learner. **Behavioral objectives** use terms such as *list, define, add,*

TABLE 6.1   Gronlund's Combined Method for Creating Objectives

General Objective

Presents and defends the research project before a group.

Specific Examples

1. Describes the project in a well-organized manner.
2. Summarizes the findings and their implications.
3. Uses display materials to clarify ideas and relationships.
4. Answers group members' questions directly and completely.
5. Presents a report that reflects careful planning.
6. Displays sound reasoning ability through presentation and answers to questions.

Source: Adapted from Norman E. Gronlund, *How to Write and Use Instructional Objectives*, 6/e, © 2000. Reproduced by permission of Pearson Education, Inc., Upper Saddle River, NJ.

or *calculate*. **Cognitive objectives,** on the other hand, emphasize thinking and comprehension, so they are more likely to include words such as *understand, recognize, create,* or *apply*. Let's look at one well-developed method of writing instructional objectives that combines specific (behavioral) and general (cognitive) ideas.

Gronlund: A Combined Approach.   Norman Gronlund (2006) believes that an objective should be stated first in general terms (*understand, solve, appreciate,* and so on). Then the teacher should clarify by listing a few sample behaviors that would provide evidence that the student has attained the objective. Look at the example in Table 6.1. The goal here really is presenting and defending a research project. The teacher does not want the student to stop with describing, summarizing, answering questions, and so on. Instead, the teacher looks at performance on these sample tasks to decide if the student can effectively present and defend. The teacher could just as well have chosen six different indicators. A teacher could never list all the behaviors that might be involved in "presenting and defending," but stating an initial, general objective along with possible evidence makes the purpose clear.

The most recent research on instructional objectives tends to favor approaches similar to Gronlund's. In addition, Terry TenBrink (2006, p. 57) suggests these criteria. Objectives should be:

1. Student-oriented (emphasis on what the student is expected to do).
2. Descriptive of an appropriate learning *outcome* (both developmentally appropriate and appropriately sequenced, with more complex objectives following prerequisite objectives).
3. Clear and understandable (not too general or too specific).
4. Observable (avoid outcomes you can't see such as "appreciating" or "realizing").

In thinking about objectives, both teachers and students must consider what is important, what is worth learning. Teachers who have clear, appropriate goals for every student often are successful in helping the students learn. The Theory into Action

THEORY INTO ACTION GUIDELINES

Developing Objectives

Avoid "word magic"—phrases that sound noble and important but say very little, such as "Students will become deep thinkers."

Examples
1. Keep the focus on specific changes that will take place in the students' knowledge of skills.
2. Ask students to explain the meaning of the objectives. If they can't give specific examples of what you mean, the objectives are not communicating your intentions to your students.

Suit the activities to the objectives.

Examples
1. If the goal is the memorization of vocabulary, give the students memory aids and practice exercises.

2. If the goal is the ability to develop well-thought-out positions, consider position papers, debates, projects, or mock trials.
3. If you want students to become better writers, give many opportunities for writing and rewriting.

Make sure your tests are related to your objectives.

Examples
1. Write objectives and rough drafts for tests at the same time; revise these drafts of tests as the units unfold and objectives change.
2. Weight the tests according to the importance of the various objectives and the time spent on each.

Guidelines should help your teachers whether they decide to make thorough use of objectives or just to prepare them for certain assignments.

Flexible and Creative Plans: Using Taxonomies

Several decades ago, a group of experts in educational evaluation led by Benjamin Bloom set out to improve college and university examinations. The impact of their work has touched education at all levels around the world (Anderson & Sosniak, 1994). Bloom and his colleagues developed a **taxonomy,** or classification system, of educational objectives. Objectives were divided into three domains: *cognitive, affective,* and *psychomotor.* A handbook describing the objectives in each area was eventually published. In real life, of course, behaviors from these three domains occur simultaneously. While students are writing (psychomotor), they are also remembering or reasoning (cognitive), and they are likely to have some emotional response to the task as well (affective).

The Cognitive Domain. The most well-known and widely used taxonomy is in the **cognitive domain**. Six basic objectives are listed in this thinking or cognitive domain (Bloom, Engelhart, Frost, Hill, & Krathwohl, 1956):

1. *Knowledge:* Remembering or recognizing something without necessarily understanding, using, or changing it.
2. *Comprehension:* Understanding the material being communicated without necessarily relating it to anything else.
3. *Application:* Using a general concept to solve a particular problem.
4. *Analysis:* Breaking something down into its parts.

5. *Synthesis:* Creating something new by combining different ideas.
6. *Evaluation:* Judging the value of materials or methods as they might be applied in a particular situation.

Updating Bloom. Bloom's taxonomy guided educators for over 40 years. It is considered one of the most significant educational writings of the twentieth century (Anderson & Sosniak, 1994). In 1995, a group of educational researchers met to discuss revising the taxonomy (Anderson & Krathwohl, 2001), and that revision is now available. The taxonomy revisers have retained the six basic levels, but they have changed the names of three to indicate the cognitive processes involved and altered the order slightly. The six cognitive processes of the revised taxonomy are *remembering* (knowledge), *understanding* (comprehension), *applying, analyzing, evaluating,* and *creating* (synthesizing). In addition, the revisers have added a new dimension to the taxonomy to recognize that cognitive processes must process something: You have to remember or understand or apply some form of knowledge. If you look at Table 6.2, you will see the result. We now have six processes or verbs: the cognitive acts of remembering, understanding, applying, analyzing, evaluating, and creating. These processes act on four kinds of knowledge: factual, conceptual, procedural, and metacognitive.

Consider how this revised taxonomy might suggest objectives for a social studies/language arts class. An objective that targets *analysis of conceptual knowledge* is:

> After reading historical account of the battle of the Alamo, the student will be able to recognize the author's point of view or bias.

An objective for *evaluating metacognitive knowledge* might be:

> Students will explain their strategies for identifying the biases of the author.

TABLE 6.2   A Revised Taxonomy in the Cognitive Domain

The Knowledge Dimension	The Cognitive Process Dimension					
	1. Remember	**2. Understand**	**3. Apply**	**4. Analyze**	**5. Evaluate**	**6. Create**
A. Factual Knowledge						
B. Conceptual Knowledge						
C. Procedural Knowledge						
D. Metacognitive Knowledge						

Source: From *A Taxonomy For Learning, Teaching, And Assessing: A Revision of Bloom's Taxonomy of Educational Objectives* by Lorin W. Anderson & David R. Krathwohl. Published by Allyn & Bacon, Boston, MA. Copyright © 2001 by Pearson Education. Reprinted by permission of the publisher.

Certain processes are more likely to be paired with certain kinds of knowledge. For example, remembering is most often used with factual and conceptual knowledge and metacognitive knowledge is more likely to be applied and analyzed than remembered. In two books, a complete and an abridged version, Anderson and Krathwohl (2001) describe the new taxonomy and give many examples of using this revised version to design lessons and assessments.

Applying the Taxonomy.   It is common in education to consider these six kinds of objectives as a hierarchy, each skill building on the previous ones, but this is not entirely accurate. Some subjects, such as mathematics, do not fit this structure very well (Kreitzer & Madaus, 1994). Still, you will hear many references to *lower-level* and *higher-level objectives*, with remembering, understanding, and applying considered lower level and the other categories considered higher level. As a rough way of thinking about objectives, this can be helpful (Gronlund, 2004, 2006).

The taxonomy of objectives can also be helpful in planning assessments because different procedures are appropriate for objectives at the various levels. Gronlund (2000) suggests that remembering factual knowledge objectives can best be measured by true-false, short-answer, matching, or multiple-choice tests. Such tests will also work with the understanding, applying, and analyzing levels of the taxonomy. For measuring evaluating and creating objectives, however, essays, reports, projects, and portfolios are more appropriate. Essay tests will also work at the middle levels of the taxonomy.

The Affective Domain.   The objectives in the taxonomy of the **affective domain,** or domain of emotional response, run from least committed to most committed (Krathwohl, Bloom, & Masia, 1964). At the lowest level, a student would simply pay attention to a certain idea. At the highest level, the student would adopt an idea or a value and act consistently with that idea. There are five basic objectives in the affective domain.

1. *Receiving:* Being aware of or attending to something in the environment. This is the I'll-listen-to-the-concert-but-I-won't-promise-to-like-it level.
2. *Responding:* Showing some new behavior as a result of experience. At this level a person might applaud after the concert or hum some of the music the next day.
3. *Valuing:* Showing some definite involvement or commitment. At this point a person might choose to go to a concert instead of a film.
4. *Organization:* Integrating a new value into one's general set of values, giving it some ranking among one's general priorities. This is the level at which a person would begin to make long-range commitments to concert attendance.
5. *Characterization by value:* Acting consistently with the new value. At this highest level, a person would be firmly committed to a love of music and demonstrate it openly and consistently.

Like the basic objectives in the cognitive domain, these five objectives are very general. To write specific learning objectives, you must state what students will actually be doing when they are receiving, responding, valuing, and so on. For example, an objective for a nutrition class at the valuing level (showing involvement or commitment) might be stated:

> After completing the unit on food contents and labeling, at least 50 percent of the class will commit to the junk-food boycott project by giving up snack foods for a month.

The Psychomotor Domain. James Cangelosi (1990) provides a useful way to think about objectives in the psychomotor domain as either voluntary muscle capabilities that require endurance, strength, flexibility, agility, or speed; or the ability to perform a specific skill. Objectives in the **psychomotor domain** should be of interest to a wide range of educators, including those in fine arts, vocational-technical education, and special education. Many other subjects, such as chemistry, physics, and biology, also require specialized movements and well-developed hand and eye coordination. Using lab equipment, the mouse on a computer, or art materials means learning new physical skills. Here are two psychomotor objectives:

> Four minutes after completing a one-mile run in eight minutes or under, your heart rate will be below 120.
>
> Use a computer mouse effectively to "drag and drop" files.

Another View: Planning from a Constructivist Perspective

Traditionally, it has been the teacher's responsibility to do most of the planning for instruction, but new ways of planning are developing. Like many recent educational innovations, these new models of planning have not been tested in large-scale carefully designed studies, but you should be aware of the possibilities. Your new teachers will certainly have studied these models in their teacher-preparation programs.

In **constructivist approaches,** planning is shared and negotiated. The teacher and students together make decisions about content, activities, and approaches. Rather than having specific student behaviors and skills as objectives, the teacher has overarching goals—"big ideas"—that guide planning. These goals are understandings or abilities that the teacher returns to again and again.

An Example of Constructivist Planning. Vito Perrone (1994) has these goals for his secondary history students. He wants his students to be able to:

1. Use primary sources, formulate hypotheses, and engage in systematic study
2. Handle multiple points of view
3. Be close readers and active writers
4. Pose and solve problems

The next step in the planning process is to create a learning environment that allows students to move toward these goals in ways that respect their individual interests and abilities. Perrone (1994) suggests identifying "those ideas, themes, and issues that provide the depth and variety of perspective that help students develop significant understandings" (p. 12). For a secondary history course, a theme might be "democracy and revolution," "fairness," or "slavery." In math or music a theme might be "patterns"; in literature, "personal identity" might be the theme. Perrone suggests mapping the topic as a way of thinking about how the theme can generate learning and understanding. An example of a topic map, using the theme of "Immigrants in the United States," is shown in Figure 6.1.

With this topic map as a guide, teacher and students can work together to identify activities, materials, projects, and performances that will support the development of the students' understanding and abilities, the overarching goals of the class. The teacher spends less time planning specific presentations and assignments and more time gathering a variety of resources and facilitating students' learning. The focus is not so

FIGURE 6.1   Planning with a Topic Map
With this map of the topic, "Immigrants in the United States," a history teacher can identify themes, issues, and ideas for study. Rather than "cover" the whole map, a few areas are examined in depth.

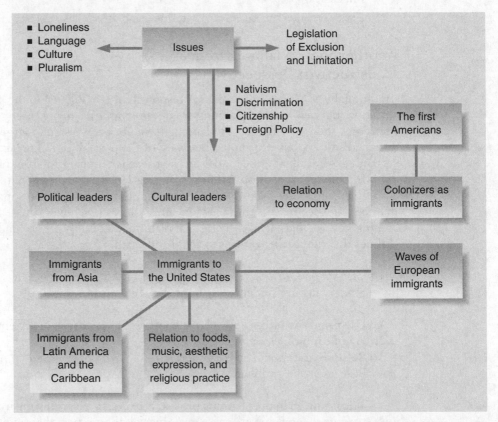

Source: From "How to Engage Students in Learning," by V. Perrone, *Educational Leadership*, February 1994, *51*(5), p. 13. Copyright 1994 by the Association for Supervision and Curriculum Development. Reprinted with permission. All rights reserved, www.ascd.org.

TABLE 6.3   Some Themes for Integrated Planning for Older Children

Courage	Time and Space
Mystery	Groups and Institutions
Survival	Work
Human Interaction	Motion
Communities of the Future	Cause and Effect
Communication/Language	Probability and Prediction
Human Rights and Responsibilities	Change and Conservation
Identity/Coming of Age	Diversity and Variation
Interdependence	Autobiography

Sources: Adapted from *Toward a Coherent Curriculum* by J. A. Beane (Ed.), 1995, Alexandria, VA: Association for Supervision and Curriculum Development; *Interdisciplinary High School Teaching* by J. H. Clarke and R. M. Agne, 1997, Boston: Allyn & Bacon; and *Teaching through Themes* by G. Thompson, 1991, New York: Scholastic.

much on students' products as on the processes of learning and the thinking behind the products.

Integrated and Thematic Plans.   Perrone's planning map shows a way to use the theme of immigrants to the United States to integrate issues in a history class. Today, teaching with themes and integrated content are major elements in planning and designing lessons and units, from kindergarten (Roskos & Neuman, 1995) through high school (Clarke & Agne, 1997). For example, a college professor and two middle school teachers (Pate, McGinnis, & Homestead, 1995) designed a unit on "Human Interactions" that included studying racism, world hunger, pollution, and air and water quality. Students researched issues by reading textbooks and outside sources, learning to use databases, interviewing local officials, and inviting guest speakers into class. Students had to develop knowledge in science, mathematics, and social studies. They learned to write and speak persuasively, and in the process raised money for hunger relief in Africa.

Elementary school students can benefit from integrated planning, too. There is no reason to work on spelling skills, then listening skills, then writing skills, and then social studies or science. All these abilities can be developed together if students work to solve authentic problems. Some ideas for integrating themes with younger children are people, friendship, communications, habitats, communities, patterns, and roots and wings (Thompson, 1991). Possibilities for older children are given in Table 6.3 above.

We turn now to the interactive phase of teaching, the lesson itself. Here, much good research has identified some elements of teaching that make a difference in student learning.

Successful Teaching: Focus on the Teacher

How would you go about identifying the keys to effective teaching? You might ask students, other principals, college professors of education, or experienced teachers to list the characteristics of good teachers. Or you could do intensive case studies of a few classrooms over a long period. You might observe classrooms, rate different teachers on certain characteristics, and then see which characteristics were associated with teachers whose students either achieved the most or were the most motivated to learn. (To do this, of course, you would have to decide how to assess achievement and motivation.) You could identify teachers whose students, year after year, learned more than students working with other teachers; then you could watch the more successful teachers and note what they do. You might also train teachers to apply several different strategies to teach the same lesson and then determine which strategy led to the greatest student learning. You could videotape teachers, then ask them to view the tapes and report what they were thinking about as they taught and what influenced their decisions while teaching. You might study transcripts of classroom dialogue to learn what helped students understand.

All these approaches and more have been used to investigate teaching. Often, researchers conduct a series of studies by making careful observations and identifying relationships between teaching and learning. The researchers then use these relationships as the basis for developing teaching approaches and testing these approaches in design experiments (Brown, 1992; Greeno, Collins, & Resnick, 1996). Let's examine some of the specific knowledge about teaching gained from these projects.

Characteristics of Effective Teachers

Some of the earliest research on effective teaching focused on the personal qualities of the teachers themselves. Researchers thought that the key to success in teaching must lie in the characteristics of teachers (Medley, 1979). Although this assumption proved incorrect—or at least incomplete—it did teach us some lessons about three teacher characteristics: knowledge, clarity, and warmth.

Teachers' Knowledge.   Do teachers who know more about their subject have a more positive impact on their students? It depends on the subject. High school students appear to learn more mathematics from teachers with degrees or significant coursework in mathematics (Wayne & Youngs, 2003). When we look at teachers' knowledge of facts and concepts in other subjects, as measured by test scores and college grades, the relationship to student learning is unclear and may be indirect. Teachers who know more facts about their subject do not necessarily have students who learn more. But teachers who know more may make clearer presentations and recognize student difficulties more readily. They are ready for any student questions and do not have to be evasive or vague in their answers. And we know from Linda Darling-Hammond's (2000) work that the quality of teachers—as measured by whether the teachers were fully certified and had a major in their teaching field—is related to student performance. Thus, knowledge is necessary but not sufficient for effective teaching because being more knowledgeable helps teachers be clearer and more organized.

Clarity and Organization.   Students discussing a teacher are likely to say things like, "Oh, she can really explain," or "He's so confusing!" When Barak Rosenshine and Norma Furst (1973) reviewed about 50 studies of teaching, they concluded that clarity was the most promising teacher behavior for future research on effective teaching. Other studies confirm the importance of clarity. Teachers who provide clear presentations and explanations tend to have students who learn more and who rate their teachers more positively. Teachers with more knowledge of the subject tend to be less vague in their explanations to the class. The less vague the teacher, the more the students learn (Land, 1987).

Planning for Clarity.   Research offers guidelines for greater clarity in teaching (Berliner, 1987; Comadena, Hunt, & Simonds, 2007; Evertson et al., 2006). When planning a lesson, teachers should try to anticipate the problems students will have with the material. Teachers' manuals and experienced teachers can help new teachers with this. You might also encourage your teachers to do the written parts of the lesson themselves to identify potential problems. Have definitions ready for new terms and prepare several relevant examples for concepts. Think of analogies that will make ideas easier to understand. Organize the lesson in a logical sequence; include checkpoints that incorporate oral or written questions or problems to make sure the students are following the explanations.

Plan a clear introduction to the lesson. Tell students what they will be learning and how they could approach it. Often teachers are vague about both the "what" and the "how." For example, in a study by Duffy, Roehler, Meloth, and Vavrus (1986), an ineffective reading teacher began her lesson on using context in reading by saying

> Today we are going to learn about context. This skill will help you in your reading. (p. 206)

This is a vague and general statement of "what" the students will learn. An effective teacher in the same study began her lesson with an explicit, precise description:

> At the end of today's lesson, you will be able to use the other words in a sentence to figure out the meaning of an unknown word. The skill is one that you use when you come to a word that you don't know and you have to figure out what the word means. (p. 206)

Being precise about "how" to do the work is even harder. One study found that teachers seldom, if ever, explain the cognitive processes they want their students to practice in a seatwork activity. Bright students figure out the right process, but slower students often guess or give up. For example, an *ineffective* teacher might introduce a seatwork activity on words with prefixes by saying, "Here are some words with prefixes. Write the meaning of each in the blanks." An *effective* teacher, on the other hand, would demonstrate how to divide the words into a prefix and a root; how to determine the meaning of the root and the prefix; and how to put the two meanings together to make sense of the whole word (Berliner, 1987).

Clarity during the Lesson.   As you observe teachers, do they make clear connections between facts or concepts by using **explanatory links** such as *because, if . . . then*, or *therefore?* For example, when a teacher says, "The Northern economy was based on manufacturing and the North had an advantage in the Civil War," students are given two facts, but no connection between them. If there is a relationship between the two ideas, it should be indicated with an explanatory link as in, "The North had an advantage in the Civil War because its economy was based on manufacturing." Explanatory links tie ideas together and make them easier to learn (Berliner, 1987). Explanatory links are also helpful in labeling visual material such as graphs, concept maps, or illustrations.

Teachers also should signal transitions from one major topic to another with phrases such as "The next area . . . ," "Now we will turn to . . . ," or "The second step is . . ." Teachers might help students follow the lesson by outlining topics, listing key points, or drawing concept maps on the board or on an overhead projector. Continually monitor the group to see if everyone is following the lesson. Look for confident nods or puzzled stares. Throughout the lesson, choose words that are familiar to the students. Define new terms and relate them to what the students already know.

Vagueness is the enemy of understanding. Encourage teachers and students to be precise. Avoid vague words and ambiguous phrases: steer clear of "the somes": *something, someone, sometime, somehow;* "the not verys": *not very much, not very well, not very hard, not very often;* and other unspecific fillers, such as *most, not all, sort of, and so on, of course, as you know, I guess, in fact, or whatever,* and *more or less.* Use specific (and, if possible, colorful) names instead of *it, them,* and *thing.* Also, refrain from using pet phrases such as *you know, like,* and *Okay?* Another idea is to have teachers record a lesson on tape to check themselves for clarity.

Warmth and Enthusiasm. As you are well aware, some teachers are much more enthusiastic than others. Studies have found that ratings of teachers' enthusiasm for their subject are correlated with student achievement gains (Rosenshine & Furst, 1973). Warmth, friendliness, and understanding seem to be the teacher traits most strongly related to student attitudes (Madsen, 2003; Hamann, Baker, McAllister, & Bauer, 2000). In other words, teachers who are warm and friendly tend to have students who like them and the class in general. But notice, these are correlational studies. The results do not tell us whether teacher enthusiasm causes student learning or whether warmth causes positive attitudes, only that the two variables tend to occur together.

The research we have looked at has identified teacher knowledge, clarity, organization, warmth, and enthusiasm as important characteristics of effective teachers. One caveat: Importance can be in the eye of the beholder. In one study, administrators and students agreed that teacher clarity was very important but differed in their views of teacher knowledge. Students rated knowledge third in importance whereas administrators rated it nineteenth (Polk, 2006). The Theory into Action Guidelines summarize the practical implications that principals and teachers can use to improve learning and teaching.

Teacher Effects

What else can the teacher do to increase student learning? Two decades of research on teacher effects points to five keys, summarized by Brophy and Good (1986).

1. Teachers do make a difference. Some teachers, year after year, have students who learn more and do better on standardized tests.

2. Teachers who make a difference take responsibility for their students' learning. These teachers have a strong sense of efficacy. They believe that they can get through to the most difficult students. If one approach doesn't work, the teachers try another way—no excuses, no giving up for teacher or student.

Characteristics of Good Teachers

Organize your lessons carefully.

Examples

1. Provide objectives that help students focus on the purpose of the lesson.
2. Begin lessons by writing a brief outline on the board, or work on an outline with the class as part of the lesson.
3. If possible, break the presentation into clear steps or stages.
4. Review periodically.

Strive for clear explanations.

Examples

1. Use concrete examples or analogies that relate to the students' own lives. Have several examples for particularly difficult points.

2. Give explanations at several levels so all students, not just the brightest, will understand.
3. Focus on one idea at a time and avoid digressions.

Communicate an enthusiasm for your subject and the day's lesson.

Examples

1. Tell students why the lesson is important. Have a better reason than "This will be on the test" or "You will need to know it next year." Emphasize the value of the learning itself.
2. Make eye contact with the students.
3. Vary your pace and volume in speaking. Use silence for emphasis.

3. These teachers make sure that class time is not wasted or lost on empty "fun" activities or unnecessary housekeeping tasks. Class management and organization make time for learning. In the next chapter, we see how important time is and how to create learning environments that minimize distractions and maximize learning.

4. Teaching is active with a great deal of time devoted to teacher–student interaction, explanation, and questioning. Less time is spent in independent seatwork or unsupervised worksheets.

5. Even though the academic focus is clear, the class environment is friendly and supportive. The teacher's enthusiasm about learning and respect for students is contagious (Brophy, 1997).

These keys have been associated with the term **direct instruction.** Weinert and Helmke (1995) describe direct instruction as having the following features:

(a) the teachers' classroom management is especially effective and the rate of student interruptive behaviors is very low; (b) the teacher maintains a strong academic focus and uses available instructional time intensively to initiate and facilitate students' learning activities; (c) the teacher insures that as many students as possible achieve good learning progress by carefully choosing appropriate tasks, clearly presenting subject-matter information and solution strategies, continuously diagnosing each student's learning progress and learning difficulties, and providing effective help through remedial instruction. (p. 138)

You can see that direct instruction applies best to the teaching of basic skills—clearly structured knowledge and essential skills—such as science facts, mathematics computations, reading vocabulary, and grammar rules (Rosenshine & Stevens, 1986). These skills involve tasks that are relatively unambiguous; they can be taught step-by-step and tested by standardized tests. The teaching approaches described above are not necessarily appropriate for objectives such as helping students to write creatively, solve complex problems, or mature emotionally. How would a teacher turn these themes into actions?

Rosenshine's Six Teaching Functions.   Rosenshine and his colleagues (Rosenshine, 1988; Rosenshine & Stevens, 1986) have identified six teaching functions based on the research on effective instruction. These could serve as a checklist or framework for teaching basic skills.

1. *Review and check the previous day's work.* Reteach if students misunderstood or made errors.

2. *Present new material.* Make the purpose clear, teach in small steps, provide many examples and nonexamples.

3. *Provide guided practice.* Question students, give practice problems, and listen for misconceptions and misunderstandings. Reteach if necessary. Continue guided practice until students answer about 80 percent of the questions correctly.

4. *Give feedback and correctives based on student answers.* Reteach if necessary.

5. *Provide independent practice.* Let students apply the new learning on their own, in seatwork, cooperative groups, or homework. The success rate during independent practice should be about 95 percent. This means that students must be well prepared for the work by the presentation and guided practice and that assignments must not be too difficult. The point is for the students to practice until the skills become overlearned and automatic, until they are confident. Hold students accountable for the work they do; check it.

6. *Review weekly and monthly to consolidate learning.* Include some review items as homework. Test often, and reteach material missed on these tests.

These six functions are not steps to be followed in a particular order, but all of them are elements of effective instruction. For example, feedback, review, or reteaching should occur whenever necessary and should match the abilities of the students. There are several other models of direct instruction, but most share these elements.

Why Does Direct Instruction Work?   What aspects of direct instruction might explain its success? Linda Anderson (1989b) suggests that lessons that help students perceive links among main ideas will help them construct accurate understandings. Well-organized presentations, clear explanations, the use of explanatory links, and reviews can all help students perceive connections among ideas. If done well, therefore, a direct instruction lesson could be a resource that students use to construct understanding. For example, reviews activate prior knowledge so the student is ready to understand. Brief, clear presentations and guided practice avoid overloading the students' information-processing systems and taxing their working memories. Numerous examples and explanations give many pathways and associations for building networks of concepts. Guided practice can also give the teacher a snapshot of the students' thinking and of their misconceptions, so these can be addressed directly as misconceptions rather than simply as "wrong answers."

Criticisms of Direct Instruction.   Critics say that direct instruction is limited to lower-level objectives and that it is based on traditional teaching methods, ignores innovative models, and discourages students' independent thinking. Some researchers claim that the direct instruction model is based on the *wrong* theory of learning. Teachers break material into small segments, present each segment clearly, and reinforce or correct, thus *transmitting* accurate understandings from teacher to student. Teacher presentations can put the students in a passive position by doing much of the cognitive work for them and may prevent students from asking or even thinking of questions (Freiberg & Driscoll, 2005). These criticisms of direct instruction echo the criticisms of behavioral learning theories.

But there is ample evidence that direct instruction and explanation can help students learn actively, not passively. For younger and less-prepared learners, student-controlled learning without teacher direction and instruction can lead to systematic deficits in the students' knowledge. Without guidance, the understandings that students construct can be incomplete and misleading (Sweller, Kirschner, & Clark, 2007; Leinhardt, 2001). Deep understanding and fluid performance—whether in dance or mathematical problem solving or reading—require models of expert performance and extensive practice with feedback (Anderson, Reder, & Simon, 1995). Guided and independent practice with feedback are at the heart of the direct instruction model.

What direct instruction cannot do is *ensure* that students understand. If badly done, it may encourage students to memorize and mimic but never to "own" the knowledge. To help students reach this goal, in the next two sections we look at teaching for understanding. The first section focuses on the subject and the second on the learning.

Teaching for Understanding: Focus on the Subject

In middle and high schools, academic subjects become more complex and more important than basic skills in teaching. It is clear that a teacher's knowledge of the subject is critical for teaching (Ball et al., 2001; Borko & Putnam, 1996). Part of that knowledge is **pedagogical content knowledge,** or knowing how to teach a subject to your particular students (Shulman, 1987). In the last decade, psychologists have made great progress understanding how students learn different subjects (Mayer, 1992; Sweller et al., 2007). Based on these findings, many approaches have been developed to teach reading, writing, science, mathematics, social studies, and all the other subjects. Below we look at a few key subjects and the controversies surrounding how to teach them.

Learning and Teaching Reading

For years, educators have debated whether students should be taught to read and write through code-based (phonics or skills) approaches that relate letters to sounds and sounds to words, or through meaning-based (whole-language, literature-based) approaches that do not dissect words and sentences into pieces, but instead focus on the meaning of the text (Barr, 2001; Carlisle, Stahl, & Birdyshaw, 2004; Goodman & Goodman, 1990; Smith, 1994; Stahl, McKenna, & Pagnucco, 1994; Symons, Woloshyn, & Pressley, 1994).

Curriculum Wars: Reading.   We woke this morning to a front-page story in the *New York Times* about the continuing reading war. Schools in Madison, Wisconsin, were refusing federal money because to accept the money, they had to adopt a phonics only approach to teaching reading (Schemo, 2007).

Advocates of **whole-language approaches** believe that learning to read is a natural process, very much like mastering your native language. Reading is a kind of guessing game in which students sample words and make predictions and guesses about meaning based on both the context of other words in the passage and their prior knowledge. Children should be immersed in a print-rich environment, surrounded by books worth reading and adults who read—to the children and for themselves. When students write, they write for an audience; their goal is to communicate effectively. Vygotsky (1978) recognized the importance of authentic writing tasks: "[W]riting should be incorporated into a task that is necessary and relevant for life. Only then can we be certain that it will develop not as a matter of hand and finger habits but as a really new and complex form of speech" (p. 118).

But is whole language the whole story? There are now three decades of research demonstrating that skill in recognizing sounds and words supports reading. Advocates of code-based approaches cite research showing that being able to identify many words as you read does not depend on using context to guess meaning. In fact, it is almost the other way around—knowing words helps you make sense of context. Identifying words as you read is a highly automatic process (Byrne, Fielding-Barnsley, & Ashley, 2000; Muter, Hulme, Snowling, & Stevenson, 2004; Vellutino, 1991). It is the poorest readers who resort to using context to help them understand meaning (Pressley, 1996). Alphabetic coding and awareness of letter sounds are essential skills for acquiring word identification, so some direct teaching of the alphabet and phonics is helpful in learning to read.

The best approach makes use of both phonics and whole language. We want children to be both fluent and enthusiastic readers and writers (National Center for Family Literacy, 2004; Pressley, 1998; Stahl & Yaden, 2004). After reviewing studies of reading instruction, Stahl, McKenna, and Pagnucco (1994) concluded "eclectic programs, which include the use of open-ended tasks and self-selected literature as in whole-language approaches but also stress an achievement orientation and phonics instruction as in more traditional approaches, seem to be effective in improving both achievement and attitude" (pp. 175–185).

Being Sensible about Reading and Writing.   The results of high-quality studies suggest that:

1. Whole-language approaches to reading and writing are most effective in preschool and kindergarten where they give children a good conceptual basis for reading and writing and improve their motivation, interest, attitude toward reading, and understanding of the nature and purposes of reading and writing (Graham & Harris, 1994; Morrow, 1992; Neuman & Roskos, 1992).

2. Phonemic awareness—the sense that words are composed of separate sounds and that sounds are combined to say words—in kindergarten and first grade predicts literacy in later grades. If children do not have phonemic awareness in the early grades, direct teaching can dramatically improve their chances of long-term achievement in literacy. Earlier is better. Preschoolers tend to profit more from phonological training than kindergarten or primary grade students (Bus & van IJzendoorn, 1999; Pressley, 1998).

3. Excellent primary school teachers use both explicit decoding-skills teaching and whole-language instruction. Reading teachers should use a balanced approach rather than stressing either a literature-based whole-language or a skills-first approach (Adams, Trieman, & Pressley, 1998; Bus & van IJzendoorn, 1999; Vellutino, 1991).

If students need help cracking the code, give them what they need. Don't let ideology get in the way. You will just send more students to private tutors, if their families can afford it. But don't forget that reading and writing are for a purpose. Surround students with good literature and create a community of readers and writers. The Center for Early Reading describes ten principles that capture this balanced approach to teaching, as shown in Table 6.4 on the next page.

Summer Setbacks. Results of many studies show that children growing up in poverty lag behind more affluent children in reading achievement. Educators have designed literally hundreds of interventions to eliminate this achievement gap. But these interventions may never be enough. Over the past decade, evidence has been mounting that students in poverty begin school about six months behind in reading compared to students from wealthier homes, but the difference between the groups grows to almost three years by sixth grade. One explanation for this growing gap is that the children from poorer homes lose ground over the summer. Even though both groups make comparable achievement gains during the school year, every summer vacation creates about a three-month reading achievement gap between poor and advantaged children. One study suggested that the four summer vacations between second and sixth grade accounted for 80% of the achievement differences between poor and advantaged students (Allington & McGill-Frazen, 2003). This truly is a case of the rich getting richer. Wealthier children have greater access to books all the time, but especially over the summer. They read more, and the more children read, the better readers they become—volume of readings matters. The question is, what can your school do to ensure that "every child has year-round access to appropriate books to read, books that they cannot wait to read" (Allington & McGill-Frazen, 2003, p. 74).

Learning and Teaching Mathematics

Some of the most compelling support for constructivist approaches to teaching comes from mathematics education. Critics of direct instruction believe that traditional mathematics instruction often teaches students an unintended lesson, that they "cannot understand mathematics," or worse, that mathematics doesn't have to make sense, you just have to memorize the formulas. Even though traditional ways of teaching mathematics have been criticized because they can lead to applying computation rules without understanding, constructivist approaches have had their critics too, as we will see next.

Curriculum Wars: Mathematics. As with reading, battles have been fought about how to teach mathematics. In 1989, the National Council of Teachers of Mathematics

TABLE 6.4   Improving the Reading Achievement of America's Children: CIERA's 10 Research-Based Principles

CIERA (the Center for the Improvement of Early Reading Achievement) has reviewed the research on learning to read and distilled the best findings into these ten principles. You can read the expanded version of the principles on its website—www.ciera.org—under free information. Reprinted by permission of CIERA.

1. **Home language and literacy experiences** support the development of key print concepts and a range of knowledge prepares students for school-based learning. Programs that help families initiate and sustain these experiences show positive benefits for children's reaching achievement.

   Examples: Joint reading with a family member, parental modeling of good reading habits, monitoring homework and television viewing.

2. **Preschool programs** are particularly beneficial for children who do not experience informal learning opportunities in their homes. Such preschool experiences lead to improved reading achievement, with some effects lasting through grade 3.

   Examples: Listening to and examining books, saying nursery rhymes, writing messages, and seeing and talking about print.

3. **Skills that predict later reading** success can be promoted in kindergarten and grade 1. The two most powerful of these predictors are letter-name knowledge and phonemic awareness. Instruction in these skills has demonstrated positive effects on primary-grade reading achievement, especially when it is coupled with letter-sound instruction.

   Examples: Encourage children to hear and blend sound through oral renditions of rhymes, poems, and songs, as well as writing messages and in journals.

4. **Primary-level instruction** that supports successful reading acquisition is consistent, well-designed, and focused.

   Examples: Systematic word recognition instruction on common, consistent letter-sound relationships and important but often unpredictable high-frequency words, such as *the* and *what*; teaching children to monitor the accuracy of their reading as well as their understanding of texts through strategies such as predicting, inferencing, clarifying misunderstandings, and summarizing; promoting word recognition and comprehension through repeated reading of text, guided reading and writing, strategy lessons, reading aloud with feedback, and conversations about texts children have read.

5. **Primary-level classroom environments** in successful schools provide opportunities for students to apply what they have learned in teacher-guided instruction to everyday reading and writing.

   Examples: Teachers read books aloud and hold follow-up discussions, children read independently every day, and children write stories and keep journals. These events are monitored frequently by teachers, ensuring that time is well spent and that children receive feedback on their efforts. Teachers design and revise these events based on information from ongoing assessment of children's strengths and needs.

6. **Cultural and linguistic diversity** among America's children reflects the variations within their communities and homes. This diversity is manifest in differences in the children's dispositions toward and knowledge about topics, language, and literacy.

TABLE 6.4 (*Continued*)

Examples: Effective instruction includes assessment, integration, and extension of relevant background knowledge and the use of texts that recognize diverse backgrounds. Build on the children's language when children are learning to speak, listen to, write, and read English. When teachers capitalize on the advantages of bilingualism or biliteracy, second language reading acquisition is significantly enhanced.

7. **Children who are identified as having reading disabilities** profit from the same sort of well-balanced instructional programs that benefit all children who are learning to read and write, including systematic instruction *and* meaningful reading and writing.

    Examples: Intensive one-on-one or small-group instruction, attention to both comprehension and word recognition processes, thoroughly individualized assessment and instructional planning, and extensive experiences with many types of texts.

8. **Proficient reading in third grade** and above is sustained and enhanced by programs that adhere to four fundamental features:

    Features: (1) deep and wide opportunities to read; (2) acquiring new knowledge and vocabulary, through wide reading and through explicit instruction about networks of new concepts; (3) emphasizing the influence on understanding of kinds of text (e.g., stories versus essays) and the ways writers organize particular texts; and (4) assisting students in reasoning about text.

9. **Professional opportunities** to improve reading achievement are prominent in successful schools and programs.

    Examples: Opportunities for teachers and administrators to analyze instruction, assessment, and achievement; to set goals for improvement; to learn about effective practices; and to participate in ongoing communities that deliberately try to understand both successes and persistent problems.

10. **Entire school staffs,** not just first-grade teachers, are involved in bringing children to high levels of achievement.

    Examples: In successful schools, reading achievement goals are clear, expectations are high, instructional means for attaining goals are articulated, and shared assessments monitor children's progress. Even though they might use different materials and technologies, successful schools maintain a focus on reading and writing and have programs to involve parents in their children's reading and homework. Community partnerships, including volunteer tutoring programs, are common.

(NCTM) published *Curriculum and Evaluation Standards* for the United States and Canada. Since that time, NCTM has released several other reports describing curriculum standards and assessment approaches for mathematics, the most recent in 2000, *Principles and Standards for School Mathematics* (http://standards.nctm.org). The goals of these publications were to make teaching consistent with the research on children's development of mathematical understandings. To do so, the NCTM recommends an end to rote memorization and drill, to be replaced by more problem solving for conceptual understanding, inquiry, and constructivist approaches to learning consistent with the theories of Piaget. These documents have been very influential. As a consequence of the recommendations, most states made long lists of mathematics learning goals for every grade. Students were encouraged to write about their thinking and come up with many different ways to solve mathematical problems, not simply memorize rules and procedures. Long division was virtually dropped from the curriculum.

But critics suggest that the NCTM standards are based on unsupported pedagogical theories and are responsible for the dismal performance of U.S. students in international comparisons such as the TIMSS. A group of 10 university professors and mathematics teachers drafted a document called *Ten Myths about Math Education and Why You Shouldn't Believe Them* (Budd et al., 2005) that criticized what they called the "fuzzy math" of the standards (for the full version of their criticism, see www.nychold.com/myths-050504.html). Critics said that students, especially those with learning disabilities, do not learn well using inquiry and discovery approaches—direct instruction often is more effective (Anderson, Reder, & Simon, 1996; Klahr & Nigram, 2004; Miller & Mercer, 1997). In addition, the ways of teaching mathematics touted by the NCTM standards are inconsistent with the ways of teaching in the top performing countries such as Singapore (Ginsburg, Leinwand, Anstrom, & Pollock, 2005).

Being Sensible about Teaching Mathematics. Recently, as with reading, some balance has appeared in the discussions of mathematics instruction. The National Council of Teachers of Mathematics (2006) issued a report called *Curriculum Focal Points for Prekindergarten through Grade 8 Mathematics* that describes three basic skills for each level in order to help teachers focus the curriculum and make sense of the many expectations in the full standards. For example, there are the over twenty expectations for children in grades 3–5 in the 2000 standards. The new curriculum suggestions that fourth grade focus on three basic skills: quick recall of multiplication and division facts and fluency with whole-number multiplication; developing an understanding of area and determining the area of two-dimensional spaces; and developing an understanding of decimals, including the relations between fractions and decimals. It appears that many of the educators who published the "10 Myths" criticisms of the previous NCTM standards are more positive about these new attempts at focus (Lewin, 2006).

Learning and Teaching Science

If you have worked with adolescents, you know that by high school, some students have developed some misconceptions about the world, such as the belief that Earth is warmer in the summer because it is closer to the sun. One key to understanding in science is for students to directly examine their own theories and confront the shortcomings (Hewson, Beeth, & Thorley, 1998). Only then can true learning and conceptual change happen. Students must go through six stages: initial discomfort with their own ideas and beliefs, attempts to explain away inconsistencies between their theories and evidence presented to them, attempts to adjust measurements or observations to fit personal theories, doubt, vacillation, and finally conceptual change (Nissani & Hoefler-Nissani, 1992). You can see Piaget's notions of assimilation, disequilibrium, and accommodation operating here. Students try to make new information fit existing ideas (assimilation), but when the fit simply won't work and disequilibrium occurs, then accommodation or changes in cognitive structures follow.

The goal of **conceptual change teaching** in science is to help students pass through these six stages of learning. The two central features of conceptual change teaching are:

1. Teachers are committed to teaching for student understanding rather than "covering the curriculum."

2. Students are encouraged to make sense of science using their current ideas. They are challenged to describe, predict, explain, justify, debate, and defend the adequacy of their understanding. Dialogue is key. Only when intuitive ideas prove inadequate can new learning take hold (Anderson & Roth, 1989).

Conceptual change teaching has much in common with cognitive apprenticeships and inquiry learning described in Chapter 3, with scaffolding and dialogue playing key roles (Shuell, 1996). The following Theory into Action Guidelines, adapted from Hewson, Beeth, and Thorley (1998), give some ideas that principals can suggest for teaching that encourages conceptual change.

THEORY INTO ACTION GUIDELINES

Conceptual Change Teaching

Encourage students to make their ideas explicit.

Examples

1. Ask students to make predictions that might contradict their naive conceptions.
2. Ask students to state their ideas in their own words, including the attractions and limitations of the ideas for them.
3. Have students explain their ideas using physical models or illustrations.

Help students see the differences among ideas.

Examples

1. Have students summarize or paraphrase each other's ideas.
2. Encourage comparing ideas by presenting and comparing evidence.

Encourage metacognition.

Examples

1. Give a pretest before starting a unit, then have students discuss their own responses to the pretest.
2. Group similar pretest responses together and ask students to discover a more general concept underlying the responses.

3. At the end of lessons, ask students: "What did you learn? What do you understand? What do you believe about the lesson? How have your ideas changed?"

Explore the status of ideas. Status is an indication of how much students know and accept ideas and find them useful.

Examples

1. Ask direct questions about how intelligible, plausible, and fruitful an idea is: Do you know what the idea means? Do you believe it? Can you achieve some valuable outcome using the idea?
2. Plan activities and experiments that support and question the students' ideas, such as showing successful applications or pointing out contradictions.

Ask students for justifications of their ideas.

Examples

1. Teach students to use terms such as *consistent, inconsistent, coherent* in giving justifications.
2. Ask students to share and analyze each other's justifications.

TABLE 6.5   One Teacher's Learning Goals for Conceptual Change Teaching

The teacher in one fifth-grade class gives these questions to her students to support their thinking about science.

1. Can you state your own ideas?
2. Can you talk about why you are attracted to your ideas?
3. Are your ideas consistent?
4. Do you realize the limitations of your ideas and the possibility they might need to change?
5. Can you try to explain your ideas using physical models?
6. Can you explain the difference between understanding an idea and believing in an idea?
7. Can you apply *intelligible* and *plausible* to your own ideas?

Source: Adapted from "Teaching Science in Fifth Grade: Instructional Goals that Support Conceptual Change," by M. E. Beeth, 1998, *Journal of Research in Science Teaching, 35*, p. 1093. Reprinted by permission of Wiley-Liss, Inc., a subsidiary of John Wiley & Sons, Inc.

How would these guidelines look in practice? One answer comes from Michael Beeth's study of a fifth-grade classroom. Table 6.5 is a list of learning goals that the teacher presents to her students.

In this classroom, the teacher typically began instruction with questions such as, "Do you have ideas? Can you talk about them? Bring them out into the open? Why do you like your ideas? Why are you attracted to them?" (Beeth, 1998, p. 1095). During her teaching she constantly asks questions that require explanation and justifications. She summarizes the students' answers, and sometimes challenges, "But do you really believe what you say?" Studies of the students in the teacher's classroom over the years show that they have a sophisticated understanding of science concepts.

A Model for Good Subject Matter Teaching

There is less accumulated evidence about teaching for understanding in school subjects, but some initial findings point to common elements in successful programs (Brophy, 1997). The emphasis is on the role of the students in constructing useful understandings as they assume more and more responsibility for learning. Brophy identified ten keys to successful teaching for understanding:

1. The curriculum emphasizes knowledge, skills, and values that will be useful outside as well as inside school.
2. Students become more expert by actually using knowledge in practical applications so that conceptual understanding and self-regulation develop simultaneously.
3. A few important topics are addressed in depth instead of "covering" the curriculum. Supporters of the constructivist approach believe (with Howard Gardner) that coverage is the enemy of understanding.
4. The content to be learned is organized around a small set of powerful or "big" ideas.
5. The teacher presents information but also scaffolds students' efforts to learn.

6. The students' role is to actively work to make sense of the information and make it their own.
7. Teaching begins with the students' prior knowledge, even if that understanding includes some misunderstanding and conceptual change must be the goal.
8. Class activities include authentic tasks that call for critical thinking and problem solving, not just memorizing.
9. Higher-order thinking skills are taught and applied as students learn subject matter, not during separate, stand-alone "thinking" activities.
10. The teacher's goal is to create a learning community where dialogue and cooperation promote student understanding of content.

The **Community of Learners** model developed by Ann Brown and Joe Campione (1996) described in Chapter 4 is an example of a teaching model that includes these ten elements. In this model, first used in the schools of Oakland, California, students are organized into small collaborative groups to research an important topic in depth. They receive direct instruction, modeling, and coaching in the learning and research strategies they will need and practice the strategies in context of doing the actual research. Jigsaw cooperative learning groups divide the material to be learned, and each student becomes an expert resource on one aspect of the topic. Students demonstrate their growing understandings in learning performances for real audiences. Evaluations of this model are very promising.

Criticisms of Constructivist Approaches to Subject Teaching

Constructivist approaches have done much to correct the excesses of tell-and-drill teaching. Some positive outcomes from constructivist teaching are better understanding of the material, greater enjoyment of literature, more positive attitudes toward school, better problem solving, and greater motivation (Harris & Graham, 1996; Palincsar, 1998). But total reliance on constructivist approaches that ignores direct teaching of skills can be detrimental for some children. Whole-language and constructivist approaches alone may not work for *all* children (Airasian & Walsh, 1997; Harris & Graham, 1996) or all kinds of learning (Sweller et al., 2007; Weinert & Helmke, 1995). If students fall behind because they lack specific skills, it would be unethical to withhold teaching and wait for those skills to "develop naturally," simply to be true to a particular philosophy. We agree with Jere Brophy (1997) that some constructivists "are being unrealistic, even romantic, in suggesting that teachers should routinely avoid transmitting knowledge and instead function only as discussion facilitators and scaffolders of learning" (p. 231).

Ernst von Glasersfeld (1995), a strong advocate of constructivist teaching in mathematics, believes that it is a misunderstanding of constructivism to say that memorization and rote learning always are useless. "There are, indeed, matters that can and perhaps must be learned in a purely mechanical way" (p. 5). Classrooms that integrate constructivist teaching with needed direct teaching of skills are especially good learning environments for students with special needs. Careful ongoing assessment of each student's abilities, knowledge, and motivations, followed by appropriate support, should ensure that no students are lost or left behind (Graham & Harris, 1994).

Beyond Models to Outstanding Teaching

Is good teaching science or art, teacher-centered lecture or student-centered discovery, the application of general theories or the invention of situation-specific practices? Is a good teacher a good explainer or a good questioner, a "sage on the stage" or a "guide by the side" of the students? These questions have and will continue to confound educational researchers for years to come. However, one thing we do know is this: When considering the impact of all of the factors in determining student achievement, the quality of classroom teaching is critical (Reeves, 2000). That, in turn, elevates the question, "What is good teaching?" to one most vital to educational leadership. What do you think? Before you answer, read the Point/Counterpoint on good teaching.

Our message for teachers is to match instructional methods to learning goals. In the early stages of learning, when students have little prior knowledge or even relevant personal experiences to provide a basis for discussion and analysis, it makes little sense to spend class time discussing and analyzing. Reading, researching, even memorizing may be needed to develop a common base of information to support discussion (Brophy, 1997). Personally, we hope you are all "sages" by the "sides" of your students.

Cautions: Where's the Learning?

As an instructional leader, you will be bombarded with claims and counterclaims about teaching innovations. Many of these programs and techniques will look promising, but it makes sense to ask, "Where's the evidence for learning? Have these innovations been tested in situations similar to your own? Do the strategies improve the bottom line, student learning and motivation? What's the evidence? How large are the gains and do they last? If the teaching approaches have not been tested, are they at least consistent with what we know about student learning and motivation? Will the teaching methods encourage student attention, cognitive investment, and long-term memory? Do they support understanding (constructivist), remembering, (cognitive-information processing), and applying/practicing (behavioral) new knowledge?"

The research support for teacher effects and direct instruction is strong and based on large-scale, carefully conducted studies. As we have seen, this work is not without its critics, but if we focus on the learning of explicit information, the research on direct instruction offers good guidance.

Turning to higher-level objectives, we would expect that the newer models of teaching for subject understanding would be best. But be aware that the research base for these approaches is thin so far. As Brophy (1997) notes, many of the instructional models advocated by intellectual leaders and position statements published by professional organizations "have yet to be tested empirically, let alone enjoy a rich accumulation of systematic evidence of effects on student outcomes" (p. 226). In other words, there is no clear evidence (beyond testimonials of advocates) that these models have worked once, much less in many different schools and settings. Slavin and Fashola (1998) are even more blunt:

Educational innovation lacks the respect for scientific evidence and independent replication that has characterized the most productive and progressive aspects of our society

POINT/COUNTERPOINT — What Is Good Teaching?

In your former education classes, you probably encountered criticisms of the scientific, teacher-centered, theory-based, lecturing *sages* on the stage. Perhaps you were even encouraged to be artistic, inventive, student-centered, questioning *guides* by the side. Now it is your responsibility as an instructional leader to supervise teachers and differentiate between good and bad instruction. So, what is it? What does it look like? What does it sound like? Let's see what the research says.

POINT

Teaching is a theory-based science.
Psychologists have spent decades studying how children think and feel, how learning occurs, what influences motivation, and how teaching affects learning. These general and abstract conceptions apply to a wide range of situations. Why should teachers have to reinvent all this knowledge? A large body of work studying real teachers in regular classrooms has identified one set of teacher characteristics and behaviors that are related to student learning: knowledge, clarity, enthusiasm, and direct or active teaching (Shuell, 1996). An effective teacher reviews, explains, checks for understanding, and reteaches if necessary, always keeping the level or difficulty and the pace just right to keep students learning. Advocates note that ignoring the direct teaching of skills can be detrimental for some children. For example, Harris and Graham (1996) describe the experiences of their daughter Leah in a whole-language/progressive education school, where the teachers successfully developed their daughter's creativity, thinking, and understanding.

> Skills, on the other hand, have been a problem for our daughter and for other children. At the end of kindergarten, when she had not made much progress in reading, her teacher said she believed Leah had a perceptual problem or a learning disability. Leah began asking what was wrong with her, because other kids were reading and she wasn't. Finally, an assessment was done. (p. 26)

The testing indicated no learning disability, strong comprehension abilities, and poor word attack skills.

Luckily, Leah's parents knew how to teach word attack skills. Direct teaching of these skills helped Leah become an avid and able reader in about six weeks.

COUNTERPOINT

Teaching is an art, a creative reflective process.
Other educators believe that the mark of an excellent teacher is not the ability to apply techniques but the artistry of being reflective—thoughtful and inventive—about teaching (Schon, 1983). Educators who adopt this view tend to be more concerned with how teachers plan, solve problems, create instruction, and make decisions than they are with the specific techniques teachers apply (Peterson & Comeaux, 1989). They believe teaching "is specific with respect to task, time, place, participants, and content, and that different subjects vary in those specifics" (Leinhardt, 2001, p. 334). Thus, teaching is so complex that it must be invented anew with every new subject and class. Critics of direct, teacher-centered teaching claim that breaking material into small segments, presenting each segment clearly, and reinforcing or correcting, is *transmitting* accurate understandings from teacher to student. The student is seen as an "empty vessel" waiting to be filled with knowledge, rather than an active constructor of knowledge (Anderson, 1989a; Berg & Clough, 1991; Davis, Maher, & Noddings, 1990).

Beware of either/or choices: In spite of the criticisms and debates, there is no one best way to teach. Different goals require different methods. Direct instruction leads to better performance on achievement tests, whereas the open, informal methods such as discovery learning or inquiry approaches are associated with better performance on tests of creativity, abstract thinking, and problem solving. In addition, the open methods are better for improving attitudes toward school and for stimulating curiosity, cooperation among students, and lower absence rates (Walberg, 1990). When the goals of teaching involve problem solving, creativity, understanding, and mastering processes, many approaches besides direct instruction should be

(Continued)

POINT/COUNTERPOINT   Continued

effective. These guidelines are in keeping with Tom Good's conclusion that teaching should become less direct as students mature and when the goals involve affective development and problem solving or critical thinking (Good, 1983).

Of course, every subject, even college English or chemistry, can require some direct instruction. In teaching when to use *who* and *whom*, or how to set up laboratory apparatus, direct instruction may be the best approach. Noddings (1990) reminds teachers that students may need some direct instruction in how to use various manipulative materials to get the possible benefits from them. Students working in

cooperative groups may need guidance, modeling, and practice in how to ask questions and give explanations. And to solve difficult problems, students may need some direct instruction in possible problem-solving strategies.

The theories you have encountered in this text should be used as cognitive tools to help you examine, inspect, and interpret the claims you will hear and read throughout your career (Leinhardt, 2001).

Reeves, D. B. (2000). *Accountability in action: A blueprint for learning organizations.* Denver, CO: Advanced Learning Press.

Reeves cites Education Trust, 1998. www.edtrust.org.

---

and economy, from medicine, technology, and engineering to agriculture. We know far more about the safety and effectiveness of our children's shampoo than we do about the reading or math programs their teachers use. Our children, our teachers, and our society deserve much better. (p. ix)

Advocates for many widely marketed practices such as whole language, integrated curriculum models, learning styles, developing multiple intelligences, and eliminating ability grouping base their arguments on their strong commitments to theories but do not have evidence that these approaches lead to learning. There is probably value in all these ideas, but be aware that clear evidence of strong connections to student learning is not readily available.

Summary

Teaching makes a difference, both for students' personal and social development and for their understanding of academic subjects. In fact, if a student has an ineffective teacher for three years in a row, it is difficult to catch up. Yet good teaching is just one element, albeit a crucial one, in a combination that produces successful student learning. Student engagement, social support, and opportunities to learn are also an important part of the mix.

It takes time and experience to become an expert teacher. These teachers have a rich store of well-organized knowledge about the many specific situations of teaching. This includes knowledge about the subjects they teach, their students, general teaching strategies, subject-specific ways of teaching, settings for learning, curriculum materials, and the goals of education.

Learning to teach is a gradual process. The concerns and problems of teachers change as they progress. During the beginning years, attention tends to be focused on survival. Maintaining discipline, motivating students, evaluating students' work, and dealing with parents are universal concerns for beginning teachers. The more experienced teacher can move on to concerns about professional growth and effectiveness with a wide range of students.

The first step in teaching is planning. Teachers engage in several levels of planning: by the year, term, unit, week, and day. All the levels must be coordinated. Accomplishing the year's plan requires breaking the work into terms, the terms into units, and the units into weeks and days. The plan determines how time and materials will be turned into activities for students. There is no single model of planning, but all plans should allow for flexibility. Most plans include instructional objectives.

An instructional objective is a clear and unambiguous description of your educational intentions for your students. Gronlund's approach suggests that an objective should be stated first in general terms, then the teacher should clarify by listing sample behaviors that would provide evidence that the student has attained the objective.

Bloom and others have developed taxonomies categorizing basic objectives in the cognitive, affective, and psychomotor domains. In real life, of course, behaviors from these three domains occur simultaneously. A taxonomy encourages systematic thinking about relevant objectives and ways to evaluate them. Six basic objectives are listed in the cognitive domain: remembering, understanding, applying, analyzing, evaluating, and creating. These processes can act on four kinds of knowledge: factual, conceptual, procedural, and metacognitive.

In teacher-centered approaches, teachers select learning objectives and plan how to get students to meet those objectives. Teachers control the "what" and "how" of learning. In contrast, planning is shared and negotiated in student-centered, or constructivist, approaches. The teacher and students together make decisions about content, activities, and approaches. Rather than having specific student behaviors as objectives, the teacher has overarching goals or "big ideas" that guide planning. Integrated content and teaching with themes are often part of the planning. Assessment of learning is ongoing and mutually shared by teacher and students.

After planning is the teaching itself. For years, researchers have tried to unravel the mystery of effective teaching. Researchers have used a variety of methods including classroom observation, case studies, interviews, experimentation with different methods, and other approaches to study teaching in real classrooms. Results of research on teacher characteristics indicate that thorough and expert knowledge of a subject, organization and clarity in presentation, and enthusiasm all play important parts in effective teaching. But no one way of teaching has been found to be right for each class, lesson, or day.

Teacher knowledge of the subject is necessary—because being more knowledgeable helps teachers be clearer and more organized—but not sufficient for effective teaching; organization and clarity are important characteristics of good teaching. Teachers who provide clear presentations and explanations tend to have students who learn more and who rate their teachers more positively. Clarity begins with planning. Tell students what they will be learning and how they could approach it. During the lesson, avoid vague language, make clear connections between facts or concepts by using explanatory links, and check often for understanding. Finally, teacher warmth, friendliness, and understanding seem to be the traits most strongly related to positive student attitudes.

In direct instruction, the teacher gives well-organized presentations, clear explanations, carefully delivered prompts, and feedback. These actions can be resources for students as they construct understanding. In student-centered approaches, the teacher designs authentic tasks, monitors student thinking, ask questions, and prods inquiry. Both kinds of teaching may be appropriate at different times.

Advocates of whole language believe children learn best when they are surrounded by good literature and read and write for authentic purposes. Advocates of a balanced approach cite extensive research indicating that skill in recognizing sounds and words—phonemic awareness—is fundamental in learning to read. Excellent primary teachers use a balanced approach combining authentic reading with skills instruction when needed.

Constructivist approaches to mathematics and science emphasize deep understanding of concepts (as opposed to memorization), discussion and explanation, and exploration of students' implicit understandings. Many educators note that the key to understanding in science is for students to directly examine their own theories and confront the shortcomings. For change to take place, students must go through six stages: initial discomfort with their own ideas and beliefs, attempts to explain away inconsistencies between their theories and evidence presented to them, attempts to adjust measurements or observations to fit personal theories, doubt, vacillation, and finally conceptual change.

Many educators feel that the careful use of direct instruction methods—well-organized presentations, clear explanations, carefully delivered prompts, and guided discovery—can be a resource for students as they construct understanding. In all cases, teaching methods should match learning. There is more research evidence for the value of direct instruction than for constructivist approaches, but the ideas from student-centered, constructivist models of teaching can be useful. To evaluate new approaches, ask if they match the principles of learning and motivation described in Chapters 4 and 5.

KEY TERMS

affective domain (204)
behavioral objectives (200)
cognitive domain (202)
cognitive objectives (201)
Community of Learners (221)
conceptual change teaching (219)

constructivist approach (205)
direct instruction (211)
explanatory links (209)
instructional objective (200)
lesson study (199)
pedagogical content knowledge (213)

phonemic awareness (214)
psychomotor domain (205)
reflective (197)
taxonomy (202)
whole-language approaches (214)

DEVELOPING YOUR PORTFOLIO

1. Develop a classroom observation form to provide feedback to teachers about the teaching and learning in the classroom. Consider each of the following:
   a. Teacher behavior
   b. Student behavior
   c. Classroom climate
   d. Teacher and principal attitudes
   e. Innovations
   f. Other important aspects of teaching and learning in the classroom

Then plan a discussion of your observations with the teacher. Be sure to describe the discussion in terms of its

a. Place—where will you talk with the teacher?

b. Structure—what will be the format and structure of your conversation?

c. Goals—what are the objectives and expected outcomes?

2. Prepare a 45-minute Parent-Teacher Organization talk about direct instruction.

a. Start by describing direct instruction.

b. Consider the pros and cons of direct instruction.

c. Contrast direct instruction with a constructivist approach to teaching.

d. Under what situations is each approach appropriate?

e. Propose and defend a balanced approach to teaching.

Remember you are speaking to parents as well as your teachers.

3. As principal, develop an induction plan for beginning teachers. Describe the elements of the plan, for example:

a. Mentors

b. In-service orientation

c. Recognition awards and activities

d. Rookie roundtables

e. Social activities

f. Relations with experienced teachers

g. Social and resource support

INSTRUCTIONAL LEADER'S TOOLBOX

Readings

Airasian, P. W., & Walsh, M. E. (1997). Constructivist cautions. *Phi Delta Kappan, 78*, 444–449.

Allington, R. L., & McGill-Franzen, A. (2003). The impact of the summer setback on the reading achievement gap. *Phi Delta Kappan, 85*(1), 68–75.

Anderson, L. W., & Krathwohl, D. R. (Eds.). (2001). *A taxonomy of teaching and learning: A revision of Bloom's taxonomy of educational objectives.* New York: Addison, Wesley, Longman.

Magnusson, S. J., & Palincsar, A. S. (1995). The learning environment as a site of science reform. *Theory into Practice, 34*, 43–50.

Nuthall, G., & Alton-Lee, A. (1990). Research on teaching and learning: Thirty years of change. *Elementary School Journal, 90*, 546–570.

Phi Delta Kappan. (January, 2006). Special section on "Math Education: Teaching for understanding," *87*, 356–376.

Phi Delta Kappan. (May, 2006). Special section on "Mathematics Education," *88*, 664–696.

Pressley, M. (1998). *Reading instruction that works: The case for balanced teaching.* New York: Guilford.

Sweller, J., Kirschner, P. A., & Clark, R. E. (2007). Why minimally guided teaching techniques do not work: A reply to commentaries. *Educational Psychologist, 42*, 115–121.

Videos

How to make homework more meaningful by involving parents, 15 minutes. Educational Consultant: Joyce Epstein.

Use homework to strengthen students' skills and make learning more meaningful. This video shows

1. Assignments that help students establish regular schedules, and demonstrate and discuss what they've learned

2. Strategies for initiating and encouraging family participation

3. Ways to follow-up assignments with class discussion and demonstration

Order from: Association for Supervision and Curriculum Development (ASCD), 125 N. West St., Alexandria, VA 22314-2798. Telephone: (703) 549-9110; FAX: (703) 549-3891. http://shop.ascd.org/category.cfm?categoryid=video

Websites

www.achieve.org/
Achieve, Inc.

www.free.ed.gov/
Federal Resources for Educational Excellence (FREE)

www.learningcommons.org/educators/library/gem.php
The Gateway to Educational Materials

www.nbpts.org/
National Board for Professional Teaching Standards

Organizations

www.aera.net
American Educational Research Association

www.cec.sped.org
Council for Exceptional Children (CEC)

www.reading.org
> International Reading Association (IRA)

www.nabe.org
> National Association for Bilingual Education

www.natcenscied.org/
> National Center for Science Education

www.ncss.org
> National Council for the Social Studies

www.ncte.org
> National Council of Teachers of English

www.nctm.org
> National Council of Teachers of Mathematics Standards

www.iste.org/standards
> National Educational Technology Standards for Teachers

www.nsta.org
> National Science Teachers Association

Classroom Management

PREVIEW: KEY POINTS

1. A main task of teaching is to enlist students' cooperation in activities that will lead to learning, and a first step in accomplishing this task is to organize the learning environment.

2. The goals of good classroom management are to make more time for learning, give all students access to learning, and support the development of self-management in students.

3. Research on effective elementary and secondary class managers shows that these teachers have carefully planned rules and procedures (including consequences) for their classes; they teach these rules and procedures early, using explanations, examples, practice, correction, and student involvement.

4. For many rule infractions, the logical consequence is "go back and do it right"; separate the deed from the doer—the problem is the behavior, not the student.

5. Once a good class environment is established, it must be maintained by encouraging student engagement and preventing management problems; "with-it-ness," overlapping, group focus, and movement management are the skills of good preventers.

6. There are several special procedures that may be helpful in maintaining positive management, including group consequences and functional assessment with behavior supports.

7. Research on discipline shows that African Americans and Latino Americans, especially males, are punished more often and more harshly than other students; consequently, these students lose time from learning as they spend time in detention or suspension. Culturally responsive classroom management might improve this situation.

8. When conflicts arise, teachers can deal more effectively with the situation if they first determine who "owns" the problem, then respond appropriately with empathetic listening or problem solving.

9. Conflicts between students, though potentially dangerous, can be the occasions for learning conflict negotiation and peer mediation strategies.

10. Communication between teacher and student is essential when problems arise; all interactions between people, even silence or neglect, communicate some meaning.

Leadership Challenge

You were hired in July as principal of Samuel Proctor Elementary School. This is your first job as principal after having been a teacher for six years. It is only the second week of school and you hear screaming when you are still halfway down the hall. "Give it back, it's MINE!" "No way—come and get it!" "I hate you!" A crashing sound follows as a table full of books hits the floor. You are surprised to hear one of your first-year teachers desperately trying to get control of the situation. You subsequently learn that the teacher has no management system—no order. Students walk around the room while the teacher is talking to the class, students interrupt when the teacher is working with a group, other students torment the class goldfish, and still others open their lunches (or other students') for a self-determined, mid-morning snack. Some students listen, but ask a million questions off the topic. Simply taking roll and introducing the first activity is a major project. Your new teacher is trying hard, but seems completely overwhelmed.

1. How would you approach the situation?
2. Which problem behaviors should the teacher tackle first?
3. Would giving rewards or administering punishments be useful in this situation? Why or why not? What specific suggestions would you give to this teacher?
4. What action would you take?

Organizing the Learning Environment

In study after study of the factors related to student achievement, classroom management stands out as the variable with the largest impact (Marzano & Marzano, 2003). Knowledge and expertise in classroom management are marks of expertise in teaching; stress and exhaustion from managerial difficulties are precursors of burnout in teaching (Emmer & Stough, 2001). What is it about classrooms that makes management so critical?

Classrooms are particular kinds of environments. They have distinctive features that influence their inhabitants no matter how the students or the desks are organized for learning or what the teacher believes about education (Doyle, 1986, 2006). Classrooms are *multidimensional*. They are crowded with people, tasks, and time pressures. Many individuals, all with differing goals, preferences, and abilities, must share resources, accomplish various tasks, use and reuse materials without losing them, move in and out of the room—the list goes on. And events occur *simultaneously*—everything happens at once. Teachers have literally hundreds of *fast-paced* exchanges with students every day. In this rapid-fire existence, events are *unpredictable*. Even when plans are carefully made and the demonstration is ready, the lesson can still be interrupted by a technology crash or a loud, angry discussion right outside the classroom. Because classrooms are *public*, the way the teacher handles these unexpected intrusions is seen and judged by all. Students are always noticing if the teacher is being "fair." What happens when a rule is broken? Finally, classrooms have *histories*. The meaning of a particular teacher's or student's actions depends in part on what has happened before. The fifteenth time a student arrives late requires a different response from the teacher than the first late arrival. In addition, the history of the first few weeks of school affects life in the class all year.

The Basic Task: Gain Their Cooperation

No productive activity can take place in a group without the cooperation of all members. This obviously applies to classrooms. Even if some students don't participate, they must allow others to do so. (We all have seen one or two students bring an entire class to a halt.) So the basic management task for teachers is to achieve order and harmony by gaining and maintaining student cooperation in class activities (Doyle, 2006). Given the multidimensional, simultaneous, fast-paced, unpredictable, public, and historical nature of classrooms, this is quite a challenge.

Gaining student cooperation means much more than dealing effectively with misbehavior. It means planning activities, having materials ready, making appropriate behavioral and academic demands on students, giving clear signals to students, accomplishing transitions smoothly, foreseeing problems and stopping them before they start, selecting and sequencing activities so that flow and interest are maintained, and much more. Also, different activities require different managerial skills. For example, loud student comments during a hip-hop reading of *Green Eggs and Ham* in an urban classroom may be indications of engagement and cooperation, not disorderly callouts (Doyle, 2006).

Obviously, gaining the cooperation of kindergartners is not the same task as gaining the cooperation of high school seniors. Jere Brophy and Carolyn Evertson (1978) identified four general stages of classroom management, defined by age-related needs. During kindergarten and the first few years of elementary school, children are learning how to go to school. They are being socialized into a new role. Direct teaching of classroom rules and procedures is important during this stage. Little learning will take place until the children master these basics. Children in the middle elementary years are usually familiar with the student role, even if they are not always perfect examples of it. Many school and classroom routines have become relatively automatic. Specific new rules and procedures for a particular activity may have to be taught directly, however. Still, at this stage teachers will spend more time monitoring and maintaining the management system than teaching it directly.

Toward the end of elementary school and the beginning of middle school, friendships and status within peer groups take on tremendous importance. Pleasing the teacher may be replaced by pleasing peers. Some students begin to test and defy authority. The management challenges at this stage are to deal productively with these disruptions and to motivate students who are becoming less concerned with teachers' opinions and more interested in their social lives. By the end of high school, the focus of most students returns to academics. By this time, unfortunately, many of the students with overwhelming behavioral problems have dropped out. At this stage the challenges are to manage the curriculum, fit academic material to students' interests and abilities, and help students become more self-managing in their learning. The first few classes each semester may be devoted to teaching particular procedures for using materials and equipment, or for keeping track of and submitting assignments. But most students know what is expected.

Managing the Learning Environment

The aim of **classroom management** is to maintain a positive, productive learning environment, relatively free of behavior problems. But order for its own sake is an empty goal. There are at least three reasons why management is important.

More Time for Learning. Almost every study examining time and learning has found a significant relationship between time spent on content and student learning (Berliner, 1988). If you time all the different activities throughout the school day, you might be surprised by how little actual teaching takes place. Many minutes each day are lost through interruptions, disruptions, late starts, and rough transitions (Karweit, 1989). So one important goal of classroom management is to expand the sheer number of minutes available for learning. This is sometimes called *allocated time*.

But simply making more time for learning will not automatically lead to achievement. To be valuable, time must be used effectively. Think back to Chapter 4. To learn, students must pay attention, process information, and practice their understanding. Time spent actively involved in specific learning tasks is often called *engaged time*, or sometimes **time on-task.** Again, however, engaged time doesn't guarantee learning. Students may be struggling with material that is too difficult or using the wrong learning strategies. When students are working with a high rate of success—really learning and understanding—the time spent is called **academic learning time.** Figure 7.1 shows how the 1,000+ hours of time mandated for school in most states can become only about 333 hours of quality academic learning time for a typical student. *Good class management increases academic learning time by keeping students actively engaged in worthwhile, appropriate learning activities.*

FIGURE 7.1   Who Knows Where the Time Goes?
The over 1,000 hours per year of instruction mandated by most states can represent only 300 or 400 hours of quality academic learning time.

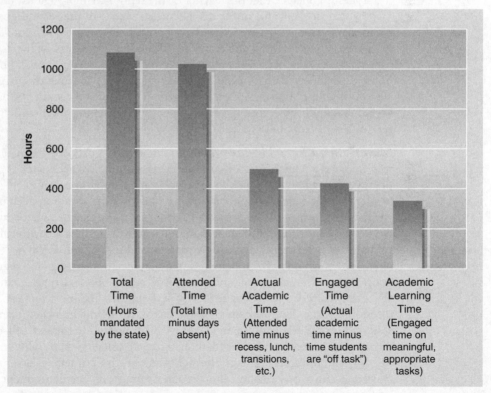

Source: From C. S. Weinstein and A. J. Mignano, Jr. *Elementary Classroom Management* (4th ed., p. 175). Published by McGraw-Hill. Copyright © 2007 by The McGraw-Hill Companies. Adapted with permission of The McGraw-Hill Companies.

Getting students engaged in learning early in their school careers can make a big difference. Several studies have shown that teachers' rating of students' on-task, persistent engagement in first grade predicts achievement test score gains and grades through fourth grade, as well as the decision to drop out of high school (Fredricks, Blumenfeld, & Paris, 2004).

Access to Learning.   Each classroom activity has its own rules for participation. Sometimes these rules are clearly stated by the teacher, but often they are implicit and unstated. And the differences are sometimes quite subtle. For example, in a reading group students may have to raise their hands to make a comment, but in a show-and-tell circle in the same class they may simply have to catch the teacher's eye. As we saw in Chapter 2, the rules defining who can talk; what they can talk about; and when, to whom, and how long they can talk are often called *participation structures.* In order to participate successfully in a given activity, students must understand the participation structure. The participation structures some students learn at home in interactions with family members do not match the participation structures of school activities. But teachers are not necessarily aware of this conflict. Instead, the teachers see that a child doesn't quite fit in, always seems to say the wrong thing at the wrong time, or is very reluctant to participate, and the teachers are not sure why. Often they blame the students for being disruptive or uncooperative, and the students conclude that the teacher or the school is simply against them.

What does this mean for management? To reach the second goal of good classroom management—giving all students access to learning—*you must make sure everyone knows how to participate in class activities.* The key is awareness. What are your rules and expectations? Are they understandable, given your students' cultural backgrounds and home experiences? What unspoken rules or values may be operating? Are your teachers clearly signaling appropriate ways to participate? For some students, particularly those with behavioral and emotional challenges, direct teaching and practicing of the important behaviors may be required (Emmer & Stough, 2001).

Management for Self-Management.   The third goal of any management system is to *help students become better able to manage themselves.* If teachers focus on student compliance, they will spend much of the teaching/learning time monitoring and correcting. Students come to see school as following rules, not constructing deep understanding of academic knowledge. And complex learning structures such as cooperative or problem-based learning require student **self-management.** Compliance with rules is not enough to make these learning structures work (McCaslin & Good, 1998).

The movement from demanding obedience to teaching self-regulation and self-control is a fundamental shift in discussions of classroom management today (Weinstein, 1999). Tom Savage (1999) says simply, "the most fundamental purpose of discipline is the development of self-control. Academic knowledge and technological skill will be of little consequence if those who possess them lack self-control" (p. 11). Through self-control, students demonstrate *responsibility*—the ability to fulfill their own needs without interfering with the rights and needs of others (Glasser, 1990). Students learn self-control by making choices and dealing with the consequences, setting goals and priorities, managing time, collaborating to learn, mediating disputes and making peace, and developing trusting relations with trustworthy teachers and classmates (Bear, 2005; Rogers & Freiberg, 1994).

Encouraging **self-management** requires extra time, but teaching students how to take responsibility is an investment well worth the effort. When elementary and secondary teachers have very effective class management systems but neglect to set student self-management as a goal, their students often find that they have trouble working independently after they graduate from these "well-managed" classes.

Creating a Positive Learning Environment: Some Research Results

What can teachers do to be good managers? For several years, researchers at the University of Texas at Austin examined classroom management quite thoroughly (Emmer & Stough, 2001; Emmer, Evertson, & Anderson, 1980; Emmer & Gerwels, 2006). Their general approach was to study a large number of classrooms, making frequent observations the first weeks of school and less-frequent visits later in the year. After several months there were dramatic differences among the classes. Some had very few management problems, while others had many. The most and least effective teachers were identified based on the quality of classroom management and student achievement in their classrooms later in the year.

Next, the researchers looked at their observation records of the first weeks of class to see how the effective teachers got started. Other comparisons were made between the teachers who ultimately had harmonious, high-achieving classes and those whose classes were fraught with problems. On the basis of these comparisons, management principles were developed. The researchers then taught these principles to a new group of teachers; the results were quite positive. Teachers who applied the principles had fewer problems; their students spent more time learning and less time disrupting; and achievement was higher. The findings of these studies are detailed in two books on classroom management (Emmer, Evertson, & Worsham, 2006; Evertson, Emmer, & Worsham, 2006). Many of the ideas in the following pages are from these books.

Rules and Procedures

At the elementary school level, teachers must lead 20 to 30 students of varying abilities through many different activities each day. Without efficient rules and procedures, a great deal of time is wasted answering the same question over and over. "My pencil broke. How can I do my math?" "I'm finished with my story. What should I do now?" "Jason hit me!" At the secondary school level, teachers must deal daily with over 100 students who use dozens of materials and often change rooms for each class. Secondary school students are also more likely to challenge teachers' authority. The effective managers studied by Emmer and Evertson and their respective colleagues (2006) had planned procedures and rules for coping with these situations.

Procedures.   How will materials and assignments be distributed and collected? Under what conditions can students leave the room? How will grades be determined? What are the special routines for handling equipment and supplies in science, art, or vocational classes? **Procedures** describe how activities are accomplished in classrooms, but they are seldom written down; they are simply the ways of getting things done in class. Weinstein (2007) and Weinstein and Mignano (2007) suggest that teachers establish procedures to cover the following areas:

1. Administrative routines, such as taking attendance
2. Student movement, such as entering and leaving or going to the bathroom
3. Housekeeping, such as watering plants or storing personal items
4. Routines for accomplishing lessons, such as how to collect assignments or return homework
5. Interactions between teacher and student, such as how to get the teacher's attention when help is needed
6. Talk among students, such as giving help or socializing

If teachers, particularly beginning teachers, are having trouble with class management, check these six areas. You might use these six areas as a framework for helping teachers think through their procedures and routines. The Theory into Action Guidelines should help principals coach their teachers.

Rules.   Statements specifying the expected and forbidden actions in class are called **rules.** They are the dos and don'ts of classroom life. Unlike procedures, rules are often written down and posted. The rules teachers set should be consistent with school rules, and also in keeping with principles of learning. For example, we know from the research on small-group learning that students benefit when they explain work to peers. They learn as they talk and teach. A rule that forbids students to help each other may be inconsistent with good learning principles. Or a rule that says, "No erasures when writing" may make students focus more on preventing mistakes than on communicating clearly in their writing (Burden, 1995; Weinstein & Mignano, 2007). Having a few general rules that cover many specifics is better than listing all the dos and don'ts. But, if specific actions are forbidden, such as chewing gum in class or smoking in the bathrooms, then a rule should make this clear (Emmer & Gerwels, 2006).

Rules for Elementary School.   Evertson and her colleagues (2006) give five examples of general rules for elementary school classes:

1. *Be polite and helpful.* This applies to behavior toward adults (including substitute teachers) and children. Examples of polite behavior include waiting your turn, saying "please" and "thank you," and not fighting or calling names.

2. *Respect other people's property.* This might include picking up litter; returning library books; not marking on walls, desks, or buses; and getting permission before using other people's things.

3. *Listen quietly while others are speaking.* This applies to the teacher and other students, in large-class lessons or small-group discussions.

4. *Do not hit, shove, or hurt others.* Make sure you give clear explanations of what you mean by "hurt." Does this apply to hurt feelings as well as hurt bodies?

5. *Obey all school rules.* This reminds students that all school rules apply in every classroom. Then students cannot claim, for example, that they thought it was okay to

THEORY INTO ACTION GUIDELINES

Rules and Procedures

Determine procedures for student upkeep of desks, classroom equipment, and other facilities.

Examples

1. Some teachers set aside a cleanup time each day or once a week in self-contained classes.
2. You might demonstrate and have students practice how to push chairs under the desk, take and return materials stored on shelves, sharpen pencils, use the sink or water fountain, assemble lab equipment, and so on.
3. In some classes a rotating monitor is in charge of equipment or materials.

Decide how students will be expected to enter and leave the room.

Examples

1. How will students know what they should do as soon as they enter the room? Some teachers have a standard assignment ("Have your homework out and be checking it over" or "Do the problem of the day").
2. Under what conditions can students leave the room? When do they need permission?
3. If students are late, how do they gain admission to the room?
4. Many teachers require students to be in their seats and quiet before they can leave at the end of class. The teacher, not the bell, dismisses class.

Establish a signal and teach it to your students.

Examples

1. In the classroom, some teachers flick the lights, sound a chord on a piano or recorder, move to the podium and stare silently at the class, use a phrase like "Eyes, please," take out their grade books, or move to the front of the class.

2. In the halls, a raised hand, one clap, or some other signal may mean "Stop."
3. On the playground, a raised hand or whistle may mean "Line up."

Set procedures for student participation in class.

Examples

1. Will you have students raise their hands for permission to speak or simply require that they wait until the speaker has finished?
2. How will you signal that you want everyone to respond at once? Some teachers raise a cupped hand to their ear. Others preface the question with "Everyone. . . ."
3. Make sure you are clear about differences in procedures for different activities: reading group, learning center, discussion, teacher presentation, seatwork, film, peer learning group, library, and so forth.
4. How many students at a time can be at the pencil sharpener, teacher's desk, learning center, sink, bookshelves, reading corner, or bathroom?

Determine how you will communicate, collect, and return assignments.

Examples

1. Some teachers reserve a particular corner of the board for listing assignments. Others write assignments in colored chalk. For younger students it may be better to prepare assignment sheets or folders, color-coding them for math workbook, reading packet, and science kit.
2. Some teachers collect assignments in a box or bin; others have a student collect work while they introduce the next activity.

For ideas about involving students in developing rules and procedures, see www.educationworld .com/a_lesson/lesson/lesson274.shtml

---

chew gum or listen to a radio in your class, even though these are against school rules, "because you never made a rule against it for us."

Whatever the rule, students need to be taught the behaviors that the rule includes and excludes. Examples, practice, and discussion will be needed before learning is complete. Many teachers you work with may think that their jobs are done when the rule is made or posted, then wonder why there are so many problems. Chances are that these teachers have not taught and practiced the rules. And, as you've seen, different activities often require different rules. This can be confusing for elementary students until they have thoroughly learned all the rules. To prevent confusion, some teachers have signs that list the rules for each activity. Then, before the activity, they post the appropriate sign (and early in the year, review the rules) as a reminder. This provides clear and consistent cues about participation structures so all students know what is expected. Of course, these rules must be explained, discussed, and practiced before the signs can have their full effect.

Rules for Secondary School. Emmer and colleagues (2006) suggest six examples of rules for secondary students:

1. *Bring all needed materials to class.* The teacher must specify the type of pen, pencil, paper, notebook, texts, and so on.

2. *Be in your seat and ready to work when the bell rings.* Many teachers combine this rule with a standard beginning procedure for the class, such as a warm-up exercise on the board or a requirement that students have paper with a proper heading ready when the bell rings.

3. *Respect and be polite to everyone.* This covers fighting, verbal abuse, and general troublemaking.

4. *Respect other people's property.* This means property belonging to the school, the teacher, or other students.

5. *Listen and stay seated while someone else is speaking.* This applies when the teacher or other students are talking.

6. *Obey all school rules.* As with the elementary class rules, this covers many behaviors and situations, so teachers do not have to repeat every school rule for their class. It also reminds the students that their teachers will be monitoring them inside and outside class.

Consequences. As soon as your teachers decide on rules and procedures, they must consider what they will do when a student breaks a rule or does not follow a procedure. It is too late to make this decision after the rule has been broken. For many infractions, the logical consequence is "go back and do it right." Students who run in the hall may have to return to where they started and walk properly. Incomplete papers can be redone. Materials left out should be put back (Charles, 2002b). Teachers can use natural or logical consequences to help students take responsibility by doing the following (Elias & Schwab, 2006):

- Separate the deed from the doer—the problem is the behavior, not the student.
- Emphasize to students that they have the power to choose their actions and avoid losing control.
- Encourage student reflection, self-evaluation, and problem solving—avoid teacher lecturing.

■ Help students identify and give a rationale for what they could do differently next time in a similar situation.

Sometimes consequences are more complicated. In their case studies of four expert elementary school teachers, Weinstein and Mignano (2007) found that the teachers' negative consequences fell into seven categories, as shown in Table 7.1. The main point here is that decisions about penalties (and rewards) must be made early on, so students know before they break a rule or use the wrong procedure what this will mean for them.

But there is a strong caution. Consequences, no matter how thoughtfully determined, will not prevent problems or guarantee learning. A consequence will work only when the students care about their relationship with the teacher or administrator asking them to follow the rules, or when the students see some value in what they are asked to do (Bodine & Crawford, 1999; Vitto, 2003). Vitto (2003) lists seven questions to judge the value of the consequences in your school:

TABLE 7.1 Seven Categories of Penalties for Students

1. *Expressions of disappointment.* If students like and respect their teacher, then a serious, sorrowful expression of disappointment may cause students to stop and think about their behavior.
2. *Loss of privileges.* Students can lose free time. If they have not completed homework, for example, they can be required to do it during a free period or recess.
3. *Time-out: Exclusion from the group.* Students who distract their peers or fail to cooperate can be separated from the group until they are ready to cooperate. Some teachers give a student a pass for 10 to 15 minutes. The student must go to another class or study hall, where the other students and teachers ignore the offending student for that time.
4. *Written reflections on the problem.* Students can write in journals, write essays about what they did and how it affected others, or write letters of apology—if this is appropriate. Another possibility is to ask students to describe objectively what they did; then the teacher and the student can sign and date this statement. These records are available if parents or administrators need evidence of the students' behavior.
5. *Visits to the principal's office.* Expert teachers tend to use this penalty rarely, but they do use it when the situation warrants. Some schools require students to be sent to the office for certain offenses, such as fighting. If a student is told to go to the office and refuses, the teacher might call the office saying the student has been sent. Then the student has the choice of either going to the office or facing the principal's penalty for "disappearing" on the way.
6. *Detentions.* Detentions can be very brief meetings after school, during a free period, or at lunch. The main purpose is to talk about what has happened. (In high school, detentions are often used as punishments; suspensions and expulsions are available as more extreme measures.)
7. *Contacting parents.* If problems become a repeated pattern, most teachers contact the student's family. This is done to seek support for helping the student, not to blame the parents or punish the student.

Source: From C. S. Weinstein and A. J. Mignano, Jr. *Elementary Classroom Management* (4th ed., pp. 350–352). Published by McGraw-Hill. Copyright © 2007 by The McGraw-Hill Companies. Adapted with permission of the McGraw-Hill Companies.

1. Does the consequence bring the teacher and student closer together or create distance in the relationship?
2. Would the consequence encourage the teacher to change his or her behavior?
3. Does the consequence and the way it is delivered model the prosocial skills that the teacher wants the student to possess?
4. Does the consequence instruct or teach appropriate behavior?
5. Does the consequence interfere with the flow of the lesson?
6. Does the consequence give the learner the choice to redirect and receive instruction?
7. Is the consequence effective? (p. 147)

Who Sets the Rules and Consequences?   Not all rules have to be stated as rules. For example, Ken, the fifth/sixth-grade teacher described in Chapter 6, works with his students to develop his class rules at the beginning of the year. Rather than specifying dos and don'ts, Ken and his students devise a "Bill of Rights" for the class, describing the rights of the students and of the teacher. These rights cover most of the situations that might need a "rule." In recent years, when Ken has had some very difficult classes, he and his students have had to establish some "laws" that protect students' rights. The rights and laws for one recent year's class are listed in Table 7.2. Developing rights and responsibilities rather than rules makes a very important point to students. "Teaching children that something is wrong *because there is a rule against it* is not the same as teaching them that there is a rule against it *because it is wrong*, and helping them to understand why this is so" (Weinstein, 1999, p. 154). Students should understand that the rules are developed so that everyone can live and learn together.

If your teachers are going to involve students in setting rules or creating a constitution, they may need to wait until they have established a sense of community in their classrooms, described in a later section of this chapter. Before students can contribute meaningfully to the class rules, they need to trust the teacher and the situation (Elias & Schwab, 2006).

Planning for Computer Uses

Many classrooms today have computers. Some classes have only one, others have several, and some classes are labs with a computer for every student. Using computers productively brings with it management challenges. Computers can be used to connect to powerful knowledge bases around the world; as tools for writing, drawing, calculating, and designing; to simulate scientific experiments or life in other times and places; to collaborate and communicate with people across the hall or across the ocean; to publish work or make presentations; and to keep track of appointments, assignments, or grades. To get the greatest benefits from computers in their classrooms, teachers must have good management systems. Table 7.3 on page 242 summarizes strategies for managing computer labs.

Most classrooms will not have a computer for every student. In fact, many have only one computer or none at all. The Theory into Action Guidelines for using computers in regular classrooms are on page 243.

TABLE 7.2 A Bill of Rights for Students and Laws to Protect those Rights

MR. KOWALSKI'S CLASS'S BILL OF RIGHTS

The right to be treated nicely, politely, respectfully, fairly, kindly, welcomed, equally.
The right to whisper when the teacher isn't talking.
The right to a two-minute break between work periods.
The right to have choices about the day's schedule.
The right to work and learn without being bothered.
The right to talk to the class without anyone else talking.
The right to choose a table.
The right to privacy.
The right to be comfortable.
The right not to have people take your things.
The right to play with anyone during recess.
The right to a snack every day.
The right to stand up for others.
The right to apologies.
The right to learn.
The right to make mistakes.
The right not to be copied.
The right to ask for help.
The right to ask questions.
The right to have fun while learning.
The right to have silence.
The right to work independently.
The right to study.
The right to have feelings.
The right to help other people at the right time.
The right to chew gum without blowing bubbles or making a mess.
The right to go outside almost every day.

LAWS TO PROTECT OUR RIGHTS

1. Follow directions the first time.
2. Speak nicely, be courteous, and respect other people, their feelings and their things. Follow the Bill of Rights.
3. Laugh at the right time for the right time.
4. Respect others' right to learn. Do not distract others. Don't be nosy. Don't yell. Remember to get quiet at countdown.
5. Talk at the right times with the right tone of voice and volume.
6. Transitions and movements are calm, quiet, careful and elegant.
7. Follow all classroom and school procedures, like: bathroom; pencil; lunch and recess; morning; dismissal; and . . .

Source: From C. S. Weinstein and A. J. Mignano, Jr. *Elementary Classroom Management* (4th ed., pp. 115–116). Published by McGraw-Hill. Copyright © 2007 by The McGraw-Hill Companies. Adapted with permission of The McGraw-Hill Companies.

TABLE 7.3   Tips for Managing a Computer Lab

All these ideas are from Cheryl Bolick and James Cooper (2006)

- Always run through a technology lesson *before* presenting it to the class—and always have a back-up lesson prepared in case the technology fails.
- Type directions for frequently used computer operations—opening programs, inserting clip art, printing documents, and so on—on index cards, laminate them, and connect them with a circle ring. Keep a set next to each computer.
- Have students turn *off* their monitors when you're giving directions.
- Appoint classroom technology managers. Consider an Attendance Manager, who takes attendance and serves as a substitute teacher helper when necessary; a Materials Manager, who passes out materials and runs errands; a Technical Manager, who helps resolve printer and computer issues; and an End-of-Class Manager, who makes sure work areas are neat—keyboards pushed in, mice straight, and programs closed—before students are dismissed.
- If you have classes filtering in and out of a computer lab each day and have little or no time to set up between classes, arrange for older students to help. Simply end your lesson five minutes early and walk the older students through the process of setting up for the next class.
- When working on lengthy technology projects, print out step-by-step instructions. Include some that say "Save your work; do not go any further until you help your neighbors reach this point." This helps less-proficient students solve problems more quickly, keeps the class at roughly the same point in the project, and fosters collaborative learning.
- Make it a class rule that students can help one another but cannot ever touch another student's computer. That way, you can be sure that learning occurs even when students help one another.
- Keep a red plastic cup at each computer. When students need help, have them place the highly visible cups on top of their monitors.
- Before students leave class, have them turn their mice upside down so the trackballs are showing. You'll lose fewer trackballs that way.
- Place different colored sticker dots on the left and the right bottom corners of each monitor. Use these to indicate which side of the screen you are talking about—very helpful when using certain programs, such as the new Kid Pix—and to determine whose turn it is if students share a computer.
- Plug all speakers into a main power bar. Turn the bar off when you're teaching and turn it on when students are working. If the room becomes too noisy, turn off the power bar to get students' attention.
- Use a Video Out card to project a monitor display onto a television screen.
- Type PLEASE WAIT FOR INSTRUCTIONS on 8 by 11 papers, laminate them, and tape one sheet to the top of every monitor. Students flip the signs to the back of the monitor *after* you've given directions.
- Create a folder in the Start menu and place any programs you use with students in that folder. Students never have to click Programs—everything they use is in one folder.
- When working in a computer lab, assign each student a computer. Students can line up in "computer lab order" in their classrooms. Seating goes very quickly when they get to the lab.
- If you're working on a network, ask your technology coordinator to set up a shared folder for Internet resources. Then, when you're planning an Internet lesson, simply save a shortcut to the Web site in that folder. During lab time, students can go to the shared folder, double click the link, and go right to the site without typing the URL. This saves time and stress for both students and teachers.

Source: From "Tips for Managing a Computer Lab, " from Cheryl Mason Bolick and J. M. Cooper, 2006. "Classroom Management and Technology," in C. Evertson and C. Weinstein (Eds.), *Handbook of Classroom Management: Research, Practice, and Contemporary Issues (Paper)*. Copyright 2006 by Taylor & Francis Group LLC - Books. Reproduced with permission of Taylor & Francis Group LLC - Books in the format Textbook via Copyright Clearance Center and Cheryl Mason Bolick, Ph.D.

THEORY INTO ACTION GUIDELINES

Using Computers: Management Issues

If you have only one computer in your classroom: Provide convenient access.

Examples

1. Find a central location if the computer is used to display material for the class.
2. Find a spot on the side of the room that allows seating and view of the screen, but does not crowd or disturb other students if the computer is used as a workstation for individuals or small groups.

Be prepared

Examples

1. Check to be sure software needed for a lesson or an assignment is installed and working.
2. Make sure instructions for using the software or doing the assignment are in an obvious place and clear.
3. Provide checklist for completing assignments.

Create "trained experts" to help with computers.

Examples

1. Train student experts and rotate experts.
2. Use adult volunteers—parents, grandparents, or older siblings.

Develop systems for using the computer.

Examples

1. Make up a schedule to ensure that all students have access to the computer and no students monopolize the time.
2. Create standard ways of saving student work.

If you have more than one computer in your classroom: Plan the arrangement of the computers to fit your instructional goals.

Examples

1. For cooperative groups, arrange so students can cluster around their group's computer.
2. For different projects at different computer stations, allow for easy rotation from station to station.

Experiment with other models for using computers.

Examples

1. *Navigator Model*—4 students per computer: One student is the (mouse and keyboard) driver, another is the "navigator." "Back-seat driver 1" manages the group's progress and "back-seat driver 2" serves as the timekeeper. The navigator attends a 10-minute to 20-minute training session in which the facilitator provides an overview of the basics of particular software. Navigators cannot touch the mouse. Driver roles are rotated.
2. *Facilitator Model*—6 students per computer: the facilitator has more experience, expertise, or training—serves as the guide or teacher.
3. *Collaborative Group Model*—7 students per computer: Each small group is responsible for creating some component of the whole group's final product. For example, one part of the group writes a report, another creates a map, and a third uses the computer to gather and graph census data.

For more ideas, see www.internet4classrooms.com/one_computer.htm

Getting Started: The First Weeks of Class

Determining rules and procedures are first steps toward having a well-managed class, but how do effective teachers gain students' cooperation in those first critical days and weeks? One study carefully analyzed the first weeks' activities of effective and ineffective elementary teachers, and found striking differences (Emmer, Evertson, & Anderson, 1980).

Effective Classroom Managers
for Elementary Students

In the effective teachers' classrooms, the very first day was well organized. Name tags were ready. There was something interesting for each child to do right away. Materials were set up. The teachers had planned carefully to avoid any last-minute tasks that might take them away from their students. These teachers dealt with the children's pressing concerns first. "Where do I put my things? How do I pronounce my teacher's name? Can I whisper to my neighbor? Where is the bathroom?" The effective teachers had a workable, easily understood set of rules and taught the students the most important rules right away. They taught the rules like any other subject, with lots of explanation, examples, and practice.

Throughout the first weeks, the effective managers continued to spend quite a bit of time teaching rules and procedures. Some used guided practice to teach procedures; others used rewards to shape behavior. Most taught students to respond to a bell or some other signal to gain their attention. These teachers worked with the class as a whole on enjoyable academic activities. They did not rush to get students into small groups or to get them started in readers. This whole-class work gave the teachers a better opportunity to continue monitoring all students' learning of the rules and procedures. Misbehavior was stopped quickly and firmly, but not harshly.

In the poorly managed classrooms, the first weeks were quite different. Rules were not workable; they were either too vague or very complicated. For example, one teacher made a rule that students should "be in the right place at the right time." Students were not told what this meant, so their behavior could not be guided by the rule. Neither positive nor negative behaviors had clear, consistent consequences. After students broke a rule, ineffective managers might give a vague criticism, such as "Some of my children are too noisy," or issue a warning, but not follow through with the threatened consequence.

In the poorly managed classes, procedures for accomplishing routine tasks varied from day to day and were never taught or practiced. Instead of dealing with these obvious needs, ineffective managers spent time on procedures that could have waited. For example, one teacher had the class practice for a fire drill the first day, but left unexplained other procedures that would be needed every day. Students wandered aimlessly and had to ask each other what they should be doing. Often the students talked to one another because they had nothing productive to do. Ineffective teachers frequently left the room. Many became absorbed in paperwork or in helping just one student. They had not made plans for how to deal with late-arriving students or interruptions. One ineffective manager tried to teach students to respond to a bell as a signal for attention, but later let the students ignore it. All in all, the first weeks in these classrooms were disorganized and filled with surprises for teachers and students alike.

Effective Classroom Managers for
Secondary Students

What about getting started in a secondary school class? It appears that many of the differences between effective and ineffective elementary school teachers hold at the secondary level as well. Again, effective managers focus on establishing rules, procedures, and expectations on the first day of class. These standards for academic work and class behavior are clearly communicated to students and consistently enforced during the first weeks of class. Student behavior is closely monitored, and infractions of the rules are dealt with quickly. In classes with lower-ability students, work cycles are shorter; students are not required to spend long, unbroken periods on one type of activity. Instead, during each period they are moved smoothly through several different tasks. In general, effective teachers carefully follow each student's progress, so students cannot avoid work without facing consequences (Emmer & Evertson, 1982).

With all this close monitoring and consistent enforcement of the rules, you may wonder if effective secondary teachers have to be grim and humorless. As any experienced teacher knows, there is much more to smile about when the class is cooperative. In fact, there is another requirement for getting started, one that was evident in the class run by the "class constitution"; establishing a climate of trust and respect that creates a community for learning.

Creating a Learning Community

Nel Noddings (1992, 1995) has written about the need to create caring educational environments where students take more responsibility for governing their school and classroom. As we saw in Chapter 5 when we discussed the need for social support, students are more intrinsically motivated when they feel that their teachers care about them (Grolnick, Ryan, & Deci, 1991). Historically, however, U.S. schools have emphasized regulating students' behavior through rules, not through relationships. But this is not true in every culture. For example, in the book, *Learning to Teach in Two Cultures*, Shimahara and Sakai (1995) observe that the Japanese approach to classroom management emphasizes such interpersonal bonds as emotional ties, relationships, and character. Success of the Japanese system "does not depend on many rules, but on a sense of trust and interdependency between the classroom teacher and his or her students and among the students" (Shimahara & Sakai, 1995, p. 79).

One approach to developing this kind of caring and mutually trusting community is David and Roger Johnson's "Three Cs" of school and classroom management. The three Cs for safe and productive schools are cooperative community, constructive conflict resolution, and civic values (Johnson & Johnson, 1999b). Classroom management begins by establishing a learning community based on cooperative approaches such as those described in Chapter 4. At the heart of the community is the idea of positive interdependence—individuals working together to achieve mutual goals. Constructive conflict resolution is essential in the community because conflicts are inevitable and even necessary for learning. Piaget's theory of development and the research on conceptual change teaching tell us that true learning requires cognitive conflict. And individuals trying to exist in groups will have interpersonal conflict—these can lead to learning too. Table 7.4 on the next page shows how academic and interpersonal conflicts can be positive forces in a learning community. At the end of this chapter we will talk more about conflict resolution in schools.

The last C is civic values: the understandings and beliefs that hold the community together. Values are learned through direct teaching, modeling, literature, group discussions, the sharing of concerns. Some teachers have a "Concerns Box," where

TABLE 7.4　Academic and Interpersonal Conflict and Learning

Conflict, if handled well, can support learning. Academic conflicts can lead to critical thinking and conceptual change. Conflicts of interest are unavoidable, but can be handled so no one is the loser.

Academic Controversy	Conflicts of Interest
One person's ideas, information, theories, conclusions, and opinions are incompatible with those of another, and the two seek to reach an agreement.	The actions of one person attempting to maximize benefits prevents, blocks or interferes with another person maximizing her or his benefits.
Controversy Procedure	*Integrative (Problem-Solving) Negotiations*
Research and prepare positions	Describe wants
Present and advocate positions	Describe feelings
Refute opposing position and refute attacks on own position	Describe reasons for wants and feelings Take other's perspective
Reverse perspectives	Invent three optional agreements that maximize joint outcomes
Synthesize and integrate best evidence and reasoning from all sides	Choose one and formalize agreement

Source: From "The Three Cs of School and Classroom Management," by D. Johnson and R. Johnson, 1999, in H. J. Freiberg (Ed.), *Beyond Behaviorism: Changing the Classroom Management Paradigm* (p. 133), Boston: Allyn & Bacon.

students can put written concerns and comments. The box is opened once a week at a class meeting and the concerns are discussed. Johnson and Johnson (1999b) give an example of a class meeting about respect. One student tells her classmates that she felt hurt during recess the day before because no one listened when she was trying to teach them the rules to a new game. The students discussed what it means to be respectful and why respect is important. Then the students shared personal experiences of times when they felt respected versus not respected.

Maintaining a Good Learning Environment

A good start is just that, a beginning. Effective teachers build on this beginning. They maintain their management system by preventing problems and keeping students engaged in productive learning activities.

Encouraging Engagement

The format of a lesson affects student involvement. In general, as teacher supervision increases, students' engaged time also increases. For example, Frick (1990) found that elementary students working directly with a teacher were on-task 97% of the time, while students working on their own were on-task only 57% of the time. This does not mean that teachers should eliminate independent work for students. It simply means that this type of activity usually requires careful monitoring.

Activities with clear steps are likely to be more absorbing because one step leads naturally to the next. When students have all the materials they need to complete a task, they tend to stay involved. If their curiosity is piqued, students will be motivated to continue seeking an answer. And students tend to be more engaged if they are involved in authentic tasks, activities that have connections to real life. Also, activities are more engaging when the level of challenge is higher and when students' interests are incorporated (Emmer & Gerwels, 2006).

Of course, teachers can't supervise every student all the time or rely on curiosity. Something else must keep students working on their own. In their study of elementary and secondary teachers, Evertson, Emmer, and their colleagues found that effective class managers at both levels had well-planned systems for encouraging accountability so that students managed their own work (Emmer et al., 2006; Evertson et al., 2006). The Theory into Action Guidelines should help principals and teachers plan strategies for effective classroom management.

THEORY INTO ACTION GUIDELINES

Encouraging Student Accountability

Make basic work requirements clear.

Examples

1. Specify and post the routine work requirements for headings, paper size, pen or pencil use, and neatness.
2. Establish and explain rules about late or incomplete work and absences. If a pattern of incomplete work begins to develop, deal with it early; speak with parents if necessary.
3. Make due dates reasonable, and stick to them unless the student has a very good excuse for lateness.

Communicate the specifics of assignments.

Examples

1. With younger students, have a routine procedure for giving assignments, such as writing them on the board in the same place each day. With older students, assignments may be dictated, posted, or given in a syllabus.
2. Remind students of coming assignments.
3. With complicated assignments, give students a sheet describing what to do, what resources are available, due dates, and so on. Older students should also be told about grading criteria.
4. Demonstrate how to do the assignment, do the first few questions together, or provide a sample worksheet.

Monitor work in progress.

Examples

1. When you make an assignment in class, make sure each student gets started correctly. If you check only students who raise their hands for help, you will miss those who think they know what to do but don't really understand, those who are too shy to ask for help, and those who don't plan to do the work at all.
2. Check progress periodically. In discussions, make sure everyone has a chance to respond.

Give frequent academic feedback.

Examples

1. Elementary students should get papers back the day after they are handed in.
2. Good work can be displayed in class and graded papers sent home to parents each week.
3. Students of all ages can keep records of grades, projects completed, and extra credits earned.
4. For older students break up long-term assignments into several phases, giving feedback at each point.

Prevention Is the Best Medicine

What else can teachers do to maintain their management systems? The ideal way to manage problems, of course, is to prevent them in the first place. In a classic study, Jacob Kounin (1970) examined classroom management by comparing effective teachers, whose classes were relatively free of problems, with ineffective teachers, whose classes were continually plagued by chaos and disruption. Observing both groups in action, Kounin found that they were not very different in the way they handled discipline once problems arose. The difference was that the successful managers were much better at preventing problems. Kounin concluded that effective classroom managers were especially skilled in four areas: "with-it-ness," overlapping activities, group focusing, and movement management. More recent research confirms the importance of these factors (Evertson, 1988; Larrivee, 2005).

With-it-ness.   It is important for teachers to demonstrate **with-it-ness,** communicating to students that they are aware of everything that is happening in the classroom, that they aren't missing anything. "With-it" teachers avoid becoming absorbed or interacting with only a few students because this encourages the rest of the class to wander. They are always scanning the room, making eye contact with individual students, so the students know they are being monitored.

These teachers prevent minor disruptions from becoming major. They also know who instigated the problem, and they make sure the right people are dealt with. In other words, they do not make what Kounin (1970) called *timing errors* (waiting too long before intervening) or *target errors* (blaming the wrong student and letting the real perpetrators escape responsibility for their behavior). If two problems occur at the same time, effective managers deal with the more serious one first. For example, a teacher who tells two students to stop whispering but ignores even a brief shoving match at the pencil sharpener communicates to students a lack of awareness (Larrivee, 2005; Woolfolk, 2008).

Overlapping and Group Focus.   Effective teachers are good at **overlapping:** keeping track of and supervising several activities at the same time. For example, a teacher may have to check the work of an individual and at the same time keep a small group working by saying, "Right, go on," and stop an incident in another group with a quick "look" or reminder (Burden, 1995; Charles, 2005).

Maintaining a **group focus** means keeping as many students as possible involved in appropriate class activities and avoiding narrowing in on just one or two students. All students should have something to do during a lesson. For example, the teacher might ask everyone to write the answer to a question, then call on individuals to respond while the other students compare their answers. Choral responses might be required while the teacher moves around the room to make sure everyone is participating. Some teachers have their students use small blackboards or colored cards for responding in groups. This lets the teacher check for understanding as well. For example, during a grammar lesson the teacher might say, "Everyone who thinks the answer is 'have run,' hold up the red side of your card. If you think the answer is 'has run,' hold up the green side" (Hunter, 1982). This is one way teachers can ensure that all students are involved and check that they all understand the material.

Movement Management.   **Movement management** means keeping lessons and the group moving at an appropriate (and flexible) pace, with smooth transitions and variety. The effective teacher avoids abrupt transitions, such as announcing a new activity before gaining the students' attention or starting a new activity in the middle of something else. In these situations, one-third of the class will be doing the new activity, many will be working on the old lesson, several will be asking other students what to do, some will be taking the opportunity to have a little fun, and most will be confused. Another transition problem Kounin (1970) noted is the *slowdown*, or taking too much time to start a new activity. Sometimes teachers give too many directions. Problems also arise when teachers have students work one at a time while the rest of the class waits and watches.

A teacher who successfully demonstrates with-it-ness, overlapping activities, group focus, and movement management tends to have a class filled with actively engaged students who do not escape his or her all-seeing eye. This need not be a grim classroom. It is more likely a busy place where students are actively learning and gaining a sense of self-worth rather than misbehaving in order to get attention and achieve status.

Student Social Skills as Prevention.   But what about the students? What can they do? When students lack social and emotional skills such as sharing materials, reading the intentions of others, or handling frustration, classroom management problems often follow. So all efforts to teach social and emotional self-regulation are steps for preventing management problems. Over the short term, educators can teach and model these skills, then give students feedback and practice using them in a variety of settings. Over the long term, teachers can help to change attitudes that value aggression over cooperation and compromise (Elias & Schwab, 2006).

Caring Relationships: Connections with School.   When students and teachers have positive, trusting relationships, many management problems are prevented. Students respect teachers who maintain their authority without being rigid, harsh, or unfair and who use creative instructional practices to "make learning fun." Students also value teachers who show academic and personal caring by acting like real people (not just as teachers), sharing responsibility, minimizing the use of external controls, including everyone, searching for students' strengths, communicating effectively, and showing an interest in their students' lives and pursuits (Elias & Schwab, 2006; Woolfolk Hoy & Weinstein, 2006). All efforts at building positive relationships and classroom community are steps toward preventing management problems. Students who feel connected with school are happier, more self-disciplined, and less likely to engage in dangerous behaviors such as substance abuse, violence, and early sexual activity (Freiberg, 2006; McNeely, Nonnemaker, & Blum, 2002).

Dealing with Discipline Problems

Every year since 1969, *Phi Delta Kappa* has published the annual Gallup Poll of the public's attitude toward public schools. From 1969 to 1999, almost every year the public identified "lack of discipline" as the number one problem facing the schools (Rose & Gallup, 1999). Since 1999, lack of funds has taken over as the top perceived problem, but lack of discipline continues to be second. Clearly, the public sees discipline as an important challenge for teachers.

Being an effective manager does not mean publicly correcting every minor infraction of the rules. This kind of public attention may actually reinforce the misbehavior. Teachers who frequently correct students do not necessarily have the best-behaved classes (Irving & Martin, 1982). The key is to know what is happening and what is important so you can prevent problems.

Most students comply quickly when the teacher gives a desist (a "stop doing that") or redirects behavior. But some students are the targets of more than their share of desists. One study found that these disruptive students seldom complied with the first teacher request to stop. Often the disruptive students responded negatively, leading to an average of 4 to 5 cycles of teacher desists and student response before the student complied (Nelson & Roberts, 2000). Emmer and colleagues (2006) and Levin and Nolan (2000) suggest seven simple ways to stop misbehavior quickly, moving from least to most intrusive:

1. *Make eye contact* with, or move closer to, the offender. Other nonverbal signals, such as pointing to the work students are supposed to be doing, might be helpful. Make sure the student actually stops the inappropriate behavior and gets back to work. If you do not, students will learn to ignore your signals.

2. Try *verbal hints* such as "name-dropping" (simply insert the student's name into the lecture), asking the student a question, or making a humorous (not sarcastic) comment such as, "I must be hallucinating. I swear I heard someone shout out an answer, but that can't be because I haven't called on anyone yet!"

3. You might also ask students *if they are aware* of the negative effects of their actions or send an "I" message, described later in the chapter.

4. If they are not performing a class procedure correctly, *remind the students* of the procedure and have them follow it correctly. You may need to quietly collect a toy, comb, magazine, or note that is competing with the learning activities, while privately informing the students that their possessions will be returned after class.

5. In a calm, unhostile way, *ask the student to state the correct rule or procedure* and then to follow it. Glasser (1969) proposes three questions: "What are you doing? Is it against the rules? What should you be doing?"

6. Tell the student in a clear, assertive, and unhostile way to *stop the misbehavior.* (Later in the chapter we will discuss assertive messages to students in more detail.) If students "talk back," simply repeat your statement.

7. *Offer a choice.* For example, when a student continued to call out answers no matter what the teacher tried, the teacher said, "John, you have a choice. Stop calling out answers immediately and begin raising your hand to answer or move your seat to the back of the room and you and I will have a private discussion later. You decide" (Levin & Nolan, 2000, p. 177).

Many teachers prefer the use of logical consequences, described earlier, as opposed to penalties. For example, if one student has harmed another, you can require the offending student to make an "Apology of Action," which includes a verbal apology plus somehow repairing the damage done. This helps offenders develop empathy and social perspective-taking as they think what would be an appropriate "repair" (Elias & Schwab, 2006).

If you or your teachers must impose penalties, the Theory into Action Guidelines taken from Weinstein and Mignano (2007) and Weinstein (2007) give ideas about how to do it. The examples are taken from the actual words of the expert teachers described in their books.

There is a caution about penalties. Never use lower achievement status (moving to a lower reading group, giving a lower grade, giving excess homework) as a punishment for breaking class rules. These actions should be done only if the benefit of the action outweighs the possible risk of harm. As Carolyn Orange (2000) notes, "Effective, caring teachers would not use low achievement status, grades, or the like as a means of discipline. This strategy is unfair and ineffective. It only serves to alienate the student" (p. 76).

Special Problems with Secondary Students

Many secondary students never complete their work. Besides encouraging student responsibility, what else can teachers do to deal with this frustrating problem? Because students at this age have many assignments and teachers have many students, both teacher and students may lose track of what has and has not been completed. It often helps to teach students how to use a daily planner. In addition, the teacher must keep accurate records. But the most important thing is to enforce the established consequences for incomplete work. Teachers should not pass a student because they know that he or she is

---

THEORY INTO ACTION GUIDELINES

Penalties

Delay the discussion of the situation until you and the students involved are calmer and more objective.

Examples

1. Say calmly to a student, "Sit there and think about what happened. I'll talk to you in a few minutes," or, "I don't like what I just saw. Talk to me during your free period today."

2. Say, "I'm really angry about what just happened. Everybody take out journals; we are going to write about this." After a few minutes of writing, the class can discuss the incident.

Impose penalties privately.

Examples

1. Make arrangements with students privately. Stand firm in enforcing arrangements.

2. Resist the temptation to "remind" students in public that they are not keeping their side of the bargain.

3. Move close to a student who must be disciplined and speak so that only the student can hear.

After imposing a penalty, reestablish a positive relationship with the student immediately.

Examples

1. Send the student on an errand or ask him or her for help.

2. Compliment the student's work or give a real or symbolic "pat on the back" when the student's behavior warrants. Look hard for such an opportunity.

Set up a graded list of penalties that will fit many occasions.

Example

1. For not turning in homework: (1) receive reminder; (2) receive warning; (3) hand homework in before close of school day; (4) stay after school to finish work; (5) participate in a teacher–student–parent conference to develop an action plan.

"bright enough" to pass. Teachers should make it clear to these students that the choice is theirs: Do the work and pass, or refuse to do the work and face the consequences.

There is also the problem of students who continually break the same rules, always forgetting materials, for example, or getting into fights, like the students described in the Principal's Perspective following. What should teachers do? Teachers should seat these students away from others who might be influenced by them; try to catch them before they break the rules. If, however, rules are broken, the teacher must be consistent in applying established consequences. Teachers should not accept promises to do better next time (Levin & Nolan, 2000). Students must be taught how to monitor their own behavior; some of the learning strategies described in Chapter 4 should be helpful. Finally, the teacher should remain friendly with the students and try to catch them in a good moment so he or she can talk to them about something other than their rule breaking. The Principal's Perspective tells how one administrator dealt with a few students who caused many problems.

A Principal's Perspective

When T. M. first started as the only administrator in a high school of approximately 500 students, his daily routine included a morning roundup of the students who failed to report to detention the day before. By mid-morning a line-up of new offenders was forming in the outer office, and by lunchtime it stretched out the door and down the hall. Student discipline consumed most of his time, and not only was this daily ritual wearing him out physically and emotionally, it was detracting from the instructional leadership issues he felt most passionately about. His frustration was captured in two questions: What was wrong with the kids at this school, and why couldn't these teachers handle much of their own discipline?

Recalling Ellen Langer's (1989) *Mindfulness* book, he suppressed the automatic administrative inclination to berate the faculty and dictate broad pupil control measures. Instead he first rigorously collected and carefully analyzed data in order to more accurately understand the problem before attempting to generate a solution. He began charting which teachers referred students to the office, during what time of the day, and for what types of infractions. Wanting to know precisely how much time he was devoting to discipline, he asked his secretary to note what time each student entered and left his office. Just two weeks of data collection revealed some startling trends. Nearly half of his day was consumed by student referrals. More surprising, though, was that a small group of students was causing the most problems. Further, it seemed these students were repeatedly referred to the office by a small number of teachers. Therefore, applying expansive solutions to these very specific problems would not only be inappropriate but would most certainly prove to be ineffective. A more focused investigation uncovered a particularly volatile mix of sophomores who simply moved from class to class through the course of a day annoying each other until they reached their breaking point at fairly predictable times. Further, he recognized that a majority of the remaining problems occurred during two exceptionally long lunch periods. By adjusting a few of the students' schedules, identifying a few others for much needed behavior intervention, and rebuilding the lunch periods, T. M. was able to reduce the time he spent on discipline by nearly 75 percent while markedly enhancing the overall learning environment of the school.

Langer, E. J. (1989). *Mindfulness.* Cambridge, MA: Perseus.
Schmoker, M. J., & Wilson, R. B. (1993). *Total quality education.* Bloomington, IN: Phi Delta Kappa.

The defiant, hostile student can pose serious problems. If there is an outbreak, the teacher should try to get out of the situation as soon as possible; everyone loses in a public power struggle. One possibility is for the teacher to give the student a chance to save face and cool down by saying, "It's your choice to cooperate or not. You can take a minute to think about it." If the student complies, they can talk later about controlling the outbursts. If the student refuses to cooperate, the teacher can tell him or her to wait in the hall until he or she gets the class started on work, and can then step outside for a private talk. If the student refuses to leave, teachers should know that they can send another class member for help from the principal or the assistant principal. Again, follow through. If the student complies before help arrives, the teacher should not let him or her off the hook. If outbursts occur frequently, the teacher might arrange a conference with the counselor, parents, or other teachers. If the problem is an irreconcilable clash of personalities, the student should be transferred to another teacher.

It sometimes is useful to keep records of the incidents by logging the student's name, words and actions, date, time, place, and teacher's response. These records may help identify patterns and can prove helpful in meeting with administrators, parents, or special services personnel (Burden, 1995). Some teachers have students sign each entry to verify the incidents.

Violence or destruction of property is a difficult and potentially dangerous problem. For teachers, the first step is to send for help and get the names of participants and witnesses. Then get rid of any crowd that may have gathered; an audience will only make things worse. The teacher should not try to break up a fight without help. Tell teachers to make sure the school office is aware of the incident; the school should have a policy for dealing with these situations.

Special Programs for Classroom Management

In some situations your teachers may want to consider using a much more formal classroom management system. Two possibilities, based on behavioral principles, are group consequences and functional assessment with positive behavior supports (introduced in Chapter 4).

Group Consequences.   A teacher can base reinforcement for the class on the cumulative behavior of all members of the class, usually by adding each student's points to a class or a team total. The **good behavior game** is an example of this approach. A class is divided into two teams. Specific rules for good behavior are cooperatively developed. Each time a student breaks one of the rules, that student's team is given a mark. The team with the fewest marks at the end of the period receives a special reward or privilege (longer recess, first to lunch, and so on). If both teams earn fewer than a preestablished number of marks, both teams receive the reward. Most studies indicate that even though the game produces only small improvements in academic achievement, it can produce definite improvements in the behaviors listed in the good behavior rules.

However, caution is needed in group approaches. The whole group should not suffer for the misbehavior or mistakes of one individual if the group has no real influence over that person (Epanchin, Townsend, & Stoddard, 1994; Jenson, Sloane, & Young, 1988). We have seen an entire class break into cheers when the teacher announced that one boy was transferring to another school. The chant "No more points! No more points!" filled the room. The "points" referred to the teacher's system of giving one point to the whole class each time anyone broke a rule. Every point meant 5 minutes of recess lost. The boy who was transferring had been responsible for many losses. He was not very popular to begin with, and the point system, though quite effective in maintaining order, had led to rejection and even greater unpopularity.

Peer pressure in the form of support and encouragement, however, can be a positive influence. **Group consequences** are recommended for situations in which students care about the approval of their peers. If the misbehavior of several students seems to be encouraged by the attention and laughter of other students, then group consequences could be helpful. Teachers might show students how to give support and constructive feedback to classmates. If a few students seem to enjoy sabotaging the system, those students may need separate arrangements.

Positive Behavior Supports: Schoolwide Programs.

Positive behavioral supports (PBS), described in Chapter 4, are required under the Individuals with Disabilities Education Act for students with disabilities and those who are being considered for special education service. PBS also can be part of a schoolwide program. At the school level, the teachers and administrators

- Agree on a common approach for supporting positive behaviors and correcting problems.
- Develop a few positively stated, specific behavioral expectations and procedures for teaching these expectations to all students.
- Identify a continuum of ways (from small and simple to more complex and stronger) to acknowledge appropriate behaviors and correct behavioral errors.
- Integrate the positive behavior support procedures with the school's discipline policy

At the classroom level, teachers are encouraged to use such preventive strategies as **precorrection,** which involves identifying the context for a student's misbehavior, clearly specifying the alternative expected behavior, modifying the situation to make the problem behavior less likely—for example, providing a cue or moving the student away from tempting distractions—then rehearsing the expected positive behaviors in the new context and providing powerful reinforcers when the behaviors occur. There is an emphasis on keeping students engaged, providing a positive focus, consistently enforcing school/class rules, correcting disruptive behavior proactively, and planning for smooth transitions (Freiberg, 2006; www.pbis.org/schoolwide.htm).

Research on schoolwide positive behavior supports is limited, but results have been good. A study comparing middle school students in a behavioral support program with students outside the program showed that program students reported more positive reinforcement for appropriate behavior. Disciplinary referrals as well as verbal and physical aggression significantly decreased. In addition, students' perceptions of school safety improved (Metzler, Biglan, Rusby & Sprague, 2001). Students in general education may benefit from positive behavior supports as well. Studies of schoolwide PBS efforts indicate decreases in disciplinary referrals (Lewis, Sugai, & Colvin, 1998;

Taylor-Green et al., 1997). In addition, Lewis & Sugai (1996) found that successful use of PBS in a general education setting benefited a student with behavioral disorders (Soodak & McCarthy, 2006).

The few pages devoted here to group consequences and PBS can offer only an introduction to these programs. If you want to allow a large-scale reward program in your school, you should probably seek more information. Remember that, applied inappropriately, external rewards can undermine the students' motivation to learn (Deci, 1975; Lepper & Greene, 1978). In addition, some people object to the use of rewards; see the Point/Counterpoint on the next page for both sides of the debate.

The Need for Communication

Communication is essential when problems arise. Communication is more than "teacher talks, student listens" or "principal talks, teacher listens." It is more than the words exchanged between individuals. We communicate in many ways. Actions, movements, voice tone, facial expressions, and many other nonverbal behaviors send messages to the students. Many times the messages the teacher intends to send are not the messages that students receive.

Message Sent, Message Received

TEACHER: Carl, where is your homework?

CARL: I left it in my dad's car this morning.

TEACHER: Again? You will have to bring me a note tomorrow from your father saying that you actually did the homework. No grade without the note.

MESSAGE CARL RECEIVES: I can't trust you. I need proof you did the work.

TEACHER: Sit at every other desk. Put all your things under your desk. Jane and Laurel, you are sitting too close together. One of you move!

MESSAGE JANE AND LAUREL RECEIVE: I expect you two to cheat on this test.

TEACHER: *(A new student comes to Ms. Lincoln's kindergarten. The child is messy and unwashed. Ms. Lincoln puts her hand lightly on the girl's shoulder.)* "I'm glad you are here." *(Ms. Lincoln's muscles tense, and she leans away from the child.)*

MESSAGE STUDENT RECEIVES: I don't like you.

In all interactions, a message is sent and a message is received. Sometimes teachers or principals believe they are sending one message, but their voices, body positions, choices of words, and gestures may communicate a different message. Students may hear the hidden message and respond to it. For example, a student may respond with hostility if he or she feels insulted by the teacher (or by another student), but may not be able to say exactly where the feeling of being insulted came from. Perhaps it was in the teacher's tone of voice, not the words actually spoken. In such cases, the teacher

POINT/COUNTERPOINT   Should Students Be Rewarded for Learning?

School districts are being held increasingly accountable for achievement results as determined by state and federal reform legislation, and principals are searching more than ever for creative ways to increase student performance. Some elect to contract with private firms to offer lucrative incentives. Others use locally designed rewards programs to lure truant students back to school or to increase effort on standardized tests. From programs as formal as the nationally recognized Jostens Renaissance to locally organized drawings for TVs, computers, and cars to simply exempting students from final exams, schools are offering more and more to students hoping to get better and better performance. But should they?

For years educators and psychologists have debated whether students should be rewarded for attendance and academic accomplishments. After all, don't laws *require* compulsory attendance and proficiency testing? In the early 1990s, Paul Chance and Alfie Kohn exchanged opinions in several issues of *Phi Delta Kappan* (March 1991; November 1992; June 1993). Then, Judy Cameron and W. David Pierce (1996) published an article on reinforcement in the *Review of Educational Research* that precipitated extensive criticisms and rebuttals in the same journal from Mark Lepper, Mark Keavney, Michael Drake, Alfie Kohn, Richard Ryan, and Edward Deci. Many of the same people exchanged opinions in the November 1999 issue of *Psychological Bulletin*. What are the arguments?

POINT

Students are punished by rewards.
Alfie Kohn (1993) argues that "applied behaviorism, which amounts to saying, 'do this and you'll get that,' is essentially a technique for controlling people. In the classroom it is a way of doing things *to* children rather than working *with* them" (p. 784). He contends that rewards are ineffective because when the praise and prizes stop, the behaviors stop too. After analyzing 128 studies of extrinsic rewards, Edward Deci, Richard Koestner, and Richard Ryan (1999) concluded that "tangible rewards tend to have a substantial effect on intrinsic

motivation, with the limiting conditions we have specified. Even when tangible rewards are offered as indicators of good performance, they typically decrease intrinsic motivation for interesting activities" (pp. 658–659).

The problem with rewards does not stop here. According to Kohn, rewarding students for learning actually makes them less interested in the material.

All of this means that getting children to think about learning as a way to receive a sticker, a gold star, or a grade—or even worse, to get money or a toy for a grade, which amounts to an extrinsic motivator for an extrinsic motivator—is likely to turn learning from an end into a means. Learning becomes something that must be gotten through in order to receive the reward. Take the depressingly pervasive program by which children receive certificates for pizzas when they have read a certain number of books. John Nicholls of the University of Illinois comments, only half in jest, that the likely consequence of this program is "a lot of fat kids who don't like to read" (p. 785).

COUNTERPOINT

Learning should be rewarding.
According to Paul Chance (1993):

Behavioral psychologists in particular emphasize that we learn by acting on our environment. As B. F. Skinner put it: "[People] act on the world, and change it, and are changed in turn by the consequences of their actions." Skinner, unlike Kohn, understood that people learn best in a responsive environment. Teachers who praise or otherwise reward student performance provide such an environment. . . . If it is immoral to let students know they have answered questions correctly, to pat students on the back for a good effort, to show joy at a student's understanding of a concept, or to recognize the achievement of a goal by providing a gold star or a certificate—if this is immoral, then count me a sinner. (p. 788)

But don't take Skinner's or Chance's word for it. After all, Skinner wasn't a building principal. The Jostens website offers testimonials from principals and teachers enjoying dramatic increases in student performance and school climate as a result of implementing their incentive program. "IT IS WORKING!! Our discipline referrals are down and our grades are improving," writes one educator. Another adds, "Little incentives do work!"

So, do rewards undermine interest? In their review of research, Cameron and Pierce (1994) conclude, "When tangible rewards (e.g., gold star, money) are offered contingent on performance on a task [not just on participation] or are delivered unexpectedly, intrinsic motivation is maintained" (p. 49). In a later review of research, Eisenberg, Pierce, and Cameron (1999) added that "reward procedures requiring specific high task performance convey a task's personal or social significance, increasing intrinsic motivation" (p. 677). Even psychologists such as Edward Deci and Mark Lepper, who suggest that rewards might undermine intrin-

sic motivation, agree that rewards can also be used positively. When rewards provide students with information about their growing mastery of a subject or when the rewards show appreciation for a job well done, then the rewards bolster confidence and make the task more interesting to the students, especially students who lacked ability or interest in the task initially. Nothing succeeds like success. As Chance points out, if students master reading or mathematics with the support of rewards, they will not forget what they have learned when the praise stops. Would they have learned without the rewards? Some would, but some might not. Would you continue working for a company that didn't pay you, even though you liked the work? Will freelance writer Alfie Kohn, for that matter, lose interest in writing because he gets paid fees and royalties?

Sources: From "Sticking Up for Rewards," by P. Chance, June 1993, *Phi Delta Kappan*, pp. 787–790. Copyright © 1993 by *Phi Delta Kappan*. Reprinted with permission of Phi Delta Kappan and the author. From "Rewards versus Learning: A Response to Paul Chance," by A. Kohn, June 1993, *Phi Delta Kappan*, pp. 783 and 785. Copyright © 1993 by Alfie Kohn. Reprinted from *Phi Delta Kappan* with the author's permission.

Founded by educators in 1988, Jostens Renaissance is a national education-focused program created to recognize and reward the academic achievements of students from elementary school through college. Renaissance schools often focus their program on four target areas:

- Increasing student attendance
- Improving overall academic performance
- Increasing graduation rates
- Creating a positive, safe school environment
   Jostens (last visited October 22, 2004). www.jostens.com/renaissance/

may feel attacked for no reason. "What did I say? All I said was. . . " The first principle of communication is that people respond to what they think was said or meant, not necessarily to the speaker's intended message or actual words.

Diagnosis: Whose Problem Is It?

Teachers may find many student behaviors unacceptable, unpleasant, or troubling. It is often difficult to stand back from these problems, take an objective look, and decide on an appropriate response. According to Thomas Gordon (2003), the key to good teacher–student relationships is determining why the teacher is troubled by a particular behavior and whose problem it is. The teacher must begin by asking who "owns" the problem. The answer to this question is critical. If it is really the student's problem, the teacher must become a counselor and supporter, helping the student find his or her own solution. But if the teacher "owns" the problem, it is the teacher's responsibility to find a solution through problem solving with the student (Larrivee, 2005).

Diagnosing who owns the problem is not always straightforward. Let's look at three troubling situations to get some practice in this skill:

1. A student writes obscene words and draws sexually explicit illustrations in a school encyclopedia.
2. A student tells you that his parents had a bad fight and he hates his father.
3. A student quietly reads a magazine in the back of the room.

Why are these behaviors troubling? If the teacher cannot accept the student's behavior because it has a serious effect on the teacher—if the teacher is blocked from reaching his or her goals by the student's action—then the teacher owns the problem. It is the teacher's responsibility to confront the student and seek a solution. A teacher-owned problem appears to be present in the first situation described above—the young pornographer—because teaching materials are damaged.

If teachers feel annoyed by the behavior because it is getting in the student's own way or because they are embarrassed for the child, but the behavior does not directly interfere with teaching, then it is probably the student's problem. The test question is: Does this student's action tangibly affect the teacher or prevent the teacher from fulfilling the role of teaching? The student who hates his father would not prevent a teacher from teaching, even though he or she might wish the student felt differently. The problem is really the student's, and he must find his own solution.

Situation 3 is more difficult to diagnose. One argument is that the teacher is not interfered with in any way, so it is the student's problem. Another argument is that teachers might find reading the magazine distracting during a lecture, so it is their problem, and they must find a solution. In a gray area such as this, the answer probably depends on how the teacher actually experiences the student's behavior. Having decided who owns the problem, it is time to act.

Counseling: The Student's Problem

Let's consider a situation in which a student finds a reading assignment "dumb." How might a teacher handle this positively?

STUDENT: This book is really dumb! Why did we have to read it?

TEACHER: You're pretty upset. This seemed like a worthless assignment to you. [Teacher paraphrases the student's statement, trying to hear the emotions as well as the words.]

STUDENT: Yeah! Well, I guess it was worthless. I mean, I don't know if it was. I couldn't exactly read it.

TEACHER: It was just too hard to read, and that bothers you.

STUDENT: Sure, I felt really dumb. I know I can write a good report, but not with a book this tough.

TEACHER: I think I can give you some hints that will make the book easier to understand. Can you see me after school today?

STUDENT: Okay.

Here the teacher used *empathetic listening* to allow the student to reach a solution. By trying to hear the student and by avoiding the tendency to jump in too quickly with advice, solutions, criticisms, reprimands, or interrogations, the teacher keeps the communication lines open. Here are a few unhelpful responses the teacher might have made:

I chose the book because it is the best example of a coming-of-age novel in our library. You will need to have read it before your English II class next year. (The teacher justifies the choice; this prevents the student from admitting that this "important" assignment is too difficult.)

Did you really read it? I bet you didn't do the work, and now you want out of the assignment. (The teacher accuses; the student hears, "The teacher doesn't trust me!" and must defend herself or himself or accept the teacher's view.)

Your job is to read the book, not ask me why. I know what's best. (The teacher pulls rank, and the student hears, "You can't possibly decide what is good for you!" The student can rebel or passively accept the teacher's judgment.)

Empathetic (active) listening can be a helpful response when students bring problems to teachers (or teachers bring problems to you). You (or the teacher) must reflect back to the person what you hear him or her saying. This reflection is more than a parroting of the words; it should capture the emotions, intent, and meaning behind them. Sokolove, Garrett, Sadker, and Sadker (1986) have summarized the components of active listening: (1) blocking out external stimuli, (2) attending carefully to both the verbal and nonverbal messages, (3) differentiating between the intellectual and the emotional content of the message, and (4) making inferences regarding the speaker's feelings.

When students realize they really have been heard and not evaluated negatively for what they have said or felt, they feel freer to trust the teacher and to talk more openly. Sometimes the true problem surfaces later in the conversation, as in the example above where reading level was the real problem for the student.

Confrontation and Assertive Discipline

Now let's assume a student is doing something that actively interferes with teaching. The teacher decides the student must stop. The problem is the teacher's. Confrontation, not counseling, is required.

"I" Messages.   Gordon (2003) recommends sending an "I" message to intervene and change a student's behavior. An **"I" message** tells a student in a straightforward, assertive, and nonjudgmental way what she or he is *doing*, how it *affects the teacher* as a teacher, and *how the teacher feels* about it. The student is then free to change voluntarily, and often does so. Here are three "I" messages taken from Larrivee (2005, pp. 120–121):

If you leave your feet in the aisles, I'm afraid someone might fall.

When you're out of your seat, it distracts the students around you. I want you to stay in your seat until this activity is over.

I was disappointed that you missed class yesterday.

The "I" messages do not have to follow a specific pattern as long as they describe how the speaker feels about a particular situation.

Assertive Discipline.   Lee and Marlene Canter (1992, 1997) suggest other approaches for dealing with a teacher-owned problem. They call their method **assertive discipline:** teachers must make their expectations clear and must follow through with established consequences. Students then have a straightforward choice: They can follow the rules or accept the consequences. Many teachers are ineffective with students because they are either wishy-washy and passive or hostile and aggressive.

The *passive style* can take several forms. Instead of telling the student directly what to do, the teacher tells, or often asks, the student to try or to think about the appropriate action. The passive teacher might comment on the problem behavior without actually telling the child what to do differently: "Why are you doing that? Don't you know the rules?" or "Sam, are you disturbing the class?" Or teachers may clearly state what should happen, but never follow through with the established consequences, giving the students "one more chance" every time. Finally, teachers may ignore behavior that should receive a response or may wait too long before responding.

A *hostile response style* involves different mistakes. Teachers may make "you" statements that condemn the student without stating clearly what the student should be doing: "You should be ashamed of the way you're behaving!" or "You never listen!" or "You are acting like a baby!" Teachers may also threaten students angrily but follow through too seldom, perhaps because the threats are too vague—"You'll be very sorry you did that when I get through with you!"—or too severe. For example, a teacher tells a student in a physical education class that he will have to sit on the bench for three weeks. A few days later the team is short one member and the teacher lets the student play, never returning him to the bench to complete the three-week sentence. Often a teacher who has been passive becomes hostile and explodes when students persist in misbehaving.

In contrast with both the passive and hostile styles, an assertive response communicates to the students that you care too much about them and the process of learning to allow inappropriate behavior to persist. Assertive teachers clearly state what they expect. To be most effective, the teachers often look into a student's eyes when speaking and address the student by name. Assertive teachers' voices are calm, firm, and confident. They are not sidetracked by accusations such as "You just don't understand!" or "You don't like me!" Assertive teachers do not get into a debate about the fairness of the rules. They expect changes, not promises or apologies.

Not all educators believe that assertive discipline is useful. Earlier critics questioned the penalty-focused approach and emphasized that assertive discipline undermined student self-management (Render, Padilla, & Krank, 1989). John Covaleskie (1992) observes: "What helps children become moral is not knowledge of the rules, or even obedience to the rules, but discussions about the reasons for acting in certain ways" (p. 56). These critics have had an impact. More recent versions of *Assertive Discipline* focus on teaching students "in an atmosphere of respect, trust, and support, how to behave responsibly" (Charles, 2002a, p. 47).

Confrontations and Negotiations.   If "I" messages or assertive responses fail and a student persists in misbehaving, teacher and student are in a conflict. Several pitfalls now loom. The two individuals become less able to perceive each other's behavior accurately. Research has shown that the angrier you get with another person, the more you see the other as the villain and yourself as an innocent victim. Because you feel the other person is in the wrong, and he or she feels just as strongly that the conflict is all your fault, very little mutual trust is possible. A cooperative solution to the problem is almost impossible. In fact, by the time the discussion has gone on a few minutes, the original problem is lost in a sea of charges, countercharges, and self-defense (Johnson & Johnson, 2003).

There are three methods of resolving a conflict between teacher and student. One is for the teacher to impose a solution. This may be necessary during an emergency, as when a defiant student refuses to go to the hall to discuss a public outbreak, but it is not a good solution for most conflicts. The second method is for the teacher to give in to the student's demands. Teachers might be convinced by a particularly compelling student argument, but again, this should be used sparingly. It is generally a bad idea to be talked out of a position, unless the position was wrong in the first place. Problems arise when either the teacher or the student gives in completely.

Gordon recommends a third approach, which he calls the "no-lose method." Here the needs of both the teacher and the students are taken into account in the solution. No one person is expected to give in completely; all participants retain respect for themselves and each other. The no-lose method is a six-step problem-solving strategy:

1. Define the problem. What exactly are the behaviors involved? What does each person want? (Use active listening to help students pinpoint the real problem.)
2. Generate many possible solutions. Brainstorm, but remember, don't allow any evaluations of ideas yet.
3. Evaluate each solution. Any participant may veto any idea. If no solutions are found to be acceptable, brainstorm again.
4. Make a decision. Choose one solution through consensus—no voting. In the end, everyone must be satisfied with the solution.
5. Determine how to implement the solution. What will be needed? Who will be responsible for each task? What is the timetable?
6. Evaluate the success of the solution. After trying the solution for a while, ask, "Are we satisfied with our decision? How well is it working? Should we make some changes?"

Many of the conflicts in classrooms are between students. These can be important learning experiences for all concerned.

Student Conflicts and Confrontations

Handling conflict is difficult for most of us; for young people it can be even harder. Given the public's concern about violence in schools, it is surprising how little we know about conflicts among students (Johnson, Johnson, Dudley, Ward, & Magnuson, 1995; Rose & Gallup, 2001). There is some evidence that in elementary schools conflicts most often center on disputes over resources (school supplies, computers, athletic equipment, or toys) and over preferences (which activity to do first or what game to play). Over twenty years ago, a large study of more than 8,000 junior and senior high students and 500 faculty from three major cities concluded that 90% of the conflicts among students are resolved in destructive ways or never resolved at all (DeCecco & Richards, 1974). The few studies since that time have reached similar conclusions. Avoidance, force, and threats seem to be the major strategies for dealing with conflict (Johnson et al., 1995).

Peer Harassment. A common form of conflict in schools involves teasing and harassment. Teachers tend to underestimate the amount of bullying and harassment in schools. For example, in one survey of eighth graders, 60% of the students said that they had been harassed by a bully, but teachers in their schools estimated the number would be about 16% (Barone, 1997). A national survey found that about 33% of sixth through tenth graders had been involved in moderate or frequent bullying (Nansel et al., 2001). The line between good-natured exchanges and hostile teasing may seem thin, but a rule of thumb is that teasing someone who is less powerful or less popular or using any racial, ethnic, or religious slur should not be tolerated. When principals or teachers are silent, students may "hear" agreement with the insult (Weinstein, 2007). Table 7.5 is a list of dos and don'ts about teasing in schools.

Violence in the Schools. "Even though violence in high schools is actually decreasing, interpersonal violence among youth is a concern for parents and teachers" (Lowry, Sleet, Duncan, Powell, & Kolbe, 1995). Every day in the United States, 8 children or youth under twenty are killed by firearms and 192 are arrested for violent crimes (CDF, 2007). Young people ages twelve to twenty-four are the most likely victims of nonfatal

TABLE 7.5   Dos and Don'ts about Teasing

Teasing has led to some tragic situations. Talk about what to do in your class.

Do:	Don't:
1. Be careful of others' feelings.	1. Tease someone you don't know well.
2. Use humor gently and carefully.	2. [If you are a boy] tease girls about sex.
3. Ask whether teasing about a certain topic hurts someone's feelings.	3. Tease about a person's body.
4. Accept teasing from others if you tease.	4. Tease about a person's family members.
5. Tell others if teasing about a certain topic hurts your feelings.	5. Tease about a topic when student has asked you not to.
6. Know the difference between friendly gentle teasing and hurtful ridicule or harassment.	6. Tease someone who seems agitated or whom you know is having a bad day.
7. Try to read others' "body language" to see if their feelings are hurt—even when they don't tell you.	7. Be thin-skinned about teasing that is meant in a friendly way.
8. Help a weaker student when he or she is being ridiculed.	8. Swallow your feelings about teasing—tell someone in a direct and clear way what is bothering you.

Source: From *Middle and Secondary Classroom Management: Lessons from Research and Practice* (3rd ed.), by C. S. Weinstein. Published by McGraw-Hill. Copyright © 2007 by The McGraw-Hill Companies. Adapted with permission of The McGraw-Hill Companies.

TABLE 7.6 **Handling a Potentially Explosive Situation**

Here are some ideas for dealing with potential danger.

- Move slowly and deliberately toward the problem situation.
- Speak privately, quietly, and calmly. Do not threaten. Be as matter-of-fact as possible.
- Be as still as possible. Avoid pointing or gesturing.
- Keep a reasonable distance. Do not crowd a student. Do not get "in the student's face."
- Speak respectfully. Use the student's name.
- Establish eye-level position.
- Be brief. Avoid long-winded statements or nagging.
- Stay with the agenda. Stay focused on the problem at hand. Do not get sidetracked. Deal with less severe problems later.

- Inform the student of the expected behavior and the negative consequence as a choice or decision for the student to make. Then withdraw from the student and allow some time for the student to decide. ("Michael, you need to return to your desk, or I will have to send for the principal. You have a few seconds to decide." The teacher then moves away, perhaps attending to other students. If Michael does not choose the appropriate behavior, deliver the negative consequences. "You are choosing to have me call the principal.") Follow through with the consequence.

Source: From *Middle and Secondary Classroom Management: Lessons from Research and Practice* (3rd ed.), by C. S. Weinstein. Published by McGraw-Hill. Copyright © 2007 by The McGraw-Hill Companies. Adapted with permission of The McGraw-Hill Companies.

violence in U.S. society, and many of these attacks happen on school property. This problem has many causes; it is a challenge for every element of society. What can the schools do? Table 7.6, taken from Weinstein (2007), has some ideas for handling potentially explosive situations.

One answer is prevention. Some Chicano gang members in Chicago reported that they turned to gang activities when their teachers insulted them, called them names, humiliated them publicly, belittled their culture, ignored them in class, or blamed all negative incidents on particular students. The students reported joining gangs for security and to escape teachers who treated them badly or expected little of them because they were Latino (Padilla, 1992; Parks, 1995). We once asked a gifted educator in an urban New Jersey high school which teachers were most effective with the really tough students. He said there are two kinds: teachers who can't be intimidated or fooled and expect their students to learn, and teachers who really care about the students. When we asked, "Which kind are you?" and he answered "Both!"

Besides prevention, schools can also establish mentoring programs, conflict resolution training, social skills training, more relevant curricula, and parent and community involvement programs (Padilla, 1992; Parks, 1995). One intervention that seems to be helpful is peer mediation.

Peer Mediation. David Johnson and his colleagues provided conflict resolution training—**peer mediation**—to 227 students in second through fifth grades. Students learned a five-step negotiating strategy:

1. Jointly define the conflict. Separate the person from the problem and the actions involved, avoid win–lose thinking, get both parties' goals clear.
2. Exchange positions and interests. Present a tentative proposal and make a case for it; listen to the other person's proposal and feelings; and stay flexible and cooperative.
3. Reverse perspectives. See the situation from the other person's point of view and reverse roles and argue for that perspective.
4. Invent at least three agreements that allow mutual gain. Brainstorm, focus on goals, think creatively, and make sure everyone has power to invent solutions.
5. Reach an integrative agreement. Make sure both sets of goals are met. If all else fails, flip a coin, take turns, or call in a third party as a mediator.

In addition to learning conflict resolution, all students in Johnson and Johnson's study were trained in mediation strategies. The role of the mediator was rotated. Every day the teacher chose two students to be the class mediators and to wear the mediator's T-shirt. Johnson and his colleagues found that students learned the conflict resolution and mediation strategies and used them successfully, both in school and at home, to handle conflicts in a more productive way. For details of the strategies, see Johnson and Johnson (1994, 2005), Miller (1994), or Smith (1993).

Peer mediation has also been successful with older students and serious problems (Sanchez & Anderson, 1990). In one program, selected gang members are given mediation training, then all members are invited to participate voluntarily in the mediation process, supervised by school counselors. Strict rules governed the process leading to written agreements signed by gang representatives. Sanchez and Anderson (1990) found that gang violence in the school was reduced to a bare minimum: "The magic of the mediation process was communication" (p. 56).

Summing It Up: Learning Environments for All Students

We have examined a number of approaches to classroom student discipline. Are some better than others? Research provides some guidance.

Research on Different Management Approaches

Emmer and Aussiker (1990) conducted a meta-analysis of three general perspectives on management: influencing students through listening and problem solving, as described by Gordon (2003); group management through class meetings and student discussion, as advocated by Glasser (1969, 1990); and control through rewards and punishments as exemplified by Canter and Canter (1997). No clear conclusions could be drawn about the impact of these approaches on student behaviors. However, some evaluations have found positive effects for Freiberg's (1999) Consistency Management program and for programs that use rewards and punishments (Lewis, 2001).

In a study conducted in Australia, Ramon Lewis (2001) found that recognizing and rewarding appropriate student behaviors, talking with students about how their behavior affects others, involving students in class discipline decisions, and providing nondirective hints and description about unacceptable behaviors were associated with students taking greater responsibility for their own learning. It is interesting that these interventions represent all three of the general approaches reviewed by Emmer and Aussiker: influence, group management, and control. Lewis also concluded that teachers sometimes find using these interventions difficult when students are aggressive and most in need of the approaches. When teachers feel threatened, it can be difficult to do what students need, but that may be the most important time to act positively.

Culturally Responsive Management

Research on discipline shows that African Americans and Latino Americans, especially males, are punished more often and more harshly than other students. These students lose time from learning as they spend more hours in detention or suspension (Gay, 2006; Monroe & Obidah, 2002; Skiba, Michael, Nardo, & Peterson, 2000). Why?

The notion that African American and Latino American students are punished more because they commit more serious offenses is not supported by the data. Instead, these students are punished more severely for minor offenses such as rudeness or defiance—words and actions that are interpreted by teachers as meriting severe punishment. One explanation is a lack of cultural synchronization between teachers and students. "The language, style of walking, glances, and dress of black children, particularly males, have engendered fear, apprehension, and overreaction among many teachers and school administrators" (Irvine, 1990, p. 27). African American students may be disciplined for behaviors that were never intended to be disruptive or disrespectful. Teachers do their students and themselves a service if they work at becoming bicultural—helping their students to learn how to function in both mainstream and home cultures, but also learning the meaning of their students' words and actions so the teachers do not misinterpret and then punish their students' unintended insults (Gay, 2006).

Culturally responsive management is simply a part of the larger concept of culturally relevant teaching. Geneva Gay (2006) sums it up:

> If the classroom is a comfortable, caring, embracing, affirming, engaging, and facilitative place for students then discipline is not likely to be much of an issue. It follows then that both classroom management and school achievement can be improved for students from different ethnic, racial, social, and linguistic backgrounds by ensuring that curriculum and instruction are culturally relevant and personally meaningful for them. (p. 364)

The teachers who seem to be most effective with these students practice culturally responsive management and have been called "warm demanders" (Irvine & Armento, 2001; Irvine & Fraser, 1998). Sometimes these **warm demanders** appear harsh to outside observers (Burke-Spero, 1999; Burke-Spero & Woolfolk Hoy, 2002). For example, results of one study indicated:

> To a person unfamiliar with African American culture of inner-city life, it could be misconstrued as intimidation or heavy handed but in the minds of these informants, discipline was directly connected to caring. In fact, all viewed lack of discipline as a sign of uncaring and an apathetic teaching force. (Gordon, 1998, p. 427)

Carla Monroe and Jennifer Obidah (2002) studied Ms. Simpson, an African American teacher working with her eighth-grade science class. She describes herself as having high expectations for academics and behavior in her classes—so much so that she believed her students perceived her as "mean." Yet she often used humor and dialect to communicate her expectations, as in the following exchange:

Ms. Simpson [addressing the class]: If you know you're going to act the fool just come to me and say, "I'm going to act the fool at the pep rally," so I can go ahead and send you to wherever you need to go. [Class laughs.]

Ms. Simpson: I'm real serious. If you know you're having a bad day, you don't want anybody touching you, you don't want nobody saying nothing to you, somebody bump into you you're going to snap—you need to come up to me and say, "I'm going to snap and I can't go to the pep rally." [The students start to call out various comments.]

Ms. Simpson: Now, I just want to say I expect you to have the best behavior because you're the most mature students in the building. Don't make me stop the pep rally and ask the eighth graders to leave.

Edward: We'll have silent lunch won't we? [Class laughs.]

Ms. Simpson: You don't want to dream about what you're going to have. [Class laughs.] OK, 15 minutes for warm ups. [The students begin their warm-up assignment.]

Many African American students may be more accustomed to a directive kind of management and discipline outside of school. Their families might say,"Put down that candy" or "Go to bed" whereas white parents might ask, "Can we eat candy before dinner?" or "Isn't it time for bed?" As H. Richard Milner (2006) says, "The question should not be which approach is right or wrong but which approach works with and connects with the students' prior knowledge and ways of knowing" (p. 498).

Listening to Students and Teachers

Recently researchers have examined students' and teachers' perceptions about classroom management (see Woolfolk Hoy & Weinstein, 2006, for a review). Good classroom management from the students' perspective requires a fair and reasonable system of classroom rules and procedures that protect and respect students. Teachers are expected to care for the students, their learning, and their personal lives, before the students will respect and cooperate with the teachers. Students want teachers to maintain order without being mean or punitive, and the students don't mind differential treatment as long as there is no racism, sexism, or favoritism. As they mature, students value choices and chances for responsibilities; they do not want to feel coerced or controlled.

Teachers, in contrast, seem to believe that students need to earn their respect, relationship, concern, and interest—in a word, their caring. Choices and autonomy come with successful student self-regulation and not before. And some teachers believe that being "mean" may be necessary, in the beginning at least, to establish authority: Don't smile until Christmas. Often with pressures on the teachers to raise test scores and maintain order come more directive and punitive control strategies.

The problem inherent in these contrasting views of good classroom management is a possible downward spiral of mistrust. Students withhold their cooperation until teachers "earn it" with their authentic caring. Teachers withhold caring until students "earn it" with respect for authority and cooperation. Marginalized students actually *expect* unfair treatment and behave defensively. Teachers get tough, grill, and punish. Students feel correct in mistrusting, and become more guarded and defiant. Teachers feel correct in mistrusting and become more controlling and punitive, and so it goes (Woolfolk Hoy & Weinstein, 2006).

This cycle is consistent with Bandura's (1997) theory of reciprocal determinism. If personal factors, behaviors, and the environment are in constant interaction, then cycles of events are progressive and self-perpetuating. For example, a new student walks into class late. The student has a tattoo and several visible pierced body parts. The student is actually anxious and hopes to do better at this new school, but the teacher's initial reaction to the late entry and dramatic appearance is a bit hostile. The student feels insulted and responds in kind, so the teacher begins to form expectations about the student, is more vigilant and less trusting, and the student decides that this school will be just as worthless as his previous one, so why bother to try. The teacher sees the student's disengagement, invests less effort in teaching him, and on and on. A challenge for instructional leaders is to help both students and teachers avoid this downward spiral of mistrust.

Communicating with Families about Classroom Management

As we discuss throughout this book, families are important partners in education. This statement applies to classroom management as well. When parents and teachers share the same expectations and support each other, they can create a more positive classroom environment and more time for learning. The Theory into Action Guidelines on the next page provide ideas for principals and teachers as they work with families and the community.

Summary

Classrooms are by nature multidimensional, full of simultaneous activities, fast-paced and immediate, unpredictable, public, and affected by the history of students' and teachers' actions. A manager must juggle all these elements every day.

Productive classroom activity requires students' cooperation. Maintaining cooperation is different for each age group. Young students are learning how to "go to school" and need to learn the general procedures of school. Older students need to learn the specifics required for working in different subjects. Working with adolescents requires teachers to understand the power of the adolescent peer group.

The goals of effective classroom management are to make ample time for learning; improve the quality of time use by keeping students actively engaged; make sure participation structures are clear, straightforward, and consistently signaled; and encourage student self-management.

The most effective teachers set rules and establish procedures for handling predictable problems. Procedures should cover administrative tasks, student movement, housekeeping, routines for running lessons, interactions between students and teachers, and interactions among students. Consequences should be established for following and breaking the rules and procedures so that the teacher and the students know what will happen. Encouraging self-management requires extra time, but teaching students how to take responsibility for their actions is an investment well worth the effort.

THEORY INTO ACTION GUIDELINES

Working with Families

Make sure families know the expectations and rules of your class and school.

Examples

1. At a Family Fun Night, have your students do skits showing the rules—how to follow them and what breaking them "looks like" and "sounds like."
2. Make a poster for the refrigerator at home that describes, in a light way, the most important rules and expectations.
3. For older students, give families a list of due dates for the major assignments, along with tips about how to encourage quality work by pacing the effort—avoiding last-minute panic.
4. Communicate in appropriate ways—use the family's first language when possible. Tailor messages to the reading level of the home.

Make families partners in recognizing good citizenship.

Examples

1. Send positive notes home when students, especially students who have had trouble with classroom management, work well in the classroom.
2. Give ideas for ways any family, even those with few economic resources, can celebrate accomplishment—a favorite food; the chance to choose a video to rent; a comment to a special person such as an aunt, grandparent, or minister; the chance to read to a younger sibling.

Identify talents in the community to help build a learning environment in your class.

Examples

1. Have students write letters to carpet and furniture stores asking for donations of remnants to carpet a reading corner.
2. Find family members who can build shelves or room dividers, paint, sew, laminate manipulative materials, write stories, repot plants, or network computers.
3. Contact businesses for donations of computers, printers, or other equipment.

Seek cooperation from families when behavior problems arise.

Examples

1. Talk to families over the phone or in their home. Have good records about the problem behavior.
2. Listen to family members and solve problems with them.

For effective classroom management, it is essential to spend the first days of class teaching basic rules and procedures. Students should be occupied with organized, enjoyable activities and learn to function cooperatively in the group. Quick, firm, clear, and consistent responses to infractions of the rules characterize effective teachers. To create a positive environment and prevent problems, teachers must take individual differences into account, maintain student motivation, and reinforce positive behavior. Successful problem preventers are skilled in four areas described by Kounin: "with-it-ness," overlapping, group focusing, and movement management. When penalties have to be imposed, teachers should impose them calmly and privately.

There are several special procedures that may be helpful in maintaining positive management, including group consequences and functional assessment with behavior supports. A teacher must use these procedures with caution, emphasizing learning and not just "good" behavior.

Research on discipline shows that African Americans and Latino Americans, especially males, are punished more often and more harshly than other students. This raises the question of culturally responsive management. Both classroom management and school achievement can be improved for students from different ethnic, racial, social, and linguistic backgrounds by ensuring that curriculum and instruction are culturally relevant and personally meaningful for them.

Communication between teacher and student is essential when problems arise. All interactions between people, even silence or neglect, communicate some meaning. Techniques such as empathetic listening, determining whether the teacher or the student "owns" the problem, assertive discipline, avoidance of passive and hostile responses, and active problem solving with students help teachers open the lines of positive communication. Students need guidance in resolving conflicts. Different strategies are useful, depending on whether the goal, the relationship, or both are important to those experiencing conflict. It can help to reverse roles and see the situation through the eyes of the other. In dealing with serious problems, prevention and peer mediation might be useful. No matter what the situation, the cooperation of families can help to create a positive learning environment in your classroom and school.

KEY TERMS

academic learning time (233)

assertive discipline (260)

classroom management (232)

culturally responsive management (265)

empathetic (active) listening (259)

good behavior game (253)

group consequences (254)

group focus (248)

"I" message (259)

movement management (249)

overlapping (248)

peer mediation (263)

precorrection (254)

procedures (235)

rules (236)

self-management (234)

time on-task (233)

warm demanders (265)

with-it-ness (248)

DEVELOPING YOUR PORTFOLIO

1. Reread the case at the beginning of this chapter and assume you are the principal in the school. Develop a plan for first working with this teacher and then consider a general policy on classroom management for Samuel Procter Elementary School. Be sure to consider the following issues:
   a. How would you approach the situation? Who should be involved?
   b. Which problem behaviors should the teacher tackle first?
   c. Would giving rewards or administering punishments be useful in this situation? Why or why not?
   d. What specific suggestions would you give to this teacher?
   e. What action would you take?
   f. Should there be a schoolwide policy?
   g. Who should be involved in the development of the school policy, if needed?
2. Write a first-of-the-year newsletter for families describing your school's rules, procedures, and discipline actions. Be sure to include the following:

   a. General school rules
   b. Policy on teacher rules in the classroom
   c. Homework requirements
   d. Policies on tardiness and absences
   e. Behavior on school property
   f. Policy on suspension and expulsion
   g. Other key aspects of a good citizen policy

   Your challenge is to be clear, firm, precise, and yet humanistic and open—not an easy task.

3. Draw a floor plan of a classroom in your school, one that could be improved in its physical arrangement.
   a. Interview the teacher about his or her learning objectives and management issues.
   b. With the teacher, redesign the classroom space (furniture, workstations, storage, and so on) so that the design supports both learning and management goals.

   Your final project should include both before and after maps of the classroom, with an explicit rationale for each change.

INSTRUCTIONAL LEADER'S TOOLBOX

Readings

Emmer, E. T., Everston, C. M., & Worsham, M. E. (2006). *Classroom management for secondary teachers* (7th ed.). Boston: Allyn & Bacon.

Evertson, C. M., Emmer, E. T., & Worsham, M. E. (2006). *Classroom management for elementary teachers* (7th ed.). Boston: Allyn & Bacon.

Herbert, E. A. (1998). Design matters: How school environment affects children. *Educational Leadership, 56*(1), 69–71.

Johnson, D., & Johnson, R. (1999). The three Cs of school and classroom management. In H. J. Freiberg (Ed.), *Beyond behaviorism: Changing the classroom management paradigm* (pp. 119–144). Boston: Allyn & Bacon.

Weinstein, C. S. (1999). Reflections on best practices and promising programs: Beyond assertive classroom discipline. In H. J. Freiberg (Ed.), *Beyond behaviorism: Changing the classroom management paradigm* (pp. 147–163). Boston: Allyn & Bacon.

Weinstein, C. S. (2007). *Middle and secondary classroom management: Lessons from research and practice* (3rd ed.). New York: McGraw-Hill.

Weinstein, C. S., & Mignano, A. (2007). *Elementary classroom management: Lessons from research and practice* (4th ed.). New York: McGraw-Hill.

Woolfolk Hoy, A., & Weinstein, C. S. (2006). Students' and teachers' perspectives on classroom management. In C. Evertson & C. S. Weinstein (Eds.), *Handbook for classroom management: Research, practice, and contemporary issues* (pp. 181–220). Mahwah, NJ: Lawrence Erlbaum.

Videos

Classroom management: A proactive approach to creating an effective learning environment, 1 hour. This video shows how teachers can minimize student behavior problems—and maximize learning—with a three-stage management plan. Planning: how to arrange a classroom, direct students' attention, and present rules. Implementing: how to provide time for practicing classroom rules and procedures including homework assignments. Maintaining: how teachers can evaluate their own management systems. #614–160ER. Association for Supervision and Curriculum Development, 125 N. West St., Alexandria, VA 22314–2798.

Discipline and the law, 29 minutes. Addresses legal questions about teachers' rights to discipline children. Available from Insight Media, 2162 Broadway, New York, NY 10024.

Websites

www.bankstreet.edu/upk/georgia.html
 Best Practices Portfolio, Office of School Readiness, Georgia

www.stophitting.com/
 Center for Effective Discipline

www.honorlevel.com
 Discipline by Design

www.ericdigests.org/1995–1/elements.htm
 The Essential Elements of Cooperative Learning in the Classroom

library.uwf.edu/eli/Education/ClassroomManagement.shtml
 Excellent tutorial on classroom management

www.disciplinehelp.com/teacher/
 Online resource for teachers identifying causes of misbehavior in school and needs of the child

www.pdkintl.org/kappan/kpollpdf.htm
 Phi Delta Kappan (see the September issue for the Annual PDK/Gallup Poll of the Public's Attitudes toward the Public Schools)

www.positivediscipline.com/
 Positive Discipline

www.proteacher.com/030000.shtml
 Proteacher On-line Community, practical classroom management tips and resources

www.nwrel.org/scpd/sirs/5/cu9.html
 Schoolwide and Classroom Discipline

www.teachnet.com/how-to/manage/
 Teachnet.com

Organizations

www.coe.uh.edu/cmcd/default.cfm
 Consistency Management and Cooperative Discipline
 H. Jerome Freiberg, University of Houston
 College of Education
 Houston, TX 77204–5872
 Phone: 713-743-8663

www.clcrc.com
 Roger T. Johnson and David W. Johnson
 The Cooperative Learning Center, 60 Peik Hall, University of Minnesota
 Minneapolis, MN 55455
 Phone: 612-624-7031

CHAPTER

8

Assessing Student Learning

PREVIEW: KEY POINTS

1. All teaching involves assessing and evaluating learning, that is, collecting information and making judgments about student performance.

2. There are two general types of tests: norm-referenced and criterion-referenced.

3. Criterion-referenced tests are scored using a fixed standard or minimum passing score whereas norm-referenced tests are scored by comparing individuals with others who have taken the same test; that is, group *norms* are used to evaluate performance.

4. When norms are used, test scores are standardized as a percentile score, grade-equivalent score, or as a standard score such as a z score, T score, or stanine scores. All good tests are reliable and valid.

5. There are three broad categories of standardized tests: achievement, diagnostic, and aptitude, each with a different purpose.

6. Achievement tests measure how much a student has learned in specific content areas; diagnostic tests identify specific learning problems; and aptitude tests measure abilities developed over many years and are used to predict how well a student will do in the future at learning unfamiliar material.

7. High-stakes, standardized testing has both positive and negative consequences; on the positive side, these tests hold teachers and students accountable, but on the negative side, they narrow the curriculum and often push students who believe they are going to fail the high school graduation test out of school.

8. Authentic assessment, portfolios, and exhibitions are alternative ways to assess and evaluate student performance in a realistic context.

9. Informal assessments, such as student journals, are ungraded (formative) assessments that gather information from multiple sources to help teachers make decisions

10. Grades and high standards have both positive and negative consequences for students, but grades do not necessarily motivate students to learn. There is a difference between working for a grade and working to learn.

Leadership Challenge

You are the principal of Washington Middle School. April, one of your beginning seventh-grade teachers, has come to you with a question. First, she shares a computer printout with you showing the results of the fall testing, including scores on a group test of intelligence for all the seventh-grade students in her class. The printouts have been distributed to all teachers in the school by the guidance department. Then she shows you notes from two parents. They want to meet with April to see their child's scores, and especially, as one parent put it, "To find out how smart Jason really is." You look at the printouts and at the parental requests, as April asks you for advice on what to do.

1. What do the intelligence test scores tell you about these students?
2. How do you suggest that April respond to the request from the parents?
3. Do you need to talk to the guidance department about the purpose of the data?
4. Do you need a school policy on testing results?

Evaluation, Measurement, and Assessment

All teaching involves assessing and evaluating learning. At the heart of assessment is judgment, making decisions based on values. In the process of evaluation, we compare outcomes and information to some set of criteria and then make judgments. Principals and teachers must make all kinds of judgments. "Should we use a different text this year? Will Sarah do better if she repeats the first grade? Should Terry get a B− or a C+ on the project? Are the students ready for the proficiency testing?"

Measurement is evaluation put in quantitative terms, the numeric description of an event or characteristic. Measurement tells how much, how often, or how well by providing scores, ranks, or ratings. Instead of saying, "Sarah doesn't seem to understand addition," a teacher might say, "Sarah answered only two of the fifteen problems correctly in her addition homework." Measurement also allows a school to compare one student's performance on one particular task with a standard or with the performances of the other students. When we think of measurement, we often think of paper-and-pencil tests. Not all the evaluative decisions made by teachers and principals involve measurement. Some decisions are based on information that is difficult to express numerically: student preferences, information from parents, previous experiences, even intuition. But measurement does play a large role in many school and classroom decisions, and, properly done, it can provide unbiased data for evaluations.

Increasingly, evaluation and measurement specialists are using the term **assessment** to describe the process of gathering information about students' learning. Assessment is broader than testing and measurement. Assessment is "any of a variety of procedures used to obtain information about student performance" (Linn & Gronlund, 2000, p. 32). Assessments can be formal, such as unit tests, or informal, such as observing who emerges as a leader in a group of teachers or students. Assessments can be designed by classroom teachers or by local, state, or national agencies such as school districts or the Educational Testing Service. And today, assessments can go well beyond paper-and-pencil exercises to observations of performances and the development of portfolios and artifacts (Popham, 2005). In this chapter, we examine formal assessments designed by groups and agencies outside the school as well as teacher-made assessment devices. Many of these assessment techniques usually involve testing and the reporting of scores, so we will start by examining two types of tests.

The answers given on any type of test have no meaning by themselves; we must make some kind of comparison to interpret test results. There are two basic types of comparison: In the first, a test score is compared to the scores obtained by other people who have taken the same test, a *norm-referenced* comparison. The second type is *criterion-referenced*. Here, the comparison is to a fixed standard or minimum passing score.

Norm-Referenced Tests

In **norm-referenced testing,** the people who have taken the test provide the *norms* for determining the meaning of a given individual's score. You can think of a norm as being the typical level of performance for a particular group. By comparing the individual's raw score (the actual number correct) to the norm, we can determine if the score is above, below, or around the average for that group. There are at least three types of

norm groups (comparison groups) in education: the class or school itself, the school district, and national samples.

Norm-referenced tests cover a wide range of general objectives rather than assessing a limited number of specific objectives. Norm-referenced tests are especially useful in measuring the overall achievement of students who have come to understand complex material by different routes. Norm-referenced tests are also appropriate when only the top few candidates can be admitted to a program.

However, norm-referenced measurement has its limitations. The results of a norm-referenced test do not tell you whether students are ready to move on to more advanced material. For instance, knowing that a student is in the top 3% of the class on a test of algebraic concepts will not tell you if he or she is ready to move on to geometry; everyone in the class may have a limited understanding of the algebraic concepts.

Nor are norm-referenced tests particularly appropriate for measuring affective and psychomotor objectives. To measure individuals' psychomotor learning, you need a clear description of standards. (Even the best gymnast in school performs certain exercises better than others and needs specific guidance about how to improve.) In the affective area, attitudes and values are personal; comparisons among individuals are not really appropriate. For example, how could we measure an "average" level of political values or opinions? Finally, norm-referenced tests tend to encourage competition and comparison of scores. Some students compete to be the best. Others, realizing that being the best is impossible, may compete to be the worst. Either goal has its casualties.

Criterion-Referenced Tests

When test scores are compared, not to those of others but to a given criterion or standard of performance, this is **criterion-referenced testing.** To decide who should be allowed to drive a car, it is important to determine just what standard of performance is appropriate for selecting safe drivers. It does not matter how your test results compare to the results of others. If your performance on the test was in the top 10% but you consistently ran through red lights, you would not be a good candidate for receiving a license, even though your score was high.

Criterion-referenced tests measure the mastery of very specific objectives. The results of a criterion-referenced test should tell parents, teachers, and principals exactly what the students can and cannot do, at least under certain conditions. For example, a criterion-referenced test would be useful in measuring the ability to add three-digit numbers. A test could be designed with 20 different problems, and the standard for mastery could be set at 17 correct out of 20. (The standard is often somewhat arbitrary and may be based on such things as the teacher's experience.) If two students receive scores of 7 and 11, it does not matter that one student did better than the other because neither met the standard of 17. Both need more help with addition.

Criterion-referenced tests, however, are not appropriate for every situation. Many subjects cannot be broken down into a set of specific objectives. Moreover, although standards are important in criterion-referenced testing, they can often be arbitrary, as you have already seen. When deciding whether a student has mastered the addition of

TABLE 8.1   Deciding on the Type of Test to Use

Norm-referenced tests may work best when you are

- Measuring general ability in certain areas, such as English, algebra, general science, or U.S. history.
- Assessing the range of abilities in a large group.
- Selecting top candidates when only a few openings are available.

Criterion-referenced tests may work best when you are

- Measuring mastery of basic skills.
- Determining if students have prerequisites to start a new unit.
- Assessing affective and psychomotor objectives.
- Providing evidence that students have met learning standards.
- Grouping students for instruction.

Source: From Anita E. Woolfolk, *Educational Psychology: Active Learning Edition*, 10/e. Published by Allyn & Bacon, Boston, MA. Copyright © 2008 by Pearson Education. Reprinted by permission of the publisher.

three-digit numbers comes down to the difference between 16 versus 17 correct answers, it seems difficult to justify one particular standard over another. Finally, at times it is valuable to know how the students in your school compare to other students at their grade level both locally and nationally. Table 8.1 offers a comparison of norm-referenced and criterion-referenced tests. You can see that each type of test is well suited for certain situations, but each also has its limitations.

What Do Test Scores Mean?

Millions of standardized tests are given every year. Most of these are norm-referenced standardized tests. **Standardized tests** are called standardized because "the same directions are used for administering them in all classrooms and standard procedures are used for scoring and interpreting them" (Carey, 1994, p. 443). Standard methods of developing items, administering the test, scoring it, and reporting the scores are all implied by the term *standardized test*.

Basic Concepts

In standardized testing, the test items and instructions have been tried out to make sure they work and then rewritten and retested as necessary. The final version of the test is administered to a **norming sample,** a large sample of subjects as similar as possible to the students who will be taking the test in school systems throughout the country. This norming sample serves as a comparison group for all students who take the test. Hence, standardized tests typically come with norms. Let's look at some of the measurements on which normative comparisons and interpretations are based.

Measurements of Central Tendency and Standard Deviation.   You have probably had a great deal of experience with means. A **mean** is simply the arithmetical average of a group of scores. The mean offers one way of measuring **central tendency,** the score that is typical or representative of the whole distribution of scores.

Two other measures of central tendency are the median and the mode. The **median** is the middle score in the distribution, the point at which half the scores are larger and half are smaller. The **mode** is the score that occurs most often. If two scores tie for the most frequent, we have a *bimodal* distribution.

The measure of central tendency gives a score that is representative of the group of scores, but it does not tell you anything about how the scores are distributed. Two groups of scores may both have a mean of 50 but be alike in no other way. One group might contain the scores 50, 45, 55, 55, 45, 50, 50; the other group might contain the scores 100, 0, 50, 90, 10, 50, 50. In both cases the mean, median, and mode are all 50, but the distributions are quite different.

The **standard deviation** is a measure of how widely the scores vary from the mean. The larger the standard deviation, the more spread out the scores in the distribution. The smaller the standard deviation, the more the scores are clustered around the mean. For example, in the distribution 50, 45, 55, 55, 45, 50, 50, the standard deviation is much smaller than in the distribution 100, 0, 50, 90, 10, 50, 50. Another way of saying this is that distributions with very small standard deviations have less variability in their scores.

Knowing the mean and the standard deviation of a group of scores gives you a better picture of the meaning of an individual score. For example, suppose you received a score of 78 on a test. You would be very pleased with the score if the mean of the test were 70 and the standard deviation were 4. In this case, your score would be 2 standard deviations above the mean, a score well above average.

Consider the difference if the mean of the test had remained at 70 but the standard deviation had been 20. In the second case, your score of 78 would be less than 1 standard deviation from the mean. You would be much closer to the middle of the group, with a score above average, but not that high. Knowing the standard deviation tells you much more than simply knowing the **range** of scores. No matter how the majority scored on the tests, one or two students may do very well or very poorly and thus make the range very large.

The Normal Distribution.   Standard deviations are very useful in understanding test results. They are especially helpful if the results of the tests form a normal distribution. You have encountered the **normal distribution** before. It is the bell-shaped curve, the most famous frequency distribution because it describes many naturally occurring physical and social phenomena. Many scores fall in the middle, giving the curve its bell shape. You find fewer and fewer scores as you look out toward the end points, or *tails*, of the distribution. The normal distribution has been thoroughly analyzed by statisticians. The mean of a normal distribution is also its midpoint. Half the scores are above the mean, and half are below it. In a normal distribution, the mean, median, and mode are all the same point.

Another convenient property of the normal distribution is that the percentage of scores falling within each area of the curve is known, as you can see in Figure 8.1.

FIGURE 8.1   The Normal Distribution
The normal distribution or bell-shaped curve has certain predictable
characteristics. For example, 68% of the scores are clustered between 1
standard deviation below and 1 standard deviation above the mean.

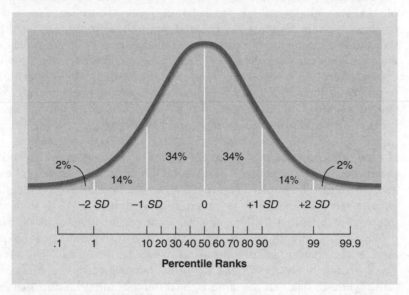

Source: From Anita E. Woolfolk, *Educational Psychology: Active Learning Edition*, 10/e.
Published by Allyn & Bacon, Boston, MA. Copyright © 2008 by Pearson Education.
Reprinted by permission of the publisher.

A person scoring within 1 standard deviation of the mean obviously has company.
Many scores pile up here. In fact, 68% of all scores are located in the area from 1 standard deviation below to 1 standard deviation above the mean. About 16% of the scores
are higher than 1 standard deviation above the mean. Of this higher group, only 2%
are better than 2 standard deviations above the mean. Similarly, only about 16% of the
scores are less than 1 standard deviation below the mean, and of that group only about
2% are worse than 2 standard deviations below. At 2 standard deviations from the mean
in either direction, the scorer has little company.

The SAT college entrance exam and the GRE test are examples of exams with
normal distributions. The mean is 500 and the standard deviation is 100. If you know
people who made scores in the 700s, you know they did very well. Only about 2% of
the people who take the test do that well, because only 2% of the scores are better than
2 standard deviations above the mean in a normal distribution.

Types of Scores

Now you have enough background for a discussion of the different kinds of scores you
may encounter in reports of results from standardized tests.

Percentile Rank Scores.   The concept of ranking is the basis for one very useful kind of score reported on standardized tests, a **percentile rank** score. In percentile ranking, each student's raw score is compared with the raw scores of the students in the norming sample. The percentile rank shows the percentage of students in the norming sample that scored at or below a particular raw score. If a student's score were the same as or better than three-quarters of the students in the norming sample, the student would score in the 75th percentile or have a percentile rank of 75. You can see that this does *not* mean that the student had a raw score of 75 correct answers or even that the student answered 75% of the questions correctly. Rather, the 75 refers to the percentage of people in the norming sample whose scores on the test were equal to or below this student's score. A percentile rank of 50 means that a student has scored as well as or better than 50% of the norming sample and has achieved an average score.

A Caution Interpreting Percentile Scores.   Differences in percentile ranks do not mean the same thing in terms of raw score points in the middle of the scale as they do at the fringes. The graph in Figure 8.2 shows Joan's and Alice's percentile scores on the fictitious Test of Excellence in Language and Arithmetic. Both students are about average in arithmetic skills. One equaled or surpassed 50% of the norming sample, the other, 60%. However, because their scores are in the middle of the distribution, this difference in percentile ranks means a raw score difference of only a few points. Their raw scores were actually 75 and 77. In the language test, the difference in percentile ranks seems to be about the same as the difference in arithmetic because one ranked at the 90th percentile and the other at the 99th. But the difference in their raw scores on the language test is much greater. It takes a greater difference in raw score points to make a difference in percentile rank at the extreme ends of the scale. On the language test the difference in raw scores is about 10 points.

Grade-Equivalent Scores.   Generally, **grade-equivalent scores** are obtained from separate norming samples for each grade level. The average of the scores of all the third graders in the norming sample defines the third-grade equivalent score. Suppose the raw-score average of the third-grade norming sample is 38. Any student who attains a raw score of 38 on that test will be assigned a grade-equivalent score of third grade. Grade-equivalent scores are generally listed in numbers such as 2.3, 3.5, 4.6, 10.5, and so on. The whole number gives the grade. The decimals stand for tenths of a year, but they are usually interpreted as months.

Suppose a student with the grade-equivalent score of 9 is a third grader. Should this student be promoted immediately? Probably not. Different forms of tests are used at different grade levels, so the third grader may not have had to answer items that would be given to ninth graders. The high score represents superior mastery of material at the third-grade level rather than a capacity for doing ninth-grade work. Even though an average ninth grader could do as well as our third grader on this particular test, the ninth grader would certainly know much more than this test covered. All the score tells us is that this third grader is well above the rest of the third graders, *not* that the child is actually equivalent to those in ninth grade. Also, grade-equivalent score units do not mean the same thing at every grade level. For example, a second grader

FIGURE 8.2 Percentile Ranking on a Normal Distribution Curve

Percentile scores have different meanings at different places on the scale. For example, a difference of a few raw score points near the mean might translate into a 10-point percentile difference, while it would take 6 or 7 points to make a 10-point percentile difference farther out of the scale.

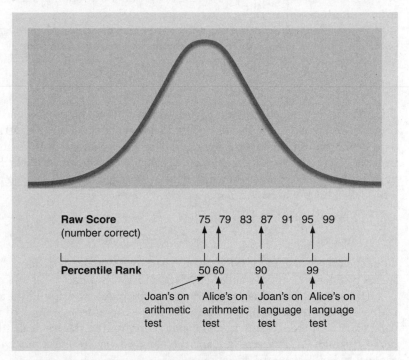

Source: From Anita E. Woolfolk, *Educational Psychology: Active Learning Edition,* 10/e. Published by Allyn & Bacon, Boston, MA. Copyright © 2008 by Pearson Education. Reprinted by permission of the publisher.

reading at the first-grade level would have more trouble in school than an eleventh grader who reads at the tenth-grade level.

Because grade-equivalent scores are misleading and are so often misinterpreted, especially by parents, most educators and psychologists strongly believe they should not be used at all. In the example above, parents of the third-grade student who is reading at the ninth-grade level might think their child can do ninth-grade work; that is a misinterpretation of the score.

Standard Scores. As you may remember, one problem with percentile ranks is the difficulty in making comparisons among ranks. A discrepancy of a certain number of raw-score points has a different meaning at different places on the scale. With standard scores, on the other hand, a difference of 10 points is the same everywhere on the scale.

Standard scores are based on the standard deviation. A very common standard score is called the **z score.** A z score tells how many standard deviations above or below the average a raw score is. In the example described earlier, in which you were fortunate enough to get a 78 on a test where the mean was 70 and the standard deviation was 4, your z score would be +2, or 2 standard deviations above the mean. If a person were to score 64 on this test, the score would be 1.5 standard deviation units *below* the mean, and the z score would be −1.5. A z score of 0 would be no standard deviations above the mean—in other words, right on the mean.

To calculate the z score for a given raw score, subtract the mean from the raw score and divide the difference by the standard deviation. The formula is:

$$z = \frac{X - \overline{X}}{SD}$$

Because it is often inconvenient to use negative numbers, other standard scores have been devised to eliminate this difficulty. The **T score** has a mean of 50 and uses a standard deviation of 10. Thus a T score of 50 indicates average performance. If you multiply the z score by 10 (which eliminates the decimal) and add 50 (which gets rid of the negative number), you get the equivalent T score as the answer. The person whose z score was −1.5 would have a T score of 35.

First multiply the z score by 10: $-1.5 \times 10 = -15$
Then add 50: $-15 + 50 = 35$

The scoring of the SAT or GRE test is based on a similar procedure. The mean of the scores is set at 500, and a standard deviation of 100 is used.

Before we leave this section on types of scores, we should mention one other widely used method. **Stanine scores** (the name comes from "standard nine") are standard scores. There are only nine possible scores on the stanine scale, the whole numbers 1 through 9. The mean is 5, and the standard deviation is 2. Each unit from 2 to 8 is equal to half a standard deviation.

Stanine scores provide a method of considering a student's rank because each of the nine scores includes a specific range of percentile scores in the normal distribution. For example, a stanine score of 1 is assigned to the bottom 4% of scores in a distribution. A stanine of 2 is assigned to the next 7%. Of course, some raw scores in this 7% range are better than others, but they all get a stanine score of 2.

Each stanine score represents a wide range of raw scores. This has the advantage of encouraging teachers and parents to view a student's score in more general terms instead of making fine distinctions based on a few points. Figure 8.3 compares the four types of standard scores we have considered, showing how each would fall on a normal distribution curve.

Interpreting Test Scores

One of the most common problems with the use of tests is misinterpretation of scores. This often happens because of the belief that numbers are precise measurements of a student's ability. No test provides a perfect picture of a person's abilities; a test is only one small sample of behavior. Two factors are important in developing good tests and interpreting results: reliability and validity.

FIGURE 8.3   Four Types of Standard Scores on a Normal Distribution Curve

Using this figure you can translate one type of standard into another.

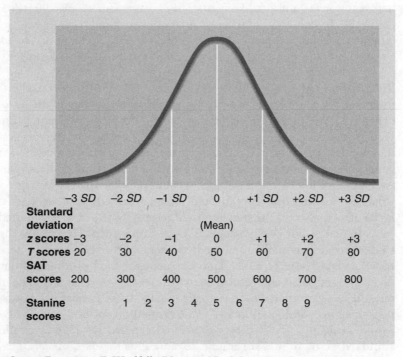

	–3 SD	–2 SD	–1 SD	0	+1 SD	+2 SD	+3 SD
Standard deviation				(Mean)			
z scores	–3	–2	–1	0	+1	+2	+3
T scores	20	30	40	50	60	70	80
SAT scores	200	300	400	500	600	700	800
Stanine scores		1 2 3	4 5 6	7 8 9			

Source: From Anita E. Woolfolk, *Educational Psychology: Active Learning Edition*, 10/e. Published by Allyn & Bacon, Boston, MA. Copyright © 2008 by Pearson Education. Reprinted by permission of the publisher.

Reliability.   If you took a standardized test on Monday, then took the same test again a week later, and you received about the same score each time, you would have reason to believe the test was reliable. If 100 people took the test one day, then repeated it the following week, and the ranking of the individual scores was about the same for both tests, you would be even more certain the test was reliable. (Of course, this assumes that no one looks up answers or studies before the second test.) A reliable test gives a consistent and stable "reading" of a person's ability from one occasion to the next, assuming the person's ability remains the same. A reliable thermometer works in a similar manner, giving you a reading of 100°C each time you measure the temperature of boiling water. Measuring a test's **reliability** in this way, by giving the test on two different occasions, indicates *stability* or *test–retest reliability*. If a group of people takes two equivalent versions of a test and the scores on both tests are comparable, this indicates *alternate-form reliability*.

Reliability can also refer to the internal consistency or the precision of a test. This type of reliability, known as *split-half reliability*, is calculated by comparing performance on half of the test questions with performance on the other half. If, for example, someone did quite well on all the odd-numbered items and not at all well on the even-numbered items, we could assume that the items were not very consistent or precise in measuring what they were intended to measure.

There are several ways to compute reliability, but all the possibilities give numbers between 0.0 and 1.0, like a correlation coefficient. Above .90 is considered very reliable; .80 to .90 is good, and below .80 is not very good reliability for standardized tests (Haladyna, 2002). The most effective way to improve reliability is to add more items to a test. Generally speaking, longer tests are more reliable than shorter ones.

True Score.   All tests are imperfect estimators of the qualities or skills they are trying to measure. There are errors in every testing situation. Sometimes the errors are in the students' favor and they score higher than their ability might warrant, because, for example, they reviewed a key section just before the test. Sometimes the errors go against students; they are sick, sleepy, or focused on the wrong material in their review. But if students could be tested over and over again without becoming tired and without memorizing the answers, their good luck and bad luck would even out, and the average of the test scores would be close to a true score. In other words, we can think of a student's true score as the mean of all the scores the student would receive if the test were repeated many times.

In reality, however, students take a test only once. That means that the score each student receives is made up of the hypothetical true score plus some amount of error. How can error be reduced so that the actual score can be brought closer to a true score? As you might guess, this returns us to the question of reliability. The more reliable the test, the less error in the score actually obtained. On standardized tests, test developers take this into consideration and make estimations of how much the students' scores would probably vary if they were tested repeatedly. This estimation is called the **standard error of measurement.** It represents the *standard deviation* of the distribution of scores from our hypothetical repeated testings. Thus, a reliable test can also be defined as a test with a small standard error of measurement. In their interpretation of tests, principals and teachers must also take into consideration the margin for error.

Confidence Interval.   Never base an opinion of a student's ability or achievement on the exact score the student obtains. Many test companies now report scores using a **confidence interval,** or "standard error band," that encloses the student's actual score. This makes use of the standard error of measurement and allows a teacher to consider the range of scores that might include a student's true score.

Let us assume, for example, that two students in your school take a standardized achievement test in Spanish. The standard error of measurement for this test is 5. One student receives a score of 79 and the other, a score of 85. At first glance, these scores seem quite different. But when you consider the standard error bands around the scores, not just the scores alone, you see that the bands overlap. The first student's true score might be anywhere between 74 and 84 (that is, the actual score of 79 plus and minus the standard error of 5). The second student's true score might be anywhere between 80 and 90. It is crucial to keep in mind the idea of standard error bands when selecting students for special programs. No child should be rejected simply because the obtained score missed the cutoff by one or two points. The student's true score might well be above the cutoff point.

Validity.   If a test is sufficiently reliable, the next question is whether it is valid, that is, does the test measure what it is suppose to measure? To have **validity,** the decisions and inferences based on the test must be supported by evidence. This means that validity is judged in relation to a particular use or purpose, that is, in relation to the actual decision being made and the evidence for that decision (Linn & Gronlund, 2000; Popham, 2005).

A test must be reliable in order to be valid. For example, if, over a few months, an intelligence test yields different results each time it is given to the same child, then by definition it is not reliable. Certainly it couldn't be a valid measure of intelligence because intelligence is assumed to be fairly stable, at least over a short period of time. However, reliability will not guarantee validity. If that intelligence test gave the same score every time for a particular child but didn't predict school achievement, speed of learning, or other characteristics associated with intelligence, then performance on the test would not be a true indicator of intelligence. The test would be reliable, but invalid.

Absence-of-Bias.   Reliability and validity have long been criteria for judging assessments. But over the past twenty years, educators and psychologists realized that another criterion should be added: absence-of-bias. **Assessment bias** "refers to qualities of an assessment instrument that offend or unfairly penalize a group of students because of the students' gender, ethnicity, socioeconomic status, religion, or other such group-defining characteristic" (Popham, 2005, p. 77). Biases are aspects of the test such as content, language, or examples that might distort the performance of a group, either for better or for worse. For example, if a reading test used passages that described boxing or football scenarios, we might expect males on average to do better than females.

Two forms of assessment bias are unfair penalization and offensiveness. The reading assessment with heavy sports content is an example of *unfair penalization;* girls may be penalized for their lack of boxing or football knowledge. *Offensiveness* occurs when a particular group might be insulted by the content of the assessment. Offended, angry students may not perform at their best.

Also, tests may not be fair because different groups have had different *opportunities to learn* the material tested. The questions asked tend to center on experiences and facts more familiar to the dominant culture than to minority-group students. Consider this test item for fourth graders described by Popham (2005, p. 336):

> My uncle's *field* is computer programming

Look at the sentences below. In which sentence does the word *field* mean the same as in the boxed sentence above?

A. The softball pitcher knew how to *field* her position.

B. They prepared the *field* by spraying and plowing it.

C. I know the *field* I plan to enter when I finish college.

D. The doctor used a wall chart to examine my *field* of vision.

Items like this are on most standardized tests. But not all families describe their work as a *field* of employment. If your parents work in professional fields such as computers, medicine, law, or education, the item would make sense, but what if your parents worked at a grocery store or a car repair shop? Are these fields? Life outside class has prepared some students, but not others for this item.

Today most standardized tests are checked carefully for assessment bias, but teacher-made tests may have biased content. It makes sense to have teachers check their tests for bias (Popham, 2005).

Types of Standardized Tests

Several kinds of standardized tests are used in schools today. One look in the cumulative folders that include testing records for individual students over several years shows the many ways students are tested in this country. There are three broad categories of standardized tests: achievement, diagnostic, and aptitude (including interest). As an instructional leader, you will probably encounter achievement and aptitude tests most frequently.

Achievement Tests: What Has the Student Learned?

The most common standardized tests given to students are **achievement tests,** which are meant to measure how much a student has learned in specific content areas such as reading comprehension, language usage, computation, science, social studies, mathematics, and logical reasoning. There are achievement tests for both individuals (for example, the Wide-Range Achievement Test; Peabody Individual Achievement Test; KeyMath Diagnostic Tests) and groups (the California, Metropolitan, SRA, or Stanford Achievement Tests; the TerraNova; and the Iowa Tests). These tests vary in their reliability and validity. Group tests can be used for screening, to identify children who might need further testing or as a basis for grouping students according to achievement levels. Individual achievement tests are given to determine a child's academic level more precisely or to help diagnose learning problems.

Using Information from a Norm-Referenced Achievement Test.   What specific information can principals and teachers expect from achievement test results? Test publishers usually provide individual profiles for each student, showing scores on each subtest. Figure 8.4 is an example of an individual profile for a fourth grader named Ken Jones, on the TERRANOVA, Second Edition. Note that the Individual Profile Report has two pages. The first page (Performance on Objectives) attempts to paint a picture of the student's mastery of different objectives in Reading, Language, Mathematics, Science, and Social Studies. For example, under Reading are the objectives of "basic understanding," "analyze text," "evaluate/extend meaning," and "identify reading strategies." Beside each objective are several different ways of reporting Ken's score.

Raw Score/Number Correct: Under the first column labeled "Student" is the number of items (out of 100) that Ken answered correctly for that objective. But

FIGURE 8.4   A Typical Score Report

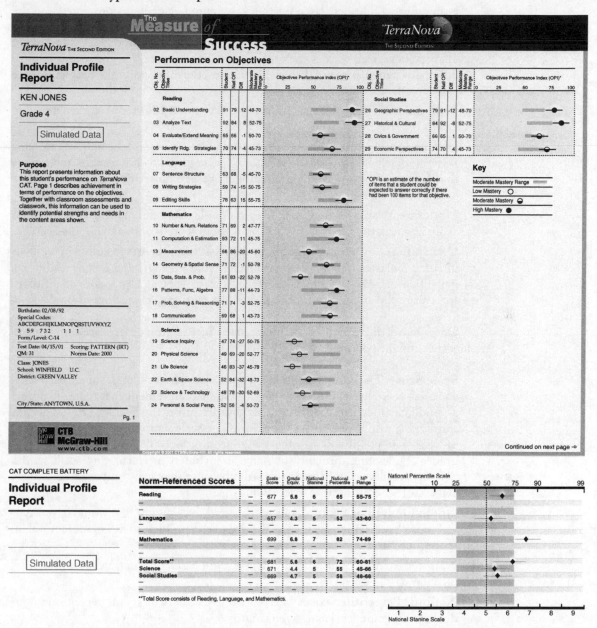

be aware, the test probably did not have 100 items to assess that objective, so this is an adjusted number based on the actual number of items presented and the number Ken got right. If there were 10 items for a particular objective and Ken got 5 of them right, his raw score for that objective would be 50. A caution: On many standardized tests, some of these specific skill areas may be measured with only a few items each, and the fewer the items, the more potential problems there can be with reliability.

National OPI: The average number correct (out of 100) for a national norming group.

Difference: The difference between the student's score and the national average: Is the student below or above the national average and by how much? You can see that Ken is 15 points below the national average on writing strategies and 15 points above on editing skills.

Moderate Mastery Range: Indicates middle-level mastery for this objective. For analyzing text, the range is 52 to 75, and Ken's score is above that range.

OPI Index Graph: On the graph to the right of the scores, a completely filled-in circle indicates high mastery (see Ken's score on analyzing text in reading), a half-filled-in circle is in the moderate mastery range (see Ken's score on sentence structure), and an empty circle indicates low mastery (science inquiry).

On page 2 of the report (Norm-Referenced Scores) Ken's scores are compared to students around the country:

Scale Score: The basic score used to derive all the other scores, sometimes called a growth score because it describes growth in achievement that typically occurs as students move through the grades. For example, the average scale score for third graders might be 585, while the average scale score for tenth graders is 714 on tests with possible scores that range from 0 to 1000 across the entire K–12 grades. Often, the difficulty of items is included in calculating scale scores. Schools are increasingly using this score because they can compare across years, classes, or schools in the district (Popham, 2005).

Grade Equivalent Score: Indicates the grade and month that would have a typical score like Ken's in each area. Beware of the problems with grade-equivalent scores described earlier.

National Stanine: This is Ken's stanine score based on a national norming sample comparison group.

National Percentile Score: This score tells us where he stands in relation to students at his grade level across the country.

National Percentile Range: The range of national percentile scores in which Ken's true score is likely to fall. You may remember from our discussion of true scores that this range, or confidence interval, is determined by adding and subtracting the standard error of the test from Ken's actual score. There is a 95% chance that Ken's true score is within this range.

Beside the scores is a graph showing Ken's national percentile and stanine scores, with the standard error bands indicated around the scores. Bands that show any overlap are probably not significantly different. When there is no overlap between bands for two test scores, we can be reasonably certain that Ken's achievement levels in these two areas are actually different. You can see that Ken's score in mathematics probably is significantly higher than his scores on reading, language, science, or social studies.

Diagnostic Tests: What Are the Student's Strengths and Weaknesses?

If teachers want to identify specific learning problems, they may need to refer to results from the various diagnostic tests that have been developed. Most **diagnostic tests** are given to students individually by a highly trained professional. The goal is usually to identify the specific problems a student is having. Achievement tests, both standardized and teacher-made, identify weaknesses in academic content areas like mathematics, computation, or reading. Individually administered diagnostic tests identify weaknesses in learning processes. There are diagnostic tests to assess the ability to hear differences among sounds, remember spoken words or sentences, recall a sequence of symbols, separate figures from their background, express relationships, coordinate eye and hand movements, describe objects orally, blend sounds to form words, recognize details in a picture, coordinate movements, and many other abilities needed to learn, remember, and communicate learning. Elementary school students are more likely than secondary school students to take diagnostic tests. High school students are more likely to take aptitude tests.

Aptitude Tests: How Well Will the Student Do in the Future?

Both achievement and aptitude tests measure developed abilities. Achievement tests may measure abilities developed over a short period of time, such as during a week-long unit on map reading, or over a longer period of time, such as a semester. **Aptitude tests** are meant to measure abilities developed over many years and to predict how well a student will do in the future at learning unfamiliar material. The greatest difference between the two types of tests is that they are used for different purposes. Achievement tests measure final performance (and perhaps give grades), and aptitude tests predict how well people will do in particular programs like college or professional school (Anastasi, 1988).

Scholastic Aptitude.   The purpose of a scholastic aptitude test, such as the SAT (Scholastic Assessment Test) or ACT (American College Testing Program) is to predict how well a student is likely to do in college. Colleges use such scores to help decide on acceptances and rejections. The SAT may have seemed like an achievement test to you, measuring what you had learned in high school. Although the test is designed to avoid drawing too heavily on specific high school curricula, the questions are very similar to achievement test questions.

Standardized aptitude tests—such as the SAT, the School and College Ability Tests (SCAT), and the Preliminary Scholastic Assessment Test (PSAT) for younger students—

seem to be reliable in predicting future achievement. Because standardized tests are less open to teacher bias, they may be even fairer predictors of future achievement than high school grades. Indeed, some psychologists believe grade inflation in high schools has made tests like the SAT even more important. Others believe that the SATs are not good predictors of success in college, particularly for women or members of cultural or ethnic minority groups. The controversy continues with some critics demanding that colleges drop tests as criteria for admission and supporters calling for improved testing.

IQ and Scholastic Aptitude.   In Chapter 3 we discussed one of the most influential aptitude tests of all, the IQ test. The IQ test as we know it could well be called a test of scholastic aptitude. The IQ score is really a standard score with a mean of 100 and a standard deviation of 15. Thus about 68% of the general population would score between +1 and −1 standard deviations from the mean, or between about 85 and 115.

A difference of a few points between two students' IQ scores should not be viewed as important. Scores between 90 and 109 are within the average range. In fact, scores between 80 and 119 are considered within the range of low average to high average. To see the problems that may arise, consider the following conversation:

> PARENT: We came to speak with you today because we are shocked at our son's IQ score. We can't believe he has only a 99 IQ when his sister scored much higher on the same test. We know they are about the same. In fact, Sam has better marks than Lauren did in the fifth grade.
>
> PRINCIPAL: What was Lauren's score?
>
> PARENT: Well, she did much better. She scored a 103!

Clearly, brother and sister have both scored within the average range. While the standard error of measurement on the WISC-IV (Weschler Intelligence Scale for Children, 4th edition) varies slightly from one age to the next, the average standard error for the total score is around 3 points. So the bands around Sam's and Lauren's IQ scores, about 96 to 102 and 100 to 106, are overlapping. Either child could have scored 100, 101, or 102.

Discussing Test Results with Families.   At times, you and your teachers will be expected to explain or describe test results to your students' families. The Theory into Action Guidelines will give principals and teachers direction.

The Dangers and Possibilities of High-Stakes Testing

Principals and teachers increasingly are expected to use standardized test scores to make judgments about students, curricula, and school performance. This trend is likely to continue. Recently enacted federal law, for example, requires each state to categorize its public schools based on results from such tests. This enhanced status of standardized

THEORY INTO ACTION GUIDELINES

Family Partnerships for Using Test Results

Be ready to explain, in nontechnical terms, what each type of score on the test report means.

Examples

1. If the test is norm-referenced, know if the comparison group was national or local. Explain that the child's score shows how he or she performed *in relation to* the other students in the comparison group.
2. If the test is criterion-referenced, explain that the child's scores show how well he or she performs in specific areas.

If the test is norm-referenced, focus on the percentile scores. They are the easiest to understand.

Examples

1. Percentile scores tell what percent of students in the comparison group made the same score or lower—higher percentiles are better and 99 is as high as you can get; 50 is average.
2. Remind parents that percentile scores do not tell the "percent correct" so scores that would be bad on a classroom test (say 65 to 75% or so) are above average—even good—as percentile scores.

Avoid using grade-equivalent scores.

Examples

1. If parents want to focus on the "grade level" of their child, tell them that high grade-equivalent scores reflect a thorough understanding of the current grade level and not the capacity to do higher grade-level work.
2. Tell parents that the same grade-equivalent score has different meanings in different subjects—reading versus mathematics, for example.

Be aware of the error in testing.

Examples

1. Encourage parents to think of the score not as a single point but as a range or band that includes the score.
2. Ignore small differences between scores.
3. Note that sometimes individual skills on criterion-referenced tests are measured with just a few (two or three) items. Compare test scores to actual class work in the same areas.

Use conference time to plan a learning goal for the child, one that families can support.

Examples

1. Have example questions, similar to those on the test, to show parents what their child can do easily and what kinds of questions he or she found difficult.
2. Be prepared to suggest an important skill to target.

---

testing requires teachers to be far more knowledgeable about every aspect of these tools. We begin with a basic question: Just how much testing is going on?

How Widespread Is Standardized Testing?

Test scores may affect "admission" to first grade, promotion from one grade to the next, high school graduation, access to special programs, placement in special education classes, teacher certification and tenure, and school funding. Because the decisions affected by test scores are so critical, many educators call this process **high-stakes testing.** The teachers we work with are frustrated that results of these high-stakes tests often come too late in the year to help them plan instruction or remediation for their current students. They also are troubled by the amount of time testing takes—to prepare for the tests and to give them. They complain that the tests cover material their curriculum does not include. Are they right?

Documented Problems with High-Stakes Testing. When so much rides on the results of a test, you would assume the test actually measured what had been taught. In the past, this match has been a problem. One group of teachers in St. Louis found that fewer than 10% of the items in their curriculum overlapped in both the textbooks and the standardized tests they were using (Fiske, 1988). Recently, the overlap between what is taught and what is tested has been improving, but it still makes sense to be aware of possible mismatches.

What about time? Studies have found that in some states, 80% of the elementary schools spend about 20% of their instructional time preparing for the end-of-grade tests (Abrams & Madaus, 2003). Studies of the actual high-stakes tests in action show other troubling consequences. Testing narrows the curriculum. In fact, after examining the results of years of testing, Lisa Abrams and George Madaus (2003) concluded that wherever high-stakes tests operate, "the exam content eventually defines the curriculum" (p. 32). For example, using the *Texas Assessment of Academic Skills* has led to curriculum changes that overemphasize what is tested and neglect other areas. In addition, it seems that the test of mathematics is also a test of reading. Students with poor reading ability have trouble with the math test, especially if their first language is not English.

Another unintended consequence of the early-warning testing in elementary school is to "push out" students who believe they are going to fail the high school graduation test. If they won't graduate anyway, they see no point in continuing to attend school (McNeil & Valenzuela, 2000). For example, in the 2000–2001 school year, about one-third of the English language learners dropped out of high school in New York. The main reason given was their inability to pass the required Regents Exam (Medina, 2002).

Accountability and High-Stakes Testing

One of the high-stakes uses for test results is to hold teachers, schools, and administrators **accountable** for student performance. For example, teacher bonuses might be tied to their students' achievement or school funding might be affected by testing results. The press for accountability that accompanies the No Child Left Behind Act (NCLB) will be with us for the foreseeable future. All 50 states have submitted plans to the Department of Education to meet the NCLB mandates. The demonstration of adequate yearly progress (AYP) by states, school districts, and schools is a key component of the requirements. Although states may define AYP in different ways, their AYP definition must apply "the same high standards of academic achievement to all public elementary and secondary school students in the state; [be] statistically valid and reliable; [and] result in continuous and substantial improvement for all students" (NCLB, 2001, sec. 111(a)(2)(c)). In addition, the AYP definition must include substantial and continuous improvement, not merely for the total aggregate of students, but for the following four groups of students: economically disadvantaged, major racial and ethnic minorities, those with disabilities, and those with limited English proficiency. These AYP objectives must be set with the goal that all students are proficient or better by the 2013–2014 school year. Schools that fail to meet their AYP objectives for two years will be identified for improvement (Linn, Baker, & Betebenner, 2002). The students in these "failing schools" can transfer. If the school's scores don't improve after three years, the school curriculum and/or staff can be replaced.

The evidence to date, however, suggests that the NCLB goals for students are unrealistic and seem likely to produce failure and demoralization rather than success and pride. The focus on achievement for all students and the special attention on those who are performing poorly are praiseworthy, but if the AYP requirements are enforced, they will result in sanctions for many schools that are making great strides in teaching students (Linn, 2003). Like most things, accountability and high-stakes testing have their benefits, but they also have costs. Is it reasonable to hold teachers and schools accountable for student achievement? The Point/Counterpoint on the next page shows that people disagree.

As you can tell from the Point/Counterpoint, high-stakes testing is a complex and controversial practice. To be valuable, testing programs must have a number of characteristics. Of course the tests used must be reliable, valid for the purposes used, and free of bias. In addition, a testing program should:

1. *Match the content standards of the district.* This is a vital part of validity.
2. *Be part of the larger assessment plan.* No one test provides all the necessary information about student achievement. It is critical that schools avoid making pass/fail decisions based on a single test.
3. *Test complex thinking*, not just skills and factual knowledge.
4. *Provide alternate assessment strategies* for students with identifiable disabilities.
5. *Provide opportunities for retesting* when the stakes are high.
6. *Include all students* in the testing, but also provide informative reports of the results that make the students' situations clear if they have special challenges or circumstances such as disabilities.
7. *Provide appropriate remediation* when students fail.
8. Make sure all students taking the test *have adequate opportunities to learn* the material being tested.
9. *Take into account the student's language.* Students who have difficulty reading or writing in English will not perform well on tests that require English.
10. *Use test results for children, not against them.* (Haladyna, 2002)

This is important, so we repeat: Standardized achievement tests must be chosen so that the items on the test actually measure knowledge gained in the classes. Also, students must have the necessary skills to take the test. If students score low on a science test, not because they lack knowledge about science but because they have difficulty reading the questions, don't speak English, or have too little time to finish, then the test is not a valid measure of science achievement for those students.

POINT/COUNTERPOINT

Should Tests Be Used to Hold Teachers Accountable?

There are two possible meanings for accountability. The first has to do with gathering information so that we can make good educational decisions about programs, policies, and resources. The second is holding someone responsible for student learning—usually the school or the teacher (Haladyna, 2002).

POINT

The public needs information.
The argument for this kind of accountability is that the public has a right to know how their schools are doing, especially because public money is used to finance schools. Testing may help to raise expectations for the lowest-performing schools and give educators the information they need to improve the programs in their schools (Doherty, 2002). And people who make decisions about which reading programs to adopt or how to allocate resources need information about student achievement. The No Child Left Behind Act of 2002 mandates annual assessment in reading and math for every student in grades 3–8. One goal is "to empower parents, citizens, educators, administrators, and policy makers with data from those annual assessments. The data will be available in annual report cards on school performance and on statewide progress. They will give parents information about the quality of their children's schools, the qualifications of teachers, and their children's progress in key subjects" (U.S.

Department of Education, *No Child Left Behind Fact Sheet*, 2002).

COUNTERPOINT

Using test scores to hold teachers and schools accountable does not make sense.
Will results of standardized tests really give parents information about the "quality of their children's schools" or the "qualifications of teachers"? If the test matches important objectives of the curriculum, is given to students who actually studied the curriculum for a reasonable period of time, is free of bias, fits the students' language capabilities, and was administered properly, then test results provide some information about the effectiveness of the school.

But studies of the actual tests in action show troubling consequences. Testing narrows the curriculum. For example, using the *Texas Assessment of Academic Skills* has led to curriculum changes that overemphasize what is tested and neglect other areas. The test of mathematics appears to also be a test of reading. Students with poor reading ability have trouble with the math test, especially if their first language is not English. And an unintended consequence of the early warning testing in elementary school is to "push out" students who leave school because they decide they are going to fail the high school graduation test—so why should they bother (McNeil & Valenzuela, 2000).

Advantages in Taking Tests—Fair and Unfair

In this section we will consider three basic issues: Are standardized tests biased against minority students? Can students gain an advantage on admissions tests through coaching? Can they be taught test-taking skills?

Bias and Fairness in Testing.   Are tests such as the individual measures of intelligence or college admissions tests fair assessments for minority group students? This is a complex question. Research on test bias shows that most standardized tests predict school achievement equally well across all groups of students. Items that might appear on the surface to be biased against minorities are not necessarily more difficult for minorities to answer correctly (Sattler, 2001). Even though standardized aptitude and achievement tests are not biased against minorities in predicting school performance, many people believe that the tests still can be unfair. Tests may not have *procedural fairness*, that is, some groups may not have an equal opportunity to show what they know on the test. Here are a few examples:

1. The language of the test and the tester is often different from the languages of the students.
2. Answers that support middle-class values are often rewarded with more points.
3. On individually administered intelligence tests, being very verbal and talking a lot is rewarded.

The above three factors favor students who feel comfortable in that particular situation. Also, tests may not be fair because different groups have had different *opportunities to learn* the material tested. The questions asked tend to center on experiences and facts more familiar to the dominant culture than to minority group students.

Stereotype Threat.   When stereotyped individuals are in situations where a stereotype applies, they bear an extra emotional and cognitive burden. The burden is the possibility of confirming the stereotype, in the eyes of others or in their own eyes. Thus, when girls are asked to solve complicated mathematics problems, for example, they are at risk of confirming widely held stereotypes that girls are inferior to boys in mathematics. It is not necessary that the individual even believes the stereotype. All that matters is that the person is *aware* of the stereotype and *cares about performing* well enough to disprove its unflattering implications (Aronson, Lustina, Good, Keough, Steele, & Brown, 1999). What are the results of stereotype threat? Recent research provides answers that should interest all educators.

In the short run, the fear that you might confirm a negative stereotype can induce test anxiety and undermine performance. In a series of experiments, Joshua Aronson, Claude Steele, and their colleagues have demonstrated that, when African American or Latino college students are put situations that induce stereotype threat, their performance suffers (Aronson & Inzlicht, 2004; Aronson & Steele, 2005). For example, African American and white undergraduate subjects in an experiment at Stanford University were told that the test they were about to take would precisely measure their verbal ability. A similar group of subjects was told that the purpose of the test was to understand the psychology of verbal problem solving and not to assess individual ability. When the test was presented as diagnostic of verbal ability, the African American students solved about half as many problems as the white students. In the nonthreat situation, the two groups solved about the same number of problems. Other studies found that anxiety and distraction were the main impediments. The African American students were more likely to be thinking about the stereotypes as they tried to work.

All groups, not just minority group students, can be susceptible to stereotype threat. In another study, the subjects were white male college students who were very strong in mathematics. One group was told that the test they were taking would help experimenters determine why Asian students performed so much better than whites on that particular test. Another group just took the test. The group that faced the stereotype threat of confirming that "Asians are better in math" scored significantly lower on the test (Aronson et al., 1999).

How does stereotype threat affect test performance? One link is anxiety. Some studies have found higher levels of anxiety among African American elementary school and middle school students compared to white students. And higher anxiety is correlated with lower scores on tests. But does stereotype threat actually cause anxiety and does anxiety actually lead to lower scores? Jason Osborne (2001) studied a large representative national sample of white, African American, and Latino high school seniors who took achievement tests and tests of anxiety at the same time. The white students scored significantly higher, but anxiety played a role in those differences. Even after controlling for prior achievement in school, anxiety explained almost one-third of the racial differences in the scores. Anxiety and distraction appeared to be the main problems in the studies of college students, too. The African American students were more likely to be thinking about the stereotypes as they tried to work (Spencer, Steele, & Quinn, 1999).

As you saw in Chapter 5, students often develop self-defeating strategies to protect their self-esteem about academics. They withdraw, claim to not care, and exert little effort; they *disidentify* or psychologically disengage from success in the domain and claim "math is for nerds" or "school is for losers." There is evidence that African Americans are more likely than whites to reject identifying with academics (Major & Schmader, 1998; Ogbu, 1997). Once students define academics as "uncool" it is unlikely they will exert the effort needed for real learning. We cannot say that all differences among scores of different groups of students are caused by stereotype threat (Sackett, Hardison, & Cullen, 2004), but the process probably plays a role.

Combating Stereotype Threat.   Stereotypes are pervasive and difficult to change. Rather than wait for changes, it may be better to acknowledge that these images exist, at least in the eyes of many, and give students ways of coping with the stereotypes. Aronson, Fried, and Good (2002) demonstrated the powerful effects of changing beliefs about intelligence. In their study, African American and white undergraduates were asked to write letters to "at-risk" middle school students to encourage them to persist in school. Some of the undergraduates were given evidence that intelligence is *improvable* and encouraged to communicate this information to their pen pals. Others were given information about multiple intelligences, but not told that these multiple abilities can be improved. The middle school students were not real, but the process of writing persuasive letters about improving intelligence proved powerful. The African American college students, and the white students to a lesser extent, who were encouraged to believe that intelligence can be improved had higher grade point averages and reported greater enjoyment of and engagement in school when contacted at the end of the next school quarter. Thus, believing that intelligence can be improved might inoculate students against the effects of stereotype threat when they take high-pressure tests.

Concern about cultural bias in testing has led some psychologists to try to develop **culture-fair** or **culture-neutral tests.** These efforts have not been very successful. On many of the so-called culture-fair tests, the performance of students from lower socioeconomic backgrounds and minority groups has been the same as or worse than their performance on the standard Wechsler and Binet Intelligence scales (Sattler, 2001).

Preparing Students for Testing.   We recently read about a sixth-grade class that used their statewide testing as an opportunity for problem-based learning (Ewy, with student authors, 1997). This class read a newspaper article about the upcoming test and

TABLE 8.2   Taking on "The Test": Problem-Based Learning

Students in a sixth-grade classroom produced this chart as they designed a program for improving their own test performance.

Problem Analysis Chart

Problem: How can we improve our performance on the IGAP test in such a way that we (1) keep improving each year, (2) set a good example for our school, (3) make preparing for IGAP more fun?

Our Ideas	Facts We Know	Our Questions	Our Action Plan
■ Pay attention in class ■ Hold fundraiser to get books and computer program ■ Look at actual IGAP book format ■ Practice: Use computer games ■ Get someone who knows how to coach IGAP: teacher, parent, friend, brother/sister ■ Tackle one subject at a time ■ Find out who wants to know	■ Test on reading, writing, and math ■ You get better when you practice ■ You might read questions wrong ■ Fill in circles ■ Writing is scored by time, spelling, sentence structure	■ When is IGAP? ■ How long is the test? ■ How long should we practice? ■ What should we practice (math, reading, writing)? ■ How many problems? ■ How is the test scored (math, reading, writing)? ■ How much time is given for math, reading, and writing? ■ How did I do on the last IGAP test?	■ Ask principal, teacher, tutor ■ Ask person who made test ■ Work with teacher to set up schedule ■ Look for resources for practice ■ Ask parents and principal to help

Source: From "Kids Take on 'the test'," by Christine Ewy & student authors, 1997, *Educational Leadership*, 54(4), p. 77. Reprinted by permission of Christine Ewy.

the less than stellar performance of the sixth graders in previous years. They took on the following problem: How could they improve their own test scores on the IGAP (Illinois Goal Assessment Program)? The students talked about why the problem was important and how to solve it, generating the problem analysis chart in Table 8.2.

Then they divided into groups to do different tasks: schedule practice times, look for resources, make up questions and interview experts, and set up a tutoring program. The result? The students met or exceeded the state reading, writing, and mathematics goals. When they moved to junior high and had to take the math placement test, these students researched the test. What are cutoff points, the possible range of scores, evaluation criteria? Perhaps you can take on a similar problem in your school. Instructional leaders can use the Theory into Action Guidelines on the next page to give teachers suggestions for helping students take tests.

Helping Students with Disabilities Prepare for High-Stakes Tests.   Erik Carter and his colleagues (2005) tested a procedure for preparing students with learning

THEORY INTO ACTION GUIDELINES

Becoming an Expert Test Taker

Use the night before the test effectively.

Examples

1. Study the night before the exam, ending with a final look at a summary of the key points, concepts, and relationships.
2. Get a good night's sleep. If you know you generally have trouble sleeping the night before an exam, try getting extra sleep on several previous nights.

Set the situation so you can concentrate on the test.

Examples

1. Give yourself plenty of time to eat and get to the exam room.
2. Don't sit near a friend. It may make concentration difficult. If your friend leaves early, you may be tempted to do so too.

Make sure you know what the test is asking.

Examples

1. Read the directions carefully. If you are unsure, ask the instructor or proctor for clarification.
2. Read each question carefully to spot tricky words, such as *not, except, all of the following but one.*
3. On an essay test, read every question first, so you know the size of the job ahead of you and can make informed decisions about how much time to spend on each question.
4. On a multiple-choice test, read every alternative, even if an early one seems right.

Use time effectively.

Examples

1. Begin working right away and move as rapidly as possible while your energy is high.
2. Do the easy questions first.
3. Don't get stuck on one question. If you are stumped, mark the question so you can return to it easily later, and go on to questions you can answer more quickly.
4. If you are unsure about a question, answer it but mark it so you can go back if there is time.
5. On a multiple-choice test, if you know you will not have time to finish, fill in all the remaining questions with the same letter if there is no penalty for guessing.
6. If you are running out of time on an essay test, do not leave any questions blank. Briefly outline a few key points to show the instructor you "knew" the answer but needed more time.

Know when to guess on multiple-choice or true-false tests.

Examples

1. Always guess when only right answers are scored.
2. Always guess when you can eliminate some of the alternatives.
3. Don't guess if there is a penalty for guessing, unless you can confidently eliminate at least one alternative.
4. Are correct answers always longer? shorter? in the middle? more likely to be one letter? more often true than false?
5. Does the grammar give the right answer away or eliminate any alternatives?

Check your work.

Examples

1. Even if you can't stand to look at the test another minute, reread each question to make sure you answered the way you intended.
2. If you are using a machine-scored answer sheet, check occasionally to be sure the number of the question you are answering corresponds to the number of the answer on the sheet.

On essay tests, answer as directly as possible.

Examples

1. Avoid flowery introductions. Answer the question in the first sentence and then elaborate.
2. Don't save your best ideas till last. Give them early in the answer.
3. Unless the instructor requires complete sentences, consider listing points, arguments, and so on by number in your answer. It will help you organize your thoughts and concentrate on the important aspects of the answer.

Learn from the testing experience.

Examples

1. Pay attention when the teacher reviews the answers. You can learn from your mistakes, and the same question may reappear in a later test.

2. Notice if you are having trouble with a particular kind of item; adjust your study approach next time to handle this type of item better.

---

disabilities, mild intellectual disabilities, and language impairments for the high-stakes test given in their state. The students were ages 15 to 19; over half were African American males and all had individual educational programs (see Chapter 3) to guide their education. None had passed the state-required achievement tests. Over six class periods, an instructor taught the students the strategies presented in Table 8.3.

TABLE 8.3 Helping Students with Learning Disabilities, Mild Intellectual Disabilities, and Language Impairments Prepare for High-Stakes Tests

Strategy	Objectives
Bubble sheet completion and timing	Fill in bubbles completely
	Be aware of how much available time is remaining
	Pace yourself when taking a test
	Answer all problems before time expires
Sorting problems	Sort problems by differentiating between easier and more difficult problems
	Complete the easy problems on a test prior to attempting the more difficult ones
	Sort problems based on similarity in content
Estimation	Estimate answers in math problems by using rounding
Substitution and backsolving	Substitute the answers provided on a multiple-choice test into the question being asked to find the one correct answer
Recopying problems	Rewrite problems in a more familiar form to make them easier to solve
Underlining and reading all answers	Identify exactly what the question is asking you to do
	Read all questions carefully to make better answer choices
	Underline key words and phrases in the question
Elimination	Eliminate absurd multiple-choice answers
	Eliminate answers with redundant or similar information
	Eliminate answers with extreme qualifiers

Source: From "Preparing adolescents with high-incidence disabilities for high-stakes testing with strategy instruction," by E. W. Carter, J. Wehby, C. Hughes, S. M. Johnson, D. R. Plank, S. M. Barton-Arwood, & L. B. Lunsford. *Preventing School Failure,* 49(2), p. 58. Reprinted with permission of the Helen Dwight Reid Educational Foundation. Published by Heldref Publications, 1319 Eighteenth St., NW, Washington, DC 20036-1802. Copyright © 2005.

The good news is that after completing the preparation program, students improved their scores significantly on the tests. But the bad news is that the increases were not large enough to bring most of the students to the passing level. The authors recommend that preparation for testing should occur much earlier for students with disabilities. The students in this study, at an average age of 16, already were discouraged. The strategies taught should be closely aligned with the specific types of problems the students will encounter on the test and should be embedded in good content instruction. Finally, these students often are anxious about the negative consequences of failing—not receiving a regular diploma, no access to college or trade school. The best way to deal with this anxiety is to better equip the students with the academic skills they will need to succeed (Carter et al., 2005).

New Directions in Standardized Testing and Classroom Assessment

As traditional standardized tests became the basis for high-stakes decisions, pressure to do well led many teachers and schools to "teach to the test." Even more troubling, say critics, the traditional tests assess skills that have no equivalent in the real world. Students are asked to solve problems or answer questions they will never encounter again; they are expected to do so alone, without relying on any tools or resources, and while working under extreme time limits. Real life just isn't like this. Important problems take time to solve and often require using resources, consulting other people, and integrating basic skills with creativity and high-level thinking (Kirst, 1991a&b; Wolf, Bixby, Glenn, & Gardner, 1991).

Authentic Assessment

In response to these criticisms, the **authentic assessment** movement was born. The goal was to create standardized tests that assess complex, important, real-life outcomes. The approach is also called *direct assessment, performance assessment,* or *alternative assessment.* These terms refer to procedures that are alternatives to traditional multiple-choice standardized tests because they directly assess student performance on "real-life" tasks (Hambleton, 1996; Worthen, 1993). Some states are developing procedures to conduct authentic assessments.

It is important to be sensible about authentic assessment. Just being different from traditional standardized tests will not guarantee that the alternative tests are better. Many questions have to be answered. Assume, for example, that a new assessment requires students to complete a hands-on science project. If the student does well on one science project, does this mean the student "knows" science and would do well on other projects? One study found that students' performance on three different science tasks was quite variable: A student who did well on the absorbency experiment, for example, might have trouble with the electricity task. Thus, it was hard to generalize about a student's knowledge of science based on just the three tasks. Many more tasks would be needed to get a good sense of science knowledge. Because authentic assessment is a new area, it will take time to develop high-quality alternative assessments for use by whole school districts or states. Until more is known, it may be best to focus on authentic assessment at the classroom level.

Authentic Classroom Tests

Authentic tests ask students to apply skills and abilities as they would in real life. For example, they might use fractions to enlarge or reduce recipes. If our instructional goals for students include the abilities to write, speak, listen, create, think critically, solve problems, or apply knowledge, then our tests should ask students to write, speak, listen, create, think, solve, and apply. How can this happen?

Many educators suggest we look to the arts and sports for analogies to solve this problem. If we think of the "test" as being the recital, exhibition, game, mock court trial, or other performance, then teaching to the test is just fine. All coaches, artists, and musicians gladly "teach" to these "tests" because performing well on these tests is the whole point of instruction. Authentic assessment asks students to perform. The performances may be thinking performances, physical performances, creative performances, or other forms.

It may seem odd to talk of thinking as a performance, but there are many parallels. Serious thinking is risky because real-life problems are not well defined. Often the outcomes of our thinking are public; others evaluate our ideas. Like a dancer auditioning for a Broadway show, we must cope with the consequences of being evaluated. Like a sculptor looking at a lump of clay, a student facing a difficult problem must experiment, observe, redo, imagine and test solutions, apply both basic skills and inventive techniques, make interpretations, decide how to communicate results to the intended audience, and often accept criticism and improve the solution (Eisner, 1999; Herman, 1997). Table 8.4 on the next page lists some characteristics of authentic tests.

The approach is also called *direct assessment* or *alternative assessment*. These terms refer to procedures that are alternatives to traditional multiple-choice standardized tests because they directly assess student performance on "real-life" tasks (Hambleton, 1996; Popham, 2005). For example, the Center for Technology in Learning of SRI International, a nonprofit science research institute, provides an online resource bank of performance-based assessments linked to the National Science Education Standards. The resource is called PALS (Performance Assessment Links in Science). Go to http://butterfly.ctl.sri.com/pals/index.html; see the performance tasks for kindergarten through twelfth grade. You can select tasks by standard and grade level. Each task comes with directions for students, a guide for administrators, and a scoring guide or rubric. Many also have examples of student work.

Performance in Context: Portfolios and Exhibitions

The concern with authentic assessment has led to the development of several new approaches based on the goal of *performance in context*. Instead of circling answers to "factual" questions on nonexistent situations, students are required to solve real problems. Facts are used in a context where they apply, for example, the student uses grammar

TABLE 8.4 Characteristics of Authentic Tests

A. Structure and Logistics
   1. Are more appropriately public; involve an audience, a panel, and so on.
   2. Do not rely on unrealistic and arbitrary time constraints.
   3. Offer known, not secret, questions or tasks.
   4. Are more like portfolios or a *season* of games (not one-shot).
   5. Require some collaboration with others.
   6. Recur—and are *worth* practicing for, rehearsing, and retaking.
   7. Make assessment and feedback to students so central that school schedules, structures, and policies are modified to support them.

B. Intellectual Design Features
   1. Are "essential"—not needlessly intrusive, arbitrary, or contrived to "shake out" a grade.
   2. Are "enabling"—constructed to point the student toward more sophisticated use of the skills or knowledge.
   3. Are contextualized, complex intellectual challenges, not "atomized" tasks, corresponding to isolated "outcomes."
   4. Involve the student's own research or use of knowledge, for which "content" is a means.
   5. Assess student habits and repertoires, not mere recall or plug-in skills.
   6. Are *representative* challenges, designed to emphasize *depth* more than breadth.
   7. Are engaging and educational.
   8. Involve somewhat ambiguous ("ill-structured") tasks or problems.

C. Grading and Scoring Standards
   1. Involve criteria that assess essentials, not easily counted (but relatively unimportant) errors.
   2. Are graded not on a "curve" but in reference to performance standards (criterion-referenced, not norm-referenced).
   3. Involve demystified criteria of success that appear to *students* as inherent in successful activity.
   4. Make self-assessment a part of the assessment.
   5. Use a multifaceted scoring system instead of one aggregate grade.
   6. Exhibit harmony with shared schoolwide aims—a *standard*.

D. Fairness and Equity
   1. Ferret out and identify (perhaps hidden) strengths.
   2. Strike a *constantly* examined balance between honoring achievement and native skill or fortunate prior training.
   3. Minimize needless, unfair, and demoralizing comparisons.
   4. Allow appropriate room for student learning styles, aptitudes, and interests.
   5. Can be—should be—attempted by *all* students, with the test "scaffolded up," not "dumbed down," as necessary.

Source: From "Teaching to the Authentic Test," by G. W. Wiggins, 1989, *Educational Leadership*, April 1989, *45*(7), p. 44. Copyright © 1989 by the Association of Supervision and Curriculum Development. Reprinted with permission. All rights reserved, www.ascd.org.

facts to write a persuasive letter to a software company requesting donations for the class computer center. The following example of a test of performance is taken from the Connecticut Core of Common Learning:

> Many local supermarkets claim to have the lowest prices. But what does this really mean? Does it mean that every item in their store is priced lower, or just some of them? How can you really tell which supermarket will save you the most money? Your assignment is to design and carry out a study to answer this question. What items and prices will you compare and why? How will you justify the choice of your "sample"? How reliable is the sample, etc.? (Wolf, Bixby, Glenn, & Gardner, 1991, p. 61)

Students completing this "test" will use mathematical facts and procedures in the context of solving a real-life problem. In addition, they will have to think critically and write persuasively.

Portfolios and exhibitions are two new approaches to assessment that require performance in context. With these new approaches, it is difficult to tell where instruction stops and assessment starts because the two processes are interwoven.

Portfolios. For years photographers, artists, models, and architects have had portfolios to display their skills and, often, to get jobs. A **portfolio** is a systematic collection of work, often including work in progress, revisions, student self-analyses, and reflections on what the student has learned (Popham, 2005). For example, one student's self-reflection is presented in Figure 8.5 on the next page. Written work or artistic pieces are common contents of portfolios, but students might also include graphs, diagrams, snapshots of displays, peer comments, audio- or videotapes, laboratory reports, and computer programs, anything that demonstrates learning in the area being taught and assessed (Belanoff & Dickson, 1991; Camp, 1990; Wolf, Bixby, Glenn, & Gardner, 1991). The Vermont Mathematics Portfolio, for example, has (a) five to seven of the student's "best pieces," including at least one puzzle, one investigation, one application, and no more than two examples of group work; (b) a letter to the portfolio examiner; and (c) a collection of other pieces of mathematics work (Abruscato, 1993). The Theory into Action Guidelines on page 303 should give principals some ideas for helping teachers use portfolios in their teaching. There is a distinction between process portfolios and final or "best work" portfolios. The distinction is similar to the difference between formative and summative evaluation. Process portfolios document learning and show progress. Best works portfolios showcase final accomplishments (Johnson & Johnson, 2002).

Exhibitions. An **exhibition** is a performance test that has two additional features. First, it is public, so students preparing exhibitions must take the audience into account; communication and understanding are essential. Second, an exhibition often requires many hours of preparation because it is the culminating experience of a whole program of study. Thomas Guskey and Jane Bailey (2001) suggest that exhibits help students understand the qualities of good work and recognize those qualities in their own productions and performances. Students also benefit when they select examples of their work

FIGURE 8.5 A Student Reflects on Learning: Self-Analysis of Work in a Portfolio
Not only has this student's writing improved, but the student has become a more self-aware and self-critical writer.

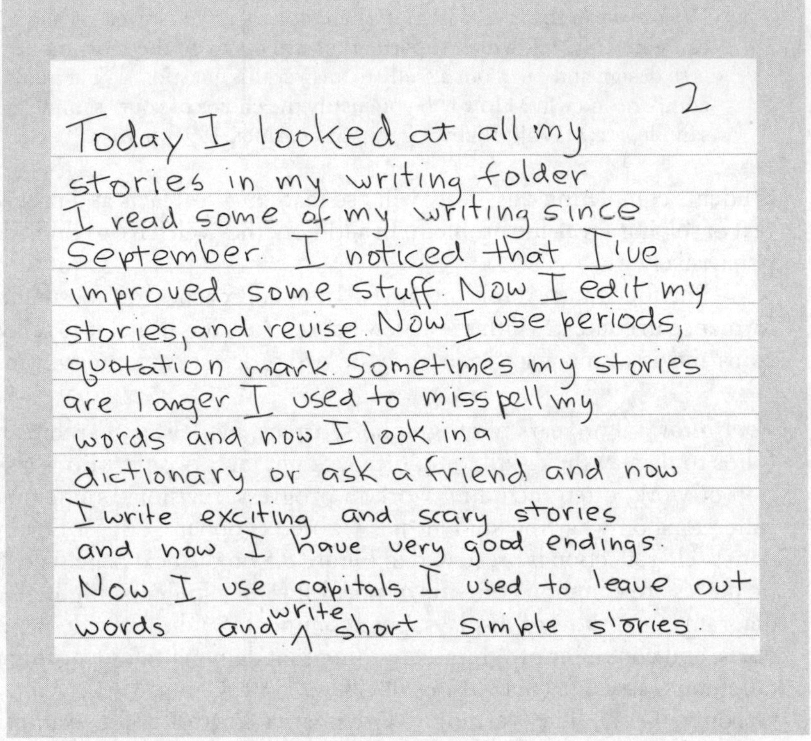
2
Today I looked at all my
stories in my writing folder
I read some of my writing since
September I noticed that I've
improved some stuff. Now I edit my
stories, and revise. Now I use periods,
quotation mark. Sometimes my stories
are langer I used to misspell my
words and now I look in a
dictionary or ask a friend and now
I write exciting and scary stories
and now I have very good endings.
Now I use capitals I used to leave out
words and write short simple stories.

Source: From "What Makes a Portfolio a Portfolio?" by F. L. Paulson, P. Paulson, and C. Meyers, 1991, *Educational Leadership*, February 1991, *48*(5), p. 63. Copyright © 1991 by the Association for Supervision and Curriculum Development. Reprinted with permission. All rights reserved, www.ascd.org.

to exhibit and articulate their reasons for the selections. Being able to judge quality can encourage student motivation by setting clear goals.

Evaluating Portfolios and Performances

Checklists, rating scales, and scoring rubrics are helpful when you assess performances because assessments of performances, portfolios, and exhibitions are criterion-referenced, not norm-referenced. In other words, the students' products and performances are compared to established public standards, not ranked in relation to other students' work (Cambourne & Turbill, 1990; Wiggins, 1991).

THEORY INTO ACTION GUIDELINES

Student Portfolios

Students should be involved in selecting the pieces that will make up the portfolio.

Examples

1. During the unit or semester, ask each student to select work that fits certain criteria, such as "my most difficult problem," "my best work," "my most improved work," or "three approaches to. . . ?"
2. For their final submissions, ask students to select pieces that best show how much they have learned.

A portfolio should include information that shows student self-reflection and self-criticism.

Examples

1. Ask students to include a rationale for their selections.
2. Have each student write a "guide" to his or her portfolio, explaining how strengths and weaknesses are reflected in the work included.
3. Include self- and peer critiques, indicating specifically what is good and what might be improved.
4. Model self-criticism of your own productions.

The portfolio should reflect the students' activities in learning.

Examples

1. Include a representative selection of projects, writings, drawings, and so forth.

2. Ask students to relate the goals of learning to the contents of their portfolios.

The portfolio can serve different functions at different times of the year.

Examples

1. Early in the year, it might hold unfinished work or "problem pieces."
2. At the end of the year, it should contain only what the student is willing to make public.

Portfolios should show growth.

Examples

1. Ask students to make a "history" of their progress along certain dimensions and to illustrate points in their growth with specific works.
2. Ask students to include descriptions of activities outside class that reflect the growth illustrated in the portfolio.

Teach students how to create and use portfolios.

Examples

1. Keep models of very well done portfolios as examples, but stress that each portfolio is an individual statement.
2. Examine your students' portfolios frequently, especially early in the year when they are just getting used to the idea. Give constructive feedback.

A Principal's Perspective

D. W. was a beginning principal at a K–6 elementary school with fourteen regular classroom teachers and approximately 300 students. Informed by the research of Doug Reeves (2000), she understood the positive correlation between the frequency of student writing and academic achievement. She knew as well that in order to be an effective instructional leader, she needed to clearly understand the academic abilities of her students and instructional aptitudes of her faculty. Inspired by Reeves, she determined that personally evaluating student writing would be an exemplary way to do both. At a faculty meeting early in the school year, she asked all of her teachers to periodically give her writing samples from their respective classes along with the scoring rubrics used to assess the work. She also asked that the teachers score the writing samples as they normally would but not reveal the score to the principal prior to her assessment. After reading each sample, she used the rubric to evaluate every student's writing and then compared her scores to those of the teacher. As it turned out, this practice not only helped her to gain a greater understanding of her students' abilities, but it also provided valuable insight about the teachers, generating critical talking points in individual conferences and faculty meetings regarding the frequency of writing assessments, the quality of the writing prompts, and the variations in scoring on rubrics. Additionally, participating as an external assessor of writing samples exemplified her commitment to being an instructional leader.

Reeves, D. B. (2000). *Accountability in action: A blueprint for learning organizations.* Denver, CO: Advanced Learning Press.

Scoring Rubrics.   A checklist or rating scale gives specific feedback about elements of a performance. **Scoring rubrics** are rules that are used to determine the quality of a student performance. It is often helpful to have students join in the development of rating scales and scoring rubrics. When students participate, they are challenged to decide what quality work looks or sounds like in a particular area. They know in advance what is expected. As students gain practice in designing and applying scoring rubrics, their work and their learning often improve. Figure 8.6 is an evaluation form for self- and peer assessment of contributions to cooperative learning groups.

Performance assessment requires careful judgment on the part of teachers and clear communication to students about what is good and what needs improving. In some ways the approach is similar to the clinical method first introduced by Binet to assess intelligence: It is based on observing the student perform a variety of tasks and comparing his or her performance to a standard. Just as Binet never wanted to assign a single number to represent the child's intelligence, teachers who use authentic assessments do not try to assign one score to the student's performance. Even if rankings, ratings, and grades have to be given, these judgments are not the ultimate goals—improvement of learning is. On page 305 are Theory into Action Guidelines for principals to help teachers develop rubrics, taken from Goodrich (1997).

Reliability, Validity, and Equity.   Because judgment plays such a central role in evaluating performances, issues of reliability, validity, and equity are critical considerations. When raters are experienced and scoring rubrics are well developed and refined, however, reliability may improve (Herman & Winters, 1994; LeMahieu, Gitomer, & Eresh, 1993).

Some of this improvement in reliability occurs because a rubric focuses the raters' attention on a few dimensions of the work and gives limited scoring levels to choose from. If scorers can give only a rating of 1, 2, 3, or 4, they are more likely to agree than if they could score based on a 100-point scale. So the rubrics may achieve reliability not because they capture underlying agreement among raters, but because the rubrics limit options and thus limit variability in scoring (Mabry, 1999).

In terms of validity, there is some evidence that students who are classified as "master" writers on the basis of portfolio assessment are judged less capable using

FIGURE 8.6　Student Self- and Peer Evaluation Form

This form will be used to assess the members of your learning group. Fill one form out on yourself. Fill one form out on each member of your group. During the group discussion, give each member the form you have filled out on them. Compare the way you rated yourself with the ways your groupmates have rated you. Ask for clarification when your rating differs from the ratings given you by your groupmates. Each member should set a goal for increasing his or her contribution to the academic learning of all group members.

Person Being Rated: _____

Write the number of points earned by the group member:
(4 = Excellent, 3 = Good, 2 = Poor, 1 = Inadequate)

_____ *On time for class.*

_____ *Arrives prepared for class.*

_____ *Reliably completes all assigned work on time.*

_____ *Work is of high quality.*

_____ *Contributes to groupmates' learning daily.*

_____ *Asks for academic help and assistance when it is needed.*

_____ *Gives careful step-by-step explanations (doesn't just tell answers).*

_____ *Builds on others' reasoning.*

_____ *Relates what is being learned to previous knowledge.*

_____ *Helps draw a visual representation of what is being learned.*

_____ *Voluntarily extends a project.*

Source: From "The Role of Cooperative Learning in Assessing and Communicating Student Learning," by D. W. Johnson and R. T. Johnson. In *ASCD 1996 Yearbook: Communicating Student Learning* (p. 41), T. Guskey (Ed.) Used by permission of the Association for Supervision and Curriculum Development. Copyright © 1996 by the Association for Supervision and Curriculum Development. Reprinted with permission. All rights reserved, www.ascd.org.

THEORY INTO ACTION GUIDELINES

Developing a Rubric

1. **Look at models:** Show students examples of good and not-so-good work. Identify the characteristics that make good ones good and the bad ones bad.
2. **List criteria:** Use the discussion of models to begin a list of what counts in quality work.
3. **Articulate gradations of quality:** Describe the best and worst levels of quality, then fill in the middle levels based on your knowledge of common problems and the not-so-good work.
4. **Practice on models:** Have your students use the rubrics to evaluate the models that you gave them in Step 1.
5. **Use self- and peer assessment:** Give students their task. As they work, stop them occasionally for self- and peer assessment.
6. **Revise:** Always give students time to revise their work based on the feedback they get in Step 5.
7. **Use teacher assessment:** Use the same rubrics students used to access their work.

Step 1 may be necessary only when you are asking students to engage in a task with which they are unfamiliar. Steps 3 and 4 are useful but time-consuming; you can do these on your own especially when you've been using rubrics for a while. A class experienced in rubric-based assessment can streamline the process so that it begins with listing criteria, after which the teacher writes out the gradations of quality, checks them with the students, makes revisions, then uses the rubrics for self-, peer, and teacher assessments.

standard writing assessment. Which form of assessment is the best reflection of enduring qualities? There is so little research on this question, it is hard to say (Herman & Winters, 1994). In addition, when rubrics are developed to assess specific tasks, the results of applying the rubric may not predict performance on anything except very similar tasks, so what do we actually know about students' learning more generally (Haertel, 1999; McMillan, 2004)?

Equity is an issue in all assessment and no less so with performances and portfolios. With a public performance there could be bias effects based on a student's appearance and speech or the student's access to expensive audio, video, or graphic resources. Performance assessments have the same potential as other tests to discriminate unfairly against students who are not wealthy or who are culturally different (McDonald, 1993). And the extensive group work, peer editing, and out-of-class time devoted to portfolios means that some students may have access to more extensive networks of support and outright help. Many students in your school will have families with sophisticated computer graphic and desktop publishing capabilities. Others may have little support from home. These differences can be sources of bias and inequity.

Informal Assessments

Informal assessments are ungraded (formative) assessments that gather information from multiple sources to help teachers make decisions (Banks, 2005). Early on in the unit, assessments should be formative (provide feedback, but not count toward a grade), saving the actual graded assessments for later in the unit when all students have had the chance to learn the material (Tomlinson, 2005). Some examples of informal assessment are student observations and checklists, questioning, journals, and student self-assessment.

Journals are very flexible and widely used informal assessments. Students usually have personal or group journals and write in them on a regular basis. In their study, Michael Pressley and his colleagues (2001) found that excellent first-grade literacy teachers used journaling for three purposes:

1. As communication tools that allowed students to express their own thoughts and ideas.
2. As an opportunity to apply what they have learned.
3. As an outlet to encourage fluency and creative expression in language usage.

Teachers may use journals to learn about their students in order to better connect their teaching to the students' concerns and interests. But often journals focus on academic learning, usually through responses to prompts. For example, Banks (2005) describes one high school physics teacher who asked his students to respond to these three questions in their journals:

1. How can you determine the coefficient of friction if you know only the angle of the inclined plane?
2. Compare and contrast some of the similarities and the differences between magnetic, electronic, and gravitational fields.

3. If you were to describe the physical concept of sound to your best friend, what music would you use to demonstrate this concept?

When he read the students' journals, the teacher realized that many of the students' basic assumptions about friction, acceleration, and velocity came from personal experiences and not from scientific reasoning. His approach to teaching had to change to reach the students. The teacher never would have known to make the changes without reading the journals (Banks, 2005).

There are many other kinds of informal assessments—keeping notes and observations about student performance, rating scales, and checklists. Every time teachers ask questions or watch students perform skills, the teachers are conducting informal assessments. One major message in this chapter is to match the type of assessment tools used to the target—what is being assessed.

Getting the Most from Traditional Tests

Even though there are many new ways of testing, students can still benefit from traditional tests. Both instruction and assessment are most effective when they are well organized and planned. When you have a good plan, you are in a better position to judge the tests provided in teacher's manuals and texts and those developed by teachers.

When to Test? Frank Dempster (1991) examined the research on reviews and tests and reached these useful conclusions for teachers:

1. Frequent testing encourages the retention of information and appears to be more effective than a comparable amount of time spent reviewing and studying the material.
2. Tests are especially effective in promoting learning if you give students a test on the material soon after they learn it, then retest on the material later. The retestings should be spaced farther and farther apart.
3. The use of cumulative questions on tests is a key to effective learning. Cumulative questions ask students to apply information learned in previous units to solve a new problem.

Unfortunately, the curriculum in many schools is so full that there is little time for frequent tests and reviews. Dempster argues that students will learn more if we "teach them less," that is, if the curriculum includes fewer topics, but explores those topics in greater depth and allows more time for review, practice, testing, and feedback (Dempster, 1993).

Judging Textbook Tests. Most elementary and secondary school texts today come complete with supplemental materials such as teaching manuals, handout masters, and ready-made tests. Using these tests can save time, but is this good teaching practice? The answer depends on your objectives for your students, the way you taught the material, and the quality of the tests provided (Airasian, 2005; McMillan, 2004). If the

TABLE 8.5 Key Points to Consider in Judging Textbook Tests

1. The decision to use a textbook test must come *after* a teacher identifies the objectives that he or she taught and now wants to assess.
2. Textbook tests are designed for the typical classroom, but since few classrooms are typical, most teachers deviate somewhat from the text in order to accommodate their pupils' needs.
3. The more classroom instruction deviates from the textbook objectives and lesson plans, the less valid the textbook tests are likely to be.
4. The main consideration in judging the adequacy of a textbook test is the match between its test questions and what pupils were taught in their classes:

   ■ Are questions similar to the teacher's objectives and instructional emphases?
   ■ Do questions require pupils to perform the behaviors they were taught?
   ■ Do questions cover all or most of the important objectives taught?
   ■ Is the language level and terminology appropriate for pupils?
   ■ Does the number of items for each objective provide a sufficient sample of pupil performance?

Source: From *Classroom Assessment: Concepts and Applications, 5/e* (p. 94), by P. Airasian. Published by McGraw-Hill. Copyright © 2005 by The McGraw-Hill Companies. Adapted with permission of The McGraw-Hill Companies.

textbook test matches your testing plan and the instruction you actually provided for your students, then it may be the right test to use. Table 8.5 gives key points to consider in evaluating textbook tests.

One aspect of assessment that affects every school is grading. Teachers are more directly involved with grading than parents, but everyone in a school is concerned about how grades affect students.

Effects of Grades and Grading on Students

When we think of grades, we often think of competition. Highly competitive classes may be particularly hard on anxious students, students who lack self-confidence, and students who are less prepared. So, although high standards and competition do tend to be generally related to increased academic learning, it is clear that a balance must be struck between high standards and a reasonable chance to succeed. Rick Stiggins (2007) encourages administrators to consider the assessment experience from the students' point of view. And that perspective differs radically for students who generally "win" at testing and those on a "losing streak," as you can see in Table 8.6 on the assessment experience for students.

Effects of Failure

It may sound as though low grades and failure should be avoided in school. But the situation is not that simple.

TABLE 8.6 The Assessment Experience

For Students on Winning Streaks	For Students on Losing Streaks
Assessment results provide	
Continual evidence of success	Continual evidence of failure
The student feels	
Hopeful and optimistic	Hopeless
Empowered to take productive action	Initially panicked, giving way to resignation
The student thinks	
It's all good. I'm doing fine.	This hurts. I'm not safe here.
See the trend? I succeed as usual.	I just can't do this . . . again.
I want more success.	I'm confused. I don't like this—help!
School focuses on what I do well.	Why is it always about what I can't do?
I know what to do next.	Nothing I try seems to work.
Feedback helps me.	Feedback is criticism. It hurts.
Public success feels good.	Public failure is embarrassing.
The student becomes more likely to	
Seek challenges.	Seek what's easy.
Seek exciting new ideas.	Avoid new concepts and approaches.
Practice with gusto.	Become confused about what to practice.
Take initiative.	Avoid initiative.
Persist in the face of setbacks.	Give up when things become challenging.
Take risks and stretch—go for it!	Retreat and escape—trying is too dangerous!
These actions lead to	
Self-enhancement	Self-defeat, self-destruction
Positive self-fulfilling prophecy	Negative self-fulfilling prophecy
Acceptance of responsibility	Denial of responsibility
Manageable stress	High stress
Feeling that success is its own reward	No feelings of success; no reward
Curiosity, enthusiasm	Boredom, frustration, fear
Continuous adaptation	Inability to adapt
Resilience	Yielding quickly to defeat
Strong foundations for future success	Failure to master prerequisites for future success

The Value of Failing?   After reviewing many years of research on the effects of fail-ure from several perspectives, Margaret Clifford (1990, 1991) concluded:

> It is time for educators to replace easy success with challenge. We must encourage stu-dents to reach beyond their intellectual grasp and allow them the privilege of learning from mistakes. There must be a tolerance for error-making in every classroom, and gradual success rather than continual success must become the yardstick by which learn-ing is judged. (1990, p. 23)

Some level of failure may be helpful for most students, especially if teachers help the students see connections between hard work and improvement. Efforts to protect students from failure and to guarantee success may be counterproductive. In fact, the more able your students are, the more challenging and important it will be to help them learn to "fail successfully" (Foster, 1981). Carol Tomlinson, an expert on dif-ferentiated instruction, puts it this way: "Students whose learning histories have caused them to believe that excellence can be achieved with minimal effort do not learn to expend effort, and yet perceive that high grades are an entitlement for them" (2005, p. 266).

So far, we have been talking about the effects of failing a test or perhaps a course. But what about the effect of failing an entire grade—that is, of being "held back"?

Retention in Grade.   Almost 20% of seniors have repeated at least one grade since kindergarten, usually in the earlier grades (Kelly, 1999). Retained students are more likely to be male, members of minority groups, and living in poverty (Beebe-Frankenberger, Bocian, MacMillan, & Gresham, 2004).

Most research finds that grade retention is associated with poor long-term out-comes such as dropping out of school, higher arrest rates, fewer job opportunities, and lower self-esteem (Jimerson, Anderson, & Whipple, 2002). In their view, students gen-erally do better academically when they are promoted. For example, in a longitudinal study of twenty-nine retained and 50 low-achieving but promoted students, Shane Jimerson (1999) found that years later, the retained students had poorer educational and employment outcomes than the promoted students. The retained students dropped out more often, had lower-paying jobs, and received lower competence ratings from employers. In addition, the low-achieving but promoted students were comparable to a control group in all employment outcomes at age 20.

Retention assumes that the students just need more time and that they have the abilities needed to catch up. But one study in California found the students retained after second grade had the same average IQ score as those targeted for more inten-sive interventions under special education requirements. In addition, about 20% of the retained group had IQ scores in the range that would qualify as having mental retardation (Beebe-Frankenberger et al., 2004), so it was probably wrong to assume that these students would benefit from the same teaching. Primary-grade students who benefit from retention tend to be more emotionally immature than their peers, but have average or above average ability (Kelly, 1999; Pierson & Connell, 1992). Even with this group, the advantage may not last. In one study that followed many students for several years, children who could have been retained, but who were promoted, did about as well as similar children who were held back, and sometimes better (Reynolds, 1992).

No matter what, students who are having trouble should get help, whether they are promoted (this is often called "social promotion") or retained. However, just covering the same material again in the same way won't solve the students' academic or social problems. As Jeannie Oakes (1999) has said, "No sensible person advocates social promotion as it is currently framed—simply passing incompetent students on to the next grade" (p. 8). The best approach may be to promote the students along with their peers, but to give them special remediation during the summer or the next year (Mantzicopoulos & Morrison, 1992; Shepard & Smith, 1989). An even better approach would be to prevent the problems before they occur by providing extra resources such as tutoring (McCoy & Reynolds, 1999).

Effects of Feedback

The results of several studies of feedback fit well with the notion of "successful" or constructive failure. These studies have concluded that it is more helpful to tell students *why* they are wrong so they can learn more appropriate strategies (Bangert-Drowns, Kulik, Kulik, & Morgan, 1991). Students often need help figuring out why their answers are incorrect. Without such feedback, they are likely to make the same mistakes again. Yet this type of feedback is rarely given. In one study, only about 8 percent of the teachers noticed a consistent type of error in a student's arithmetic computation and informed the student (Bloom & Bourdon, 1980).

What are the identifying characteristics of effective written feedback? With older students (late elementary through high school), written comments are most helpful when they are personalized and when they provide constructive criticism. This means the teacher should make specific comments on errors or faulty strategies, but balance this criticism with suggestions about how to improve, and with comments on the positive aspects of the work (Butler & Nisan, 1986; Elawar & Corno, 1985). Working with sixth-grade teachers, Elawar and Corno (1985) found that feedback was dramatically improved when the teachers used these four questions as a guide: "What is the key error? What is the probable reason the student made this error? How can I guide the student to avoid the error in the future? What did the student do well that could be noted?" (p. 166). Here are some examples of teachers' written comments that proved helpful (Elawar & Corno, 1985, p. 164):

> Juan, you know how to get a percent, but the computation is wrong in this instance. . . . Can you see where? (Teacher has underlined the location of errors.)

> You know how to solve the problem—the formula is correct—but you have not demonstrated that you understand how one fraction multiplied by another can give an answer that is smaller than either $\left(\frac{1}{2} \times \frac{1}{2} = \frac{1}{4} \right)$.

These comments should help students correct errors and should recognize good work, progress, and increasing skill.

Grades and Motivation

If you are relying on grades to motivate students, you had better think again (Smith, Smith, & De Lisi, 2001). The assessments your school gives should support students' motivation to learn—not just to work for a grade. But is there really a difference between working for a grade and working to learn? The answer depends in part on how a grade is determined. Your teachers can use grades to motivate the kind of learning you intend students to achieve in your course. If they test only at a simple but detailed level of knowledge, you may force students to choose between complex learning and a good grade. But when a grade reflects meaningful learning, working for a grade and working to learn become the same thing. Finally, even though high grades may have some value as rewards or incentives for meaningful engagement in learning, low grades generally do not encourage greater efforts. Students receiving low grades are more likely to withdraw, blame others, decide that the work is "dumb," or feel responsible for the low grade but helpless to make improvements. They give up on themselves or on school (Tomlinson, 2005). Rather than give a failing grade, teachers might consider the work incomplete and give students support in revising or improving. Maintain high standards and give students a chance to reach them (Guskey, 1994; Guskey & Bailey, 2001).

Another effect on motivation occurs in high schools in the race for valedictorian. Sometimes, students and parents find clever ways to move ahead of the competition— but the strategies have little to do with learning. As Tom Guskey and Jane Bailey (2001) note, when a valedictorian wins by a 1/1,000 of decimal point, how meaningful is the learning behind the difference? Some high schools now name multiple valedictorians— as many as meet the highest standards of the school—because they believe that the educators' job is "not to *select* talent, but, rather, to *develop* talent" (Guskey & Bailey, 2001, p. 39). Principals can help teachers with grading by suggesting the Theory into Action Guidelines on the next page.

Summary

All teaching involves assessing and evaluating student learning. At the heart of assessment is judgment, making decisions based on values and goals. In the process of evaluation, we measure results and compare outcomes to some set of criteria. Test results have no meaning by themselves; we must make some kind of comparison to interpret them. There are two basic types of comparison: in the first, a test score is compared to the scores obtained by other people who have taken the same test, a norm-referenced comparison. The second type is criterion-referenced. Here, the comparison is to a fixed standard or minimum passing score.

Increasingly, standardized tests are given to students. These tests are called standardized because they have standard methods of developing items, administering the test, scoring it, and reporting the scores. The final version of the test is administered to a large sample of subjects as similar as possible to the students who will be taking the test in school systems throughout the country. This norming sample serves as a comparison group for all students who take the test. Test scores of individuals and groups are compared to the mean (average score) and distribution in the norming sample. To

THEORY INTO ACTION GUIDELINES

Grading

Avoid reserving high grades and high praise for answers that simply conform to those in the textbook.

Examples

1. Give extra points for correct and creative answers.
2. Withhold your opinions until all sides of an issue have been explored.
3. Reinforce students for disagreeing in a rational, productive manner.
4. Give partial credit for partially correct answers.

Make sure each student has a good chance to be successful, especially at the beginning of a new task.

Examples

1. Pretest students to make sure they have prerequisite abilities.
2. When appropriate, provide opportunities for students to retest to raise their grades, but make sure the retest is as difficult as the original.
3. Consider failing efforts as "incomplete" and encourage students to revise and improve.

Balance written and oral feedback.

Examples

1. Consider giving short, lively written comments with younger students and more extensive written comments with older students.

2. When the grade on a paper is lower than the student might have expected, be sure the reason for the lower grade is clear.
3. Tailor comments to the individual student's performance; avoid writing the same phrases over and over.
4. Note specific errors, possible reasons for errors, ideas for improvement, and work done well.

Make grades as meaningful as possible.

Examples

1. Tie grades to the mastery of important objectives.
2. Give ungraded assignments to encourage exploration.
3. Experiment with performances and portfolios.

Base grades on more than just one criterion.

Examples

1. Use essay questions as well as multiple-choice items on a test.
2. Grade oral reports and class participation.

make comparisons easy the scores are also standardized using percentile scores, z scores, stanine scores, or T scores. For example, a T score of 60 for an individual means that the person has scored one standard deviation above the mean score for the normative sample. Other comparisons such as grade-equivalent scores are useful to principals and teachers as they make assessments about progress.

No test provides a perfect picture of a person's or group's ability or progress. Two critical features of any test are its reliability and validity; that is, does the test measure the results consistently, and does it measure what it is suppose to measure? At a minimum all tests should be reliable and valid. Achievement tests are designed to measure what a student has learned in a specific content area whereas diagnostic tests measure a student's strengths and weaknesses, often to plan a course of action that will help the student learn and progress. Elementary school students are more likely than secondary school students to take diagnostic tests. High school students are more likely to take aptitude tests such as the SAT or IQ tests, which are meant to measure abilities developed over many years and to predict how well a student will do in the future.

Today, many important decisions about students, teachers, and schools are based in part on the results of standardized tests; in fact, the No Child Left Behind Act requires each state to create content standards in reading and mathematics and standardized tests to measure student learning and knowledge in those areas. Because the decisions affected by test scores are so critical, many educators call this process high-stakes testing. But most standardized tests have been criticized as being biased against minority students. Culture-fair tests are difficult to find. There is, however, evidence that students can prepare for standardized tests and learn test-taking skills. Another criticism of traditional forms of testing is that such tests are merely samples of performance at one particular point in time; they fail to capture the student's potential for future learning. An alternative view of cognitive assessment is based on the assumption that the goal of assessment is to reveal potential for learning and to identify the psychological and educational interventions that will help the person realize this potential. Ungraded (formative) informal assessments, such as journals, student observations, and self-assessments, gather information from multiple sources to help teachers make decisions about student progress.

As the public and government demanded greater accountability in education and as traditional standardized tests became the basis for high-stakes decisions, pressure to do well led many teachers and schools to "teach to the test." Even more troubling, say critics, the traditional tests assess skills that have no equivalent in the real world. In response to these criticisms, the authentic assessment movement was born. The goal was to create standardized tests that assess complex, important, real-life outcomes. The approach is also called direct assessment, performance assessment, or alternative assessment. Similarly, new approaches to classroom assessment include authentic classroom tests that ask students to apply skills and abilities as they would in real life.

The concern with authentic assessment has led to the development of several new approaches based on the goal of performance in context. For example, a portfolio is a purposeful collection of student work that demonstrates the student's efforts, progress, and achievements. The collection usually includes student participation in selecting contents, the criteria for judging merit, and evidence of student self-reflection. Portfolios include work in progress, revisions, student self-analyses, and reflections on what the student has learned, but the issues of reliability, validity, and equity remain important in assessment using such alternative means of testing.

High standards, a competitive class atmosphere, and a large percentage of lower grades are associated with increased absenteeism and dropout rates, especially for disadvantaged students. It may sound as though low grades and failure should be avoided in school, but the situation is not that simple. Failure can have both positive and negative effects on subsequent performance, depending on the situation and the personality of the students. For example, it is helpful to tell students *why* they are wrong so they can learn more appropriate strategies. Without such feedback, students are likely to make the same mistakes again, yet this type of feedback is rarely given. If teachers test only at a simple but detailed level of knowledge, they may force their students to choose between higher aspects of learning and a good grade; however, when a grade reflects meaningful learning, working for a grade and working to learn become the same thing. Finally, although high grades may have some value as rewards or incentives for meaningful engagement in learning, low grades generally do not encourage greater efforts. Ultimately, the task of the school is not to *identify* talent, but, rather, to *develop* it.

KEY TERMS

accountable (290)

achievement tests (284)

aptitude tests (287)

assessment (273)

assessment bias (283)

authentic assessment (298)

authentic tests (299)

central tendency (276)

confidence interval (282)

criterion-referenced testing (274)

culture-fair (culture-neutral) tests (294)

diagnostic tests (287)

exhibition (301)

grade-equivalent scores (278)

high-stakes testing (289)

informal assessments (306)

mean (276)

measurement (273)

median (276)

mode (276)

normal distribution (276)

norm groups (274)

norming sample (275)

norm-referenced testing (273)

percentile rank (278)

portfolio (301)

range (276)

reliability (281)

scoring rubric (304)

standard deviation (276)

standard error of measurement (282)

standard scores (279)

standardized tests (275)

stanine scores (280)

T score (280)

validity (283)

z score (279)

DEVELOPING YOUR PORTFOLIO

1. Based on the case at the beginning of this chapter, work with your teachers to develop a policy on sharing standardized test results with parents. Be sure that your policy is clear, precise, and can be included in a written statement to the parents of students in your school. As you draft your statement, address the following issues:
   a. School philosophy on the meaning and use of standardized test scores
   b. Brief description of the tests taken
   c. Guidance for interpreting the scores appropriately
   d. Parents' role in preparing their children for testing
   e. The role of teachers and the principal in meeting with parents about test results
   f. Any other information useful to the parents in your school
2. Analyze the state report card results for your school over the past few years (or, if there are no

report card results, compile and use standardized test scores).
   a. Identify specific areas of students' strengths and weaknesses.
   b. Develop a report to your faculty that is informative but not accusatory.
   c. Then jointly devise a plan with your teachers for capitalizing on the strengths and improving the areas of weakness.
3. Investigate how four other schools are using authentic assessment. Work with a teacher to develop a supplemental authentic assessment plan for a unit of study in your curriculum.
   a. Specify the components of the assessment process, for example, portfolios, exhibitions, projects, presentations, and so on.
   b. Specify the rubrics for evaluating each component.
   c. Discuss how your plan for authentic assessment will be used in grading.

INSTRUCTIONAL LEADER'S TOOLBOX

Readings

Airasian, P. W. *Classroom assessment: Concepts and applications* (5th ed.). New York: McGraw-Hill.

Aronson, J. (2002). *Improving academic achievement: Impact of psychological factors on education.* San Diego: Academic Press.

Aschbacher, P. (1997). New directions in student assessment [Special Issue]. *Theory into Practice, 36*(4), 194–272.

Ewy, C., & student authors. (1997). Kids take on "the test." *Educational Leadership, 54*(4), 76–78.

Goodrich, H. (1997). Understanding rubrics. *Educational Leadership, 54*(4), 14–17.

Haertel, E. H. (1999). Performance assessment and educational reform. *Phi Delta Kappa, 80,* 662–666.

Kelly, K. (1999). Retention vs. social promotion: Schools search for alternatives. *Harvard Education Letter, 15*(1), 1–3.

Sheppard, L., Hammerness, K., Darling-Hammond, L., & Rust, F. (2005). Assessment. In L. Darling-Hammond & J. Bransford (Eds.), *Preparing teachers for a changing world: What teachers should learn and be able to do* (pp. 275–326). San Francisco: Jossey-Bass.

Tomlinson, C. (2005, Summer). Differentiated Instruction. *Theory into Practice, 44*(3) (special issue).

Websites

electronicportfolios.com/portfolios.html
 Alternative Assessment and Electronic Portfolios
www.ericdigests.org/1996-3/testing.htm
 Assessment and Testing: Measuring Up to Expectations
mailer.fsu.edu/~jflake/assess.html
 Authentic Assessment
www.eric.ed.gov/ERICDocs/data/ericdocs2sql/content_storage_01/0000019b/80/15/15/e8.pdf
 Authentic Mathematics Assessment
www.ericdigests.org/pre-9218/case.htm
 The Case for Authentic Assessment
www.ericdigests.org/1996-1/creating.htm
 Creating Meaningful Performance Assessments

www.ericdigests.org/1997-4/young.htm
 A Developmental Approach to Assessment of Young Children
www.ericdigests.org/1997-1/grading.html
 Grading Students
www.ericdigests.org/1998-1/development.htm
 Guidelines for the Development and Management of Performance Assessments
www.ericdigests.org/1999-4/tests.htm
 Helping Children Master the Tricks and Avoid the Traps of Standardized Tests
www.ericdigests.org/1996-1/study.htm
 Making the A: How to Study for Tests
www.eric.ed.gov/ERICDocs/data/ericdocs2sql/content_storage_01/0000019b/80/16/cf/e7.pdf
 Norm- and Criterion-Referenced Testing
www.eric.ed.gov/ERICDocs/data/ericdocs2sql/content_storage_01/0000019b/80/23/40/b5.pdf
 On Standardized Testing
www.ncrel.org/skrs/areas/as0cont.htm
 Pathways to School Improvement—Assessment
www.ericdigests.org/1996-3/portfolios.htm
 Portfolios for Assessment and Instruction
nces.ed.gov/timss/
 TIMSS

Organizations

www.makingstandardswork.com/
 Center for Performance Assessment
www.ets.org
 Educational Testing Service
www.mcrel.org
 Mid-continent Research for Education and Learning
www.cse.ucla.edu/
 National Center for Research on Evaluation, Standards, and Student Testing
www.ncrel.org/sdrs/
 Pathways to School Improvement—Assessment
pals.sri.com/
 Performance Assessment Links in Science
www.PAREonline.net
 Practical Assessment Research and Evaluation

Assessing and Changing School Culture and Climate

PREVIEW: KEY POINTS

1. School culture and school climate are two ways to capture the feel or atmosphere of the school workplace.

2. Organizational culture is a pattern of shared orientations that binds the unit together and gives it a distinctive identity.

3. School culture can be examined at four levels: tacit assumptions, core values, shared norms, artifacts.

4. Schools can create cultures that encourage learning and improvement among all participants.

5. One such culture is a culture of academic optimism.

6. School climate is a relatively enduring quality of the school environment that is experienced by teachers, influences their behavior, and is based on their collective perceptions of behavior.

7. School climate can be viewed using a personality metaphor and measured in terms of the openness of interactions among teachers and between teachers and the principal.

8. School climate can also be examined using a health metaphor and measured in terms of healthy interactions among students, teachers, and administrators.

9. Change is characteristic of all organizations, but change can be random or directed.

10. Schools have the potential to become learning organizations that solve their own problems.

11. An organizational development model can provide guidelines for changing school climate.

Leadership Challenge

You are the principal of an urban high school in the Northeast. About one-third of your students are minority and another 14% are newly arrived immigrants to this "ethnically rich" community. The diversity of the school and community makes your job a challenging one. You are committed to improving the school; among your goals are increasing the graduation rates, increasing the number of students heading to college, and in general, making the high school a place where students want to be rather than have to be. You are in the middle of your third year, and although the job is difficult and demands long hours, you feel like you are making a difference. Most of the teachers seem reasonably content and you believe that they are receptive to your initiatives. Yet, you have a nagging suspicion that things are not quite right at Martin Luther King Jr. High School. Little things keep happening that give you pause—teachers leaving early, teachers skipping meetings, teachers not attending extracurricular activities. You decide to systematically examine the climate of your school. What you find shocks you. The teachers describe the schoolwork environment in much more negative terms than you do. They question your leadership. Morale is low. The academic emphasis in the school is poor. The climate is closed. At least that is what your teachers say.

1. You are dismayed and surprised, but what do you do?
2. Where do you begin?

Think about it. Later in the chapter we will describe what principal Elbert Gibbs did.

The School Workplace

A collective sense of identity emerges in organizations as members interact and transform the workplace into a distinctive institution. There are many common terms used to refer to this indigenous feel of the organization: *ecology, milieu, setting, tone, field, character, atmosphere, culture,* and *climate.* All are used to refer to the internal quality of the organization as experienced by its members, but *organizational culture* and *organizational climate* are the two concepts that have captured the attention of scholars and researchers.

These two approaches to examining the collective identity of the workplace, culture and climate, come from different intellectual traditions. Scholars of organizational culture tend to use the qualitative and ethnographic techniques of anthropology and sociology to examine the character or atmosphere of organizations. They are interested in thick, rich descriptions and understanding how the elements of culture fit together. In contrast, scholars of climate use quantitative techniques and multivariate analyses to find patterns of perceived behavior in organizations. Their background and training are more likely to be in multivariate statistics and psychology or social psychology rather than in ethnography and anthropology or sociology. Moreover, these researchers tend to be more interested in how climate influences organizational outcomes. The goal of studying climate is often to determine effective strategies of change and the impact that organizations have on groups and individuals.

Both perspectives, climate and culture, are attempts to understand the influence of social context on organizational life. Thus, both should be useful to instructional leaders as they grapple with how social conditions in the school affect teaching and learning. Which perspective is better? You be the judge. Our position is that both frameworks are useful; the concepts are complements rather than alternatives.

Organizational Culture

There is no single accepted definition of *organizational culture*. At one level everyone agrees that culture refers to the social context of the organization and that different organizations have different cultures. The idea that groups and organizations have certain things that are shared or held in common that make them distinctive is also generally accepted. But what are the critical shared elements? Some argue that they are the customs, rituals, and traditions of the organizations; others argue they are the implicit values and norms that evolve in work groups; and still others maintain they are the shared meanings that are created as members interact with each other in organizations. Indeed organizational culture has been defined from all these perspectives. The notion of culture accentuates the need for stability, consistency, and meaning in organizational life (Schein, 1992). It's useful to think of **organizational culture** as a pattern of shared orientations that binds the organization together and gives it a distinctive identity (Hoy & Miskel, 2008).

Levels of Culture

Culture manifests itself at different levels of abstraction. One way to begin to disentangle the concept is to examine these levels of culture. The levels range from very visible and tangible aspects that are concrete to deeply held, basic assumptions that are unconscious, tacit, and abstract (Schein, 1992). In-between the fairly concrete artifacts and the abstract basic assumptions are informal norms and core values. The levels of analysis at which culture can be analyzed are pictured in Figure 9.1 on the next page.

FIGURE 9.1 Levels of Culture

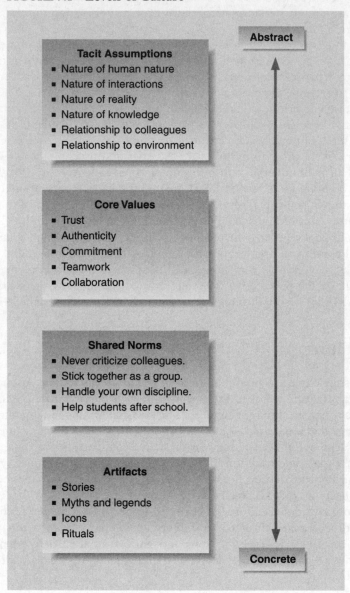

Culture as Tacit Assumptions. At its most abstract level, culture is the collective manifestation of **tacit assumptions.** Such assumptions have become unconscious, basic premises about human nature, social relationships, truth, reality, and environment; they are taken for granted—and they are highly resistant to change. The pattern of basic assumptions that has developed within the organization to cope with its problems of external adaptation and internal integration is its culture. When the pattern has worked well enough to be considered valid, it is taught to new members as the correct way to perceive, think, feel, and solve fundamental organizational problems.

Culture as a set of tacit assumptions defines for its members what to pay attention to, what things mean, how to react emotionally to what is going on, and what actions to take in different situations (Schein, 1992, 1999). Consider a school that has a strong culture with the following basic assumptions:

- Relationships among teachers are primarily group oriented and shared decisions are determined through debate, which necessitates conflict and the testing and sharing of ideas.
- Teachers are highly motivated and competent.
- All teachers are evaluated by the same fair standards.
- Teachers view the school as a big family; they accept, respect, and take care of each other.

These basic assumptions give rise to shared values of cooperation, expertise, openness, fairness, and respect, a school culture where an effective program of instructional improvement is possible.

Any challenge or questioning of basic assumptions can lead to anxiety and defensiveness. Schein (1992, 1999) explains that the shared basic assumptions making up the culture of a group can be conceived of—at both the individual and group levels—as psychological defense mechanisms that protect the individual and group and permit them to function. Thus change is very difficult. Moreover, because the basic assumptions of an organization are often unconscious, distortions of information are quite possible. For example, if we believe that people will take advantage of us whenever they have a chance, we interpret events in ways that confirm that assumption. A principal's visit is seen as an opportunity to exploit weaknesses rather than help. Further, if this belief is not only a personal one but one that is shared and is part of the organizational culture, teachers will discuss with others how they have been taken advantage of during the principal's visits, and the beliefs are reconfirmed. If beliefs are individual and idiosyncratic, they can be corrected more easily because the group will not reinforce them. But when the beliefs are part of the culture, they become mutually reinforced and the culture is validated.

Culture as Core Values.   As groups emerge, they also develop a set of common, core values that are central to behavior; such values define, in broad terms, ideas organizational members need to embrace if they are to "fit in" and be successful. **Values** are abstract conceptions of the desirable. If we ask teachers to explain why they do the things they do, we may begin to discover the central values of the school. Shared values define the basic character of the school and give the school a distinctive identity. When teachers know what their school stands for, they know what standards should be upheld and make decisions consistent with those standards. Values are on a higher level of abstraction than norms, which are also common expectations of how teachers should behave. Values deal with ideals and ends, while norms deal with the specific means to achieve those ends. In other words, values define the ends of human conduct and norms distinguish the legitimate and illegitimate means to accomplish those ends.

William Ouchi's (1981) book on successful Japanese corporations was one of the first analyses of organizational culture. Ouchi argued that the key to success in organizations was not so much a matter of technology as it was culture; in fact, he identified the core values of successful U.S. and Japanese organizations, which included the following: trust, commitment, cooperation, teamwork, egalitarianism, and intimacy. Notice that these are fairly abstract values of the organization. There are competing values that are embodied in organizational actions such as competition, loyalty, democracy, expertise, innovation, and impersonality. Schools develop their own culture; that is, schools develop a core of common values that members embrace and that guide their behavior.

We expect, for example, that instructional leadership will be most effective in a culture that is imbued with such values as openness, authenticity, cooperation, collegiality, and innovation. On the other hand, a school culture that values competition, impersonality, correctness, and hierarchy will likely make the improvement of teaching and learning more difficult. But how do shared values develop in schools? There is no easy or simple answer. Leadership can help. If a principal, for example, can convince teachers to act based on trust and collegiality and if such actions are perceived as successful, then the perceived value that trust and collegiality are "good" gradually starts a process of cognitive transformation. Over time this transformation can lead to a common set of shared values or beliefs, but the process will proceed only if the actions continue to work well (Schein, 1992, 1999, 2004).

In strong cultures, core values are held intensely, shared widely, and guide organizational behavior; however, the content as well as the strength of culture are important. Each school has a set of core values that undergirds behavior. If improvement is to be successful, the core values must be consistent with authentic principal practices.

Culture as Shared Norms.   The next level of analysis for culture is in terms of the informal norms. **Norms** are the unwritten and informal expectations that teachers learn as they become socialized into the school. Norms are expectations, not behavior. Becoming a member of a group means learning the important informal expectations of behavior for the group. Norms are universal and guide group activity. Make no mistake; norms affect behavior. The stronger the norms, the more constraining they are on behavior. Although norms are less abstract than values and tacit assumptions, they often are not obvious. In fact, it is sometimes difficult to surface the important norms of a group because members are reluctant to talk about them unless they are confident the information will not be held against them: In fact, many groups have a norm against revealing the important unofficial expectations to outsiders.

Norms are communicated to members by stories and significant events in the history of the school that vividly depict what the organization stands for. New teachers quickly learn the shared norms of the group, which are critical elements of the informal organization. Norms influence the way teachers dress and interact, the way they respond to authority, and the way they balance their own interests with those of the organization. In brief, norms are the informal rules that govern behavior in schools.

Although there are few, if any, universal norms for teachers, common ones exist in many schools. For example, "Handle your own discipline problems," and "Don't criticize other teachers to students," are two typical norms found in many schools. Examples of other norms that are more idiosyncratic are: "Don't rock the boat," "Innovate, try new ideas," "Support your fellow teachers even when they are wrong," "Never let students out of class before the bell rings," "Change your bulletin boards frequently," and "Don't criticize the principal in public." Norms are enforced by such informal sanctions as invitations to participate in special events (positive) and ostracism (negative). Teachers develop their own distinctive expectations for each other in their schools. Do teachers prize contentious debate or courteous restraint? Are playful and relaxed interactions appropriate, or are interactions structured and formal? Groups develop norms to answer such questions (Bolman & Deal, 2003). In brief, the shared norms of the work group define a major slice of the culture of a school.

Culture as Artifacts. At the most basic and concrete level, the shared perspectives of which we speak are the things that members see, hear, and feel that make the organization distinctive. **Artifacts** include aspects of the physical environment (buildings, layout, classrooms, lounges, and so on) as well as the language, activities, and ceremonies that have become a routine part of organizational life. Although artifacts are easy to observe, they are sometimes difficult to decipher (Schein, 1999) because they are infused with meanings that come from that special group. For example, in one school informality may be a sign of inefficiency and fooling around, but in another school informality represents independent and efficient interaction among committed professionals.

There are many artifacts that are useful in understanding the culture of a school. Stories are narratives that become part of the school culture; they are based on true events, but often combine truth and fiction. The story of the heroic principal who supports a teacher even at risk of losing his or her job becomes retold and elaborated to embody the supportive norms that exist between the principal and teacher. Some stories are **myths;** that is, they communicate an unquestioned belief that cannot be demonstrated by the facts. Legends are stories that have become institutionalized. They have been repeated and elaborated in ways that add to the importance of the event. They capture what the organization has come to value. People who do extraordinary things that capture the essence of the culture become legends and heroes. The principal who stood by his teacher and overcame great pressure from parents becomes the focus for cohesiveness, loyalty, and commitment in a school. The stories of heroes and legends provide insight into the core values of an organization.

Icons and rituals are important artifacts because they also indirectly communicate the culture of the school. Logos, mottoes, and trophies are icons that offer a glimpse of the school culture. **Rituals** are the routine ceremonies and rites that are visible examples of what is valued in the school. Beyer and Trice (1987) identify four rites that are typical of most organizations: rites of passage, degradation, enhancement, and integration. For example, the faculty lounge, coffee groups, and parties provide activities that bind the group together and make it a unique whole. Rites of enhancement are often seen in formal assemblies as the school recognizes the teacher of the year or the debate team champions. Such ceremonies reinforce appropriate behavior and signal what the school values. New teachers go through a series of rites of passage as they are assigned difficult classes, lunch duty, and after-school detention. They quickly learn to cope and discover the appropriate "way to do things around here."

Artifacts are observable and fairly concrete, but their meanings are often obscured. Only with time in the organization can one learn the meanings of the artifacts of a particular school. Stories, myths, legends, rituals, and icons typically embody the informal norms, core values, and basic assumptions of the organization. These latter elements of school culture are less obvious, but provide a fuller picture.

In summary, a school's culture can be examined at four levels: artifacts, shared norms, core values, and tacit assumptions. Although artifacts are most concrete, they sometimes are difficult to decipher. At the other extreme, tacit assumptions are most abstract and difficult to identify, but they most clearly capture the meanings of events and relationships in organizations. Core values and shared norms are at the middle range of abstraction and also give meaning and understanding to the culture of the school. A thorough understanding of culture requires a comprehension of all four levels. In other words, to understand the culture of a school, one must comprehend the meanings and the shared orientations of the school: its artifacts, norms, values, and basic assumptions.

Functions of Culture

Although there is no one best culture for all schools, strong cultures promote cohesiveness, loyalty, and commitment, which in turn reduce the propensity for members to leave the organization (Mowday, Porter, & Steers, 1982). Moreover, Robbins (1998) summarizes a number of important functions performed by the organization's culture:

1. Culture has a boundary-defining function; it creates distinctions among organizations.
2. Culture provides the organization with a sense of identity.
3. Culture facilitates the development of commitment to the group.
4. Culture enhances stability in the social system.
5. Culture is the social glue that binds the organization together; it provides the appropriate standards for behavior.
6. Culture serves to guide and shape the attitudes and behavior of organizational members.

It is important to remember, however, that a strong culture can be either functional or dysfunctional; that is, it can promote or impede effectiveness.

Common Elements of Culture

At the core of any organizational culture is a set of shared values. Several studies (Chatman & Jehn, 1994; O'Reilly, Chatman, & Caldwell, 1991) have suggested that there are seven basic elements that shape the culture of most organizations:

1. *Innovation:* the degree to which employees are expected to be creative and take risks
2. *Stability:* the degree to which activities focus on the status quo rather than change
3. *Attention to detail:* the degree to which there is concern for precision and detail

4. *Outcome orientation:* the degree to which management emphasizes results
5. *People orientation:* the degree to which management decisions are sensitive to individuals
6. *Team orientation:* the degree of emphasis on collaboration and teamwork
7. *Aggressiveness:* the degree to which employees are expected to be competitive rather than easygoing

The culture of most organizations can be mapped by using these elements to describe the values that are dominant. Schein (1999), however, provides three cautions. First, cultures are deep, not superficial; thus, if you assume that you can manipulate it, you are likely to fail. Second, culture is broad because it is formed by beliefs and assumptions about daily life in organizations; hence, deciphering culture is a challenge. Third, culture is stable because it provides meaning and makes life predictable; consequently, changing it is difficult.

Some General Propositions about School Culture

Without question school culture is complex, symbolic, and contextual. Much of what occurs in schools can be understood and interpreted only in the unique context of the school's culture. Bolman and Deal (2003) summarize the complexities and difficulties of understanding organizational activities.

1. The most important aspect of any organizational event is not what happened but what it means. *Events are often not what they seem.*
2. What an event means is often not clear because the activity must be interpreted in the context, and events have multiple meanings because people interpret them differently. *Meaning is elusive.*
3. Because events are typically ambiguous or uncertain, it is difficult to understand what happened, why it happened, and what will happen next. *Events are often puzzles: The future is problematic.*
4. The greater the ambiguity and uncertainty in events, the more difficult it is to use rational approaches to solve problems. *Rational decision making is limited as a process to solve organizational problems.*
5. When organizational members are confronted with ambiguity and uncertainty, they create symbols and stories to resolve conflict, provide understanding, and create hope. *Explanations are invented both to resolve conflict and to create positive outcomes.*
6. The importance of many organizational events rests with what the event expresses, not what it produces. *Myths, rituals, ceremonies, and sagas often give people the meanings that they seek.*

The implications of these propositions for principals are clear. The principal must be part of the culture in order to understand it. Significant events should never be accepted at face value; their meanings must be interpreted in terms of the values and norms of the school and from the points of view of different organizational members. Given the uncertainty and ambiguity of school life, rational responses to school problems are only part of the solution. The symbolic aspects of actions are often more important than the content of the action. For example, it is not so much what a principal says or does when working with teachers but how it is done and what it means. A talk to a teacher about a difficult student can be seen as a judgment of poor teaching or an opportunity to solve a mutual problem; the meaning of the event depends on the shared norms and values of the group. Principals need to be creative in their ability to develop stories and explanations that ameliorate conflict. Humor and play are also important aspects of instructional leadership that reduce tension and encourage creativity (Bolman & Deal, 2003). Finally, the rituals, stories, and sagas of a school are important to help teachers give meaning and value to their work.

Although there is no one culture that is best for every school, there are some tacit assumptions that facilitate the process of improvement of instruction. Consider the following set of basic assumptions that Schein (1992) suggests is at the heart of a learning culture:

- Teachers and students are proactive problem solvers and learners.
- Solutions to problems derive from a pragmatic search; knowledge is found in many forms—scientific research, experience, trial and error, and clinical research in which teachers and principals work things out together.
- Teachers have good intentions and are amenable to change and improvement.
- Creativity and innovation are central to student learning.
- Both individualism and teamwork are important aspects of human interaction.
- Information and communication are central to the well-being of the school.
- Diversity is a resource that has the potential to enhance learning.
- Productive learning is enhanced by both challenge and support.
- The world is a complex field of interconnected forces in which multiple causation is more likely than simple causation.

Schools anchored with such assumptions have created learning cultures that encourage improvement among all participants.

A Culture of Academic Optimism

One important perspective of school culture is academic optimism—shared beliefs about the potentials of students to succeed. Such optimism is a function of collective efficacy, faculty trust, and academic emphasis of the school. These three collective properties are similar in both nature and function but also in their potent and positive impact on student achievement; in fact, all three properties work together in a unified fashion to create a positive school culture that is called *academic optimism* (Hoy, Tarter, & Woolfolk Hoy, 2006a, 2006b; McGuigan & Hoy, 2006; Smith & Hoy, in press). Many conceptions treat optimism as a cognitive characteristic (Peterson, 2000; Snyder et al., 2002). The current conception of academic optimism, however, includes cognitive (efficacy), affective (trust), and behavioral components (academic emphasis).

Academic optimism is a collective set of beliefs about strengths and capabilities in schools that paints a rich picture of human agency in which optimism is the overarching idea that unites efficacy and trust with academic emphasis. A school culture permeated with such beliefs has a sense of the possible.

- **Collective efficacy** is the shared belief that the faculty can make a positive difference in student learning; *the faculty believes in itself.*
- **Faculty trust in students and parents** is the belief that teachers, parents, and students can cooperate to improve learning, that is, *the faculty believes in its students.*
- **Academic emphasis** is the enacted behavior of these beliefs, that is, *the faculty focuses on student success in academics.*

Thus, a school with high academic optimism defines a culture in which the faculty believes: *it can* make a difference, *students can* learn, and academic performance *can be* achieved (Hoy, Tarter, & Woolfolk Hoy, 2006a, 2006b). These three aspects of collective optimism interact in a reciprocal way with each other (see Figure 9.2). For example, faculty trust in parents and students increases a sense of collective efficacy, but collective efficacy in turn reinforces the trust. Similarly, when the faculty trusts parents, teachers believe they can demand higher academic standards without fear that parents will undermine them, and emphasis on high academic standards in turn strengthens the faculty trust in parents and students. Finally, when the faculty as a whole believes it can organize and execute actions needed to have a positive effect on student achievement, it will stress academic achievement, and academic emphasis will in turn support a strong sense of collective efficacy. In brief, all three aspects of academic optimism are in transactional relationships with each other and interact to create a culture of academic optimism in the school workplace.

Several factors underscore the utility of a culture of academic optimism. The term *optimism* itself suggests learning possibilities; a pessimistic school workplace can change. Faculty can learn to be optimistic. Academic optimism gains its name from the conviction that its composite properties all express an optimistic perspective and are malleable.

FIGURE 9.2   Reciprocal Relationships among the Three Aspects of Academic Optimism

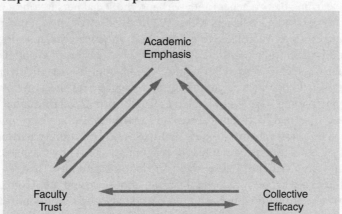

Administrators and teachers have reason to be optimistic—they are empowered to make a difference. Neither the faculty nor their students have to be irretrievably trapped by socioeconomic factors that breed a sense of hopelessness and cynicism. The research is encouraging. Academic optimism can and does have strong positive impact on school achievement, even controlling for socioeconomic factors, previous success, and other demographic variables (Hoy, Tarter, & Woolfolk Hoy, 2006a, 2006b; McGuigan & Hoy, 2006; Smith & Hoy, in press).

How can leaders build a culture of academic optimism in their schools? We suspect the general way to enhance the academic optimism of a school is to improve its component parts. The one goal that virtually everyone shares for schools is academic achievement of students. The reform and accountability movements have promoted a press toward the academic achievement of all students (No Child Left Behind, 2002). The focus of schooling is clear—it is an academic one. A push for academic achievement, however, in an environment where teachers do not feel efficacious is a recipe for frustration and failure. The challenge is to create school conditions in which teachers believe *they are up to the task and so are their students.* How might this be done? Principals lead a school by example. Celebrate the achievements of students and faculty, especially the academic ones. An emphasis on the honor roll, national honor societies, and extraordinary academic accomplishments of all kinds are examples of behaviors that foster academics. This may be an old list, but combined with building efficacy and trust, these activities take on new and added strength.

Collective efficacy is grounded in Bandura's social cognitive theory (Bandura, 1997); thus, we turn to his sources of efficacy for ideas about how to build collective efficacy in schools. The sources of self-efficacy are mastery experiences, vicarious experiences, social persuasion, and affective states, each of which communicates information that influences teacher perceptions about the school (Bandura, 1993, 1997; Goddard, Hoy, & Woolfolk Hoy, 2004; Pajares, 1997). For example, consider a school with a poor graduation rate. A neighboring district has implemented a successful and effective program for at-risk students. The principal can orchestrate the transfer of the neighbor's success to his or her school. In so doing, the school is using a self-regulatory process informed by the vicarious learning of its teachers and, perhaps, the social persuasion of leaders. Modeling success and persuading teachers to believe in themselves and their capabilities is also a good route to improve collective efficacy and enhance academic optimism (Bandura, 1997; Goddard, Hoy, & Woolfolk Hoy, 2004; Hoy, Tarter, & Woolfolk Hoy, 2006b).

There is some research on family and community involvement in schools (cf., Epstein, 1989); however, there is little systematic research on how to build trust in students and parents in schools. Such trust can be promoted through interchanges, both formal and informal, between parents and teachers. Using vicarious learning, for example, a school can respond to a lack of trust and community participation in school activities by emulating the practices of magnet schools known for their parental cooperation and involvement. These examples demonstrate how changes in social perceptions influence what actions organizations choose to pursue. Collective perceptions about efficacy, academic emphasis, and trust shape the school's norms and can be developed through experiences that convey their value and utility.

A caveat is in order: Interventions should be supportive of all three aspects of optimism. Some ways of enhancing academic emphasis, such as more competitive grading and greater punishment for failure, may well undermine the development of trust among teachers, students, and parents. Similarly, an emphasis on developing trust could come as a result of diminishing standards and rewarding students for merely adequate work by providing only positive feedback. Constructive criticism is essential for academic growth.

The research on individual optimism suggests some ideas about encouraging a culture of optimism in schools. Peterson (2000) found that optimism is thwarted by stress; hence, decreasing stress should support optimism. Principals can lower teacher stress by increasing their agency through appropriate participation in decisions that affect their school lives (Hoy & Tarter, 2004).

Teachers learn from models because the observation of successful performance in others promotes an acquisition of their beliefs and actions. The most effective models are those who seem competent, powerful, prestigious, and similar to the observer (Pintrich & Schunk, 2002). Vicarious and observational learning are other sources of optimism. Teachers can serve as models for each other, and the way school problems are discussed should convey the possibilities for resolution rather than defeatism. Novice teachers should hear optimistic approaches to teaching from their colleagues rather than a sense of passive helplessness in teachers' lounges and school hallways (Hoy, Tarter, & Woolfolk Hoy, 2006b).

In sum, a culture of academic optimism gets administrators and faculty over a wall of learned pessimism and futility. Academic optimism creates a culture with collective beliefs and norms that view teachers as capable, students as willing, parents as supportive, and academic success as achievable. You can get a sense of the academic optimism of your school; use the scales found on the website (www.coe.ohio-state.edu/whoy) to measure collective efficacy, faculty trust, and academic emphasis. Then average the three standard scores for an index of the academic optimism of your school. Academic optimism is only one perspective, albeit an important one, for viewing the culture of a school; there are others. For example, a culture of trust (Hoy, 2002; Hoy & Tschannen-Moran, 2003) or a culture of control (Hoy, 2001) are other useful lenses that principals may want to apply to examine their school culture and to plan for improvement (see Hoy & Miskel, 2008).

Organizational Climate

Another aspect of the school context that sets the scene for effective instructional leadership is organizational climate. Teachers' performances in schools are in part determined by the climate in which they work. **Organizational climate** is a general concept that refers to teachers' perceptions of the school's work environment; it is affected by the formal organization, informal organization, and politics, all of which, including climate, affect the motivations and behavior of teachers. Simply stated, the set of internal characteristics that distinguishes one school from another and influences the behavior of its members is the organizational climate of the school. More specifically, climate is a relatively enduring quality of the school environment that is experienced by teachers, influences their behavior, and is based on their collective perceptions (Hoy & Miskel, 2005).

As we have suggested earlier, *climate* and *culture* both refer to the atmosphere of the school. Culture is a broader construct than climate, and exists at a higher level of abstraction than climate; indeed, climate can be considered a manifestation of culture. Culture refers to shared *beliefs* and climate refers to basic patterns of *behavior* that exist in organizations. Admittedly there is not a huge difference between shared assumptions, values, and norms and shared perceptions of behavior, but the distinction is a useful one. School climate is a little more manageable in some respects. For example, climate can be conceived and measured from a variety of perspectives, several of which are described and discussed in this chapter. Each provides the principal with a valuable set of conceptual capital to analyze, understand, and improve teaching and learning.

Organizational Climate: Open to Closed

Probably the best-known conceptualization and measurement of the organizational climate of a school was developed by Andrew W. Halpin and Don B. Croft (1962) in their pioneering study of elementary schools. As they visited and observed schools, they were struck by the dramatic differences they found in the "feel" of the schools. Halpin (1966) described the marked contrasts as follows:

> In one school the teachers and the principal are zestful and exude confidence in what they are doing. They find pleasure in working with each other; this pleasure is transmitted to students. . . . In a second school the brooding discontentment of teachers is palpable; the principal tries to hide his incompetence and his lack of direction behind a cloak of authority. . . . And the psychological sickness of such a faculty spills over on the students who, in their own frustration, feed back to teachers a mood of despair. A third school is marked by neither joy nor despair, but by hollow ritual . . . in a strange way the show doesn't seem to be for real. (p. 131)

These stark differences in the feel of schools led Halpin and Croft (1962) to a systematic attempt to conceptualize and measure school climate. They viewed the climate of the school in terms of its personality, that is, just as individuals have personalities, schools have organizational climates. Two general sets of social behavior were mapped: principal–teacher interactions and teacher–teacher interactions. The principal's leadership can influence teacher behavior, but so can group behavior affect the principal's behavior; hence, the leadership of the principal, the nature of the teacher group, and their mutual interaction became the key components for identifying the social climate of schools. In all, eight dimensions of teacher–teacher and teacher–principal behavior were identified as Halpin and Croft (1962) developed an instrument to measure the organizational climate of elementary schools, the Organizational Climate Description Questionnaire (**OCDQ**).

A Revised OCDQ

The original OCDQ spawned hundreds of studies in the 1960s and 1970s (Anderson, 1982). But times and conditions have changed dramatically since the first appearance of the OCDQ. Many of the items no longer measure what they were intended to measure; some of the subtests are no longer valid; the reliabilities of some of the subtests are low; and time has rendered many of the items irrelevant to contemporary school organizations (Hoy & Miskel, 2001). Consequently, it should come as no surprise that the OCDQ has been revised and updated for use in today's schools. The original OCDQ was designed for use only in elementary schools, but revised versions have been formulated and tested for elementary (Hoy & Clover, 1986), middle (Hoy & Sabo, 1998), and high schools (Hoy, Tarter, & Kottkamp, 1991). Regardless of level, the conceptual foundations of the instruments are similar; they are based on the openness of professional interactions. Although we will describe only the revised Organizational Climate Description Questionnaire for elementary schools (OCDQ-RE), reliable versions for use in middle and high schools are available. All the climate instruments describe the behavior of principals as they interact with their teachers and the behavior of teachers as they interact with their colleagues.

Principal Behavior.   The first element of school climate is the principal's style of interacting with teachers. Three key aspects of principal–teacher interactions set the tone for life in schools—supportive, directive, and restrictive principal behavior.

1. *Supportive* behavior reflects genuine concern for teachers. Principals respect the professional expertise of their teachers and treat them as colleagues. Assisting teachers, complimenting teachers, providing constructive criticism, and concern for their personal welfare are examples of supportive behavior.

2. *Directive* behavior is starkly task-oriented with little attention to the personal needs of teachers. The principal's behavior is direct and controlling: Teachers are closely observed, criticized, and constrained. Communication is downward with little attention to feedback from teachers. In brief, directive principal behavior is autocratic, rigid, and controlling.

3. *Restrictive* behavior is burdensome. Principals overload teachers with unnecessary work—too many committees, too much paperwork, and too much busywork. The principal hinders rather than facilitates teachers' work.

Teachers' Behavior.   The second key element of school climate is the teachers' behavior in school. Teachers do not react to the school organization as isolated individuals but as members of a teacher work group; they are part of the informal organization. As they work in school, they interact with other teachers and form ideas that have important consequences for their behavior. Three important dimensions of teacher interactions are postulated to have major influence on the climate of the school: collegial, intimate, and disengaged teacher behavior.

1. *Collegial* behavior is supportive professionalism among teachers. Teachers are pleased with their school; they accept and support each other and feel a sense of accomplishment in their teaching. Above all, teachers are professionals who respect the competence and dedication of their colleagues.

2. *Intimate* behavior is close personal relations among teachers both inside and outside the school. Teachers' closest friends are often teachers in their school; they talk and confide in each other.

3. *Disengaged* behavior is a general sense of alienation and separation among teachers in the school. There is little cohesiveness among teachers. They bicker with

TABLE 9.1   Sample Items for Each Dimension of the OCDQ-RE

Principal Behavior	Teacher Behavior
Supportive Behavior	**Collegial Behavior**
■ The principal uses constructive criticism.	■ Teachers help and support each other.
■ The principal compliments teachers.	■ Teachers respect the professional competence of their colleagues.
■ The principal listens to and accepts teachers' suggestions.	■ Teachers accomplish their work with vim, vigor, and pleasure.
Directive Behavior	**Intimate Behavior**
■ The principal monitors everything teachers do.	■ Teacher socialize with each other.
■ The principal rules with an iron fist.	■ Teachers' closest friends are other faculty members at this school.
■ The principal checks lesson plans.	■ Teachers have parties for each other.
Restrictive Behavior	**Disengaged Behavior**
■ Teachers are burdened with busywork.	■ Faculty meetings are useless.
■ Routine duties interfere with the job of teaching.	■ There is a minority group of teachers who always oppose the majority.
■ Teachers have too many committee requirements.	■ Teachers ramble when they talk at faculty meetings.

A copy of the entire instrument is found in Appendix D.

each other and ramble when they talk in meetings. Teachers are simply going through the motions; they are not productive in group efforts or team building.

These six features are the key elements for developing school climates. But specifically how are these dimensions of climate measured? How are the profiles determined? What do the profiles mean?

Interpreting the OCDQ-RE.   All items are simple descriptive statements of interactions in schools. Teachers are asked to describe the extent to which each item characterizes his or her school. The responses to each item are made on a four-point scale: rarely occurs, sometimes occurs, often occurs, and very frequently occurs. Sample items for each of the dimensions of the OCDQ-RE are summarized in Table 9.1 and a copy of the instrument is found in Appendix D (p. 360).

Using factor-analytic techniques and a sample of seventy elementary schools, forty-four items were identified that measured six dimensions of school climate (Hoy, Tarter, & Kottkamp, 1991). The six aspects, taken together, map a profile of the climate of each school. Scores for all subtests and schools were standardized so that the mean score was 500 and the standard deviation was 100. Then the scores are interpreted as one would SAT or GRE scores. A score of 500 is a school with average openness whereas one with a score of 600 is quite open—more than 1 standard deviation better than an average school. For example, the profiles of the climates for two hypothetical schools might be plotted as indicated in Figure 9.3. The school climate profiled with

FIGURE 9.3   **Contrasting School Climate Profile**

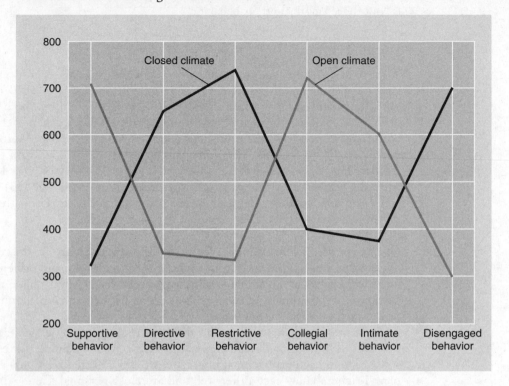

the gray line in the figure reflects an open school climate with a supportive, nondirective, and nonrestrictive principal and a collegial, engaged, intimate faculty committed to the teaching–learning task. The other school, indicated by the black line, represents a closed school climate with a directive, restrictive, and nonsupportive principal and suspicious (noncollegial), disengaged, and distant teachers.

Elementary school climate rests on two general factors of openness (Hoy & Clover, 1986; Hoy & Tarter, 1997b). Specifically, openness in faculty relations is characterized by teacher interactions that are meaningful and tolerant (low disengagement); that are friendly, close, and supportive (high intimacy); and that are enthusiastic, accepting, and mutually respectful (high collegial relations). Openness in principal behavior is characterized by avoiding the assignment of meaningless routines and burdensome duties to teachers (low restrictiveness); by giving flexibility and freedom to teachers to act independently (low directiveness); and by giving teachers respect and support in both personal and professional matters (high supportiveness). In general, this factor depicts a functional flexibility and openness in the principal's leadership behavior.

The conceptual underpinnings of the OCDQ-RE are consistent and clear. The instrument has two general factors: one a measure of openness of teacher interactions and the other a measure of openness of teacher–principal relations. Organizational climate is a description of the perceptions of the faculty. Some may question whether a climate is open or closed just because the teachers perceive it to be. Whether or not it really is cannot be answered and is probably irrelevant. Teachers' perceptions of what is "out there" motivate their behavior.

Climate Types

These two openness factors are relatively independent. That is, it is quite possible to have open faculty interactions and closed principal ones or vice versa. Thus, theoretically, four contrasting types of school climate are possible. First, both factors can be open, producing a congruence between the principal's and teachers' behavior. Second, both factors can be closed, producing a congruence of closedness. Moreover, there are two incongruent patterns. The principal's behavior can be open with the faculty, but teachers may be closed with each other; or the principal may be closed with teachers, while the teachers are open with each other (see Figure 9.3 on page 333). Table 9.2 provides a summary of the patterns of the four climate prototypes. Using this information, it is possible to sketch a behavioral picture of each climate.

Open Climate.   The distinctive features of the **open climate** are the cooperation and respect that exist within the faculty and between the faculty and principal. This combination suggests a climate in which the principal listens and is open to teacher suggestions, gives genuine and frequent praise, and respects the professional competence of the faculty (high supportiveness). Principals also give their teachers freedom to perform without close scrutiny (low directiveness) and provide facilitating leadership behavior devoid of bureaucratic trivia (low restrictiveness). Similarly, teacher behavior supports open and professional interactions (high collegial relations) among the faculty. Teachers know each other well and are close personal friends (high intimacy). They cooperate and are committed to their work (low disengagement). In brief, the behavior of both the principal and the faculty is open and authentic.

Engaged Climate.   The **engaged climate** is marked, on the one hand, by ineffective attempts of the principal to control and, on the other, by high professional performance of the teachers. The principal is rigid and autocratic (high directiveness) and respects

TABLE 9.2   Prototypic Profiles of School Climate

	Climate Type			
Climate Dimension	Open	Engaged	Disengaged	Closed
Supportive	High	Low	High	Low
Directive	Low	High	Low	High
Restrictive	Low	High	Low	High
Collegial	High	High	Low	Low
Intimate	High	High	Low	Low
Disengaged	Low	Low	High	High

neither the professional competence nor the personal needs of the faculty (low supportiveness). Moreover, the principal hinders the teachers with burdensome activities and busywork (high restrictiveness). The teachers, however, ignore the principal's behavior and conduct themselves as professionals. They respect and support each other, are proud of their colleagues, and enjoy their work (highly collegial). Moreover, the teachers not only respect each other's competence but they like each other as people (high intimacy), and they cooperate with each other as they engage in the task at hand (high engagement). In short, the teachers are productive professionals in spite of weak principal leadership; the faculty is cohesive, committed, supportive, and open.

Disengaged Climate.   The **disengaged climate** stands in stark contrast to the engaged climate. The principal's behavior is open, concerned, and supportive. The principal listens and is open to teachers (high supportiveness), gives the faculty freedom to act on their professional knowledge (low directiveness), and relieves teachers of most of the burdens of paperwork and committee assignments (low restrictiveness). Nonetheless, the faculty is unwilling to accept the principal. At worst, the faculty actively works to immobilize and sabotage the principal's leadership attempts; at best, the faculty simply ignores the principal. Teachers not only do not like the principal but they neither like nor respect each other as friends (low intimacy) or as professionals (low collegial relations). The faculty is simply disengaged from the task. In sum, although the principal is supportive, concerned, flexible, facilitating, and noncontrolling (i.e., open), the faculty is divisive, intolerant, and uncommitted (i.e., closed).

Closed Climate.   The **closed climate** is virtually the antithesis of the open climate. The principal and teachers simply appear to go through the motions, with the principal stressing routine trivia and unnecessary busywork (high restrictiveness) and the teachers responding minimally and exhibiting little commitment (high disengagement). The principal's ineffective leadership is further seen as controlling and rigid (high directiveness) as well as unsympathetic, unconcerned, and unresponsive (low supportiveness). These misguided tactics are accompanied not only by frustration and apathy but also by a general suspicion and lack of respect of teachers for each other as either friends or professionals (low intimacy and noncollegial relations). Closed climates have principals who are nonsupportive, inflexible, hindering, and controlling and a faculty that is divisive, intolerant, apathetic, and uncommitted. These four school climate types are pictured in Figure 9.4 on the next page.

The OCDQ: Some Implications

A basic assumption of our analysis of instructional leadership is that a school's organizational climate is closely related to its improvement practices. The collective perceptions of teachers about their work environment influence their motivations and behaviors in the classroom. An open climate, with its authentic interpersonal relations, seems likely to produce a situation where constructive change can succeed. The closed climate, on the other hand, presents an environment of hostility, suspicion, and inauthenticity where the improvement of instruction is doomed to failure. Improving teaching and learning simply will not work in a closed climate; in fact, in such schools it seems futile to attempt to improve the teaching–learning process. If the climate of a school is

FIGURE 9.4   Typology of School Climates

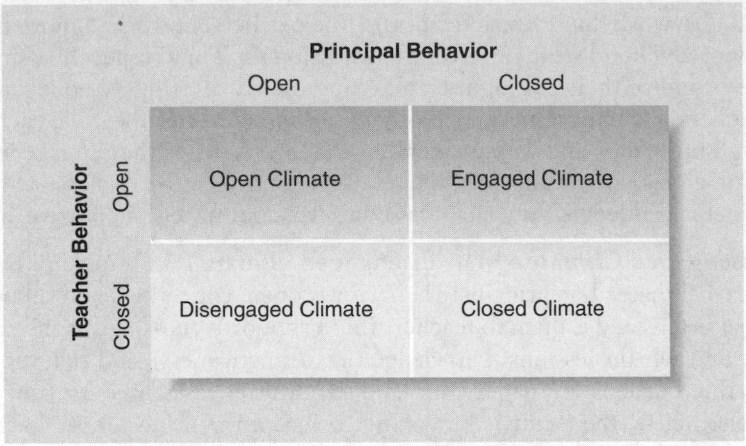

closed, the first task is to change it. Such change requires a cooperative effort between the teachers and principal; in fact, the principal's leadership is a key to improving the climate. Trust and openness are necessary conditions for effective school improvement.

Research on school climates consistently supports the conclusion that the school's openness and its emotional tone are related in predictable ways. Openness is associated with less student alienation, lower student dropout rates, and more student satisfaction with schools (Finkelstein, 1998; Hoy, 1972; Mullins, 1983). Moreover, open schools are generally more effective than closed ones, and teachers are more involved in decision making (Hoy, Tarter, & Kottkamp, 1991; Hoy & Sabo, 1998). Openness and teacher commitment and teacher loyalty (Hoy, Tarter, & Kottkamp, 1991; Reiss & Hoy, 1998) are also positively associated.

Open organizational relations also have positive consequences in schools because they facilitate the process of improving instruction. No climate can guarantee effective teaching and learning because school climate in and of itself cannot make a poor program good or a weak teacher strong, but an open school climate can provide the necessary atmosphere for reflection, cooperation, change, and improvement. There are three separate OCDQ measures for school climates, one for elementary schools (Hoy & Tarter, 1997b), another for middle schools (Hoy & Tarter, 1997a; Hoy & Tarter, 1997b), and one for high schools (Hoy, Tarter, & Kottkamp, 1991). There are no copyright restrictions for the use of any of the instruments for research or school improvement; in fact, they are all available at www.coe.ohio-state.edu/whoy. Simply log on, download the instrument, and use it.

Open school climates likely increase faculty trust (Hoy, Smith, & Sweetland, 2002) and enhance perceptions of fairness in school (Hoy & Tarter, 2004). But schools also face a countervailing pressure to control student behavior with coercive rules. In fact, there is quite a bit of discussion today about zero tolerance for rule breaking in schools. Is such a policy a good idea? How might it affect the school climate? The Point/Counterpoint examines both sides of the issue.

POINT/COUNTERPOINT   Is Zero Tolerance a Good Idea?

With the very visible violence in schools today, some districts have instituted "zero-tolerance" policies for rule breaking. One result? Two eight-year-old boys in New Jersey were suspended for making "terrorist threats." They had pointed paper guns at their classmates while playing. Do zero-tolerance policies make sense?

POINT

Zero tolerance means zero common sense.
An Internet search using the keywords "*zero-tolerance*" and "*schools*" will locate a wealth of information about the policy, much of it against. For example, in the August 29, 2001, issue of *Salon*, Johanna Wald wrote an article entitled "The Failure of Zero Tolerance." Here are two examples she cites:

A 17-year-old honors student in Arkansas begins his senior year with an even more ominous cloud over his head. His college scholarship is in danger because of a 45-day sentence to an alternative school. His offense? An arbitrary search of his car by school officials in the spring revealed no drugs, but a scraper and pocketknife that his father had inadvertently left there the night before when he was fixing the rearview mirror. Despite anguished pleas of extenuating circumstances by the desperate father, the school system has so far adamantly insisted that automatic punishments for weapon possession in school are inviolate.

Upon her release on bail, the National Merit scholar jailed and banned from her graduation for leaving a kitchen knife in her car commented, "They're taking away my memories." Indeed, for all of the pious talk about the need for "consequences" for students' actions, officials justifying these excesses seem curiously oblivious to the long-term impact of taking away the memories, dreams, and futures of a generation of students.

There are many other stories available on the Web. In researching this Point/Counterpoint, I read of a six-year-old boy in Colorado who was suspended in 1997 for giving another child a lemon drop candy. The suspension was justified using the school's zero-tolerance drug policy. Students have been suspended for playing with squirt guns, carrying key ring fobs that look like guns, using their fingers as pretend guns in a game, and drawing pictures of guns.

A 2001 Associated Press story, "ABA Recommends Dropping Zero-Tolerance in Schools," announced that the leadership of the American Bar Association voted to recommend ending zero-tolerance school policies. The article quotes a report that accompanied the resolution against zero tolerance adopted by the ABA's policymaking House of Delegates: "Zero-tolerance has become a one-size-fits-all solution to all of the problems that schools confront" (Associated Press, February 21, 2001, available online at www.cnn.com/2001/fyi/teachers.ednews/02/21/zero.tolerance.ap/). On this website, you can post your views about zero tolerance.

COUNTERPOINT

Zero tolerance is necessary for now.
The arguments for zero tolerance focus on school safety and the responsibilities of schools and teachers to protect the students and themselves. Of course, many of the incidents reported in the news seem like overreactions to childhood pranks or worse, overzealous application of zero tolerance to innocent mistakes or lapses of memory. But how do school officials separate the innocent from the dangerous? For example, it has been widely reported that Andy Williams (the boy who killed two classmates in Santee, California) assured his friends before the shootings that he was only joking about "pulling a Columbine."

In response to the girl who missed her graduation ceremony because school authorities found a knife in her car, Mike Gallagher (2001), a journalist writing for NewsMax.com, said:

I certainly understand the reason behind the e-mails of protest I received from Americans who think this is a case that went too far. It sure was a shame that this

(Continued)

POINT/COUNTERPOINT   Continued

high-schooler, by all accounts a great student and fine young lady, had to miss the excitement of her commencement ceremony. But I argued that rules are rules, and zero-tolerance weapons policies were created because of parents' demands that schools be safe.

Gallagher went on to describe a tragic event in Japan where eight young children were killed in school by a madman wielding a knife just one inch longer than the one found in the student's car.

On January 13, 2003, I read a story in *USA Today* by Gregg Toppo entitled "School Violence Hits Lower Grades: Experts Who See Violent Behavior in Younger Kids Blame Parents, Prenatal Medical Problems and an Angry Society; Educators Search for Ways to Cope." The story opened with these examples: a second grader in Indiana takes off his shoe and attacks his teacher with it; a Philadelphia kindergartner hits a pregnant teacher in the stomach; and an eight-year-old in Maryland threatens to use gasoline (he knew exactly where he would pour it) to burn down his suburban elementary school. Toppo noted, "Elementary school principals and safety experts say they're seeing more violence and aggression than ever among their youngest students, pointing to what they see as an alarming rise in assaults and threats to classmates and teachers" (p. A2). Toppo cited statistics indicating that, although the incidence of school violence has decreased overall, attacks on elementary school teachers have actually increased.

The late Albert Shanker (1995), long-time president of the American Federation of Teachers, said:

[S]chools must teach not only English and mathematics and reading and writing and history, but also teach that there are ways of behaving in society that are unacceptable. And when we sit back and tolerate certain types of behaviors, we are teaching youngsters that certain types of behaviors are acceptable, which eventually will end up with their being in jail or in poverty for the rest of their lives.

Organizational Climate: Healthy to Unhealthy

Another framework for defining and measuring the social climate of a school is the organizational health of a school. The idea of positive health in an organization is not new, and it calls attention to factors that facilitate growth and development as well as to conditions that impede positive organizational dynamics. It is likely that the state of health of a school can tell us much about the probable success of change initiatives.

Matthew Miles (1969) defines a healthy organization as one that survives and adequately copes over the long haul as it continuously develops and extends its surviving and coping abilities. Implicit in this definition is that healthy organizations deal successfully with disruptive outside forces while effectively directing their energies toward the major goals and objectives of the organization. Operations on a given day may be effective or ineffective, but the long-term prognosis in healthy organizations is favorable.

All social systems, if they are to grow and develop, must satisfy the four basic conditions of adaptation, goal attainment, integration, and latency (Parsons, Bales, & Shils, 1953). In other words, organizations must successfully solve four basic problems:

1. The problem of acquiring sufficient resources and accommodating to their environments

2. The problem of setting and implementing goals
3. The problem of maintaining solidarity and cohesiveness within the system
4. The problem of creating and preserving the unique values of the system

Thus, organizations must be concerned with the instrumental needs of goal achievement as well as the expressive and developmental needs of its participants. Healthy organizations meet both sets of needs. All formal organizations, including schools, exhibit three distinct levels of responsibility and control over these needs—the technical, managerial, and institutional levels.

The technical level produces the basic organizational product. In schools, the technical function is the teaching–learning process. Teachers and principals are professionals who are directly responsible for student learning. Educated students are the product of schools, and the entire technical function revolves around the problems associated with effective teaching and student learning.

The managerial level mediates and controls the internal efforts of the organization. The chief managerial function is the administrative process, a process that is qualitatively different from teaching. Principals are the prime administrative officers in schools. They must find ways to develop teacher loyalty and trust, motivate teacher effort, coordinate their work, and improve their instruction. The administration services the technical system in two important ways: first, it mediates between the teachers and students and parents; and second, it procures the necessary resources for effective teaching. Thus, teacher needs should be a basic concern of the administration.

The institutional level connects the organization with its environment. It is important for schools to have legitimacy and backing in the community. Principals and teachers need this support to perform their respective functions in a harmonious fashion without undue pressure and interference from individuals and groups outside the school.

This broad framework provides the integrative scheme for conceptualizing and measuring the **organizational health** of a school. Specifically, a healthy organization is one in which the technical, managerial, and institutional levels are in harmony; the organization meets its needs and successfully copes with disruptive outside forces as it directs its energies toward its mission.

Dimensions of Organizational Health

Seven specific aspects of organizational health are viewed as crucial dimensions of the interaction patterns of life in schools: institutional integrity, principal influence, consideration, initiating structure, resource support, morale, and academic emphasis. These critical components meet both the task and social needs of the social system, and they represent each of the three levels of responsibility and control within the school.

1. Institutional integrity refers to the school's ability to adapt to its environment in a way that maintains the educational integrity of its programs. Teachers are protected from unreasonable community and parental demands. The school is not vulnerable to the whims of the public. Neither a few vocal parents nor select citizens' groups can affect the operation of the school when their demands are not consistent with the educational programs. The board of education and the administration are successful in enabling the school to cope with destructive outside forces.

2. Principal influence refers to the principal's ability to affect the decisions of superiors. Being able to persuade superiors, get additional support, and not be impeded by the hierarchy are important facets of leadership. In fact, a key to effective leadership is the ability to influence superiors while at the same time not becoming overly dependent on them.

3. Consideration refers to the principal's leader behavior that is friendly and open. This aspect of behavior reflects behavior indicative of respect, mutual trust, colleagueship, and support. Consideration does not denote a superficial or calculative affability; it expresses a genuine concern for teachers as colleagues and professionals.

4. Initiating structure refers to the principal's behavior in specifying the work relationships with teachers. The principal clearly defines the work expectations, the standards of performance, and the methods of procedure. The principal's behavior is task-oriented, and the work environment is structured and achievement-oriented. Like consideration, initiating structure is a major dimension of effective leadership performance.

5. Resource support refers to providing teachers with the basic materials they need to do an outstanding teaching job. Instructional materials and supplies are readily available. If extra or supplementary materials are needed or requested, they are quickly supplied. In brief, teachers have access to the materials that they need.

6. Morale refers to a collective sense of friendliness, openness, and trust within the faculty. The teachers form a cohesive unit that is enthusiastic about teaching. They like each other, they like their jobs, they help each other, and they are proud of their school.

7. Academic emphasis refers to the extent to which the school is driven by a quest for academic excellence. High but attainable standards of academic performance are set, and an orderly, serious learning environment exists. The press for academic achievement is supported by administrators, teachers, and students alike. Teachers believe in their students, and students respond with vigor. Academic success is respected as a major accomplishment among students themselves. Good grades and scholarship earn praise and admiration from students as well as teachers.

These seven aspects of teacher and principal patterns of interaction form the framework for defining and measuring the organizational health of schools. The elements of the organizational health framework are summarized in Table 9.3.

TABLE 9.3   The Dimensions and Levels of Organizational Health Inventory

Institutional Level—School–Community Relations
- Institutional integrity

Managerial Level—Administrators
- Principal influence
- Consideration
- Initiating structure
- Resource support

Technical Level—Teachers
- Morale
- Academic emphasis

TABLE 9.4   Sample Items for Each Dimension of the OHI*

Institutional Level (School)

Institutional Integrity
- Teachers are protected from unreasonable community and parental demands.
- The school is open to the whims of the public.**

Managerial Level (Administration)

Principal Influence
- The principal is able to influence the actions of his or her superiors.
- The principal is impeded by superiors.**

Consideration
- The principal is friendly and approachable.
- The principal looks out for the personal welfare of faculty members.

Initiating Structure
- The principal lets faculty members know what is expected of them.
- The principal maintains definite standards of performance.

Resource Support
- Teachers receive necessary classroom supplies.
- Supplementary materials are available for classroom use.

Technical Level (Teachers)

Morale
- There is a feeling of trust and confidence among the staff.
- Teachers in this school are cool and aloof to each other.**

Academic Emphasis
- The learning environment is orderly and serious.
- This school set high standards for academic performance.

---

*A copy of the entire instrument is found on the website (www.coe.ohio-state.edu/whoy).

**These items are scored in reverse.

Organizational Health Inventory (OHI-S)

The Organizational Health Inventory is a descriptive questionnaire, not unlike the OCDQ, that measures these seven patterns of behavior. The **OHI** is administered to the professional staff of the school, and teachers are asked to describe the extent to which each item characterizes their school along a four-point scale: rarely occurs, sometimes occurs, often occurs, and very frequently occurs. Examples of the items of the health inventory for high schools (OHI-S), grouped by subtest, are listed in Table 9.4.

The OHI-S is a valid and the reliable instrument to measure the organizational health of secondary schools (Hoy & Feldman, 1999; Hoy, Tarter, & Kottkamp, 1991). To facilitate the interpretation of school health, school scores are standardized so the mean score is 500 and the standard deviation is 100. Then the scores are interpreted as one would SAT or GRE scores. A climate score of 500 is a school with average health while one with a score of 610 is quite healthy, more than 1 standard deviation better

FIGURE 9.5   School Health Profiles

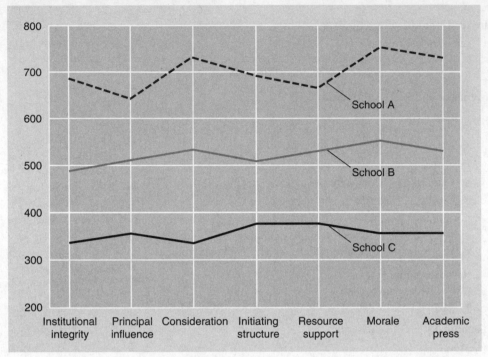

than an average school. Profiles for three schools are graphed in Figure 9.5. School A represents a school with a healthy climate—all dimensions of health are substantially above the mean; School C, in contrast, is below the mean in all aspects of health; and School B is a typical school, about average on all dimensions.

The subtests of the OHI-S are modestly correlated with each other; that is, if a school scores high on one subtest, there is some tendency to score higher on some of the other subtests. Furthermore, factor analysis of the subtests demonstrated that one general factor explained most of the variation among the subtests, a factor we called school health. High schools array themselves along a continuum with a few schools having profiles of very healthy organizations, a few having very unhealthy profiles, and most schools having somewhat mixed profiles in between the extremes. An index of health can be developed by simply adding the standard scores of the seven subtests; the higher the sum, the healthier the school dynamics.

We sketch below a behavioral picture for each of the poles of the continuum, that is, the prototypes for very healthy and unhealthy school climates.

Healthy School Climate.   Where there is a **healthy school climate,** the school is protected from unreasonable community and parental pressures. The board successfully resists all narrow efforts of vested interest groups to influence policy. The principal of a healthy school provides dynamic leadership, leadership that is both task-oriented and relations-oriented. Such behavior is supportive of teachers and yet provides direction and maintains high standards of performance. Moreover, the principal has influence with his or her superiors as well as the ability to exercise independent thought and action. Teachers in a healthy school are committed to teaching and learning. They set high but achievable goals for students; they maintain high standards of performance; and the learning environment is orderly and serious. Furthermore, students work hard on academic matters, are highly motivated, and respect other students who achieve academically. Classroom supplies and instructional materials are accessible if needed. Finally, in a healthy school, teachers like each other, trust each other, are enthusiastic about their work, and identify positively with the school. They are proud of their school.

Unhealthy School Climate.   When there is an unhealthy school climate, the school is vulnerable to destructive outside forces. Teachers and administrators are bombarded by unreasonable demands from parental and community groups. The school is buffeted by the whims of the public. The principal does not demonstrate leadership; that is, the principal provides little direction or structure, exhibits limited consideration and support for teachers, and has virtually no ability to influence the action of superiors. Morale of teachers is low. Teachers feel good neither about each other nor about their jobs. They act aloof, suspicious, and defensive. Finally, there is little press for academic excellence. Neither students nor teachers believe that academic matters are serious and important. Indeed, academically oriented students are ridiculed by their peers and are viewed as threats by their teachers.

The OHI: Some Implications

The OHI is a useful tool for several reasons. First, it reliably measures seven key dimensions of the organizational health of schools. Second, the conceptual underpinnings of the OHI are consistent with setting an atmosphere for improving teaching and learning. Third, a healthy school climate facilitates student achievement in schools (Hoy & Hannum, 1997; Hoy & Sabo, 1998).

Research findings using the OHI are encouraging. As one would expect, the healthier the organizational dynamics, the greater the degree of faculty trust in the principal, trust in colleagues, and trust in the organization itself. Not surprisingly, too, there is a strong correlation between the openness and health of schools; open schools are healthy schools and healthy schools are open ones (Hoy, Tarter, & Kottkamp, 1991; Hoy & Sabo, 1998). The research also strongly supports the importance of organizational health as a pivotal aspect of school life. In general, school health is positively associated with student achievement, school quality, overall school effectiveness, teacher participation, effective leadership, and a strong culture (Hoy & Sabo, 1998; Hoy, Tarter, & Kottkamp, 1991).

Healthy organizational dynamics also have positive consequences because they facilitate teaching and learning. Although such an environment cannot guarantee high achievement, it does provide an atmosphere conducive to improvement of instruction. Moreover, the characteristics of healthy schools have many of the attributes stressed in the effective-school literature: an orderly and serious environment, high but attainable goals, visible rewards for academic achievement, principals who are dynamic leaders, and a cohesive unit based on mutual trust.

In sum, organizational health is another functional framework for analyzing important aspects of the character of life in schools. The OHI is a practical tool for assessing the health of a school. Like openness in school climate, healthy organizational dynamics are necessary conditions for an effective program of improvement. The principal must first have a positive climate; if it is lacking, it must be developed. Although we have described the OHI for high schools (see www.coe.ohio-state.edu/whoy), there are versions of the instruments for elementary and middle schools (Hoy & Tarter, 1997b). Recently, an organizational climate index (OCI) has been created that combines key elements of both the OCDQ and the OHI into one instrument (Hoy, Smith, & Sweetland, 2002). There are no copyright restrictions for use of any of the instruments for research or school improvement; in fact, they are available at www.coe.ohio-state.edu/whoy. Simply log on, download the instrument, copy it, and use it.

Changing School Climate

We have described several frameworks for examining school context. It should be clear that improvement of instruction is most likely in school climates that are open in interactions and healthy in organizational dynamics and where there is strong collective efficacy. Moreover, we have offered a set of instruments that enables teachers and principals to assess the organizational climate of their schools. What happens when the climates are closed and unhealthy? Embarking immediately on a program of improvement of instruction with teachers working cooperatively with principals is difficult and usually counterproductive. Indeed, it seems futile for principals and teachers to attempt any authentic plan to improve instruction that involves cooperation, trust, and respect in such climates. At best, such attempts will be meaningless rituals, and at worst they provide opportunities for the administration and teachers to punish and blame each other. If the school setting is inappropriate, changing *it* is the first business of the day.

Some Assumptions about Change in Schools

Before we proceed any further, we think it is useful to examine some basic assumptions about organizations and change to which we subscribe (Hoy & Tarter, 1997a):

1. *Change is a characteristic of all organizations.* Organizations are in a constant state of flux. Change can be random or a resource harnessed for improvement, but it cannot be eliminated.
2. *Change has direction.* Change can be progressive or regressive or aimless.
3. *Organizational learning is possible.* Schools can develop their own learning processes to solve their problems. Principals and teachers have the potential to learn how to solve problems together.
4. *Schools can be learning organizations.* Schools can become places where professionals can continually expand their capacity to create the results that they desire, where emergent patterns of thinking are nurtured, where collective aspiration is liberated, and where people are constantly learning how to learn. (Senge, 1990)

A Principal's Perspective: The Case of Martin Luther King Jr. High School

Martin Luther King Jr. High School is on an old campus in an urban community in the Northeast on the corridor between New York City and Philadelphia. It is the only high school in Urban Park and enrolls a little over 1,200 students. Other potential students in the town are enrolled in Orthodox Jewish schools, and there is a large Catholic population that sends many of its children to St. Polycarp High School. While the school has its supporters in the town, it doesn't lack detractors. Urban Park is an ethnically rich small city of 45,000. The African American population has remained a stable population of about a quarter of the district. About 14% of the population is newly arrived Russians and Indians, and another 8% or so are Hispanic. A unique aspect of this urban community is its proximity to a major public university; consequently, about 20% of the students in the school are children of faculty, graduate students, and staff. By and large, however, this is a working-class community with great diversity and financially pressed to support its schools.

Elbert Gibbs is a dynamic and youthful administrator. People meeting him are struck by his physical fitness; he jogs daily on the high school track, usually with student athletes after school. Gibbs was a former high school football player who earned athletic scholarships through college. After college he became a successful high school teacher for several years before returning to the state university to pursue his master's degree in educational administration. He earned his principalship by dint of hard work as an assistant principal for three years in a nearby urban center. Elbert is on the fast track. In his course work at the university, Gibbs found the literature on school climate, culture, and change intriguing. He decided to do a systematic analysis of his high school.

Let's take a look at King High. First, we examine the climate profiles as described by Gibbs. In other words, the following profile is the way Gibbs and his teachers responded to the OHI and the OCDQ-RS. He sought to maintain his objectivity in filling out the forms. Gibbs also had his teachers answer the same instruments at a faculty meeting. He took pains to get a frank response from the teachers by absenting himself from the meeting and insisting that teachers provide candid responses to the anonymous questionnaires. They rather enjoyed the activity. A comparison of the climate profiles as perceived by the teachers and Gibbs is summarized below:

	Principal	Faculty
Institutional Integrity	540	420
Initiating Structure	560	555
Consideration	540	505
Principal Influence	510	465
Resources Allocation	500	445
Academic Emphasis	530	455
Morale	520	480
Overall Health	529	485
Supportive	555	490
Directive	480	540
Engaged	510	515
Frustrated	465	542
Over Openness	533	481

The process of building a healthy and open school climate can naturally transform the school into a learning organization where teacher professionals continually learn how to learn. Such organizations are functional for the improvement of teaching and student learning. We have included an actual case to illustrate one strategy for changing school climate.

A Problem

A quick glance at the profiles signals discrepancy. Gibbs describes a much healthier and open school climate than his teachers. Who is right? It doesn't matter; the problem is the discrepancy in views. Gibbs see his behavior as much more positive and open than his teachers do. For example, on every dimension of health he describes the school higher than the teachers. Similarly, on every OCDQ measure, he describes the school as more open than his teachers. Starkly, the difference between Gibbs and the faculty is that he sees an above average climate and they see one below average. What's happening?

Identifying and solving a problem call for different strategies. Gibbs has used climate instruments to identify the problem. That's the easy part. What to do and how to change the organization are other matters. Gibbs has to discover the root of the discrepancy: that is, why the teachers describe his behavior as more directive and less supportive than he thinks it is. There are only two aspects of school climate on which Gibbs and his faculty agree. Both judge the teachers to be slightly above average in their engagement, and both agree that the principal initiates structure and action to solve problems. But after that, there is not much agreement. Why does the faculty perceive most interactions in the school as much less positive than Gibbs? For example, why is it that the faculty doesn't see the supportive leadership that Gibbs is trying to model? Why does the faculty describe the climate as basically unhealthy when Gibbs sees it as healthy? Does Gibbs suffer from unrealistic optimism? The principal cannot solve this problem alone because it is an interaction issue. It may be a question of misperception. But who is misperceiving?

An Organizational Development Model

What is a good strategy for developing healthy and open learning organizations? One potentially useful way to change school climate is a collaborative effort on the part of all those concerned, often called an **organizational development model.** This approach addresses both individual and organizational needs, and is a planned effort to make both the individual and institution more productive (Hanson & Lubin, 1995). The approach is useful for principals who want to improve the climate of their school. In order to be successful, this strategy requires that administrators and teachers recognize difficulties, take responsibility for their solution, and develop and implement action plans. In the case at hand, the objective is to have teachers and the principal recognize that a challenge exists. Identifying a problem—discrepancies between the principal's and the teachers' perception of the social interactions in the workplace—was made possible by using the climate instruments described earlier in this chapter.

Before proceeding further, we outline and begin to apply the steps in an organizational development approach (Hoy & Tarter, 1997a):

1. *Identify the problem*—discrepancies in the climate profiles.

2. *Establish a problem-solving team*—usually the teachers in the school. To change climate, teachers must be involved.

3. *The team takes on the problem*—the teachers and principal come to an understanding of the difficulty. Teachers examine the data with the principal and express a willingness to resolve the troubling issues. They must understand the situation and see the need for change.

4. *Diagnosis of the problem*—the team diagnoses the causes of the problem.

5. *Develop an action plan*—the team develops an action plan by examining alternatives and consequences, and then selecting a course of action.

6. *Implement action plan*—put the plan into action.

7. *Evaluate*—assess the consequences of the plan by collecting new data and evaluating discrepancies.

Back to Martin Luther King Jr. High School

Principal Elbert Gibbs was startled by the school climate data. The teachers view the school as much more negative than he does. This discrepancy in perceptions defines the problem, which Gibbs has identified. Now, he needs to join forces with his teachers and involve them in organizational problem solving. Does this mean that he should involve all the teachers in the school? Perhaps, but especially those who want to be part of the process and have something to say should be involved. Over the long run, the goal is to routinely have all teachers participate in decision making and organizational problem solving, that is, to create a learning organization. Over the short run, however, the problem is to put together a team to begin the process.

One way to get interested teachers involved is to use an in-service workshop. Most schools have a day or two throughout the year for such activities, and Martin Luther King Jr. High School (MLKHS) is no exception.

First, teachers need to understand the ideas of health and openness and how they are measured. In a faculty this large, the information can be presented efficiently at the workshop with accompanying overheads and handouts to simplify the explanation. Our own experience is that teachers are very receptive to the climate ideas, especially because data about their school are available; the results of the OCDQ and the OHI are intriguing. An explanation of school climate and its measures can be done in a half day. That is, by the end of the morning of an in-service day, teachers should be able to interpret overheads of profiles of school climates.

Next, teachers are ready to look at the profile of their own school as they have described it. In this school the teachers' score for overall health is 485 (below average) and school openness is 481 (below average). From the teachers' vantage point, this is an unhealthy school and its climate is closed. There are major discrepancies between the teachers and principal on institutional integrity (420 | 540), on principal influence (465 | 510), on resources allocation (445 | 500), on academic emphasis (455 | 530), on supportiveness (490 | 555), and on directiveness (540 | 480). These are major differences in views. What's happening here? Both the teachers and principal need to know.

The principal must discover why the teachers saw his behavior as less supportive and more directive than he did. Gibbs admitted to the faculty that he was puzzled by the results because he thought his relationship with the faculty was better than the teacher data suggested. Although he was perplexed, he was willing to examine his own values and choices in this open forum. This is not to say he was comfortable in doing so. Most principals are not, and he was no exception. But he felt he needed to continue what he started, an analysis of the school climate. There was no turning back. He believed that he needed to have an open mind toward his own as well as his faculty's behavior. He knew there were risks, but he wanted a platform of openness and trust to build a more effective school, one in which the improvement of instruction was a primary goal.

Actually, the problem-solving process seemed daunting. There were, after all, almost sixty professionals on the faculty, and the faculty had judged the school climate to be deficient. The thing that bothered Gibbs more than anything else was the low academic emphasis that the teachers believed existed in the school. While troubled by the teacher frustration and his reported directive leadership, the lack of academic emphasis hurt his professional pride. He wanted this school to be an important sequence in the education of all students, but minorities especially. Gibbs and the teachers must seek explanations and avoid blaming or scapegoating. Was the problem real or imagined? Of course it was real, and the teachers recognized it.

At the next faculty meeting, Gibbs and his teachers had an open conversation about the causes of the discrepancies. With overheads and charts at his disposal, Gibbs took 20 minutes to review the health profiles of MLKHS and then opened the meeting for discussion. Let's listen in:

> **GIBBS:** I was surprised that you believe that parents are too obtrusive and there is too much community pressure. I don't just let people wander the halls, but I do want a lot of parental involvement in the school. I think it helps us to do our work.
>
> **FACULTY MEMBER:** I have spent a considerable part of my adult life learning the skills of teaching. I appreciate help, but generally parents interfere; they don't help, they get in the way.
>
> **GIBBS:** What do you mean? Give me an example.
>
> **FACULTY MEMBER:** I have a master's in history from the university and I have taught history for fourteen years. I am interested in teaching students how to evaluate evidence, how to think. Parents want me to talk about the unique contributions of their group. Do you think the Multicultural Fair idea was our idea?
>
> **GIBBS:** Well, I think multiculturalism is a good idea. After all, we have a multicultural school.
>
> **FACULTY MEMBER:** We know that! But it's outside interference we resent. We think we should control those kinds of decisions, not outsiders. That's why our scores on institutional integrity differ from yours.
>
> **GIBBS:** What do you think I can do? Parents have a right to come into the school.

FACULTY MEMBER: Of course they have a right to come in. But they are not here to write curriculum.

(Long period of silence.)

GIBBS: Well, well . . . we need to talk about this some more. I am beginning to understand why we responded to the items on institutional integrity differently. That's useful. But what really surprised me, and I don't understand, was our wholly different views of my leadership. I think of myself as being a lot more supportive and more open than you give me credit for.

(Long period of silence.)

FACULTY MEMBER: Well, we do think of you as supportive, but we get too many directives. You are always dropping in on our classes unannounced. You are always telling us what to do like we are students not teachers. It's just too much.

GIBBS: Give me an example.

FACULTY MEMBER: We need more freedom to make the decisions that we need to make. You're an old history teacher, and I am a veteran English teacher. Why do you think you know more about teaching composition than I do?

GIBBS: I never said I did.

FACULTY MEMBER: Maybe, but you sure act like it. Here's what I mean: I am struggling in class with one of the slower students trying to teach him the skills of writing simple sentences, and I am making progress. And you suggest that I should give the students more freedom to develop their ideas. That's not a bad idea in itself. But you just don't understand what's happening in the class. To be candid, I sometimes find your supervision obtrusive and irritating.

GIBBS: We need to talk about this later.

ANOTHER FACULTY MEMBER: I agree with Wally. You need to treat us more as colleagues and less as employees. We like you and you work hard. But so do we. You don't see us as equals. We feel like hired help.

GIBBS: I don't want to hurt your feelings, but when things go wrong, I take the heat. I am sorry you feel as you do, but I do respect you.

FACULTY MEMBER: You asked for some examples, and you got them. What are you going to do?

GIBBS: Well, I'll have to think about this. I asked for your interpretations, you have given them, but frankly, it's hard for me not to be defensive. We have some work to do.

This little exchange should give you a flavor of the kind of conversation that may occur. A close analysis of the conversation shows that the principal himself sees a difference in his status and he indirectly communicates it ("I'm the one accountable"). Teachers are seeking more autonomy, and some teachers feel the principal doesn't respect their abilities. In other parts of the dialogue, it also became obvious that teachers felt that occasionally Gibbs's observations of their performance were critical but nei-ther insightful nor constructive. These were some of the reasons for the discrepancies between Gibbs's perception of his leadership style and the faculty's perceptions.

At this point, Gibbs needs a plan of action. Sixty professionals in a faculty meet-ing just is not the right format to get at the root causes of the discrepancies. Gibbs de-cided to ask for volunteers to work on the problems exposed by the climate analysis. Between volunteers (and all were included) and appointees the principal put together a task force of twelve veteran teachers who were willing to work to improve the climate of the school. After the task force was appointed, Gibbs went to the superintendent and requested a modest stipend for the teachers. Gibbs argued that use of the climate mea-sures served two important purposes. First, it got the faculty to engage in organizational problem solving, and second it provided a useful vehicle for administrative assessment. The superintendent agreed to support Gibbs's foray into school improvement and or-ganizational problem solving. To that end, she underwrote the cost for three Saturday morning work sessions.

What are the causes of the discrepancies? The first Saturday, the principal and teachers decided to develop a series of rival explanations for the differences in percep-tions. The teachers had to be willing to take some risks in articulating their position without fear of reprisal. The teachers were divided into three groups and each devel-oped an explanation of what was happening. The principal and his assistant were not part of any group. But nonetheless, Gibbs and his assistant also developed a tentative explanation of the data. After a couple of hours, the group as a whole reassembled and the four explanations were presented and compared. After comparing the explanations, the faculty agreed to devote the next session to trying to reconcile differences.

The next session opened with a brief recapitulation of the teachers' perspective on the climate data. The teachers saw the parents as having entirely too much access to the school; ultimately, they claimed that the parents interfered rather than helped. The faculty didn't mind parent participation in education, but they expected the principal to be a better gatekeeper. Parents were going directly to the teachers with their con-cerns and demands. There was agreement that Gibbs needed to serve as a buffer be-tween community groups and the teachers. Growing out of conversations of the kind that we have just heard, the teachers suggested that, if Gibbs were less directive, they would be less frustrated. The teachers saw themselves being drafted for too many ac-tivities. In fact, many were suspicious of his latest climate venture; they saw it as just an-other drain on their time that would be fruitless. A number of teachers also offered that busywork, such as written, formal lesson plans that go unreviewed, be eliminated. They suggested a committee on paperwork whose charge was to reduce paperwork wherever feasible. For his part, Gibbs still did not agree with the explanation of his faculty, but he respected the faculty's judgment and agreed that something needed to be done and he would do it.

Although Gibbs believed he had adequate support from central, the teachers complained that he had little influence in getting them the things that they needed to improve their work. Making copies was always a problem; it took a long time to get class sets of materials; supplementary materials were simply not forthcoming. Gibbs saw it differently. He almost always got what he requested from the superintendent, as long as it was within reason. He believed that she respected his opinions and efforts.

Gibbs was not sure the teachers understood the limited resources of the district; this was not a wealthy suburban district.

The teachers agreed that academic emphasis at MLKHS was below average. They saw little respect among students for academics. Football was king, closely followed by indifference. The teachers felt they were only being realistic in lowering their expectations of student performance. In fact, a good many teachers believed that most students simply couldn't do the work. They had difficulty getting students to do homework, not to mention classroom discipline problems. Gibbs, however, was unaware that for at least half the teachers, student homework and apathy were problems. Gibbs was probably misled by the orderly appearances of the halls and the good relations he had with students. It was not that Gibbs thought MLKHS was an academic powerhouse. Clearly, it was not. But he believed that compared to other urban high schools, his was above average.

On the measures of both directive and frustrated behavior of the principal, there were sharp discrepancies between Gibbs and the faculty. By and large, the teachers believed that his observations of their classroom teaching were intrusive and authoritarian. He didn't visit the classrooms often, but when he did, he always had many directives for improvement. The teachers resented the style if not the substance of his comments. The teachers resented the formal sign-in and sign-out required of all teachers. The teachers resented the extreme formalization in the school: forms for parking, for library materials, for audio/visual equipment, about grade distribution, and more: repetitive absentee forms, lateness forms, lunch forms, and a form for virtually anything out of the ordinary was required. Teachers believed the forms for the most part unnecessary. Gibbs saw the forms as a necessary way to monitor things.

If nothing else, the teachers and Gibbs were now communicating openly with each other and explaining their positions. Gibbs was interested but he was unconvinced on many issues. The teachers, for their part, enjoyed letting Gibbs know how they felt. They believed that he was interested in them and the school and eventually would come around. At least he was open and not too defensive.

How do we develop constructive plans for reducing discrepancies and improving climate? This is the time for the teachers and the principal to work together to forge a realistic plan. There is no one best way to do this, but in the current case the principal and teachers decided to each work on the plan independently and then come back together (much in the same manner as they had framed the causes of the problem) to propose a school improvement plan.

The faculty task force met on yet another Saturday morning to discuss and formulate an improvement plan. In response to the analysis of problem causes, the principal offered the following:

1. Gibbs suggested that the teachers report all instances of parental interference to his office. Gibbs would monitor the reports and try to buffer the teachers from the parents.

2. Gibbs was genuinely concerned about the appearance of heavy-handedness in his administration, and he proposed two immediate actions. He would review the amount of paperwork and reduce it dramatically, if possible. He respected his faculty and conceded that they should have more independence in decision making. In fact, he proposed that a leadership cabinet be formed composed of all the department chairs and administrators to share in decision making in the school.

3. Gibbs was still perplexed by the faculty's low student expectation; he rationalized that if it was as bad as his teachers said, the school needed some strong direct leadership. Here was his dilemma: How could he work with teachers to improve the academic climate and simultaneously remain indirect? He turned to his teachers for advice in this matter.

4. Gibbs promised that he would make himself more readily available to the faculty. He also pledged that, in the future, his criticism would be constructive and helpful. He concluded by reaffirming confidence and admiration for his faculty and pointed out the one area in which there was virtual agreement: the commitment of the teachers to the school.

5. Finally, Gibbs was concerned about the academic seriousness of the school. This was a good school in a community that supported education. He was shocked to find his teachers did not share his perception of the academic climate. He vowed to address the issue on a number of fronts. First, a series of meetings with his faculty were necessary to discover the origin of the faculty's mediocre assessment of the academic emphasis at MLKHS.

The faculty for its part came in with the following set of recommendations:

1. The teachers proposed that Gibbs become involved as a liaison between teachers and parents. They recommended that department chairs together with Gibbs and the executive committee of the PTA meet regularly to address and mollify parental concerns.

2. The teachers proposed a system of peer coaching to improve the teaching process. They also asked that they be given more input into future in-service meetings. They wanted teachers to be more directly involved, and administrators less, in improving instruction. After all, they reasoned, their job was teaching, and the principal's job was administration.

3. Because MLKHS was not a large school, the faculty asked for more informal consultation. They didn't want more meetings, just more influence and information.

4. The teachers recommended that a committee of teachers be appointed to streamline the bureaucratic procedures—eliminate forms.

5. The teachers recommended that a schoolwide policy be established on homework and tutorials. The honor society would be approached and asked to do volunteer tutoring a few afternoons a week.

6. Finally, the faculty commended the principal for his concern and action in trying to improve the school workplace.

After the suggestions and recommendations were enumerated and discussed, Gibbs and the faculty were concerned about the number of different issues that surfaced and the time needed to confront them. Gibbs for his part admitted that he was unrealistically optimistic and the whole exercise provided him with a reality check. The teachers, on the other hand, were a little afraid that if they tried to do too much, nothing would be accomplished. They needed a reasonable plan that was realistic and attainable.

There was, however, an inherent dilemma in their suggestions: They wanted greater involvement and more interaction but fewer meetings and less administrative work. They agreed to be idealistic and yet pragmatic. The following aspects were key elements of their eventual plan:

1. A committee of teachers would work with the principal to find ways to reduce administrative trivia and paperwork.

2. Gibbs and the teachers agreed that department chairs, the executive committee of the PTA, and Gibbs would meet regularly to address community concerns.

3. Gibbs agreed with the teachers that a system of peer coaching should be initiated.

4. Teachers agreed to combine classes on occasion so that they could serve as teaching models and coaches for each other.

5. Department chairs would work out the details. Gibbs turned over the next three professional in-service days to the teachers and department chairs; they would plan and conduct the in-service days.

6. The faculty and Gibbs agreed that a leadership cabinet composed of department chairs and elected teachers should be formed to share in the governance of the school. Gibbs agreed to consult with the faculty cabinet concerning all matters in which teachers had a personal stake and professional knowledge.

7. Gibbs suggested and the teachers agreed that the faculty would have complete independence in planning the programs for the three in-service days of professional development next year.

Clearly, this plan is not a set of step-by-step procedures to be accomplished in a rigid way. To the contrary, the plan is a set of accepted guidelines and commitments. The teachers and principal realize that their plan requires increased effort. It is ironic that a major goal of the plan is to reduce unnecessary busywork, yet the cost of involvement, professional control, and autonomy is more work to do. The faculty is committed to the plan, even though they know it will be more work—but, they believe, meaningful work.

How successful would this plan be? That is an empirical question. In six months, two activities would occur to assess its effectiveness. First, the OCDQ and OHI would be administered and scored, and then the principal and faculty would revisit the climate and changes at MLKHS.

Just to keep things in perspective, let us review what has happened at MLKHS. The morning of the first day was spent explaining, discussing, and interpreting the climate frameworks, their measures, and the school profiles. In the afternoon, the teachers were confronted with the openness and health profiles of MLKHS. After some discussion of those profiles and agreement on what they meant, the principal introduced his perception of the school profile, which diverged dramatically from that of the faculty. The discrepancies led to a frank, open discussion between the principal and teachers culminating in the formation of three teacher groups to develop tentative explanations about the causes of the discrepancies in perceptions. After working in small groups for an hour or so, the teachers reconvened and shared their explanations, coming to a rough consensus about the causes of the discrepancy.

The next day was spent formulating a plan to reduce the discrepancies and improve the health and openness of the school. These two in-service days should be thought of as a beginning of a continuous program of improvement and problem solving. Even if these educators are successful in developing the school climate they all desire, periodic monitoring of climate is a wise course. The two goals of this process were first, the climate of the school is improved and the stage is set for effective supervision, and second, group problem solving and organizational learning become natural elements of school life.

Summary

Organizational culture and climate are two complementary ways to capture the feel or working atmosphere of schools. Culture is the shared set of beliefs and values that binds the organization together and gives it a distinctive identity. The culture of the school can be viewed from four vantage points—tacit assumptions, core values, shared norms, artifacts—all of which contribute to a full understanding of school culture. Schools can create cultures that encourage learning and improvement of instruction or those that discourage such outcomes. A culture of academic optimism is one that enhances the improvement of instruction and learning. Beliefs about academic optimism are social perceptions that provide school norms, which are strengthened rather than depleted through their use. Administrators are well advised to cultivate a culture of efficacy, trust, and academic emphasis to improve teaching and learning in their schools. Finally, significant events should never be accepted at face value; their meanings must be interpreted in terms of the values and norms of the school and from the points of view of different organizational members.

School climate is a relatively enduring quality of the school environment that is experienced by teachers, influences their behavior, and is based on their collective perceptions of dominant patterns of school behavior. Whereas culture is the shared beliefs and values of the school, climate refers to perceptions of the basic patterns of behavior that exist in schools. Although values and behavior should be related, they are not the same. School climate was conceptualized and measured from two perspectives: the openness and health of interpersonal relations. The OCDQ-RE is an instrument to measure the openness of interactions among teachers and administrators, while the OHI is an inventory to gauge the health of the interactions among students, teachers, and administrators. Both instruments give a reliable snapshot of school climate and are useful in attempts to improve the teaching–learning environment.

Organizations are in a constant state of flux. Their change can be progressive, regressive, or aimless. Schools can develop their own learning procedures to solve their problems. They can become places where teachers and principals can continually expand their capacity to create the results that they desire, where emergent patterns of thinking are nurtured, where collective aspiration is liberated, and where people are constantly learning how to learn.

We concluded this chapter with an example of how one principal used the climate frame and measures as bases for organizational change. Using an organizational development approach, we identified a climate problem, established a problem-solving team, diagnosed the potential problem causes, developed an action plan, and set the stage for effective school improvement.

KEY TERMS

academic emphasis (327)

academic optimism (326)

artifacts (323)

closed climate (335)

collective efficacy (327)

consideration (340)

disengaged climate (335)

engaged climate (334)

faculty trust in students and
  parents (327)

healthy school climate (342)

initiating structure (340)

institutional integrity (339)

morale (340)

myths (323)

norms (322)

OCDQ (330)

OHI (341)

open climate (334)

organizational climate (329)

organizational culture (319)

organizational development
  model (346)

organizational health (339)

principal influence (340)

resource support (340)

rituals (323)

tacit assumptions (320)

values (321)

DEVELOPING YOUR PORTFOLIO

1. Determine the organizational climate of your school by using both the OHI and OCDQ.

   a. First you respond to each instrument.

   b. Then have the faculty of your school respond to each.

   c. Develop two profiles of the climate: yours and the faculty's.

   d. Compare the two profiles and speculate on the reasons for any differences.

   e. Develop a two-year plan of action for improving the school climate.

2. Describe the organizational culture of your school.

   a. Be sure and include a description of the norms and values for each of the following areas: innovation, stability, attention to detail, outcome orientation, people orientation, team orientation, and aggressiveness. Provide examples of the consequences of each.

   b. Also identify any other shared values that make your school distinctive and give examples.

   c. Use the questionnaires found on the website (www.coe.ohio-state.edu/whoy) to measure collective efficacy, faculty trust, and academic emphasis, and then average the measures to gauge the academic optimism of the school.

   d. Critique your school's organizational culture; that is, discuss its strengths and weaknesses.

   e. Finally, develop a two-year plan of action for improving the school culture.

3. Over a two-year period, develop a series of in-service activities to improve the collective efficacy of the school. In particular, make sure that your activities are directed toward developing

   a. mastery experiences;

   b. vicarious experiences;

   c. verbal persuasion;

   d. affective states.

Clearly explain how your plan will address each of these sources of collective efficacy, then develop an evaluation plan to assess the effectiveness of your in-service activities.

INSTRUCTIONAL LEADER'S TOOLBOX

Readings

Bandura, A. (1997). *Self-efficacy: The exercise of control*. New York: Freeman.

Cohen, M. D., & Sproull, L. S. (Eds.). (1996). *Organizational learning*. Thousand Oaks, CA: Sage.

Hoy, W. K., & Sabo, D. (1998). *Quality middle schools: Open and healthy*. Thousand Oaks, CA: Corwin.

Hoy, W. K., & Tarter, C. J. (1997). *The road to open and healthy schools: A handbook for change, elementary edition*. Thousand Oaks, CA: Corwin.

Hoy, W. K., Tarter, C. J., & Kottkamp, R. (1991). *Open schools/healthy schools: Measuring organizational climate*. Beverly Hills, CA: Sage.

Hoy, W. K., Tarter, C. J., & Woolfolk Hoy, A. (2006). Academic optimism of schools: A force for student achievement. *American Educational Research Journal, 43*, 425–446.

McGuigan, L. & Hoy, W. K. (2006). Principal leadership: Creating a culture of academic optimism to improve achievement for all students. *Leadership and Policy in Schools, 5*, 203–229.

Ouchi, W. (1981). *Theory z*. Reading, MA: Addison-Wesley.

Schein, E. H. (1992). *Organizational culture and leadership* (2nd ed.). San Francisco: Jossey-Bass.

Schein, E. H. (1999). *The corporate culture*. San Francisco: Jossey-Bass.

Senge, P. M. (1990). *The fifth discipline: The art and practice of the learning organization*. New York: Doubleday.

Senge, P. M., Cambron-McCabe, N. H., Lucas, T., Kleiner, A., Dutton, J., & Smith, B. (2000). *Schools that learn*. New York: Doubleday.

Senge, P. M., Kleiner, A., Roberts, C., Rossi, R., & Smith, B. J. (1994). *The fifth discipline fieldbook*. New York: Bantam Doubleday Dell.

Websites

www.coe.ohio-state.edu/whoy
Climate instruments
www.infed.org/thinkers/senge.htm
Learning organizations
www.ncrel.org/rural/
Resources for educators in rural areas
www.ncrel.org/sdrs/
Pathways to school improvement
www.tnellen.com/ted/tc/schein.html
Organizational culture

Organizations

www.aom.pace.edu
Academy of Management
www.teachingforchange.org/
Teaching for change
www.ucea.org
University Council for Educational Administration

APPENDIX A

Conducting a Job Interview

Here is a collection of questions* to use in selecting teachers. We have grouped the questions around a number of typical topics.

Questions about why applicant wants a position in your school system

1. Why do you want this position?
2. Why do you want to work in this district?
3. What do you know about our school/school system?

Questions about the applicant's conceptions of good teaching

1. Do you remember your favorite or best elementary or high school teacher? Tell me what there was about him/her that you admire.
2. What makes a good teacher?
3. Why would you be a good teacher? What are your strengths? Weaknesses?

Questions about the applicant's beliefs/goals/philosophy

1. What do you hope to achieve with your students?
2. If there were only one skill or concept that you could get them to learn, what would it be and why?
3. Why did you want to become a teacher?
4. What is your stance on (be familiar with the initiatives of the school or district to identify issues that might come up):
   - Inclusion?
   - Whole language versus phonics?
   - Using concrete rewards to motivate students?
   - Involving families and the community in your classroom?
   - Integrated curriculum?
5. If you were to be on an advisory committee for your college to improve the preparation of teachers, what would you suggest and why?
6. What current trends in public education please you? Displease you?

Questions about the applicant's skills/abilities

1. What is the best lesson you have taught? What made it good?
2. What has been your best experience in the classroom so far? What made it good?
3. What support do you need to make you successful?
4. Tell me about all your experiences in working with children in addition to your student teaching.
5. What has happened in your student teaching experience that you felt you were not well prepared for and how did you handle it? What would you do differently now that you have had this experience?

Questions about the applicant's classroom management skills

1. What are the challenging aspects of classroom management for you?
2. What was your most challenging discipline problem so far and how did you handle it?
3. Here is a specific situation (interviewer describes a student who challenges your authority or refuses to follow rules or do work). What would you do?
4. How will you establish rapport with students and motivate them?

Questions about the applicant's instructional strategies

1. How do you accommodate different student abilities and learning styles in your teaching?
2. How do you make accommodations for students with special needs and challenges?
3. How would you involve families and the community in your classroom?
4. Based on what you know so far, would you prefer to work alone and be responsible for smaller numbers of students or collaborate with other teachers and be responsible for larger numbers of students?
5. What role does technology play in your teaching?

*Thanks to Dr. Harry Galinsky, former superintendent of Paramus, NJ, and Superintendent of the Year, and Dr. Michael DiPaola, former superintendent of Pitman, NJ, and Associate Professor of Education at the College of William and Mary, for their questions and suggestions.

357

APPENDIX B

Guidelines for Helping Beginning Teachers

- Schedule an orientation for beginning teachers.
- Develop a mentoring system for beginning teachers.
- Provide teachers with an appropriate mix of courses, students, and facilities; beginning teachers deserve good classrooms and the requisite supplies.
- If possible, provide a light load for beginning teachers. For example, keep the number of preparations for new high school teachers to two or three at most.
- Make sure that extracurricular duties are not overly demanding for beginning teachers. Protect your beginning teachers.
- Provide both social and work-related activities (e.g., team teaching, cooperative instruction, etc.) for beginning teachers. Encourage beginning teachers to interact with each other. Develop a "Rookie Roundtable," a regular meeting of beginning teachers focused on typical problems.
- Develop a newsletter that reports on the accomplishments of all teachers, but highlight those of beginning teachers.
- Avoid formal classroom evaluation by the principal of beginning teachers, and instead have colleagues coach, monitor, provide feedback on strengths and weaknesses, and develop opportunities for practice and feedback in a nonthreatening environment.
- Plan some in-service programs specifically for beginning teachers; find out what your beginning teachers need and want and help them get it.
- Have beginning teachers meet regularly with their mentors to identify and share problems before they become serious.
- Celebrate accomplishments. Plan and schedule events for experienced and beginning teachers such as luncheons, parties, and award recognition.
- Provide for joint planning, cooperative teaching, committee assignments, and other cooperative activities between new and experienced teachers.
- Provide opportunities for new teachers to observe master teachers at work.

APPENDIX C

Guidelines for Observing Classroom Behavior

Student–Teacher Relations

- What is the evidence of organization and clarity in teacher presentations?
- How enthusiastic is the teacher?
- How does the teacher demonstrate care, warmth, and empathy, and how does he or she nurture students?
- How does the teacher motivate students?
- What is the evidence that the teacher listens to and responds to individual student's needs, interests, and concerns?
- How does the teacher encourage respect for other students and their views?
- How does the teacher encourage and build on student discussions?
- What is the evidence that the teacher is concerned with the social–emotional development of students?

The Teaching–Learning Process

- To what extent is the teacher concerned with comprehension and application of knowledge? Analysis, synthesis, and evaluation?
- To what extent does the teacher use inquiry approaches?
- Which instructional methods did the students find most interesting?
- What is the evidence of student learning?
- How does the teacher use real-life examples to stimulate interest, illustrate, and integrate the concepts being taught?
- What instructional techniques are used to motivate divergent thinking?
- How does the teacher integrate different instructional activities?
- How does the teacher prevent frustration and confusion?
- To what extent and how is learning reinforced?
- To what extent and how does the teacher use groups?

Classroom Management

- What student behaviors were acceptable and unacceptable in class?
- How does the teacher effectively use classroom space?
- What did you like and dislike about the physical environment of the classroom?
- How does the teacher enlist student cooperation?
- Are the rules of the classroom known and used by students?
- What activities encourage student engagement? Prevent management problems?
- How is conflict managed?
- What is the evidence that a positive learning context exists?
- What is the evidence that students are developing responsibly and managing themselves?

OCDQ-RE

DIRECTIONS: The following are statements about your school.* Please indicate the extent to which each statement characterizes your school by circling the appropriate response.

RO = Rarely Occurs   SO = Sometimes Occurs
O = Often Occurs   VFO = Very Frequently Occurs

1. The teachers accomplish their work with vim, vigor, and pleasure	RO	SO	O	VFO
2. Teachers' closest friends are other faculty members at this school	RO	SO	O	VFO
3. Faculty meetings are useless	RO	SO	O	VFO
4. The principal goes out of his/her way to help teachers	RO	SO	O	VFO
5. The principal rules with an iron fist	RO	SO	O	VFO
6. Teachers leave school immediately after school is over	RO	SO	O	VFO
7. Teachers invite faculty members to visit them at home	RO	SO	O	VFO
8. There is a minority group of teachers who always oppose the majority	RO	SO	O	VFO
9. The principal uses constructive criticism	RO	SO	O	VFO
10. The principal checks the sign-in sheet every morning	RO	SO	O	VFO
11. Routine duties interfere with the job of teaching	RO	SO	O	VFO
12. Most of the teachers here accept the faults of their colleagues	RO	SO	O	VFO
13. Teachers know the family background of other faculty members	RO	SO	O	VFO
14. Teachers exert group pressure on nonconforming faculty members	RO	SO	O	VFO
15. The principal explains his/her reasons for criticism to teachers	RO	SO	O	VFO
16. The principal listens to and accepts teachers' suggestions	RO	SO	O	VFO
17. The principal schedules the work for the teachers	RO	SO	O	VFO
18. Teachers have too many committee requirements	RO	SO	O	VFO
19. Teachers help and support each other	RO	SO	O	VFO
20. Teachers have fun socializing together during school time	RO	SO	O	VFO
21. Teachers ramble when they talk at faculty meetings	RO	SO	O	VFO
22. The principal looks out for the personal welfare of teachers	RO	SO	O	VFO
23. The principal treats teachers as equals	RO	SO	O	VFO
24. The principal corrects teachers' mistakes	RO	SO	O	VFO
25. Administrative paperwork is burdensome at this school	RO	SO	O	VFO
26. Teachers are proud of their school	RO	SO	O	VFO
27. Teachers have parties for each other	RO	SO	O	VFO
28. The principal compliments teachers	RO	SO	O	VFO

29. The principal is easy to understand	RO	SO	O	VFO
30. The principal closely checks classroom (teacher) activities	RO	SO	O	VFO
31. Clerical support reduces teachers' paperwork	RO	SO	O	VFO
32. New teachers are readily accepted by colleagues	RO	SO	O	VFO
33. Teachers socialize with each other on a regular basis	RO	SO	O	VFO
34. The principal supervises teachers closely	RO	SO	O	VFO
35. The principal checks lesson plans	RO	SO	O	VFO
36. Teachers are burdened with busy work	RO	SO	O	VFO
37. Teachers socialize together in small, select groups	RO	SO	O	VFO
38. Teachers provide strong social support for colleagues	RO	SO	O	VFO
39. The principal is autocratic	RO	SO	O	VFO
40. Teachers respect the professional competence of their colleagues	RO	SO	O	VFO
41. The principal monitors everything teachers do	RO	SO	O	VFO
42. The principal goes out of his/her way to show appreciation to teachers	RO	SO	O	VFO

*OCDQ instruments for all levels are available at www.coe.ohio-state.edu/whoy

Administering the OCDQ-RE Instrument

The OCDQ-RE is best administered as part of a faculty meeting. It is important to guarantee the anonymity of the teacher respondent; teachers are not asked to sign the questionnaire and no identifying code is placed on the form. Most teachers do not object to responding to the instrument, which takes less than ten minutes to complete. It is probably advisable to have someone other than an administrator collect the data. It is important to create a nonthreatening atmosphere where teachers give candid responses. All of the health and climate instruments follow the same pattern of administration.

REFERENCES

Abi-Nader, J. (1991). Creating a vision of the future: Strategies for motivating minority students. *Phi Delta Kappan, 72*, 546–549.

Abrams, I. M., & Madaus, G. F. (2003). The lessons of high stakes testing. *Educational Leadership, 61*(32), 31–35.

Abruscato, J. (1993). Early results and tentative implications from the Vermont Portfolio Project. *Phi Delta Kappan, 74*, 474–477.

Ackerman, B. P., Brown, E. D., & Izard, C. E. (2004). The relations between contextual risk, earned income, and the school adjustment of children from economically disadvantaged families. *Developmental Psychology, 40*, 204–216.

Ackerman, B. P., & Brown, E. D. (2006). Income poverty, poverty co-factors, and the adjustment of children in elementary school. In R. V. Kail (Ed.), *Advances in child development and behavior* (Vol. 34, pp. 91–129). New York: Elsevier.

Adams, M. J., Treiman, R., & Pressley, M. (1998). Reading, writing, and literacy. In I. Sigel & A. Renninger (Eds.), *Handbook of child psychology: Child psychology in practice* (Vol. 4, pp. 275–355). New York: Wiley.

Ainley, M., Hidi, S., & Berndorf, D. (2002). Interest, learning, and the psychological processes that mediate their relationship. *Journal of Educational Psychology 94*, 545–561.

Airasian, P. W. (2005). *Classroom assessment: Concepts and applications* (5th ed.). New York: McGraw-Hill.

Airasian, P. W., & Walsh, M. E. (1997). Constructivist cautions. *Phi Delta Kappan, 78*, 444–449.

Albanese, M. A., & Mitchell, S. A. (1993). Problem-based learning: A review of literature on its outcomes and implementation issues. *Academic Medicine, 68*, 52–81.

Alberto, P., & Troutman, A. C. (2006). *Applied behavior analysis for teachers: Influencing student performance* (7th ed.). Saddle River, NJ: Prentice-Hall/Merrill.

Alderman, M. K. (1985). Achievement motivation and the preservice teacher. In M. Alderman & M. Cohen (Eds.), *Motivation theory and practice for preservice teachers* (pp. 37–49). Washington, DC: ERIC Clearinghouse on Teacher Education.

Alderman, M. K. (2004). *Motivation for achievement: Possibilities for teaching and learning.* Mahwah, NJ: Lawrence Erlbaum.

Alexander, P. A. (1996). The past, present, and future of knowledge research: A reexamination of the role of knowledge in learning and instruction. *Educational Psychologist, 31*, 89–92.

Alexander, P. A., & Murphy, P. K. (1998). The research base for APA's learner-centered psychological principles. In N. Lambert & B. McCombs (Eds.), *How students learn: Reforming schools through learner-centered education.* Washington, DC: American Psychological Association.

Allington, R. L., & McGill-Frazen, A. (2003). The impact of summer setback on the reading achievement gap. *Phi Delta Kappan, 85*(1), 68–75.

Alloy, L. B., & Seligman, M. E. P. (1979). On the cognitive component of learned helplessness and depression. *The Journal of Learning & Motivation, 13*, 219–276.

Alloway, T. P., Gathercole, S. E., & Pickering, S. J. (2006). Verbal and visuo-spatial short-term and working memory in children: Are they separable? *Child Development, 77*, 1698–1716.

Allport, G. (1954). *The nature of prejudice.* Cambridge, MA: Addison-Wesley.

American Association for the Advancement of Science (AAAS). (1993). *Benchmarks for science literacy.* Washington, DC: Author.

Ames, C. (1992). Classrooms: Goals, structures, and student motivation. *Journal of Educational Psychology, 84*, 261–271.

Ames, R., & Lau, S. (1982). An attributional analysis of student help-seeking in academic settings. *Journal of Educational Psychology, 74*, 414–423.

Anastasi, A. (1988). *Psychological testing* (6th ed.). New York: Macmillan.

Anderman, E. M., & Maehr, M. L. (1994). Motivation and schooling in the middle grades. *Review of Educational Research, 64*, 287–310.

Anderman, L. H. (2004). Student motivation across subject-area domains. *Journal of Educational Research, 97*(6), 283–285.

Anderson, C. S. (1982). The search for school climate: A review of the research. *Review of Educational Research, 52*, 368–420.

Anderson, C. W., Holland, J. D., & Palincsar, A. S. (1997). Canonical and sociocultural approaches to research and reform in science education: The story of Juan and his group. *Elementary School Journal, 97*, 359–384.

Anderson, C. W., & Roth, K. J. (1989). Teaching for meaningful and self-regulated learning of science. In J. Brophy (Ed.), *Advances in research on teaching* (Vol. 1, pp. 265–306). Greenwich, CT: JAI Press.

Anderson, J. R. (1993). Problem solving and learning. *American Psychologist, 48*, 35–44.

Anderson, J. R. (1995). *Cognitive psychology and Its implications* (4th ed.). New York: Freeman.

Anderson, J. R., Reder, L. M., & Simon, H. A. (1995). Applications and misapplication of cognitive psychology to mathematics education. (Unpublished manuscript). Retrieved from http://www.psy.cmu.edu/~mm4b/misapplied.html

Anderson, J. R., Reder, L. M., & Simon, H. A. (1996). Situated learning and education. *Educational Researcher, 25*, 5–11.

Anderson, L. M. (1989a). Learners and learning. In M. Reynolds (Ed.), *Knowledge base for be-gin-ning teachers* (pp. 85–100). New York: Pergamon.

Anderson, L. M. (1989b). Classroom instruction. In M. Reynolds (Ed.), *Knowledge base for beginning teachers* (pp. 101–116). New York: Pergamon.

Anderson, L. W., & Krathwohl, D. R. (Eds.). (2001). *A taxonomy for learning, teaching, and assessing: A revision of Bloom's taxonomy of educational objectives.* New York: Addison, Wesley, Longman.

Anderson, L. W., & Sosniak, L. A. (Eds.). (1994). *Bloom's Taxonomy: A forty-year retrospective. Ninety-third yearbook for the National Society for the Study of Education: Part II.* Chicago: University of Chicago Press.

Anderson, P. J., & Graham, S. M. (1994). Issues in second-language phonological acquisition among children and adults. *Topics in Language Disorders, 14*, 84–100.

Angier, N., & Chang, K. (2005, January 24). Gray matter and the sexes: Still a scientific gray area. *The New York Times*, A1+.

Arends, R. I. (2004). *Learning to teach* (6th ed.). New York: McGraw-Hill.

Armbruster, B. B., & Anderson, T. H. (1981). Research synthesis on study skills. *Educational Leadership, 39*, 154–156.

Aronson, E. (2000a). Building empathy, compassion and achievement in the jigsaw classroom. In J. Aronson & D. Cordova, *Improving education: Classic and contemporary lessons from psychology.* Mahwah, NJ: Erlbaum.

Aronson, E. (2000b). *Nobody left to hate: Teaching compassion after Columbine.* New York: Worth.

Aronson, E., & Patnoe, S. (1997). *Cooperation in the classroom: The Jigsaw method.* New York: Longman.

Aronson, J. (2002). *Improving academic achievement: Impact of psychological factors on education.* San Diego: Academic Press.

Aronson, J., Fried, C. & Good, C. (2002). Reducing the effects of stereotype threat on African American college students by shaping theories of intelligence. *Journal of Experimental Social Psychology, 38*, 113–125.

Aronson, J., & Inzlicht, M. (2004). The ups and downs of attributional ambiguity: Stereotype vulnerability and the academic self-knowledge of African American college students. *Psychological Science, 15*, 829–836.

Aronson, J., Lustina, M. J., Good, C., Keough, K., Steele, C. M., & Brown, J. (1999). When white men can't do math: Necessary and sufficient factors in stereotype threat. *Journal of Experimental Social Psychology, 35*, 29–46.

Aronson, J., & Steele, C. M. (2005). Stereotypes and the fragility of human competence, motivation, and self-concept. In C. Dweck & E. Elliot (Eds.), *Handbook of competence and motivation.* New York: Guilford.

Ashcraft, M. H. (2002). *Cognition* (3rd ed.). Upper Saddle River, NJ: Prentice-Hall.

Ashcraft, M. H. (2006). *Cognition* (4th ed.). Upper Saddle River, NJ: Prentice-Hall.

Association for the Gifted (2001). *Diversity and developing gifts and talents: A national action plan.* Arlington, VA: Author.

Atkinson, J. W. (1964). *An introduction to motivation.* Princeton, NJ: Van Nostrand.

Atkinson, R. K., Levin, J. R., Kiewra, K. A., Meyers, T., Atkinson, L. A., Renandya, W. A., & Hwang, Y. (1999). Matrix and mnemonic text-processing adjuncts: Comparing and combining their components. *Journal of Educational Psychology, 91*, 242–257.

Au, K. H. (1980). Participation structures in a reading lesson with Hawaiian children: Analysis of a culturally appropriate instructional event. *Anthropology and Education Quarterly, 11*, 91–115.

Au, K. T., Knightly, L. M., Jun, S., & Oh, J. S. (2002). Overhearing a language during childhood. *Psychological Science, 13*, 238–243.

Ausubel, D. P. (1963). *The psychology of meaningful verbal learning.* New York: Grune & Stratton.

Avramidis, E., Bayliss, P., & Burden, R. (2000). Student teachers' attitudes toward the inclusion of children with special education needs in the ordinary school. *Teaching & Teacher Education, 16,* 277–293.

Baddeley, A. D. (2006). Working memory: An overview. In S. J. Pickering (Ed.), *Working memory and education.* New York: Elsevier.

Bailey, S. M. (1993). The current status of gender equity research in American schools. *Educational Psychologist, 28,* 321–339.

Baker, S. K., & Gersten, R. (2006). Teaching practice and the reading growth of first-grade English learners: Validation of an instrument. *The Elementary School Journal, 106,* 199–219.

Ball, D. L., Lubienski, S. T., & Mewborn, D. S. (2001). Research on teaching mathematics: The unsolved problem of teachers' mathematical knowledge. In V. Richardson (Ed.), *Handbook of research on teaching* (4th ed., pp. 433–456). Washington, DC: American Educational Research Association.

Bandura, A. (1982). Self-efficacy mechanisms in human agency. *American Psychologist, 37,* 122–147.

Bandura, A. (1986). *Social foundations of thought and action.* Englewood Cliffs, NJ: Prentice-Hall.

Bandura, A. (1993). Perceived self-efficacy in cognitive development and functioning. *Educational Psychologist, 28,* 117–148.

Bandura, A. (1997). *Self-efficacy: The exercise of control.* New York: Freeman.

Bangert-Drowns, R. L., Kulik, C. C., Kulik, J. A., & Morgan, M. (1991). The instructional effect of feedback in test-like events. *Review of Educational Research, 61,* 213–238.

Banks, J. A. (1997). *Teaching strategies for ethnic studies* (6th ed.). Boston: Allyn & Bacon.

Banks, J. A. (2002). *An introduction to multicultural education* (3rd ed.). Boston: Allyn & Bacon.

Banks, S. R. (2005). *Classroom assessment: Issues and practice.* Boston: Allyn & Bacon.

Barkley, R. A. (2003). Attention-deficit disorder. In E. J. Marsh & R. A. Barkley (Eds.), *Child psychopathology* (2nd ed., pp. 75–143). New York: Guilford.

Barnhill, G. P. (2005). Functional behavioral assessment in schools. *Intervention in School & Clinic, 40,* 131–143.

Baron, R. A. (1998). *Psychology* (4th ed.). Boston: Allyn & Bacon.

Barone, F. J. (1997). Bullying in school: It doesn't have to happen. *Phi Delta Kappan, 79,* 80–82.

Barr, R. (2001). Research on the teaching of reading. In V. Richardson (Ed.), *Handbook of research on teaching* (4th ed., pp. 390–415). Washington, DC: American Educational Research Association.

Bartlett, F. C. (1932). *Remembering: A study in experimental and social psychology.* New York: Macmillan.

Basow, S. A., & Rubin, L. R. (1999). Gender influences on adolescent development. In N. G. Johnson, M. C. Roberts, & J. Worell (Eds.), *Beyond appearance: A new look at adolescent girls* (pp. 25–52). Washington, DC: American Psychological Association.

Battistich, V., Solomon, D., & Delucci, K. (1993). Interaction processes and student outcomes in cooperative groups. *The Elementary School Journal, 94,* 19–32.

Bauer, S. (2007, January 25). More public schools dividing boys, girls. *Houston Chronicle.*

Baumeister, R., Campbell, J. D., Krueger, J. I., & Vohs, K. D. (2003). Does high self-esteem cause better performance, interpersonal success, happiness, or healthier lifestyles? *Psychological Science in the Public Interest, 4*(1), 1–44.

Baumeister, R. F., & Leary, M. R. (1995). The need to belong: Desire for interpersonal attachments as a fundamental human motivation. *Psychological Bulletin, 117,* 497–529.

Beane, J. A. (1991). Sorting out the self-esteem controversy. *Educational Leadership, 49*(1), 25–30.

Bear, G. G. (with Cavalier, A. R., & Manning, M. A.). (2005). *Developing self-discipline and preventing and correcting misbehavior.* Boston: Pearson/Allyn & Bacon.

Becker, W. C., Engelmann, S., & Thomas, D. R. (1975). *Teaching 1: Classroom management.* Chicago: Science Research Associates.

Beebe-Frankenberger, M., Bocian, K. L., MacMillan, D. L., & Gresham, F. M. (2004). Sorting second grade students with academic deficiencies: Characteristics differentiating those retained in grade from those promoted to third grade. *Journal of Educational Psychology, 96,* 204–215.

Beeth, M. E. (1998). Teaching science in fifth grade: Instructional goals that support conceptual change. *Journal of Research in Science Teaching, 35,* 1091–1101.

Belanoff, P., & Dickson, M. (1991). *Portfolios: Process and product.* Portsmouth, NH: Heinemann, Boynton/Cook.

Bennett, C. I. (1999). *Comprehensive multicultural education: Theory and practice* (4th ed.). Boston: Allyn & Bacon.

Berg, C. A., & Clough, M. (1991). Hunter lesson design: The wrong one for science teaching. *Educational Leadership, 48*(4), 73–78.

Bergin, D. (1999). Influences on classroom interest. *Educational Psychologist, 34,* 87–98.

Berieter, C. (1997). Situated cognition and how I overcame it. In D. Kirshner & J. A. Whitson (Eds.), *Situated cognition: Social, semiotic, and psychological perspectives* (pp. 281–300). Mahwah, NJ: Lawrence Erlbaum.

Berk, L. E. (2001). *Awakening children's minds: How parents and teachers can make a difference.* New York: Oxford University Press.

Berk, L. E. (2005). *Infants, children, and adolescents* (5th ed.). Boston: Allyn & Bacon.

Berk, L. E. (2007). *Development through the life span* (4th ed.). Boston: Allyn & Bacon.

Berliner, D. (1987). But do they understand? In V. Richardson-Koehler (Ed.), *Educators' handbook: A research perspective* (pp. 259–293). New York: Longman.

Berliner, D. (1988). Simple views of effective teaching and a simple theory of classroom instruction. In D. Berliner & B. Rosenshine (Eds.), *Talks to teachers* (pp. 93–110). New York: Random House.

Berlyne, D. (1966). Curiosity and exploration. *Science, 153,* 25–33.

Betancourt, H., & Lopez, S. R. (1993). The study of culture, ethnicity, and race in American psychology. *American Psychologist, 48,* 629–637.

Beyer, J. M., & Trice, H. M. (1987). How an organization's rites reveal its culture. *Organizational Dynamics, 15,* 4–24.

Bialystok, E. (2001). *Bilingualism in development: Language, literacy, and cognition.* New York: Cambridge University Press.

Bialystok, E., Majumder, S., & Martin, M. M. (2003). Developing phonological awareness: Is there a bilingual advantage? *Applied Linguistics, 24,* 27–44.

Blair, C. (2006). How similar are fluid cognition and general intelligence? A developmental neuroscience perspective on fluid cognition as an aspect of human cognition. Main article with commentaries. *Behavioral & Brain Sciences, 29,* 109–160.

Bleeker, M. M., & Jacobs, J. E. (2004). Achievement in math and science: Do mothers' beliefs matter twelve years later? *Journal of Educational Psychology, 96*(1), 97–109.

Bloom, B. S., Engelhart, M. D., Frost, E. J., Hill, W. H., & Krathwohl, D. R. (1956). *Taxonomy of educational objectives. Handbook I: Cognitive domain.* New York: David McKay.

Bloom, R., & Bourdon, L. (1980). Types and frequencies of teachers' written instructional feedback. *Journal of Educational Research, 74,* 13–15.

Blumenfeld, P. C., Puro, P., & Mergendoller, J. R. (1992). Translating motivation into thoughtfulness. In H. Marshall (Ed.), *Redefining student learning: Roots of educational change* (pp. 207–240). Norwood, NJ: Ablex.

Bodine, R., & Crawford, D. (1999). *Developing emotional intelligence: Behavior management and conflict resolution in schools.* Champaign, IL: Research Press.

Bolman, L. G., & Deal, T. E. (2003). *Reframing organizations: Artistry, choice, and leadership* (3rd ed.). San Francisco: Jossey-Bass.

Borko, H., & Livingston, C. (1989). Cognition and improvisation: Differences in mathematics instruction by expert and novice teachers. *American Educational Research Journal, 26,* 473–498.

Borko, H., & Putnam, R. (1996). Learning to teach. In D. Berliner & R. Calfee (Eds.), *Handbook of educational psychology* (pp. 673–708). New York: Macmillan.

Borman, G. D., & Overman, L. T. (2004). Academic resilience in mathematics among poor and minority students. *The Elementary School Journal, 104,* 177–195.

Braddock, J., II, & Slavin, R. E. (1993). Why ability grouping must end: Achieving excellence and equity in American education. *Journal of Intergroup Relations, 20*(2), 51–64.

Brannon, L. (2002). *Gender: Psychological perspectives* (3rd ed.). Boston: Allyn & Bacon.

Bransford, J. D., Brown, A. L., & Cocking, R. R. (2002). *How people learn: Brain, mind, experience, and school.* Washington, DC: National Academy Press.

Bransford, J., Derry, S., Berliner, D., & Hammerness, K. (2005). Theories of learning and their roles in teaching. In L. Darling-Hammond (Ed.), *Preparing teachers for a changing world: What teachers should learn and be able to do* (pp. 40–87). San Francisco: Jossey-Bass.

Bredderman, T. (1983). Effects of activity-based elementary science on student outcomes: A qualitative synthesis. *Review of Educational Research, 53,* 499–518.

Bronfenbrenner, U., McClelland, P., Wethington, E., Moen, P., & Ceci, S. (1996). *The state of Americans: This generation and the next.* New York: Free Press.

Brophy, J. E. (1983). Conceptualizing student motivation to learn. *Educational Psychologist, 18,* 200–215.

Brophy, J. E. (1985). Teacher-student interaction. In J. Dusek (Ed.), *Teacher expectancies.* Hillsdale, NJ: Lawrence Erlbaum.

Brophy, J. E. (1988). On motivating students. In D. Berliner & B. Rosenshine (Eds.), *Talks to teachers* (pp. 201–245). New York: Random House.

Brophy, J. E. (1997). Effective teaching. In H. Walberg & G. Heartel (Eds.), *Psychology and educational practice* (pp. 212–232). Berkeley, CA: Mc-Cutchan.

Brophy, J. (2003). An interview with Jere Brophy by B. Gaedke & M. Shaughnessy. *Educational Psychology Review, 15*, 199–211.

Brophy, J. E., & Evertson, C. (1978). Context variables in teaching. *Educational Psychologist, 12*, 310–316.

Brophy, J. E., & Good, T. (1986). Teacher behavior and student achievement. In M. Wittrock (Ed.), *Handbook of research on teaching* (3rd ed.) (pp. 328–375). New York: Macmillan.

Brophy, J. E., & Kher, N. (1986). Teacher socialization as a mechanism for developing student motivation to learn. In R. Feldman (Ed.), *Social psychology applied to education* (pp. 256–288). New York: Cambridge University Press.

Brown, A. L. (1987). Metacognition, executive control, self-regulation, and other more mysterious mechanisms. In F. Weinert & R. Kluwe (Eds.), *Metacognition, motivation, and understanding* (pp. 65–116). Hillside, NJ: Lawrence Erlbaum.

Brown, A. L. (1992). Design experiments: Theoretical and methodological challenges in creating complex interventions in classroom settings. *Journal of the Learning Sciences, 2*, 141–178.

Brown, A. L. (1997). Transforming schools into communities of thinking and learning about serious matters. *American Psychologist, 52*, 399–413.

Brown, A. L., Bransford, J., Ferrara, R., & Campione, J. (1983). Learning, remembering, and understanding. In P. Mussen (Ed.), *Handbook of child psychology* (Vol. 3). New York: Wiley.

Brown, A. L., & Campione, J. C. (1996). Psychological theory and the design of innovative learning environments: On procedures, principles, and systems. In L. Schauble & R. Glaser (Eds.), *Innovations in learning: New environments for education* (pp. 289–325). Mahwah, NJ: Lawrence Erlbaum.

Bruer, J. T. (1999). In search of brain-based education. *Phi Delta Kappan, 80*, 648–657.

Bruner, J. S. (1966). *Toward a theory of instruction.* New York: Norton.

Bruner, J. S., Goodnow, J. J., & Austin, G. A. (1956). *A study of thinking.* New York: Wiley.

Bruning, R. H., Schraw, G. J., Norby, M. M., & Ronning, R. R. (2004). *Cognitive psychology and instruction* (4th ed.). Columbus, OH: Merrill.

Bruning, R. H., Schraw, G. J., & Ronning, R. R. (1999). *Cognitive psychology and instruction* (3rd ed.). Columbus, OH: Merrill.

Budd, K., Carson, E., Garelick, B., Klein, D., Milgram, R. J., Raimi, R. A., et al. (2005). 10 Myths about math education and why you shouldn't believe them [Electronic version]. Retrieved February 28, 2007, from http://www.nychold.com/myths-050504 .html#bottom

Burden, P. R. (1995). *Classroom management and discipline: Methods to facilitate cooperation and instruction.* White Plains, NY: Longman.

Burke-Spero, R. (1999). Toward a model of *civitas* through an ethic of care: A qualitative study of preservice teachers' perceptions about learning to teach diverse populations (Doctoral dissertation, The Ohio State University, 1999). *Dissertation Abstracts International, 60*, 11A, 3967.

Burke-Spero, R., & Woolfolk Hoy, A. (2002). *The need for thick description: A qualitative investigation of developing teacher efficacy.* Unpublished manuscript, University of Miami.

Bus, A. G., & van IJzendoorn, M. H. (1999). Phonological awareness and early reading: A meta-analysis of experimental training studies. *Journal of Educational Psychology, 91*, 403–414.

Buss, D. M. (1995). Psychological sex differences: Origin through sexual selection. *American Psychologist, 50*, 164–168.

Butler, R., & Neuman, O. (1995). Effects of task and ego achievement goals on help-seeking behaviors and attitudes. *Journal of Educational Psychology, 87*, 261–271.

Butler, R., & Nisan, M. (1986). Effects of no feedback, task-related comments, and grades on intrinsic motivation and performance. *Journal of Educational Psychology, 78*, 210–224.

Butzin, S. M. (2007). NCLB: Fix it, don't nix it. *Phi Delta Kappan, 88*(10), 768–769.

Byrne, B., Fielding-Barnsley, R., & Ashley, L. (2000). Effects of preschool phoneme identity training after six years: Outcome level distinguished from rate of response. *Journal of Educational Psychology, 92*, 659–667.

Byrnes, J. P. (1996). *Cognitive development and learning in instructional contexts.* Boston: Allyn & Bacon.

Byrnes, J. P., & Fox, N. A. (1998). The educational relevance of research in cognitive neuroscience. *Educational Psychology Review, 10*, 297–342.

Calderhead, J. (1996). Teacher: Beliefs and knowledge. In D. Berliner & R. Calfee (Eds.), *Handbook of educational psychology* (pp. 709–725). New York: Macmillan.

Calderhead, J., & Robson, M. (1991). Images of teaching: Student teachers' early conceptions of classroom practice. *Teaching & Teacher Education, 7*, 1–8.

Callahan, C. M., Tomlinson, C. A., & Plucker, J. (1997). *Project START using a multiple intelligences model in identifying and promoting talent in high-risk students.* Storrs, CT: National Research Center for Gifted and Talented. University of Connecticut Technical Report.

Cambourne, B., & Turbill, J. (1990). Assessment in whole-language classrooms: Theory into practice. *Elementary School Journal, 90,* 337–349.

Cameron, J., & Pierce, W. D. (1994). Reinforcement, reward, and intrinsic motivation: A meta-analysis. *Review of Educational Research, 64,* 363–423.

Cameron, J., & Pierce, W. D. (1996). The debate about rewards and intrinsic motivation: Protests and accusations do not alter the results. *Review of Educational Research, 66,* 39–52.

Camp, R. (1990, Spring). Thinking together about portfolios. *The Quarterly of the National Writing Project, 27,* 8–14.

Canfield, J. (1990). Improving students' self-concepts. *Educational Leadership, 48*(1), 48–50.

Cangelosi, J. S. (1990). *Designing tests for evaluating student achievement.* New York: Longman.

Canter, L. (1988). Let the educator beware: A response to Curwin and Mendler. *Educational Leadership, 46*(2), 71–73.

Canter, L. (1989). Assertive discipline—More than names on the board and marbles in a jar. *Phi Delta Kappan, 71*(1), 41–56.

Canter, L., & Canter, M. (1997). *Lee Canter's assertive discipline: Positive behavior management for today's classrooms.* Santa Monica, CA: Lee Canter & Associates.

Capa, .Y. (2005). Novice teachers' sense of efficacy. (Doctoral dissertation, The Ohio State University, Columbus, OH).

Caprara, G. V., Barbaranelli, C., Borgogni, L., & Steca, P. (2003). Efficacy beliefs as determinants of teachers' job satisfaction. *Journal of Educational Psychology, 95,* 821–832.

Carey, L. M. (1994). *Measuring and evaluating school learning* (2nd ed.). Boston: Allyn & Bacon.

Carlisle, J. F., Stahl, S. A., & Birdyshaw, D. (Eds.). (2004, November). Lessons from research at the Center for the Improvement of Early Reading Achievement (Special issue). *Elementary School Journal, 105*(2).

Carnegie Council on Adolescent Development. (1995). *Great transitions: Preparing adolescents for a new century.* New York: Carnegie Corporation of New York.

Carney, R. N., & Levin, J. R. (2000). Mnemonic instruction, with a focus on transfer. *Journal of Educational Psychology, 92,* 783–790.

Carney, R. N., & Levin, J. R. (2002). Pictorial illustrations *still* improve students' learning from text. *Educational Psychology Review, 14,* 5–26.

Carroll, J. B. (1997). The three-stratum theory of cognitive abilities. In D. P. Flanagan, J. L. Genshaft, & P. L. Harrison (Eds.), *Contemporary intellectual assessment: Theories, tests, and issue*s (pp. 122–130). New York: Guilford.

Carter, E. W., Wehby, J., Hughes, C., Johnson, S. M., Plank, D. R., Barton-Arwood, S. M., & Lunsford, L. B. (2005). Preparing adolescents with high-incidence disabilities for high-stakes testing with strategy instruction. *Preventing School Failure, 49*(2), 55–62.

Castle, S., Deniz, C. B., & Tortora, M. (2005). Flexible grouping and student learning in a high-needs school. *Education & Urban Society, 37,* 139–150.

Cattell, R. B. (1963). Theory of fluid and crystallized intelligence: A critical experiment. *Journal of Educational Psychology, 54,* 1–22.

Cattell, R. B. (1987). *Intelligence: Its structure, growth, and action.* New York: Elsevier.

CDF. (2007). Each day in America [Electronic Version]. Children's Defense Fund. Retrieved August 6, 2007, from http://www.childrensdefense.org/site/PageServer? pagename=research_national_data_each_day

Ceci, S. J., & Williams, W. M. (1997). Schooling, intelligence, and income. *American Psychologist, 52,* 1051–1058.

Chance, P. (1993). Sticking up for rewards. *Phi Delta Kappan, 74,* 787–790.

Charles, C. M. (2002a). *Essential elements of effective discipline.* Boston: Allyn & Bacon.

Charles, C. M. (2002b). *Building classroom discipline* (7th ed.). Boston: Allyn & Bacon.

Charles, C. M. (2005). *Building classroom discipline* (8th ed.). Boston: Allyn & Bacon.

Chatman, J. A., & Jehn, K. A. (1994). Assessing the relationship between industry characteristics and organizational culture: How different can you be? *Academy of Management Journal, 37*(3), 522–553.

Clark, C. M., & Peterson, P. L. (1986). Teachers' thought processes. In M. Wittrock (Ed.), *Handbook of research on teaching* (3rd ed., pp. 255–296). New York: Macmillan.

Clark, C. M., & Yinger, R. (1988). Teacher planning. In D. Berliner & B. Rosenshine (Eds.), *Talks to teachers* (pp. 342–365). New York: Random House.

Clarke, J. H., & Agne, R. M. (1997). *Interdisciplinary high school teaching.* Boston: Allyn & Bacon.

Clifford, M. M. (1990). Students need challenge, not easy success. *Educational Leadership, 48*(1), 22–26.

Clifford, M. M. (1991). Risk taking: Empirical and educational considerations. *Educational Psychologist, 26,* 263–298.

Cobb, P., & Bowers, J. (1999). Cognitive and situated learning: Perspectives in theory and practice. *Educational Researcher, 28*(2), 4–15.

Codell, E. R. (2001). *Educating Esme: Diary of a teacher's first year.* Chapel Hill, NC: Algonquin Books.

Coffield, F., Moseley, D., Hall, E., & Ecclestone, K. (2004). *Learning styles and pedagogy in post-16 learning: A systematic and critical review.* Trowbridge, Witlshire, England: The Learning and Skills Research Centre.

Cognition and Technology Group at Vanderbilt (CTGV). (1990). Anchored instruction and its relations to situated cognition. *Educational Researcher, 19*(6), 2–10.

Cognition and Technology Group at Vanderbilt (CTGV). (1993). Anchored instruction and situated learning revisited. *Educational Technology, 33*(3), 52–70.

Cognition and Technology Group at Vanderbilt (CTGV). (1996). Looking at technology in context: A framework for understanding technology and educational research. In D. Berliner & R. Calfee (Eds.), *Handbook of educational psychology* (pp. 807–840). New York: Macmillan.

Cohen, E. G. (1986). *Designing groupwork: Strategies for the heterogeneous classroom.* New York: Teachers College Press.

Cohen, M. D., & Sproull, L. S. (Eds.). (1996). *Organizational learning.* Thousand Oaks, CA: Sage.

Coladarci, T. (1992). Teachers' sense of efficacy and commitment to teaching. *Journal of Experimental Education, 60,* 323–337.

Cole, M. (1985). The zone of proximal development: Where culture and cognition create each other. In J. V. Wertsch (Ed.), *Culture, communication, and cognition: Vygotskian perspectives* (pp. 146–161). Cambridge: Cambridge University Press.

Coleman, J. S. (1966). *Equality of educational opportunity.* Washington, DC: U.S. Government Printing Office.

Collins, A., Brown, J. S., & Holum, A. (1991). Cognitive apprenticeship: Making thinking visible. *American Educator, 15*(3), 38–39.

Collins, A., Brown, J. S., & Newman, S. E. (1989). Cognitive apprenticeship: Teaching the crafts of reading, writing, and mathematics. In L. B. Resnick (Ed.), *Knowing, learning, and instruction: Essays in honor of Robert Galser* (pp. 453–494). Hillsdale, NJ: Lawrence Erlbaum.

Comadena, M. E., Hunt, S. K., & Simonds, C. J. (2007). The effects of teacher clarity, nonverbal immediacy, and caring on student motivation, affective and cognitive learning. *Communication Research Reports, 24,* 241–248.

Comer, J. P., Haynes, N. M., & Joyner, E. T. (1996). The school development program. In J. P. Comer, N. M. Haynes, E. T. Joyner, & M. Ben-Avie (Eds.), *Rallying the whole village: The Comer process for reforming education* (pp. 1–26). New York: Teachers College Press.

Committee on Increasing High School Students' Engagement and Motivation to Learn (2004). *Engaging schools: Fostering high school students' motivation to learn.* Washington, DC: The National Academies Press.

Connell, R. W. (1996). Teaching the boys: New research on masculinity and gender strategies. *Teachers College Record, 98,* 206–235.

Conway, P. F., & Clark, C. M. (2003). The journey inward and outward: A re-examination of Fuller's concerns-based model of teacher development. *Teaching & Teacher Education, 19,* 465–482.

Cooke, B. L., & Pang, K. C. (1991). Recent research on beginning teachers: Studies of trained and untrained novices. *Teaching & Teacher Education, 7,* 93–110.

Cooper, H., & Valentine, J. C. (Eds.). (2001, Summer). Homework. *Educational Psychologist, 36*(3) (special issue).

Cooper, H. M., Valentine, J. C., Nye, B., & Kindsay, J. J. (1999). Relationships between five after-school activities and academic achievement. *Journal of Educational Psychology, 91,* 369–378.

Cordova, D. I., & Lepper, M. R. (1996). Intrinsic motivation and the process of learning: Beneficial effects of contextualization, personalization, and choice. *Journal of Educational Psychology, 88,* 715–730.

Corno, L. (1995). The principles of adaptive teaching. In A. Ornstein (Ed.), *Teaching: Theory into practice* (pp. 45–67). Boston: Allyn & Bacon.

Corno, L. (2000). Looking at homework differently. *Elementary School Journal, 100,* 529–548.

Corno, L., & Snow, R. E. (1986). Adapting teaching to individual differences in learners. In M. Wittrock (Ed.), *Handbook of research on teaching* (3rd ed., pp. 605–629). New York: Macmillan.

Council of Chief State School Officers. (1996). *Interstate School Leader Licensure Consortium: Standards for school leaders.* Washington, DC: Author.

Covaleskie, J. F. (1992). Discipline and morality: Beyond rules and consequences. *Educational Forum, 56*(2), 56–76.

Covey, S. R. (2004). *The 7 habits of highly effective people: Powerful lessons in personal change.* New York: Free Press.

Covington, M. V. (1992). *Making the grade: A self-worth perspective on motivation and school reform.* New York: Holt, Rinehart, & Winston.

Covington, M. V., & Mueller, K. J. (2001). Intrinsic versus extrinsic motivation: An approach/avoidance reformulation. *Education Psychology Review, 13,* 157–176.

Covington, M. V., & Omelich, C. L. (1987). "I knew it cold before the exam": A test of the anxiety-blockage hypothesis. *Journal of Educational Psychology, 79,* 393–400.

Cowley, G., & Underwood, A. (1998, June 15). Memory. *Newsweek,* 48–54.

Craik, F. I. M., & Lockhart, R. S. (1972). Levels of processing: A framework for memory research. *Journal of Verbal Learning & Verbal Behavior, 11,* 671–684.

Crawford, J. (1996). *Best evidence: Research foundations of the bilingual education act.* Washington, DC: National Clearinghouse for Bilingual Education.

Cremin, L. (1961). *The transformation of the school: Progressivism in American education, 1876–1957.* New York: Vintage.

Crisci, P. E. (1986). The Quest National Center: A focus on the prevention of alienation. *Phi Delta Kappa, 67,* 440–442.

Crocker, J., & Park, L. E. (2004). Reaping the benefits of pursuing self-esteem without the costs. *Psychological Bulletin, 130,* 392–414.

Crone, D. A., & Horner, R. H. (2003). *Building positive behavior support systems in schools: Functional behavioral assessment.* New York: Guilford.

Cummins, J. (1994). The acquisition of English as a second language. In K. Spangenberg-Urbschat & R. Prichard (Eds.), *Kids come in all languages: Reading instruction for ESL students* (pp. 36–62). Newark, DE: International Reading Association.

Curwin, R. L., & Mendler, A. N. (1988). Packaged discipline programs: Let the buyer beware. *Educational Leadership, 46*(2), 68–71.

Daley, T. C., Whaley, S. E., Sigman, M. D., Espinosa, M. P., & Neumann, C. (2003). IQ on the rise: The Flynn Effect in rural Kenyan children. *Psychological Science, 14*(3), 215–219.

Darley, J. M., Glucksberg, S., & Kinchla, R. (1991). *Psychology* (5th ed.). Englewood Cliffs, NJ: Prentice-Hall.

Darling-Hammond, L. (2000). Teacher quality and student achievement: A review of state policy evidence. *Educational Policy Analysis Archives, 8,* 1–48. Available at http://epaa.asu.edu/epaa/v8n1/

Darling-Hammond, L., & Youngs, P. (2002). Defining "highly qualified teachers": What does "scientifically-based research" actually tell us? *Educational Researcher, 31*(9), 13–25.

Davis, R. B., Maher, C. A., & Noddings, N. (Eds.). (1990). *Constructivist views on the teaching and learning of mathematics.* Monograph 4 of the National Council of Teachers of Mathematics, Reston, VA.

Deaux, K. (1993). Commentary: Sorry, wrong number: A reply to Gentile's call. *Psychological Science, 4,* 125–126.

DeCecco, J., & Richards, A. (1974). *Growing pains: Uses of school conflicts.* New York: Aberdeen.

deCharms, R. (1976). *Enhancing motivation.* New York: Irvington.

Deci, E. L. (1975). *Intrinsic motivation.* New York: Plenum.

Deci, E. L., Koestner, R., & Ryan, R. M. (1999). A meta-analytic review of experiments examining the effects of extrinsic rewards on internal motivation. *Psychological Bulletin, 125,* 627–668.

Deci, E. L., & Ryan, R. M. (1985). *Intrinsic motivation and self-determination in human behavior.* New York: Plenum.

Deci, E. L., & Ryan, R. M. (Eds.). (2002). *Handbook of self-determination research.* Rochester, NY: University of Rochester Press.

Deci, E. L., Vallerand, R. J., Pelletier, L. G., & Ryan, R. M. (1991). Motivation and education: The self-determination perspective. *Educational Psychologist, 26,* 325–346.

De Corte, E., Greer, B., & Verschaffel, L. (1996). Mathematics teaching and learning. In D. Berliner & R. Calfee (Eds.), *Handbook of educational psychology* (pp. 491–549). New York: Macmillan.

Dee, J. R., & Henkin, A. B. (2002). Assessing dispositions toward cultural diversity among preservice teachers. *Urban Education, 37*(1), 22–40.

De Kock, A., Sleegers, P., & Voeten, M. J. M. (2004). New learning and the classification of learning environments in secondary education. *Review of Educational Research, 74,* 141–170.

Delpit, L. (1995). *Other people's children: Cultural conflict in the classroom.* New York: The New Press.

Delpit, L. (2003). Educators as "seed people": Growing a new future. *Educational Researcher, 7*(32), 14–21.

Dempster, F. N. (1991). Synthesis of research on reviews and tests. *Educational Leadership, 48*(7), 71–76.

Dempster, F. N. (1993). Exposing our students to less should help them learn more. *Phi Delta Kappan, 74,* 432–437.

Derry, S. J. (1992). Beyond symbolic processing: Expanding horizons for educational psychology. *Journal of Educational Psychology, 84,* 413–419.

Deutsch, M. (1949). An experimental study of the effects of cooperation and competition upon group processes. *Human Relations, 2,* 199–231.

Dewey, J. (1910). *How we think.* Boston: D.C. Heath.

Dewey, J. (1913). *Interest and effort in education.* Cambridge, MA: Houghton Mifflin.

DeZolt, D. M., & Hull, S. H. (2001). Classroom and school climate. In J. Worrell (Ed.), *Encyclopedia of women and gender* (p. 265). San Diego: Academic Press.

Dingfelder, S. F. (2005). Closing the gap for Latino patients. *Monitor on Psychology, 36*(1), 58–61.

Diller, L. (1998). *Running on ritalin.* New York: Bantam Books.

DiVesta, F. J., & Gray, G. S. (1972). Listening and note-taking. *Journal of Educational Psychology, 63,* 8–14.

Doggett, A. M. (2004). ADHD and drug therapy: Is it still a valid treatment? *Child Health Care, 8,* 69–81.

Doherty, K. M. (2002, July 12). Assessment. Education Week on the Web. Retrieved August 5, 2002, from http://edweek.org/context/topics/issuespage.cfm?id=41

Dole, J. A., Duffy, G. G., Roehler, L. R., & Pearson, P. D. (1991). Moving from the old to the new: Research on reading comprehension instruction. *Review of Educational Research, 61,* 239–264.

Dolezal, S. E., Welsh, L. M., Pressley, M., & Vincent, M. (2003). How do nine third-grade teachers motivate their students? *Elementary School Journal, 103,* 239–267.

Doll, B., Zucker, S., & Brehm, K. (2005). *Resilient classrooms: Creating healthy environments for learning.* New York: Guilford.

Doyle, W. (1986). Classroom organization and management. In M. C. Wittrock (Ed.), *Handbook of research on teaching* (3rd ed., pp. 392–431). New York: Macmillan.

Doyle, W. (2006). Ecological approaches to classroom management. In C. Evertson & C. Weinstein (Eds.), *Handbook of classroom management: Research, practice, and contemporary issues* (pp. 97–126). Mahwah, NJ: Lawrence Erlbaum.

Driscoll, M. P. (1994). *Psychology of learning for instruction.* Boston: Allyn & Bacon.

Driscoll, M. P. (2005). *Psychology of learning for instruction* (3rd ed.). Boston: Allyn & Bacon.

Duffy, G., Roehler, L. R., Meloth, M. S., & Vavrus, L. G. (1986). Conceptualizing instructional explanation. *Teaching & Teacher Education, 2,* 197–214.

Duke, D. L. (1993). How a staff development program can rescue at-risk students. *Educational Leadership, 50,* 28–30.

Duncan, G. J., & Brooks-Gunn, J. (2000). Family poverty, welfare reform, and child development. *Child Development, 71,* 188–196.

Dunn, K., & Dunn, R. (1978). *Teaching students through their individual learning styles.* Reston, VA: National Council of Principals.

Dunn, R., Beaudry, J. S., & Klavas, A. (1989). Survey of research on learning styles. *Educational Leadership, 47*(7), 50–58.

Dunn, R., Dunn, K., & Price, G. E. (1989). *Learning Style Inventory (LSI): An inventory for identification of how individuals in grades 3 through 12 prefer to learn.* Lawrence, KS: Price Systems.

Dunn, R., & Griggs, S. A. (Eds.). (2003). *Synthesis of the Dunn and Dunn learning-style model research: Who, what, when, where, and so what?* New York: St. John's University's Center for the Study of Learning and Teaching Styles.

Dweck, C. S. (1999). *Self-theories: Their role in motivation, personality, and development.* Philadelphia: Psychology Press.

Dweck, C. S. (2000). *Self-theories: Their role in motivation, personality, and development.* Philadelphia: Routledge Press.

Dweck, C. S. (2002). The development of ability conceptions. In A. Wigfield & J. Eccles (Eds.), *The development of achievement motivation.* San Diego: Academic Press.

Dweck, C. S., & Bempechat, J. (1983). Children's theories on intelligence: Consequences for learning. In S. Paris, G. Olson, & W. Stevenson (Eds.), *Learning and motivation in the classroom* (pp. 239–256). Hillsdale, NJ: Erlbaum.

Ebmeier, H. (2003). How supervision influences teacher efficacy and commitment: An investigation of a path model. *Journal of Curriculum & Supervision, 18,* 110–141.

Eccles, J., & Wigfield, A. (1985). Teacher expectations and student motivation. In J. Dusek (Ed.), *Teacher expectancies* (pp. 185–226). Hillsdale, NJ: Lawrence Erlbaum.

Echevarria, M. (2003). Anomalies as a catalyst for middle school students' knowledge construction and scientific reasoning during science inquiry. *Journal of Educational Psychology, 95,* 357–374.

Eisenberg, R., Pierce, W. D., & Cameron, J. (1999). Effects of rewards on intrinsic motivation—Negative, neutral, and positive: Comment on Deci, Koestner, and Ryan (1999). *Psychological Bulletin, 125,* 677–691.

Eisner, E. W. (1999). The uses and limits of performance assessments. *Phi Delta Kappan, 80,* 658–660.

Elawar, M. C., & Corno, L. (1985). A factorial experiment in teachers' written feedback on student homework: Changing teacher behavior a little rather than a lot. *Journal of Educational Psychology, 77,* 162–173.

Elias, M. J., & Schwab, Y. (2006). From compliance to responsibility: Social and emotional learning and classroom management. In C. Evertson & C. S. Weinstein (Eds.), *Handbook for classroom management: Research, practice, and contemporary issues.* Mahwah, NJ: Lawrence Erlbaum.

Emmer, E. T., & Aussiker, A. (1990). School and classroom discipline programs: How well do they work? In O. Moles (Ed.), *Student discipline strategies: Research and practice* (pp. 105–142). Albany, NY: SUNY Press.

Emmer, E. T., & Evertson, C. M. (1982). Effective classroom management at the beginning of the school year in junior high school classes. *Journal of Educational Psychology, 74,* 485–498.

Emmer, E. T., Evertson, C. M., & Anderson, L. M. (1980). Effective classroom management at the beginning of the school year. *Elementary School Journal, 80,* 219–231.

Emmer, E. T., Evertson, C., & Worsham, M. (2006). *Classroom management for middle and high school teachers* (7th ed.). Boston: Allyn & Bacon.

Emmer, E. T., & Gerwels, M. C. (2006). Classroom management in middle school and high school classrooms. In C. Evertson & C. S. Weinstein (Eds.), *Handbook for classroom management: Re-*

search, practice, and contemporary issues. Mahwah, NJ: Lawrence Erlbaum.

Emmer, E. T., & Stough, L. M. (2001). Classroom management: A critical part of educational psychology with implications for teacher education. *Educational Psychologist, 36,* 103–112.

Entwisle, D. R., Alexander, K., & Olson, L. (1997). *Children, schools, and inequality.* Boulder, CO: Westview Press.

Epanchin, B. C., Townsend, B., & Stoddard, K. (1994). *Constructive classroom management: Strategies for creating positive learning environments.* Pacific Grove, CA: Brooks/Cole.

Epstein, J. L. (1989). Family structure and student motivation. In R. E. Ames & C. Ames (Eds.), *Research on motivation in education: Volume 3: Goals and cognitions* (pp. 259–295). New York: Academic Press.

Epstein, J. L., & MacIver, D. J. (1992). *Opportunities to learn: Effects on eighth graders of curriculum offerings and instructional approaches.* (Report No. 34). Baltimore: Center for Research on Elementary and Middle Schools, Johns Hopkins University.

Evans, G. W. (2004). The environment of childhood poverty. *American Psychologist, 59,* 77–92.

Evensen, D. H., Salisbury-Glennon, J. D., & Glenn, J. (2001). A qualitative study of six medical students in a problem-based curriculum: Toward a situated model of self-regulation. *Journal of Educational Psychology, 93,* 659–676.

Evertson, C. M. (1988). Managing classrooms: A framework for teachers. In D. Berliner & B. Rosenshine (Eds.), *Talks to teachers* (pp. 54–74). New York: Random House.

Evertson, C. M., Emmer, E. T., & Worsham, M. E. (2006). *Classroom management for elementary teachers* (7th ed.). Boston: Allyn & Bacon.

Ewy, C., & student authors. (1997). Kids take on "the test." *Educational Leadership, 54*(4), 76–78.

Farnham-Diggory, S. (1994). Paradigms of knowledge and instruction. *Review of Educational Research, 64,* 463–477.

Fass, S., & Cauthen, N. K. (2006). *Who are America's poor children?* National Center for Children in Poverty, Columbia University. Retrieved May 25, 2007, from http://www.nccp.org/publications/pub_684.html

Fennema, E., & Peterson, P. (1988). Effective teaching for boys and girls: The same or different? In D. Berliner & B. Rosenshine (Eds.), *Talks to teachers* (pp. 111–127). New York: Random House.

Fenstermacher, G. D., & Richardson, V. (2005). On making determinations of quality in teaching. *Teachers College Record, 107,* 186–213.

Ferguson, A. A. (2000). *Bad boys: Public schools and the making of black masculinity.* Ann Arbor: University of Michigan Press.

Ferguson, D. L., Ferguson, P. M., & Bogdan, R. C. (1987). If mainstreaming is the answer, what is the question? In V. Richardson-Koehler (Ed.), *Educators' handbook: A research perspective* (pp. 394–419). New York: Longman.

Ferrer, E., & McArdle, J. J. (2004). An experimental analysis of dynamic hypotheses about cognitive abilities and achievement from childhood to early adulthood. *Developmental Psychology, 40,* 935–952.

Feshbach, N. (1997). Empathy: The formative years— Implications for clinical practice. In A. Bohart & L. Greenberg (Eds.), *Empathy reconsidered: New directions in psychotherapy* (pp. 33–59). Washington, DC: American Psychological Association.

Feshbach, N. (1998). Aggression in the schools: Toward reducing ethnic conflict and enhancing ethnic understanding. In P. Trickett & C. Schellenbach (Eds), *Violence against children in the family and the community* (pp. 269–286). Washington, DC: American Psychological Association.

A Field Trip to the Sea [Computer software] (1999). Hazelton, PA: Sunburst Software.

Finkel, D., Reynolds, C. A., McArdle, J. J., Gatz, M., & Pederscn, N. L. (2003). Latent growth curve analyses of accelerating decline in cognitive abilities in adulthood. *Developmental Psychology, 39,* 535–550.

Finkelstein, R. (1998). The effects of organizational health and pupil control ideology on the achievement and alienation of high school students. (Unpublished doctoral dissertation, St. Johns University, Queens, NY).

Fiske, E. B. (1988, April 10). America's test mania. *The New York Times* (Education Life Section), pp. 16–20.

Fitzgerald, J. (1995). English-as-a-second-language learners' cognitive reading process: A review of the research in the United States. *Review of Educational Research, 62,* 145–190.

Fives, H. R., Hamman, D., & Olivarez, A. (2005, April). Does burnout begin with student teaching? Analyzing efficacy, burnout, and support during the student-teaching semester. Paper presented at the Annual Meeting of the America Educational Research Association, Montreal, CA.

Flammer, A. (1995). Developmental analysis of control beliefs. In A. Bandura (Ed.), *Self-efficacy in changing societies* (pp. 69–113). New York: Cambridge University Press.

Flavell, J. H., Green, F. L., & Flavell, E. R. (1995). *Young children's knowledge about thinking.* Monographs of the Society for Research in Child Development, *60*(1) (Serial No. 243).

Floden, R. E., & Klinzing, H. G. (1990). What can research on teacher thinking contribute to teacher preparation? A second opinion. *Educational Researcher, 19*(4), 15–20.

Ford, D. Y. (2000). *Infusing multicultural content into the curriculum for gifted students.* (ERIC EC Digest #E601). Arlington, VA: ERIC Clearinghouse on Disabilities and Gifted Education.

Foster, W. (1981, August). *Social and emotional development in gifted individuals.* Paper presented at thc Fourth World Conference on Gifted and Talented, Montreal.

Franklin, J. (2007). Achieving with autism: Dispelling common misconceptions is essential for success. *Education Update, 49*(7), 1–9.

Fredricks, J. A., Blumenfeld, P. C., & Paris, A. H. (2004). School engagement: Potential of the concept, state of the evidence. *Review of Educational Research, 74,* 59–109.

Freiberg, H. J. (Ed.). (1999). *Beyond behaviorism: Changing the classroom management.* Boston: Allyn & Bacon.

Freiberg, H. J., & Driscoll, A. (2005). *Universal teaching strategies* (4th ed.). Boston: Allyn & Bacon.

Freiberg, J. (2006). Research-based programs for preventing and solving discipline problems. In C. Evertson & C. S. Weinstein (Eds.), *Handbook for classroom management: Research, practice, and contemporary issues.* Mahwah, NJ: Lawrence Erlbaum.

Frick, T. W. (1990). Analysis of patterns in time: A method of recording and quantifying temporal relations in education. *American Educational Research Journal, 27,* 180–204.

Friend, M. (2008). *Special education: Contemporary perspectives for school professionals* (7th ed.). Boston: Allyn & Bacon.

Friend, M., & Bursuck, W. D. (2006). *Including students with special needs: A practical guide for classroom teachers* (4th ed.). Boston: Allyn & Bacon.

Fuchs, L. S., Fuchs, D., Hamlett, C. L., & Karns, K. (1998). High-achieving students' interactions and performance on complex mathematical tasks as a function of homogeneous and heterogeneous pairings. *American Educational Research Journal, 35,* 227–268.

Furrer, C., & Skinner, E. (2003). Sense of relatedness as a factor in children's academic engagement and performance. *Journal of Educational Psychology, 95*(11), 148–161.

Gagné, E. D. (1985). *The cognitive psychology of school learning.* Boston: Little, Brown.

Gagné, E. D., Yekovich, C. W., & Yekovich, F. R. (1993). *The cognitive psychology of school learning* (2nd ed.). New York: HarperCollins.

Galambos, S. J., & Goldin-Meadow, S. (1990). The effects of learning two languages on metalinguistic development. *Cognition, 34,* 1–56.

Gallagher, M. (2001, June 11). More on zero-tolerance schools. Retrieved October 23, 2007, from http://www.newsmax.com/archives/articles/2001/6/11/123253.shtml

Gamoran, A. (1987). The stratification of high school learning opportunities. *Sociology of Education, 60,* 135–155.

Gamoran, A., & Mare, R. D. (1989). Secondary school detracking and educational inequity: Compensation, reinforcement, or neutrality? *American Journal of Education, 106*(3), 385–415.

Garcia, E. E. (1992). "Hispanic" children: Theoretical, empirical, and related policy issues. *Educational Psychology Review, 4,* 69–94.

Garcia, E. (2002). *Student cultural diversity: Understanding the meaning and meeting the challenge.* Boston: Houghton Mifflin.

Gardner, H. (1983). *Frames of mind: The theory of multiple intelligences.* New York: Basic Books.

Gardner, H. (1991). *The unschooled mind: How children think and how schools should teach.* New York: Basic Books.

Gardner, H. (1993). *Multiple intelligences: The theory in practice.* New York: Basic Books.

Gardner, H. (1998). Reflections on multiple intelligences: Myths and messages. In A. Woolfolk (Ed.), *Readings in educational psychology* (2nd ed., pp. 61–67). Boston: Allyn & Bacon.

Gardner, H. (1999, August). Who owns intelligence? Invited address at the Annual Meeting of the American Psychological Association, Boston.

Gardner, H. (2000). *Intelligence reframed: Multiple intelligences for the 21st century.* New York: Basic Books.

Gardner, H. (2003, April 21). Multiple intelligence after twenty years. Paper presented at the American Educational Research Association, Chicago.

Gardner, R., Brown, R., Sanders, S., & Menke, D. J. (1992). "Seductive details" in learning from text. In K. A. Renninger, S. Hidi, & A. Krapp (Eds.), *The role of interest in learning and development* (pp. 239–254). Hillsdale, NJ: Lawrence Erlbaum.

Garmon, A., Nystrand, M., Berends, M., & LePore, P. C. (1995). An organizational analysis of the effects of ability grouping. *American Educational Research Journal, 32,* 687–715.

Garnets, L. (2002). Sexual orientations in perspective. *Cultural Diversity & Ethnic Minority Psychology, 8,* 115–129.

Garrison, J. (1995). Deweyan pragmatism and the epistemology of contemporary social constructivism. *American Educational Research Journal, 32,* 716–740.

Gathercole, S. E., Pickering, S. J., Ambridge, B., & Wearing, H. (2004). The structure of working memory from 4 to 15 years of age. *Developmental Psychology, 40,* 177–190.

Gay, G. (2000). *Culturally responsive teaching: Theory, research, and practice.* New York: Teachers College Press.

Gay, G. (2006). Connections between classroom management and culturally responsive teaching. In C. Evertson & C. S. Weinstein (Eds.), *Handbook for classroom management: Research, practice, and contemporary issues.* Mahwah, NJ: Lawrence Erlbaum.

Geary, D. C. (2006). Development of mathematical understanding. In D. Kuhn & R. S. Siegler (Eds.), *Handbook of child psychology* (Vol. 2, *Cognition, Perception, and Language,* pp. 777–810). New York: Wiley.

Gergen, K. J. (1997). Constructing constructivism: Pedagogical potentials. *Issues in Education: Contributions from Educational Psychology, 3,* 195–202.

Gershoff, E. T., Aber, J. L., Raver, C. C., & Lennon, M. C. (2007). Income is not enough: Incorporating material hardship into models of income associations with parenting and child development. *Child Development, 78,* 70–95.

Gersten, R. (1996a). The language-minority students in transition: Contemporary instructional research. *The Elementary School Journal, 96,* 217–220.

Gersten, R. (1996b). Literacy instruction for language-minority students: The transition years. *The Elementary School Journal, 96,* 217–220.

Gersten, R. (Ed.). (2006). Scientific research on instruction of English Language Learners: The beginnings. *The Elementary School Journal.* (special issue).

Ginsburg, A., Leinwand, S., Anstrom, T., & Pollock, E. (2005). *What the United States can learn for Singapore's world-class mathematics system (and what Singapore can learn from the United States): An exploratory study.* Washington, DC: American Institutes for Research.

Glasser, W. (1969). *Schools without failure.* New York: Harper & Row.

Glasser, W. (1990). *The quality school: Managing students without coercion.* New York: Harper & Row.

Glickman, C. D. (2002). *Leadership for learning: How to help teachers succeed.* Alexandria, VA: Association for Supervision and Curriculum Development

Goddard, R. D., Sweetland S. R., & Hoy, W. K. (2000). Academic emphasis of urban elementary schools and student achievement: A multi-level analysis. *Educational Administration Quarterly, 36,* 683–702.

Goddard, R. G., Hoy, W. K., & Woolfolk Hoy, A. (2004). Collective efficacy: Theoretical development, empirical evidence, and future directions. *Educational Researcher, 33,* 3–13.

Goleman, D. (1995). *Emotional intelligence.* New York: Bantam.

Gonzalez, V. (1999). *Language and cognitive development in second language learning: Educational implications for children and adults.* Boston: Allyn & Bacon.

Gonzalez, V., Brusca-Vega, R., & Yawkey, T. (1997). *Assessment and instruction of culturally diverse students with or at-risk of learning problems: From research to practice.* Boston: Allyn & Bacon.

Good, T. L. (1983). Classroom research: A decade of progress. *Educational Psychologist, 18,* 127–144.

Good, T. L., & Brophy, J. E. (2003). *Looking in classrooms* (9th ed.). New York: Allyn & Bacon/ Longman.

Good, T. L., & Brophy, J. (2008). *Looking in classrooms* (10th ed.). Boston: Allyn & Bacon.

Goodenow, C. (1993). Classroom belonging among early adolescents: Relationships to motivation and achievement. *Journal of Early Adolescence, 13,* 21–43.

Goodman, K. S. (1986). *What's whole in whole language: A parent-teacher guide.* Portsmouth, NH: Heinemann.

Goodman, Y. M., & Goodman, K. S. (1990). Vygotsky in a whole-language perspective. In L. Moll (Ed.), *Vygotsky and education: Instructional implications and applications of sociohistorical psychology* (pp. 223–250). New York: Cambridge University Press.

Goodrich, H. (1997). Understanding rubrics. *Educational Leadership, 54*(4), 14–17.

Gordon, E. W. (1991). Human diversity and pluralism. *Educational Psychologist, 26,* 99–108.

Gordon, J. A. (1998). Caring through control: Reaching urban African American youth. *Journal for a Just and Caring Education, 4,* 418–440.

Gordon, T. (2003). *Teacher Effectiveness Training: The program proven to help teachers bring out the best in students of all ages.* New York: Random House.

Graham, S. (1991). A review of attribution theory in achievement contexts. *Educational Psychology Review, 3,* 5–39.

Graham, S. (1994). Motivation in African Americans. *Review of Educational Research, 64,* 55–117.

Graham, S. (1995). Narrative versus meta-analytic reviews of race differences in motivation. *Review of Educational Research, 65,* 509–514.

Graham, S. (1996). How causal beliefs influence the academic and social motivation of African-American children. In G. G. Brannigan (Ed.), *The enlightened educator: Research adventures in the schools* (pp. 111–126). New York: McGraw-Hill.

Graham, S., & Harris, K. R. (1994). The effects of whole language on children's writing: A review of literature. *Educational Psychologist, 29,* 187–192.

Graham, S., & Weiner, B. (1996). Theories and principles of motivation. In D. Berliner & R. Calfee (Eds.), *Handbook of educational psychology* (pp. 63–84). New York: Macmillan.

Gredler, M. E. (2005). *Learning and instruction: Theory and practice.* Columbus, OH: Merrill/Prentice-Hall.

Greeno, J. G., Collins, A. M., & Resnick, L. B. (1996). Cognition and learning. In D. Berliner & R. Calfee (Eds.), *Handbook of educational psychology* (pp. 15–46). New York: Macmillan.

Gregorc, A. F. (1982). *Gregorc style delineator: Development, technical, and administrative manual.* Maynard, MA: Gabriel Systems.

Grigorenko, E. L., & Sternberg, R. J. (2001). Analytical, creative, and practical intelligence as predictors of self-reported adaptive functioning: A case study in Russia. *Intelligence, 29,* 57–73.

Grolnick, W. S., Gurland, S. T., Jacob, K. F., & Decourcey, W. (2002). The development of self-determination in middle childhood and adolescence. In A. Wigfield & J. Eccles (Eds.), *Development of achievement motivation* (pp. 147–171). New York: Academic Press.

Grolnick, W. S., Ryan, R. M., & Deci, E. L. (1991). Inner resources for school achievement: Motivational mediators of children's perceptions of their parents. *Journal of Educational Psychology, 83*, 508–517.

Gronlund, N. E. (2004). *Writing instructional objectives for teaching and assessment* (7th ed.). Columbus: OH: Prentice Hall/Merrill.

Gronlund, N. E. (2006). *Assessment of student achievement* (8th ed.). Boston: Allyn & Bacon.

Gross, M. U. M. (1992). The use of radical acceleration in cases of extreme intellectual precocity. *Gifted Child Quarterly, 36*, 91–99.

Grossman, H., & Grossman, S. H. (1994). *Gender issues in education.* Boston: Allyn & Bacon.

Guilford, J. P. (1988). Some changes in the Structure-of-Intellect model. *Educational and Psychological Measurement, 48*, 1–4.

Guilfoyle, C. (2006). NCLB: Is there life beyond testing? *Educational Leadership, 64*(3), 8–13.

Gutierrez, R., & Slavin, R. E. (1992). Achievement effects of the nongraded elementary school: A best evidence synthesis. *Review of Educational Research, 62*, 333–376.

Gurian, M., & Henley, P. (2001). *Boys and girls learn differently: A guide for teachers and parents.* San Francisco: Jossey-Bass.

Guskey, T. R. (1994). Making the grade: What benefits students? *Educational Leadership, 52*(2), 14–21.

Guskey, T. R., & Bailey, J. M. (2001). *Developing grading and reporting systems for student learning.* Thousand Oaks, CA: Corwin.

Gustafsson, J-E., & Undheim, J. O. (1996) Individual differences in cognitive functioning. In D. Berliner & R. Calfee (Eds.), *Handbook of educational psychology* (pp. 186–242). New York: Macmillan.

Guthrie, J. T., & Alao, S. (1997). Designing contexts to increase motivations of reading. *Educational Psychologist, 32*, 95–105.

Gutman, L. M., Sameroff, A., & Cole, R. (2003). Academic growth curve trajectories from 1st grade to 12th grade: Effects of multiple social risk factors and preschool child factors. *Developmental Psychology, 39*, 777–790.

Haertel, E. H. (1999). Performance assessment and educational reform. *Phi Delta Kappan, 80*, 662–666.

Hakuta, K. (2000). Points on SAT-9 Performance and Proposition 227. Retrieved from http://www.stanford.edu/hakuta/SAT9/SAT9 2000/bullets.htm

Hakuta, K., Bialystok, E., & Wiley, E. (2003). Critical evidence: A test of the critical period for second language acquisition. *Psychological Science, 14*, 31–38.

Hakuta, K., Butler, Y. G., & Witt, D. (2000). *How long does it take English learners to attain proficiency?* Berkeley, CA: University of California Linguistic Minority Reserch Report 2000–1.

Hakuta, K., & Gould, L. J. (1987). Synthesis of research on bilingual education. *Educational Leadership, 44*(6), 38–45.

Haladyna, T. H. (2002). *Essentials of standardized achievement testing: Validity and accountability.* Boston: Allyn & Bacon.

Halford, J. M. (1999). A different mirror: A conversation with Ronald Takaki. *Educational Leadership, 56*(7), 8–13.

Hall, J. W. (1991). More on the utility of the keyword method. *Journal of Educational Psychology, 83*, 171–172.

Hallahan, D. P., & Kauffman, J. M. (2006). *Exceptional learners* (10th ed.). Boston: Allyn & Bacon.

Hallahan, D. P., Lloyd, J. W., Kauffman, J. M., Weiss, M. P., & Martinez, E. A. (2005). *Learning disabilities: Foundations, characteristics, and effective teaching.* Boston: Allyn & Bacon.

Halpern, D. F. (2000). *Sex differences in cognitive abilities.* Mahwah, NJ: Lawrence Erlbaum.

Halpern, D. F. (2004). A cognitive-process taxonomy for sex differences in cognitive abilities. *Current Directions in Psychological Science, 13*, 135–139.

Halpin, A. W. (1966). *Theory and research in administration.* New York: Macmillan.

Halpin, A. W., & Croft, D. B. (1962). *The organization climate of schools.* Contract #SAE 543–8639. U.S. Office of Education, Research Project.

Hamann, D. L., Baker, D. S., McAllister, P. A., & Bauer, W. I. (2000). Factors affecting university music students' perceptions of lesson quality and teaching effectiveness. *Journal of Research in Music Education, 48*, 102–113.

Hambleton, R. K. (1996). Advances in assessment models, methods, and practices. In D. C. Berliner & R. C. Calfee (Eds.), *Handbook of educational psychology* (pp. 899–925). New York: Macmillan.

Hamers, J. F., & Blanc, M. H. A. (2000). *Bilinguality and bilingulism* (2nd ed.). Cambridge, England: Cambridge University Press.

Hamman, D., Berthelot, J., Saia, J., & Crowley, E. (2000). Teachers' coaching of learning and its relation to students' strategic learning. *Journal of Educational Psychology, 92*, 342–348.

Hamre, B. K., & Pianta, R. C. (2001). Early teacher–child relationships and the trajectory of children's school outcomes through eighth grade. *Child Development, 72*, 625–638.

Hansen, R. A. (1977). Anxiety. In S. Ball (Ed.), *Motivation in education*. New York: Academic Press.

Hanson, P. G., & Lubin, B. (1995). *Answers to questions most frequently asked about organizational development.* Thousand Oaks, CA: Sage.

Hardman, M. L., Drew, C. J., & Egan, M. W. (2005). *Human exceptionality: Society, school, and family* (8th ed.). Boston: Allyn & Bacon.

Harp, S. F., & Mayer, R. E. (1998). How seductive details do their damage: A theory of cognitive interest in science learning. *Journal of Educational Psychology, 90,* 414–434.

Harris, K. R., & Graham, S. (1996). Memo to constructivist: Skills count too. *Educational Leadership, 53*(5), 26–29.

Harris, P. L. (2006). Social cognition. In D. Kuhn & R. Siegler (Eds.), *Handbook of child psychology* (6th ed., Vol. 2). New York: Wiley.

Hawkins, M. R. (2004). Researching English language and literacy development in schools. *Educational Researcher, 33*(3), 14–25.

Henderson, M. (1996). *Helping your students get the most from homework* [brochure]. Chicago: National Parent-Teacher Association.

Herman, J. (1997). Assessing new assessments: How do they measure up? *Theory into Practice, 36,* 197–204.

Herman, J., & Winters, L. (1994). Portfolio research: A slim collection. *Educational Leadership, 52*(2), 48–55.

Hernshaw, L. S. (1987). *The shaping of modern psychology: A historical introduction from dawn to present day.* London: Routledge & Kegan Paul.

Hess, F. M., & Petrilli, M. J. (2004). The politics of No Child Left Behind: Will the coalition hold? *Boston University Journal of Education, 185*(3), 13–25.

Hess, F. M., & Rotherham, A. J. (2007). NCLB and the competitiveness agenda: Happy collaboration or a collision course? *Phi Delta Kappan, 88,* 344–352.

Hewson, P. W., Beeth, M. E., & Thorley, N. R. (1998). Teaching for conceptual change. In B. J. Fraser & K. G. Tobin (Eds.), *International handbook of science education* (pp. 199–218). New York: Kluwer.

Hickey, D. T. (2003). Engaged participation vs. marginal non-participation: A stridently sociocultural model of achievement motivation. *The Elementary School Journal, 103*(4), 401–429.

Hilgard, E. R. (1996). Perspectives on educational psychology. *Educational Psychology Review, 8,* 419–431.

Hill, K. T., & Eaton, W. O. (1977). The interaction of test anxiety and success-failure experiences in determining children's arithmetic performance. *Developmental Psychology, 13,* 205–211.

Hill, K. T., & Wigfield, A. (1984). Test anxiety: A major educational problem and what can be done about it. *The Elementary School Journal, 85,* 105–126.

Hill, W. F. (2002). *Learning: A survey of psychological interpretations* (7th ed.). Boston: Allyn & Bacon.

Hiroto, D. S., & Seligmen, M. E. P. (1975). Generality of learned helplessness in man. *Journal of Personality and Social Psychology, 31,* 311–327.

Hirsch, E. D., Jr. (1996). *The schools we need—and why we don't have them.* New York: Doubleday.

Hmelo-Silver, C. E. (2004). Problem-based learning: What and how do students learn? *Educational Psychology Review, 16,* 235–266.

Hofer, B. K., & Pintrich, P. R. (1997). The development of epistemological theories: Beliefs about knowledge and knowing and their relation to learning. *Review of Educational Research, 67,* 88–140.

Hogan, T., Rabinowitz, M., & Craven, J. A., III. (2003). Representation in teaching: Inferences from research of expert and novice teachers. *Educational Psychologist, 38,* 235–247.

Horgan, D. D. (1995). *Achieving gender equity: Strategies for the classroom.* Boston: Allyn & Bacon.

Horn, J. L. (1998). A basis for research on age differences in cognitive capabilities. In J. J. McArdle & R. W. Woodcock (Eds.), *Human cognitive theories in theory and practice* (pp. 57–87). Mahwah, NJ: Lawrence Erlbaum.

Hoy, W. K. (1972). Dimensions of student alienation and characteristics of public high schools. *Interchange, 3,* 38–51.

Hoy, W. K. (2001). The pupil control studies: A historical, theoretical, and empirical analysis. *Journal of Educational Administration, 39,* 424–441.

Hoy, W. K. (2002). Faculty trust: A key to student achievement. *Journal of School Public Relations, 23*(2), 88–103.

Hoy, W. K., & Clover, S. I. R. (1986). Elementary school climate: A revision of the OCDQ. *Educational Administration Quarterly, 22,* 93–110.

Hoy, W. K., & Feldman, J. (1999). Organizational health profiles for high schools. In J. Freiberg (Ed.), *School climate: Measuring, sustaining, and improving* (pp. 84–103). Philadelphia: Falmer Press.

Hoy, W. K., & Hannum, J. (1997). Middle school climate: An empirical assessment of organizational health and student achievement. *Educational Administration Quarterly, 33,* 290–311.

Hoy, W. K., & Miskel, C. G. (2001). *Educational administration: Theory, research, and practice* (6th ed.). New York: McGraw-Hill.

Hoy, W. K., & Miskel, C. G. (2005). *Educational administration: Theory, research, and practice* (7th ed.). New York: McGraw-Hill.

Hoy, W. K., & Miskel, C. G. (2008). *Educational administration: Theory, research, and practice* (8th ed.). New York: McGraw-Hill.

Hoy, W. K., & Sabo, D. J. (1998). *Quality middle schools: Open and healthy.* Thousand Oaks, CA: Corwin Press.

Hoy, W. K., Smith, P. A., & Sweetland, S. R. (2002). The development of the organizational climate index for high schools: Its measure and relationship to faculty trust. *High School Journal, 86*(2), 38–49.

Hoy, W. K., & Tarter, C. J. (1997a). *The road to open and healthy schools: A handbook for change, secondary edition.* Thousand Oaks, CA: Corwin Press.

Hoy, W. K., & Tarter, C. J. (1997b). *The road to open and healthy schools: A handbook for change, elementary edition.* Thousand Oaks, CA: Corwin Press.

Hoy, W. K., & Tarter, C. J. (2004). Organizational justice in schools: No justice without trust. *International Journal of Educational Management, 18,* 250–259.

Hoy, W. K., Tarter, C. J., & Kottkamp, R. (1991). *Open schools/healthy schools: Measuring organizational climate.* Beverly Hills, CA: Sage.

Hoy, W. K., Tarter, C. J., & Woolfolk Hoy, A. (2006a). Academic optimism of schools. In Wayne K. Hoy & Cecil Miskel (Eds.), *Contemporary issues ineducational policy and school outcomes* (pp. 135–156). Greenwich, CT: Information Age.

Hoy, W. K., Tarter, C. J., & Woolfolk Hoy, A. (2006b). Academic optimism of schools: A force for student achievement. *American Educational Research Journal, 43,* 425–446.

Hoy, W. K., & Tschannen-Moran, M. (2003). The conceptualization and measurement of faculty trust in schools. In Wayne K. Hoy & Cecil Miskel (Eds.), *Studies in leading and organizing schools* (pp. 181–207). Greenwich, CT: Information Age.

Hoy, W. K., & Woolfolk, A. E. (1990). Organizational socialization of student teachers. *American Educational Research Journal, 27,* 279–300.

Hoy, W. K., & Woolfolk, A. E. (1993). Teachers' sense of efficacy and the organizational health of schools. *The Elementary School Journal, 93,* 355–372.

Hulbert, A. (2005, April 3). Boy problems: The real gender crisis in education starts with the Y chromosome. *The New York Times Magazine,* pp. 13–14.

Hung, D. W. L. (1999). Activity, apprenticeship, and epistemological appropriation: Implications from the writings of Michael Polanyi. *Educational Psychologist, 34,* 193–205.

Hunt, E. (2000). Let's hear it for crystallized intelligence. *Learning and Instruction, 12,* 123–129.

Hunter, M. (1982). *Mastery teaching.* El Segundo, CA: TIP Publications.

Hunter, M. (1995). Mastery teaching. In J. H. Block, S. T. Evertson, & T. R. Guskey (Eds.), *School improvement programs* (pp. 181–204). New York: Scholastic.

Hyde, J. S. (2005). The gender similarities hypothesis. *American Psychologist, 60,* 581–592.

Irvine, J. J. (1990). *Black students and school failure: Policies, practices, and prescriptions.* New York: Praeger.

Irvine, J. J., & Armento, B. J. (2001). *Culturally responsive teaching: Lesson planning for elementary and middle grades.* New York: McGraw-Hill.

Irvine, J. J., & Fraser, J. W. (1998, May). Warm demanders. *Education Week.* Retrieved September 4, 2004, from http://www.edweek.org/ew/ewstory.cfm?slug=35irvine.h17&keywords=Irvine

Irving, O., & Martin, J. (1982). Withiness: The confusing variable. *American Educational Research Journal, 19,* 313–319.

Irwin, J. W. (1991). *Teaching reading comprehension* (2nd ed.). Boston: Allyn & Bacon.

Jagacinski, C. M., & Nicholls, J. G. (1987). Competence and affect in task involvement and ego involvement: The impact of social comparison information. *Journal of Educational Psychology, 76,* 107–114.

James, W. (1912). *Talks to teachers on psychology: And to students on some of life's ideals.* New York: Holt.

Jennings, J., & Rentner, D. S. (2006). Ten big effects of the No Child Left Behind Act on public schools. *Phi Delta Kappan, 88*(2), 110–113.

Jenson, W. R., Sloane, H. N., & Young, K. R. (1988). *Applied behavior analysis in education: A structured teaching approach.* Englewood Cliffs, NJ: Prentice-Hall.

Jimerson, S. R. (1999). On the failure of failure: Examining the association between early grade retention and education and employment outcomes during late adolescence. *Journal of School Psychology, 37,* 243–272.

Jimerson, S. R., Anderson, G. E., & Whipple, A. D. (2002). Winning the battle and losing the war: Examining the relation between grade retention and dropping out of high school. *Psychology in the Schools, 39,* 441–457.

Jimenez, R. (2000). Literacy and identity development of Latina/o students who are successful English readers: Opportunities and obstacles. *American Educational Research Journal, 37,* 971–1000.

Johnson, A. (2008). *Short guide to action research* (3rd ed.) Boston: Allyn & Bacon.

Johnson, D. W., & Johnson, R. (1994). *Learning together and alone: Cooperation, competition, and individualization* (4th ed.). Boston: Allyn & Bacon.

Johnson, D. W., & Johnson, R. (1999a). *Learning together and alone: Cooperation, competition, and individualization* (5th ed.). Boston: Allyn & Bacon.

Johnson, D. W., & Johnson, R. (1999b). The three Cs of school and classroom management. In H. J. Freiberg (Ed.), *Beyond behaviorism: Changing the classroom management paradigm* (pp. 119–144). Boston: Allyn & Bacon.

Johnson, D. W., & Johnson, R. (2002). *Meaningful assessment: A manageable and cooperative process.* Boston: Allyn & Bacon.

Johnson, D. W. & Johnson, R. (2003). *Reaching out: Interpersonal effectiveness and self-actualization* (8th ed.). Boston: Allyn & Bacon.

Johnson, D. W., & Johnson, R. (Eds.). (2005). Peace education. *Theory into Practice, 44* (special issue).

Johnson, D. W., Johnson, R., Dudley, B., Ward, M., & Magnuson, D. (1995). The impact of peer mediation training on the management of school and home conflicts. *American Educational Research Journal, 32,* 829–844.

Jones, E. D., & Southern, W. T. (1991). Conclusions about acceleration: Echoes of a debate. In W. Southern & E. Jones (Eds.) *The academic acceleration of gifted children* (pp. 223–228). New York: Teachers College Press.

Jones, M. S., Levin, M. E., Levin, J. R., & Beitzel, B. D. (2000). Can vocabulary-learning strategies and pair-learning formats be profitably combined? *Journal of Educational Psychology, 92,* 256–262.

Kagan, S. (1994). *Cooperative learning.* San Juan Capistrano, CA: Kagan Cooperative Learning.

Kanaya, T., Scullin, M. H. & Ceci, S. J. (2003). The Flynn effect and U.S. policies: The impact of rising IQ scores on American society via mental retardation diagnoses. *American Psychologist, 58,* 1–13.

Karweit, N. (1989). Time and learning: A review. In R. E. Slavin (Ed.), *School and classroom organization* (pp. 69–95). Hillsdale, NJ: Erlbaum.

Kazdin, A. E. (2001). *Behavior modification in applied settings* (6th ed.). Belmont, CA: Wadsworth.

Keefe, J. W. (1982). Assessing student learning styles: An overview. In *Student learning styles and brain behavior.* Reston, VA: National Association of Secondary School Principals.

Keefe, J. W., & Monk, J. S. (1986). *Learning style profile: Examiner's manual.* Reston, VA: National Association of Secondary School Principals.

Kelly, K. (1999). Retention vs. social promotion: Schools search for alternatives. *Harvard Education Letter, 15*(1), 1–3.

Keogh, B. K., & MacMillan, D. L. (1996). Exceptionality. In D. Berliner & R. Calfee (Eds.), *Handbook of educational psychology* (pp. 311–330). New York: Macmillan.

Kerckhoff, A. C. (1986). Effects of ability grouping in British secondary schools. *American Sociological Review, 51,* 842–858.

Keyser, V., & Barling, J. (1981). Determinants of children's self-efficacy beliefs in an academic environment. *Cognitive Therapy & Research, 5,* 29–40.

Kiewra, K. A. (1985). Investigating notetaking and review: A depth of processing alternative. *Educational Psychologist, 20,* 23–32.

Kiewra, K. A. (1988). Cognitive aspects of autonomous note taking: Control processes, learning strategies, and prior knowledge. *Educational Psychologist, 23,* 39–56.

Kiewra, K. A. (1989). A review of note-taking: The encoding storage paradigm and beyond. *Educational Psychology Review, 1,* 147–172.

Kindsvatter, R., Wilen, W., & Ishler, M. (1988). *Dynamics of effective teaching.* New York: Longman.

King, A. (1990). Enhancing peer interaction and learning in the classroom through reciprocal questioning. *American Educational Research Journal, 27,* 664–687.

King, A. (2002). Structuring peer interactions to promote high-level cognitive processing. *Theory into Practice, 41,* 31–39.

Kirschner, P. A., Sweller, J., & Clark, R. E. (2006). Why minimal guidance during instruction does not work: An analysis of the failure of constructivist, discovery, problem-based experiential and inquiry- based teaching. *Educational Psychologist, 41*(2), 75–86.

Kirst, M. (1991a). Interview on assessment issues with Lorrie Shepard. *Educational Researcher, 20*(2), 21–23.

Kirst, M. (1991b). Interview on assessment issues with James Popham. *Educational Researcher, 20*(2), 24–27.

Klahr, D., & Nigram, M. (2004). Equivalence of learning paths in early science instruction: Effects of direct instruction and discovery learning. *Psychological Science, 15*, 661–667.

Koeppen, K. E. (1998). The experiences of a secondary social studies student teacher: Seeking security by planning for self. *Teaching & Teacher Education, 14*, 401–411.

Kohn, A. (1993). Rewards versus learning: A response to Paul Chance. *Phi Delta Kappan, 74*, 784–785.

Kohn, A. (2002). How not to teach values. In L. Abbeduto (Ed.), *Taking sides: Clashing on controversial issues in educational psychology* (pp. 138–153). Guilford, CT: McGraw-Hill/Duskin.

Kolb, D. (1985). *Learning Styles Inventory* (Rev. ed.). London: McBer.

Kornhaber, M., Fierros, E., & Veenema, S. (2004). *Multiple intelligences: Best ideas for research and practice*. Boston: Allyn & Bacon.

Kounin, J. S. (1970). *Discipline and group management in classrooms*. New York: Holt, Rinehart & Winston.

Krathwohl, D. R., Bloom, B. S., & Masia, B. B. (1964). *Taxonomy of educational objectives. Handbook II: Affective domain*. New York: David McKay.

Krauss, M. (1992). Statement of Michael Krauss, representing the Linguistic Society of America. In U.S. Senate, *Native American Languages Act of 1991: Hearing before the Select Committee on Indian Affairs* (pp. 18–22). Washington, DC: U.S. Government Printing Office.

Kreitzer, A. E., & Madaus, G. F. (1994). Empirical investigations of the hierarchical structure of the taxonomy. In L. W. Anderson & L. A. Sosniak (Eds.), *Bloom's taxonomy: A forty-year retrospective. Ninety-third yearbook for the National Society for the Study of Education: Part II* (pp. 64–81). Chicago: University of Chicago Press.

Krueger, T. (1997). Oral communication skills necessary for successful teaching: The students' perspective. *Educational Research Quarterly, 21*(2), 13–26.

Kulik, J. A., & Kulik, C. C. (1997). Ability grouping. In N. Colangelo & G. Davis (Eds.), *Handbook of gifted education* (2nd ed., pp. 230–242). Boston: Allyn & Bacon.

Labaree, D. F. (1997). *How to succeed in schools without really trying: The credentials race in American education*. New Haven, CT: Yale University Press.

Lachter, J., Forster, K. I., & Ruthruff, K. I. (2004). Forty-five years after Broadbent (1958): Still no identification without attention. *Psychological Review, 111*, 880–913.

Ladson-Billings, G. (1990). Like lightning in a bottle: Attempting to capture the pedagogical excellence of successful teachers of black students. *Qualitative Studies in Education, 3*, 335–344.

Ladson-Billings, G. (1992). Culturally relevant teaching: The key to making multicultural education work. In C. A. Grant (Ed.), *Research and multicultural education* (pp. 106–121). London: Falmer Press.

Ladson-Billings, G. (1994). *The dream keepers*. San Francisco: Jossey-Bass.

Ladson-Billings, G. (1995). But that is just good teaching! The case for culturally relevant pedagogy. *Theory into Practice, 34*, 161–165.

Landrum, T. J., & Kauffman, J. M. (2006). Behavioral approaches to classroom management. In C. M. Evertson & C. S. Weinstein (Eds.), *Handbook of classroom management: Research, practice, and contemporary issues*. Mahwah, NJ: Lawrence Erlbaum.

Lane, K., Falk, K., & Wehby, J. (2006). Classroom management in special education classrooms and resource rooms. In C. M. Evertson & C. S. Weinstein (Eds.), *Handbook of classroom management: Research, practice, and contemporary issues*. Mahwah, NJ: Lawrence Erlbaum.

Langer, E. J. (1989). *Mindfulness*. Cambridge, MA: Perseus.

Language Development and Hypermedia Group. (1992). "Open" software design: A case study. *Educational Technology, 32*, 43–55.

Larrivee, B. (1985). *Effective teaching behaviors for successful mainstreaming*. New York: Longman.

Larrivee, B. (2005). *Authentic classroom management: Creating a learning community and building reflective practice*. Boston: Allyn & Bacon.

Lashley, T. J., II, Matczynski, T. J., & Rowley, J. B. (2002). *Instructional models: Strategies for teaching in a diverse society* (2nd ed.). Belmont, CA: Wadsworth/Thomson Learning.

Lave, J. (1997). The culture of acquisition and the practice of understanding. In D. Kirshner & J. A. Whitson (Eds.), *Situated cognition: Social, semiotic, and psychological perspectives* (pp. 17–35). Mahwah, NJ: Lawrence Erlbaum.

Lave, J., & Wenger, E. (1991). *Situated learning: Legitimate peripheral participation*. Cambridge, MA: Cambridge University Press.

Lee, R. M. (2005). Resilience against discrimination: Ethnic identity and other group orientation as protective factors for Korean Americans. *Journal of Counseling Psychology, 52,* 36–44.

Leinhardt, G. (2001). Instructional explanations: A commonplace for teaching and location for contrasts. In V. Richardson (Ed.), *Handbook of research on teaching* (4th ed., pp. 333–357). Washington, DC: American Educational Research Association.

LeMahieu, P., Gitomer, D. H., & Eresh, J. T. (1993). Portfolios in large-scale assessment: Difficult but not impossible. (Unpublished manuscript, University of Delaware).

Leming, J. S. (1981). Curriculum effectiveness in value/moral education. *Journal of Moral Education, 10,* 147–164.

Lepper, M. R. (1988). Motivational considerations in the study of instruction. *Cognition & Instruction, 5,* 289–309.

Lepper, M. R., & Greene, D. (1978). *The hidden costs of rewards: New perspectives on the psychology of human motivation.* Hillsdale, NJ: Lawrence Erlbaum.

Levin, J. R. (1994). Mnemonic strategies and classroom learning: A twenty-year report card. *The Elementary School Journal, 94,* 235–254.

Levin, J. R., & Nolan, J. F. (2000). *Principles of classroom management: A professional decision-making model.* Boston: Allyn & Bacon.

Lewin, T. (2006, September 13). Report urges changes in the teaching of math in U.S. schools. *The New York Times,* p. 1+.

Lewis, A. C. (2007). How well has NCLB worked? How do we get the revisions we want? *Phi Delta Kappan, 88*(5), 353–358.

Lewis, R. (2001). Classroom discipline and student responsibility: The students' view. *Teaching & Teacher Education, 17,* 307–319.

Lewis, T. J., & Sugai, G. (1996). Functional assessment of problem behavior: A pilot investigation of the comparative and interactive effects of teacher and peer social attention on students in general education settings. *School Psychology Quarterly, 11,* 1–19.

Lewis, T. J., Sugai, G., & Colvin, G. (1998). Reducing problem behavior through a school-wide system of effective behavioral support: Investigation of a school-wide social skills training program and contextual interventions. *School Psychology Review, 27,* 446–459.

Liben, L. S., & Signorella, M. L. (1993). Gender-schematic processing in children: The role of initial interpretations of stimuli. *Developmental Psychology, 29,* 141–149.

Lickona, T. (2002). Character education: Seven crucial issues. In L. Abbeduto (Ed.), *Taking sides: Clashing on controversial issues in educational psychology* (pp. 130–137). Guilford, CT: McGraw-Hill/Duskin.

Linn, M. C., & Hyde, J. S. (1989). Gender, mathematics, and science. *Educational Researcher, 18,* 17–27.

Linn, R. L. (2003). Accountability: Responsibility and reasonable expectations. *Educational Researcher, 32*(7), 3–13.

Linn, R. L., Baker, E. L., & Betebenner, D. W. (2002). Accountability systems: Implications of the requirements of the No Child Left Behind Act of 2001. *Educational Researcher, 31*(6), 3–16.

Linn, R. L., & Gronlund, N. E. (2000). *Measurement and assessment in education* (8th ed.). Columbus, OH: Merrill.

Locke, E. A., & Latham, G. P. (1990). *A theory of goal setting and task performance.* Englewood Cliffs, NJ: Prentice-Hall.

Locke, E. A., & Latham, G. P. (2002). Building a practically useful theory of goal setting and task motivation: A 35-year odyssey. *American Psychologist, 57,* 705–717.

Lorch, R. F., Lorch, E. P., Ritchey, K., McGovern, L., & Coleman, D. (2001). Effects of headings on text summarization. *Contemporary Educational Psychology, 26,* 171–191.

Loveless, T. (1999). Will tracking reform social equity? *Educational Leadership, 56*(7), 28–32.

Lovett, M. W., Lacerenza, L., Borden, S. L., Frijters, J. C., Steinbach, K. A., & De Palma, M. (2000). Components of effective remediation for developmental disabilities: Combining phonological and strategy-based instruction to improve outcomes. *Journal of Educational Psychology, 92,* 263–283.

Lowenstein, G. (1994). The psychology of curiosity: A review and reinterpretation. *Psychological Bulletin, 117,* 75–98.

Lowry, R., Sleet, D., Duncan, C., Powell, K., & Kolbe, L. (1995). Adolescents at risk for violence. *Educational Psychology Review, 7,* 7–40.

Lucas, S. R., & Berends, M. (2002). Sociodemographic diversity, correlated achievement, and de facto tracking. *Sociology of Education, 75,* 328–348.

Maag, J. W., & Kemp, S. E. (2003). Behavioral intent of power and affiliation: Implications for functional analysis. *Remedial & Special Education, 24,* 57–64.

Mabry, L. (1999). Writing to the rubrics: Lingering effects of traditional standardized testing on direct writing assessment. *Phi Delta Kappan, 80,* 673–679.

Madsen, K. (2003). The effect of accuracy of instruction, teacher delivery, and student attentiveness on musicians' evaluation of teacher effectiveness. *Journal of Research in Music Education, 51,* 38–51.

Magnusson, S. J., & Palincsar, A. S. (1995). The learning environment as a site of science reform. *Theory into Practice, 34,* 43–50.

Major, B., & Schmader, T. (1998). Coping with stigma through psychological disengagement. In J. Swim & C. Stangor (Eds.), *Stigma: The target's perspective* (pp. 219–241). New York: Academic Press.

Mandlebaum, L. H., Russell, S. C., Krouse, J., & Gonter, M. (1983). Assertive discipline: An effective classwide behavior management program. *Behavior Disorders, 8*(4), 258–264.

Manning, M. L., & Baruth, L. G. (1996). *Multicultural education of children and adolescents* (2nd ed.). Boston: Allyn & Bacon.

Mantzicopoulos, P., & Morrison, D. (1992). Kindergarten retention: Academic and behavioral outcomes through the end of second grade. *American Educational Research Journal, 29,* 182–198.

Marinova-Todd, S., Marshall, D., & Snow, C. (2000). Three misconceptions about age and L2 learning. *TESOL Quarterly, 34*(1), 9–34.

Marsh, H. W., Walker, R., & Debus, R. (1991). Subject-specific components of academic self-concept and self-efficacy. *Contemporary Educational Psychology, 16,* 331–345.

Marshall, H. H. (1996). Implications of differentiating and understanding constructivist approaches. *Journal of Educational Psychology, 31,* 235–240.

Marshall, H. H. (Ed.). (1992). *Redefining student learning: Roots of educational change.* Norwood, NJ: Ablex.

Martin, C. L., & Little, J. K. (1990). The relation of gender understanding to children's sex-typed preferences and gender stereotypes. *Child Development, 61,* 1427–1439.

Marzano, R. J. (2003). *What works in schools: Translating research into action.* Alexandria, VA: Association of Supervision and Curriculum Development.

Marzano, R. J., & Marzano, J. S. (2003, September). The key to classroom management. *Educational Leadership, 61*(1), 6–13.

Maslow, A. H. (1968). *Toward a psychology of being* (2nd ed.). New York: Van Nostrand.

Maslow, A. H. (1970). *Motivation and personality* (2nd ed.). New York: Harper & Row.

Mason, D. A., & Good, T. L. (1993). Effects of two-group and whole-class teaching on regrouped elementary students' mathematics achievement. *American Educational Research Journal, 30,* 328–360.

Mayer, J. D., & Cobb, C. D. (2000). Educational policy on emotional intelligence: Does it make sense? *Educational Psychology Review, 12,* 163–183.

Mayer, J. D., & Salovey, P. (1997). What is emotional intelligence? In P. Salovey & D. Sluyter (Eds.), *Emotional development, emotional literacy, and emotional intelligence.* New York: Basic Books.

Mayer, R. E. (1992). Cognition and instruction: Their historic meeting within educational psychology. *Journal of Educational Psychology, 84,* 405–412.

Mayer, R. E. (1996). Learners as information processors: Legacies and limitations of educational psychology's second metaphor. *Journal of Educational Psychology, 31,* 151–161.

Mayer, R. E. (2004). Should there be a three-strikes rule against discovery learning? A case for guided methods of instruction. *American Psychologist, 59,* 14–19.

Mayer, R. E., & Massa, L. J. (2003). Three facets of visual and verbal learners: Cognitive ability, cognitive style, and learning preference. *Journal of Educational Psychology, 95,* 833–846.

Mayer, R. E., & Wittrock, M. C. (1996). Problem-solving transfer. In D. Berliner & R. Calfee (Eds.), *Handbook of educational psychology* (pp. 47–62). New York: Macmillan.

McCaslin, M., & Good, T. L. (1998). Moving beyond management as sheer compliance: Helping students to develop goal coordination strategies. *Educational Horizons, 76,* 169–176.

McCaslin, M., & Hickey, D. T. (2001). Self-regulated learning and academic achievement: A Vygotskian view. In B. Zimmerman & D. Schunk (Eds.), *Self-regulated learning and academic achievement. Theoretical perspectives* (2nd ed., pp. 227–252). Mahwah, NJ: Lawrence Erlbaum.

McClelland, D., Atkinson, J. W., Clark, R. W., & Lowell, E. L. (1953). *The achievement motive.* New York: Appleton-Century-Crofts.

McClelland, D., & Pilon, D. (1983). Sources of adult motives in patterns of parent behavior in early childhood. *Journal of Personality & Social Psychology, 44,* 564–574.

McClelland, D. C. (1985). *Human motivation.* Glenview, IL: Scott, Foresman.

McClelland, D. C. (1993). Intelligence is not the best predictor of job performance. *Current Directions in Psychological Science, 2,* 5–6.

McCoach, D. B., Kehle, T. J., Bray, M. L., & Siegle, D. (2001). Best practices in the identification of gifted students with learning disabilities. *Psychology in the Schools, 38,* 403–411.

McCormack, S. (1989). Response to Render, Padilla, and Krank: But practitioners say it works! *Educational Leadership, 46*(6),77–79.

McCoy, A. R., & Reynolds, A. J. (1999). Grade retention and school performance: An extended investigation. *Journal of School Psychology, 37,* 273–298.

McCutcheon, G., & Milner, H. R. (2002). A contemporary study of teacher planning in a high school. *Teachers & Teaching: Theory and Practice, 8,* 81–94.

McDonald, J. P. (1993). Three pictures of an exhibition: Warm, cool, and hard. *Phi Delta Kappan, 6,* 480–485.

McGuigan, L., & Hoy, W. K. (2006). Principal leadership: Creating a culture of academic optimism to improve achievement for all students. *Leadership & Policy in Schools, 5,* 203–229.

McLoyd, V. C. (1998). Economic disadvantage and child development. *American Psychologist, 53,* 185–204.

McMillan, J. H. (2004). *Classroom assessment: Principles and practice for effective instruction* (3rd ed.). Boston: Allyn & Bacon.

McNeely, C. A., Nonnemaker, J. M., & Blum, R. W. (2002). Promoting school connectedness: Evidence from the National Longitudinal Study of Adolescent Health. *Journal of School Health, 72*(4), 138–146.

McNeil, L. M., & Valenzuela, A. (2000). *The harmful impact of the TAAS system of testing in Texas: Beneath the accountability rhetoric.* Cambridge, MA: Harvard University Civil Rights Project. Retrieved from www.law.harvard.edu/groups/civilrights/testing.html

Mears, T. (1998, April 12). Saying 'Si' to Spanish. *Boston Globe.*

Medina, J. (2002, June 23). Groups say Regents Exam push immigrants to drop out. *The New York Times,* p. A28.

Medley, D. M. (1979). The effectiveness of teachers. In P. Peterson & H. Walberg (Eds.), *Research on teaching: Concepts, findings, and implications* (pp. 11–27). Berkeley, CA: McCutchan.

Meece, J. L., & Kurtz-Costes, B. (2001). Introduction: The schooling of ethnic minority children and youth. *Educational Psychologist, 36,* 1–7.

Meichenbaum, D., Burland, S., Gruson, L., & Cameron, R. (1985). Metacognitive assessment. In S. Yussen (Ed.), *The growth of reflection in children* (pp. 1–30). Orlando, FL: Academic Press.

Meijer, A. M., & van den Wittenboer, G. L. H. (2004). The joint contribution of sleep, intelligence and motivation to school performance. *Personality & Individual Differences, 37,* 95–106.

Mendell, P. R. (1971). Retrieval and representation in long-term memory. *Psychonomic Science, 23,* 295–296.

Metzler, C. W., Biglan, A., Rusby, J. C., & Sprague, J. R. (2001). Evaluation of a comprehensive behavior management program to improve schoolwide positive behavior support. *Education & Treatment of Children, 24*(4), 448–470.

Miles, M. B. (1969). Planned change and organizational health: Figure and ground. In F. D. Carver & T. J. Sergiovanni (Eds.), *Organizations and Human Behavior* (pp. 375–391). New York: McGraw-Hill.

Miller, E. (1994). Peer mediation catches on, but some adults don't. *Harvard Education Letter, 10*(3), 8.

Miller, G. A. (1956). The magical number seven, plus or minus two: Some limits on our capacity for processing information. *Psychological Review, 63,* 81–97.

Miller, G. A., Galanter, E., & Pribram, K. H. (1960). *Plans and the structure of behavior.* New York: Holt, Rinehart & Winston.

Miller, P. H. (2002). *Theories of developmental psychology* (4th ed.). New York: Worth.

Miller, S. P., & Mercer, C. D. (1997). Educational aspects of mathematics disabilities. *Journal of Learning Disabilities, 30,* 47–56.

Mills, J. R., & Jackson, N. E. (1990). Predictive significance of early giftedness: The case of precocious reading. *Journal of Educational Psychology, 82,* 410–419.

Milner, H. R. (2006). Classroom management in urban classrooms. In C. Evertson & C. Weinstein (Ed.), *Handbook of classroom management: Research, practice, and contemporary issues* (pp. 491–522). Mahwah, NJ: Lawrence Erlbaum.

Mitchell, M. (1993). Situational interest: Its multifaceted structure in the secondary school mathematics classroom. *Journal of Educational Psychology, 85*, 424–436.

Moll, L. C., Amanti, C., Neff, D., & Gonzalez, N. (1992). Funds of knowledge: Using a qualitative approach to connect homes and classrooms. *Theory into Practice, 31*, 132–141.

Monroe, C. R., & Obidah, J. E. (2002, April). *The impact of cultural synchronization on a teacher's perceptions of disruption: A case study of an African American middle school classroom.* Paper presented at the American Educational Research Association, New Orleans.

Morine-Dershimer, G. (2006). Instructional planning. In J. Cooper (Ed.), *Classroom teaching skills* (7th ed., pp. 20–54). Boston: Houghton Mifflin.

Morris, C. G. (1991). *Psychology: An introduction* (7th ed.). Englewood Cliffs, NJ: Prentice-Hall.

Morris, P. F. (1990). Metacognition. In M. W. Eysenck (Ed.), *The Blackwell dictionary of cognitive psychology* (pp. 225–229). Oxford, UK: Basil Blackwell.

Morrow, L. M. (1992). The impact of a literature-based program on literacy achievement, use of literature, and attitudes of children from minority backgrounds. *Reading Research Quarterly, 27*, 251–275.

Morrow, L. M., & Weinstein, C. (1986). Encouraging voluntary reading: The impact of a literature program on children's use of library centers. *Reading Research Quarterly, 21*, 330–346.

Moshman, D. (1982). Exogenous, endogenous, and dialectical constructivism. *Developmental Review, 2*, 371–384.

Moshman, D. (1997). Pluralist rational constructivism. *Issues in Education: Contributions from Educational Psychology, 3*, 229–234.

Mowday, R. T., Porter, L. W., & Steers, R. M. (1982). *Employee-organizational linkages: The psychology of commitment, absenteeism, and turnover.* New York: Academic Press.

Mullins, T. (1983). *Relationships among teachers' perceptions of principal's style, teachers' loyalty to the principal, and teachers' zone of acceptance.* Unpublished doctoral dissertation, Rutgers University, New Brunswick, NJ.

Mullis, I. V. S., Martin, M. O., Gonzalez, E. J., & Kennedy, A. M. (2003). *PIRLS 2001 International Report: IEA's study of reading literacy achievement in primary schools* Boston: International Study Center, Boston College.

Mullis, I. V. S., Martin, M. O., & Foy, P. (2005). *A developmental project to report TIMSS 2003 mathe-matics achievement in cognitive domains.* Chestnut Hill, MA: TIMSS & PIRLS International Study Center.

Murdock, S. G., O'Neill, R. E., & Cunningham, E. (2005). A comparison of results and acceptability of functional behavioral assessment procedures with a group of middle school students with emotional/behavioral disorders (E/BD). *Journal of Behavioral Education, 14*, 5–18.

Murphy, P. K., & Alexander, P. A. (2000). A motivated exploration of motivation terminology. *Contemporary Educational Psychology, 25*, 3–53.

Muter, V., Hulme, C., Snowling, M. J., & Stevenson, J. (2004). Phonemes, rimes, vocabulary, and grammatical skills as foundation of early reading development: Evidence from a longitudinal study. *Developmental Psychology, 40*, 665–681.

Myers, D. G. (2008). *Exploring psychology* (7th ed.). New York: Worth.

Mullins, T. (1983). Relations among teachers' perceptions of the principal's style, teachers' loyalty to the principal, and teachers' zone of acceptance. (Unpublished Doctoral Dissertation, Rutgers University, New Brunswick, NJ).

Nansel, T. R., Overbeck, M., Pilla, R. S., Ruan, W. J., Simons-Morton, B., & Schiedt, P. (2001). Bullying behavior among U.S. youth: Prevalence and association with psychosocial adjustment. *Journal of the American Medical Association, 285*(16), 2094–2100.

National Alliance of Black School Educators. (2002). *Addressing over-representations of African American students in special education: The prereferral intervention process.* Arlington, VA: Council for Exceptional Education.

National Center for Family Literacy. (2004). *Report of the National Early Literacy Panel.* Washington, DC: National Institute for Literacy.

National Council of Teachers of Mathematics (NCTM). (1989). *Curriculum and evaluation standards for school mathematics.* Reston, VA: Author.

National Council of Teachers of Mathematics (NCTM). (2006). *Curriculum focal points for prekindergarten through grade 8 mathematics: A quest for coherence.* Reston, VA: Author.

National Research Council, Institute of Medicine. (2004). *Engaging schools: Fostering high school students' motivation to learn.* Washington, DC, The National Academies Press.

Naveh-Benjamin, M. (1991). A comparison of training programs intended for different types of test-anxious students: Further support for an information-processing model. *Journal of Educational Psychology, 83*, 134–139.

Naveh-Benjamin, M., McKeachie, W. J., & Lin, Y. (1987). Two types of test-anxious students: Support for an information processing model. *Journal of Educational Psychology, 79*, 131–136.

Needles, M., & Knapp, M. (1994). Teaching writing to children who are underserved. *Journal of Educational Psychology, 86*, 339–349.

Neisser, U., Boodoo, G., Bouchard, A., Boykin, W., Brody, N., Ceci, S. J., Halpern, D. F., Loehlin, J. C., Perloff, R., Sternberg, R. J., & Urbina, S. (1996). Intelligence: Knowns and unknowns. *American Psychologist, 51*, 77–101.

Nelson, J. R., & Roberts, M. L. (2000). Ongoing reciprocal teacher-student interactions involving disruptive behaviors in general education classrooms. *Journal of Emotional and Behavioral Disorders, 4*, 147–161.

Nelson, T. O. (1996). Consciousness and meta-cognition. *American Psychologist, 51*, 102–116.

Neuman, S. B., & Roskos, K. (1992). Literacy objects as cultural tools: Effects on children's literacy behaviors in play. *Reading Research Quarterly, 27*, 255–275.

Newcombe, N., & Baenninger, M. (1990). The role of expectations in spatial test performance: A meta-analysis. *Sex Roles, 16*, 25–37.

Nicholls, J. G., & Miller, A. (1984). Conceptions of ability and achievement motivation. In R. Ames & C. Ames (Eds.), *Research on motivation in education. Volume 1: Student Motivation* (pp. 39–73). New York: Academic Press.

Nissani, M., & Hoefler-Nissani, D. M. (1992). Experimental studies of belief dependence of observations and of resistance to conceptual change. *Cognition & Instruction, 9*, 97–111.

No Child Left Behind Act of 2001. (2002). Pub. L. No. 107–110, 115 Stat. 1925.

Noddings, N. (1990). Constructivism in mathematics education. In R. Davis, C. Maher, & N. Noddings (Eds.), *Constructivist views on the teaching and learning of mathematics* (pp. 7–18). Monograph 4 of the National Council of Teachers of Mathematics, Reston, VA.

Noddings, N. (1992). *The challenge to care in schools: An alternative approach to education.* New York: Teachers College Press.

Noddings, N. (1995). Teaching themes of care. *Phi Delta Kappan, 76*, 675–679.

Nungester, R. J., & Duchastel, P. C. (1982). Testing versus review: Effects on retention. *Journal of Educational Psychology, 74*, 18–22.

Nylund, D. (2000). *Treating Huckleberry Finn. A new narrative approach to working with kids diagnosed ADD/HDD.* San Francisco: Jossey-Bass.

Oakes, J. (1990). *Multiplying inequities: The effects of race, social class, and tracking on opportunities to learn mathematics and science.* Santa Monica, CA: Rand.

Oakes, J. (1999). Promotion or retention: Which one is social? *Harvard Education Letter, 15*(1), 8.

Oakes, J., & Wells, A. S. (1998). Detracking for high student achievement. *Educational Leadership, 55*(6), 38–41.

Oakes, J., & Wells, A. S. (2002). Detracking for high student achievement. In L. Abbeduto (Ed.), *Taking sides. Clashing views and controversial issues in educational psychology* (2nd ed., pp. 26–30). Guilford, CT: McGraw-Hill Duskin.

O'Donnell, A. M., & O'Kelly, J. (1994). Learning from peers: Beyond the rhetoric of positive results. *Educational Psychology Review, 6*, 321–350.

Ogbu, J. U. (1997). Understanding the school performance of urban blacks: Some essential background knowledge. In H. Walberg, O. Reyes, & R. P. Weissberg (Eds.), *Children and youth: Interdisciplinary perspectives* (pp. 190–240). Norwood, NJ: Ablex.

Ogbu, J. U. (1999). Beyond language: Ebonics, Proper English, and identity in a Black-American speech community. *American Educational Research Journal, 36*, 147–184.

Okagaki, L. (2001). Triarchic model of minority children's school achievement. *Educational Psychologist, 36*, 9–20.

O'Neil, J. (1990). Link between style, culture proves divisive. *Educational Leadership, 48*(2), 8.

Ong, W., Allison, J., & Haladyna, T. M. (2000). Student achievement of third graders in comparable single-age and multiage classrooms. *Journal of Research in Childhood Education, 14*, 205–215.

Orange, C. (2000). *25 biggest mistakes teachers make and how to avoid them.* Thousand Oaks, CA: Corwin.

Orange, C. (2005). *44 smart strategies for avoiding classroom mistakes.* Thousand Oaks, CA: Corwin.

O'Reilly, C. A. I., Chatman, J. A., & Caldwell, D. (1991). People and organizational culture: A Q-sort approach to assessing person-organization fit. *Academy of Management Journal, 34*(3), 487–516.

Ormrod, J. E. (1999). *Human learning* (3rd ed.). Upper Saddle River, NJ: Merrill/Prentice-Hall.

Ortony, A., Clore, G. L., & Collins, A. (1988). *The cognitive structure of emotions.* Cambridge: Cambridge University Press.

Osborne, J. W. (2001). Testing stereotype threat: Does anxiety explain race and sex differences in achievement? *Contemporary Educational Psychology, 26,* 291–310.

Ouchi, W. (1981). *Theory Z.* Reading, MA: Addison-Wesley.

Padilla, F. M. (1992). *The gang as an American enterprise.* New Brunswick, NJ: Rutgers University Press.

Pai, Y., & Adler, S. A. (2001). *Cultural foundations of education* (3rd ed.). Upper Saddle River, NJ: Merrill.

Pajares, F. (1997). Current directions in self-efficacy research. In M. L. Maehr & P. R. Pintrich (Eds.), *Advances in motivation and achievement* (Vol. 10, pp. 1–49). Greenwich, CT: JAI Press.

Pajares, F. (2000, April). Seeking a culturally attentive educational psychology. Paper presented at the annual meeting of the American Educational Research Association, New Orleans. Retrieved May 23, 2005, from http://www.emory.edu/EDUCATION/mfp/AERA2000Discussant.html

Palincsar, A. S. (1998). Social constructivist perspectives on teaching and learning. In J. T. Spence, J. M. Darley, & D. J. Foss (Eds.), *Annual Review of Psychology* (pp. 345–375). Palo Alto, CA: Annual Reviews.

Palincsar, A. S., & Brown, A. L. (1989). Classroom dialogues to promote self-regulated comprehension. In J. Brophy (Ed.), *Advances in research on teaching* (Vol. 1, pp. 35–67). Greenwich, CT: JAI Press.

Palincsar, A. S., Magnusson, S. J., Marano, N., Ford, D., & Brown, N. (1998). Designing a community of practice: Principles and practices of the GIsML community. *Teaching & Teacher Education, 14,* 5–19.

Panksepp, J. (1998). Attention deficit hyperactivity disorders, psychostimulants, and intolerance of playfulness: A tragedy in the making? *Current Directions in Psychological Science, 7,* 91–98.

Paris, S. G., Byrnes, J. P., & Paris, A. H. (2001). Constructing theories, identities, and actions of self-regulated learners. In B. J. Zimmerman & D. H. Schunk (Eds.), *Self-regulated learning and academic achievement: Theoretical perspectives* (2nd ed., pp. 253–287). Mahwah, NJ: Lawrence Erlbaum.

Paris, S. G., & Cunningham, A. E. (1996). Children becoming students. In D. Berliner & R. Calfee (Eds.), *Handbook of educational psychology* (pp. 117–146). New York: Macmillan.

Paris, S. G., Lipson, M. Y., & Wixson, K. K. (1983). Becoming a strategic reader. *Contemporary Educational Psychology, 8,* 293–316.

Parks, C. P. (1995). Gang behavior in the schools: Myth or reality? *Educational Psychology Review, 7,* 41–68.

Parsons, T., Bales, R. F., & Shils, E. A. (1953). *Working papers in the theory of action.* New York: Free Press.

Pashler, H. (2006). How we learn. *APS Observer, 19*(3), 22–24.

Pate, P. E., McGinnis, K., & Homestead, E. (1995). Creating coherence through curriculum integration. In M. Harmin, *Inspiring active learning: A handbook for teachers* (pp. 62–70). Alexandria, VA: Association for Supervision and Curriculum Development.

Patterson, C. J. (1995). Lesbian mothers, gay fathers, and their children. In A. R. D'Augelli & C. J. Patterson (Eds.), *Lesbian, gay, and bisexual identities over the lifespan: Psychological perspectives* (pp. 262–290). New York: Oxford University Press.

Paulman, R. G., & Kennelly, K. J. (1984). Test anxiety and ineffective test taking: Different names, same construct? *Journal of Educational Psychology, 76,* 279–288.

Paulson, F. L., Paulson, P. R., & Meyer, C. A. (1991). What makes a portfolio a portfolio? *Educational Leadership, 48*(5), 60–63.

Payne, K. J., & Biddle, B. J. (1999). Poor school funding, child poverty, and mathematics achievement. *Educational Researcher, 28*(6), 4–12.

Pelham, W. E. (1981). Attention deficits in hyperactive and learning-disabled children. *Exceptional Education Quarterly, 2,* 13–23.

Pekrun, R., Goetz, T., Titz, W., & Perry, R. P. (2002). Academic emotions in students' self-regulated learning and achievement. A program of qualitative and quantitative research. *Educational Psychologist, 37,* 91–105.

Perner, J. (2000). Memory and theory of mind. In E. Tulving & F. I. M. Craik (Eds.), *The Oxford handbook of memory* (pp. 297–312). New York: Oxford.

Perrone, V. (1994). How to engage students in learning. *Educational Leadership, 51*(5), 11–13.

Perry, N. E., VandeKamp, K., & Mercer, L. (2000, April). Investigating teacher–student interactions that foster self-regulated learning. In N. E. Perry (Chair), Symposium conducted at the meeting of the American Educational Research Association, New Orleans.

Peterson, C. (2000). The future of optimism. *American Psychologist, 55*, 44–55.

Peterson, P. L., & Comeaux, M. A. (1989). Assessing the teacher as a reflective professional: New perspectives on teacher evaluation. In A. Woolfolk (Ed.), *Research perspectives on the graduate preparation of teachers* (pp. 132–152). Englewood Cliffs, NJ: Prentice-Hall.

Phillips, D. (1997). How, why, what, when, and where: Perspectives on constructivism and education. *Issues in Education: Contributions from Educational Psychology, 3*, 151–194.

Piaget, J. (1971). *Biology and knowledge.* Edinburgh, UK: Edinburgh Press.

Piaget, J. (1985). *The equilibrium of cognitive structures: The central problem of intellectual development* (T. Brown & K. L. Thampy, Trans.). Chicago: University of Chicago Press.

Pierson, L. H., & Connell, J. P. (1992). Effect of grade retention on self-system processes, school engagement, and academic performance. *Journal of Educational Psychology, 84*, 300–307.

Pigge, F. L., & Marso, R. N. (1997). A seven-year longitudinal multi-factor assessment of teaching concerns development through preparation and early years of teaching. *Teaching and Teacher Education, 13*, 225–235.

Pintrich, P. R. (2003). A motivational science perspective on the role of student motivation in learning and teaching. *Journal of Educational Psychology, 95*, 667–686.

Pintrich, P. R., Marx, R. W., & Boyle, R. A. (1993). Beyond cold conceptual change: The role of motivational beliefs and classroom contextual factors in the process of conceptual change. *Review of Educational Research, 63*, 167–199.

Pintrich, P. R., & Schunk, D. H. (2002). *Motivation in education: Theory, research, and applications* (2nd ed.). Columbus, OH: Merrill.

Pintrich, P. R., & Zusho, A. (2002). The development of academic self-regulation: The role of cognitive and motivational factors. In A. Wigfield & J. Eccles (Eds.), *Development of achievement motivation* (pp. 249–284). San Diego: Academic Press.

Polk, J. A. (2006). Traits of effective teachers. *Arts Education Policy Review, 107*(4), 23–29.

Polson, P. G., & Jeffries, R. (1985). Instruction in general problem-solving skills: An analysis of four approaches. In J. Segal, S. Chipman, & R. Glaser (Eds.), *Thinking and learning skills* (Vol. 1, pp. 417–455). Mahwah, NJ: Lawrence Erlbaum.

Popham, W. J. (2002). *Classroom assessment: What teachers need to know.* Boston: Allyn & Bacon.

Popham, W. J. (2005). *Classroom assessment: What teachers need to know* (4th ed.). Boston: Allyn & Bacon.

Portes, A., & Hao, L. (1998). E pluribus unum: Bilingualism and loss of language in the second generation. *Sociology of Education, 71*, 269–294.

Prawat, R. S. (1992). Teachers' beliefs about teaching and learning: A constructivist perspective. *American Journal of Education, 100*, 354–395.

Prawat, R. S. (1996). Constructivism, modern and postmodern. *Issues in Education: Contributions from Educational Psychology, 3*, 215–226.

Pressley, M. (1996, August). Getting beyond whole language: Elementary reading instruction that makes sense in light of recent psychological research. Paper presented at the annual meeting of the American Psychological Association, Toronto.

Pressley, M. (1998). *Reading instruction that works: The case for balanced teaching.* New York: Guilford.

Pressley M., Allington, R., Wharton-McDonald, R., Block, C., & Morrow, L. (2001). *Learning to read: Lessons from exemplary first-grade teachers.* New York: Guilford.

Public Agenda Foundation. (1994). *First things first: What Americans expect from public schools.* New York: Author.

Puncochar, J., & Fox, P. W. (2004). Confidence in individual and group decision-making: When "Two Heads" are worse than one. *Journal of Educational Psychology, 96*, 582–591.

Purdie, N., Hattie, J., & Carroll, A. (2002). A review of the research on interventions for attention deficit hyperactivity disorder: What works best? *Review of Educational Research, 72*(1), 61–82.

Rachlin, H. (1991). *Introduction to modern behaviorism* (3rd ed.). New York: Freeman.

Raffini, J. P. (1996). *150 ways to increase intrinsic motivation in the classroom.* Boston: Allyn & Bacon.

Raudenbush, S., Rowen, B., & Cheong, Y. (1992). Contextual effects on the self-perceived efficacy of high school teachers. *Sociology of Education, 65*, 150–167.

Recht, D. R., & Leslie, L. (1988). Effect of prior knowledge on good and poor readers' memory of text. *Journal of Educational Psychology, 80*, 16–20.

Reeve, J. (1996). *Motivating others: Nurturing inner motivational resources.* Boston: Allyn & Bacon.

Reeve, J., Deci, E. L., & Ryan, R. M. (2004). Self-determination theory: A dialectical framework for understanding the sociocultural influences on motivation and learning: Big theories revisited (Vol. 4, pp. 31–59). Greenwich, CT: Information Age.

Reeves, D. B. (2000). *Accountability in action: A blueprint for learning organizations.* Denver, CO: Advanced Learning Press.

Reis, S. M., Kaplan, S. N., Tomlinson, C. A., Westberg, K. L., Callahan, C. M., & Cooper, C. R. (2002). Equal does not mean identical. In L. Abbeduto (Ed.), *Taking sides: Clashing on controversial issues in educational psychology* (pp. 31–35). Guilford, CT: McGraw-Hill/Duskin.

Reis, S. M., & Renzulli, J. S. (2004). Current research on the social and emotional development of gifted and talented students: Good news and future possibilities. *Psychology in the Schools, 41,* 119–130.

Reisberg, D., & Heuer, F. (1992). Remembering the details of emotional events. In E. Winograd & U. Neisser (Eds.), *Affect and accuracy in recall: Studies of "flashbulb" memories.* Cambridge, England: Cambridge University Press.

Reiss, F., & Hoy, W. K. (1998). Faculty loyalty: An important but neglected concept in the study of schools. *Journal of School Leadership, 8,* 4–21.

Render, G. F., Padilla, J. N. M., & Krank, H. M. (1989). What research really shows about assertive discipline. *Educational Leadership, 46*(6), 72–75.

Renninger, K. A., Hidi, S., & Krapp, A. (Eds.). (1992). *The role of interest in learning and development.* Hillsdale, NJ: Lawrence Erlbaum.

Renzulli, J. S., & Reis, S. M. (1991). The schoolwide enrichment model: A comprehensive plan for the development of creative productivity. In N. Colangelo & G. Davis (Eds.), *Handbook of gifted education.* (pp. 111–141). Boston: Allyn & Bacon.

Renzulli, J. S., & Reis, S. M. (2003). The schoolwide enrichment model: Developing creative and productive giftedness. In N. Colangelo, & G. A. Davis, (Eds.), *Handbook of gifted education* (pp. 184–203). Boston: Allyn & Bacon.

Resnick, L. B. (1981). Instructional psychology. *Annual Review of Psychology, 32,* 659–704.

Resnick, L. B., & Nolan, K. (1995). Where in the world are world-class standards? *Educational Leadership, 52*(6), 6–11.

Reynolds, A. (1992). Grade retention and school adjustment: An explanatory analysis. *Educational Evaluation & Policy Analysis, 14*(2), 101–121.

Ricciardelli, L. A. (1992). Bilingualism and cognitive development: Relation to threshold theory. *Journal of Psycholinguistic Research, 21,* 301–316.

Richardson, T. M., & Benbow, C. P. (1990). Long-term effects of acceleration on the social-emotional adjustment of mathematically precocious youths. *Journal of Educational Psychology, 82,* 464–470.

Riding, R. J. (2001). The nature and effects of cognitive style. In R. J. Sternberg & L. Zhang (Eds.), *Perspectives on thinking, learning, and cognitive styles* (pp. 47–72). Mahwah, NJ: Lawrence Erlbaum.

Rivkin, S. G., Hanushek, E. A., & Kain, J. F. (2001). *Teachers, schools, and academic achievement.* Amherst, MA: Amherst College.

Robbins, S. P. (1998). *Organizational behavior: Concepts, controversies, applications.* Upper Saddle River, NJ: Prentice Hall.

Roberts, R. D., Zeidner, M., & Matthews, G. (2001). Does emotional intelligence meet traditional standards for an intelligence? Some new data and conclusions. *Emotion, 1,* 196–231.

Robinson, A., & Clinkenbeard, P. R. (1998). Giftedness: An exceptionality examined. In J. T. Spence, J. M. Darley, & D. J. Foss (Eds.), *Annual Review of Psychology* (pp. 117–139). Palo Alto, CA: Annual Reviews.

Robinson, D. H. (1998). Graphic organizers as aids to test learning. *Reading Research & Instruction, 37,* 85–105.

Robinson, D. H., & Kiewra, K. A. (1995). Visual argument: Graphic outlines are superior to outlines in improving learning from text. *Journal of Educational Psychology, 87,* 455–467.

Rogers, C. R., & Freiberg, H. J. (1994). *Freedom to learn* (3rd ed.). Columbus, OH: Merrill.

Rogoff, B. (1998). Cognition as a collaborative process. In W. Damon (Series Editor) & D. Kuhn & R. S. Siegler (Volume Eds.), *Handbook of child psychology: Volume 2* (5th ed., pp. 679–744). New York: Wiley.

Rogoff, B., Turkanis, C. G., & Bartlett, L. (2001). *Learning together: Children and adults in a school community.* New York: Oxford.

Rose, L. C., & Gallup, A. M. (1999). The 31st annual Phi Delta Kappa/Gallup Poll of the public's attitude toward the public schools. *Phi Delta Kappan, 81*(1), 41–58.

Rose, L. C., & Gallup, A. M. (2001). The 33rd annual Phi Delta Kappa/Gallup Poll of the public's attitude toward the public schools. *Phi Delta Kappan, 83*(1), 41–58.

Rosenshine, B. (1988). Explicit teaching. In D. Berliner & B. Rosenshine (Eds.), *Talks to teachers* (pp. 75–92). New York: Random House.

Rosenshine, B., & Furst, N. (1973). The use of direct observation to study teaching. In R. Travers (Ed.), *Second handbook of research on teaching.* Chicago: Rand McNally.

Rosenshine, B., & Stevens, R. (1986). Teaching functions. In M. Wittrock (Ed.), *Handbook of research on teaching* (3rd ed.) (pp. 376–391). New York: Macmillan.

Roskos, K., & Neuman, S. B. (1995). Two beginning kindergarten teachers' planning for integrated literacy instruction. *The Elementary School Journal, 96*, 195–215.

Ross, J. A. (1998). The antecedents and consequences of teacher efficacy. *Advances in Research on Teaching, 7*, 49–73.

Ross, J. A., Cousins, J. B., & Gadalla, T. (1996). Within teacher predictors of teacher efficacy. *Teaching & Teacher Education, 12*, 385–400.

Rubin, B. (Ed.). (2006). Detracking and heterogeneous grouping. *Theory into Practice, 45*(1) (special issue).

Rueda, R., & Moll, L. C. (1994). A sociocultural perspective on motivation. In F. O'Neil Jr. & M. Drillings (Eds.), *Motivation: Theory and research* (pp. 117–137). Hillsdale, NJ: Lawrence Erlbaum.

Rumelhart, D., & Ortony, A. (1977). The representation of knowledge in memory. In R. Anderson, R. Spiro, & W. Montague (Eds.), *Schooling and the acquisition of knowledge* (pp. 99–135). Hillsdale, NJ: Lawrence Erlbaum.

Rummel, N., Levin, J. R., & Woodward, M. M. (2003). Do pictorial mnemonic text-learning aids give students something worth writing about? *Journal of Educational Psychology, 95*, 327–334.

Ruopp, F., & Driscoll, M. (1990, January/February). Access to algebra. *Harvard Education Letter, 6*(A), 4–5.

Ryan, R. M., & Deci, E. L. (1996). When paradigms clash: Comments on Cameron and Pierce's claim that rewards do not undermine intrinsic motivation. *Review of Educational Research, 66*, 33–38.

Ryan, R. M., & Deci, E. L. (2000). Intrinsic and extrinsic motivation: Classic definitions and new directions. *Contemporary Educational Psychology, 25*, 54–67.

Sabers, D. S., Cushing, K. S., & Berliner, D. C. (1991). Differences among teachers in a task characterized by simultaneity, multidimensionality, and immediacy. *American Educational Research Journal, 28*, 68–87.

Sackett, P. R., Hardison, C. M., & Cullen, M. J. (2004). On interpreting stereotype threat as accounting for African American–White differences on cognitive tests. *American Psychologist, 59*(1), 7–13.

Sadker, D., & Sadker, D. (2000). *Teachers, schools, and society* (5th ed.). New York: McGraw-Hill.

Sadker, M., Sadker, D., & Klein, S. (1991). The issue of gender in elementary and secondary education. *Review of Research in Education, 17*, 269–334.

Sagvolden, T. (1999). Attention deficit/hyperactive disorder. *European Psychologist, 4*, 109–114.

Sanchez, F., & Anderson, M. L. (1990, May). Gang mediation: A process that works. *Principal*, 54–56.

Sanders, W. L., & Rivers, J. C. (1996). *Cumulative and residual effects of teachers on student academic achievement.* Knoxville: University of Tennessee Value-Added Research and Assessment Center.

Sattler, J. (2001). *Assessment of children* (4th ed. rev.). San Diego: Jerome M. Sattler.

Savage, T. V. (1999). *Teaching self-control through management and discipline.* Boston: Allyn & Bacon.

Savin-Williams, R. C., & Diamond, L. M. (2004). Sex. In R. M. Lerner & L. Steinberg (Eds.), *Handbook of adolescent psychology* (2nd edition, pp. 189–231). New York: Wiley.

Scales, P., & McEwin, C. K. (1994). *Growing pains: The making of America's middle school teachers.* Columbus, OH: National Middle School Association and the Center for Early Adolescence.

Scardamalia, M., & Bereiter, C. (1996). Adaptation and understanding: A case for new cultures of schooling. In S. Vosniado, E. De Corte, R. Glasse, & H. Mandl (Eds.), *International perspectives on the design of technology-supported learning environments* (pp. 149–163). Hillsdale, NJ: Lawrence Erlbaum.

Schein, E. H. (1992). *Organizational culture and leadership* (2nd ed.). San Francisco: Jossey-Bass.

Schein, E. H. (1999). *The corporate culture.* San Francisco: Jossey-Bass.

Schein, E. H. (2004). *Organizational culture and leadership* (3rd ed.). San Francisco: Wiley.

Schemo, D. J. (2007, March 9). Federal-local clash in war over teaching reading. *The New York Times*, p. A16.

Schiefele, U. (1991). Interest, learning, and motivation. *Educational Psychologist, 26*, 299–324.

Schon, D. (1983). *The reflective practitioner.* New York: Basic Books.

Schraw, G., & Lehman, S. (2001). Situational interest: A review of the literature and directions for future research. *Educational Psychology Review, 13,* 23–52.

Schraw, G., & Moshman, D. (1995). Metacognitive theories. *Educational Psychology Review, 7,* 351–371.

Schunk, D. H. (2000). *Learning theories: An educational perspective* (3rd ed.). Columbus, OH: Merrill/Prentice-Hall.

Schunk, D. H. (2004). *Learning theories: An educational perspective* (4th ed.). Columbus, OH: Merrill/Prentice-Hall.

Seligman, M. E. P. (1975). *Helplessness: On depression, development, and death.* San Francisco: Freeman.

Semb, G. B., & Ellis, J. A. (1994). Knowledge taught in school: What is remembered? *Review of Educational Research, 64,* 253–286.

Senge, P. M. (1990). *The fifth discipline: The art and practice of the learning organization.* New York: Doubleday.

Senge, P. M., Cambron-McCabe, N. H., Lucas, T., Kleiner, A., Dutton, J., & Smith, B. (2000). *Schools that learn.* New York: Doubleday.

Senge, P. M., Kleiner, A., Roberts, C., Rossi, R., & Smith, B. J. (1994). *The Fifth discipline fieldbook.* New York: Bantam Doubleday Dell.

Serpell, R. (1993). Interface between sociocultural and psychological aspects of cognition. In E. Forman, N. Minick, & C. A. Stone (Eds.), *Contexts for learning: Sociocultural dynamics in children's development* (pp. 357–368). New York: Oxford University Press.

Shanker, A. (1995, May 15). Restoring the connection between behavior and consequences. In *Vital speeches of the day.* Washington, DC: America Federation of Teachers.

Shavelson, R. J. (1987). Planning. In M. Dunkin (Ed.), *The international encyclopedia of teaching and teacher education* (pp. 483–486). New York: Pergamon Press.

Sheets, R. H. (2005). *Diversity pedagogy: Examining the role of culture in the teaching-learning process.* Boston: Allyn & Bacon.

Shepard, L. A., & Smith, M. L. (1989). Academic and emotional effects of kindergarten retention. In L. Shepard & M. Smith (Eds.), *Flunking grades: Research and policies on retention* (pp. 79–107). Philadelphia: Falmer Press.

Sherman, A. (1994). *Wasting America's future: The Children's Defense Fund report on the costs of child poverty.* Boston: Beacon Press.

Shimahara, N. K., & Sakai, A. (1995). *Learning to teach in two cultures.* New York: Garland.

Shipley, J., & Wescott, M. C. (2000). *Systems check: School improvement resource guide.* Seminole, FL: Jim Shipley & Associates.

Shoda, Y., Mischel, W., & Peake, P. K. (1990). Predicting adolescent cognitive and self-regulatory competencies from preschool delay of gratification. *Developmental Psychology, 26,* 978–986.

Shuell, T. J. (1986). Cognitive conceptions of learning. *Review of Educational Research, 56,* 411–436.

Shuell, T. J. (1996). Teaching and learning in a classroom context. In D. Berliner & R. Calfee (Eds.), *Handbook of educational psychology* (pp. 726–764). New York: Macmillan.

Shulman, L. S. (1987). Knowledge and teaching: Foundations of the new reform. *Harvard Educational Review, 19*(2), 4–14.

Siegel, J., & Shaughnessy, M. F. (1994). Educating for understanding: An interview with Howard Gardner. *Phi Delta Kappan, 75,* 536–566.

Siegler, R. S. (1993). Adaptive and non-adaptive characteristics of low-income children's mathematical strategy use. In B. Penner (Ed.), *The challenge in mathematics and science education: Psychology's response* (pp. 341–366). Washington, DC: American Psychological Association.

Sigler, R. S. (1998). *Children's thinking* (3rd ed.). Upper Saddle River, NJ: Prentice-Hall.

Skiba, R. J., Michael, R. S., Nardo, A. C., & Peterson, R. (2000). *The color of discipline: Sources of racial and gender disproportionality in school punishment* (Report #SRS1). Bloomington, IN: Indiana Education Policy Center.

Skinner, B. F. (1950). Are theories of learning necessary? *Psychological Review, 57,* 193–216.

Slater, L. (2002, February 3). The trouble with self-esteem. *The New York Times Magazine,* pp. 44–47.

Slavin, R. E. (1987). Ability grouping and student achievement in elementary schools: A best-evidence synthesis. *Review of Educational Research, 57,* 293–336.

Slavin, R. E. (1995). *Cooperative learning* (2nd ed.). Boston: Allyn & Bacon.

Slavin, R. E., & Fashola, O. S. (1998). *Show me the evidence: Proven and promising programs for America's schools.* Thousand Oaks, CA: Corwin.

Slavin, R. E., Karweit, N. L., & Madden, N. A. (1989). *Effective programs for students at risk.* Boston: Allyn & Bacon.

Smith, C. B. (Moderator) (1994). *Whole language: The debate.* Bloomington, IN: EDINFO Press.

Smith, J. D., & Caplan, J. (1988). Cultural differences in cognitive style development. *Developmental Psychology, 24*, 46–52.

Smith, J. K., Smith, L. F., & DeLisi, R. (2001). *Natural classroom assessment.* Thousand Oaks, CA: Corwin.

Smith, P. A., & Hoy, W. K. (2007). Academic optimism and student achievement in urban elementary schools. *Journal of Educational Administration, 45*, 550–568.

Snider, V. E. (1990). What we know about learning styles from research in special education. *Educational Leadership, 48*(2), 53.

Snowman, J. (1984). Learning tactics and strategies. In G. Phye & T. Andre (Eds.), *Cognitive instructional psychology* (pp. 243–275). Orlando, FL: Academic Press.

Snyder, C. R., Shorey, H. S., Cheavens, J., Pulvers, K. M., Adams, V. H., III, & Wiklund, C. (2002). Hope and academic success in college. *Journal of Educational Psychology, 94*, 820–826.

Soar, R. S., & Soar, R. M. (1979). Emotional climate and management. In P. Peterson & H. Walberg (Eds.), *Research on teaching: Concepts, findings, and implications* (pp. 97–119). Berkeley, CA: McCutchan.

Sokolove, S., Garrett, J., Sadker, D., & Sadker, M. (1986). Interpersonal communications skills. In J. Cooper (Ed.), *Classroom teaching skills: A handbook* (pp. 233–278). Lexington, MA: Heath.

Solomon, D., Battistich, V., Watson, M., Schaps, E., & Lewis, C. (2000). A six-district study of educational change: Direct and mediated effects of the Child Development Project. *Social Psychology of Education, 4*, 3–51.

Soodak, L. C., & McCarthy, M. R. (2006). Classroom management in inclusive settings. In C. M. Evertson & C. S. Weinstein (Eds.), *Handbook of classroom management: Research, practice, and contemporary issues.* Mahwah, NJ: Lawrence Erlbaum.

Spearman, C. (1927). *The abilities of man: Their nature and measurement.* New York: Macmillan.

Spelke, E. S. (2005). Sex differences in intrinsic aptitude for mathematics and science?: A critical review. *American Psychologist, 60*, 950–958.

Spelling, M. (2007, January). Building on results: A blueprint for strengthening the *No Child Left Behind Act.* Washington, DC: U.S. Department of Education. Available online at: www.ed.gov/policy/elsec/leg/nclb/buildingonresults.html.

Spencer, S. J., Steele, C. M., & Quinn, D. M. (1999). Stereotype threat and women's math performance. *Journal of Experimental Social Psychology, 35*, 4–28.

Spiro, R. J., Feltovich, P. J., Jacobson, M. L., & Coulson, R. L. (1991). Cognitive flexibility, constructivism, and hypertext: Random access instruction for advanced knowledge acquisition in ill-structured domains. *Educational Technology, 31*(5), 24–33.

Stahl, S. A. (2002). Different strokes for different folks? In L. Abbeduto (Ed.), *Taking sides: Clashing on controversial issues in educational psychology* (pp. 98–107). Guilford, CT: McGraw-Hill/Duskin.

Stahl, S. A., McKenna, M. C., & Pagnucco, J. R. (1994). The effects of whole-language instruction: An update and a reappraisal. *Educational Psychologist, 29*, 175–185.

Stahl, S. A., & Yaden, D. B., Jr. (2004). The development of literacy in preschool and primary grades: Work by the Center for the Improvement of Early Reading Achievement. *The Elementary School Journal, 82*, 141–166.

Stainback, S., & Stainback, W. (1992). Schools as inclusive communities. In W. Stainback & S. Stainback (Eds.), *Controversial issues confronting special education: Divergent perspectives* (pp. 29–43). Boston: Allyn & Bacon.

Stanovich, K. E. (1994). Constructivism in reading. *Journal of Special Education, 28*, 259–274.

Stanovich, K. E. (1998). Cognitive neuroscience and educational psychology: What season is it? *Educational Psychology Review, 10*, 419–426.

Steinberg, L. (2005). *Adolescence* (7th ed.). New York: McGraw-Hill.

Stepien, W., & Gallagher, S. (1993). Problem-based learning: As authentic as it gets. *Educational Leadership, 50*(7), 25–28.

Sternberg, R. J. (1985). *Beyond IQ: A triarchic theory of human intelligence.* New York: Cambridge University Press.

Sternberg, R. J. (1997). *Successful intelligence.* New York: Plume.

Sternberg, R. J. (2000). *Handbook of human intelligence.* New York: Cambridge University Press.

Sternberg, R. J. (2001). Beyond *g:* The theory of successful intelligence. In R. J. Sternberg & E. L. Grigorenko (Eds.), *The general factor of intelligence: How general is it?* (pp. 447–479). Mahwah, NJ: Lawrence Erlbaum.

Sternberg, R. J. (2004). Culture and intelligence. *American Psychologist, 59*, 325–338.

Sternberg, R. J., & Detterman, D. L. (Eds.). (1986). *What is intelligence? Contemporary viewpoints on its nature and definition.* Norwood, NJ: Ablex.

Sternberg, R. J., & Wagner, R. K. (1993). The g-ocentric view of intelligence and job performance is wrong. *Current Directions in Psychological Science, 2,* 1–5.

Sternberg, R. J., Wagner, R. K., Williams, W. M., & Horvath, J. A. (1995). Testing common sense. *American Psychologist, 50,* 912–927.

Stevenson, H. W., & Stigler, J. (1992). *The learning gap.* New York: Summit Books.

Stiggins, R. (2007). Assessment through the students' eyes. *Educational Leadership, 64*(8), 22–26.

Stipek, D. J. (1996). Motivation and instruction. In D. Berliner & R. Calfee (Eds.), *Handbook of educational psychology* (pp. 85–109). New York: Macmillan.

Stipek, D. J. (2002). *Motivation to learn* (4th ed.). Boston: Allyn & Bacon.

Stodolsky, S. S. (1988). *The subject matters: Classroom activity in math and social studies.* Chicago: University of Chicago Press.

Stormont, M., Stebbins, M. S., & Holliday, G. (2001). Characteristics and educational support needs of underrepresented gifted adolescents. *Psychology in the Schools, 38,* 413–423.

Stumpf, H. (1995). Gender differences on tests of cognitive abilities: Experimental design issues and empirical results. *Learning & Individual Differences, 7,* 275–288.

Suzuki, B. H. (1983). The education of Asian and Pacific Americans: An introductory overview. In D. Nakanishi & M. Hirano-Nakanishi (Eds.), *The education of Asian and Pacific Americans: Historical perspectives and prescriptions for the future* (pp. 1–14). Phoenix: Oryx Press.

Svoboda, J. S. (2001). Review of *Boys And Girls Learn Differently.* The Men's Resource Network. Retrieved May 18, 2002, from www.themenscenter.com/reviews/Swoboda/boysandgirls.htm

Swanson, H. L. (1990). The influence of metacognitive knowledge and aptitude on problem solving. *Journal of Educational Psychology, 82,* 306–314.

Swanson, H. L. (2001). Research on interventions for adolescents with learning disabilities: A meta-analysis of outcomes related to higher-order processing. *The Elementary School Journal, 101,* 332–348.

Swanson, H. L., O'Conner, J. E., & Cooney, J. B. (1990). An information processing analysis of expert and novice teachers' problem solving. *American Educational Research Journal, 27,* 533–556.

Swartz, B., Wasserman, E., & Robbins, S. (2002). *Psychology of learning and behavior* (5th ed.). New York: Norton

Sweller, J., Kirschner, P. A., & Clark, R. E. (2007). Why minimally guided teaching techniques do not work: A reply to commentaries. *Educational Psychologist, 42,* 115–121.

Symons, S., Woloshyn, V., & Pressley, M. (1994). The scientific evaluation of the whole language approach to literacy development. *Educational Psychologist, 29*(4) (special issue).

Taylor, J. B. (1983). Influence of speech variety on teachers' evaluation of reading comprehension. *Journal of Educational Psychology, 75,* 662–667.

Taylor-Green, S., Brown, D., Nelson, L., Longton, J., Gassman, T., Cohen, J., Swartz, J., Horner, R. H., Sugai, G., & Hall, S. (1997). School-wide behavioral support: Starting the year off right. *Journal of Behavioral Education, 7,* 99–112.

TenBrink, T. D. (2006). Assessment. In J. Cooper (Ed.), *Classroom teaching skills* (8th ed., pp. 55–78). Boston: Houghton Mifflin.

Tharp, R. G. (1989). Psychocultural variables and constants: Effects on teaching and learning in schools. *American Psychologist, 44,* 349–359.

Thompson, G. (1991). *Teaching through themes.* New York: Scholastic.

Thurstone, L. L. (1938). Primary mental abilities. *Psychometric Monographs,* No. 1.

Tobias, S. (1985). Text anxiety: Interference, defective skills, and cognitive capacity. *Educational Psychologist, 20,* 135–142.

Tochon, F., & Munby, H. (1993). Novice and expert teachers' time epistemology: A wave function from didactics to pedagogy. *Teaching & Teacher Education, 9,* 205–218.

Tomlinson, C. (2005). Grading and differentiation: Paradox or good practice? *Theory into Practice, 44,* 262–269.

Tomlinson-Keasey, C. (1990). Developing our intellectual resources for the 21st century: Educating the gifted. *Journal of Educational Psychology, 82,* 399–403.

Toppo, G. (2003, January 13). School violence hits lower grades. *USA Today,* p. A2.

Torrance, E. P. (1986). Teaching creative and gifted learners. In M. Wittrock (Ed.), *Handbook of research on teaching* (3rd ed., pp. 630–647). New York: Macmillan.

Toth, E., Klahr, D., & Chen, Z. (2000). Bridging research and practice: A cognitively based classroom intervention for teaching experimentation to elementary school children. *Cognition & Instruction, 18,* 423–459.

Trautwein, U., & Koller, O. (2003). The relationship between homework and achievement—Still much of a mystery. *Educational Psychology Review*, *15*, 115–145.

Tschannen-Moran, M., & Woolfolk Hoy, A. (2001). Collaborative learning: A memorable model. *Teacher Educator, 37*, 148–165.

Tschannen-Moran, M., & Woolfolk Hoy, A. (2007). The differential antecedents of self-efficacy beliefs of novice and experienced teachers. *Teaching and Teacher Education, 23*, 944–956.

Tschannen-Moran, M., Woolfolk Hoy, A., & Hoy, W. K. (1998). Teacher efficacy: Its meaning and measure. *Review of Educational Research, 68*, 202–248.

Umbreit, J. (1995). Functional analysis of disruptive behavior in an inclusive classroom. *Journal of Early Intervention, 20*(1), 18–29.

Urdan, T. C., & Maehr, M. L. (1995). Beyond a two-goal theory of motivation and achievement: A case for social goals. *Review of Educational Research, 65*, 213–243.

U.S. Bureau of the Census. (2003). *Statistical abstract of the United States* (123rd ed.). Washington, DC: U.S. Government Printing Office.

Valentine, J. C., DuBois, D. L., & Cooper, H. (2004). The relations between self-beliefs and academic achievement: A systematic review. *Educational Psychologist, 39*, 111–133.

van der Mass, H. L. J., Dolan, C. V., Grasman, R. P. P. P., Wicherts, J. M., Huizenga, H. M., & Raijmakers, M. E. J. (2006). A dynamic model of general intelligence: The positive manifold of intelligence by mutualism. *Psychological Review, 113*, 842–861.

van Kraayenoord, C. F., Rice, D., Carroll, A., Dillon, L., & Hill. A. (2001). *Attention deficit hyperactivity disorder: Impact and implications for Queensland* (Volume 1: Executive Summary). Bisbane, Australia: Queensland Disability Council.

Van Meter, P. (2001). Drawing construction as a strategy for learning form text. *Journal of Educational Psychology, 93*, 129–140.

Van Meter, P., Yokoi, L., & Pressley, M. (1994). College students' theory of note-taking derived from their perceptions of note-taking. *Journal of Educational Psychology, 86*, 323–338.

Vasquez, J. A. (1990). Teaching to the distinctive traits of minority students. *The Clearing House, 63*, 299–304.

Vaughn, S., Mathes, P., Linan-Thompson, S., Cirino, P., Carlson, C., Pollard-Durodola, S., et al. (2006). Effectiveness of English intervention for first-grade English Language Learners at risk for reading problems. *The Elementary School Journal, 107*, 153–180.

Veenman, S. (1984). Perceived problems of beginning teachers. *Review of Educational Research, 54*, 143–178.

Veenman, S. (1997). Combination classes revisited. *Educational Research & Evaluation, 65*(4), 319–381.

Vellutino, F. R. (1991). Introduction to three studies on reading acquisition: Convergent findings on theoretical foundations of code-oriented versus whole-language approaches to reading instruction. *Journal of Educational Psychology, 83*, 437–443.

Vera, A. H., & Simon, H. A. (1993). Situated action: A symbolic interpretation. *Cognitive Science, 17*, 7–48.

Vispoel, W. P., & Austin, J. R. (1995). Success and failure in junior high school: A critical incident approach to understanding students' attributional beliefs. *American Educational Research Journal, 32*, 377–412.

Vitto, J. M. (2003). *Relationship-driven management: Strategies that promote student motivation.* Thousand Oaks, CA: Corwin.

von Glaserfeld, E. (1995). A constructivist approach to teaching. In L. Steffe & J. Gale (Eds.), *Constructivism in education* (p. 5). Hillsdale, NJ: Lawrence Erlbaum.

von Glaserfeld, E. (1997). Amplification of a constructivist perspective. *Issues in Education: Contributions from Educational Psychology, 3*, 203–210.

Vroom, V. (1964). *Work and motivation.* New York: Wiley.

Vygotsky, L. S. (1978). *Mind in society: The development of higher mental process.* Cambridge, MA: Harvard University Press.

Vygotsky, L. S. (1997). *Educational psychology* (R. Silverman, Trans.). Boca Raton, FL: St. Lucie.

Wade, S. E., Schraw, G., Buxton, W. M., & Hayes, M. T. (1993). Seduction of the strategic reader: Effects of interest on strategies and recall. *Reading Research Quarterly, 28*, 3–24.

Walberg, H. J. (1990). Productive teaching and instruction: Assessing the knowledge base. *Phi Delta Kappan, 72*, 470–478.

Wang, A. Y., & Thomas, M. H. (1995). Effects of keywords on long-term retention: Help or hindrance? *Journal of Educational Psychology, 87*, 468–475.

Wang, A. Y., Thomas, M. H., & Ouellette, J. A. (1992). Keyword mnemonic and retention of second-language vocabulary words. *Journal of Educational Psychology, 84*, 520–528.

Wang, M. C., Haertel, G. D., & Walberg, H. J. (1993). Toward a knowledge base for school learning. *Review of Educational Research, 63*, 249–294.

Wang, M. C., Haertel, G. D., & Walberg, H. J. (1997). Learning influences. In H. Walberg & G. Heartel (Eds.), *Psychology and educational practice* (pp. 199–211). Berkeley, CA: McCutchan.

Wayne, A. J., & Youngs, P. (2003). Teacher characteristics and student achievement gains: A review. *Review of Educational Research, 73*, 89–122.

Webb, N. (1985). Verbal interaction and learning in peer-directed groups. *Theory into Practice, 24*, 32–39.

Webb, N., Farivar, S. H., & Mastergeorge, A. M. (2002). Productive helping in cooperative groups. *Theory into Practice, 41*, 13–20.

Webb, N., & Palincsar, A. (1996). Group processes in the classroom. In D. C. Berliner & R. C. Calfee (Eds.), *Handbook of educational psychology* (pp. 841–876). New York: Macmillan.

Wenger, E. (1998) *Communities of practice: learning, meaning, and identity.* New York: Cambridge University Press.

Weiner, B. (1986). *An attributional theory of motivation and emotion.* New York: Springer.

Weiner, B. (1992). *Human motivation: Metaphors, theories, and research.* Newbury Park, CA: Sage.

Weiner, B. (1994). Ability versus effort revisited: The moral determinants of achievement evaluation an achievement as a moral system. *Educational Psychologist, 29*, 163–172.

Weiner, B. (2000). Interpersonal and intrapersonal theories of motivation from an attributional perspective. *Educational Psychology Review, 12*, 1–14.

Weiner, B., & Graham, S. (1989). Understanding the motivational role of affect: Life span research from an attributional perspective. *Cognition & Emotion, 4*, 401–419.

Weiner, B., Russell, D., & Lerman, D. (1978). Affective consequences of causal ascriptions. In J. H. Harvey, W. J. Ickes, & R. F. Kidd (Eds.), *New directions in attribution research* (Vol. 2). Hillsdale, NJ: Erlbaum.

Weinert, F. E., & Helmke, A. (1995). Learning from wise mother nature or big brother instructor: The wrong choice as seen from an educational perspective. *Educational Psychologist, 30*, 135–143.

Weinstein, C. S. (1999). Reflections on best practices and promising programs: Beyond assertive classroom discipline. In H. J. Freiberg (Ed.), *Beyond behaviorism: Changing the classroom management paradigm* (pp. 147–163). Boston: Allyn & Bacon.

Weinstein, C. S. (2007). *Secondary classroom management: Lessons from research and practice* (3rd ed.). New York: McGraw-Hill.

Weinstein, C. S., & Mignano, A. (2007). *Elementary classroom management: Lessons from research and practice* (4th ed.). New York: McGraw-Hill.

Weiss, G., & Hechtman, L. T. (1993). *Hyperactive children grow up: ADHD in children, adolescents, and adults* (2nd ed.). New York: Guilford.

Wentzel, K. R. (1999). Social-motivational processes and interpersonal relations: Implications for understanding motivation in school. *Journal of Educational Psychology, 91*, 76–97.

Wheelock, A. (1992). *Crossing the tracks: How untracking can save America's schools.* New York: New Press.

Whitehead, A. N. (1929). *The aims of education.* New York: Macmillan.

Wigfield, A., & Eccles, J. (1989). Test anxiety in elementary and secondary school students. *Educational Psychologist, 24*, 159–183.

Wigfield, A., & Eccles, J. (2002). The development of competence beliefs, expectancies for success, and achievement values from childhood through adolescence. In A. Wigfield & J. Accles (Eds.), *Development of achievement motivation* (pp. 91–120). San Diego: Academic Press.

Wiggins, G. (1991). Standards, not standardization: Evoking quality student work. *Educational Leadership, 48*(5), pp. 18–25.

Wiggins, G. (1993). Assessment, authenticity, context, and validity. *Phi Delta Kappan, 75*, 200–214.

Willcutt, E. G., Pennington, B. F., Boada, R., Ogline, J. S., Tunick, R. A., Chabildas, N. A., and Olson, R. K. (2001). A comparison of the cognitive deficits in reading disability and attention-deficit/hyperactivity disorder. *Journal of Abnormal Psychology, 110*, 157–172.

Williams, G. C., Wiener, M. W., Markakis, K. M., Reeve, J., & Deci, E. L. (1993). Medical student motivation for internal medicine. *Annals of Internal Medicine, 9*, 327–333.

Willingham, W. W., & Cole, N. S. (1997). *Gender and fair assessment.* Mahwah, NJ: Lawrence Erlbaum.

Willoughby, T., Porter, L., Belsito, L., & Yearsley, T. (1999). Use of elaboration strategies by grades two, four, and six. *The Elementary School Journal, 99*, 221–231.

Windschitl, M. (2002). Framing constructivism in practice as the negotiation of dilemmas: An analysis of the conceptual, pedagogical, cultural, and political challenges facing teachers. *Review of Educational Research, 72*(2), 131–175.

Winerip, M. (2005, June 29). Test scores are up. So why isn't everybody cheering? *The New York Times.*

Wingate, N. (1986). Sexism in the classroom. *Equity & Excellence, 22,* 105–110.

Winner, E. (2000). The origins and ends of giftedness. *American Psychologist, 55,* 159–169.

Wintergerst, A. C., DeCapua, A., & Itzen, R. C. (2001). The construct validity of one learning styles instrument. *System, 29,* 385–403.

Wittrock, M. (Ed.). (1986). *Handbook of research on teaching* (3rd ed.). New York: Macmillan.

Wittrock, M. C. (1992). An empowering conception of educational psychology. *Educational Psychologist, 27,* 129–142.

Wolf, D., Bixby, J., Glenn, J., III, & Gardner, H. (1991). To use their minds well: New forms of student assessment. *Review of Research in Education, 17,* 31–74.

Wolters, C. A., Yu, S. L., & Pintrich, P. R. (1996). The relation between goal orientation and students' motivational beliefs and self-regulated learning. *Learning & Individual Differences, 8,* 211–238.

Wood, S. E., & Wood, E. G. (1999). *The world of psychology* (3rd ed.). Boston: Allyn & Bacon.

Woods, B. S., & Murphy, P. K. (2002). Thickening the discussion: What can William James tell us about constructivism? *Educational Theory, 52,* 443–449.

Woolfolk, A. E. (2008). *Active learning edition: Educational psychology* (10th ed.). Boston: Allyn & Bacon.

Woolfolk, A. E., & Hoy, W. K. (1990). Prospective teachers' sense of efficacy and beliefs about control. *Journal of Educational Psychology, 82,* 81–91.

Woolfolk, A. E., Rosoff, B., & Hoy, W. K. (1990). Teachers' sense of efficacy and their beliefs about managing students. *Teaching & Teacher Education, 6,* 137–148.

Woolfolk Hoy, A., & Burke-Spero, R. (2005). Changes in teacher efficacy during the early years of teaching: A comparison of four measures. *Teaching & Teacher Education, 21,* 343–356.

Woolfolk Hoy, A., & Tschannen-Moran, M. (1999). Implications of cognitive approaches to peer learning for teacher education. In A. O'Donnell & A. King (Eds.), *Cognitive perspectives on peer learning* (pp. 257–284). Mahwah, NJ: Lawrence Erlbaum.

Woolfolk Hoy, A., & Weinstein, C. S. (2006). Students' and teachers' perspectives about classroom management. In C. Evertson & C. S. Weinstein (Eds.), *Handbook for classroom management: Research, practice, and contemporary issues* (pp. 181–219). Mahwah, NJ: Lawrence Erlbaum.

Worthen, B. R. (1993). Critical issues that will determine the future of alternative assessment. *Phi Delta Kappan, 74,* 444–457.

Wright, S. C., & Taylor, D. M. (1995). Identity and the language of the classroom: Investigating the impact of heritage versus second language instruction on personal and collective self-esteem. *Journal of Educational Psychology, 87,* 241–252.

Yarhouse, M. A. (2001). Sexual identity development: The influence of valuative frameworks on identity synthesis. *Psychotherapy, 38*(3), 331–341.

Yee, A. H. (1992). Asians as stereotypes and students: Misperceptions that persist. *Educational Psychology Review, 4,* 95–132.

Yerkes, R. M., & Dodson, J. D. (1908). The relation of strength of stimulus to rapidity of habit formation. *Journal of Comparative Neurology, 18,* 459–482.

Young, A. J. (1997). I think, therefore I'm motivated: The relations among cognitive strategy use, motivational orientation, and classroom perceptions over time. *Learning & Individual Differences, 9,* 249–283.

Zeidner, M. (1995). Adaptive coping with test situations. *Educational Psychologist, 30,* 123–134.

Zigmond, N., Jenkins, J., Fuchs, D., Deno, S., & Fuchs, L. S. (1995). When students fail to achieve satisfactorily: A reply to Leskey and Waldron. *Phi Delta Kappan, 77,* 303–306.

Zimmerman, B. J. (1995). Self-efficacy and educational development. In A. Bandura (Ed.), *Self-efficacy in changing societies* (pp. 202–231). New York: Cambridge University Press.

NAME INDEX

SUBJECT INDEX